Apple Pro Training Series

Pages, Numbers, and Keynote

Mark Wood

Apple Pro Training Series: Pages, Numbers, and Keynote
Mark Wood

Peachpit Press
www.peachpit.com

To report errors, please send a note to errata@peachpit.com.
Peachpit Press is a division of Pearson Education.

Apple Series Editor: Lisa McClain
Editor: Bob Lindstrom
Production Editor: Maureen Forys, Happenstance Type-O-Rama
Technical Editor: Michael E. Cohen
Apple Reviewer: Raj Saklikar
Apple Project Manager: Debra Otterstetter
Technical Review: Klark Perez
Copy Editor: Darren Meiss
Proofreader: Darren Meiss
Compositor: Cody Gates, Happenstance Type-O-Rama
Indexer: Jack Lewis
Cover Illustration: Paul Mavrides
Cover Production: Cody Gates, Happenstance Type-O-Rama

ISBN 13: 978-0-13-398706-5
ISBN 10: 0-13-398706-X
9 8 7 6 5 4 3 2 1
Printed and bound in the United States of America

For meritocracy, family, and friends,
Let Reason shine.

—Mark Wood

Acknowledgments Firstly, to Apple and Brenda Brierley for suggesting that I might be the man for the job, and then to Raj Saklikar for agreeing.

From my first contact with Peachpit, their professionalism and commitment was clear and welcoming. I'd like to thank everyone involved in the production of this book, but special mention must be made to Michael E. Cohen, Darren Meiss, and Klark Perez for reviewing the lessons and translating my occasional British colloquialisms. To Bob Lindstrom, your guidance to write freely was a tremendous gift. And to Lisa McClain, thank you so much for your calm sagacity in steering this project.

Additional thanks to: Dr. Chris Cottam and Dr. Mat Cottam for their mathematical insights; and Ray Walmsley, PIVA, and the members of Leek Kansen Ryu Kempo Ju-Jitsu Academy for granting me permission to photograph them.

Finally, to Jonathan, Catherine, and Hilary for your support and understanding, as I worked the hours away.

88
76
54
71
29
30
95
66

Contents at a Glance

Table of Contents

Exploring Pages, Numbers, and Keynote

Publishing with Pages

Working with iPad, Mac, and iCloud Apps

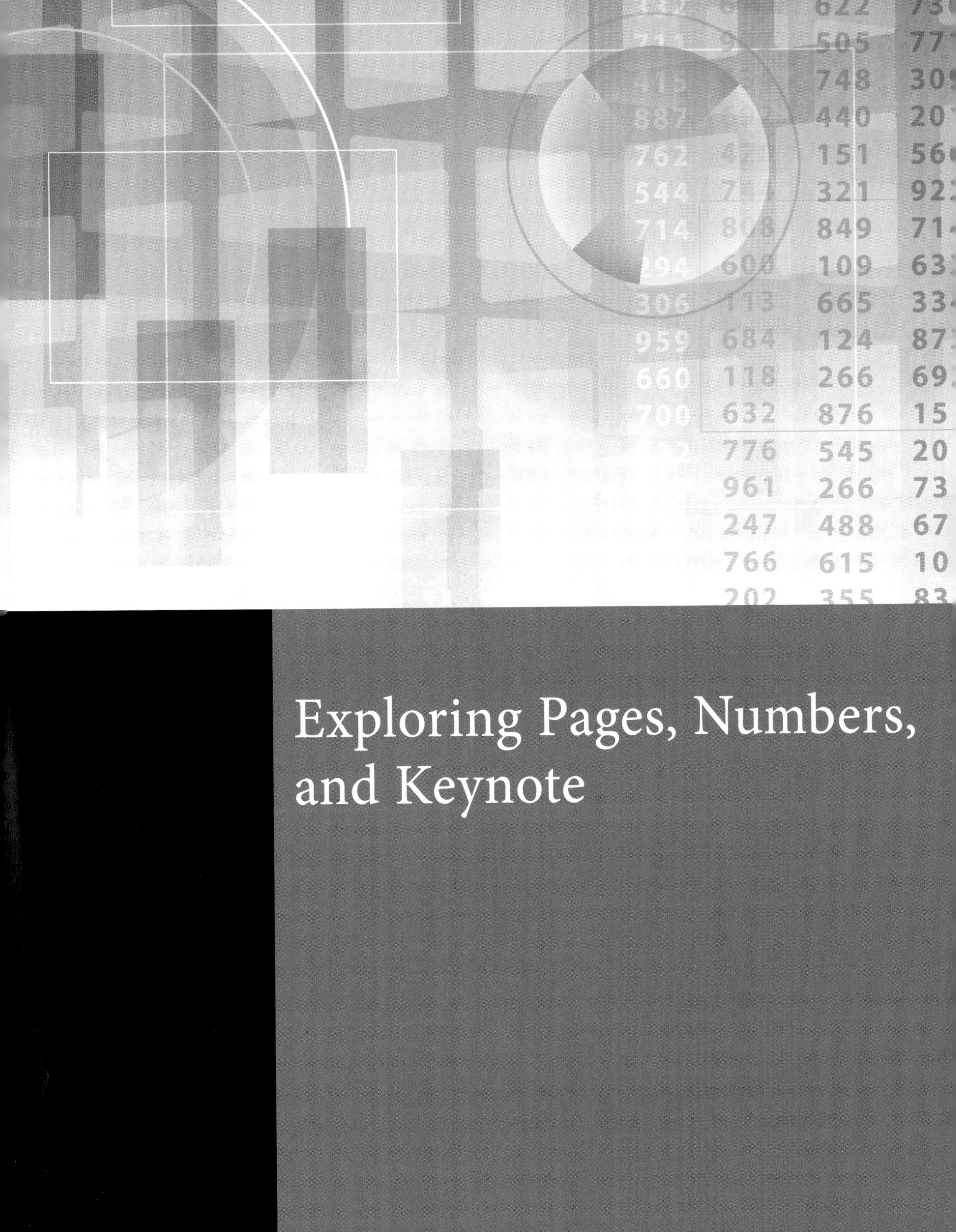

Exploring Pages, Numbers, and Keynote

1

Lesson File	APTS_Pages_Numbers_Keynote.zip
Goals	Understand learning methodology and structure of material
	Download and install lesson files

Lesson 1

Getting Started

Welcome to the Apple-certified guide to Pages, Numbers, and Keynote.

Whether you are using it for self-study or in a class, this guide will lead you through a series of lessons that begin with a solid overview of all three applications, and then explore Pages, Numbers, and Keynote in greater depth.

You will explore how to be more productive when creating letters, brochures, business cards, or posters in Pages. You will use Numbers to analyze budgets, track personnel, and create fantastic charts and graphs to illustrate data. In Keynote you will make cinema-quality presentations to communicate ideas, share recorded versions of slideshows, and use the timing and rehearsal tools to make timely, well-paced presentations.

These three programs, originally released as the iWork suite, are now separately available for OS X and iOS. You can even use them on iCloud via a web browser.

However, all versions of Pages, Numbers, and Keynote are designed to work together seamlessly. For example, you could start preparing a letter on an iPad using Pages for iOS and then complete the task on Pages for Mac.

Learning Methodology

This book is the official Apple curriculum for training in Pages, Numbers, and Keynote as used in Apple Authorized Training Centers worldwide. It can also be used in self-paced study. The downloadable lesson files focus on practical, real-world projects that increase in complexity throughout the book.

Beginning with Lesson 1, "Getting Started," is best as it covers how to download and install the lesson files.

Lesson 2, "Discovering Common Features" takes you on a quick tour through all three applications on OS X, highlighting the similarities in their interfaces and formatting tools. Lesson 2 is essential reading if you're unfamiliar with these applications and highly advisable reading for everyone else, as there are important new features to discover. Subsequent lessons expand on the topics introduced in Lesson 2. Because you may not wish to learn about all three productivity applications just now, this book covers Pages, Numbers, and Keynote separately. If making presentations is your immediate need, for instance, once you've reached the end of Lesson 2, you may want to jump directly to Lesson 12, "Outlining a Presentation," and work sequentially to Lesson 15, "Rehearsing and Delivering a Presentation."

The aim throughout the course is to give you a concise but comprehensive insight into the Apple productivity applications by working through real-world scenarios and exercises. The exercises are based on the needs of three fictitious characters who use Pages, Numbers, and Keynote for different reasons. In working through the lessons, you may identify real-world tasks you need to perform and discover solutions to your own productivity questions.

Understanding Course Structure

This book is divided into five sections:

- An overview, "Exploring Pages, Numbers, and Keynote"
- Pages for Mac
- Numbers for Mac
- Keynote for Mac
- Working with iPad, Mac, and iCloud Apps

Each of the 17 lessons investigates a different aspect of document creation taught in the following order.

Publishing with Pages

You will use Pages to create a report; import text from Microsoft Word; and add charts, graphs, web links and rich media to your document. You will format text and apply style sheets, as well as create a table of contents and manage headers and footers.

Furthermore, you'll use Pages as a page layout tool to create brochures, posters, and business cards. You will learn how to design and produce polished documents, and then publish them electronically and in print.

Organizing and Illustrating Data Using Numbers

Numbers is a great application for organizing and analyzing data. You will use Numbers to create a budget planner for a new business. This exercise will highlight some of the 250 available functions. Table and cell formatting options will teach you how to use interactive sliders, checkboxes, steppers, and pop-up menus to keep data input under control. You'll also use charts, text and photos to illustrate technical information.

Make Compelling Presentations with Keynote

In Keynote, you'll develop presentations by organizing and sequencing ideas. You'll modify Apple-designed templates to create new slide designs. Then you'll quickly build and add logos, photos, charts, and animation for your presentation. Using presenter view to display a timer and speaker notes, you will rehearse your show before delivering it in a variety of formats.

Working with iPad, Mac, and iCloud Apps

Like the OS X versions, the iOS versions of Pages, Numbers, and Keynote share similar functions. You will access documents using the iOS apps to edit text, photos, and data. You will create presentations entirely within Keynote for iOS, and review font and template considerations across all three applications.

iCloud is a great place to store, share, and review documents. Productivity can be enhanced using collaborative workflows. This section illustrates those workflows—for example, by developing a report on an iPad and sharing it on iCloud, where it can be modified in a web browser before being transferred to OS X. In another example, you will transfer an OS X Numbers document to an iOS device, using that device as a light, convenient tool for data entry.

System Requirements

This book is written for Pages v.5.5, Numbers v.3.5, and Keynote v.6.5 for OS X Yosemite or later. For the iOS versions, iOS 8.1 or later is required. To use Pages, Numbers, and Keynote on iCloud, you will need an iCloud account and one of these browsers: Safari 6.0.3 or later, Chrome 27.0.1 or later, or Internet Explorer 9.0.8 or later. Creating an iCloud account is covered in Lesson 17.

You must install Pages, Numbers, and Keynote on your Mac to work through to Lesson 15. Lessons 16 and 17 require that Pages, Numbers, and Keynote are installed on your iOS device.

In working through this book, having a good working knowledge of your Mac and its operating system helps. You don't have to be an expert, but knowing how to use the standard menus to open, save, and close files, along with how and where files are stored will help you focus on learning Pages, Numbers, and Keynote.

Because Apple productivity applications are designed to work seamlessly between Mac, iOS devices, and iCloud, using finger gestures to zoom, rotate, and navigate have become increasingly important. Trackpads are built into MacBook computers and can be purchased for Mac mini, iMac, and Mac Pro systems. If you have a trackpad, you may want to familiarize yourself with gestures. Here's how:

1 Choose Apple menu > System Preferences.

2 Click the Trackpad icon.

3 Review the gesture options in the three tabs: Point & Click, Scroll & Zoom, and More Gestures.

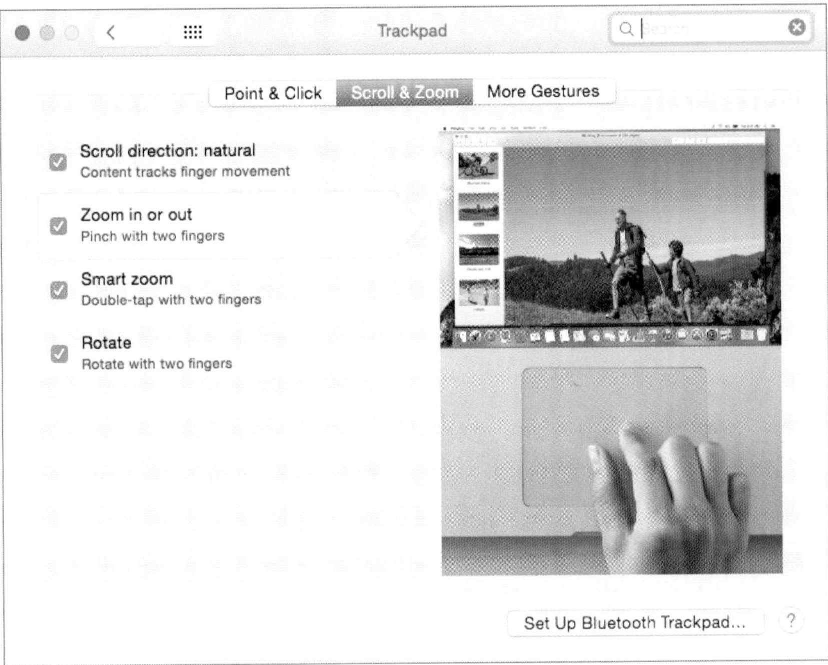

4 After reviewing the gesture options, close System Preferences.

If you want to learn more about your Mac and its operating system, consult the Help Center.

1 In the Dock, open Finder by clicking its icon.

2 Choose Help > Mac Help Center. Review the listed topics.

Downloading and Installing Lesson Files

You will need to download the lesson files before you move on to Lesson 2. If you are working with the printed edition of this book, the access code is provided on the card at the back of the book. If you are working with an electronic book version, the access code is on your "Where Are the Lesson Files?" page at the back of your electronic book.

> **NOTE ▶** If you purchase or redeem a code for the electronic version of the book directly from Peachpit, the lesson files will appear automatically on the Lesson & Update Files tab without the need to redeem an additional code.

1. Go to www.peachpit.com/redeem, and enter your access code.
2. Click Redeem Code and sign in or create a Peachpit.com account.

   The downloadable files will be listed on your Account page on the Lesson & Update Files tab.
3. Click the lesson file link APTS Pages Numbers Keynote.zip and download the file to your Downloads folder.
4. In the Dock, click the Downloads icon.
5. Click Reveal In Finder.
6. If necessary, double-click APTS Pages Numbers Keynote.zip to open it, and then drag the APTS Pages Numbers Keynote folder to your desktop.

   The APTS Page Numbers Keynote folder contains folders for each lesson.

About Apple Training and Certification

Apple Pro Training Series: Pages, Numbers, and Keynote is part of the official training series for Apple applications. Apple Certified Pro status is offered to those who pass the certification exams offered separately in Pages, Numbers, and Keynote. These exams test knowledge and performance.

Working through this book and practicing the skills outlined will help you prepare for the certification exams. However, you may prefer to learn in an instructor-led setting. Apple offers training courses in Apple Authorized Training Centers throughout the world. Taught by Apple Certified Trainers, these courses outline concepts, while providing hands-on experience and expert help.

Apple Certified Pro status will:

- Differentiate yourself and your business
- Gain recognition for technical competency
- Build credibility with clients and employers
- Increase visibility and enhance your reputation in a competitive marketplace
- Publicize your certifications on the Apple Certified Professionals Registry
- Display your personalized certificate and a logo that distinguishes you as an Apple Certified professional

Additional Resources

Apple Pro Training Series: Pages, Numbers, and Keynote is not intended as a comprehensive reference manual. All the applications feature reference guides through their respective Help menus. For more information about Pages, Numbers, and Keynote, refer to these resources:

- Companion Peachpit Press website: As the applications evolve, lessons may be updated, and additional training resources might be posted. Visit www.peachpit.com/apts.pnk.
- The Apple website: www.apple.com

2

Lesson Files

APTS Pages Numbers Keynote > Lesson_02 > ju-jitsu-grading.pages

APTS Pages Numbers Keynote > Lesson_02 > ju-jitsu-grading-print.pages

APTS Pages Numbers Keynote > Lesson_02 > ju-jitsu-register.numbers

APTS Pages Numbers Keynote > Lesson_02 > ju-jitsu-presentation.key

APTS Pages Numbers Keynote > Lesson_02 > ju-jitsu-club-logo.ai

APTS Pages Numbers Keynote > apts-pnk-photolibrary

Time

This lesson takes approximately 90 minutes to complete.

Goals

Understand the basic features of Pages, Numbers, and Keynote

Open, save, close, and manage documents

Navigate the template windows

Edit text, photos, and layout

Switch between Pages, Numbers, and Keynote

Lesson **2**

Discovering Common Features

Software applications help us organize data, write reports, and present information. In these areas, Pages, Numbers, and Keynote are ideal with clean and uncluttered interfaces that offer you powerful editing tools.

For their new separately available releases, Pages, Numbers, and Keynote were redesigned to simplify creating stunning documents, spreadsheets, and presentations. Sharing with iCloud is built in, so you can automatically keep documents up to date across your Mac, iPad, iPhone, and even the web.

In this lesson, you'll look at the features and functions of Pages, Numbers, and Keynote for Mac OS X. The applications share similar and sometimes identical interface controls for manipulating text, shapes, and rich media. You'll start by examining these common elements, touching on the basic skills you will build on in later lessons.

This lesson shows how a Ju-Jitsu club might use the apps. You will update three documents for the club and create a newsletter in Pages, produce a register of students in Numbers, and build a short presentation about the martial arts using Keynote. You will then modify headings, colors, and pictures.

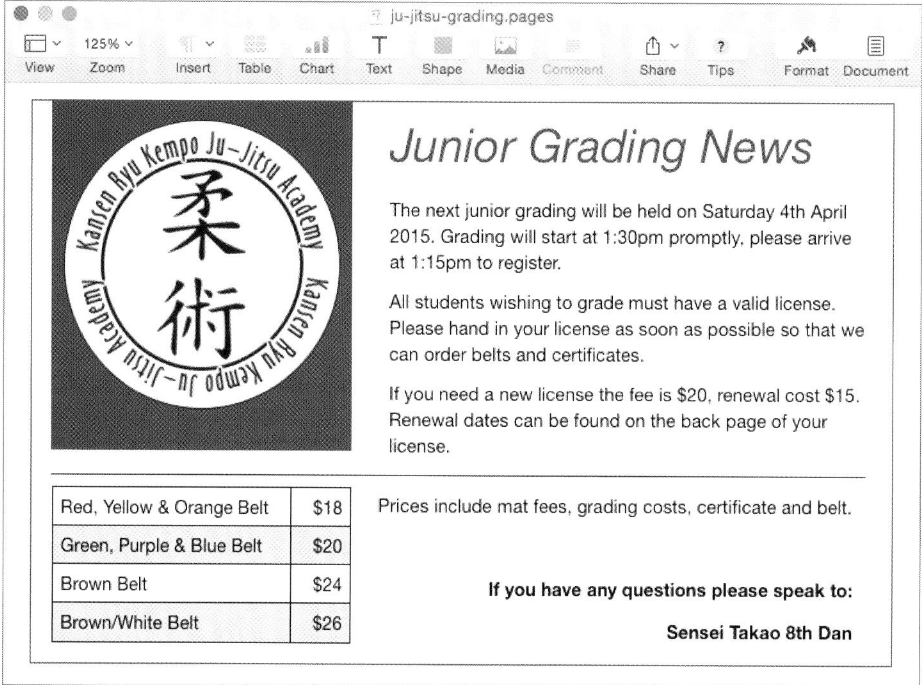

Before You Start

Make sure you have worked through Lesson 1—and downloaded and installed the lesson files as described—before beginning this lesson. Also, you are advised to close all your open documents and applications—including Pages, Numbers, Keynote, and iPhoto—before you begin this lesson.

Opening Pages, Numbers, and Keynote

Let's start by opening Pages on the Mac. This can be done in one of four ways:

- Open your Applications folder, and then double-click the Pages application file.
- In the Dock, click the Pages icon. If it's not there, you can drag the Pages application icon from your Applications folder into the Dock.

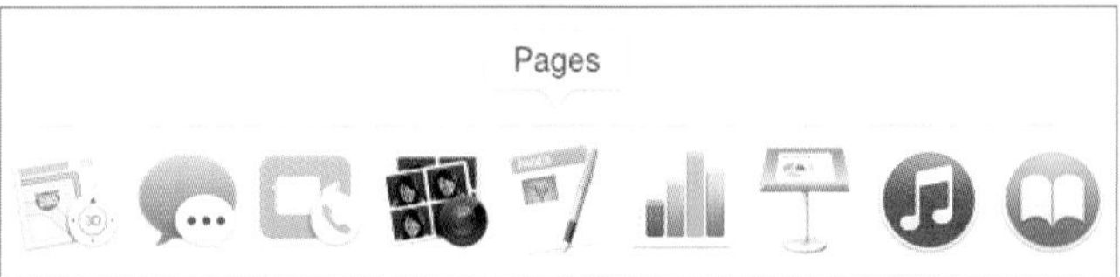

- Double-click any Pages project file.

- Use Launchpad to open Pages.

Swapping Between Open Applications

First, let's look at a way to swap from Pages to Numbers to Keynote and back again using your computer keyboard. You'll be jumping between these apps quite a lot in this lesson.

1 Open Numbers and Keynote using one of the methods described in the preceding section.

2 Press Command-Tab.

3 While holding down the Command key, press the Tab key several times. Notice that each of your open applications and the Finder are highlighted.

4 Use Command-Tab to swap to Pages.

NOTE ▶ Using this keyboard shortcut makes swapping between applications easy, but other options are available for swapping between active applications, including Mission Control. You can learn more about Mission Control in Apple Help.

Choosing Themes

When you need to write a report, balance a budget, or make a presentation, Pages, Numbers, and Keynote are loaded with useful templates customized for those purposes. You can modify them to create your own designs and save them as personalized templates for future use.

1 In Pages, choose File > New.

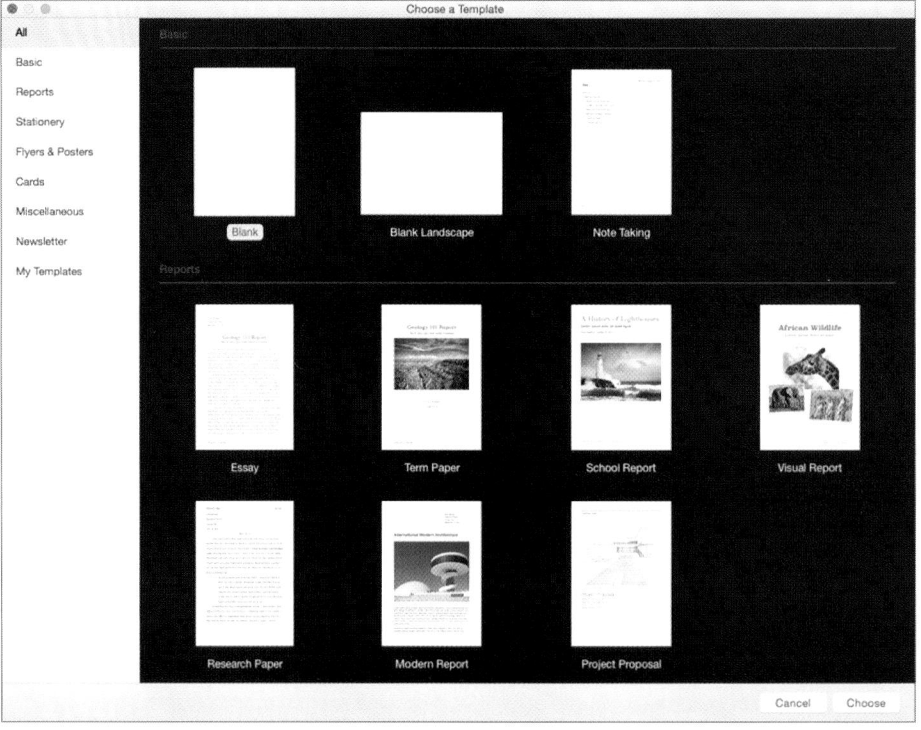

2 Browse through the available templates.

Use the panel on the left side of the templates window to review the subsections, such as Basic, Reports, and Stationery. Feel free to open any of the templates.

NOTE ▶ Pages documents fall loosely into two categories: word processing and page layout. It makes sense to start with a template in the most appropriate template category for the task at hand.

3. Open a template by double-clicking its icon; or in the template window, selecting the icon and clicking Choose.

4. When you are ready to move on, close all the open documents you have created by choosing File > Close.

   If you've made changes to your documents, a Save As dialog appears.

5. If prompted, click Delete.

   Alternatively, if you want to save your work, click Save and use the "Save as" option to save your work to the desktop.

6. Switch to Numbers, and choose File > New.

7. Browse through the Numbers templates. Note each of the subsections, such as Personal Finance and Business.

   TIP Using Numbers templates is a great way to learn about functions and formulas because many templates have calculations built into their tables.

8. Close any open Numbers documents.

   If you've made changes to your documents, a Save As dialog appears.

9. If prompted, click Delete or Save.

10. Swap to Keynote. Choose File > New to browse the themes.

    In Keynote the templates are called themes. The window is organized into two tabs: Standard and Wide. If you've previously customized templates, you'll see a third tab called My Themes.

    TIP Most presentations would use Standard. Wide is appropriate for widescreen 16:9 ratio displays. Keynote lets you customize the width and height of your slides, so they can be square if you want.

11 Close any Keynote documents you may have opened.

12 If prompted, click Delete or Save.

Editing Text in Pages

You are learning about the common ground across Pages, Numbers, and Keynote. Let's now look at a Pages window. You will find that Numbers and Keynote share many of its features.

In this exercise you will update a Pages document and use styles to quickly duplicate some formatting.

1 In the Finder, open the APTS Pages Numbers Keynote > Lesson_02 folder.

2 Double-click **ju-jitsu-grading.pages** to open it in Pages.

This document contains two versions of a notice about grading at a Ju-Jitsu club. Although the notice could easily be distributed electronically, this notice will be printed.

NOTE ▶ To make printing more economical, a design can be repeated more than once on a single sheet of paper. The business card templates in Pages are a good example because they include several copies of the same card on a single page. The grading notice could be printed on US Letter paper and then cut in two.

3 In the toolbar, click the Format icon, which looks like a paintbrush.

The Format inspector opens (or closes).

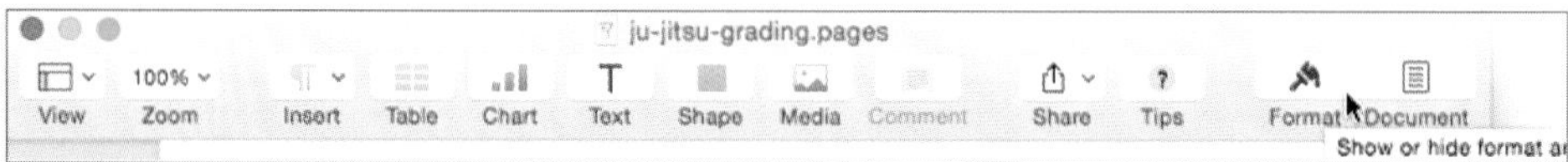

When nothing is selected, the Format inspector asks you to select an object or text item to format.

Pages, Numbers, and Keynote interfaces are all context aware, so you have to select objects or text to see their respective tools.

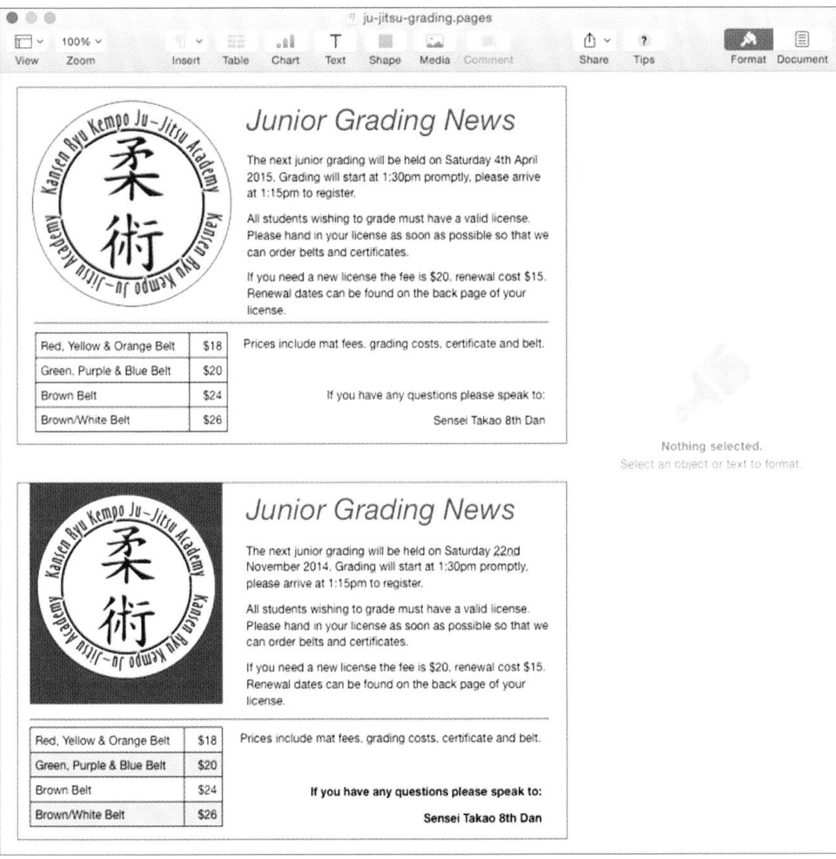

4 In the upper notice in the line "Junior Grading News," triple-click the word "Junior" to select all three words in that line. The Format inspector displays the tools for formatting text.

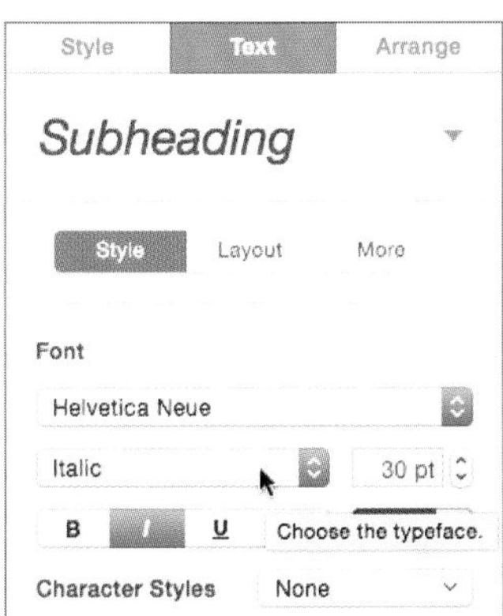

5 In the Text Inspector typeface pop-up menu, choose Condensed Black.

The Text tab of the Format inspector places an asterisk next to the Subheading menu, and an Update button appears.

6 Click Update.

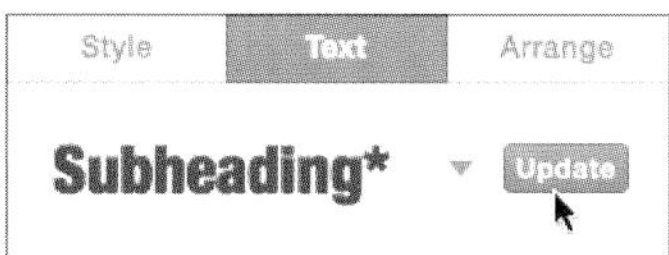

The words "Junior Grading News" are changed in both versions of the artwork. Using style sheets is a real time-saver. You'll be using them in most of these lessons. If you haven't previously used style sheets, now is a great time to start.

7 In the opening paragraph, drag across the words "Saturday 4th April 2015" to select them.

8 Choose Edit > Copy.

9 In the second grading notice, select the words "Saturday 22nd November 2014."

10 Choose Edit > Paste to replace the older dates with the new ones.

TIP Using copy and paste is a good way to update a few items, but for longer documents with more items, consider using Edit > Find > Find.

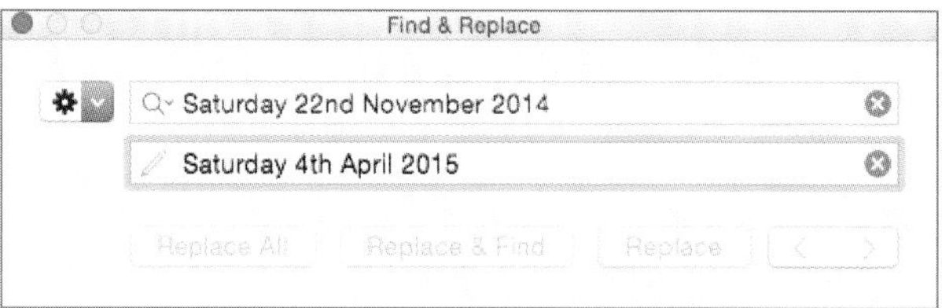

Customizing Your Workspace

You have seen that Pages has a simple, clean interface with very few buttons that might bamboozle you. The same is true of Numbers and Keynote. But sometimes having additional controls in full view is helpful. Let's take a closer look at the default toolbar and how you can customize it.

1 In the toolbar, click the View button and choose Show Page Thumbnails.

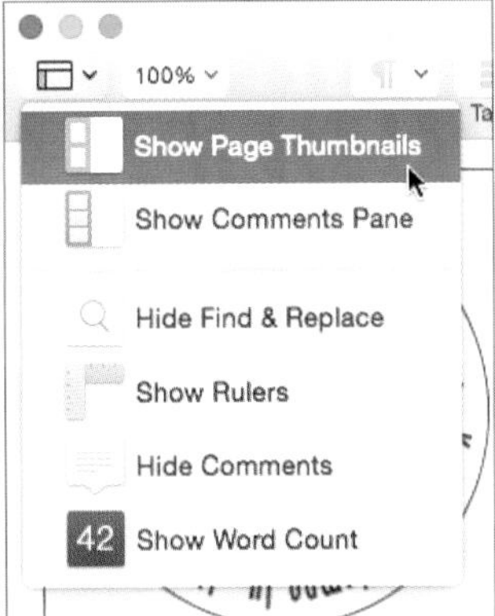

TIP Page thumbnails are a quick way to navigate long documents. Double-clicking a page icon will take you straight to that page.

2 Place your pointer over other icons in the toolbar to see a help tag that describes them. You'll explore all these items later.

3 Click the Tips icon, and then select items in the document to see different help tags.

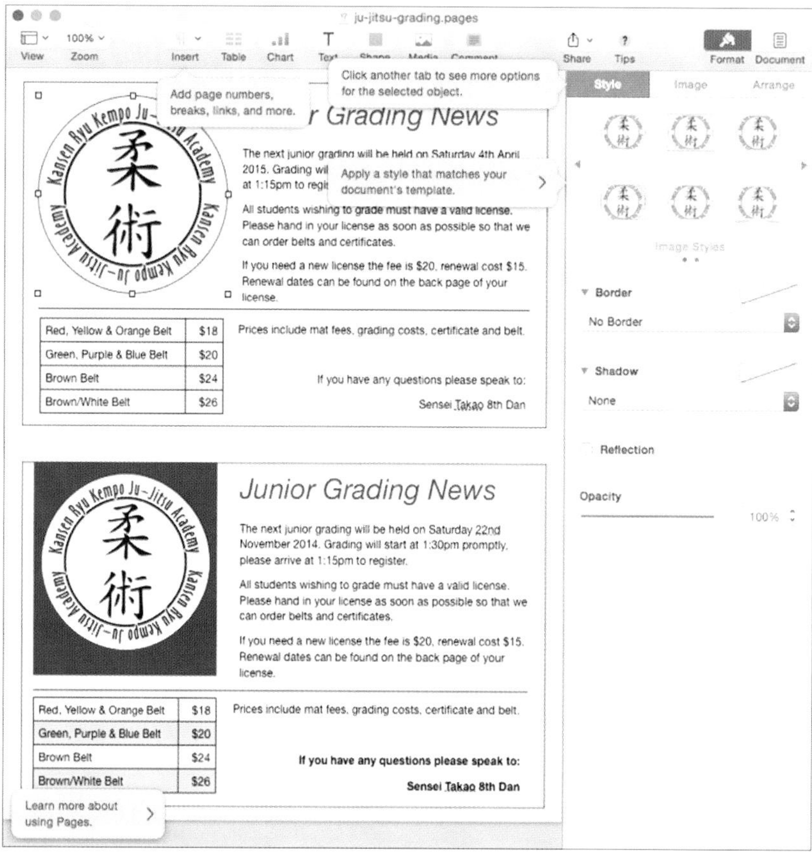

You can turn on coaching tips while you become familiar with Pages, Numbers, and Keynote.

NOTE ▶ The iOS versions of Pages, Numbers, and Keynote also have coaching tips.

4 Click the Tips icon to switch off coaching tips.

5 In the toolbar, Control-click the gray background area and choose Customize Toolbar from the shortcut menu that appears.

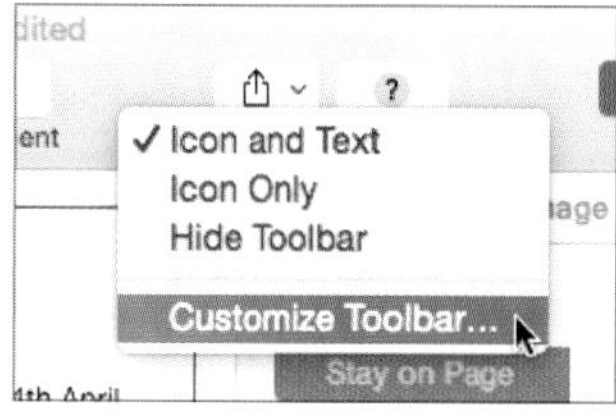

6 Drag the Copy Style and Paste Style items to the toolbar.

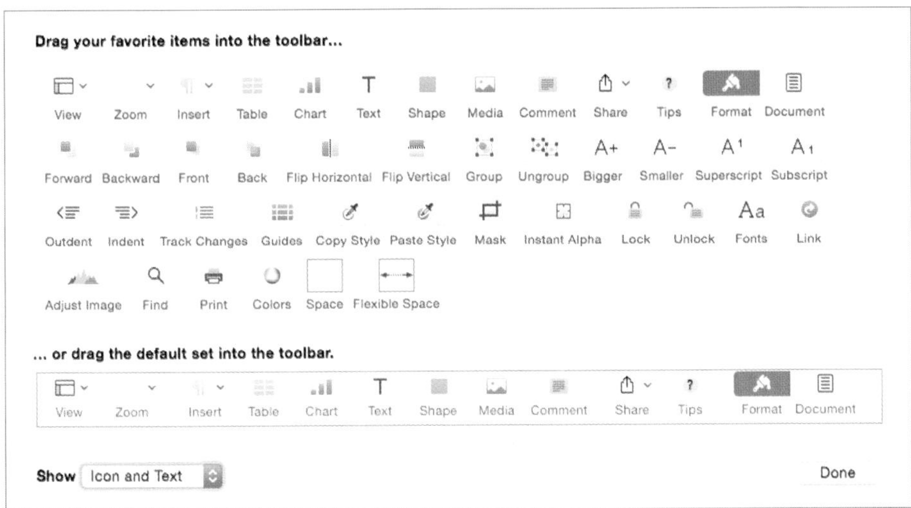

TIP Many Apple applications allow you to customize the toolbar. Reviewing the custom icons is a neat way get an overview of an application's features.

7 When you have finished adding items to the toolbar, click Done.

8 To the far right of the toolbar, click the Document icon.

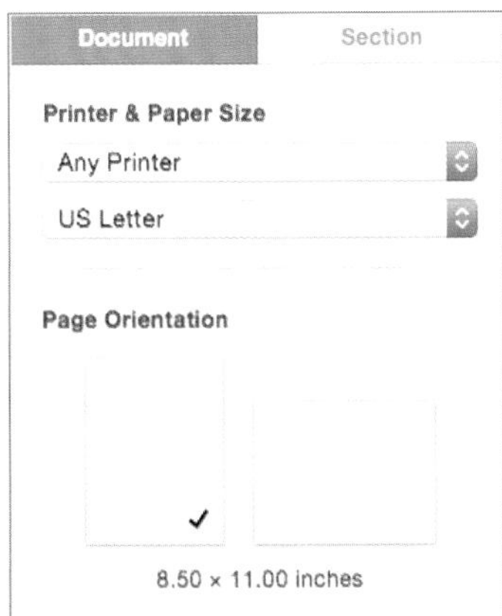

In the Document inspector, you can set the printer, paper size, and document orientation. It's also where you set document margins and section options.

TIP When you set printer options, choose the printer before setting the paper size. Then you will see a full list of paper sizes available on the selected printer. When the Printer pop-up menu is set to Any Printer, only generic page sizes are shown.

Repeating Image Styles

You've taken your first look at paragraph styles in Pages and will dig deeper into text style options later, but now let's copy and paste image styles.

1 At the top left of the document, click the Ju-Jitsu logo at the upper left of the document.

2 In the toolbar, click Format, and then in the Style tab, from the Shadow pop-up menu, choose Contact Shadow. Feel free to adjust the Blur, Offset, and Opacity settings.

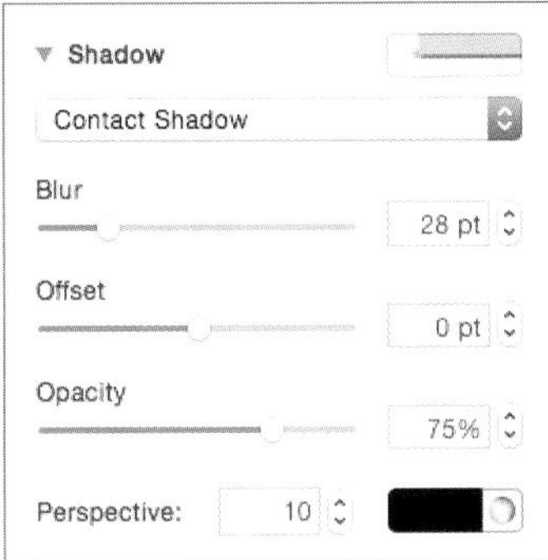

You see lots of image attributes you can adjust, but for now let's just use the Contact Shadow.

3 With the logo still selected, click the Copy Style button you added to the toolbar.

4 Click the second logo, being sure not to select the red background.

5 Click the Paste Style button.

All the attributes you applied to the first logo are applied to the second logo. Applying several image attributes to logos or photos using Copy Style and Paste Style is a quick way to repeat image styles.

TIP Copying and pasting styles also works on text.

Saving a Document

We haven't yet discussed saving your work. That's because Pages has been automatically saving in the background as you worked. The autosaves happen every five minutes or so, creating multiple versions of your document.

You can choose File > Save when you want to create a version of your document in addition to the autosave versions.

1 Choose File > Revert To > Browse All Versions.

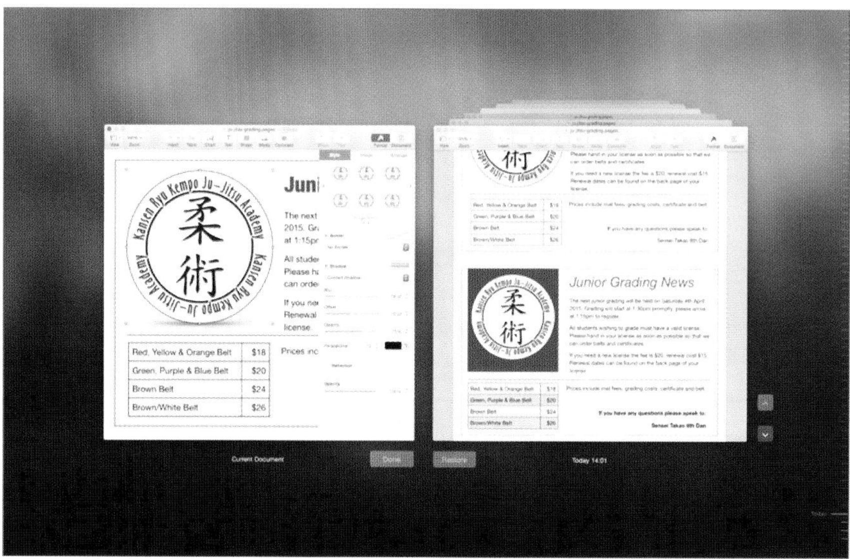

Pages swaps to a window very much like Apple's Time Machine. Clicking through the windows on the right, or dragging the scrolling times and dates bar, allows you to review earlier versions of your documents. At this point, unless you've been saving the ju-jitsu-grading.pages document, you will see only one prior version of your document.

To replace your current document with an earlier version, you would choose Restore.

To duplicate a previous version as a new document, you would Option-click Restore a Copy.

2 Click Done to return to Pages with the latest version of your document.

NOTE ▸ The Revert To menu in Pages, Numbers, and Keynote may also show Last Saved, where any changes you made to a document since you last saved it are deleted; or Last Opened, where any changes made since you last opened a document are deleted.

3 Click the document title "ju-jitsu-grading.pages."

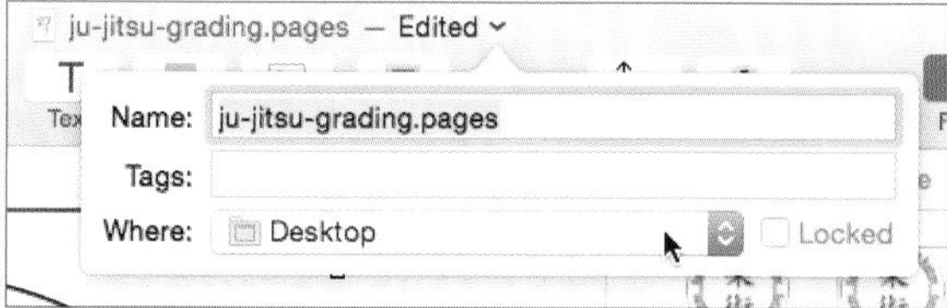

In the popover that appears, you can do three things:

- Rename a document, using the Name field.
- Tag a document. Tags first appeared in OS X Mavericks. Tags are also known as keywords.
- Move a document using the Where pop-up menu. Choose iCloud to move a document to iCloud. Choose Other to open a Finder window and move a document to any location on your drives or network.

NOTE ▶ This pop-up menu combines two items found under the File menu: Rename and Move To.

4 In the Tags field, type *Ju-Jitsu, Jiu Jitsu, Martial Arts, Grading.*

Adding tags or keywords is a great way to catalog your work. In this example adding an alternative spelling of Jiu Jitsu and the broader label Martial Arts would help other people locate the grading document when doing a search.

NOTE ▶ A tag or keyword can be several words set between commas. Therefore in these examples Jiu Jitsu and Martial Arts are single keywords.

5 Click anywhere in the document window to close the popover.

6 Choose File > Duplicate to make a new copy of the open document.

A copy of the document is created with the entire name, ju-jitsu-grading copy, selected.

7 In the Name field, change the document name to *ju-jitsu-grading finished.*

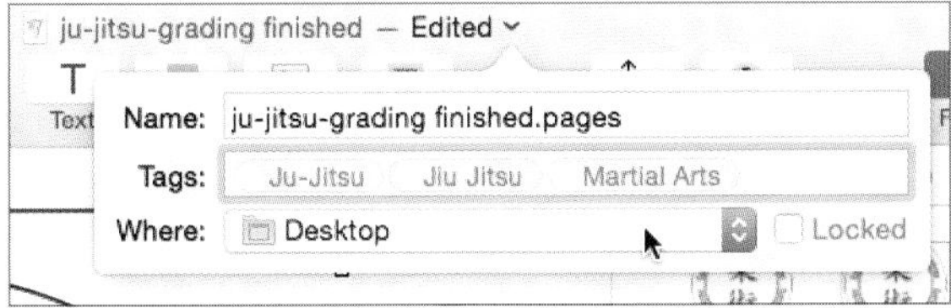

NOTE ▶ Duplicate is similar to the Save As function used in other applications.

8 Choose File > Close, and repeat the command, if necessary, to close all open Pages documents.

Distributing Your Work

You can share your work in Pages, Numbers, and Keynote using several methods. Some are unique to a single application. For example, Keynote can output a slideshow as a movie file. You'll later take a deeper look at the sharing options for each application; but for now, let's take a brief look at Pages.

NOTE ▶ Sharing via iCloud is described in Lesson 17.

1 Choose File > Open, and navigate to Lesson_02.

2 Double-click **ju-jitsu-grading-print.pages** to open a black-and-white version of the grading notice.

3 Choose File > Export To > PDF.

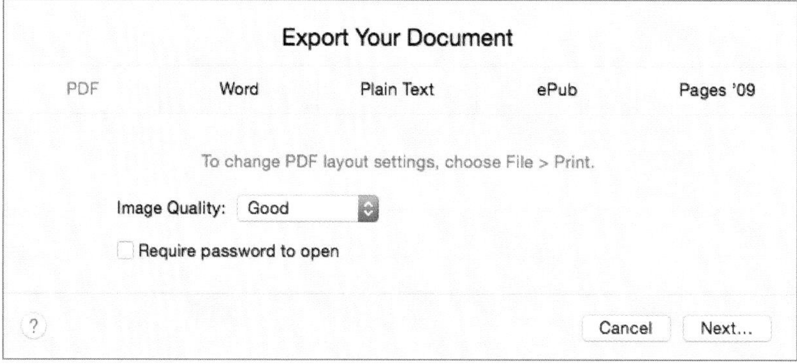

The Export Your Document dialog has five tabs: PDF, Word, Plain Text, EPUB, and Pages '09.

NOTE ▶ The File > Export To menu allows you to jump directly to any of the export options, but the same Export Your Document dialog opens.

4 In the Image Quality pop-up menu, choose Best.

Printing a document using Best does not resample or compress the artwork.

TIP To reduce the size of a file for emailing, choose Good. However, some loss of image quality may occur when you choose this option.

5 Select the "Require password to open" checkbox.

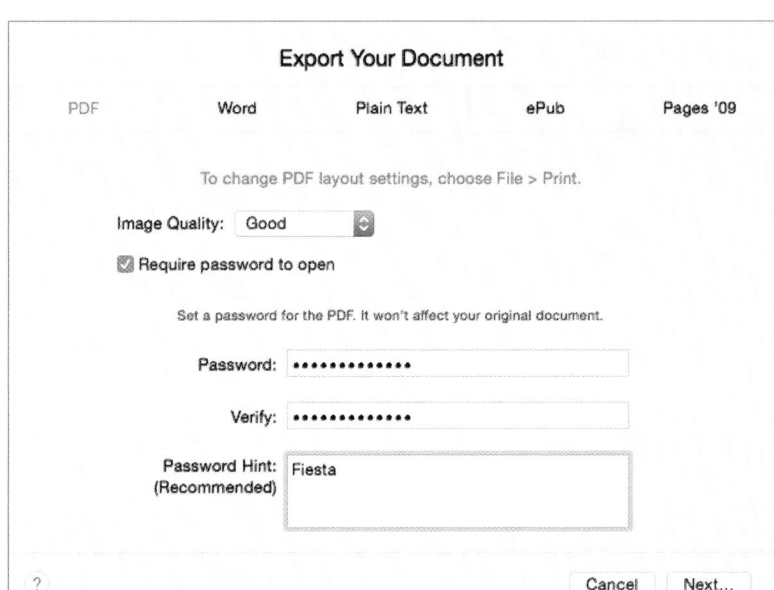

6 Set a password (and verify it) and a password hint, and then click Next.

7 Use the Finder to save the PDF to your desktop.

When the export is complete, you are returned to Pages.

8 Choose File > Export To > PDF to open the Export Your Document dialog again.

9 Click the tabs for Word, Plain Text, ePub, and Pages '09. Take note of the following options:

- The Word tab allows you to create password protection, and in the Advanced Options you can choose from the current Word .docx or older .doc (Word 1997–2004 compatible) formats.
- Saving as plain text removes all formatting.

- In ePub, the current document can't be saved as it's in Page Layout mode. You'll look at making an ePub in Lesson 7.
- Pages '09 creates a copy of a document compatible with the previous version of Pages. Both Numbers and Keynote can also export to the '09 versions.

10 Click Cancel to return to Pages.

Printing from Pages

Even in the connected world of iPads and the Internet, sometimes you need to print a document. Pages has postcard templates you can use to create stunning printouts, and it just so happens that the grading notice you've been working on must be handed out in class.

The OS X print options allow you to send a PDF straight to Apple iBooks, email, and more.

1 Choose > File > Print to open the Print dialog.

2 Click Show Details to view the print options.

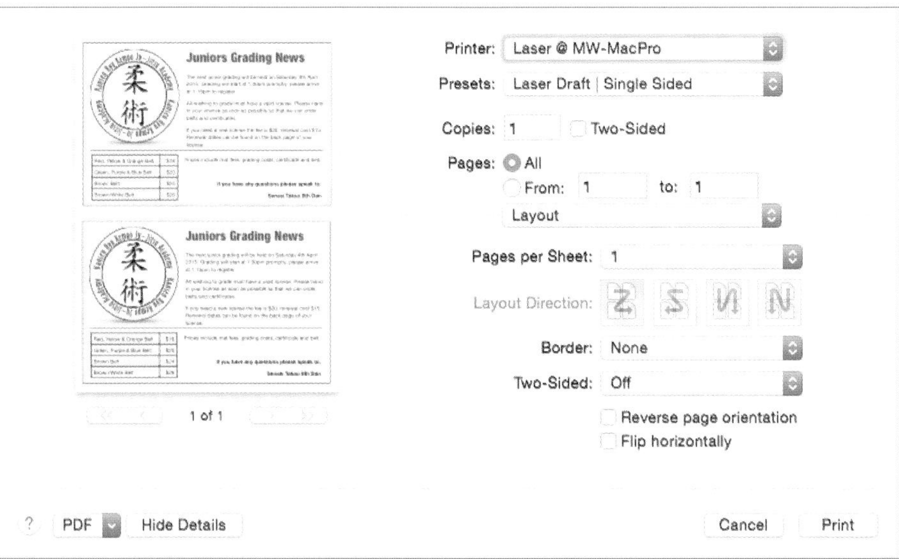

Printers vary, so once you've chosen a printer the remaining options still need to be set.

TIP Once your printer settings are configured properly, you can save them as a preset. Presets save you the trouble of configuring these options every time you print.

3 In the lower left of the print dialog, choose PDF > Mail PDF.

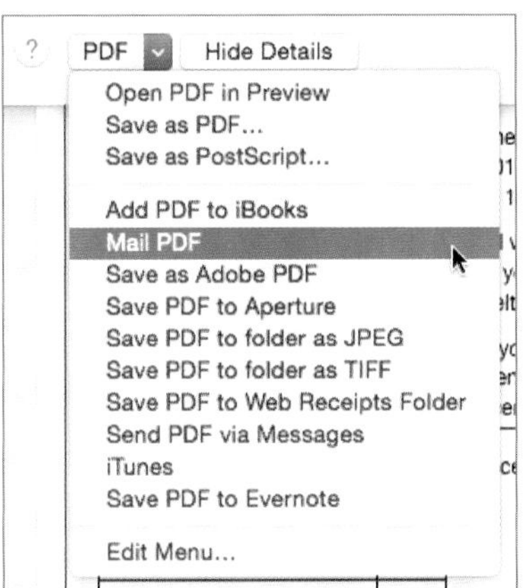

OS X runs a script that attaches a PDF copy of the document to an email. Several PDF creation scripts are available. You will explore a few of them in later lessons.

4 For this exercise, close the Mail message without sending or saving it.

NOTE ▶ You've been saving and exporting files to the desktop. Unless you really want to keep them there, you can delete them.

Working with Tables

Many of the features and techniques you use in Pages can be applied to both Numbers and Keynote. This section takes a look at tables and charts in Numbers. When you need heavy data crunching, Numbers has you covered, but tables and charts are also found in Pages and Keynote.

1 In the Finder, open the folder APTS Pages Numbers Keynote > Lesson_02.

2 Double-click **ju-jitsu-register.numbers** to open the file in Numbers.

3 In the toolbar, use View to change the document magnification to 125% (or higher) so you can more clearly see the list of student names.

4 Click the cell containing the Last Name heading.

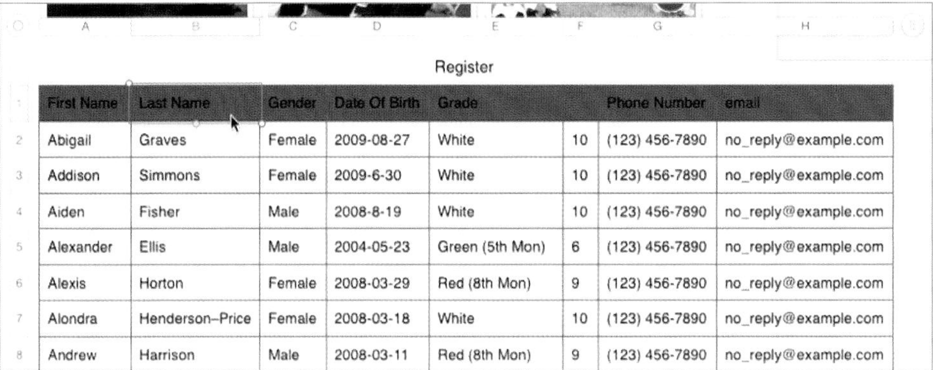

Register

First Name	Last Name	Gender	Date Of Birth	Grade		Phone Number	email
Abigail	Graves	Female	2009-08-27	White	10	(123) 456-7890	no_reply@example.com
Addison	Simmons	Female	2009-6-30	White	10	(123) 456-7890	no_reply@example.com
Aiden	Fisher	Male	2008-8-19	White	10	(123) 456-7890	no_reply@example.com
Alexander	Ellis	Male	2004-05-23	Green (5th Mon)	6	(123) 456-7890	no_reply@example.com
Alexis	Horton	Female	2008-03-29	Red (8th Mon)	9	(123) 456-7890	no_reply@example.com
Alondra	Henderson-Price	Female	2008-03-18	White	10	(123) 456-7890	no_reply@example.com
Andrew	Harrison	Male	2008-03-11	Red (8th Mon)	9	(123) 456-7890	no_reply@example.com

Two bars appear, one horizontal labeled with letters, and a vertical one labeled with numbers. These are the column and row references.

5 Move your pointer over the reference for column B. A small triangle appears.

6 Click the disclosure triangle to reveal a menu for that column.

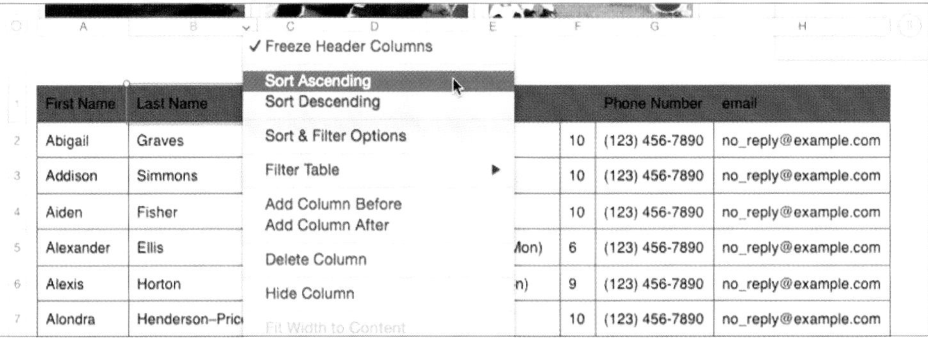

7 Choose Sort Ascending to list the students alphabetically by last name.

You can apply the same principle to sort the students by age.

8 Click the reference number 1 to select row 1.

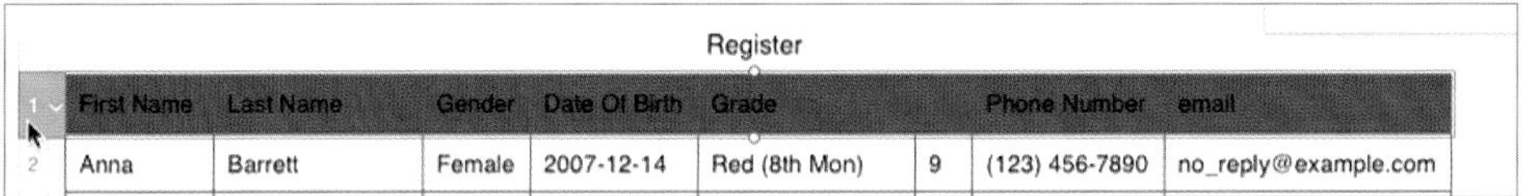

Register

First Name	Last Name	Gender	Date Of Birth	Grade		Phone Number	email
Anna	Barrett	Female	2007-12-14	Red (8th Mon)	9	(123) 456-7890	no_reply@example.com

Clicking a reference for a row or column selects all the cells in that row or column.

9 In the toolbar, click the Format icon to open the Format inspector.

10 In the Text tab, set the text color to White and the typeface to Bold to make the column header easier to read.

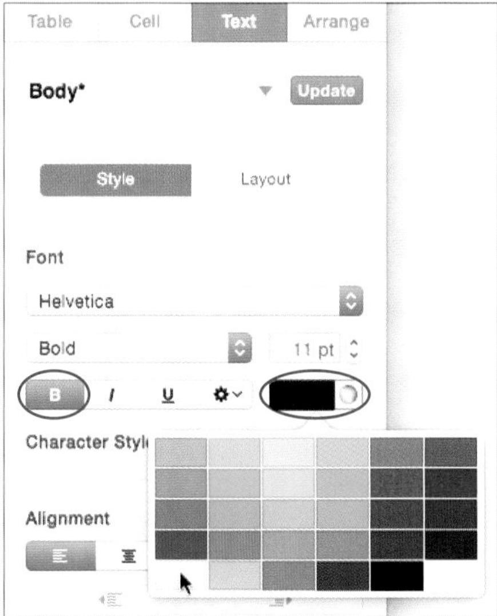

11 Click the reference header for column F, and open the column menu.

12 Choose Delete Column.

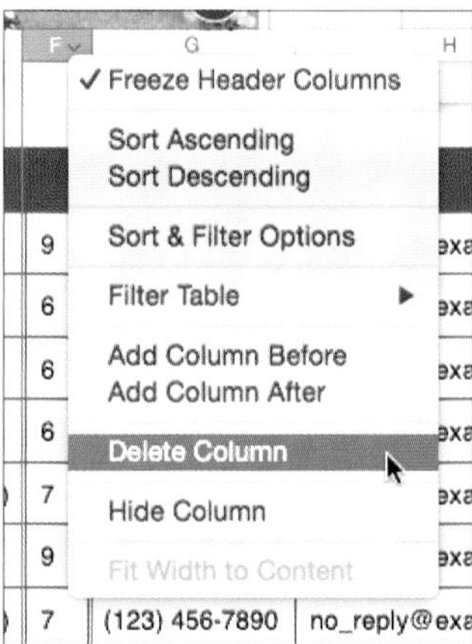

13 Click the reference header for row 2.

14 From the Row menu, choose Add Row Above.

First Name	Last Name	Gender	Date Of Birth
		Female	2009-08-27
		Female	2009-6-30
		Male	2008-8-19
		Male	2004-05-23
		Female	2008-03-29
		Female	2008-03-18
		Male	2008-03-11
		Male	2008-02-25

✓ Freeze Header Rows
Add Row Above
Add Row Below
Add Header Row Above
Convert to Header Row
Delete Row
Hide Row
Fit Height to Content
Sort & Filter Options
Search With Google
Add to iTunes as a Spoken Track
Add to Evernote

15 Double-click cell A2 to select it. It's currently blank. Double-clicking enables you to edit the cell contents.

16 Type the letter *a*.

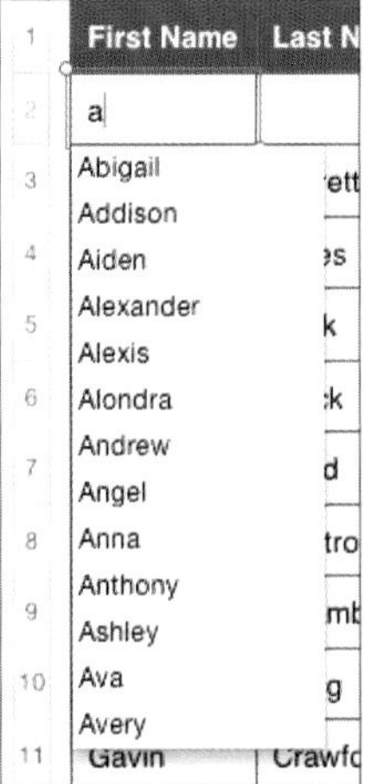

All the previously entered first names beginning with "a" now appear as a list. You can select one of these names or type in one of your own.

NOTE ▶ If this list doesn't appear as expected, choose Numbers > Preferences > General, and select the Automatically Detect Lists checkbox.

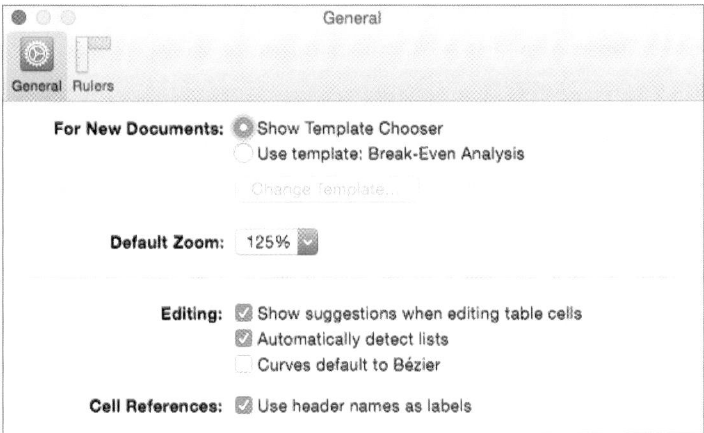

17 Click cell E2, which already has the word "White" in it.

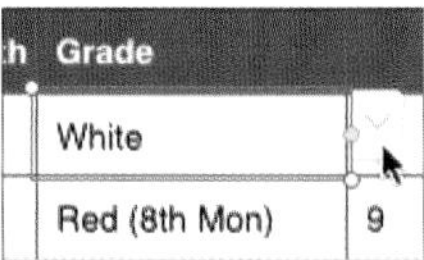

This cell was made using the pop-up menu data format.

NOTE ▸ Interactive formats such as pop-up menus for data entry are available only in Numbers. They include checkbox and slider formatting for cells. These offer a simple way to add data.

18 Click the disclosure triangle next to cell E2. From the menu that appears, choose a different grade for this student.

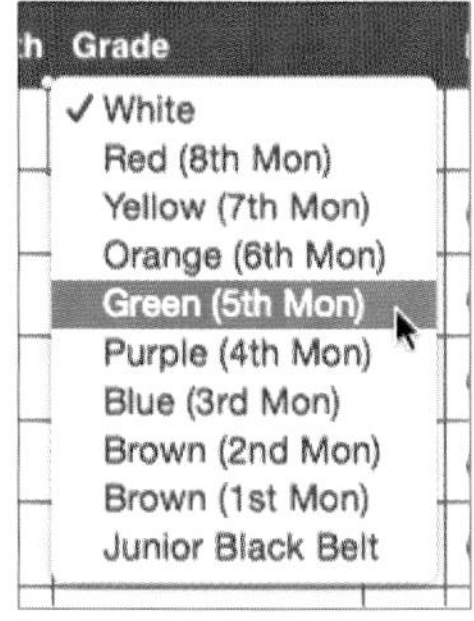

Illustrating Data Using Charts

Charts are another feature shared across Pages, Numbers, and Keynote. As a quick introduction to charts, you will generate a pie chart using the data on the grade levels of the Ju-Jitsu students.

If the file **ju-jitsu-register.numbers** is already open, skip to step 3. If not, do the following:

1. In the Finder, open the folder APTS Pages Numbers Keynote > Lesson_02.
2. Double-click the file **ju-jitsu-register.numbers** to open it.
3. Scroll around the document to see the pie chart and grades table.

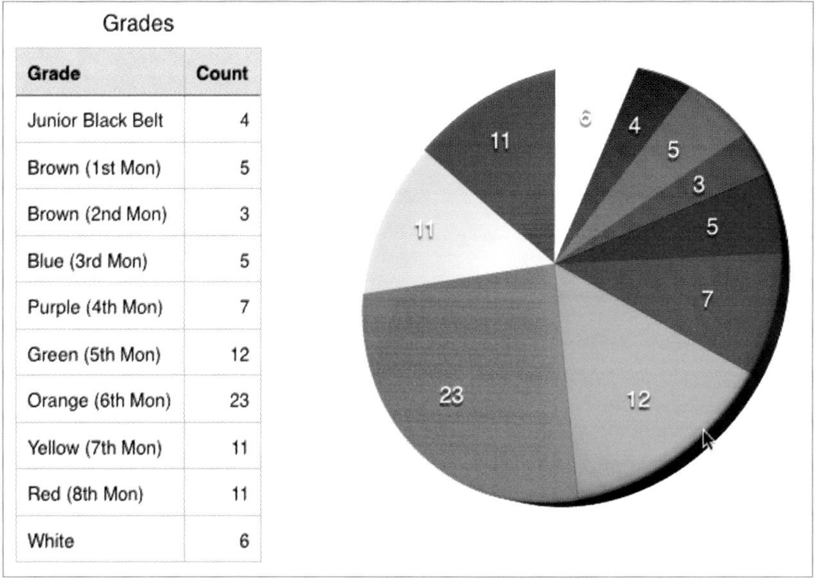

Grades

Grade	Count
Junior Black Belt	4
Brown (1st Mon)	5
Brown (2nd Mon)	3
Blue (3rd Mon)	5
Purple (4th Mon)	7
Green (5th Mon)	12
Orange (6th Mon)	23
Yellow (7th Mon)	11
Red (8th Mon)	11
White	6

4. Click the Count column to view the cell references.
5. Click cell B2 to select it, and then Shift-click cell B11 to select cells B2 through B11.

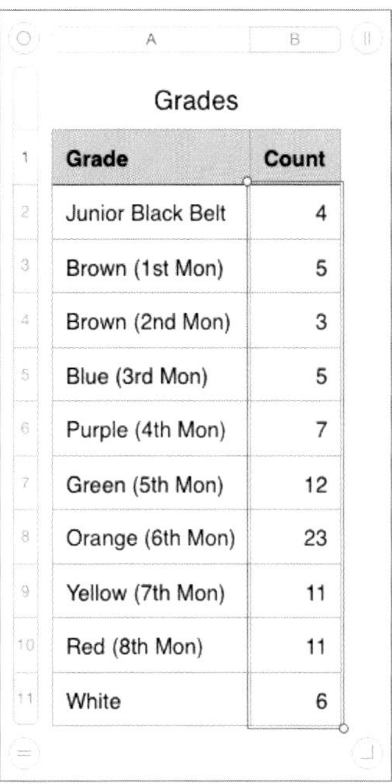

Grades

Grade	Count
Junior Black Belt	4
Brown (1st Mon)	5
Brown (2nd Mon)	3
Blue (3rd Mon)	5
Purple (4th Mon)	7
Green (5th Mon)	12
Orange (6th Mon)	23
Yellow (7th Mon)	11
Red (8th Mon)	11
White	6

6 In the toolbar, click the Chart icon.

7 In the 3D tab, click the pie chart icon.

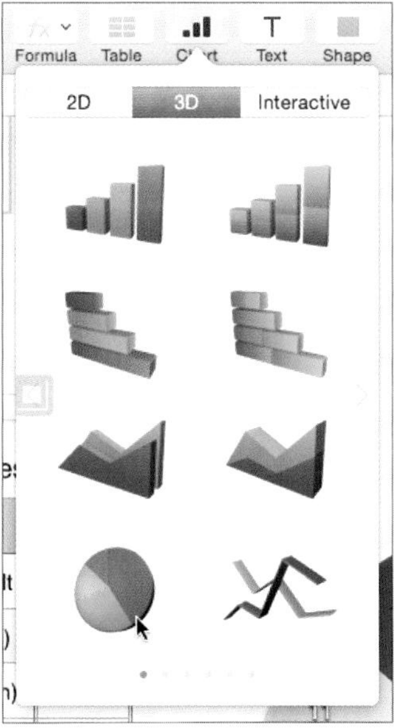

A pie chart is rendered using the data selected. You'll now use the Format inspector to modify the chart.

8 In the Format inspector, click the Wedges tab. In the Value Data Format pop-up menu, choose Same As Source Data.

The pie chart values now displays a count of the grades, which is currently four junior black belts and five white belts.

In the original pie chart, the wedges are colored to match the grade colors.

9 Select the pie chart you made, and drag inside the circle overlay to rotate the chart in 3D.

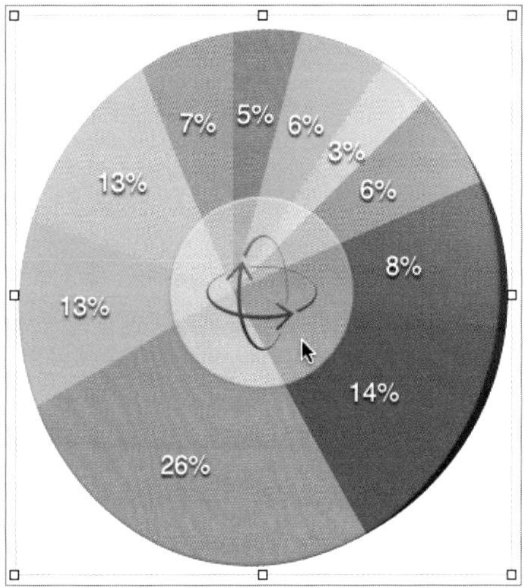

10 Scroll to the register of students table, and click the bottom row.

Beneath the reference bar for row 88, you'll see an icon with two parallel lines.

11 Drag the icon beneath the row 88 reference bar. Doing so allows you to add more rows. Add three new rows.

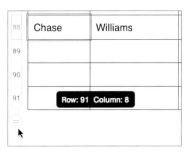

88	Chase	Williams
89		
90		
91		

Row: 91 Column: 8

TIP Use the similar icon found to the right of the column reference bar to drag out additional columns.

12 Scroll back to the pie chart. You now have eight white belts, assuming that you added three new rows.

Try changing the grading of some of the students to see the values in the pie charts change.

NOTE ▶ The grade values are found in column E of the Register table.

To discover what's driving the pie chart, you need to look at the cells in the Grades table.

13 Click the Grades table to select it, then double-click cell B2.

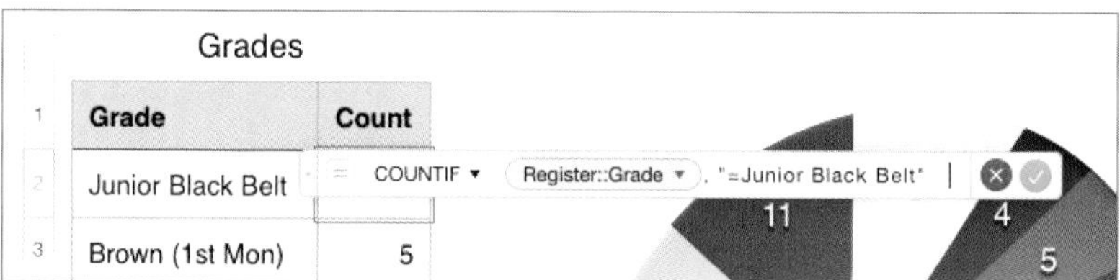

The cell contains a function that tells Numbers to "count if the grade column in the student register contains the words "Junior Black Belt."

14 Close the Formula Editor.

15 Double-click other cells in column B of the Grades table to see how the function is modified for each grade. Click away from the Formula Editor to dismiss it.

TIP When a cell containing a function is selected, the Format inspector shows a list of functions, along with a description and examples.

You'll now add a formula, over in the Register table.

16 Click the Register table to select it, and then click cell A89.

17 Press the = (equals) key to add a function.

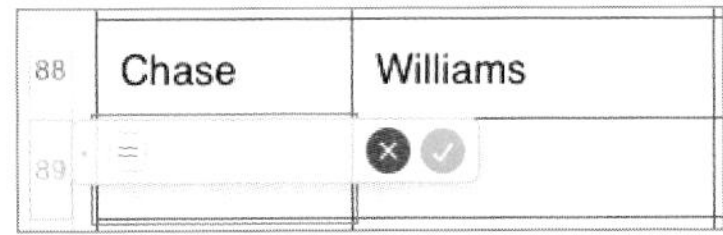

18 In the toolbar, click the Formula icon, and choose Count.

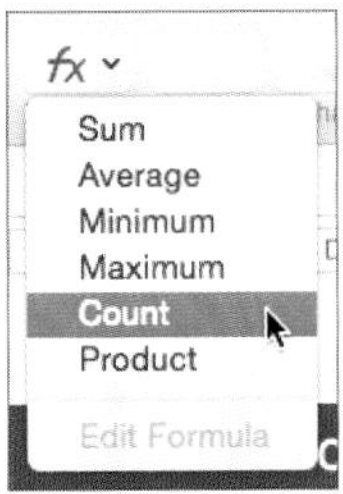

19 In the Formula Editor, click the green checkmark to accept it.

Numbers automatically counts the number of entries in column A and adds the value to cell A89.

If you were to add more students to the register above row 88, they would be added to the Count value.

NOTE ▶ Although you can copy and paste tables and charts to and from Pages, Numbers, and Keynote, some features found in Numbers, such as pop-up menus, are removed when you paste to Pages or Keynote.

Adding Comments

As you work on a document in Pages, Numbers, or Keynote, leaving a few production notes is often useful for others who will be using the document, or for jogging your memory when you later return to the document. Comments are designed to do just that. What is more, when sharing a document with a group of people your collaborators can add their comments, too.

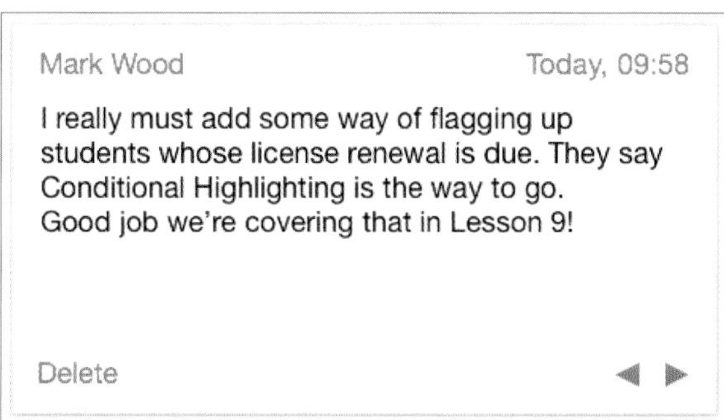

1 Open the file **ju-jitsu-register.numbers**, if necessary.

2 In the toolbar, choose View > Hide Comments.

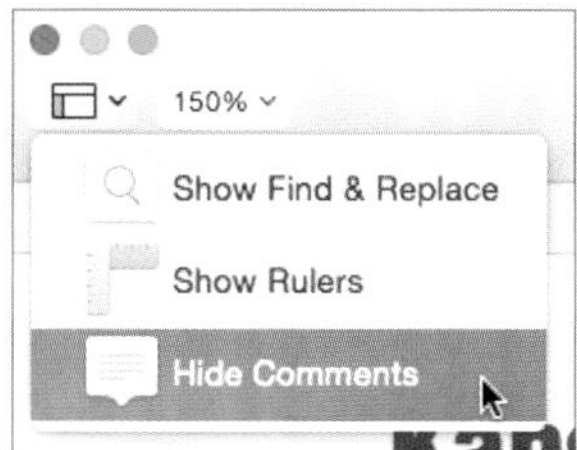

The comment disappears. When comments are visible, they will appear in prints.

3 In the toolbar, choose View > Show Comments.

4 Click a blank area in the Numbers canvas to make sure that nothing is selected.

5 In the toolbar, click the Comment icon.

A colored note appears showing who created the comments and when.

NOTE ▶ If you have not used this feature in your installation of Numbers, you are first asked for permission to use your contacts in comments, and then asked for an author name to use with comments.

6 Type a comment.

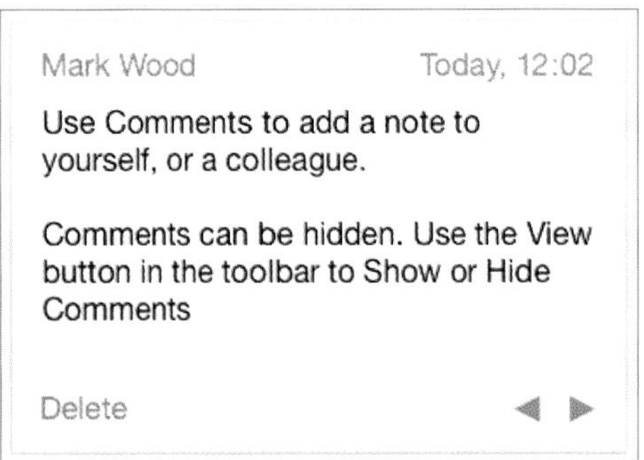

7 At the top of the Register table, you can see three photographs. One is a placeholder image showing a game of soccer. Click the soccer placeholder image to select it.

8 In the toolbar, click the Comment icon and type a quick note.

This time the comment is applied directly to the selected object.

TIP Comments can be applied to a single word or groups of words.

Adding Photos

The Numbers document **ju-jitsu-register.numbers** has three photos in it. All three started out as image placeholders, but now only one needs updating.

Placeholder images can be replaced using the Media Browser, which contains photos from Apple Photos, iPhoto, or Aperture, depending on which applications are installed on your system.

NOTE ▸ Apple Photos is available only for OS X Yosemite and later.

To access the photographs required, you'll have to open the apts-pnk-photolibrary.

1. To open the iPhoto application, open your Applications folder and then double-click the iPhoto application file

2. In iPhoto, choose File > Switch to Library.

3. Open the folder APTS Pages Numbers Keynote.

4. Double-click **apts-pnk-photolibrary**.

   iPhoto will quit and restart using the new album, apts-pnk-photolibrary.

   NOTE ▸ To return to your original iPhoto library, choose File > Switch to Library, and in the dialog, double-click your iPhoto library.

5. Press Command-Tab to switch to Numbers.

6 Click the circular button in the lower right of the soccer placeholder image to open the Media Browser.

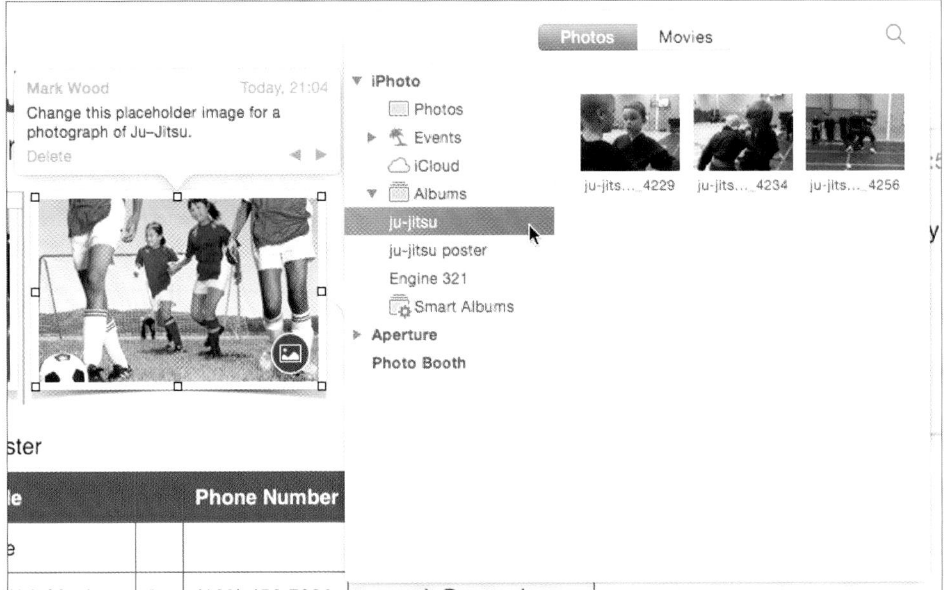

7 In the Photos tab, you can view your iPhoto library. Select the ju-jitsu album.

8 Select a photo to replace the placeholder.

9 Double-click the new photo to open pan and zoom options.

10 Drag the slider to zoom in to the photo.

11 Drag the photo to move it inside its frame.

12 Click Done to close the zoom options.

13 Choose View > Show Adjust Image to open the Adjust Image dialog.

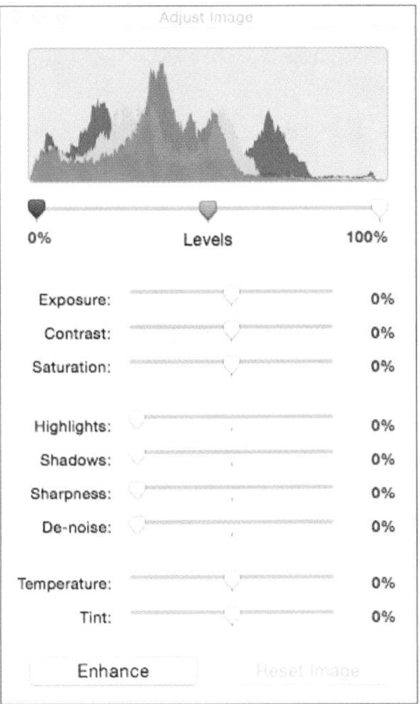

14 With the photo selected, click Enhance to quickly improve the appearance of the image.

TIP For added finesse in image enhancement, you can drag the sliders to alter tone and color.

15 Close the Adjust Image window when you're ready to move on.

Adjusting Layouts

Pages, Numbers, and Keynote can be used to lay out graphics, text, and images and create great designs. Let's explore these features in Keynote.

1 In Keynote, choose File > Open. Locate the folder APTS Pages Numbers Keynote > Lesson_02, and open it.

2 Double-click **ju-jitsu-presentation.key** to open it in Keynote.

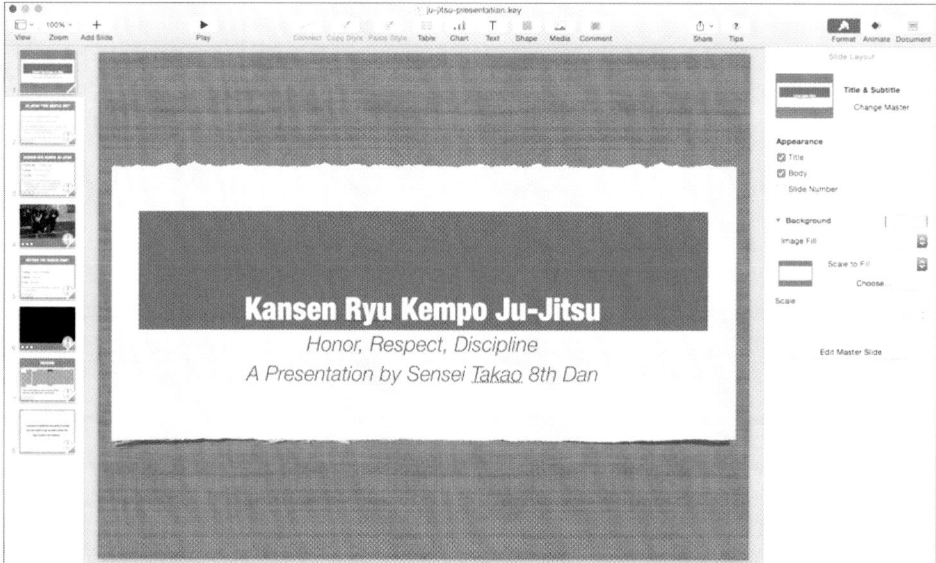

3 Check the View menu to make sure that Navigator is chosen.

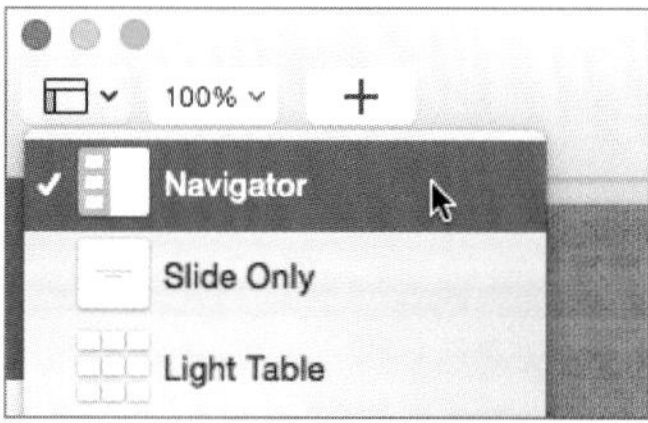

4 In the navigator, click the thumbnail for slide 1.

You're going to add a logo to this slide.

5 Choose Insert > Choose and navigate to the APTS Pages Numbers Keynote > Lesson_02 folder.

6 Double-click the file **ju-jitsu-club-logo.ai** to insert it.

The logo looks OK, but the green background is distracting. Let's remove it.

7 With the logo selected, in the Format inspector, click the Image tab.

8 Click the Instant Alpha button.

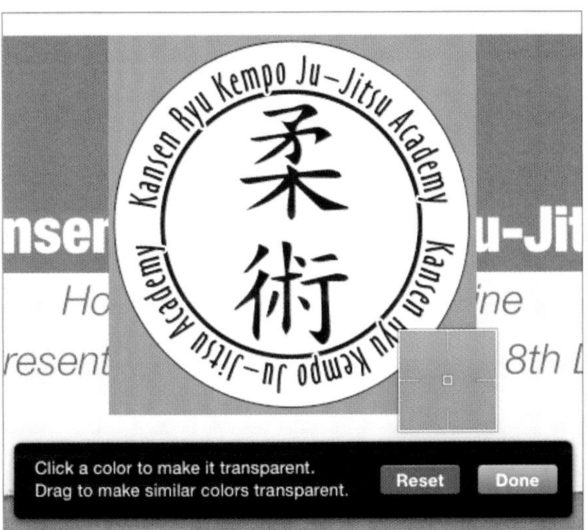

A dialog appears under the logo to indicate that if you click a color it will become transparent.

9 Click the green background of the logo. Then click Done to close the Instant Alpha window.

The logo background is now transparent, and you can move it into place.

TIP To make the logo look more authentic, in the Format inspector's Style tab, drag the Opacity slider to 95%.

10 Drag the logo upward, and position it above the words, "Kansen Ryu Kempo Ju-Jitsu."

TIP You can scale the logo by dragging the edges of the selection.

11 Choose Arrange > Lock to prevent the logo from being moved accidentally.

Under the logo are the words "Kansen Ryu Kempo Ju-Jitsu."

12 Rapidly click the word "Kansen" three times. Three clicks will select entire paragraphs, while double-clicking selects a single word.

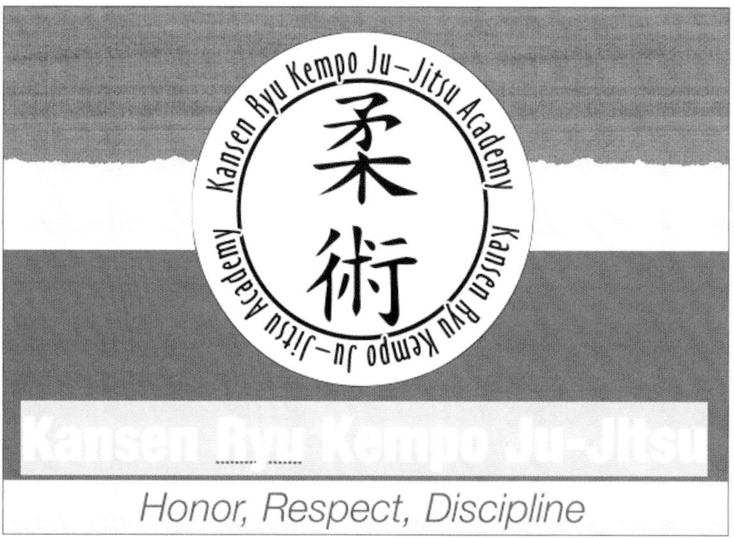

13 Hold down the Command key and press the Plus or Minus keys to make the text larger or smaller.

14 In the navigator, click the thumbnail for slide 7.

The brown rectangles are misaligned. You can use the Align and Distribute controls to fix this.

15 Carefully Shift-click each of the brown rectangles to select them.

16 Choose Arrange > Align Objects > Top.

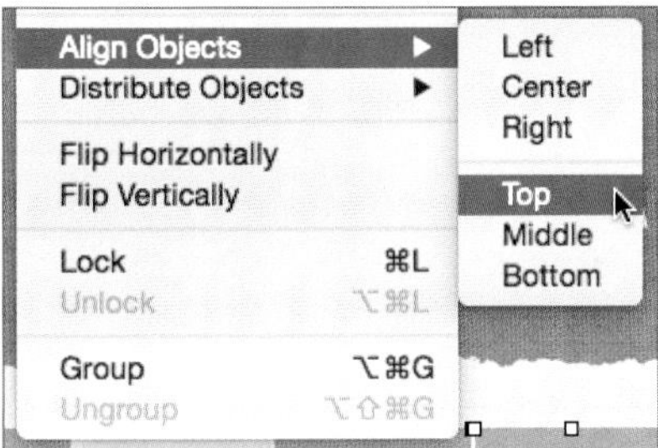

The rectangles line up nicely. Now let's sort out the spacing.

17 Choose Arrange > Distribute Objects > Horizontally to even out the spacing.

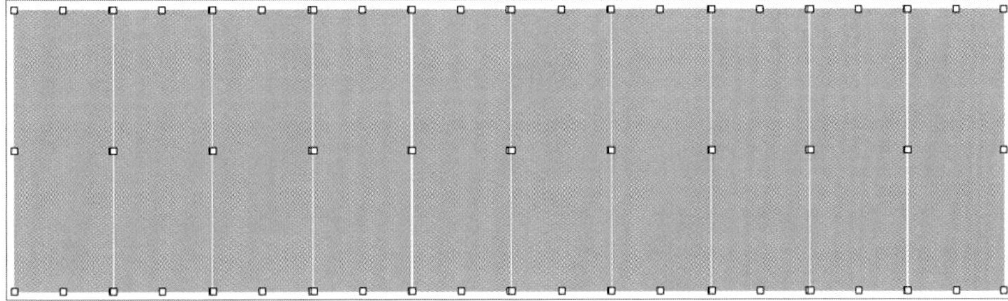

Trimming a Movie Clip

Pages, Numbers, and Keynote all support rich media, such as movies and audio. The Ju-Jitsu presentation has two videos: one on slide 4 and a second on slide 6.

In slide 4, you can see a frame from the movie, but slide 6 just displays a big black rectangle. Let's investigate.

1 Use the navigator in Keynote to jump to slide 6, and click the black rectangle to select it.

   Because this rectangle represents a video clip, the play movie icon appears, and the Format inspector shows a tab labeled Movie.

   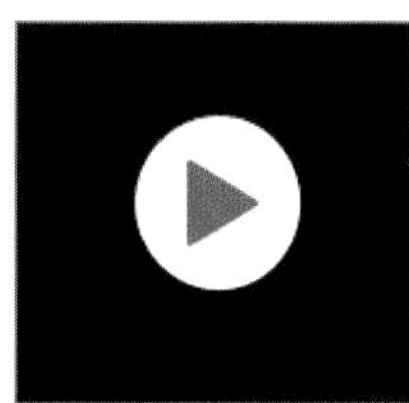

2 In the Movie tab, drag the Poster Frame slider to the right.

   TIP If you can't see the Poster Frame section in the inspector, click the disclosure triangle next to Edit Movie.

   As you drag, frames from the video appear. Notice that whichever frame you choose becomes the poster image for the movie.

   Now let's trim a few seconds off the end of the movie.

3 Set the end frame to approximately 24 seconds by dragging the end frame slider to the left.

   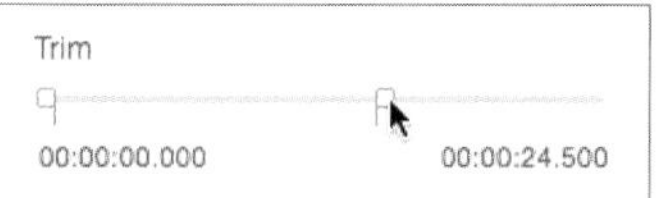

TIP To prevent a movie from playing automatically, select the "Start movie on click" checkbox at the bottom of the Movie inspector.

4 Click the Movie tab controls to play, fast forward, and rewind the video.

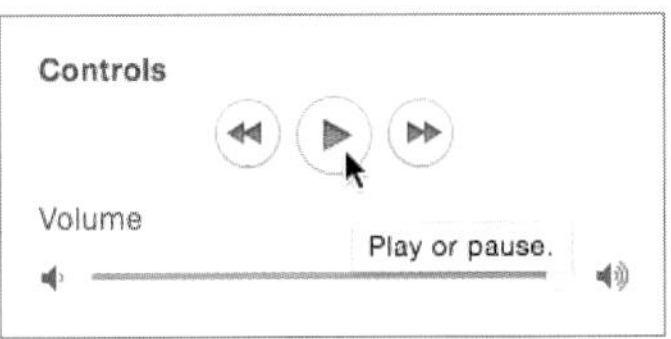

5 To view the entire presentation, navigate to slide 1, and in the toolbar, click Play.

6 Press Esc to exit the slideshow.

You'll learn more about Keynote in Lessons 12 to 15.

Securing Your Files

You may want to lock your files to prevent other people from viewing your work. Pages, Numbers, and Keynote share the same control for setting document passwords.

1 Choose File > Set Password.

2 Type a password (and verify it) and a password hint in the appropriate data fields.

NOTE ▶ In this lesson there is no need to have Keychain remember the password.

Require a password to open this presentation:

Password:

Verify:

Password Hint:
(Recommended)

Remember this password in my keychain

Cancel Set Password

3 Click Set Password.

4 To remove a password, choose File > Change Password.

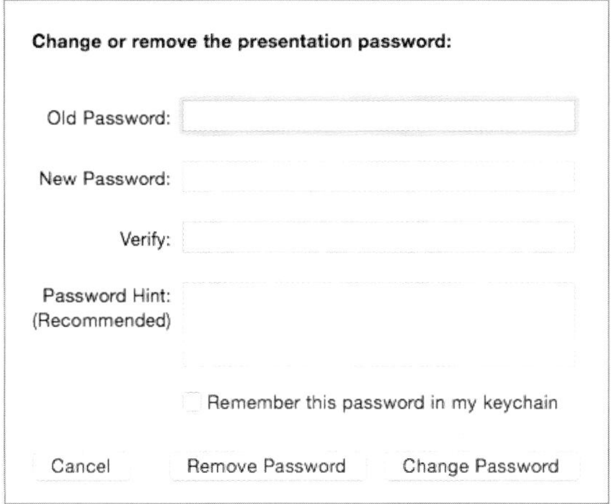

5 Enter the current password in the Old Password data field, and then click Remove Password.

6 To change a password, choose File > Change Password.

7 Enter the current password in the Old Password field, then enter a new password in the New Password field and reenter it in the Verify field; add a password hint if you wish.

8 Click Change Password to accept the changes.

Lesson Review

1. How do you choose a template?
2. How can images found in the Media Browser can be placed in Pages, Numbers, and Keynote?
3. True or false? Tables in Keynote can contain functions.
4. Although Pages, Numbers, and Keynote save your work automatically, why would you want to manually save Versions of your work?
5. What kinds of shadow can be applied to an object in Numbers?

Answers

1. By choosing File > New in either Pages, Numbers, or Keynote, templates (or themes, as they are called in Keynote) are presented. By default, the Template Chooser displays all the currently installed templates and themes. Double-clicking one of these will select it. However, the application preferences can be set to always open a document created from a specific template.
2. Images can be dragged from the Media Browser onto a document. To replace a placeholder image, click the placeholder icon on the image, and select a replacement image from the Media Browser.
3. Table cells in Pages, Numbers, and Keynote can all contain functions.
4. Manually saving your work creates Versions that you can revert to at any time, enabling you to restore a previous state of your document, spreadsheet, or presentation.
5. Drop, Contact, and Curved are the types of shadow that can be applied in all three applications.

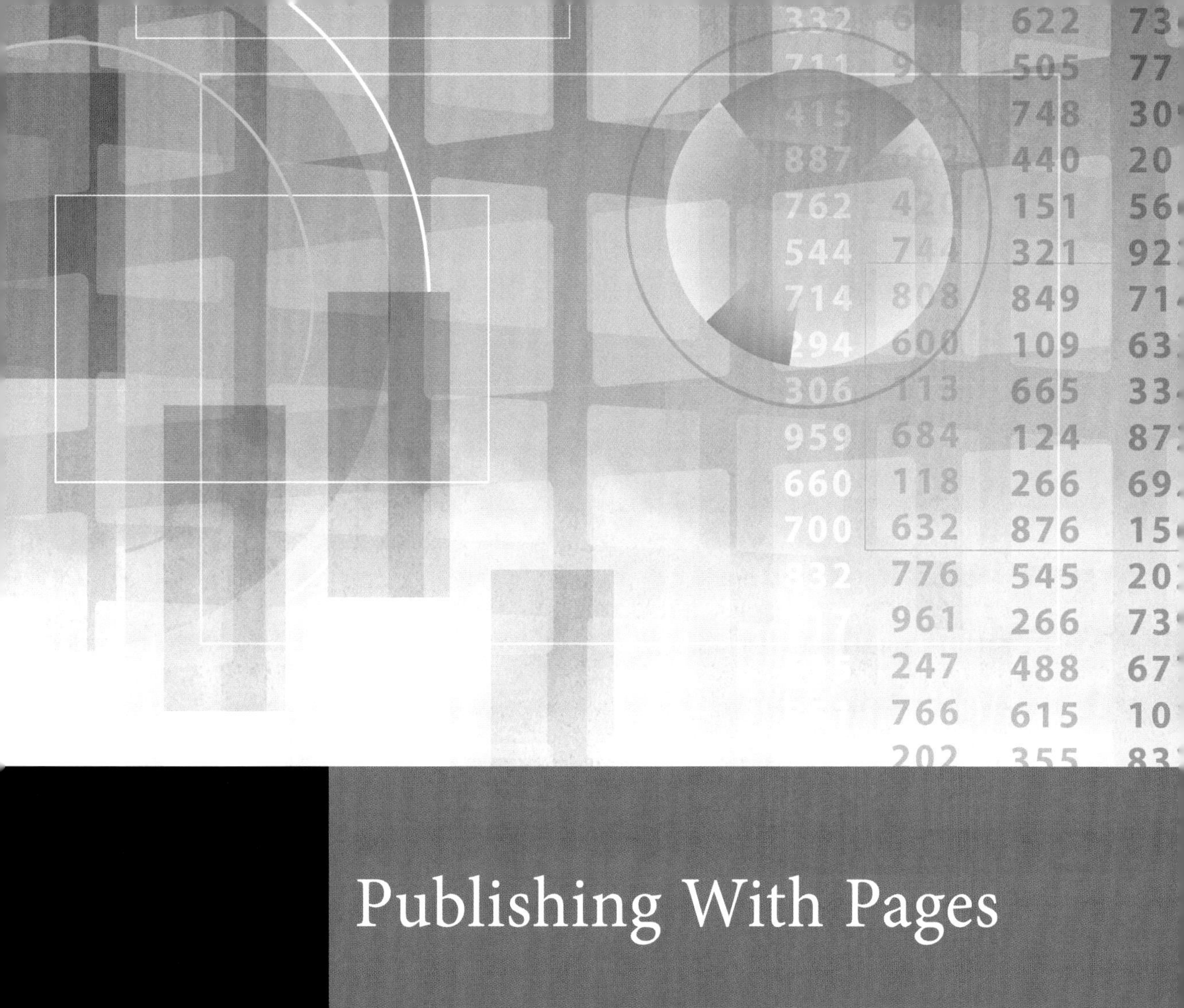

Publishing With Pages

3

Lesson Files

APTS Pages Numbers Keynote > Lesson_03 > report.pages

APTS Pages Numbers Keynote > Lesson_03 > contents.pages

APTS Pages Numbers Keynote > Lesson_03 > header.pages

APTS Pages Numbers Keynote > Lesson_03 > rafiq.doc

APTS Pages Numbers Keynote > Lesson_03 > sl-logo.pdf

Time

This lesson takes approximately 60 minutes to complete.

Goals

Create and open a document

Align text and images

Manage text formatting styles

Create a table of contents

Manage headers and footers

Save and manage documents

Lesson 3

Approaches to Word Processing

Pages makes word processing easy, providing an uncluttered interface in which you can start writing quickly. This lesson explores the importance of style sheets, sectioned documents, and a broad range of available options to structure your thoughts in words and streamline your workflow.

The focus here is on word processing, rather than using Pages as a page layout tool. In word processing mode, Pages conveniently adds new pages to the body of a document as you type.

In this lesson, you will work with long documents and explore options to manage their formatting in ways that keep you productive and frown free.

Creating a New Document Using a Template

In this exercise you're going to set up an engineering report for a fictitious character called Sophia Larkinson. You'll start by creating a new document using a template.

1 Choose File > New, and in the Choose a Template window, select Reports. Double-click the Project Proposal template to open it.

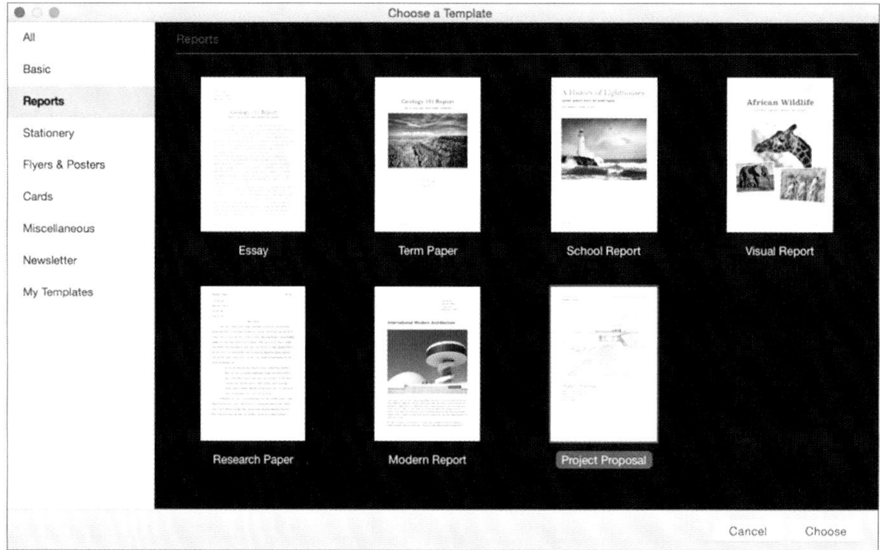

This is an ideal template; let's see what is included.

2 In the toolbar, click the View icon, and choose Show Page Thumbnails.

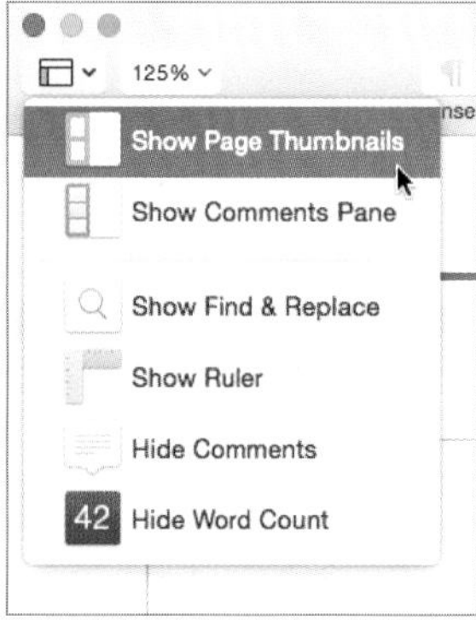

The template has three pages.

3 Click each page thumbnail to jump to its corresponding page.

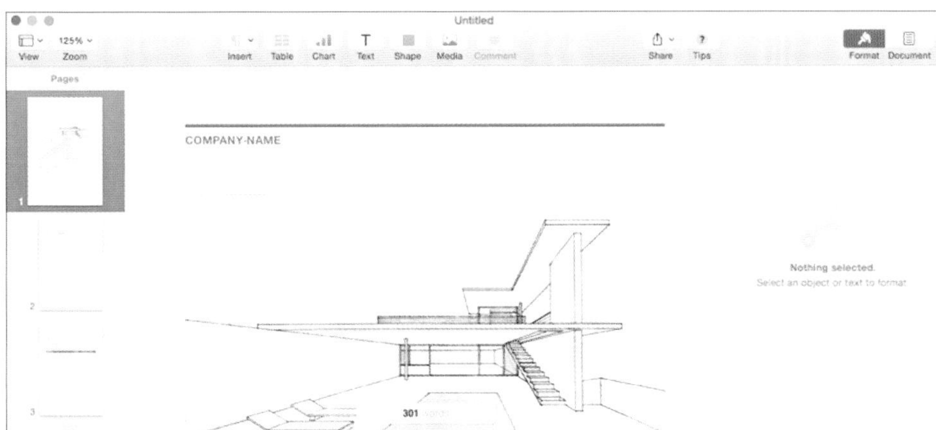

Page 1 is a cover page, page 2 is an executive summary, and page 3 is a budget with a table. Let's modify the template design to suit the project.

4 Save your document. At the top of the document window, click the word "untitled." Change the title to *sl-report*, and save it to the desktop. Leave the sl-report document open.

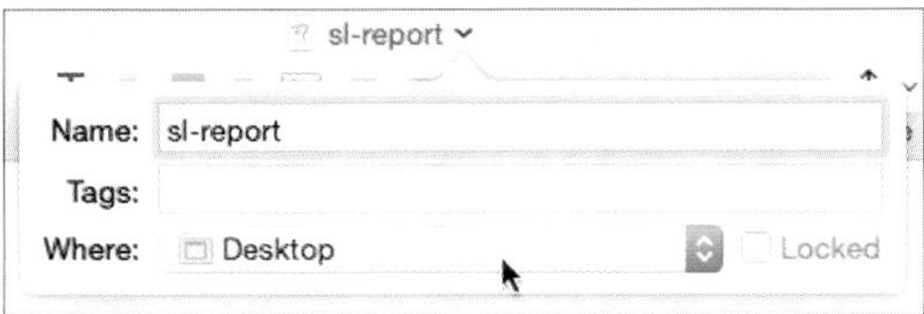

Customizing Page Design

Templates give you a head start on a project, but the documents you create from templates often need some customizing. To do this, you will add a logo and color scheme to your report design, as you begin to use style sheets.

1 Return to page 1 by clicking the page thumbnail or scrolling to the page in the main document window.

2 At the top of page 1, click the blue line to select it. Press Delete.

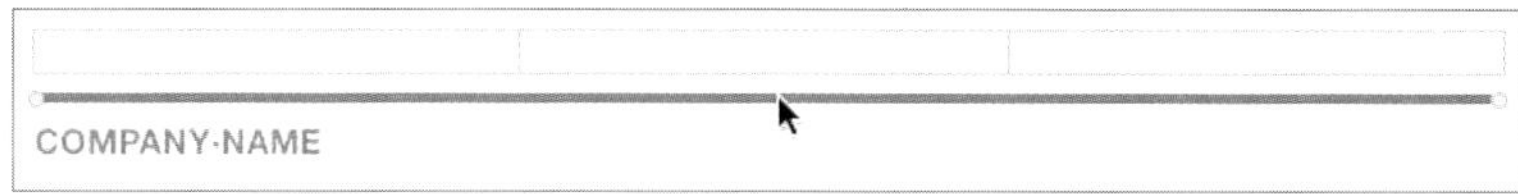

3 At the top of page 1, click the words “COMPANY NAME” to select the text field. Press Delete.

You’ll now add a logo in the space you created.

4 Click a blank part of the document page to make sure nothing is selected.

5 Choose Insert > Choose and navigate to APTS Pages Numbers Keynote > Lesson_03 > sl-logo.pdf.

Sophia’s logo appears on the page. It’s a vector graphic so it can be made bigger or smaller without altering its sharpness.

6 Drag the logo to position it at the top of the page. The yellow guides that appear help you center the logo.

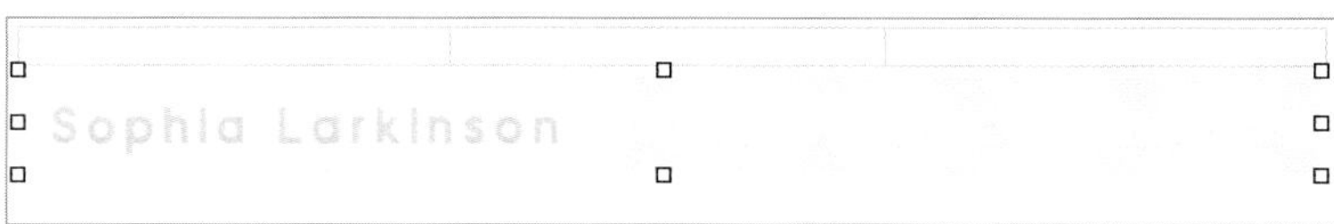

7 Scale the logo by dragging the selection handles.

NOTE ▶ The Constrain Proportions option—found in the Arrange tab of the Format inspector—is selected by default for placed images such as photos or logos. Having this option selected retains the image proportions and prevents images from being stretched out.

8 With the logo selected, choose Arrange > Section Masters > Move Object to Section Master. In the same menu, deselect Make Master Objects Selectable.

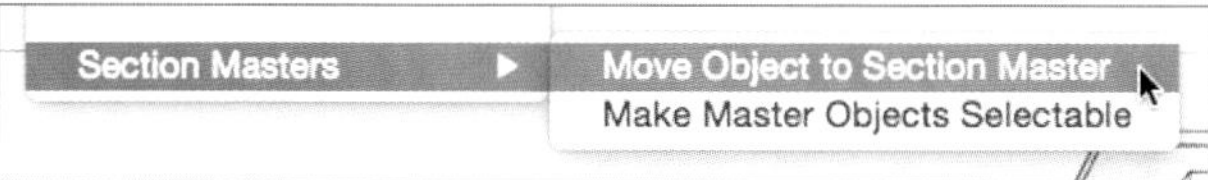

Objects moved to a section master appear on every page built using that master. Sophia's logo will now appear on every page of this section. Deselecting "Make Master Objects Selectable" prevents the logo from accidentally being moved.

9 Go to page 2. Delete the words "COMPANY NAME" that obscure Sophia's logo.

Page 2 is looking good, but the four headings should be green. Let's fix that.

10 Select the heading "Objective." The style selected is called Heading 2.

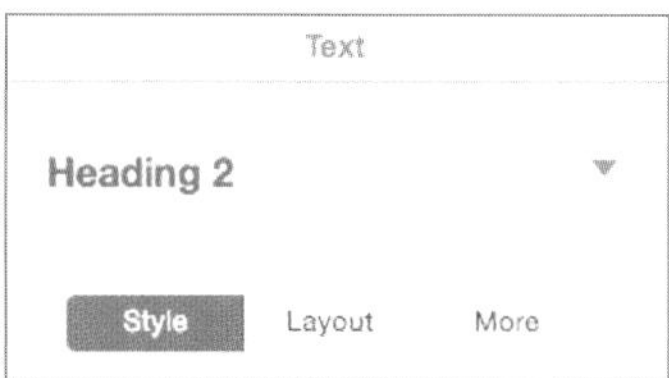

The Format inspector displays the style attributes. Make sure you are on the Style tab.

11 Open the Colors window by clicking the multicolored ball, not the color swatch next to it.

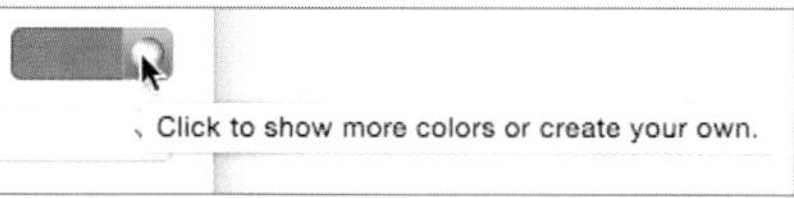

You'll see a small eyedropper icon in the lower part of the Colors window. You are going to use it to choose a new color for Heading 2, but first let's zoom in a bit.

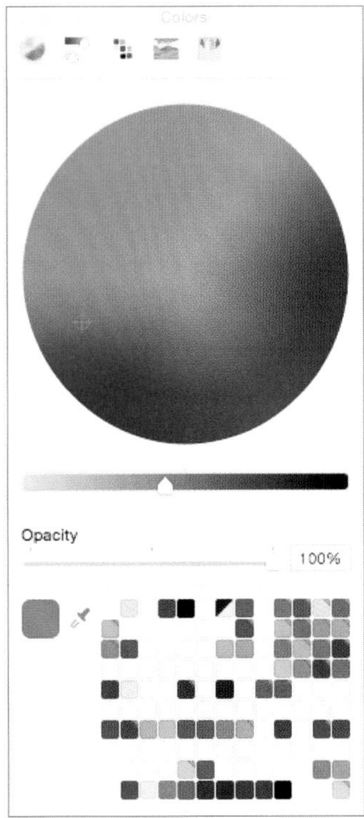

12 In the toolbar, set the Zoom menu to 400%. Scroll your document so that the word "Sophia" in the logo is clearly visible.

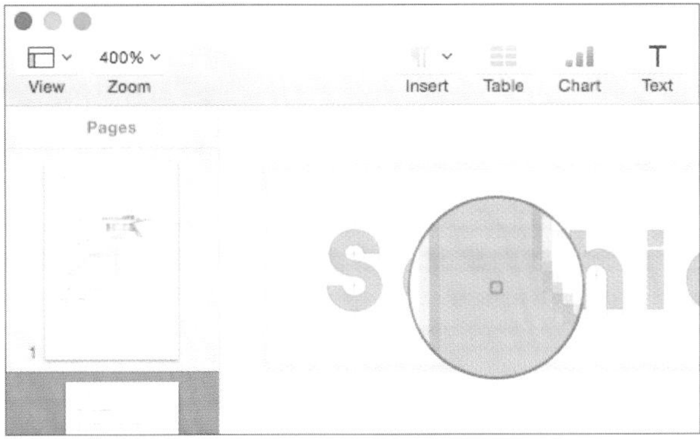

13 In the Colors window, click the eyedropper and carefully move the magnify pointer over the green lettering in the logo and click. Doing so samples the green color.

Look in the Format inspector. The label for Heading 2 now has an asterisk next to it. This is how a style sheet lets you know that changes were made to a style.

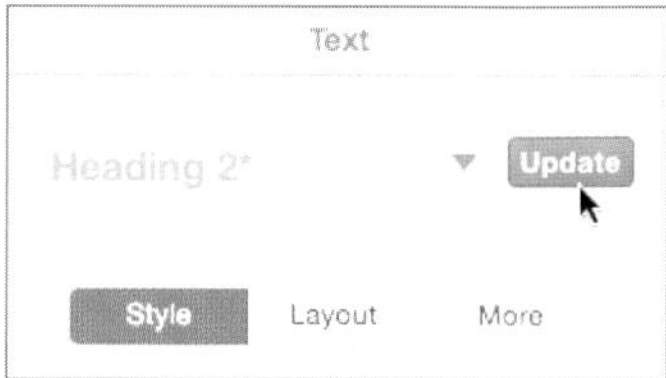

14 Click Update.

All instances of the Heading 2 style are updated. Imagine a 10,000-word report with hundreds of instances of heading styles. Rather than having to find each heading and change it by hand, you now know a better, faster way to do this.

15 Choose View > Zoom > Fit Page to see the style change on the entire page.

Style sheets have a lot more to discover, but this is a great demonstration of their productivity-boosting superpower.

16 Choose File > Close.

Creating and Applying Styles

Structuring a long document often involves developing a hierarchy of headings, starting with a title, followed by sections, chapters, subsections, and so on. The choice of structure may be entirely in your hands, or you may be following a set of rules established by others. The way to implement a solid structure is to use styles consistently.

1 Open APTS Pages Numbers Keynote > Lesson_03 > **report.pages**.

This document has developed the engineering report a little further. Take a moment to skim through the pages to see the change. The document contains lots of text and headings, but you have more work to do.

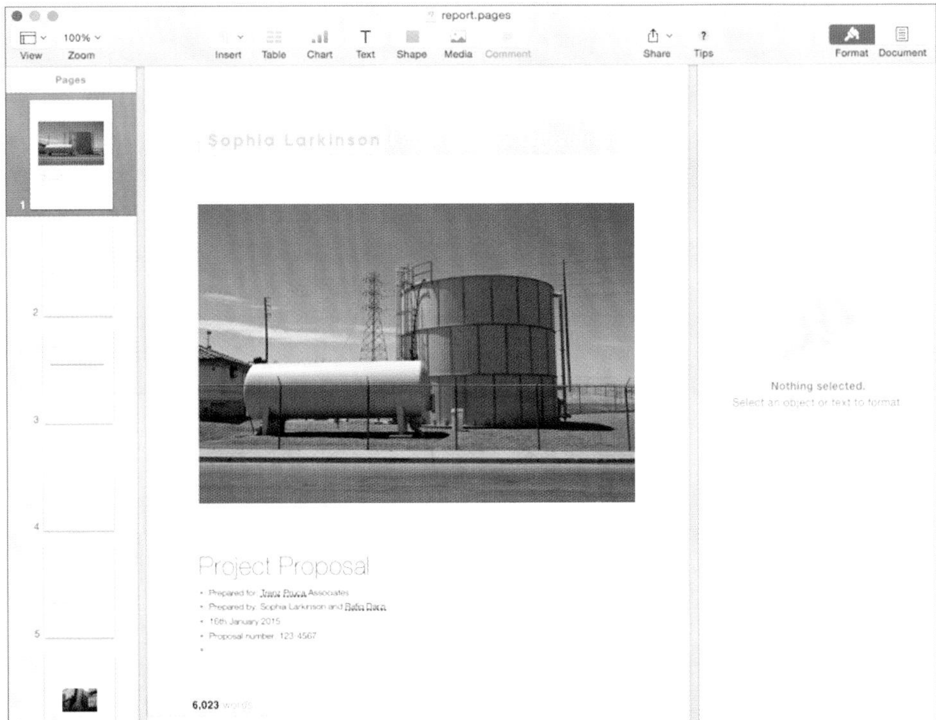

2 Click the page thumbnails to jump to page 2. Press Command-0 to zoom the document to actual size.

NOTE ▶ The magnification value of actual size will depend on the resolution of your display.

At the top of the page you'll find a heading called "Executive Summary." Farther down the page is another larger heading, "Project Outline." They are both Heading styles.

NOTE ▶ Setting a style is sometimes called *style tagging*. Style sheets are found in a vast range of applications, and the terminology used can vary by application.

This is a good time to mention that we are dealing with paragraph styles. There are character, list, and object styles, too. To help illustrate this, we'll reveal the invisibles.

3 Choose View > Show Invisibles.

Every keystroke appears. In addition to all the letters and punctuation marks, lots of little blue characters are also visible.

Between each word is a blue dot that represents a space. The symbol that looks like a backward P is a return. In word processing and typesetting, any sequence of characters followed by a carriage return is considered a paragraph.

Budget¶

Initial·Estimates¶

Rafiq·Darzi·will·confirm·the·figures,·before·we·commence·stage·one.·Sociis·mauris·in·integer,·a·dolor·netus·non·dui·aliquet,·sagittis·felis·sodales,·dolor·sociis·mauris,·vel·eu·libero·cras.·Faucibus·at.·Arcu·habitasse·elementum·est,·ipsum·purus·pede·porttitor·class,·ut·adipiscing,·aliquet·sed·auctor,·imperdiet·arcu·per·diam·dapibus·libero·duis.·Enim·eros·in·vel,·volutpat·nec·pellentesque·leo,·temporibus·nec.¶

In this figure, the first line with just a single word is a paragraph, and so is the subheading, and so is the first block of text that we'd normally consider a paragraph.

NOTE ► Paragraph styles apply themselves to whole paragraphs. Character styles can be applied to a word or word within a paragraph.

4 Triple-click the "Project Outline" heading.

In the Format inspector, you'll see this has been styled as a Heading.

5 In the Format inspector, change the attributes of Heading to:

- ▶ Font Family—Helvetica Neue
- ▶ Typeface—Thin
- ▶ Font Size—21pt
- ▶ Alignment—Centered

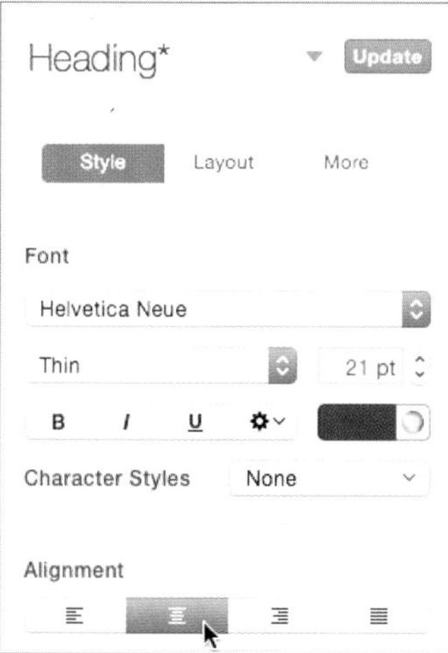

An asterisk appears next to the Heading style label.

6 Click the Update button.

7 Look through the document to verify that the Heading styles have been updated, except those on page 5. That's because the Heading style has not been applied on that page.

8 Navigate to page 5. Click anywhere in the words "Stage Two Proposal."

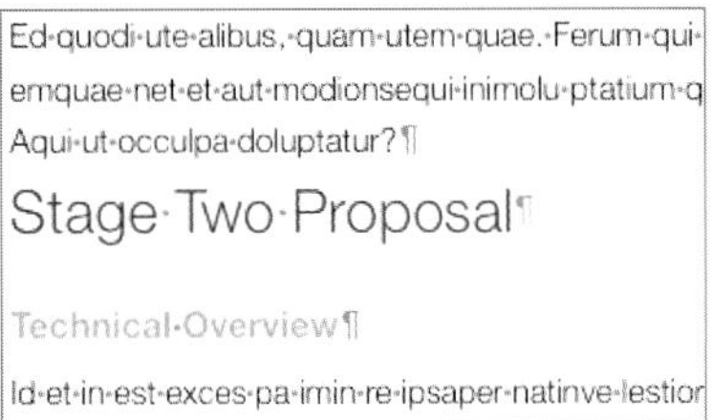

These words were tagged with the Body style and modified to look like a heading. You need to apply the Heading style.

9 In the Format inspector, from the Paragraph Styles menu, choose Heading.

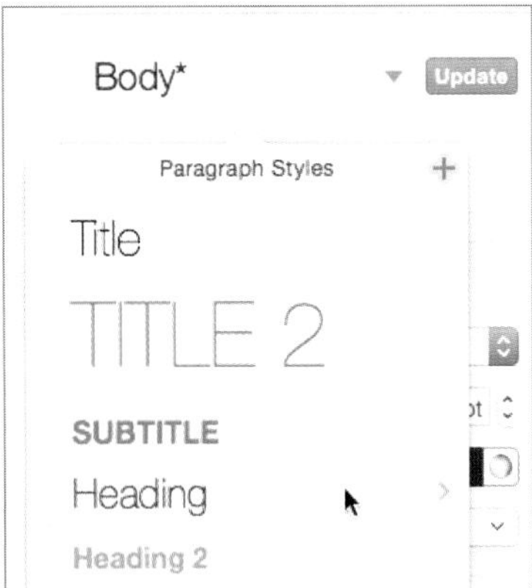

NOTE ▸ Just because something looks like it's been styled doesn't always mean that a style sheet was applied. You can publish Pages documents in a variety of formats, including EPUB. EPUBs rely on style sheets to create their structures.

Saving Styles for Bullets and Lists

Sometimes you are given style guidelines that dictate how to format bullets and lists. Pages has several formats to choose from, whether you are following guidelines set by others or creating your own.

Page 2 has a bullet list on it. It's OK as it is, but let's make it clearer and create a new style sheet for the list.

1 On Page 2 of **report.pages**, drag to select all the bulleted text.

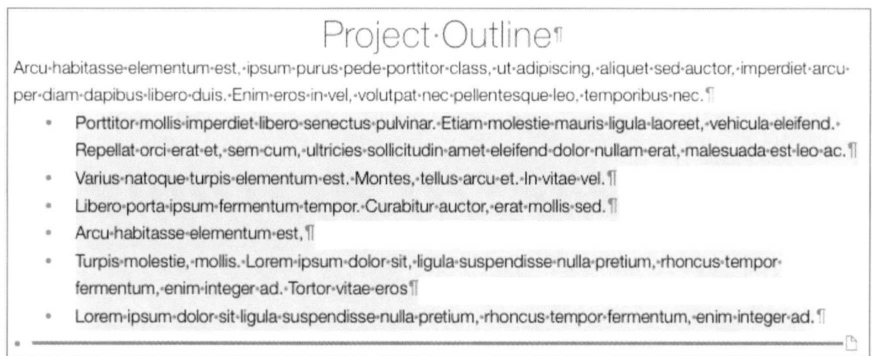

The Format inspector shows the current attributes of the bullet list. You can change some of these values to create a better-looking list.

2 Set the Spacing attributes to:

- Before Paragraph—6 pt
- After Paragraph—3 pt
- Spacing—1.3 (adjusts the line spacing; historically referred to as *leading*)

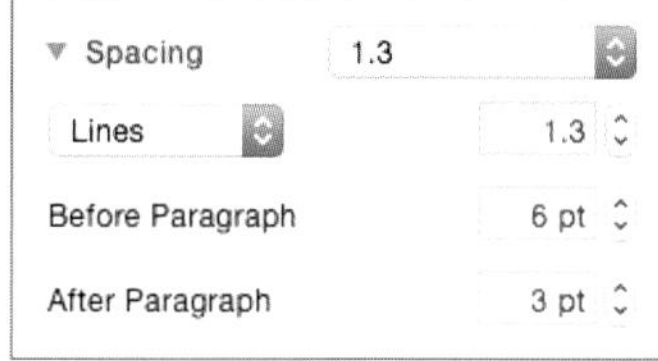

Adding space before and after each of the bullets helps separate them visually. The bullet points with two lines now stand out.

3 In Bullets & Lists, change the pop-up menu under the label from Text Bullets to Numbers. Set the following:

- Indent—Set Number to 0.25 in, and Text to 0.25 in.
- Change the number format to lowercase roman numerals.

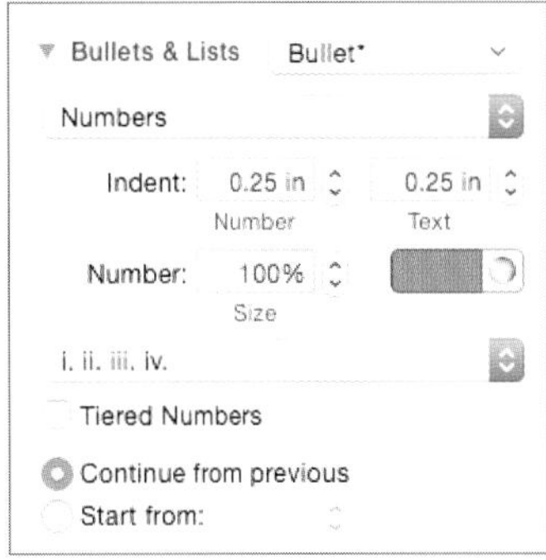

The Bullet style now has an asterisk next to it.

4 In Bullets & Lists, click the List Styles pop-up menu, currently labeled Bullet*.

5 From the List Styles pop-up menu, click the Add (+) button to create a new list style based on the bullet options set in the current selection.

6 Name the list *Roman Bullet*.

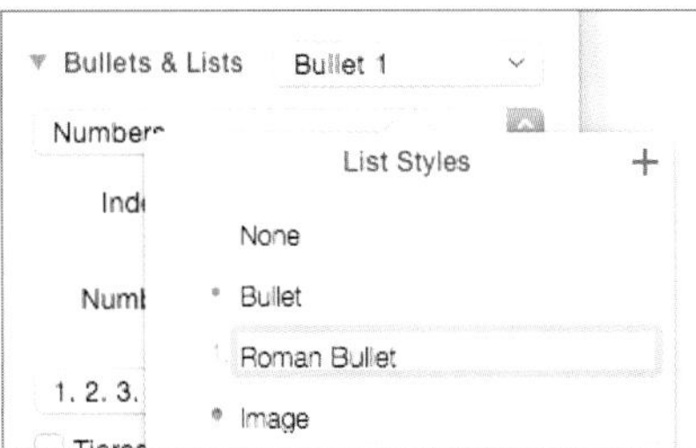

NOTE ▶ You can use several different methods to create and apply styles; though other methods work, the methods described here suit most purposes.

7 Choose File > Close.

Making a Table of Contents

When a document runs to dozens of pages, creating a table of contents is a great idea but hardly a new one. In this exercise, you will use style sheets to quickly create a table of contents.

1 Open APTS Pages Numbers Keynote > Lesson_03 > **contents.pages**.

   You'll continue to work on Sophie's engineering report. In this version, all the styles have been applied. You can verify this by clicking each of the text elements to see which paragraph style is applied.

2 Move to page 1. Click immediately beneath the proposal number text, "Proposal number: 123-4567." Choose Edit > Insert > Section Break.

   This step splits the document, putting the cover and content pages into their own sections. Sections can be used to split a long document into chapters.

3 Click in the middle of page 2, and choose Insert > Table of Contents > Section.

   Doing so builds a table of contents based on the following sections, excluding the cover page.

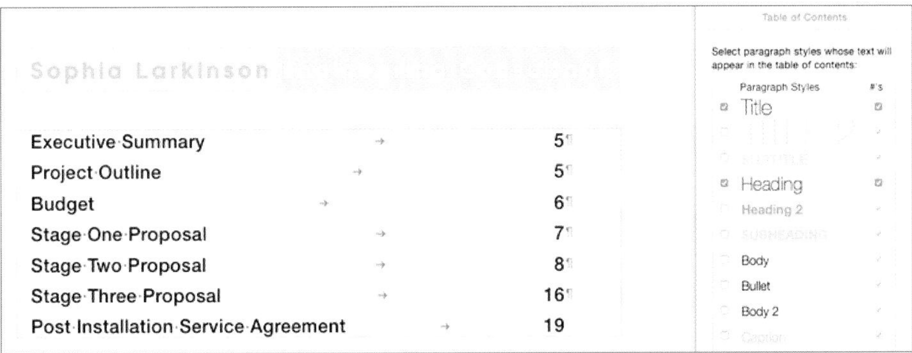

   A table of contents is added to page 2. You'll build it using Title and Heading styles. Let's also add Heading 2 items.

4 Select the checkbox to the left of Heading 2 to add the style to the contents table.

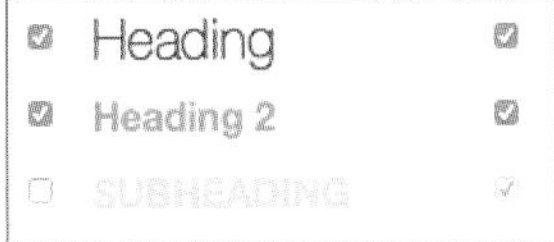

5 To the right of Heading 2 is another checkbox. Try selecting and deselecting this box, you'll see that it adds a page number to the table of contents. Let's select that checkbox.

You now have a table of contents, but it needs some formatting.

6 In the first line of the table of contents, click anywhere on the line containing the words "Executive Summary."

All instances of the heading are selected in the table.

7 In the Format inspector, click the Text tab to move to it.

8 Let's change the type attributes to make the text look better. Try these settings:

- Font Family—Helvetica Neue
- Typeface—Thin
- Font Size—18 pt
- Spacing—1.0 Single
- Before Paragraph—18 pt
- After Paragraph—10 pt

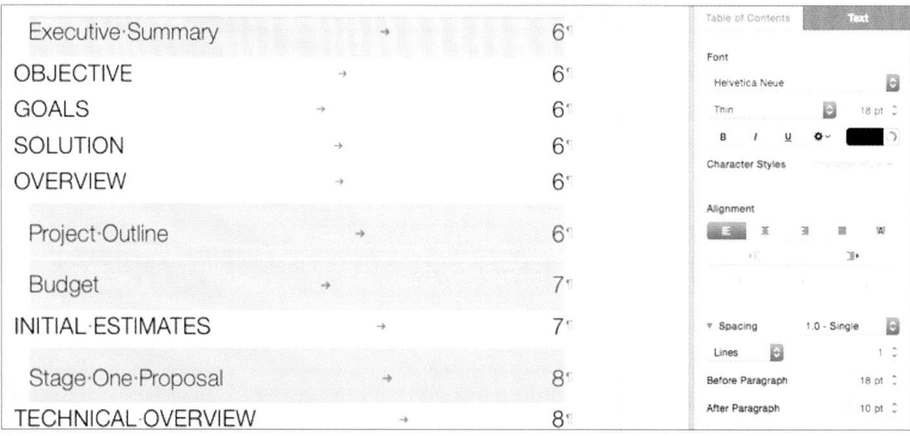

TIP White space is your friend in page design. Thoughtful use of the spaces between letters and paragraphs makes documents easier to read.

At the bottom of the Text inspector you'll set some leader dots.

9 In Tabs, change the Leader setting from None to the series of dots.

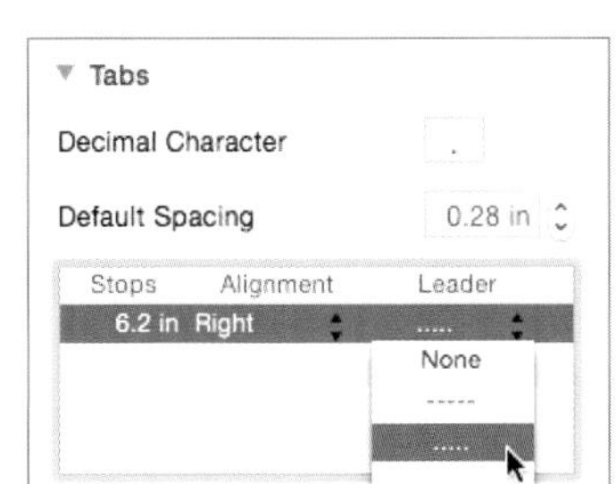

The leaders help lead the eye from the content item to its page number.

10 In the second line of the table of contents, click anywhere on the line containing the word "Objective."

All instances of heading 2 are selected.

11 Change the type attributes. Try these settings:

- Font Family—Helvetica Neue
- Typeface—Light
- Font Size—12 pt
- Spacing—1.0 Single
- Before Paragraph—12 pt
- After Paragraph—6 pt
- Set the Leader to dots.

Some additional formatting is required to inset these secondary headers.

12 In the Text inspector set the Indents to:

- First—0.5 in
- Left—0 in
- Right—0 in

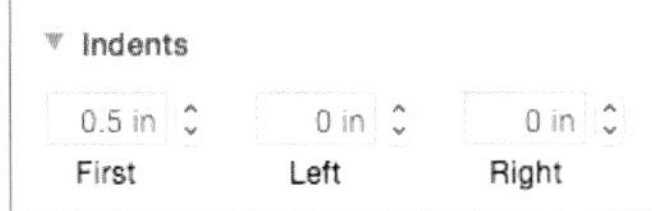

This formatting makes a much stronger looking table of contents. Better still, when you add or remove words in your document that cause the headings to move to different pages, the numbers on the table of contents will automatically update!

13 Close the **contents.pages** document.

Managing Headers and Footers

Headers and footers are found, as the names suggest, at the top and bottom of a document page. In Pages, many templates include these elements.

You are going to use headers and footers to add page numbers, page count, and dates to a document.

1 Open APTS Pages Numbers Keynote > Lesson_03 > **header.pages**.

   You will recognize the engineering report you've been working on.

2 Navigate to the contents on page 2.

3 In the Executive Summary content item, position the pointer over the page number.

   The pointer changes to a pointing hand icon because in Pages the table of contents has hyperlinks in it.

4 Click the number 4 to go to page 4.

5 Choose View > Zoom > Fit Page to display the whole page.

6 Move the pointer to the top of the screen above the Sophia Larkinson logo. Three conjoined boxes appear; this is the header.

7 Move the pointer to the bottom of the page. The three boxes that appear indicate the footer. Click the middle box of the footer to open a pop-up menu. Click Insert Page Number, and from the pop-up menu, choose a numbering format.

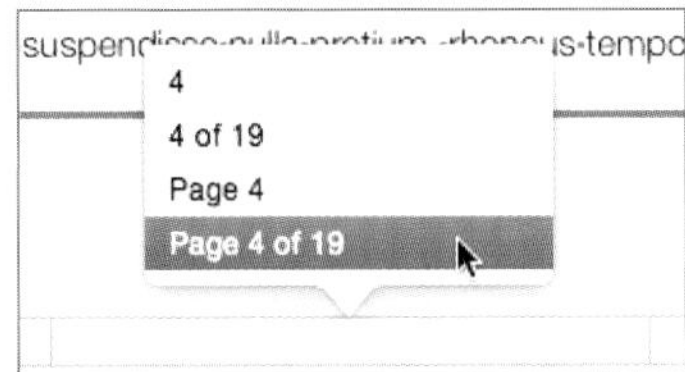

TIP When creating legal documents, best practice is to choose a page number format option that includes the total number of pages, such as Page 1 of 80.

8 Click in the leftmost footer box, and type *Prepared by SL*. Press the Spacebar.

9 Choose Insert > Date and Time to automatically set the current date and time.

10 Click the date and time you just added to the footer. In the menu that appears, you can choose the date format, or set a different date for the document.

11 To set a different date, in the lower right of the menu, click the calendar icon. The menu expands to a navigable calendar, in which you can choose a new date and time.

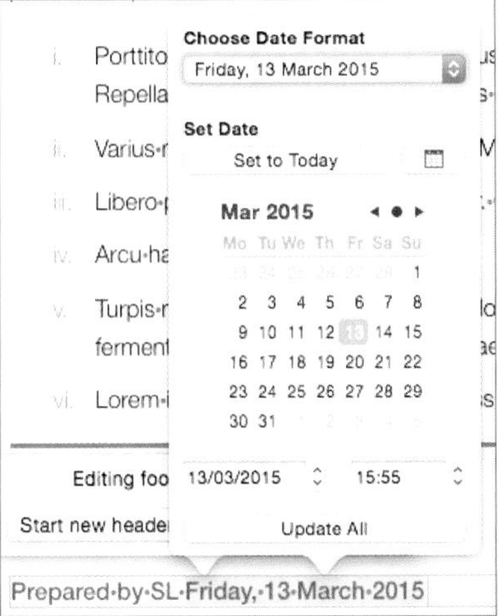

NOTE ▸ Changing the date and time here will not affect the time stamp on the Pages document, as this is set by your computer's clock.

12 Leave the **header.pages** document open.

Changing the Page Order

In a word processing document such as this one, you can use sections to divide a document into chapters, and then use page thumbnails to reorder the sections. Later, you'll learn how to rearrange pages in a page layout document.

The **header.pages** document should be open. It already has one section, and you're now going to add a few more.

1 Go to page 4. Click to the left of the heading, Executive Summary. Choose Insert > Section Break.

  You've started to divide the document. You'll now divide or section the report again.

2 Go to page 7. Click to the left of the Stage One heading. Choose Insert > Section Break.

3 In the toolbar, click the View icon and choose Show Page Thumbnails (if they are not already visible). Click the thumbnail for page 1.

  The thumbnail is highlighted, and a yellow box encloses the selection. Pages 2 to 4 are also a section.

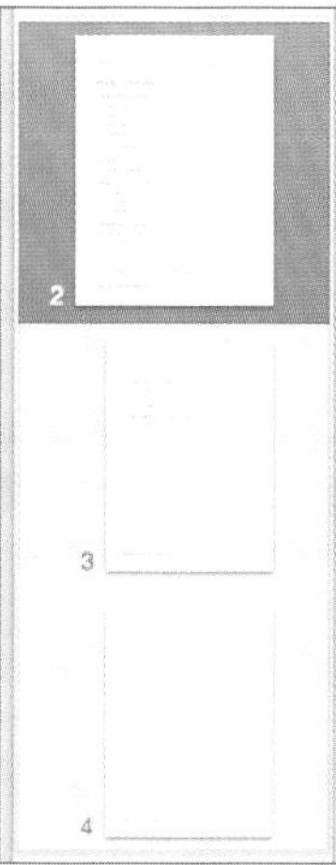

4 Click the thumbnail for page 5. Again, it is selected but now the yellow box extends to page 7. This marks the third section of this document.

Let's move this section to the end of the document.

5 Click anywhere inside the yellow box, and drag the section to the bottom of the page thumbnail window.

NOTE ▶ The page numbering and the table of contents will automatically update.

Tables of contents in Pages are built using one of the following criteria: Entire Document, This Section, or Until the Next Table of Contents.

6 Go to page 1. This is a cover page that doesn't need a page number in the footer. In the footer, select the page numbering. Press Delete to remove it.

Because the cover page is in its own section, edits made to its header or footer will affect only the cover page section.

TIP Creating sections allows you to associate that section with new headers and footers, page numbers, or page background.

You have access to a few more options for controlling page numbers when using sections.

7 In the toolbar, click the Document icon, and then click the Section tab.

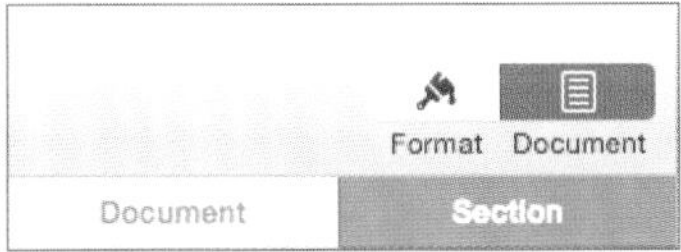

In the Section inspector, you can hide the headers and footers on the first page of a section, a useful option when dealing with cover pages. You've already removed the page number from the cover, but normally a cover page isn't labeled as page 1. So let's fix that now.

8 In the footer of page 2, double-click the page numbering. Make sure that all the text is selected, and then choose Insert > Page Number to replace the selected text with a single number.

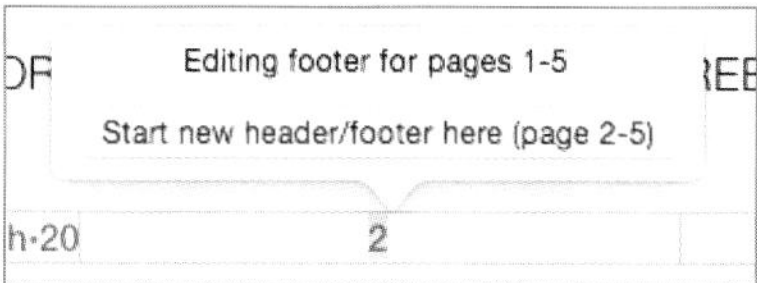

Sometimes prefaces and tables of contents are labeled in Roman numerals rather than Arabic numbers.

9 Go to page 2, the table of contents. In the Section inspector, set the following:

- Format—Roman numerals
- Start at: 1

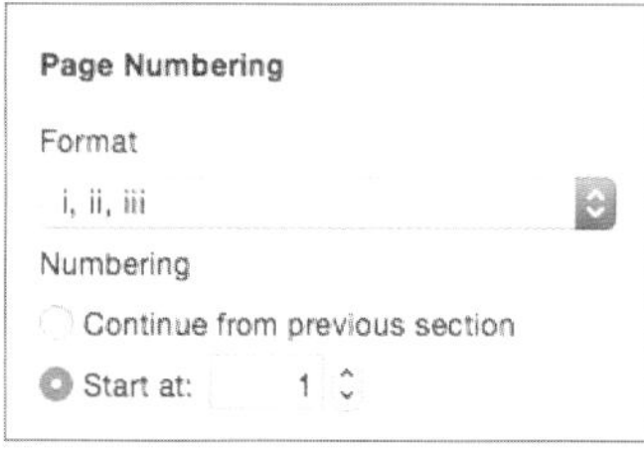

10 Now go to page 5. It's the start of a new section, so it has retained the Arabic numbering you applied earlier.

11 Leave the document open. Remember autosave has been hard at work in the background, but to save a version of your document explicitly, so you can revert to that version later, choose File > Save.

Keeping Headers with the Following Paragraph

You've taken quite a journey through the realm of word processing so far, but there's one other feature that will help keep you stress free.

Generally speaking, headings go in front of (and stay with) the paragraphs that follow it. You wouldn't want a heading at the bottom of one page and the paragraphs it introduces on the next page. Fortunately, you can stop this from happening.

1. In the **header.pages** document, select an instance of the Heading style, such as the words "Stage One Proposal" on page 4.

2. In the toolbar, click Format.

3. In the Text inspector, click the More tab.

   In the More tab, you can control pagination, page breaks, hyphenation rules, and which paragraph style comes next.

4. Set the following:

   - Keep lines on same page.
   - Keep with next paragraph—Doing so will keep the header on the same page as the paragraph that follows it.
   - Start paragraph on a new page—A great way to automatically push chapter titles to a new page.
   - Prevent widow & orphan lines—This prevents the first or last line of a paragraph from appearing on a separate page. Note that it's not strictly necessary for the heading you're currently formatting.
   - Remove paragraph hyphenation—When the last word on a line doesn't fit, selecting this checkbox will force the entire word to the next line, thereby preventing unnecessary hyphenation.

TIP If you want to justify a paragraph—that is, to align both the left and right edges of the text column—do not select "Remove paragraph hyphenation." But, you should attempt to justify a column only when it has more than five words in a line.

5 From the Following Paragraph Style pop-up menu, choose Heading 2.

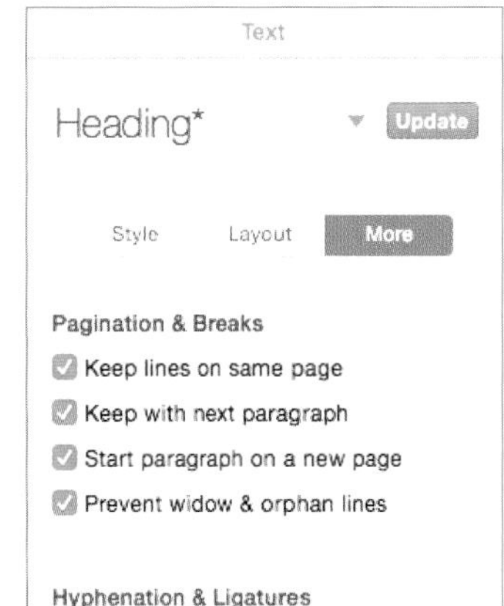

Now when you press Return after adding a heading, the following paragraph will automatically format to Heading 2 style. You'll now add the same kind of automatic formatting to Heading 2.

6 Click an instance of Heading 2 style, such as "Technical Overview" on page 4.

7 In the Text inspector, click Heading 2.

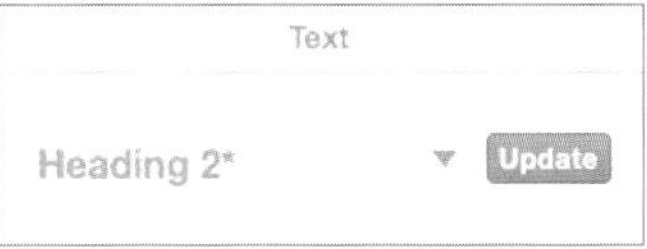

8 In the More tab of the Text inspector, select the following checkboxes:

- Keep lines on same page.
- Keep with next paragraph.
- Prevent widow & orphan lines.
- Remove paragraph hyphenation.

9 From the Following Paragraph Style pop-up menu, choose Body.

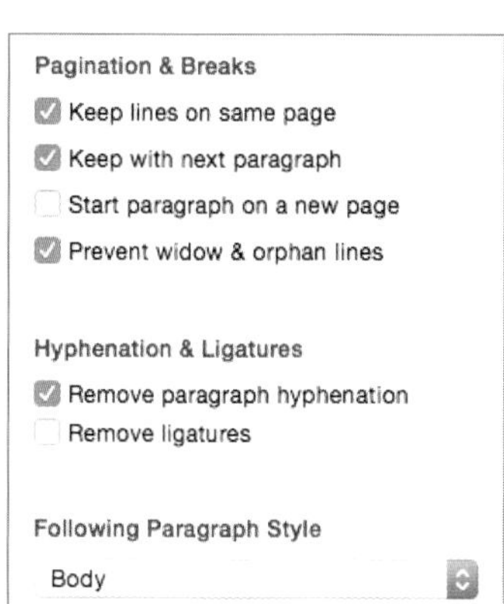

10 Click Update to save and apply the changes you made to the Heading 2 style.

With these options saved, when you press Return after applying the Heading style, the next paragraph will automatically be set to Heading 2. When you press Return after entering a title for Heading 2, the next paragraph will automatically be set to Body style.

Applying Keyboard Shortcuts to Paragraph Styles

Paragraph styles can be applied using keyboard shortcuts. In the Project Proposal you've been working on, you might want to apply these styles regularly. To speed the process, you can set keyboard shortcuts for them.

1 Click an instance of Heading style, such as "Stage One Proposal" on page 4.

2 In the inspector, click the Heading style.

3 In the pop-up menu, click the > symbol next to Heading.

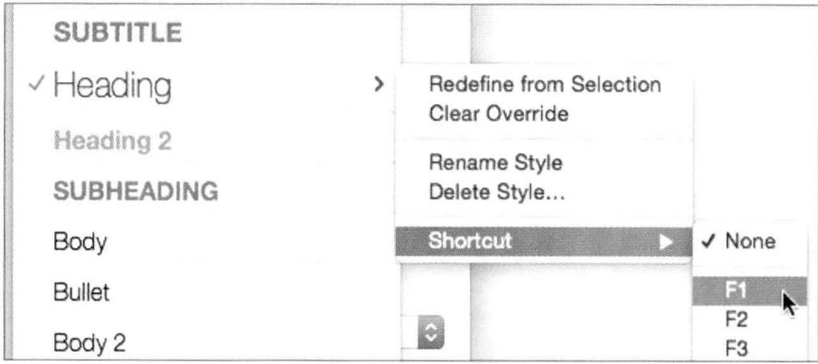

4 In the menu that appears, choose Shortcut.

A submenu of the function keys appears.

5 Choose F1.

Pressing the F1 key will now apply the Heading style to any selected text. Using the preceding steps, the remaining function keys, can be assigned to other paragraph styles.

Saving to Word and PDF Formats

After shaping your thoughts and getting them down in Pages, you need to share your work. To that end, Pages can save to a variety of formats. In this exercise, you'll save your document in Word format, so that colleagues can open your document in Microsoft Word. And you'll also look at Adobe's Portable Document Format (PDF).

1 In the **header.pages** document, choose File > Export To > Word.

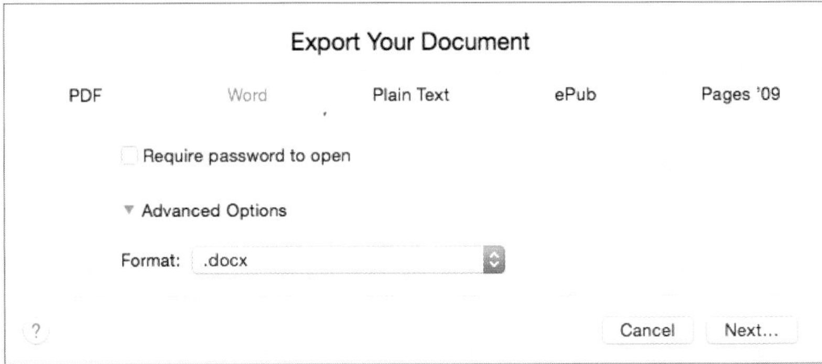

2 The Export Your Document window appears. Click the disclosure triangle next to Advanced Options.

3 In the Format menu, change the setting from .docx to .doc (Word 1997–2004 compatible). This format provides the greatest compatibility with older versions of Word.

Pages does a very good job of translating into Word format, but you may still want to make some changes. Some things are changed or lost in translation.

4 Click Next and save your document to the desktop.

Pages can export a copy of a document to Word, which is great for collaborative working; but when you've painstakingly formatted a document and you want a perfect copy to share with the world, choose PDF to maintain the highest fidelity to your original formatting.

5 In the **header.pages** document, choose File > Export To > PDF.

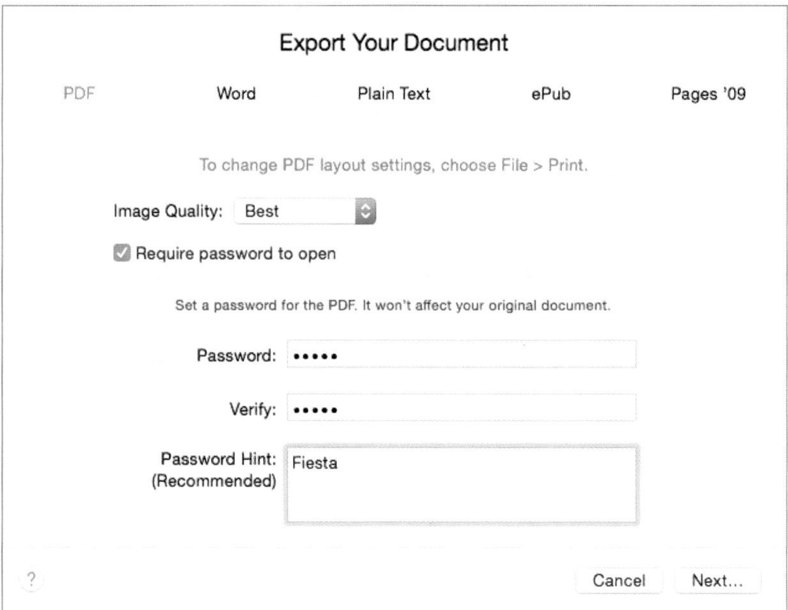

TIP If file size isn't an issue, set Image Quality to Best. In Best quality, no down sampling of photos or graphics is performed; so your work will look its best!

6 Select "Require password to open" if you want to add some security to the PDF. Fill in the required fields, click Next, and save the PDF to your desktop.

7 Close the **header.pages** document.

Opening and Editing a Word Document

When you open a Word file in Pages, a new document is created leaving the original document untouched. Once open in Pages, the former Word document may be edited just like any other Pages file.

In this exercise you will open a Word document, address any file translation issues that have arisen, and tidy up the document formatting.

1 Choose File > Open, and navigate to the APTS Pages Numbers Keynote > Lesson_03 folder to open **rafiq.doc**.

   The document opens in Pages with no problems. What is not immediately obvious, however, is that the styles used in the Word document have been brought over to Pages. You can verify that by selecting parts of the text.

2 Click a word in the first paragraph block.

   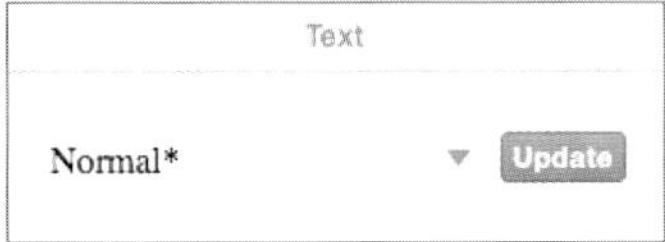

   In the Text inspector, you can see that the Normal style is applied, but that overrides have been made as indicated by the asterisk next to the style name.

3 In the Text inspector, click the Normal paragraph style. In the menu that appears, locate the Normal style and click the > symbol to display a submenu.

   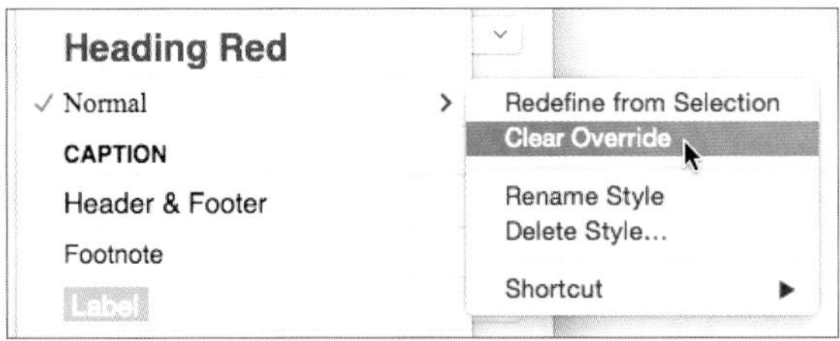

4 Choose Clear Override, which changes the Normal style from a serif typeface to a sans serif typeface.

   TIP It's OK to leave style overrides in place. Alternatively, you could update a style.

You may want to iron out style conflicts when you import a Word document. The conversion from Word has also added some new styles into Pages.

5. At the top of the document, click the words "Rafiq Darzi." In the Text inspector, notice that a Sender Name style is applied. This is a style created by Word.

6. In the Text inspector's style submenu, choose Clear Override to change the font size.

   When working collaboratively, agreeing on a set of styles to use is wise. If a document is shared among several people, each using a different set of styles, those styles will be added to the document, which may cause style conflicts.

   TIP If your style sheet menu grows excessively long, you can delete extraneous styles to reduce the file size.

7. Click any word in Rafiq's document. In the Text inspector, open the Style menu, and choose the Addressee style.

8. From the style submenu, choose Delete Style.

   A window appears asking which style you'd like to replace the Addressee style you are about to delete.

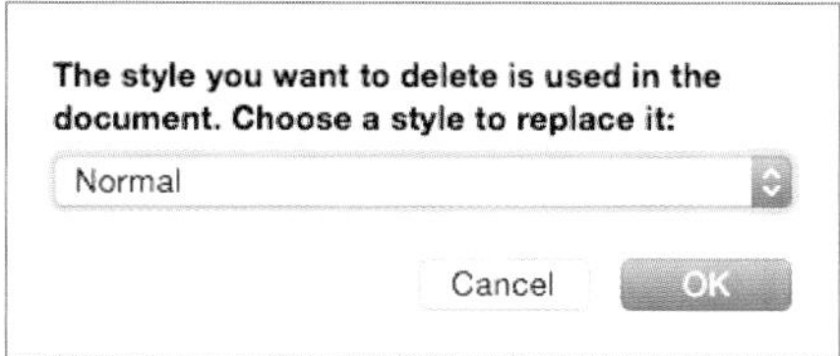

9. Choose Normal to replace all instances of the Addressee style with the Normal style (although style overrides may still be in place).

10. In the Text inspector, open the Paragraph Styles menu. Drag the Normal style to the top of the menu to reorder its place in the menu.

    TIP Reordering the Paragraph Styles menu is a good way to keep your often-used styles at the top of the menu.

Tabulating Text

Rafiq's document contains a set of budget figures that don't line up properly. One way to address this would be to use a table to tidy things up, but in this exercise you'll use tabs instead.

1 Choose View > Show Invisibles, if necessary.

2 In the toolbar, click the View icon, and choose Show Ruler.

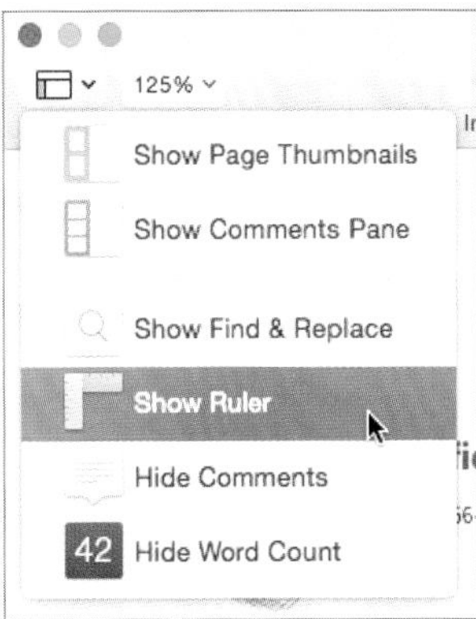

You are going to add tab stops to reformat the budget figures.

3 Drag to select all the text elements of the budget.

¶
Description → Quantity → Unit·Price → Cost¶
Item·1→55 → $ → 100 → $ → 5,500¶
Item·2→13 → $ → 90 → $ → 1,170¶
Item·3→25 → $ → 50 → $ → 1,250¶
→ → → ¶
Total→ → → $ → 7,920¶
¶

4 Click the ruler at the top of the document window, somewhere around the 2-inch mark, to add a tab stop.

5 Carefully drag the tab stop along the ruler to move the word "Quality" and the numbers 55, 13, and 25 to the left or right. Position the stop near the 2.2-inch mark.

6 Click the ruler to the right of the first tab stop to add a second stop.

7 Drag the new tab stop on the ruler to the 3.2-inch mark

By moving the tab to the right, you create space to avoid jumbling up the figures.

Let's add two more stops using a different method.

8 In the Text inspector, choose Layout. Under Tabs, click the Add (+) button in the lower left.

A tab has been added. Double-click the Stops value and change it to 3 in.

9 Click the Add (+) button again. Set the fourth tab to 4 in.

Setting the Tabs options in the Text inspector is a great way to control tab positioning, and to add leaders and change alignment.

10 Change the alignment of all four tabs to Center. You may need to adjust the positioning of the tab stops to prevent overlapping.

11 Change the tab stop positions by dragging their positions on the ruler, or by changing their values in the Text inspector in Tabs.

TIP To remove a tab stop, drag it out of the ruler, or select it in the inspector and click the Remove (–) button in Tabs.

The budget list still does look right because the text has too many tabs. A tab isn't needed between the dollar sign and its number value.

12 In the Unit Price column, click once just to the left of the figure 100. Now press Delete. Repeat this operation for all the other dollar values.

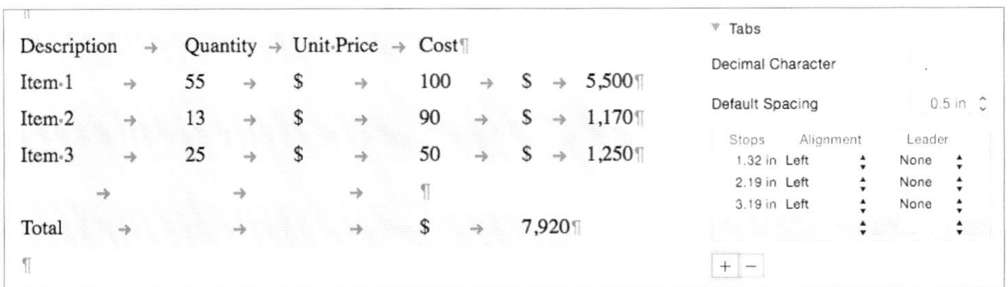

The budget now looks a lot better. The columns of figures line up, greatly improving legibility.

Lesson Review

1. How do you repeat a logo on every page of a Pages document?
2. If you need to send a document to someone who is not using Pages, which format would you choose to preserve the layout of the document?
3. Describe how to reorder pages in word processing mode in Pages.
4. Describe a way to add tab stops to a document.
5. Describe how to delete an unwanted paragraph style in Pages.
6. How do you control the vertical spaces between paragraphs?

Answers

1. To make a logo appear on every page of a document, you can position a logo on a page and then choose Arrange > Section Masters > Move Object to Section Master. Note that when a document has multiple sections, this step must be repeated for each section.
2. PDF format preserves document layout.
3. In word processing mode, only sections can be reordered, so to move individual pages they would have to be on different sections.
4. To add tab stops you need to select the text you want to format, and then:
   - Use the document ruler to add stops by clicking the ruler, and dragging the stops into position.

     or

   - Click the Add (+) button in the Tabs section of the Format inspector.
5. To delete an unwanted style, click any style in the Inspector. In the submenu that appears, click the > symbol next to the style you want to delete. Another submenu appears. Choose Delete Style. You'll be prompted to choose a style to replace the one you are deleting. All text in Pages has a style applied.
6. To control the vertical space between paragraphs, in the Style tab of the Text inspector, set Spacing Before Paragraph and After Paragraph to the required values.

4

Lesson Files APTS Pages Numbers Keynote > Lesson_04 > 2009_report.pages

Time This lesson takes approximately 60 minutes to complete.

Goals

Use tables to calculate and compare values

Add charts to present data

Create bulleted and numbered lists

Review a document

Add footnotes and endnotes

Lesson **4**

Working with Charts and Data

Pages, like Numbers and Keynote, can handle data intelligently: Tables can be used to run calculations, and charts can display and readily update statistical information. What you learn about tables and charts in this lesson can be applied to Numbers and Keynote, though Numbers does have some extra table formatting control not found in Pages or Keynote.

In this lesson, you'll also look at how you can review a document to check spelling and grammar, and look up word definitions.

You'll work with a single document that was created using the version of Pages found in iWork '09—updating that document before adding a list, table, or chart.

Opening a Pages '09 Document

The current version of Pages maintains backward compatibility with the previous release, Pages '09. When opening a Pages '09 document, you have two options for converting the document to the latest version of Pages.

1 In the Finder, locate the APTS Pages Numbers Keynote > Lesson_04 folder.

2 Double-click **2009_report.pages** to open it in Pages without any warnings that it was created in Pages '09.

3 Choose File > Save, and click Upgrade.

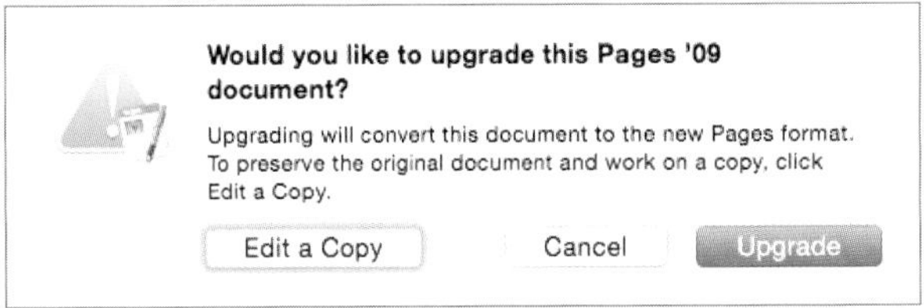

Alternatively, to preserve the original Pages '09 document, click Edit a Copy. Pages will duplicate the original document and upgrade it before opening it in Pages.

NOTE ▶ To open a Pages '08 document, you must first open it in Pages '09.

Using a Table to Add Data

Tables are a great way to organize information, such as work schedules or action plans. In Pages, Numbers, and Keynote, tables automatically detect the format of the data being added. In this exercise, you'll investigate the power of automatic data detection.

1 Go to page 5 of **2009_report.pages**, titled “budget.”

2 Click at the end of the line that ends with the word “restoration,” and press Return.

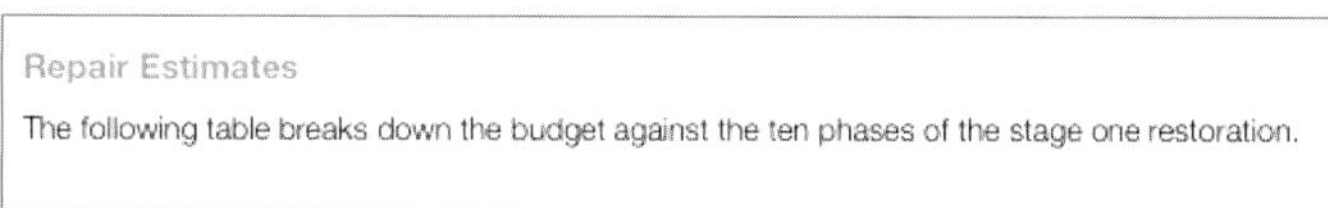

3 In the toolbar, click the Table icon. In the dialog that opens, click the table in the lower left.

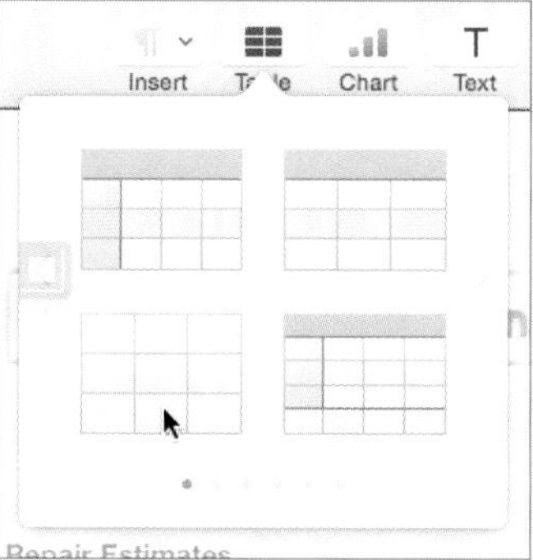

A simple table is added to the page. Now you’ll format it.

4 Click row header 1 to open a pop-up menu. Choose Add Header Row Above.

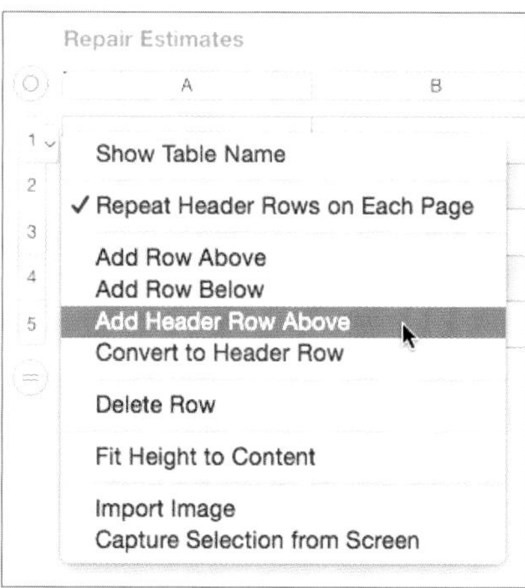

5 Click cell B1, type *Phase Number*, and press Tab to move to cell C1. In cell C1, type *Description*, and press Tab again to move to the next cell; and in cell D1, type *Budget*.

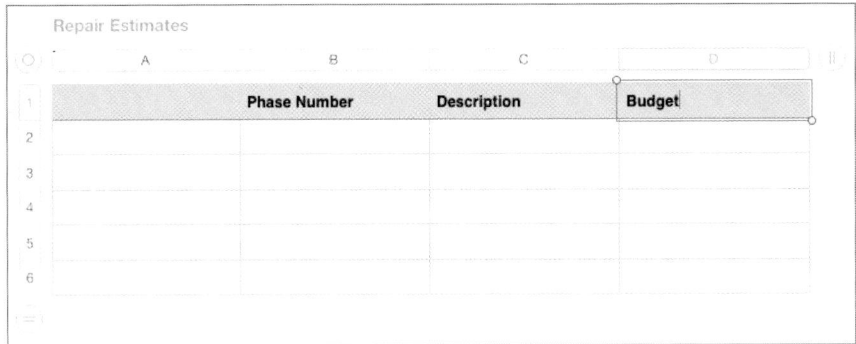

6 In the row reference column, click the symbol beneath the number 6 to open a control.

7 Click the arrows to change the number of rows to 14.

NOTE ▶ Alternatively, you can double-click the number 6, type *14*, and then press Return.

8 Click cell A2, and type *January*.

9 Move the pointer over the lower border of cell A2. A yellow handle appears, intersecting the cell border.

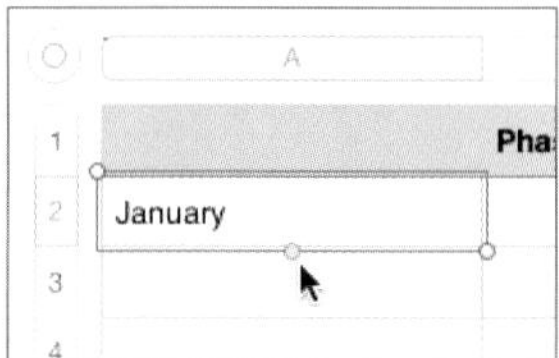

10 Drag the yellow handle down to row 13. All the months of the year appear.

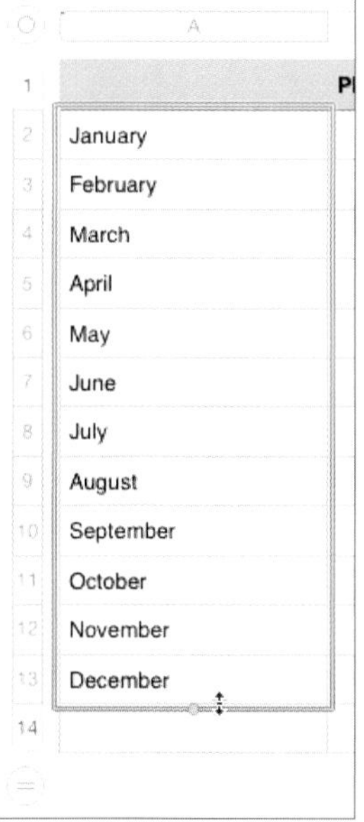

11 Click cell B2, and type *Phase 1*. Move your pointer so that the yellow handle intersecting the cell border appears.

12 Drag the yellow handle down to row 13. A sequence is created from Phase 1 to Phase 12.

The table automatically detects the numeral 1 after the text component in the cell, which causes the auto-sequence.

NOTE ▸ If you typed *1 Phase*, placing the number before the text, the auto-sequence is not created.

13 Click cell C2. Type *Blurb*. Repeat the steps described previously to drag the contents of cell C2 down to cell C13.

This time the only the word “Blurb” was repeated. No special data format was detected because the cell contains only text.

14 Click cell D2, and type $7000. Drag the yellow handle to repeat $7000 in column D down to row 13.

By typing the dollar sign, you are setting the data format to currency.

15 Click cell D2, and type *5000*. Click cell D4, and type *12000*.

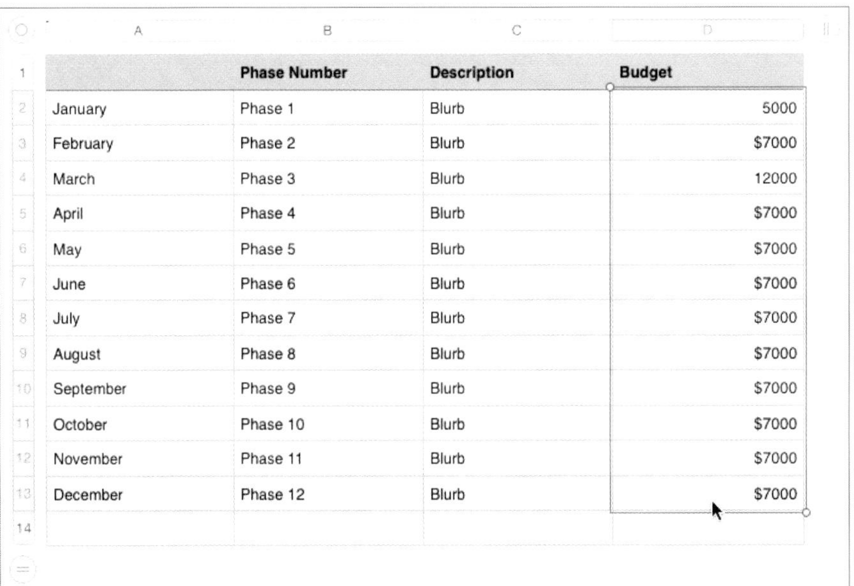

	A	B	C	D
1		**Phase Number**	**Description**	**Budget**
2	January	Phase 1	Blurb	5000
3	February	Phase 2	Blurb	$7000
4	March	Phase 3	Blurb	12000
5	April	Phase 4	Blurb	$7000
6	May	Phase 5	Blurb	$7000
7	June	Phase 6	Blurb	$7000
8	July	Phase 7	Blurb	$7000
9	August	Phase 8	Blurb	$7000
10	September	Phase 9	Blurb	$7000
11	October	Phase 10	Blurb	$7000
12	November	Phase 11	Blurb	$7000
13	December	Phase 12	Blurb	$7000
14				

You now need to let Pages know that the values 5000 and 12000 are also meant to be dollar amounts.

16 Click cell D2, and Shift-click cell D13 to select all the number values in column D.

17 In the Cell inspector, change the data format to Currency. Select the Thousands Separator checkbox, and set the Decimals value to 2.

The values in column D are set to dollars with two decimal points.

TIP In the Currency menu, you can choose a different currency.

NOTE ▶ Tables in Pages, Numbers, and Keynote are set to detect data automatically; but to manually format cells, select them and in the Cell inspector choose another data format.

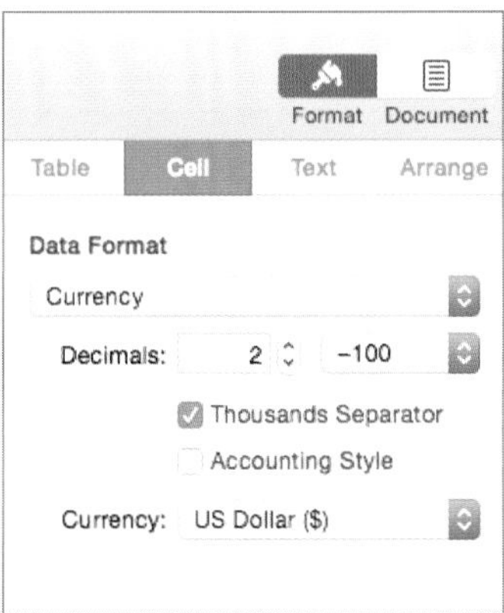

Formatting Tables

You're currently working with a simple table containing a variety of data formats. You will now create a formula to add up the budget figures in column D.

1 Click the cell reference bar for row 14, and from the pop-up menu, choose Convert to Footer Row.

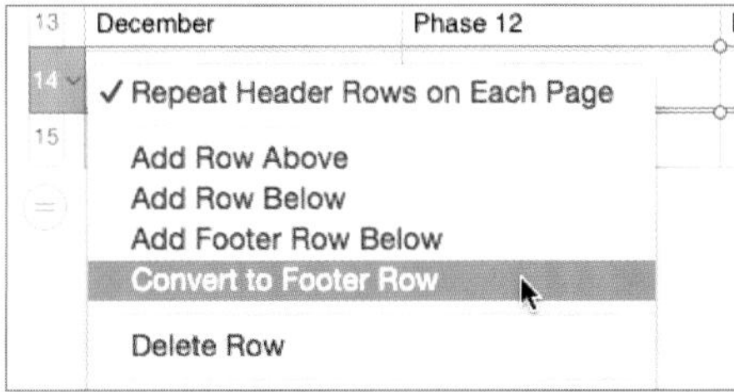

Footer rows are often used to total columns in accountancy style spreadsheets. You'll now add a totalizer in the footer row.

2 Double-click cell D14. Press the = (equals) key. The Formula Editor appears.

3 Click cell D2

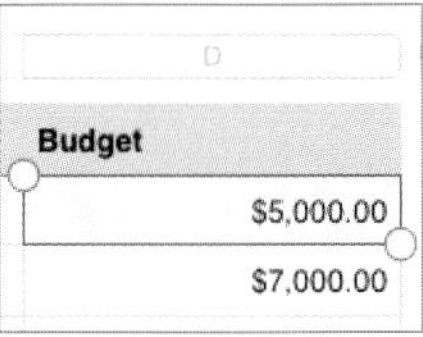

The cell is now highlighted with two handles in opposite corners.

4 Click the handle in the lower right of the cell, and drag it down to cell D13 to quickly place all the figures into a formula. Click the checkmark to run the calculation.

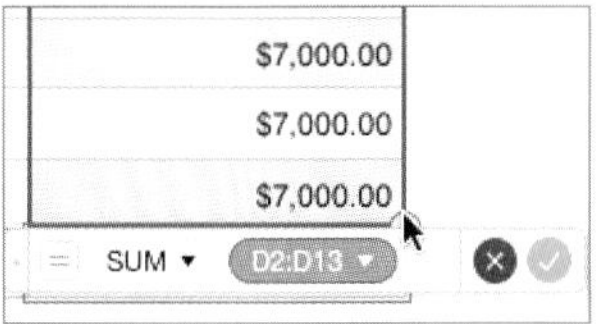

TIP Another way to set this calculation would be to double-click cell D14, type the formula *=sum(d2:d13)*, and then press Return.

5 Click the table handle icon at the top left of the table.

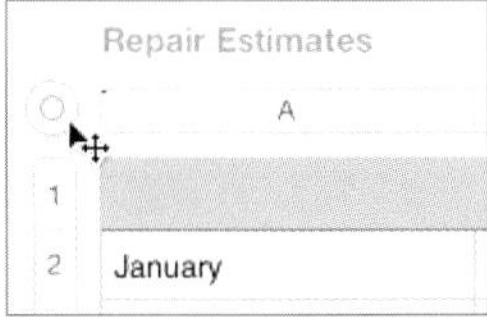

How and where you click a table affects which edits you can perform.

6 In the Layout tab of the Text inspector, change the Text Inset to 6 pt.

7 In the Table inspector, locate Row & Column Size. Click the Fit button for Column.

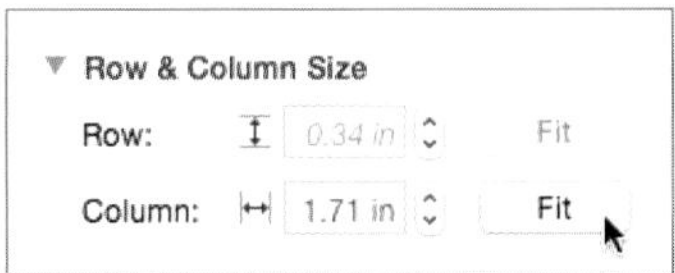

The table shrinks to fit the cell contents. Graphically the table is too narrow, so let's stretch it out a little.

Where you click a table affects the available editing options. If a table is first selected by carefully clicking its outside edge, selection handles appear. Doing this can be tricky. If a cell is selected, the table selection handles won't be available. To make selection handles appear, click the table handle icon.

8 With the table selection handles active, drag the side of the table to the right. The whole table stretches, giving the cell contents more space.

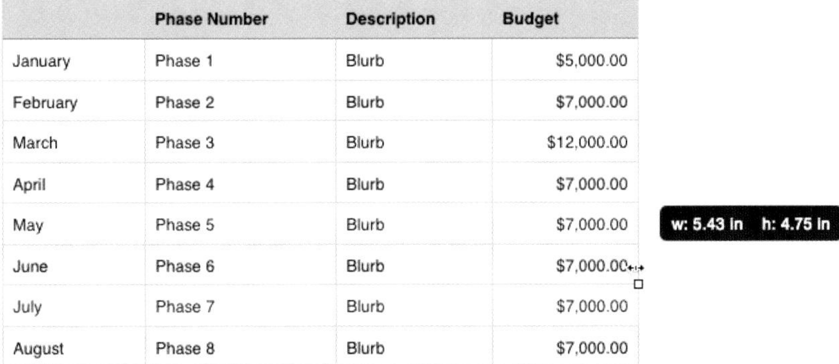

	Phase Number	Description	Budget
January	Phase 1	Blurb	$5,000.00
February	Phase 2	Blurb	$7,000.00
March	Phase 3	Blurb	$12,000.00
April	Phase 4	Blurb	$7,000.00
May	Phase 5	Blurb	$7,000.00
June	Phase 6	Blurb	$7,000.00
July	Phase 7	Blurb	$7,000.00
August	Phase 8	Blurb	$7,000.00

Don't drag the table edge too close to the edge of the document page because you'll need some extra space later.

The Description column could be wider still.

9 Move your pointer to the division between the header references for columns C and D. Drag the dividing line to the right to make column C wider.

You can also set precise measurements for column width and row height.

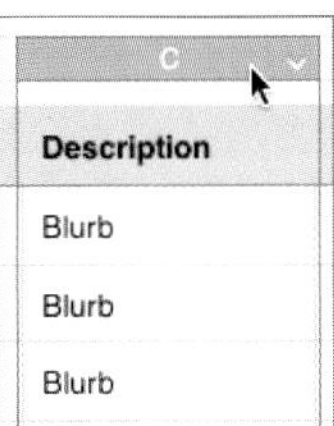

10 Click the reference bar for column C. In the Table inspector, in the Column data field, type *2 in*. Doing this adds clarity to the table layout.

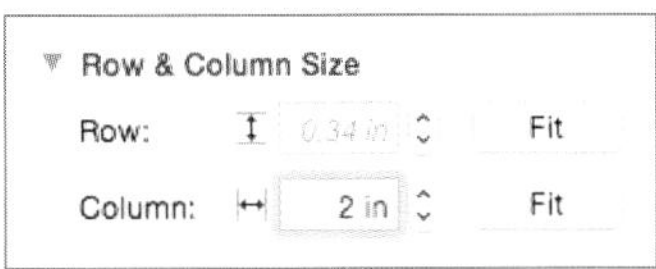

Creating List Structures

Tables are ideal when you need to sort data and run calculations; but when you simply need to create a hierarchy of ideas, tiered numbered lists are a great solution. On pages 3 and 4 of the 2009_report document you'll find an outline plan. Let's format it using tiered numbers.

1 Select the text on page 3, starting with the paragraph beginning, "The mounting," through to the paragraph on page 4 beginning, "Mud ring."

The mounting that support the steam dome is presently stored within the museum's top shed, these mounts are semi restored and require finishing and re-assembly upon the boiler.¶

Firebox. The firebox could be transferred to the museum's larger workshop for safe keeping, we recommend overhauling the tank cover including finish painting it, following this work it could be refitted to the engine.¶

Mud ring. The mud ring is stripped of paint and disassembled, it was found to be in quite poor condition and is in need of quite extensive work. ¶

2 In the Text inspector, locate Bullets & Lists. Set the bullet type to Numbers, use standard Arabic numerals, and select Tiered Numbers.

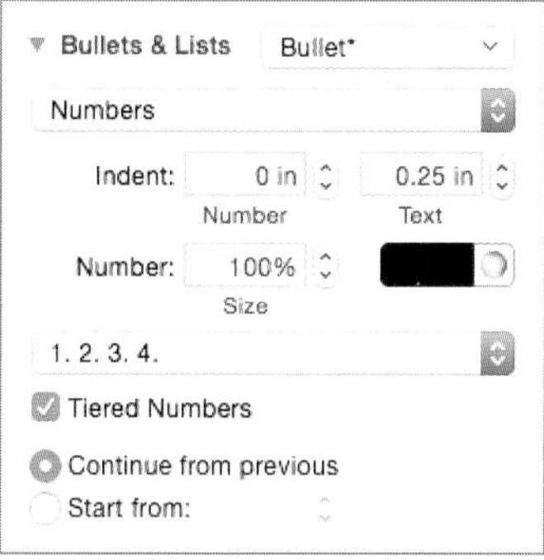

NOTE ▶ The " Continue from previous" button is selected. If a document has more than one list and you want each list to start at 1, select the "Start from" option and type *1* in its field.

Each paragraph now starts with a number. To create a tiered list, the paragraphs must be indented.

3 Click the word "Firebox," listed as paragraph number 2.

4 In the Text inspector, click the Increase Indent button.

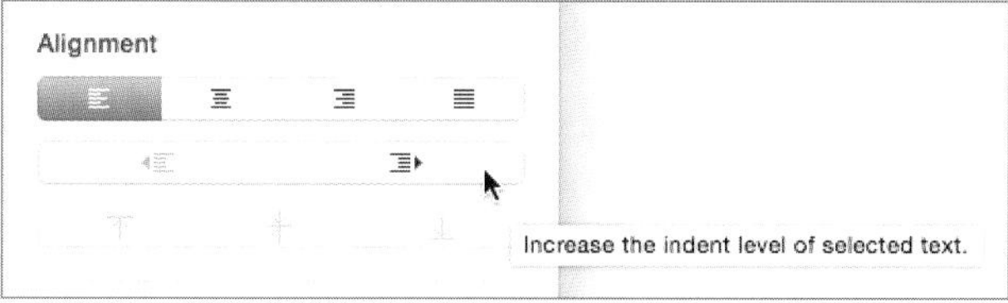

The paragraph is indented and labeled 1.1.

5 Click the word "Cab," now listed as paragraph 2. In the Text inspector, indent the paragraph.

The Cab paragraph is indented and labeled 1.2.

NOTE ▶ If you were to indent paragraph 1.2 again, it would be renamed 1.1.1.

6 Click the number 3 to select the entire bullet paragraph.

> 3. The hand rail well is complete and fitted, it will however need a new set of brackets as the ones currently fitted are badly made copies and do not properly sit, and will vibrate loose as and when the engine is back in service.¶

7 Drag the number 3 upward. A blue horizontal line appears. Move the blue line above list item 1.

NOTE ▶ Bullets can be dragged left or right to change their indent levels.

The bulleted list updates the numbering using the new order. This function allows topics to be typed randomly and later structured for sequence and hierarchy.

8 Choose File > Save to save a version of **2009_report.pages**.

Presenting Data Using Charts

Charts help illustrate data. They can highlight trends or show the breakdown of a budget. Like Numbers, Pages can create charts; but there are some differences in how you use it to add and edit charts. Generally, Numbers has greater data-crunching flexibility. In this exercise, you will create a line chart in Pages to illustrate the cash flow for a fictitious restoration project.

1 In the **2009_report.pages** document, go to page 6 and find two tables: Cash Flow by Month and Annual Totals.

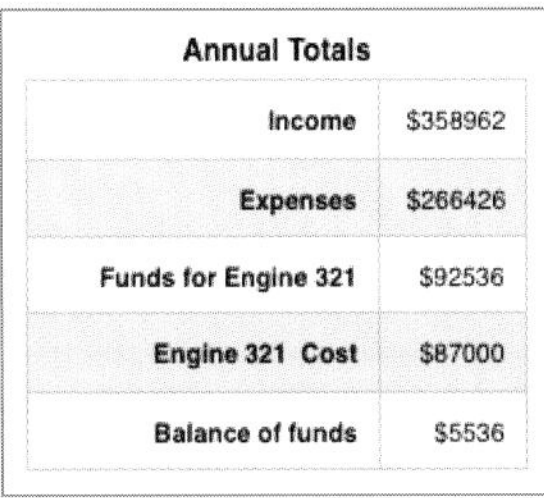

Annual Totals	
Income	$358962
Expenses	$266426
Funds for Engine 321	$92536
Engine 321 Cost	$87000
Balance of funds	$5536

The annual totals show a balance of $5536 so you have sufficient funds for the fictitious restoration project. What is less clear is the monthly balance of funds.

Profit	$805	$312	$26129	$3207	$3450	$3005	$6395	$1895	$614	$28910	$2398	$15416
321 Budget	$5000	$7000	$12000	$7000	$7000	$7000	$7000	$7000	$7000	$7000	$7000	$7000

Look at the Profit and 321 Budget lines at the bottom of the Cash Flow by Month table. In several of the months, you won't have enough money to pay the restoration bill. Line charts are often used to display trends or patterns like this. Let's make one.

2 In the toolbar, click the Chart icon. In the dialog, select the 2D line chart.

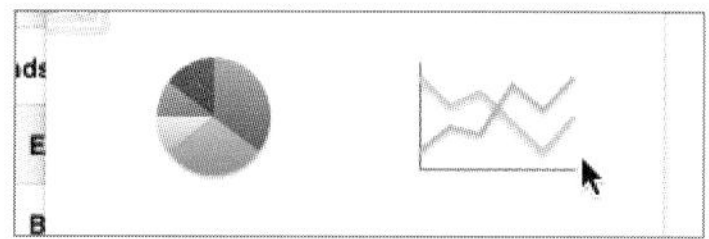

A chart appears with placeholder data. You will replace this with data from a table.

3 Move the chart if necessary so that it doesn't obscure any tables.

You'll resize the chart later.

NOTE ▸ You have other methods for creating charts in Numbers.

4 In the Cash Flow by Month table, select rows 1, 7, and 8 by Command-clicking the reference headers for those rows.

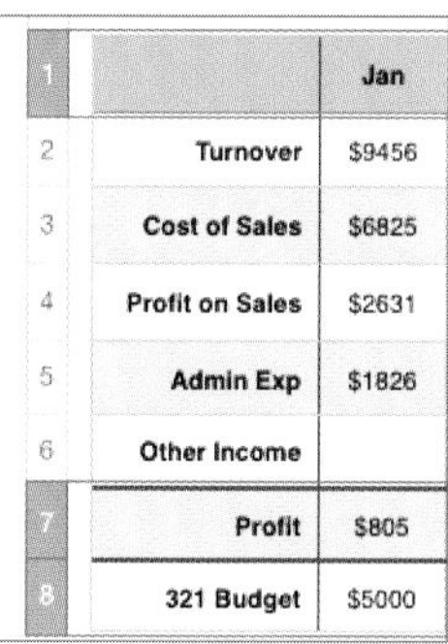

1		Jan
2	Turnover	$9456
3	Cost of Sales	$6825
4	Profit on Sales	$2631
5	Admin Exp	$1826
6	Other Income	
7	Profit	$805
8	321 Budget	$5000

5 Choose Edit > Copy.

6 Select the line chart to display the Edit Chart Data button.

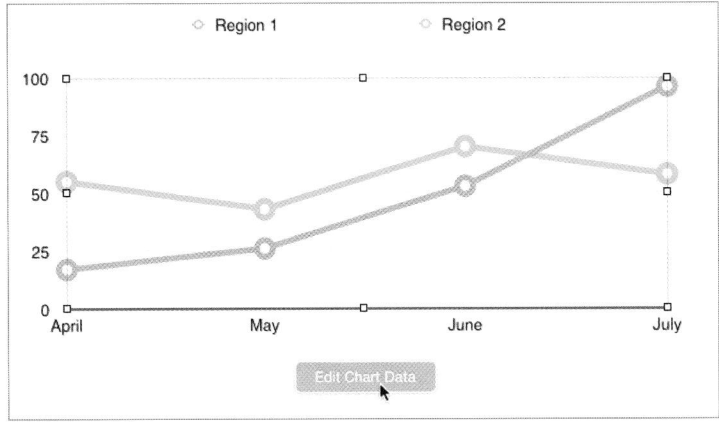

7 Click the Edit Chart Data button to open a new table dialog.

You will paste the copied data into this table, but first you need to select fields in the new table.

8 Select the first three rows of the Chart Data table by Command-clicking each row header.

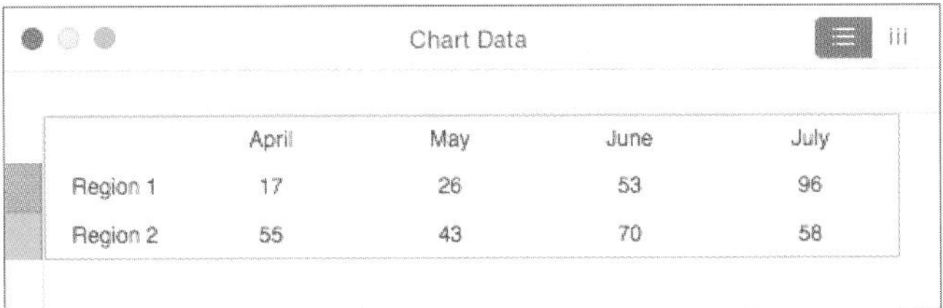

Chart Data

	April	May	June	July
Region 1	17	26	53	96
Region 2	55	43	70	58

9 Choose Edit > Paste. The Chart Data dialog populates with the table data you copied.

You may want to resize the Chart Data window to see all the data.

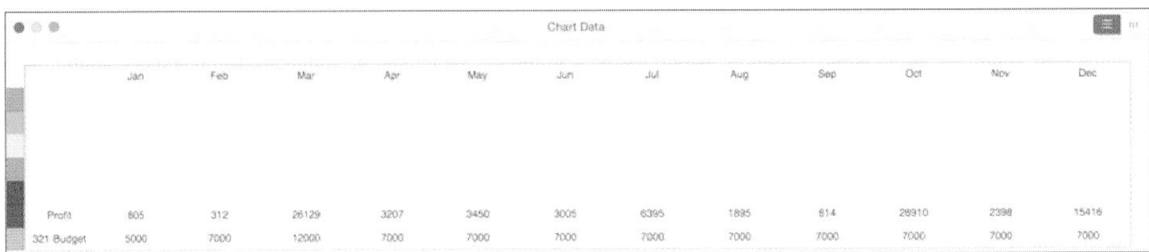

Chart Data

	Jan	Feb	Mar	Apr	May	Jun	Jul	Aug	Sep	Oct	Nov	Dec
Profit	805	312	26129	3207	3450	3005	6395	1895	614	28910	2398	15416
321 Budget	5000	7000	12000	7000	7000	7000	7000	7000	7000	7000	7000	7000

The paste operation added extra rows. Let's remove them now.

10 Command-click the header for each of the blank rows. Press Backspace to delete the blank rows.

You now have a 2D line chart created in Pages.

To edit the chart data, you click the Edit Chart Data button and change the figures. This method differs from Numbers in which you change data in the original table to automatically update any chart created from it.

11 Select the chart, and drag the selection handles to change its width and height.

NOTE ► The selection handles are the small squares that appear in the corners and in the middle of three sides of the selected chart.

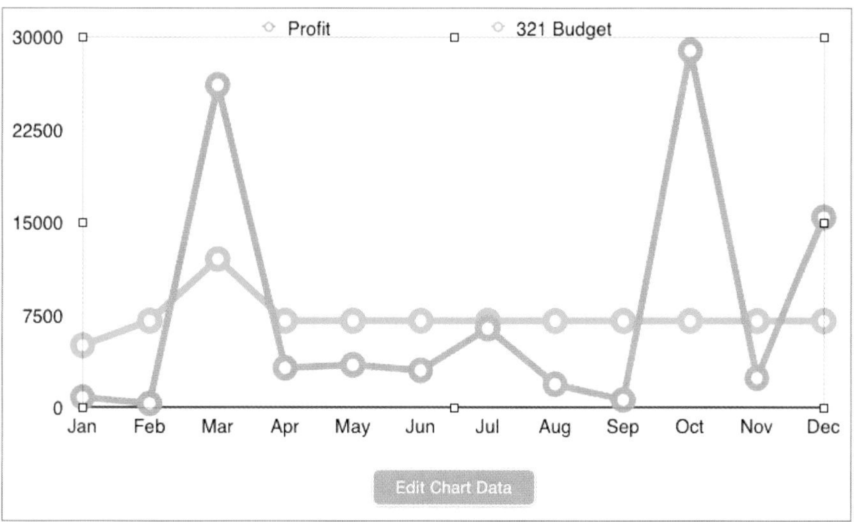

12 Drag the chart into clear space on the page.

NOTE ► Other page elements move as you reposition the chart. This is caused by text wrap options, which are covered in Lesson 5.

The line chart now displays the difference between income and expenditure. In the next exercise, you will change the labeling to display selective information.

Creating Chart Styles

You can choose from many types of charts. By default, placeholder data has generic labels. In the chart you created, the x-axis is now marked in months; the y-axis displays the correct figures, but has no dollar units. You will change that now.

In this set of exercises, you'll change many of the format options for charts, learning techniques you can apply in Numbers and Keynote.

1 In the Format inspector, click the Axis tab, and then click the Value (Y) tab.

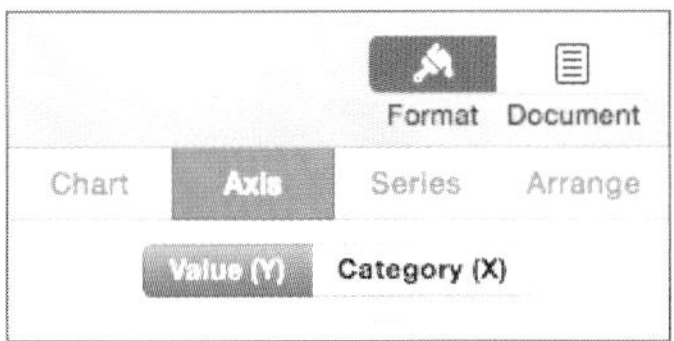

2 In the Value Labels section, change the format to Currency. Set Decimals to 0, and Currency to US Dollar ($). Select or deselect the Thousands Separator checkbox to suit yourself.

3 In the Format inspector, click the Series tab. Change the Data Symbols to squares and set their Size to 11.

With five data symbols to choose from (and the ability to scale them), you can customize your charts.

Although this chart doesn't call for them, feel free to experiment with Value Labels and Trendlines in the Series pane.

4 In the Format inspector, click the Axis tab, and then click the Category (X) tab.

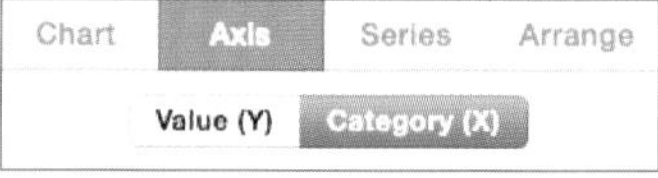

5 Change the Gridlines to dots.

6 In the Format inspector, click the Chart tab.

7 In Chart Options, select Title.

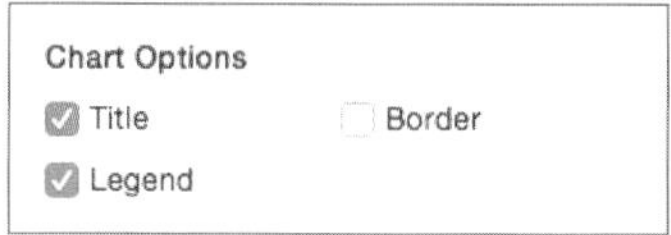

The legend and title overlap, so let's move the legend.

8 Click to deselect the table, if necessary, and then drag the legend beneath the chart.

9 Double-click the title, and type *Cash Flow*.

Giving charts and tables specific titles helps identify what's what.

TIP In the Chart Title tab in the inspector, you can set a different font style.

The chart now displays the key information required. As a finishing touch, let's change the chart colors.

10 With the chart selected, click the green data line.

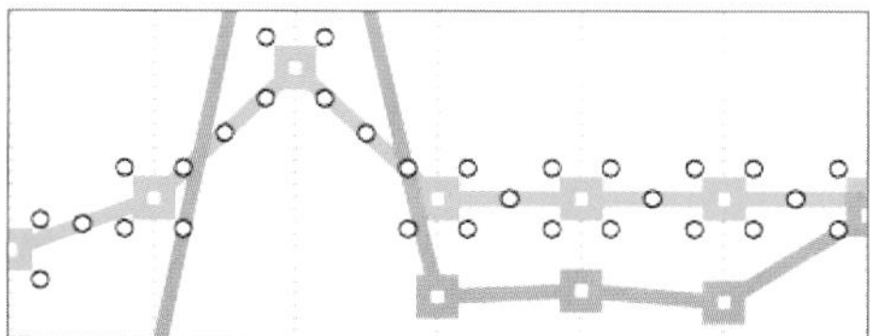

11 In the Style tab of the inspector, click the color wheel for Stroke to open the Colors window.

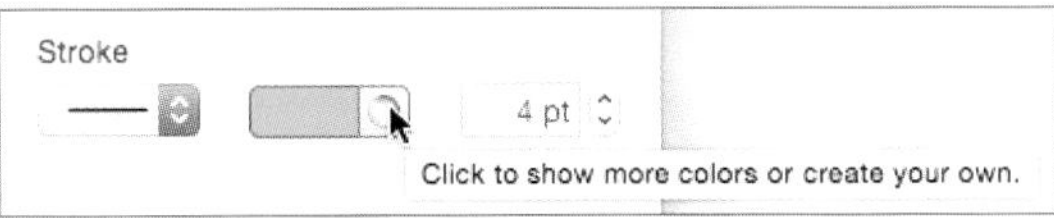

12 Click the eyedropper icon.

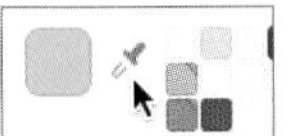

Your pointer changes to an eyedropper.

13 Click the dark green of the Sophia Larkinson logo. The data symbols change color.

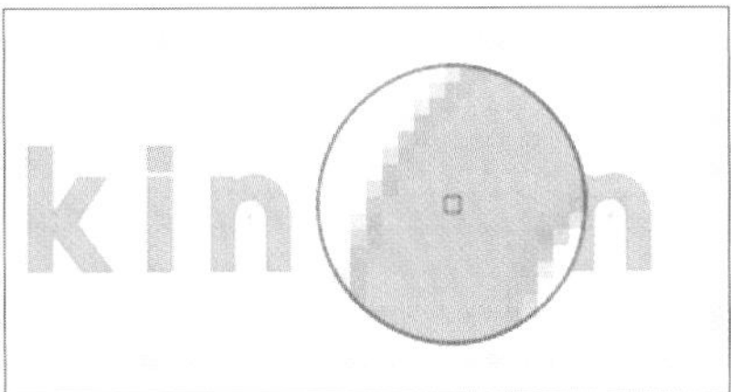

14 In the Connection Line options, click the color wheel button. In the Colors window, resample the dark green of the logo.

The chart's green now matches Sophia's business signature color.

Pages, Numbers, and Keynote can make great-looking charts. There are lots of options to explore, so that you can display your data clearly and quickly.

Using Footnotes and Endnotes

Pages can add footnotes or endnotes, which appear at the bottom of a page or at the end of a document or section, depending on the options you set.

NOTE ► For research projects that require a bibliography, EndNote can be purchased. It is an application that enables you to search, organize, and share your findings. You can access EndNote within Pages as you write.

In this exercise, you'll use Pages to add footnotes to the **2009_report.pages** document.

NOTE ▶ You can't use footnotes and endnotes in the same Pages document.

1 Go to page 2 of the 2009_report. In the Solution subsection, click after the term "modern paints."

Solution

All the paints and materials used for the work list
preservation. The applications of modern paints,
current state of the engine negate the need for fu

2 Choose Insert > Footnote, and type *safe and tough*.

A footnote is placed at the bottom of the page, numbered 1.

3 Click at the end of the Background paragraph.

4 Choose Insert > Footnote, and type *TBA*.

Because the second footnote insertion comes before the first footnote in the reading order it is labeled 1.

NOTE ▶ By default, footnotes and endnotes are numbered continuously throughout a document using Arabic numerals, but you can change this.

5 Select the footnote, TBA.

6 In the Text inspector, set the type to Bold.

Only the selected footnote's font style changes. When you want to change the formatting of every footnote in a document, perform the following steps.

7 Choose Edit > Deselect All.

8 Click a footnote.

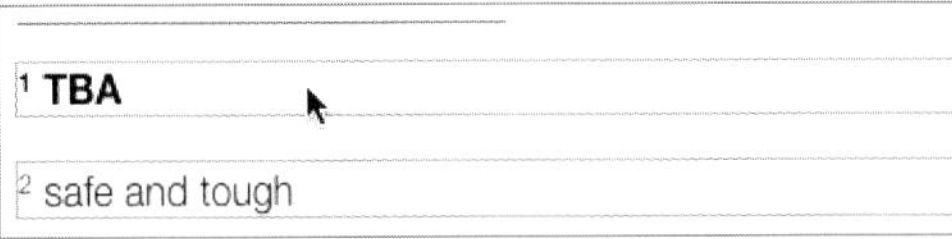

All the footnotes show blue selection lines. Any change made to the font or typeface will now affect every footnote in the document.

9 In the Text inspector, change the type size and style to 6pt italic.

All the footnotes change. Now you'll change the footnotes to endnotes.

10 In the Footnotes inspector, change the Type pop-up menu to Document Endnotes.

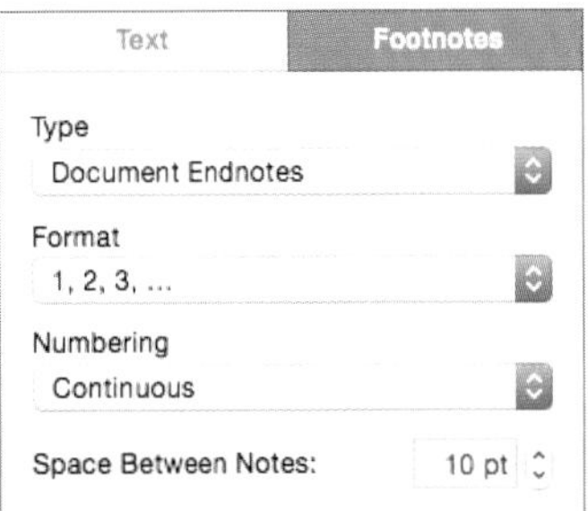

The footnotes that were on page 2 move to the end of the document.

NOTE ▶ Use the Footnotes inspector to change the numbering format and sequence. If a document is sectioned, you can choose to have endnotes appear at the end of each section, and the endnote numbering starts from 1 in each section.

Checking a Document for Errors

Pages will help you stay error free by checking spelling and grammar as you write. You can also check a word's definition with a couple of clicks.

1 Choose Edit > Spelling and Grammar > Check Spelling While Typing.

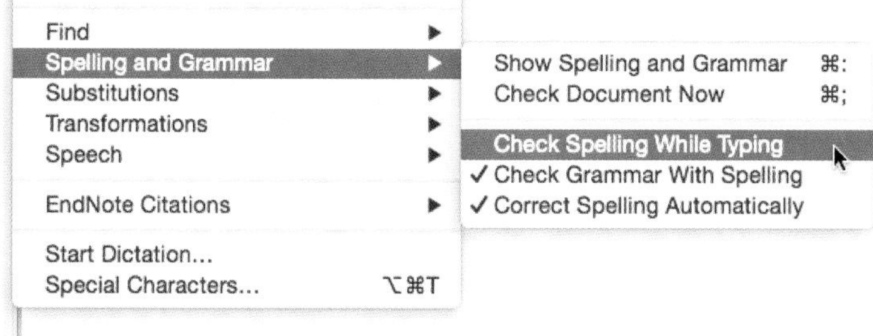

2 Go to page 3. In bullet number 5, the word "warrent" is misspelled, as indicated by a red dotted line.

3 Click at the end of the word "warrent" to display some spelling suggestions.

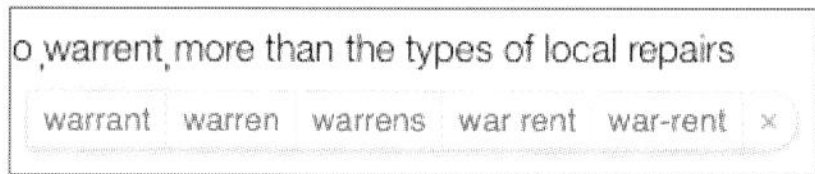

4 Click the × at the end of the spelling suggestions to close the suggestion bubble without correcting the spelling.

5 Control-click the misspelling of warrant.

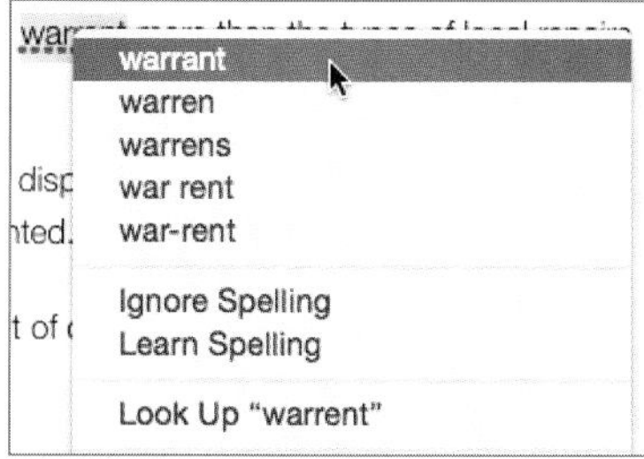

The shortcut menu that appears offers spelling suggestions, and options to ignore a misspelled word or to learn its spelling.

6 Choose “warrant” to set the correct spelling.

7 Control-click the word “warrant” and choose Look Up “warrant” from the shortcut menu.

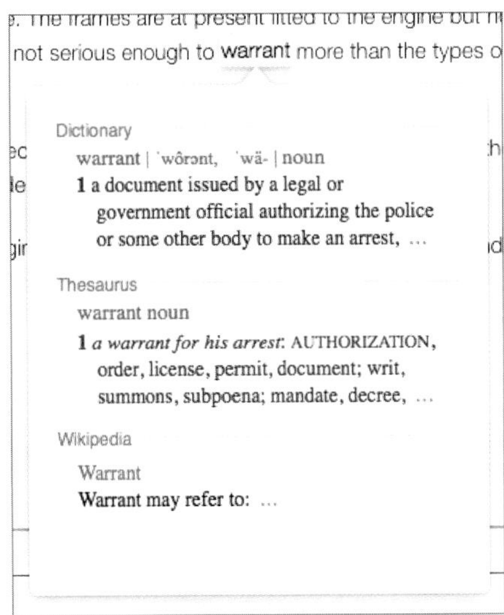

A popover appears with dictionary, thesaurus, and Wikipedia entries.

8 Click the word “Thesaurus” to open the dictionary application. It has extended definitions and hyperlinks to help you further research the selected word.

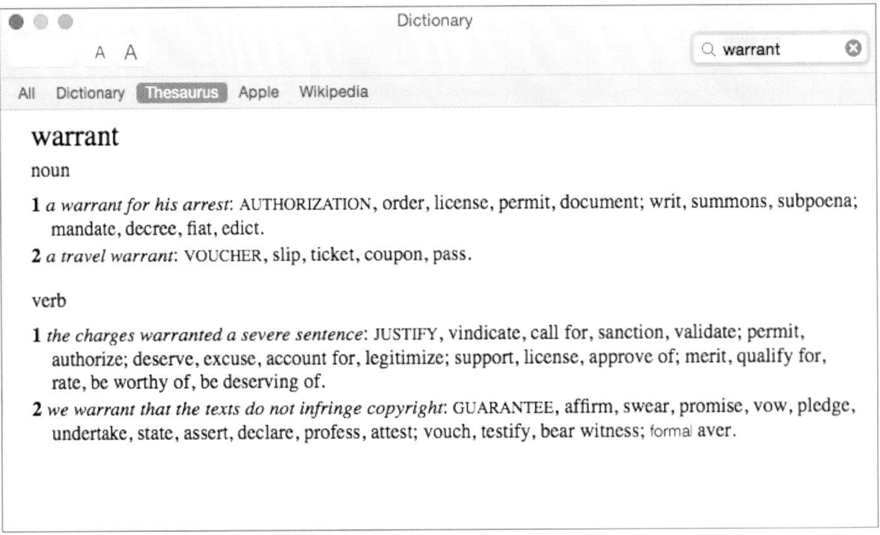

9 Close the Dictionary window to return to Pages.

NOTE ▶ A green dotted line under a word or words indicates a possible grammar or punctuation error.

Although you are working with Pages, the spelling suggestions are generated by the operating system. The dictionary and autocorrect preferences can be set in Pages, but they affect all applications that use autocorrection.

10 Choose Edit > Substitutions > Show Substitutions.

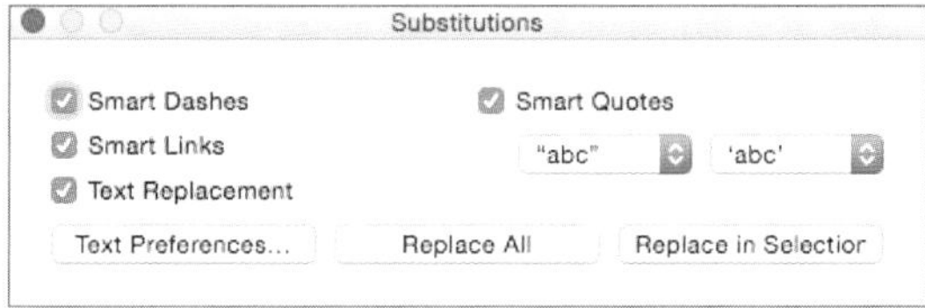

In the Substitutions window, you can set the following options:

Convert double hyphens (--) to dashes (—).

Convert straight quotes to curly quotes.

Auto-detect website addresses (URLs) and email addresses and turn them into links.

Select or deselect your preferred options.

11 Click the Text Preferences button.

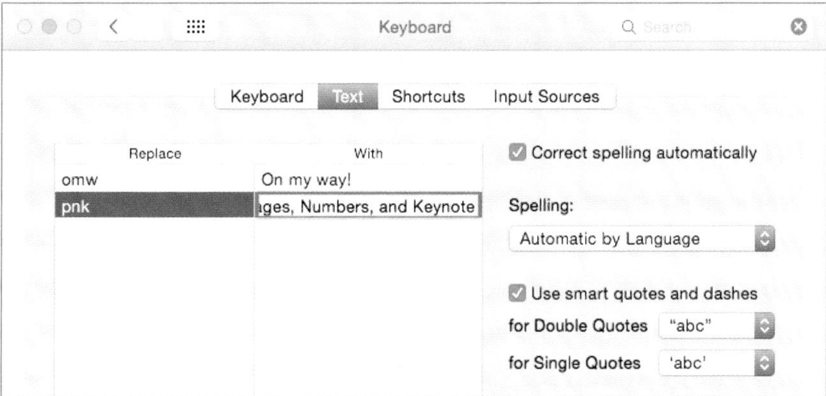

The System Preferences open in the Text pane of the Keyboard preferences. Any changes made here are applied systemwide.

By default, Spelling is set to Automatic by Language. If you were writing for someone in England, you might change the language to British English so that, for example, any instances of the U.S. English spelling of "color" would be marked as misspelled, or autocorrected to "colour" as you type.

TIP Click the Add (+) button at the lower left of Text preferences to add a new "replace with" option. Imagine the time saved if an author who was writing a book about Pages, Numbers, and Keynote could replace a typed "pnk" with "Pages, Numbers, and Keynote" as a preference. So, every time he typed "pnk" the title of the book would automatically appear.

12 Close System Preferences and return to Pages.

13 Choose Edit > Spelling and Grammar > Check Correct Spelling Automatically. Make sure this default setting is selected.

14 Type *teh*. Pages automatically changes this to "the."

TIP If you actually want to spell a word as *teh*, or any other word that otherwise autocorrects, type the word, but don't press the Spacebar. When the spelling suggestion appears, click the × to reject the autocorrection.

NOTE ▸ Clicking the Replace All button sets substitution preferences across a whole document. Clicking the "Replace in Selection" button affects only a text selection. Closing the Substitution dialog without choosing one of these options does not affect existing text.

Lesson Review

1. In Pages, how do you edit the data in a chart?
2. You have written a list in Pages, and selected Tiered Numbers in the inspector. Describe two ways to indent list items.
3. You have placed footnotes on the last page of a Pages document containing several chapters. The Footnote inspector has been set to Section Endnotes. What steps are required to place the endnotes at the end of each chapter?
4. A budget was created using a table in Pages. The currency format defaulted to U.S. Dollars. How do you change the currency to Chinese Yuan?
5. As you type, URL references are automatically being created. How do you turn off this function?

Answers

1. Select the chart and click the Edit Chart Data button.
2. Use the Increase Indent or Decrease Indent buttons in the Format inspector; or drag the button number left or right.
3. Start a new section for each chapter.
4. Select the cell ranges. Use the Format inspector's cell options to change the currency.
5. Choose Edit > Substitutions > Show Substitutions. Deselect Smart Links.

5

Lesson Files

APTS Pages Numbers Keynote > Lesson_05 > agata-brochure.pages

APTS Pages Numbers Keynote > Lesson_05 > sl-report-rd-reviewed.pages

Time

This lesson takes approximately 60 minutes to complete.

Goals

Understand the difference between page layout and word processing

Add, move, and delete pages in page layout mode

Change text wrap options

Adjust a photograph in Pages

Create shape styles

Format tables

Track changes in a document

Lesson **5**

Designing a Brochure

You can make word-processed documents look stunning by applying style sheets to shape and order content. Great page layout can be done in Pages' word-processing mode, but this lesson introduces how you can use page layout mode as a design tool.

Whether you decide to design in word-processing or page layout mode depends on your project's requirements. In the following exercises, you will learn which options best suit a particular job.

This lesson explores shape styles, image adjustments, and text wrap features, all important design tools. However, concentrating on page layout sometimes closes your mind to the meaning of words on a page, so use Pages' review tools to share your work for peer comment before publishing.

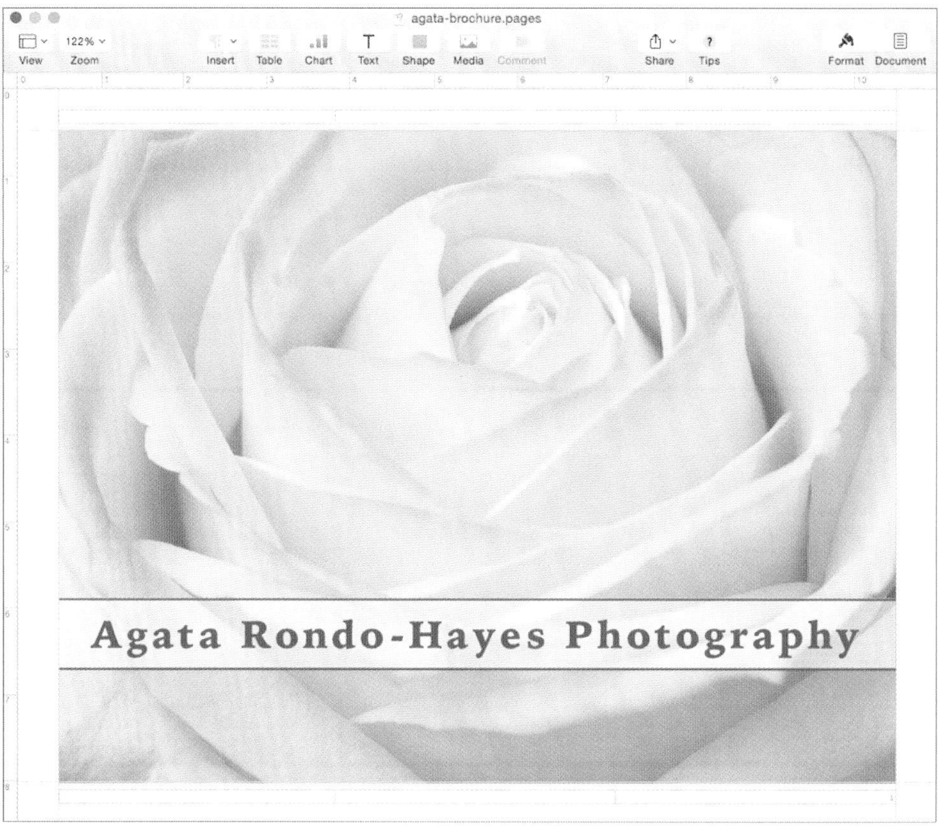

Changing to Page Layout

In page layout mode, every page is an open canvas. You can add text boxes, photos, and graphics and then freely move them around the page. Objects can be layered by stacking photos over text boxes and vice versa.

Throughout this lesson you'll develop a brochure design for a fictitious photographer. Your first step is to modify a document created from the newsletter template.

1 In Pages, choose File > New. In the Template chooser, double-click Serif Newsletter to open it.

2 Click the body text to select it. This placeholder text flows from page 1 to page 2. Scroll through each page to see the text flow.

Ac dolor ac adipiscing amet bibendum nullam, lacus molestie ut libero nec, diam et, pharetra sodales, feugiat ullamcorper id tempor id vitae. Mauris pretium aliquet, lectus tincidunt. Porttitor mollis imperdiet libero senectus pulvinar. Etiam molestie mauris ligula laoreet, vehicula eleifend. Repellat orci erat et, sem cum, ultricies sollicitudin amet eleifend dolor nullam erat, malesuada est leo ac. Varius natoque turpis elementum est. Duis montes, tellus lobortis lacus amet arcu et. In vitae vel, wisi at, id praesent bibendum libero faucibus porta egestas, quisque praesent ipsum fermentum tempor. Curabitur auctor, erat mollis sed, turpis vivamus a dictumst congue magnis. Aliquam amet ullamcorper dignissim molestie, mollis. Tortor vitae tortor eros wisi facilisis.
Class aptent taciti sociosqu ad per inceptos lobortis.

3 In the toolbar, click the Document icon. Click the Document tab, and change the Page Orientation from portrait to landscape.

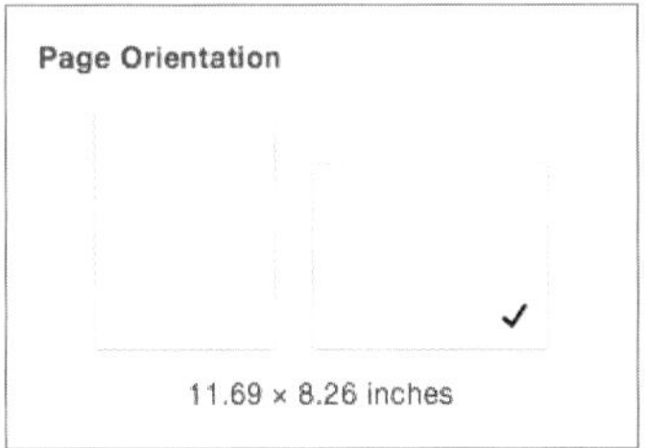

The text reflows. On page 2 the blue sidebar now sits on the text.

NOTE ▶ Landscape orientation works well for visually rich subjects such as photography, but it requires more design work to make the layout look right.

4 Choose View > Show Layout to display document margins and the header and footer boxes.

5 Choose View > Show Invisibles (if the menu shows Hide Invisibles, they are already enabled).

Turning on Show Invisibles allows you to see more of the document's structure, at least while learning about Pages.

6 In the Document inspector, change the left and right margins to 0.5 in.

The margin moves, as does the placeholder text. Other objects on the page remain fixed. Two types of objects are on the page.

The Serif Newsletter has been created from a word-processed template. You will change it to page layout mode so that you can freely change the page order, and also to learn how word-processing and page layout documents differ. In doing so the placeholder text will disappear.

NOTE ▶ When you convert a word-processing document to a page layout, Pages deletes any existing body text (text that's not placed in a text box, such as the placeholder text in the Serif Newsletter).

7 Choose View > Show Ruler. Note that the ruler runs across the top and left side of the document.

Guides can be dragged from the ruler to create a layout design.

8 In the Document inspector, deselect the Document Body checkbox.

Document Body

A warning dialog appears.

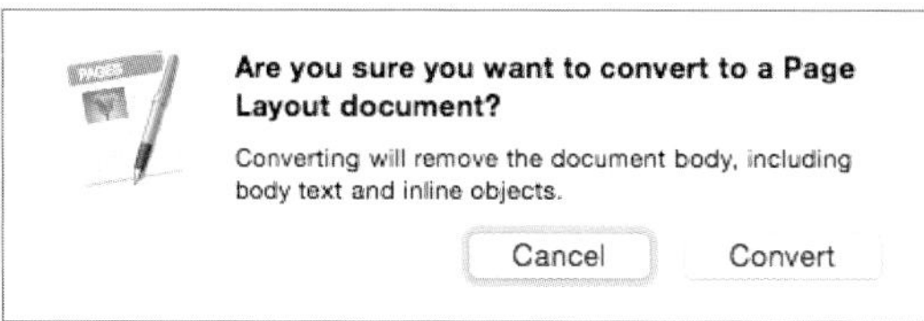

9 Click Convert. The placeholder text disappears, but the text boxes and photos remain.

TIP Any objects that are set to move in line with text are deleted when converting to page layout. If you want to save body text, copy and paste it into text boxes before conversion.

In the Document inspector, the document margins are dimmed. In page layout mode, objects can be placed anywhere on the page. Also note that the ruler now runs vertically and horizontally.

10 In the Document inspector, set the header and footer to 0.25 in.

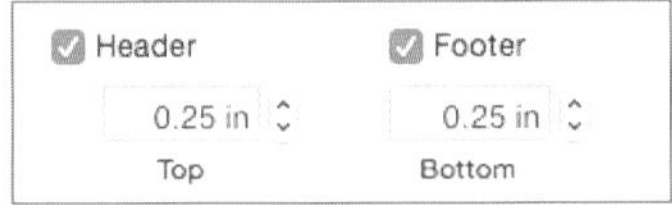

In page layout mode, the vertical placement of the header and footer can be changed, but not their widths; that's why you changed the document margins to 0.5 in in step 6.

11 Go to page 1.

You'll place two guides here. In page layout mode, vertical guides are page-specific.

12 Point at the vertical ruler to the left and drag right to obtain a vertical guide. Keep dragging until the guide aligns with the left edge of the header, at 0.5 in.

13 Drag a second guide to the right edge of the header, at 10.5 in.

TIP Use guides to set margins in page layout mode. Margins can be visually pleasing and may be required for print use.

14 On page 2, click the text box starting with the words "Class aptent."

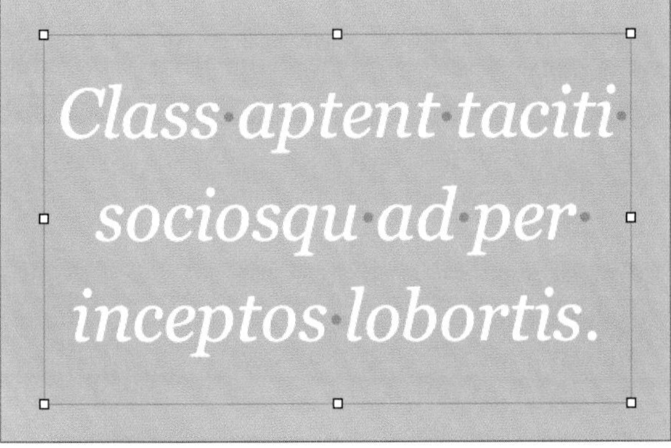

15 Drag the text box to freely position it anywhere on the page. Then click the blue box on page 2.

Small gray crosses appear in the corners of the blue box to indicate that this item is locked. Locked objects can't be moved.

16 With the blue box selected, choose Arrange > Unlock.

The blue box can now be repositioned and sized, and its layer order can be changed.

Many graphic art applications use layers, and in layout mode, Pages behaves like a graphics-oriented application. Think of layers like sheets of acetate. Some layers can be completely opaque and fill a document page. If such a layer were on top of a stack of layers, only the top layer would be visible. In the Serif Newsletter, the white text sits on top of the blue box in the layer order.

17 With the blue box still selected, choose Arrange > Bring to Front.

18 In the Arrange pane of the Format inspector, click the Backward button several times.

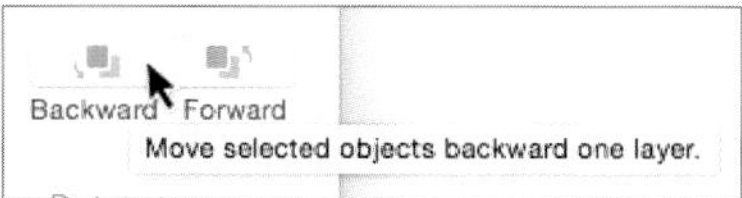

The blue box moves back a layer with each click of the button. Use the Forward button to bring the blue box to the top of the layer order.

19 Choose File > Convert to Word Processing.

Converting to word processing only adds a document body, so no warnings about losing text appear.

20 Choose File > Convert to Page Layout. In the dialog that appears, click Convert.

21 Choose File > Save. Title your document *Layout*, and save it to your desktop.

By working in page layout, you've been able to experience a little of the design potential of Pages by changing layer order and freely positioning elements on a page.

Making a Logotype

Pages includes several type formatting options you can use to transform a few words into a professional logo.

1 On page 1 of your layout document, double-click the word "Newsletter."

2 In the Format inspector's Text pane, change the type size to 24 pt.

3 Type *Agata Rhondo-Hayes Photography*, replacing the placeholder "Newsletter".

The text appears in capital letters. Let's change this.

4 Triple click the word "Agata" to select the entire line.

5 Choose Format > Font > Capitalization> None. The text changes to the case you typed.

TIP If you're not sure whether your heading should be all caps, small caps, or title case, type in lowercase only. The Capitalization settings can change lowercase to any other case, but not vice versa.

6 Choose Edit > Deselect All. Now click the logo's text box. Drag the edges of the selection to the document's vertical margins.

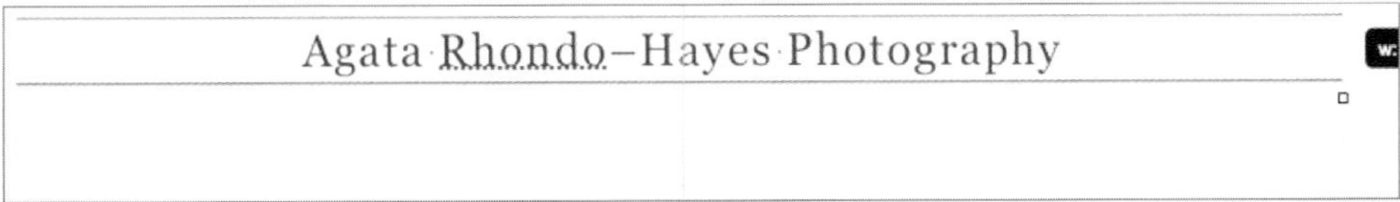

7 In the Text inspector's Style pane, change the font to Iowan Old Style.

TIP Apple lists all the available iOS fonts on its website (search for *iOS fonts*). If you are working across Apple platforms, choosing an iOS font ensures that your work will match on both OS X and iOS devices.

8 In the Text inspector's Layout pane, change the Border & Rules settings to a line width of 1 pt and an offset of –3 pt. Leave the Position so that lines appear above and below the text.

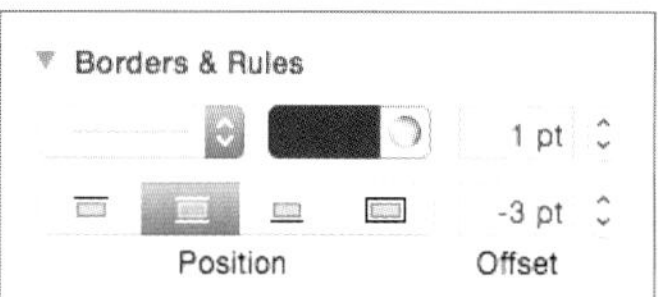

The borders can be moved in relation to the text. They always extend to the end of the text box. To make lines shorter, you can drag the edges of the text box inward.

9 Triple-click the word "Rhondo" to select the entire line.

10 In the Text inspector, click the Style tab.

11 Hold down the Command key and press the + (plus) or – (minus) key to make your text bigger or smaller. A type size around 33 pt works well for this brochure.

12 In the Text inspector, click the Show Advanced Options button (looks like a gear).

13 In the Advanced Options popover, change the Character Spacing to 10%.

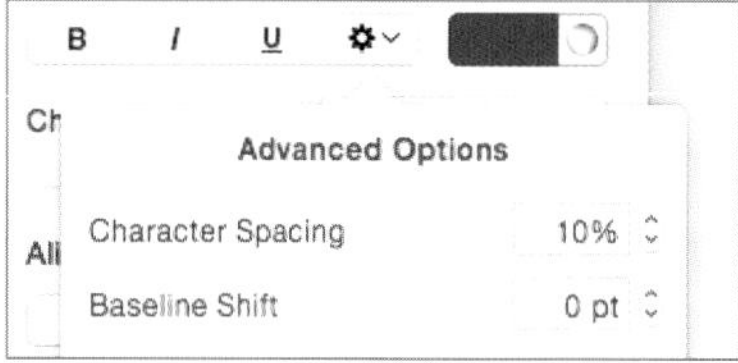

NOTE ▶ The Advanced Options popover also includes settings for capitalization.

Designers may find fault with the character spacing, but the logotype now has more impact.

14 In the inspector, click Update.

The Title style is now set to match the logo type and is ready to be applied when needed.

15 Save and close your document.

Changing Page Order

Using page layout mode, you can easily reorder the pages of a document and add and subtract pages as needed. Unlike in word-processing mode, in page layout mode you cannot flow text from one page to another.

In this exercise you will move and add pages to your brochure design.

1 Open APTS Pages Numbers Keynote > Lesson_05 > **agata-brochure.pages.**

2 In the toolbar, choose View > Show Page Thumbnails.

3 Drag the thumbnail for page 2 to the bottom of the thumbnails area.

Page 2 now becomes page 7. Because it is the address page, having it at the end of the document makes sense.

4 Click the thumbnail for the new page 2. It shows a guitar player.

In the lower right of the page is the page number (2).

5 In the toolbar, click the Document icon. In the Section inspector, deselect the "Match previous section" checkbox.

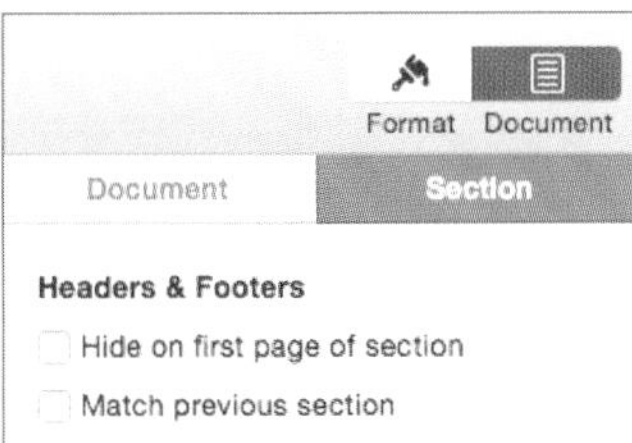

6 In the Section inspector, set the page numbering to "Start at" 1.

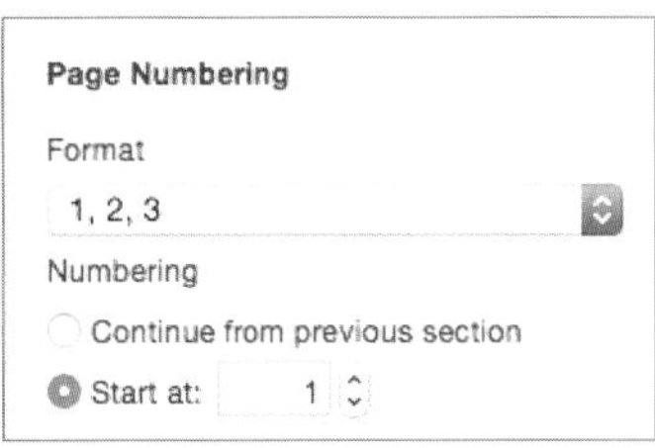

Page 2 changes to page 1. By deselecting "Match previous section," you can delete the page number in the footer of page 1 without deleting the numbers from every page in the brochure.

7 Go to page 1. In the footer, select the number 1 and delete it.

Page 1 has a logo placed on it, but it's been pushed out of view by a text wrap that's been placed on the flower photograph.

8 Drag the flower photograph on page 1 upward.

The photographer's logo appears. Text wraps can be very useful, but turn this one off.

NOTE ▶ Take care not to double-click the flower. If you do, image mask options will appear. If this happens, in the mask dialog, click Done to return to the required selection.

9 With the photo selected, click the Format inspector's Arrange tab. Set the Text Wrap pop-up menu to None.

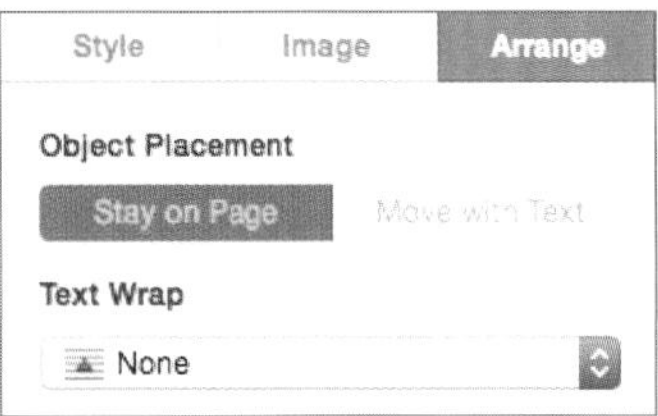

NOTE ▶ The Object Placement options are dimmed because "Move with Text" does not work in page layout mode.

10 In the Arrange pane, click the Backward button twice to place the photograph behind the logo.

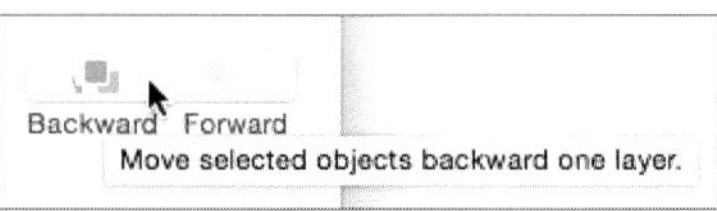

11 Drag the photograph's selection handles to scale the image so that it touches all four guides.

The page looks good, but the logo type could stand out a little more.

12 Click the logo text box to select it. In the Format inspector's Style pane, locate the Fill options. Change the Fill to Color Fill.

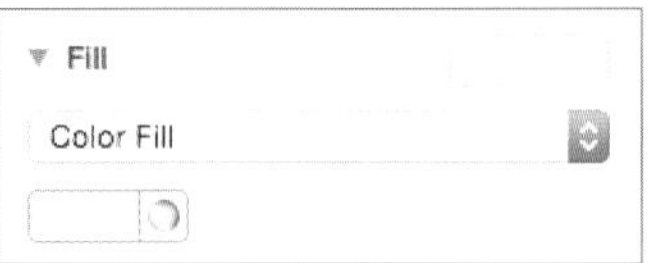

Click the color pop-up and the white swatch.

13 The text box fills with a solid white color. If necessary, scale the text box so that no white shows above or below the border lines.

As a finishing touch, you'll change the opacity of the white fill.

14 In the Fill options, click the color wheel button to open the Colors window.

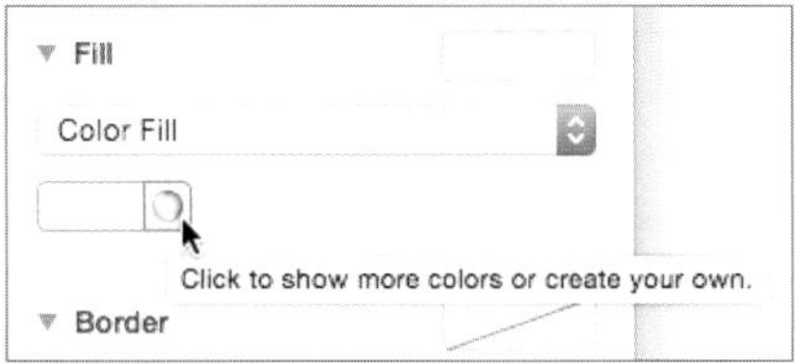

15 In the Colors window, in the Opacity data field, type *50*.

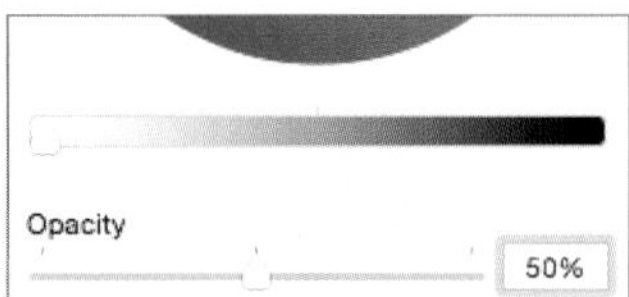

NOTE ▶ Don't drag the Opacity slider at the bottom of the Style inspector because doing so alters the text and background.

Your brochure cover is complete.

16 Choose File > Save, and leave the document open.

Enhancing Images

Pages, Numbers, and Keynote share common image-editing capabilities. In this exercise, you will enhance a black-and-white photograph of a guitar player. Working with a black-and-white photo is a good way to see some of the image adjustments in action.

1 In **agata-brochure.pages**, go to page 2. Click the guitar player photograph.

2 Choose View > Show Adjust Image to open the Adjust Image window.

The photograph is a little too dark. The best adjustments for correcting this are the Levels sliders. These control the points at which an image turns white or black, and where the middle gray is set. The ideal way to understand their function is to use them.

3 Drag the middle slider to the left to lighten the middle tones of the image.

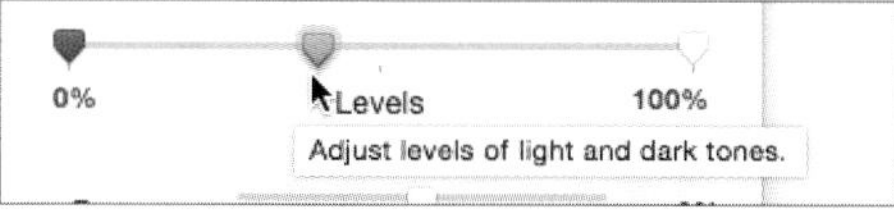

Moving the middle slider, also known as gamma, is often a pro photographer's best correction. Notice how the guitar player's jacket and shirt change as you move the middle slider.

4 Drag the white slider to the left to about 75%.

Depending on your screen's brightness, this is the point where the gray background turns to white. The white slider sets the point where grays turn to white. The black slider sets the point where grays turn to black.

The Adjust Image window is packed with powerful enhancement controls. Exposure makes the whole image lighter or darker. Saturation boosts or reduces color, so it's not needed on this photograph. Contrast? It affects contrast.

5 Drag the Highlights slider to 1%, and the Shadows slider to 50%.

Highlights:	1%
Shadows:	50%

Adjusting the Highlights returns some tone back to the guitar player's face, while the Shadows adjustment lightened the darkest tones. The subtle adjustment to the highlights may be hard to see, but cranking it too much will make the photograph look artificial.

Every image is different, so every image might not need adjustment; but it's good to know that Pages, Numbers, and Keynote all leverage the power of Core Image processing.

Now try adjusting the image sharpness. This adjustment is never going to fix a blurred photo, but as you'll see it can add a little definition.

6 Drag the Sharpness slider to 12%. Leave De-noise set to 0%.

Sharpness:	12%
De-noise:	0%

Increasing the percentage of sharpness can make photographs appear sharper, but should be used only in moderation because too much sharpness creates halos at the edges of tone changes. To see this, you could drag the Sharpness slider all the way to the right.

De-noise will smooth out pixel patterns that can occur when shooting in dark places. Try dragging the De-noise slider to the right and watch as the photograph becomes a little blurred.

NOTE ▶ Temperature and Tint settings are designed to correct color photographs. Dragging the Temperature slider makes a photo more orange or more blue—warmer or cooler in photography terms. The Tint slider allows you to correct the magenta or green color cast found in artificial light. For example, energy saving light bulbs can make people look a little green. You can drag the Tint slider to correct this.

7 If you experimented with the settings, click Reset Image to remove your adjustments. Choose Edit > Undo to reapply your adjustments.

TIP Clicking the Enhance button performs a base level quick fix that is worth trying before making manual adjustments. If Enhance doesn't produce an ideal result, you can click Reset Image to return the image to its original state.

8 Close the Adjust Image window.

Creating Shape Styles

In Lesson 3, you learned about the power of style sheets. However, those style concepts also can be extended to entire text boxes.

1 In **agata-brochure.pages**, go to page 3. Triple-click the text to select it.

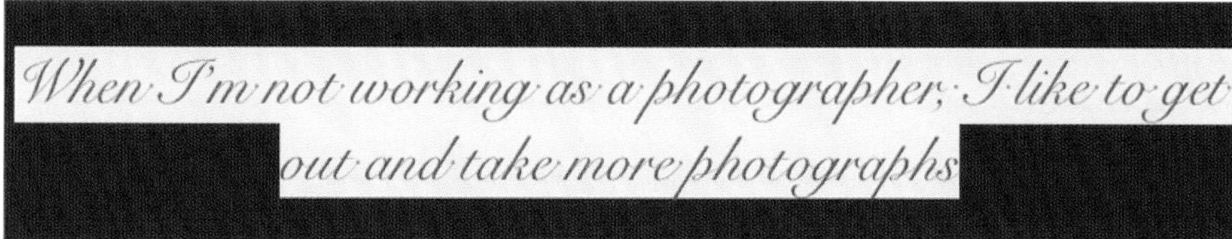

2 In the Text inspector's Layout pane, set Text Inset to 40 pt.

By default, text aligns to the edges of a text box. Changing the inset makes for a stronger design, by creating space around the words, they stand out more effectively.

3 In the Text inspector's Style pane, click the color wheel button to open the Colors window.

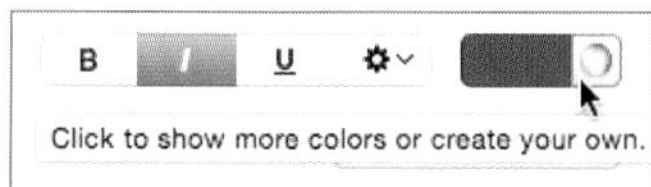

The Colors window is set to the selected text's current color.

4 Click the eyedropper icon, and then click the light gray beach area of the Yosemite Valley photograph to change the text color.

Picking colors from an associated image creates color harmonies in page designs. This same method was used to style the text box on page 4.

5 Close the Colors window.

6 Go to page 4, and click the text box to select it.

Much of the formatting has been done for you. Tab through the Format inspector to see which options have been applied. The text box looks good, but a shadow effect would make it stand out even more.

7 In the Style inspector, from the Shadow pop-up menu, choose Curved Shadow. Change the Offset to 7 pt, the Opacity to 21%, and the Angle to 7° to apply a subtle shadow.

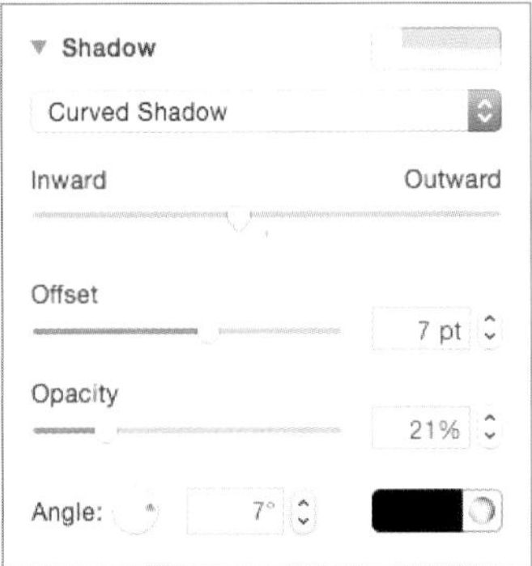

8 In the Style inspector, in Shape Styles, click the right arrow to move to a blank window. Click the + (plus) button.

The text box formatting, including the text style, has been added to the Shape Styles.

9 Go to page 5, and click the gray text box.

10 In the inspector's Shape Styles, locate the style you just created. Click the new shape style to apply it to the gray text box.

Formatting Table Styles

Lesson 4 covered the data-crunching power of tables. This exercise moves from mechanics to aesthetics. You'll apply formatting to a table and create a style for future use.

1 In **agata-brochure.pages**, go to page 6. Click the reference header for row 5.

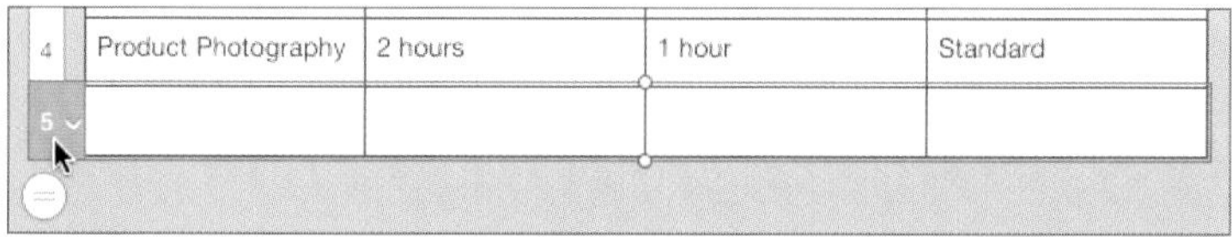

2 With row 5 selected, choose Format > Table > Merge Cells to merge the columns in Row 5.

NOTE ▶ Merging cells can change the operation of table functions, so it is not recommended in tables with calculations.

3 Select the second paragraph in the text box on page 6, beginning with "†Expenses." Choose Edit > Cut.

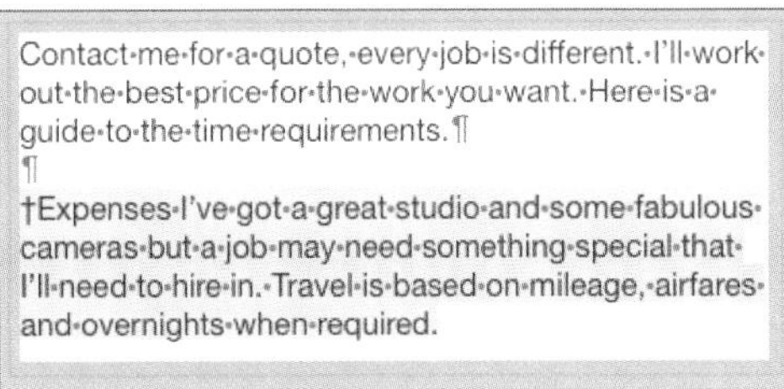

4 Click the merged cell. The text insertion cursor appears.

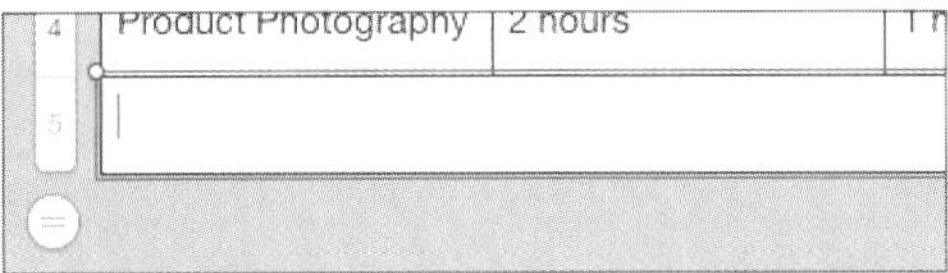

5 Choose Edit > Paste. The text is pasted into the cell and spans the entire width of the table.

6 Click cell B1, and then Shift-click cell D4, to select that block of cells. In the Text inspector, change the Alignment to centered.

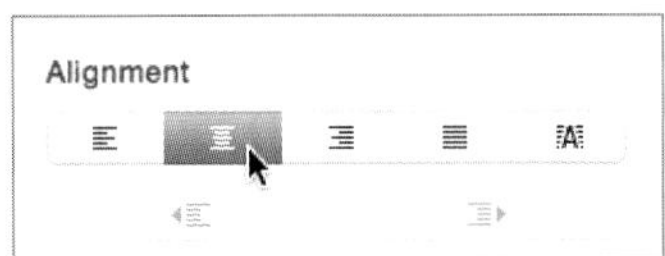

The table now looks clearer, but the headers could be emphasized.

7 Click the reference header for row 1 to select the row. In the Text inspector, change the typeface to 11 pt Condensed Bold.

8 Click the reference header for column A. Change the typeface to 11 pt Condensed Bold.

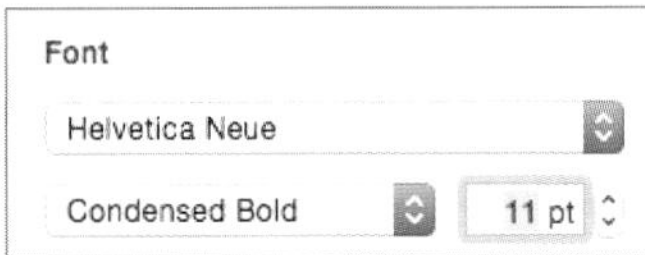

NOTE ▶ The merge cell does not change.

9 Click the reference header for row 1, and from the pop-up menu, choose Add Row Above.

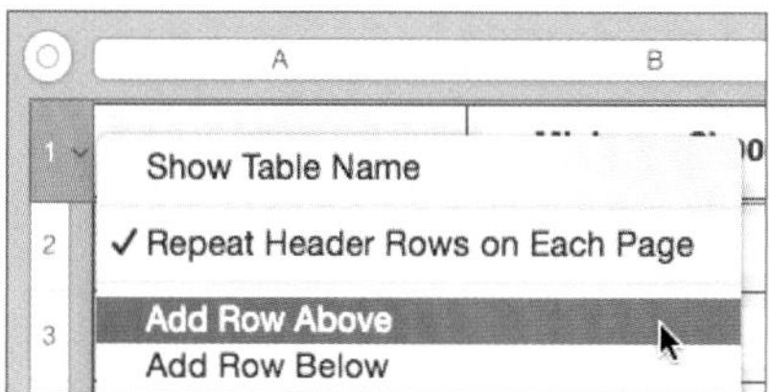

The new row has four columns, but you'll use it to contain a paragraph of text that will span the table.

10 Select the new row, and choose Format > Table > Merge Cells.

11 Select the remaining text in the text box, beginning with "Contact me." Cut and paste this text into row 1.

Later you will change the cell appearance in rows 1 and 2 to make them look like merged cells, without actually merging them.

NOTE ► If you delete the extra paragraph returns in row 1, the cell automatically shrinks to fit the text.

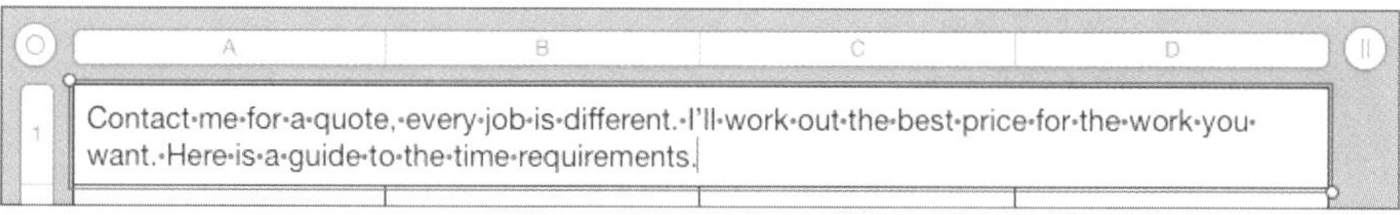

12 At the upper left of the table, click the table handle to select it.

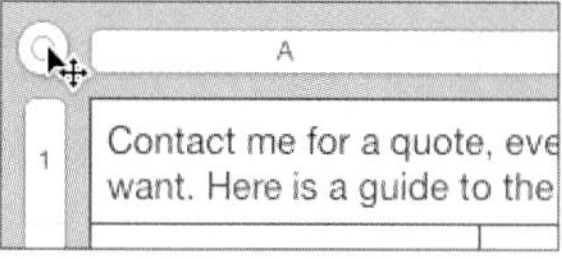

13 Drag the right edge of the table to make the table 7 inches wide.

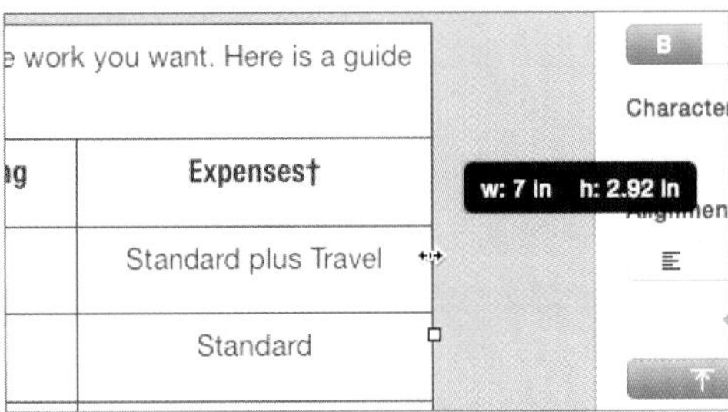

When you're formatting pages, tables are useful because they can be resized and repositioned to enhance page design.

You may have noticed that the table is light brown, but the text has a white background. This has been done to highlight the difference between the cell fill color and the text background color.

14 With the table selected, from the Layout tab of the Text inspector, click the background color pop-up, and select none.

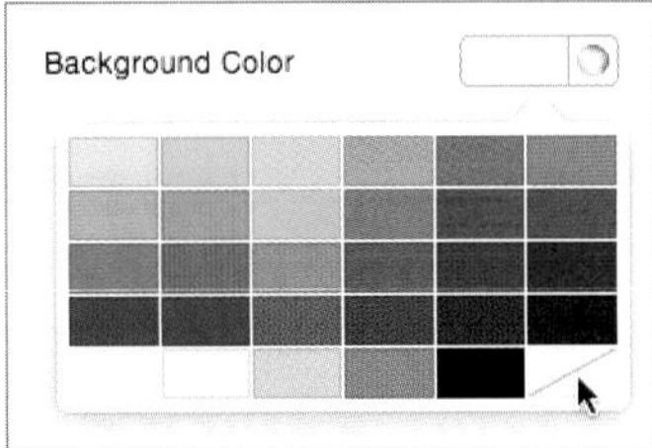

15 Click the reference header for row 1, and then Shift-click the reference header for row 2 to select both rows.

16 In the inspector, click the Cell tab. Click the Inside Borders button, and then change the Border pop-up menu to No Border to apply the change.

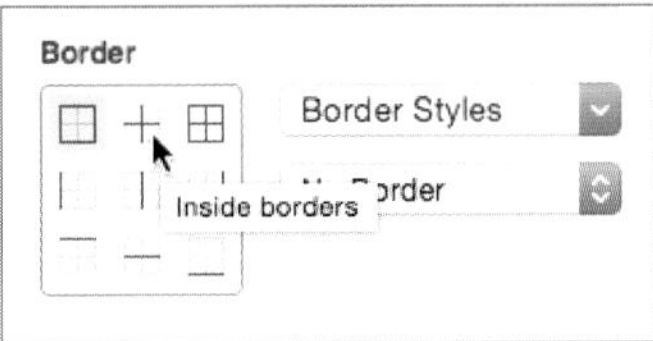

The inside borders disappear. No cells were merged, which presents another option for formatting tables.

NOTE ▸ Tables can be saved in Table Styles, but headers and footers are included in the style, and these have not been set for this table.

17 With the table selected, in the Table inspector, move to a blank window in Table Styles, and click the + (plus) button.

A new table style is created and applied to the table.

NOTE ▸ The inside borders disappeared from the table when this preference was added to the table style. Borders can be reapplied as style overrides.

You may wish to add header rows and columns to the table (as explained in Lesson 4) and then format your table using the methods described in this exercise. With a little experimentation, you will find your ideal way to create and manage tables.

18 Choose File > Save.

Preparing for Print

In print shops, pages are not printed edge-to-edge; they are printed with a border and then trimmed to the final document size. If you want images to print edge-to-edge, the printable area has to be larger than the final trim size, a feature known as *bleed*. Unfortunately, Pages doesn't have a direct way of creating a bleed, but you will learn how to create one in Lesson 7.

In this exercise you'll adjust an image mask so that Agata's brochure won't require a bleed.

TIP ▸ If you are using a print shop, discuss their requirements in the early stages of document planning to avoid wasted time and costly mistakes.

To keep things simple and avoid a lengthy description of reprographics, the brochure has 0.5-inch borders, but the photograph on page 5 touches the edge of the document.

1 In **agata-brochure.pages**, go to page 5. Double-click the photograph to open the Image Mask control.

   The image runs off the right side of the page.

2 Drag the lower-right corner of the selection to the guide set at 10 in. Click Done to close the Image Mask control.

   Doing so reshapes the image mask. Take care not to change the height of the mask.

   If your intention is to print this brochure at a print shop, at least one more page is required. Almost without exception, multipage documents are printed in multiples of four pages using a system called *imposition*.

   In the next steps, you'll use two methods for adding pages in page layout mode and then learn how to delete an unwanted page.

3 With the thumbnail for page 5 selected, choose Insert > Page.

   A blank page appears; an alternative method would be to duplicate an existing page and modify it.

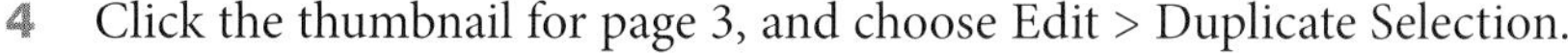

4 Click the thumbnail for page 3, and choose Edit > Duplicate Selection.

TIP ▶ The duplicate page can be modified, which can be a time-saver compared to starting a page from scratch. The photo page of Yosemite could be duplicated several times, then the photos swapped to quickly create a portfolio and edit captions.

This document now has nine pages, rather than the eight required.

5 Click the thumbnail for the blank page. Press Backspace to delete it.

6 Go to page 8, which should be the address page.

Because this is a print version of the brochure, you'll switch off the live hyperlink.

7 Click the URL, www.example.com. In the popover, click Edit, and then click Remove.

The underline disappears from the URL, which indicates that the URL is no longer clickable as a link.

To prepare the document to send to a print shop, you'll export it as a PDF

NOTE ▶ There are various subtypes of PDF. Not every print shop can process the PDFs created by the Pages export option, which is another reason to discuss your project in advance with your chosen print shop.

8 Choose File > Export To > PDF. Select Best image quality. Do not set password security.

9 Click Next, and save the PDF to your desktop.

Taking Part in a Document Review

You have been working on the look and feel of a brochure, and not concentrating on the brochure's text. For many people, designing layout and checking spelling and grammar are not done simultaneously.

For that reason, sharing your Pages document for review is a good idea, and it's not difficult. You'll learn how to collaborate using iCloud in Lesson 17. However, you can use other methods to share a Pages document such as email or posting on a shared network.

Comments, markups, and changes are labeled with user names. Here's how to verify the author name currently being used for tracking changes and adding comments on your copy of Pages.

1 With Pages open, choose Pages > Preferences, and in the General tab locate the Author field.

2 If necessary, change the Author name (usually this would be your name).

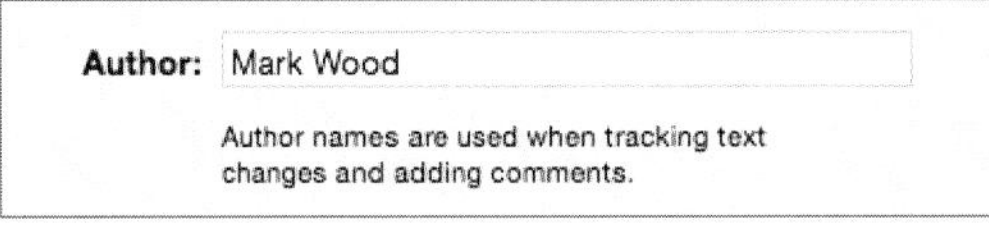

Adding Comments

Here's how to mark up a document in a review.

1 With **agata-brochure.pages** open, choose Edit > Track Changes.

The review toolbar appears (beneath the toolbar).

Because the brochure is a page layout document, the only collaborative review tools are highlights and comments. Later you'll work with tracked changes in a word-processing document.

Your colleague will also need to enable Track Changes on her Mac. Because you may not be able to review the text with a colleague right now, let's cover what you need to do both as a reviewer and the reviewed.

2 Click the icon at the left of the review bar to show or hide comments and changes. Leave the pane hidden for now.

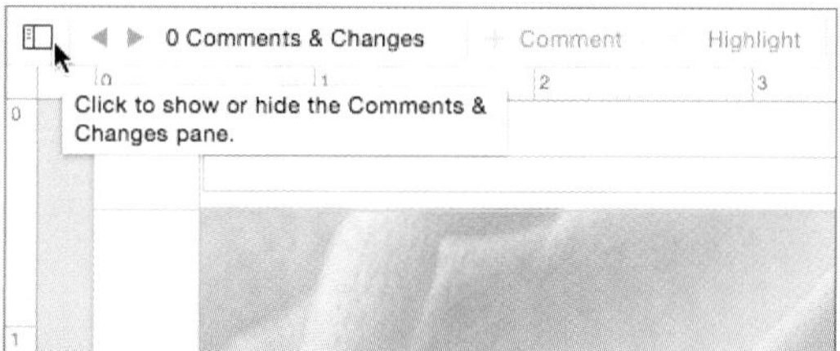

3 Go to page 3. Select the words "as a photographer." In the review toolbar, click the Comment button, and then type a comment.

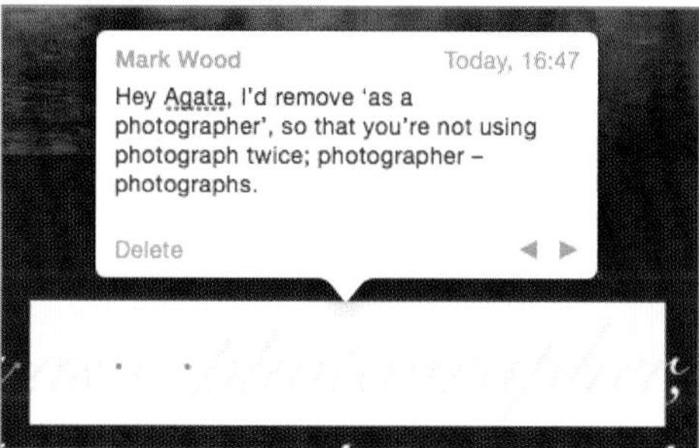

By default the comments are highlighted in yellow. This may be your favorite color, but it makes the highlighted words hard to see.

4 In the review toolbar, from the Action (gear) pop-up menu, choose Author Color > Blue to change the color of your comments.

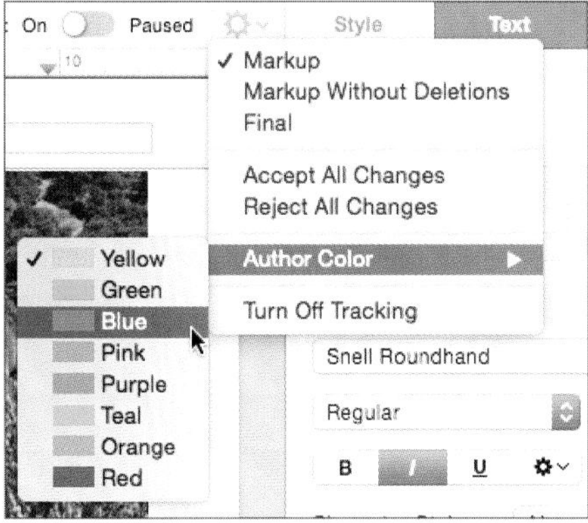

NOTE ▶ You could also select text and add a highlight, which highlights the text without any comment.

5 Go to page 8. In the address, triple-click the phone number. Then, click the Comment button, and type a comment.

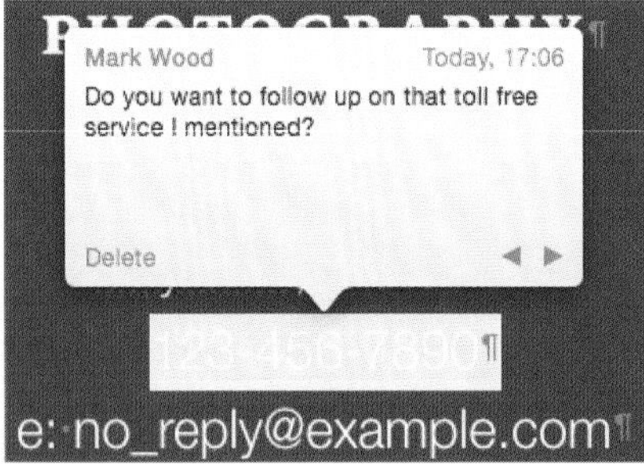

6 The review toolbar shows two comments. Click the arrow buttons to jump to the preceding or following comment. In a comment's popover, you can click Delete to remove the comment.

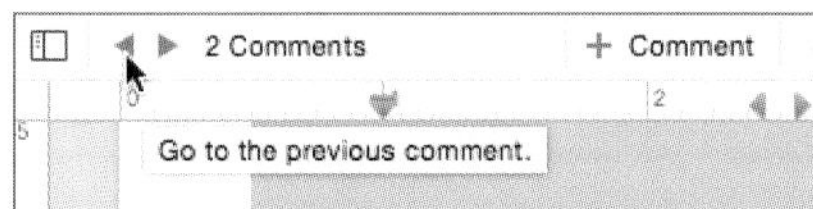

7 Close the **agata-brochure.pages** document.

Reviewing Tracked Changes

If you receive a document in which a colleague has Track Changes enabled, and he has deleted or amended text, those changes will be listed in the review pane. You can choose to accept or reject the edits. To experience this, you'll now open a word-processing document that's been amended with Track Changes switched on.

1 Open APTS Pages Numbers Keynote > Lesson_05 > **sl-report-rd-reviewed.pages.**

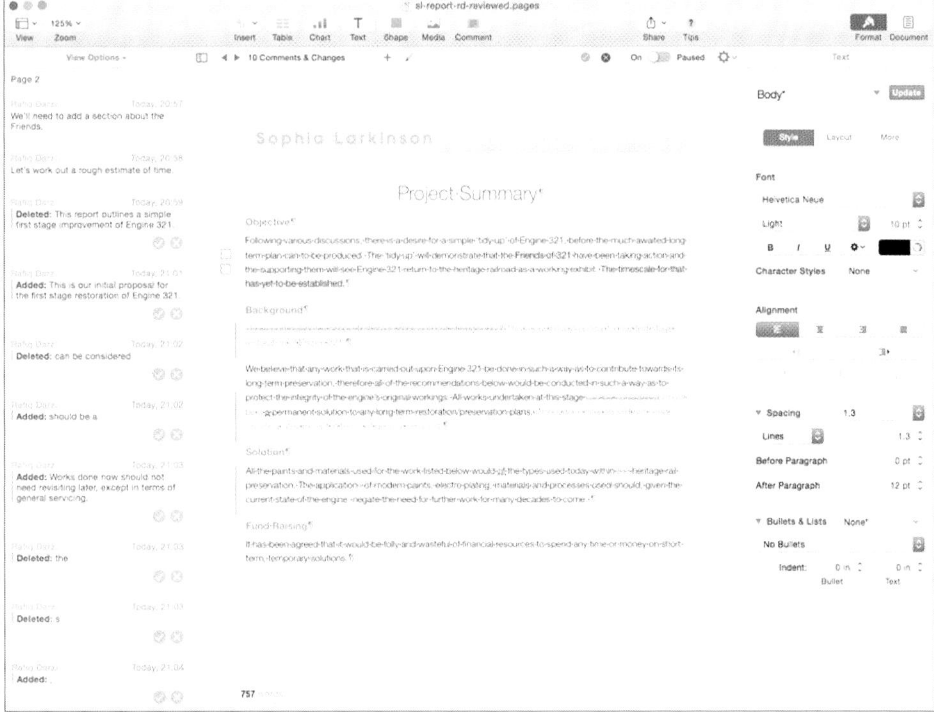

The document opens with changes and comments visible. You'll work through the changes and accept and reject them. You'll also amend the document to see how your edits are displayed with Track Changes turned on.

2 Click the first comment in the review sidebar.

A connection line appears linking the comment to a box in line with the text or object to which it is applied.

Beneath the first comment box is a second box, in line with the second comment.

3 Click the second box. The connection line links back to the comment in the sidebar.

The third and fourth changes are linked; the reviewer has deleted a sentence and added a new one.

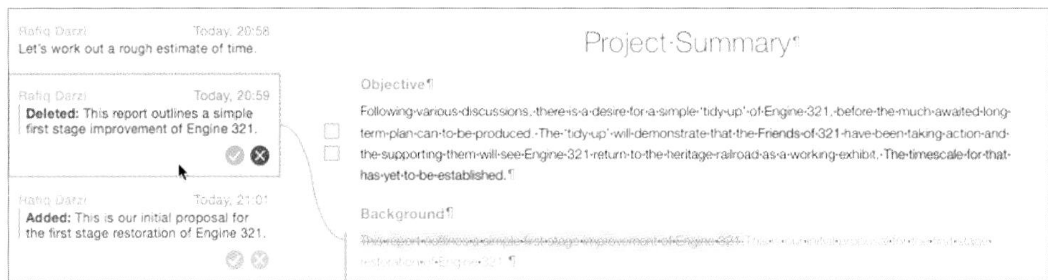

4 In the review sidebar, click the third change.

A line connects the change to its occurrence on the page.

5 Click the green checkmark to accept this change.

6 Click the fourth change, and accept this change.

This is the process for reviewing changes. Now you'll amend a few words to see how those changes are tracked.

7 Zoom in to 200% to more clearly see the text.

The next step suggests an amendment, but feel free to make your own edits.

8 In the Background section, locate the line beginning with "long-term preservation," and select ", therefore a".

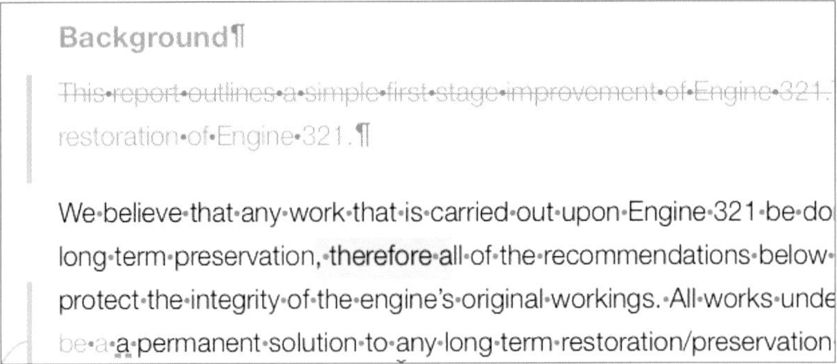

9 Type . *A* (period space A). Your changes are listed in the review sidebar to accept or reject as you see fit.

If a document has multiple reviewers, you can filter to see a specific reviewer's changes.

10 At the top of the review sidebar, click the View Options pop-up menu.

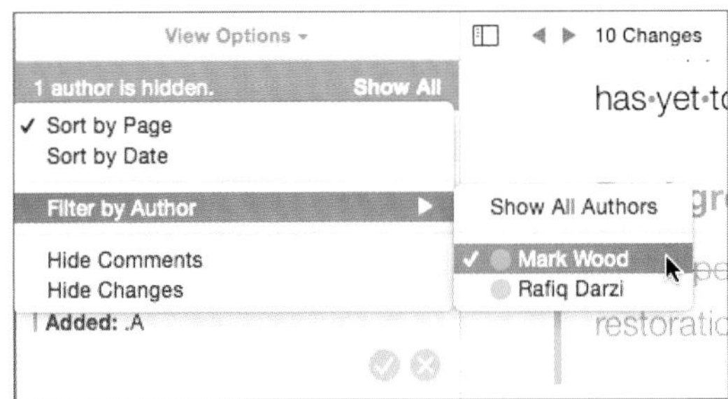

11 Choose Filter by Author > [your review name].

The changes and comments list now shows only those changes you made.

12 Choose View Options > Filter by Author > Show All Authors to display all the comments and changes once again.

NOTE ▶ The review toolbar has a switch labeled On and Paused. You may wish to pause tracking while you make changes.

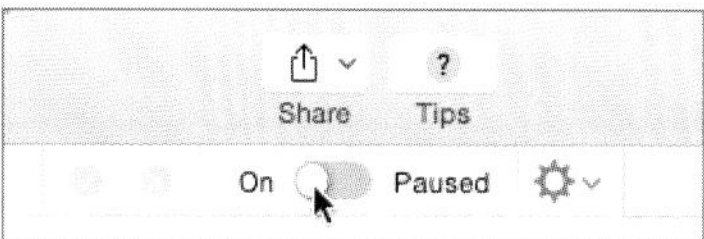

Next to the pause switch is an action menu. You can use it to change how tracked changes are displayed. For example, choosing Markup Without Deletions hides any text that was deleted with Track Changes enabled. The deleted text is preserved; to display it, choose Markup.

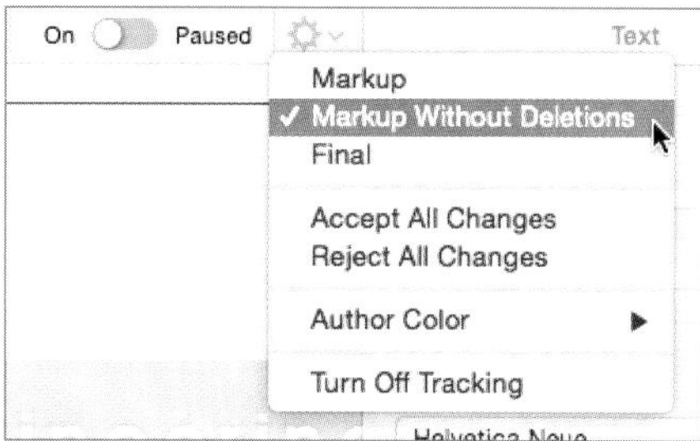

You have been working through the options available for document review. Pages makes it easy to comment, mark up, and track changes.

13 Choose Edit > Turn Off Tracking. A dialog appears.

If you're done reviewing, you can click Accept All Changes, which honors any changes you rejected or accepted individually. If you suspect there's more reviewing to be done, click Cancel and run through the review again.

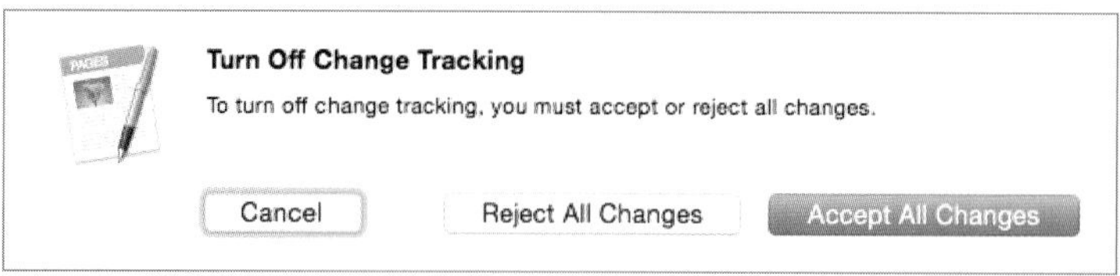

NOTE ▶ You can also choose Accept All Changes or Reject All Changes from the review toolbar Action pop-up menu.

14 Choose File > Close to end this lesson.

Lesson Review

1. Which Pages features are available only in a word-processing document?
2. In the Adjust Image window, describe how to make a photograph lighter or darker.
3. Which option moves text away from the edges of a text box?
4. How do you reshape an image mask?
5. In a page layout document, how do you add extra pages?

Answers

1. Document body, document margins, moving objects with text, and text flowing continuously across multiple pages.
2. Using the middle slider in Levels is a great way to lighten or darken an image. In addition, you can use Exposure, Contrast, Highlights, and Shadows.
3. Text Inset, found in the Text inspector's Layout pane, moves text away from the edges of a text box, or table cell.
4. Double-click an image, so that the Image Mask control appears. Drag a corner of the image mask to reshape it, and then click Done.
5. Choose Insert > Page to add a page following the current one. Repeat this operation until you have the required number of pages.

6

Lesson Files

APTS Pages Numbers Keynote > Lesson_06 > agata-postcard.pages

APTS Pages Numbers Keynote > Lesson_06 > ju-jitsu-poster.pages

APTS Pages Numbers Keynote > Lesson_06 > ju-jitsu-club-logo.pdf

APTS Pages Numbers Keynote > Lesson_06 > agata-logo.pages

APTS Pages Numbers Keynote > Lesson_06 > elegant-business-cards.template

Time

This lesson takes approximately 60 minutes to complete.

Goals

Position objects and guides precisely

Create a business card and a poster from a template

Format objects and text as placeholders

Save documents as templates

Understand the concept of printable area

Share and manage templates

Lesson **6**

Building Promotional Materials

Lesson 5 took a deep look at how you can use Pages to lay out multipage documents. In this lesson, you'll use page layout mode to create business cards, posters, and postcards.

Rather than creating a multipage document, you will build multiple documents on a page. Trim marks are required when several designs are set on a single page. You will learn how to create trim marks so that you can generate printable documents from scratch.

You'll also insert placeholders for text and images so you can save pages as templates you can apply to recurring tasks.

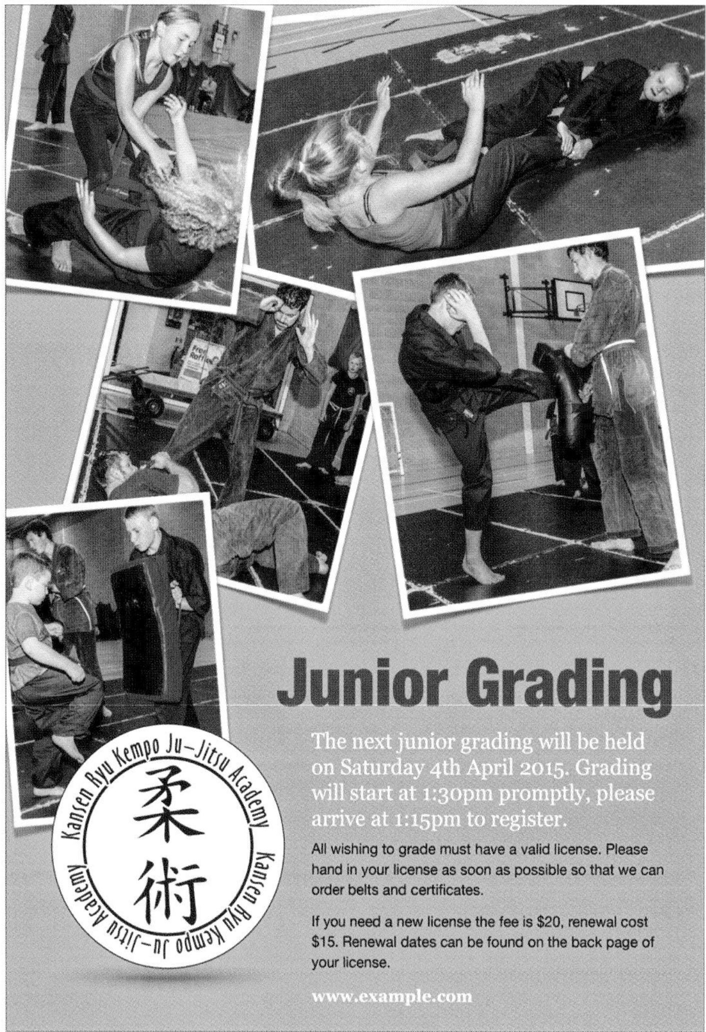

Creating Business Cards

Pages installs with several business card templates. While the dimensions of business cards vary, this lesson describes ways to design custom-sized documents using a template or from scratch. In this exercise, you will modify a document created from a template and learn how trim marks are placed.

1 In Pages, choose File > New. In the Template Chooser, in Stationery, select Elegant Business Cards.

2 Scroll to the bottom of page 1. Check that the label reads "Avery 5371."

It's a two-page document; the Avery number for page two should be 5881. If you're working outside the USA, you might have templates for different labels. If the labels for your Elegant Business Cards are not Avery 5371 and Avery 5881, you will need to complete the additional exercise that follows.

If your document uses Avery 5371 and Avery 5881, jump to the "Customizing Your Layout" section.

Additional Steps to Load the Required Template

You need to complete the four steps in this exercise only if the required template is not installed on your computer.

1 Open APTS Pages Numbers Keynote > Lesson_06 > **elegant-business-cards.template**.

2 When prompted, click Add to Template Chooser.

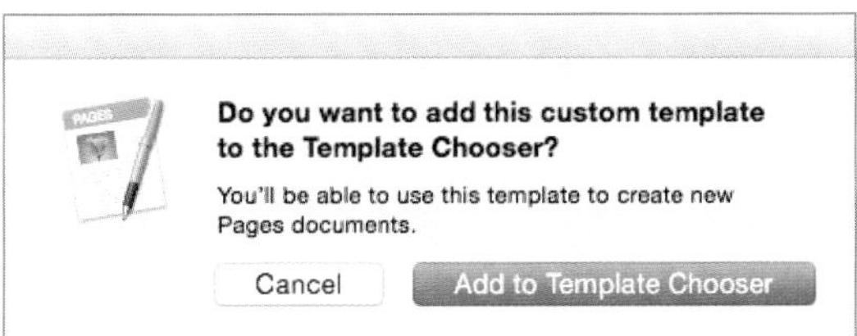

3 In Pages, choose File > New. In the Template Chooser, in My Templates, select elegant-business-cards.

A document is created using the same template used in this lesson.

4 Close the Untitled document that was created from the incorrect template.

Customizing Your Layout.

The Elegant Business Cards design looks compatible with the visual identity of our fictitious photographer.

This is a page layout document; you'll need to add some guides.

1 In the toolbar, choose View > Show Rulers.

2 On page 1, drag a horizontal guide to the center of each of the lines underscoring the placeholder text, "Company Name."

TIP Zooming in to 200% or higher may help you place the guides more accurately.

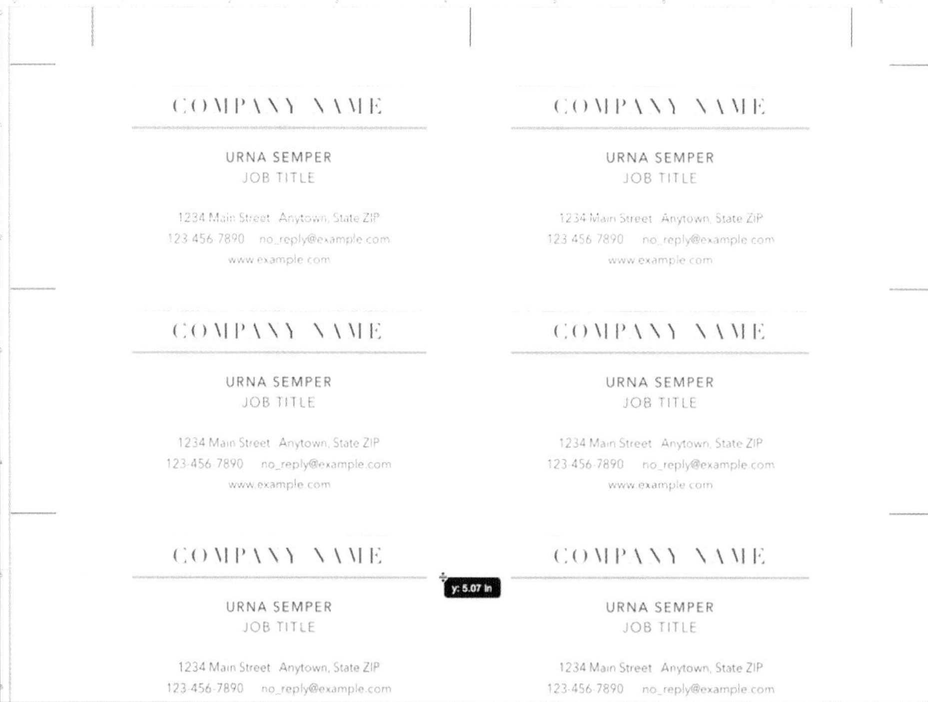

You could type the business card details ten times to complete the sheet, but let's use a more efficient method.

3 At the top of the page, select the first text box that contains the job title and address. Choose Edit > Cut.

This useful information is now on your Clipboard, ready to be pasted into the document later. The remaining duplicates of the job title and address can be deleted.

4 Choose Edit > Select All to select all the text placeholders, and then press Backspace to delete them.

5 Choose Edit > Paste. The address placeholder appears back in position. You'll now modify this single instance of the business card and later duplicate the new improved business card design.

Agata already has a logo design, and copying and pasting it from an existing document is a simple task.

6 Open APTS Pages Numbers Keynote > Lesson_06 > **agata-logo.pages**. Select the text box, "Agata Rhondo-Hayes Photography." Choose Edit > Copy to copy the text.

7 Return to the business card document, and choose Edit > Paste.

The photographer's logo you copied from the **agata-logo.pages** document appears, but it fills the page. You'll need to scale and position the text box and change its font size. To ensure that the logo is scaled and positioned properly, you'll type new values into the Format inspector.

8 Triple-click the logo's text to select it. Use the Text inspector to change the font size to 10 pt.

9 In the Arrange pane of the inspector, set the logo's Size and Position as follows:

- Size Width: 3.9 in
- Size Height: 0.56 in
- Position X: 0.55 in
- Position Y: 0.7 in

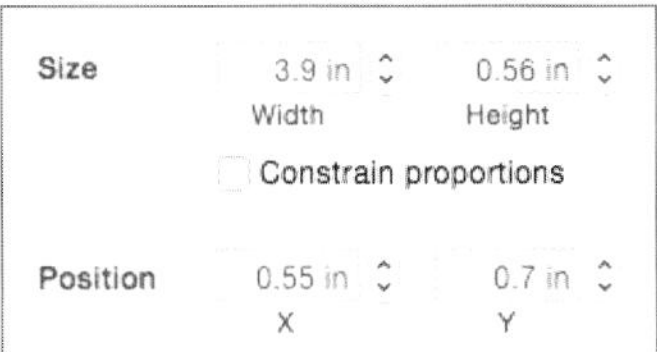

NOTE ▸ In most projects, scaling and positioning objects requires a mix of dragging selections and handles and entering values into the inspector's data fields.

TIP ▸ To scale the logo's border lines appropriately, in the inspector, change the Borders and Rules value to 1 pt.

10 Click the logo text box. Shift-click the address text box. Choose Arrange Group.

11 Option-drag the grouped text boxes to the right.

Position the duplicate business card artwork using the alignment guides. When the artwork is in place, first release the mouse button and then release the Option key.

NOTE ▸ Alignment guides are enabled by default. If they don't appear, check Pages > Preferences. In the Rulers tab, make sure both Alignment Guide options are selected.

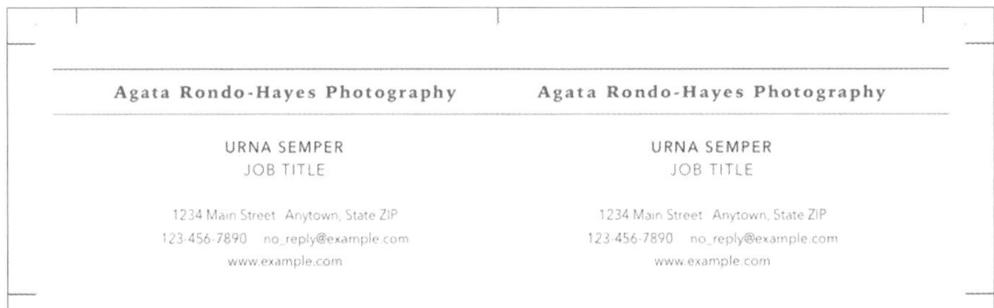

TIP ▸ Shift-drag an object to constrain its movement to straight horizontal, vertical, or diagonal lines.

12 Select both copies of the business card, and then Option-drag the artwork down to the second row.

13 Repeat this operation until all five rows contain copies of the business cards.

Agata Rondo-Hayes Photography URNA SEMPER JOB TITLE 1234 Main Street Anytown, State ZIP 123-456-7890 no_reply@example.com www.example.com	**Agata Rondo-Hayes Photography** URNA SEMPER JOB TITLE 1234 Main Street Anytown, State ZIP 123-456-7890 no_reply@example.com www.example.com
Agata Rondo-Hayes Photography URNA SEMPER JOB TITLE 1234 Main Street Anytown, State ZIP 123-456-7890 no_reply@example.com www.example.com	**Agata Rondo-Hayes Photography** URNA SEMPER JOB TITLE 1234 Main Street Anytown, State ZIP 123-456-7890 no_reply@example.com www.example.com
Agata Rondo-Hayes Photography URNA SEMPER JOB TITLE 1234 Main Street Anytown, State ZIP 123-456-7890 no_reply@example.com www.example.com	**Agata Rondo-Hayes Photography** URNA SEMPER JOB TITLE 1234 Main Street Anytown, State ZIP 123-456-7890 no_reply@example.com www.example.com
Agata Rondo-Hayes Photography URNA SEMPER JOB TITLE 1234 Main Street Anytown, State ZIP 123-456-7890 no_reply@example.com www.example.com	**Agata Rondo-Hayes Photography** URNA SEMPER JOB TITLE 1234 Main Street Anytown, State ZIP 123-456-7890 no_reply@example.com www.example.com
Agata Rondo-Hayes Photography URNA SEMPER JOB TITLE 1234 Main Street Anytown, State ZIP 123-456-7890 no_reply@example.com www.example.com	**Agata Rondo-Hayes Photography** URNA SEMPER JOB TITLE 1234 Main Street Anytown, State ZIP 123-456-7890 no_reply@example.com www.example.com

Avery 5371

TIP You can press the arrow keys to nudge the artwork into place.

That's one method for duplicating artwork on a single sheet. Before moving to the next exercise, however, let's look at the trim marks included in the business card template.

14 Click the white space just above the logo text box.

Small crosses appear, which indicate that a shape has been locked.

Agata Rondo-Hayes Photography
Agata Rondo-Hayes Photography
URNA SEMPER
JOB TITLE
URNA SEMPER
JOB TITLE

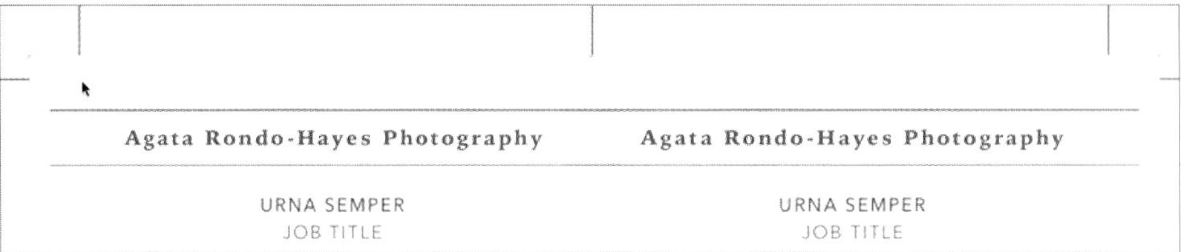

15 Choose Arrange > Unlock. The shape appears as a selection and fills the space behind all ten business cards.

16 Press Backspace to delete the shape.

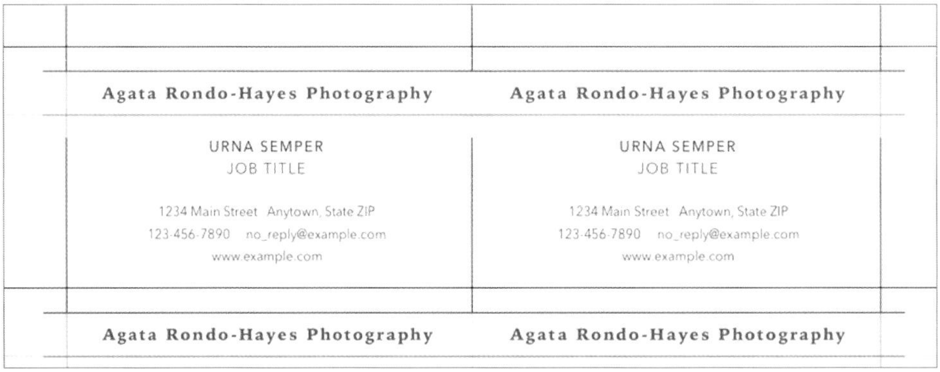

Agata Rondo-Hayes Photography
Agata Rondo-Hayes Photography
URNA SEMPER
JOB TITLE
1234 Main Street Anytown, State ZIP
123-456-7890 no_reply@example.com
www.example.com
URNA SEMPER
JOB TITLE
1234 Main Street Anytown, State ZIP
123-456-7890 no_reply@example.com
www.example.com
Agata Rondo-Hayes Photography
Agata Rondo-Hayes Photography

The trim marks are displayed as lines. Previously, these marks were partially obscured by the white shape. Later in this lesson, you will create these trim marks in a postcard project.

17 Choose File > Close to close all your open Pages documents.

Making Posters

A good poster is eye-catching, drawing the viewer to digest a simple message. That's an easy statement to make, but it's harder to execute. Fortunately, Pages templates help give you a head start.

By creating a document from a template, you'll find many design elements in place, leaving you to change the placeholder text and images, to change colors and fonts, and to make the design your own.

1 Choose File > New, and from Flyers & Posters, select the School Poster Small template.

   The photos are placeholders; let's replace those using the Media Browser.

2 In the upper-left photo, click the placeholder icon to open the Media Browser.

3 In the Media Browser, select the ju-jitsu poster album. Locate and select the photo ju-jitsu-9.

   The Media Browser closes, and the photo replaces the placeholder.

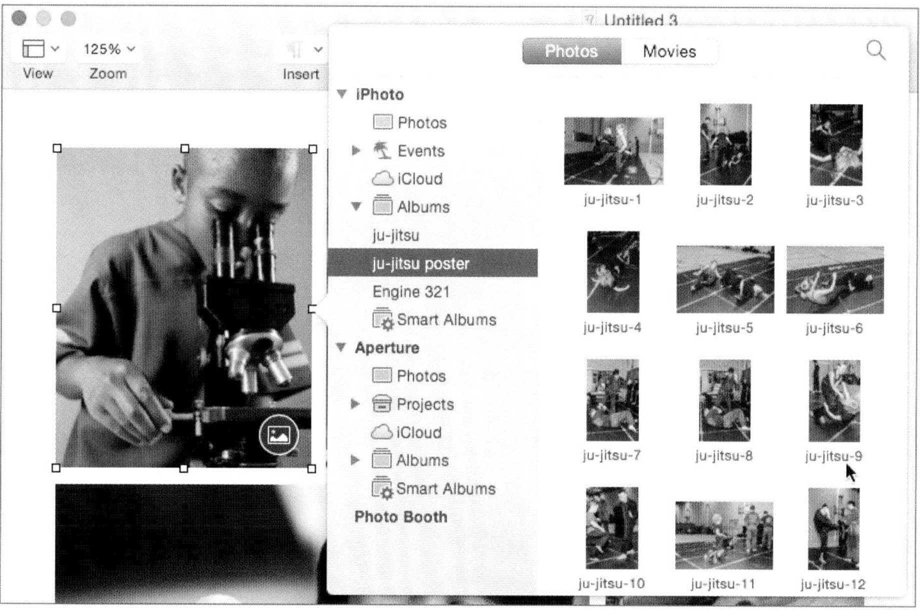

4 Repeat step 3 to replace all the placeholder images, using different photos from the ju-jitsu poster album.

NOTE ▸ You'll later resize the image masks so don't worry if the photos crop poorly.

Rotating images and logos can make a design look informal. To rotate a photo, text box, or shape, you use the Rotate options.

5 Click a photo to select it, and then in the Arrange inspector, change the Rotate Angle.

Experiment by clicking or dragging inside the circle icon. Alternatively you can type a value into the Rotation Angle field.

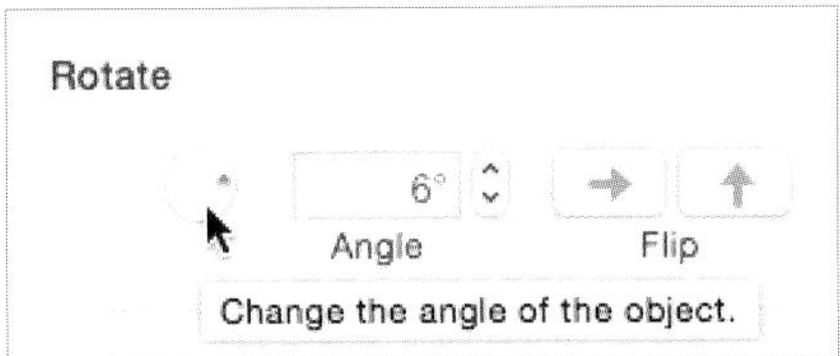

The aim is to practice repositioning objects on the page.

6 Double-click a photo to reshape the image mask to better frame an image.

You can repeat steps 5 and 6 for all the images on the poster if you wish. But, resolving a design takes time—adjusting the relative size of image to text and working with color—and though this is very important, let's move things along by opening a more fully developed version of the poster.

7 Close the document you've been working on.

8 Open APTS Pages Numbers Keynote > Lesson_06 > **ju-jitsu-poster.pages.**

9 Shift-click each of the photos to select them. In the Style inspector, select the Picture Frame image style to attach a frame to all the images.

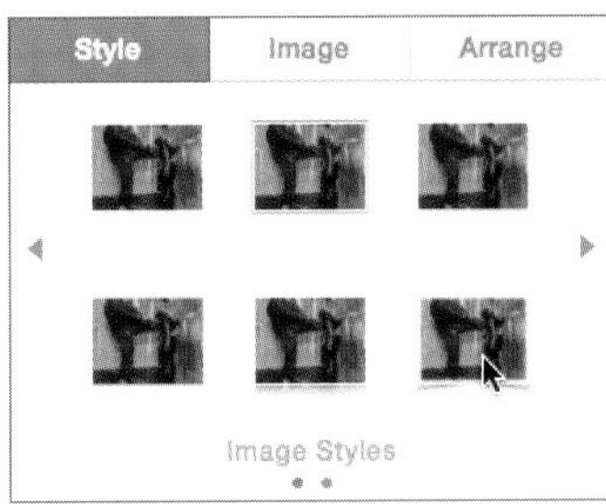

TIP ▶ You can scale picture frames in the inspector to improve your design.

10 Click near the edge of the green shape box to the lower-right of the poster. Make sure you haven't selected the text box

11 Choose Arrange > Unlock.

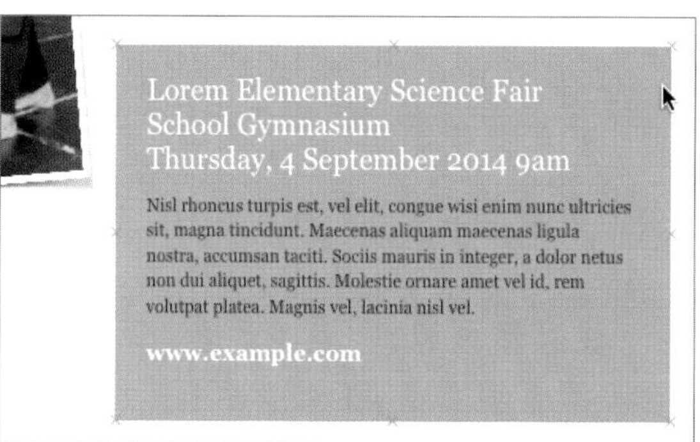

12 In the Style inspector, click the yellow shape style.

Sensei Takao's favorite color works well in this design. Take care when choosing yellows, though, as they can be hard to read onscreen and in print.

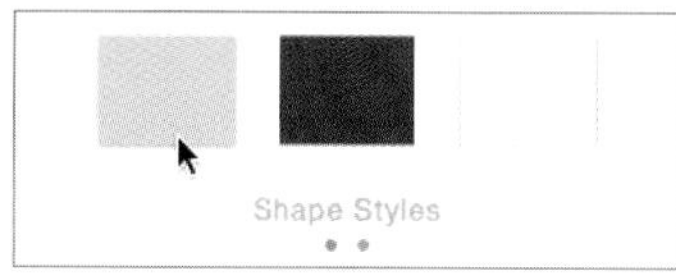

13 Scale the yellow shape to fill the entire poster background by dragging the selection handles to scale up the shape.

TIP ▶ Zoom out to see the whole page, which makes scaling the yellow shape easier.

NOTE ▶ The poster design touches all four document edges. Some printers, including numerous inkjet printers, can print edge-to-edge; but many printers, especially those used in print shops, require that page designs include a margin. You'll learn the process for producing edge-to-edge designs in the next exercise.

Let's complete the poster.

14 Reposition the text box containing "Lorem Elementary Spring Science Fair." Scale and drag the text box so that that it's fully visible.

The Lorem Elementary text box contains two text placeholders, one for each line.

NOTE ▶ As you reposition and reshape the text box, some of the placeholder text may become hidden. For example, in the line "Spring Science Fair," the word "Fair" is going to disappear. This isn't a problem for placeholder text.

15 Select "Spring Science Fair," and press Backspace to delete it.

16 Select "Lorem Elementary," and replace the text by typing *Junior Grading*.

17 Choose Insert > Choose, and select APTS Pages Numbers Keynote > Lesson_06 > **ju-jitsu-club-logo.pdf**.

A text wrap is automatically applied, so the text boxes have been disrupted.

18 In the Arrange inspector, from the Text Wrap pop-up menu, choose None.

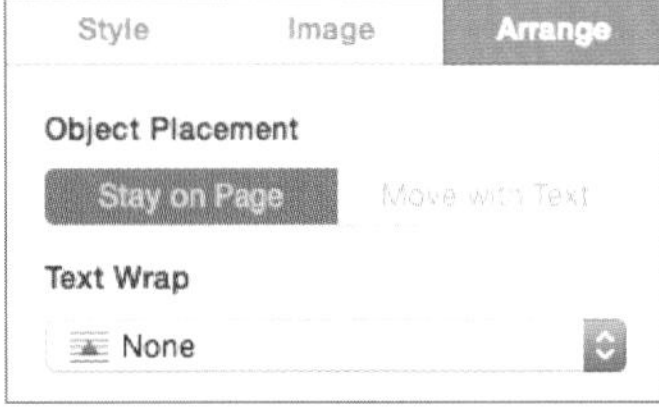

The logo can be positioned in the lower-left of the poster.

With all elements placed on the poster, some additional scaling and repositioning will help complete your design.

19 Close your poster document.

Starting with a Blank Canvas

Templates with design elements already in place are very useful, but sometimes it's best to start with a blank template. Agata, our fictitious photographer, needs a postcard template design. In this exercise, you'll draw on concepts introduced in the previous lessons to build a custom template.

The following exercises require that you develop a postcard design with front and back artwork that could be uploaded to an online print service.

To begin this process, you will set the document size and add crop marks to the postcard artwork.

1 In Pages, choose File > New. In the Template Chooser, select the Blank Landscape template.

2 Choose File > Convert to Page Layout > Convert.

3 In the Document inspector, deselect the Header and Footer checkboxes.

   These elements are not needed for the postcard; so to keep things tidy, they're best turned off.

   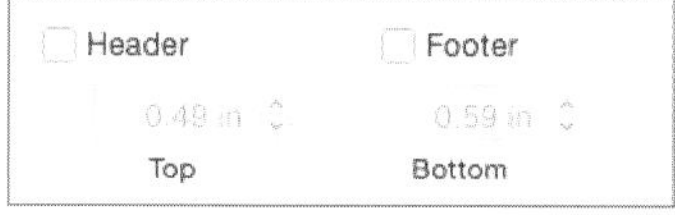

   NOTE ▶ You can set the paper size in the Document inspector. When your project calls for edge-to-edge printing, options such as Borderless Printing may be available for your Mac computer's printer. More significantly, the paper sizes available to you will be displayed in the paper size menu once a printer is chosen. In this exercise, however, setting the paper size is not important.

4 In the toolbar, click the Shape icon, and then click the square shape.

   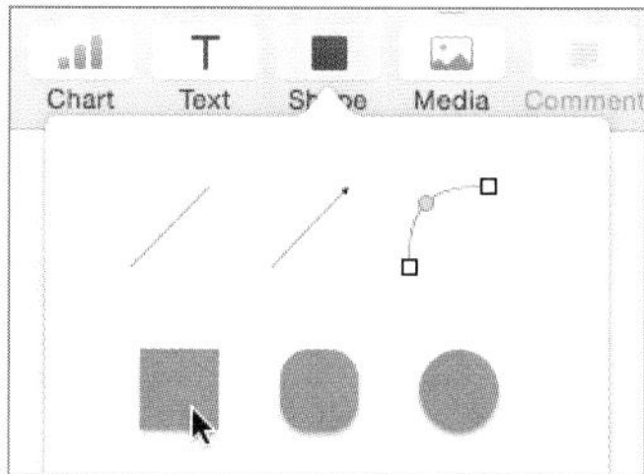

5 In the Arrange tab of the Format inspector, set the Size Width and Height to 6 in by 4 in, respectively.

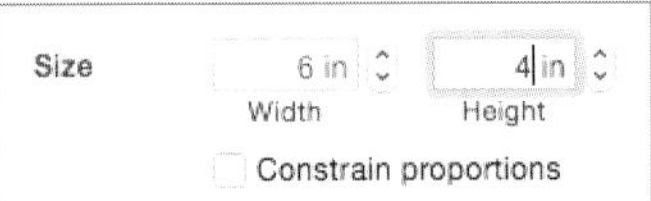

This postcard will be 6 x 4 inches, hence, the dimensions given. Of course, you can substitute other values depending on the finished postcard size you want.

6 Using the alignment guides, drag the shape to the center of the page.

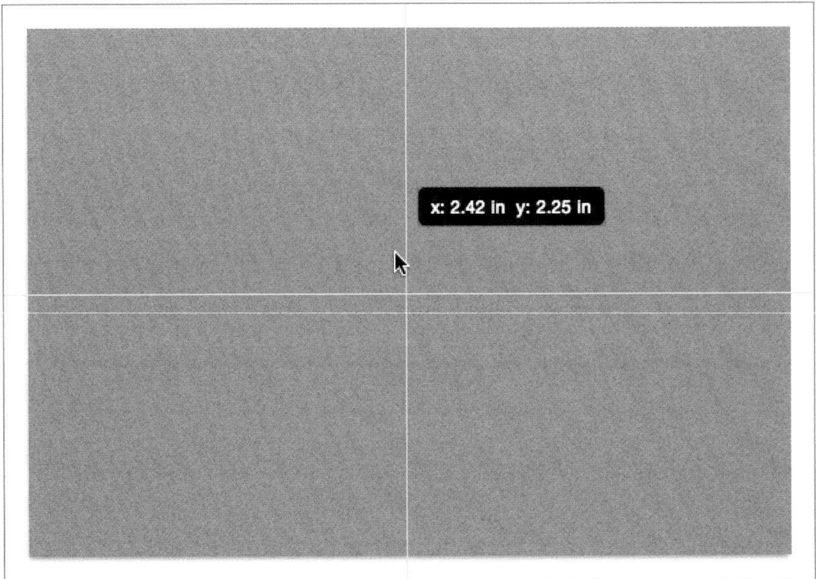

7 Press Command-R. This shows and hides the rulers. Make sure the rulers are visible.

8 In the toolbar, click the Shape icon, and then choose the line tool.

You'll use the line tool to create crop marks for the postcard.

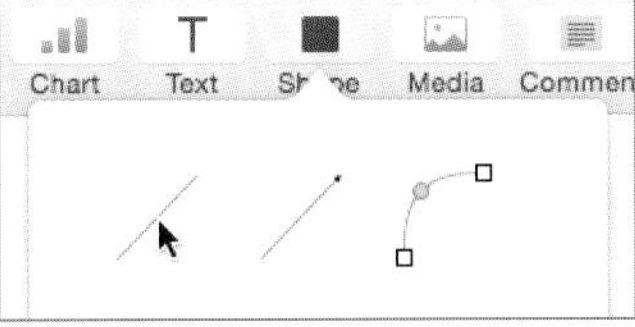

9 Drag the end points of the line to align with the left edge of the picture box.

Take care not to move the rectangle shape. You can choose Edit > Undo to correct any mistakes.

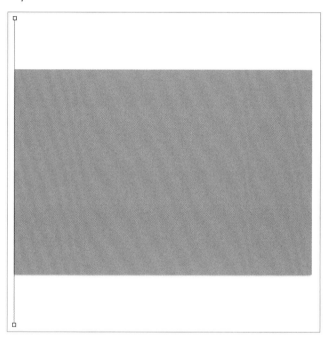

10 Extend the line above and below the rectangle shape. The line should be approximately 6 inches long.

11 Choose Edit > Duplicate Selection to copy the line, and then drag the duplicate line to the right edge of the rectangle.

12 Choose Edit > Duplicate Selection. This time move the end points of the line to align with the upper edge of the rectangle.

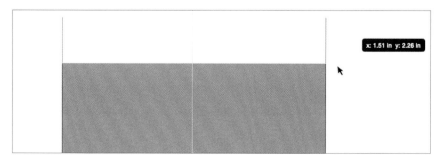

13 Drag the end points of the horizontal line out equally on both sides of the rectangle to extend its length to approximately 8 inches.

14 Press Command-D. Drag the duplicate line to the lower edge of the rectangle.

You now have lines that will become your crop marks. Let's set the bleed area, the bit of the print that will be trimmed off after the print run is complete.

15 Click the rectangle to select it. In the Format inspector, change the Size Width and Height to 6.25 in and 4.25 in.

16 Drag the rectangle to center it on the page. The rectangle represents the *bleed area*, because it extends the artwork an eighth of an inch beyond the crop marks and therefore "bleeds" off the edge.

NOTE ▶ In metric measures, a bleed is usually 3mm on all sides.

17 Choose Arrange > Bring to Front.

You will now complete the crop mark process.

18 In the Style inspector, set the shape Fill to white with No Border.

If a drop shadow appears, choose None from the Shadow menu, also found in the Style inspector.

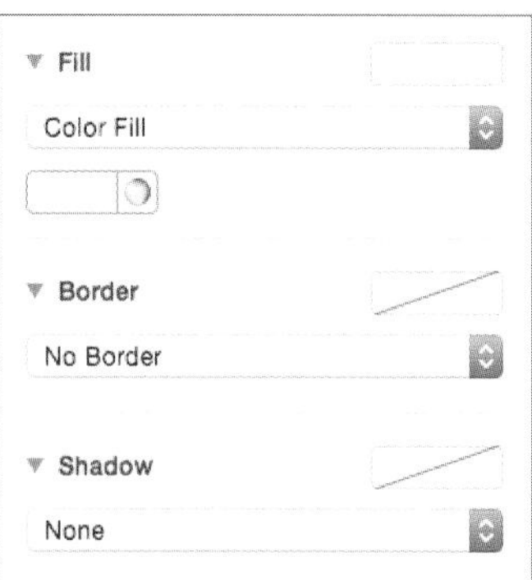

19 Choose Edit > Select All, and then press Command-L to lock all the objects in place.

NOTE ▶ The keyboard shortcut to lock elements is Command-L. To unlock elements, select the required item and press Command-Option-L.

You've now created the trim marks for a 6-inch x 4-inch postcard. This method can be applied in a myriad of ways to create labels, delegate badges, and so on.

20 In the toolbar, click the View icon and choose Show Page Thumbnails.

21 Click the thumbnail for page 1, and press Command-D to duplicate the page.

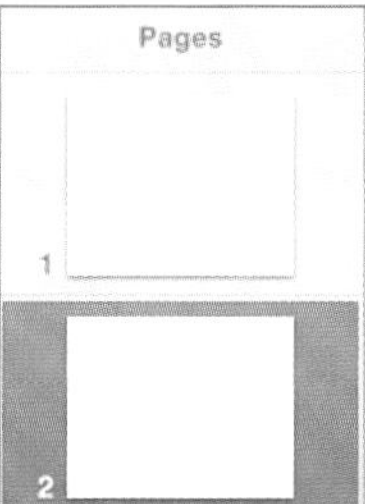

You now have created the front and back of the postcard, complete with crop marks.

22 Close the open document.

Defining Placeholder Images

For this exercise, you'll start with a version of the postcard design that has the front and back already in place. The techniques used to execute this were covered in earlier lessons, so you're not missing any super user tips!

In this exercise, you will learn how to convert an image to a media placeholder.

1 Open APTS Pages Numbers Keynote > Lesson_06 > **agata-postcard.pages**.

2 Go to page 1.

In addition to crop marks, two guides have been added to this postcard version. When working with a full-bleed design, it is easy to position objects poorly. The guides obscure the crop marks, but they are very useful.

NOTE ▶ In reprographics, the terms *crop marks* and *trim marks* mean similar things. For this exercise we'll use the term *crop marks*.

3 Click the horizontal ruler. Drag a guide to align with the upper set of crop marks.

4 Click the vertical ruler. Drag a guide to align with the leftmost set of crop marks.

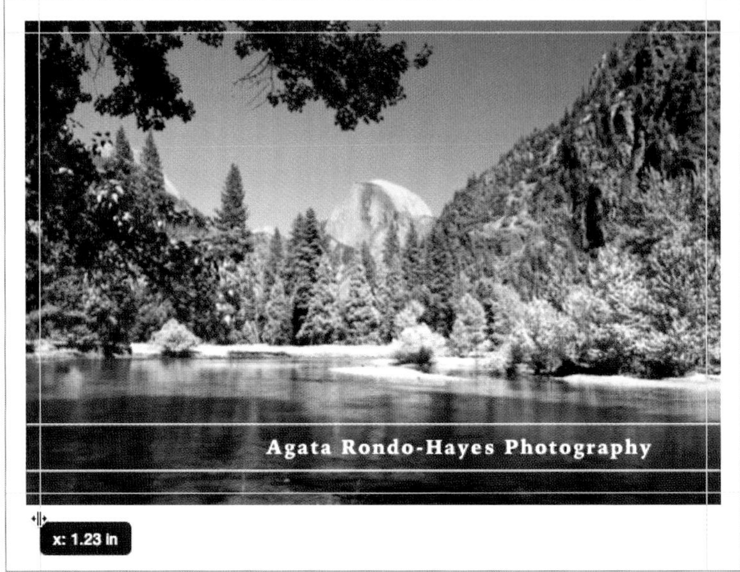

The guides will help you visualize the printable area. Notice that the photograph extends beyond the printing area to create a bleed.

5 Select the photograph. Choose Format > Advanced > Define as Media Placeholder.

In the lower right of the photo, the Media Placeholder button appears, indicating the new status of the photograph.

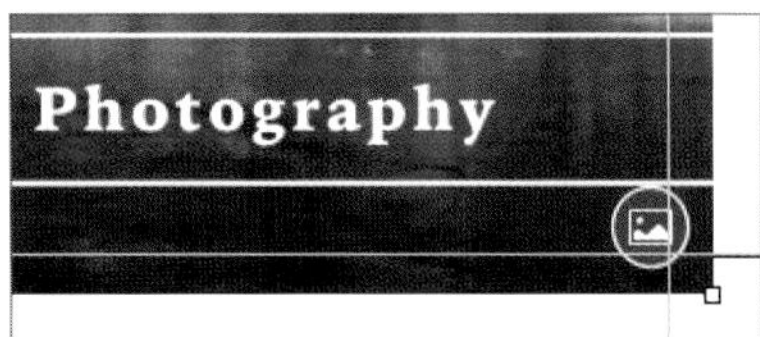

6 Click the Media Placeholder button. The Media Browser appears, allowing you to replace the placeholder with any image currently stored in the library of your Apple photo application, which could be Photos, iPhoto, or Aperture.

NOTE ▶ To change the media placeholder into a standard photo, choose Format > Advanced and deselect Define as Media Placeholder.

Defining Placeholder Text

You have learned how to create a media placeholder, so now you'll convert a standard text box to placeholder text. Once this document is saved as a custom template, any document created from that template will have preformatted placeholder text.

1 Go to page 2 of **agata-postcard.pages**.

This page has two text boxes. The address text box has been locked because it is a permanent feature in this design.

2 Triple-click the upper text box to select it.

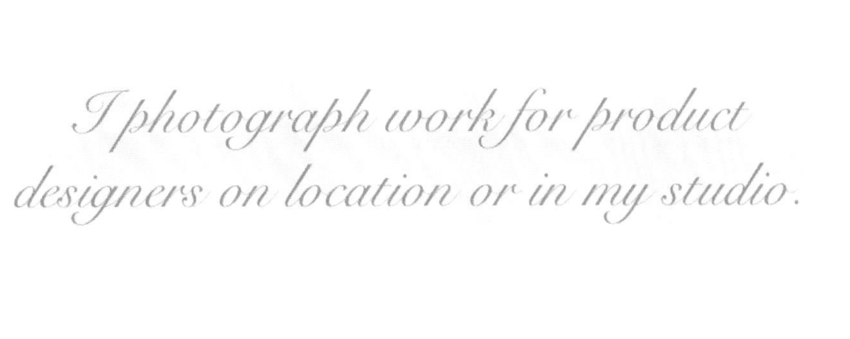

3 Choose Format > Advanced > Define as Placeholder Text.

The text selection color changes to indicate that it is now placeholder text.

NOTE ▶ A single word or group of words can be converted to placeholders. Also, placeholder text can be converted to standard text by choosing Format > Advanced, and deselecting Define as Placeholder Text.

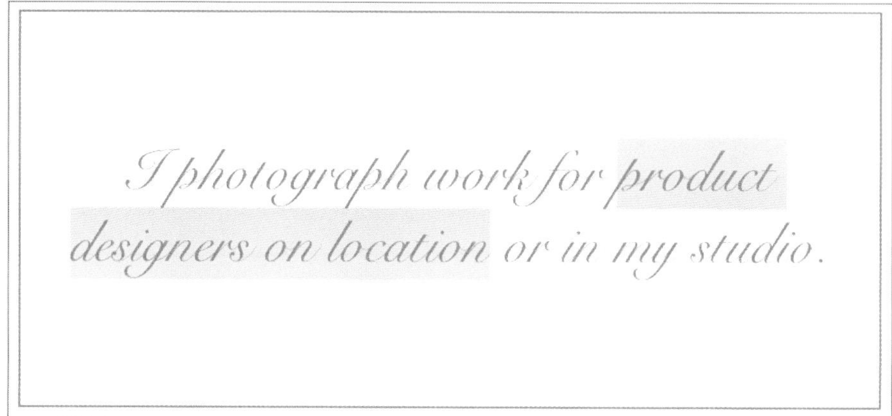

4 Choose File > Save.

Saving Designs as Templates

With all your design work completed and the placeholders created, you can save your work as a template for future use. You have two methods for saving templates: Save a template to a location of your choice, or add the template straight into your Template Chooser.

1 With **agata-postcard.pages** open, choose File > Save as Template.

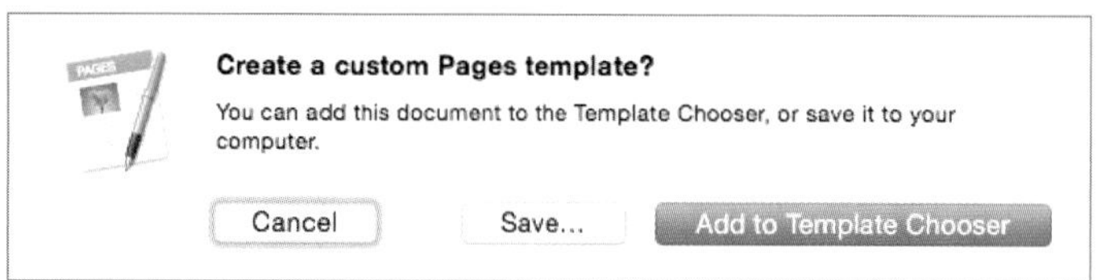

All the design work you have done, including converting elements to placeholders, will be saved as a custom template. This means you won't have to start from scratch every time you create a 6x4-inch postcard. Later, you'll choose Add to Template Chooser to add the template to your Template Chooser, but first let's imagine that you need to share this template with a colleague.

2 In the "Create a custom Pages template" dialog, click Save.

3 In the Save window, save the template to your desktop.

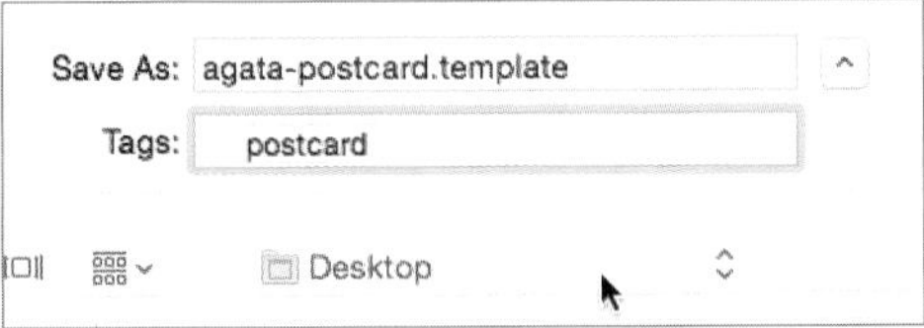

You now have a template file on your desktop. You can share this template with a colleague. To do so, you can file share it.

Imagine that you have just received a Pages template from a colleague, and it's sitting on your desktop. This is how you add a template to your Template Chooser.

4 In the Finder, navigate to your desktop. Double-click **agata-postcard.template**.

5 In the dialog that appears, click Add to Template Chooser.

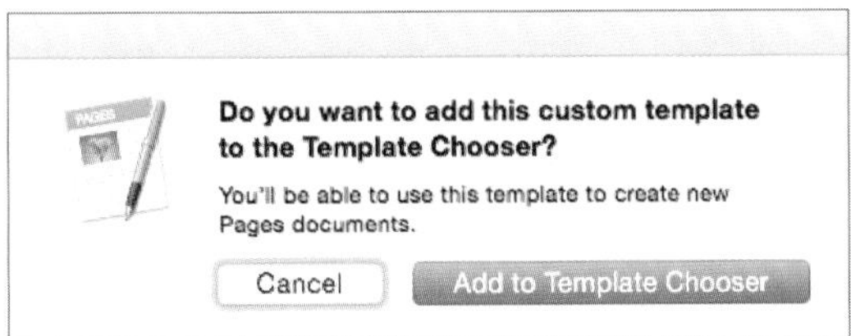

The template is placed in the My Templates section of the Template Chooser.

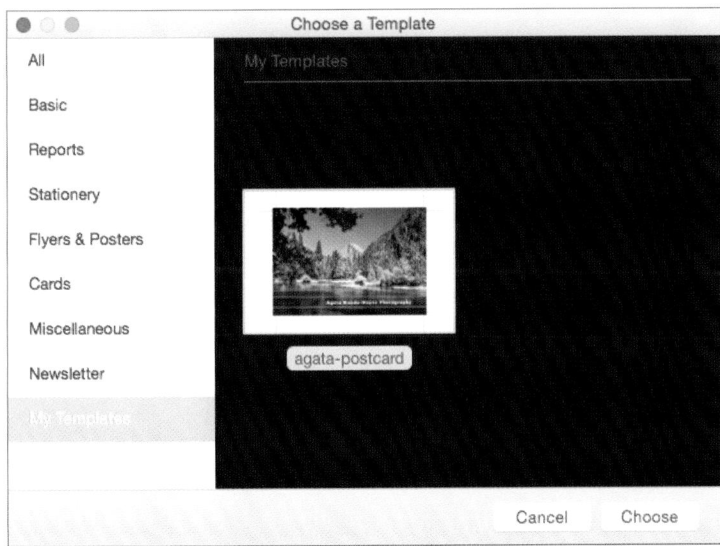

NOTE ▶ Alternatively, you could choose File > Save as Template, and click Add to Template Chooser.

6 Choose Pages > Preferences.

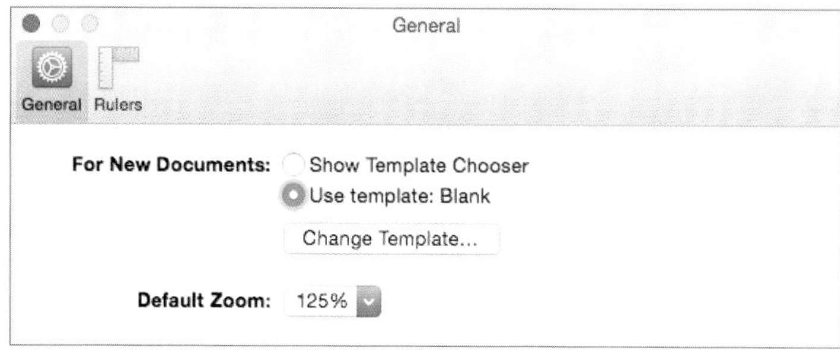

7 In the General pane, select "Use template: Blank" to open a new Pages document as a blank word-processing document, which is a basic template with little formatting in place.

8 Click the Change Template button to open the Template Chooser.

This allows you to choose a template that Pages will always open with, such as your letterhead or a report template.

9 Click Cancel.

NOTE ▶ To delete a template, open the Template Chooser. Control-click the template you wish to remove, and from the shortcut menu, choose Delete.

10 In the General pane, choose Show Template Chooser to return to the default settings.

11 Close the preferences.

12 Close any open Pages documents.

Lesson Review

1. Which features in Pages, Numbers, and Keynote help you to position objects accurately?
2. For print use, when a design has elements that extend beyond the page edges, what steps can you take to remove an unwanted border?
3. In page layout mode, how can you ensure that an object will not be selected accidentally?
4. Describe how to create a Pages template you can share.
5. In Pages, you have repositioned a photo closer to a text box. The type inside the text box jumps out of position. When you move the photo away from the text box, the type falls back into position. How do you move the photo closer to the text box and not move the text box?
6. How do you simultaneously change the border settings on multiple objects?

Answers

1. Alignment guides and the X and Y position values in the Arrange inspector help you to position objects accurately.
2. To remove a border when printing, do one of the following:

   Use a printer capable of borderless printing.

   or

   Print the design on a larger paper size than the artwork and trim to the desired size.

   (In addition to this, if available, you could choose Shrink To Fit in the Print dialog. The resulting print will be smaller than the design and will need trimming.)
3. Select the object and choose Arrange > Lock, or press Command-L. Locking is not available for objects set to move with text.
4. Choose File > Save as Template, and in the dialog click Save.
5. With the photo selected, in the Arrange Inspector, change Text Wrap to None.
6. Shift-click all the required objects. In the inspector, change the border options.

7

Lesson Files

APTS Pages Numbers Keynote > Lesson_07 > engine321_report.pages

APTS Pages Numbers Keynote > Lesson_07 > engine321-movie.m4v

APTS Pages Numbers Keynote > Lesson_07 > railroad-audio.m4a

APTS Pages Numbers Keynote > Lesson_07 > pie-chart.m4v

Time

This lesson takes approximately 75 minutes to complete.

Goals

Create and apply character styles

Export a document to ePub format

Insert audio and video media into Pages

Lesson 7

Creating Rich Media ePubs

Pages makes creating ePubs easy. The electronic publication format is a free and open e-book standard set by the International Digital Publishing Forum.

The Apple iBooks application can be used to read ePubs, but some non-Apple devices use proprietary e-book standards. Fortunately, should you wish to convert a Pages-created ePub to another e-book format, free conversion software for Mac OS X is available.

In this lesson you will prepare a Pages document and export it to ePub format. Because you have to be running OS X Yosemite or later to use Pages 5.5, you'll be able to open your ePub in iBooks to check out your handiwork.

Preparing a Document for ePub

Any Pages document in word processing mode can be exported to ePub, but a few pre-export checks and modifications will help produce an ePub that will display reliably on multiple platforms and reading applications.

1 Open APTS Pages Numbers Keynote > Lesson_07 > **engine321_report.pages**.

This document is ready to be printed or distributed as a PDF. You'll protect this original version of the document by duplicating it before making changes.

2 Choose File > Duplicate.

3 Press Command-S. Save the duplicate file to the desktop, as *engine321_epub.pages*.

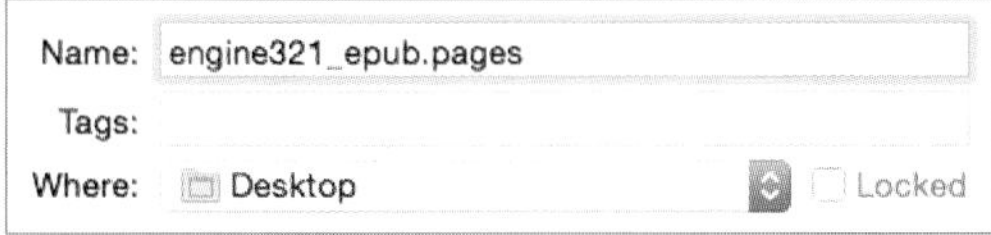

4 In the Document inspector, deselect Ligatures.

Because ePubs can contain hyperlinks, disabling ligatures is prudent. Hyperlinks make a world of sense on a platform that can open webpages and launch email. The automatic formatting of a URL with a ligature may prevent the link from working.

Several photographs were already placed in the report. They were scaled down to the required size, so they no longer need higher resolution to display them at larger sizes.

5 Choose File > Advanced > Reduce File Size.

Choosing Reduce File Size resamples images, so any photographs with high resolutions will be downsized to reduce file size and enable shorter download times.

6 Navigate to page 1.

When exporting to ePub you have the option of using the first page as a cover. The report has a cover design created in Pages.

TIP Photos can have a variety of mask shapes. The cover design uses circular masks. To mask a photo with an alternative shape, choose Format > Image > Mask with Shape.

7 Drag a selection rectangle around the elements in the top right of the cover page.

You will use these elements to create an icon that looks like a gear. Pages, Numbers, and Keynote have graphics features that allow you to make simple logos and illustrations.

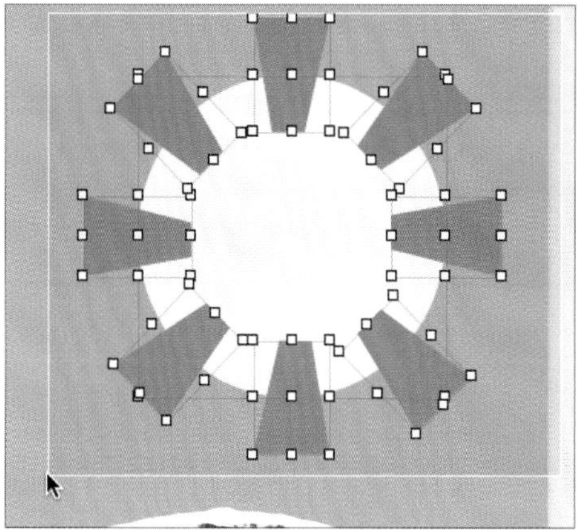

8 Look at the inspector. In Object Placement, "Stay on Page" is selected.

NOTE ▶ All the text boxes and photos on the cover page have been set to "Stay on Page," which allows shapes to overlap the top and bottom of the page. This would not be possible if "Move with Text" were selected.

Dragging to select the graphic at the top of the page also selected the page background, even though it is locked.

9 Shift-click the green page background to deselect it.

10 In the Arrange inspector, click Subtract.

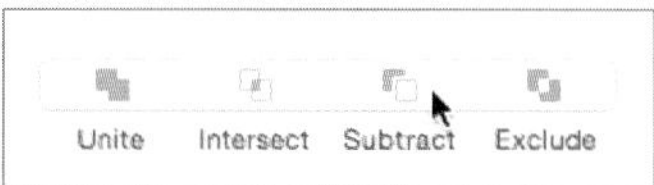

A single shape is created for a simple logo. This graphic can be colored or outlined, but for now you'll reshape it.

11 Choose Format > Shapes and Lines > Make Editable.

Instructions appear describing how you can modify the graphic. Feel free to experiment by toggling between straight and curved lines. Also try adding new points to a line.

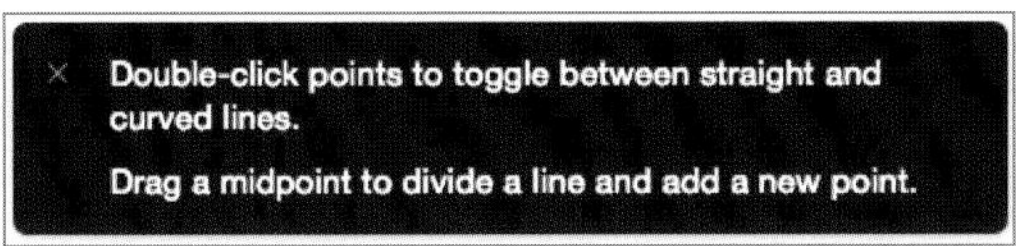

12 Click away from the graphic to deselect it.

The cover is complete, but other graphics in the report need attention.

Working with Inline Graphics

Because ePubs allow text to reflow freely, any photos or graphics placed in the body of a document need to reflow along with the text. If they are not set to reflow, the pictures won't stay with the associated text when a user changes font size in his e-reader, or changes from a landscape to a portrait display.

1 Navigate to page 10.

You are going to use inline graphic options to identify where a photo is anchored to connect it to associated text.

2. Click the picture on page 10 to select it.

   A blue line with a circle at the top appears at the end of the paragraph before the photo.

   This blue line is an anchor. In the Document inspector, the photo is set to "Move with Text," which is ideal, but moving the anchor point ensures that you have control over the text and image flow. This process is made easier when you can see the otherwise hidden formatting characters.

3. Choose View > Show Invisibles. All the spaces and paragraph returns appear.

4. With your insertion point at the anchor point, press Return twice.

5. Drag the photo down, so that the anchor sits on the second carriage return. Doing so allows you to control where graphics and photos are located in the flow of text.

   Adding the extra carriage returns creates space around graphics and photos in ePubs. However, be aware that many ePub readers do not honor text wrap settings.

TIP As an alternative to using carriage returns to create empty space, you can create a white shape larger than the picture, and position the picture over it so the white area provides a border. Then group the picture with the white shape so that the image includes its own surrounding white space.

NOTE ▶ The preceding step is not strictly necessary. A second photo placed in the report has been set to "Move with Text" but has no extra carriage returns. Later when you view the ePub you can decide whether or not to add extra space around images in the future.

Creating Character Styles

Throughout these Pages lessons, the importance of using paragraph and list styles has been emphasized. But you have one type of text style yet to discover: character styles. Let's use them to emphasize all instances of the words "Engine 321" in the report.

Unlike paragraph styles, character styles can be applied to a single word or groups of words between returns.

1 With engine321_epub.pages open, choose Edit > Find > Find. The search field may contain terms from a previous search. If so, click the × to clear the field.

2 From the Find pop-up menu, choose Find.

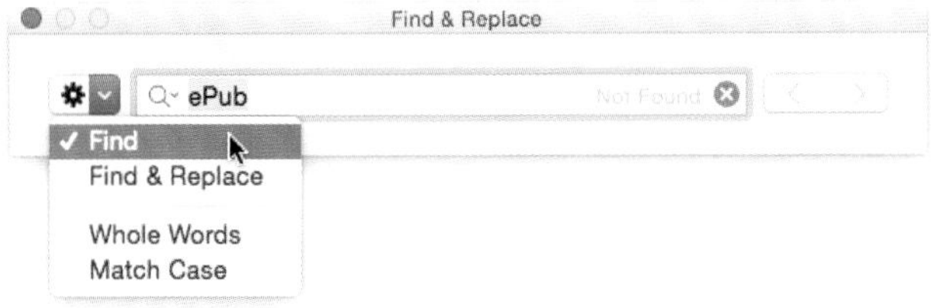

Rather than manually locating and changing each instance of "Engine 321" in the report, you're going to use Find & Replace to search for and change them.

3 In the search field, type *Engine 321*. Seven instances of "Engine 321" are found.

The first instance is on the cover of the report.

4 Click the right-pointing arrow in the Find & Replace window to go to the second instance of "Engine 321."

Objective¶

Following·various·discussions,·there·is·a·desire·for·a·simple·'tidy·up'·of·Engine·321·before·the·much·awaited·long·term·plan·can·to·be·produced.·The·'tidy·up'·will·demonstrate·that·the·Friends·of·321·have·been·taking·action·and·the·supporting·them·will·see·Engine·321·return·to·the·heritage·railroad·as·a·working·exhibit.·The·timescale·for·that·has·yet·to·be·established.¶

You are going to create a new character style and use the Find & Replace feature to speed up the formatting process.

5 Select this second instance of "Engine 321." In the inspector, change the font to Bold Italic.

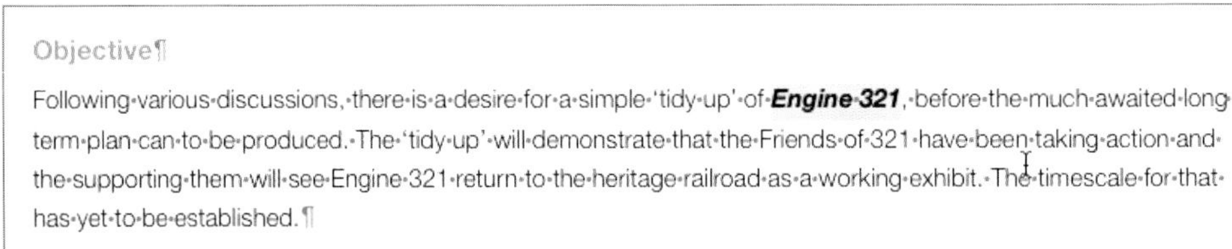

Objective¶

Following·various·discussions,·there·is·a·desire·for·a·simple·'tidy·up'·of·***Engine·321***,·before·the·much·awaited·long·term·plan·can·to·be·produced.·The·'tidy·up'·will·demonstrate·that·the·Friends·of·321·have·been·taking·action·and·the·supporting·them·will·see·Engine·321·return·to·the·heritage·railroad·as·a·working·exhibit.·The·timescale·for·that·has·yet·to·be·established.¶

The text is formatted but is not a character style yet.

6 In the inspector, in the Character Styles pop-up menu click the Add (+) button to define the selected text as a new character style.

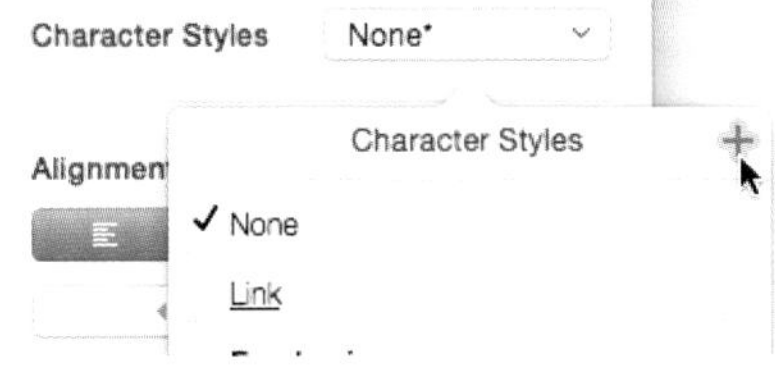

7 In the name field for the new style, type *Engine 321*.

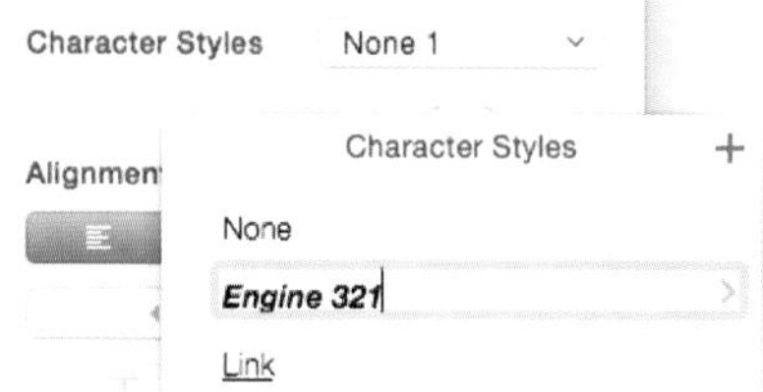

With the character style defined, you can change the format of all instances of the text "Engine 321."

8 Click the Find & Replace window to reactivate it. Click the right arrow to go to the next instance of "Engine 321."

9 Select the highlighted instance of Engine 321. From the Character Styles pop-up menu, choose Engine 321.

10 Reactivate the Find & Replace window, and jump to the next instance of "Engine 321."

11 From the Character Styles pop-up menu, choose Engine 321.

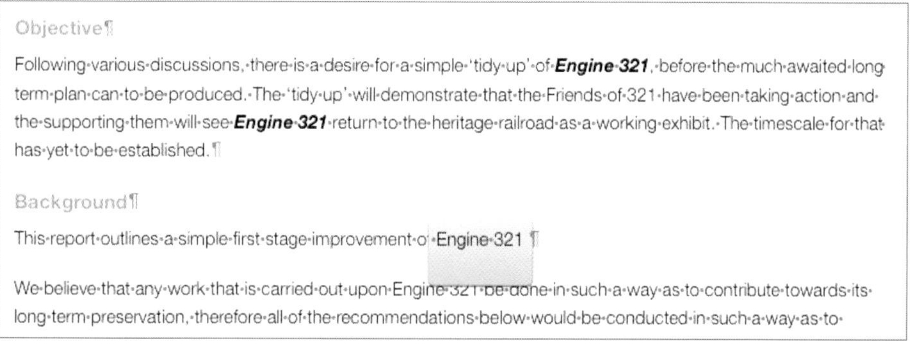

12 Repeat steps 10 and 11 to change the remaining instances of Engine 321, if you wish.

TIP Character styles can be created to emphasize phone numbers or to format book titles, and help you apply those formats consistently and conveniently. Adding all forms of style as you type is probably best, but the Find function can leap to the rescue as needed.

13 Close the Find & Replace window.

Adding Movies to Pages

The ePub 3.0 format added the ability to embed video and audio content into ePub files. OS X and iOS devices support ePub 3.0, but for users of older e-reader apps that don't support the new format, any video included in an ePub will, at best, appear as a still photo. Furthermore, audio files may be completely invisible, not to mention inaudible.

For the greatest backward compatibility, you can create a duplicate version of your ePub that doesn't include video or audio clips.

1 Navigate to page 8 of engine321_epub.pages.

2 Click to place the insertion point at the end of the first paragraph, and press Return twice to create the space in which to insert a video file.

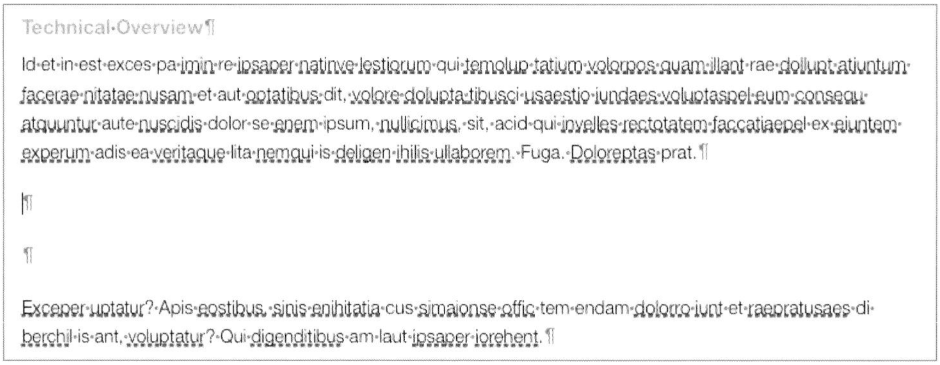

Technical Overview

Id et in est exces pa imin re ipsaper natinve lestiorum qui temolup tatium volorpos quam illant rae dollupt atiuntum facerae nitatae nusam et aut optatibus dit, volore dolupta tibusci usaestio iundaes voluptaspel eum consequ atquuntur aute nuscidis dolor se enem ipsum, nullicimus, sit, acid qui invelles rectotatem faccatiaepel ex eiuntem experum adis ea veritaque lita nemqui is deligen ihilis ullaborem. Fuga. Doloreptas prat.

Exceper uptatur? Apis eostibus, sinis enihitatia cus simaionse offic tem endam dolorro iunt et raepratusaes di berchil is ant, voluptatur? Qui digenditibus am laut ipsaper iorehent.

3 Locate the insertion point at the first carriage return beneath the paragraph.

Doing so ensures the padding is above and below the media you are about to place.

4 Choose Insert > Choose, and then navigate to APTS Pages Numbers Keynote > Lesson_07.

5 Double-click **pie-chart.m4v**. A media box appears set in line with the text. If necessary, drag the media box down so that the text anchor is correctly positioned.

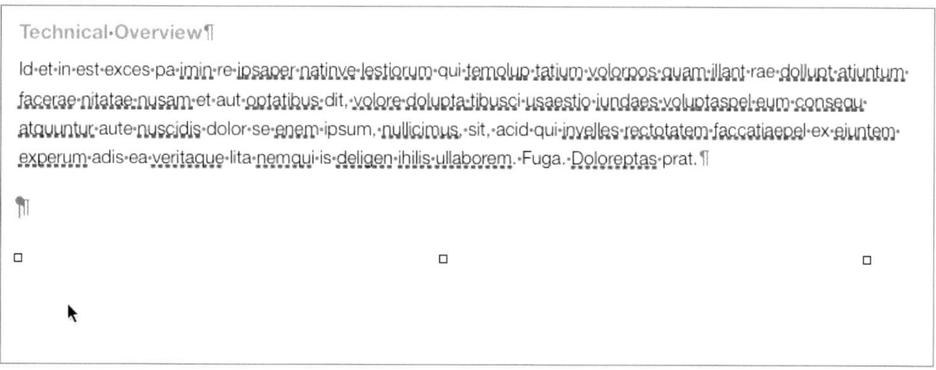

You've placed one video, and you'll add one more. There is no upper limit to the amount of media you can add, but all media, especially video, may increase the ePub file size to the point where readers won't want to download it.

6 Navigate to page 9. With the insertion point placed at the end of the second paragraph, press Return twice.

7 Choose Insert > Choose and double-click the file **engine321-movie.m4v**.

This time the media box has an image in it—the first frame of the movie. If necessary, you can drag the media box down so that the text anchor is correctly positioned.

8 Go back to page 8, which contains a pie chart movie.

The media box is blank (because the first frame of the movie is blank), which makes it look broken. Let's fix that.

9 Click the media box for **pie-chart.m4v**.

10 In the Movie inspector, in the Edit Movie section, drag the Poster Frame slider to the right, until you find a frame that represents the chart.

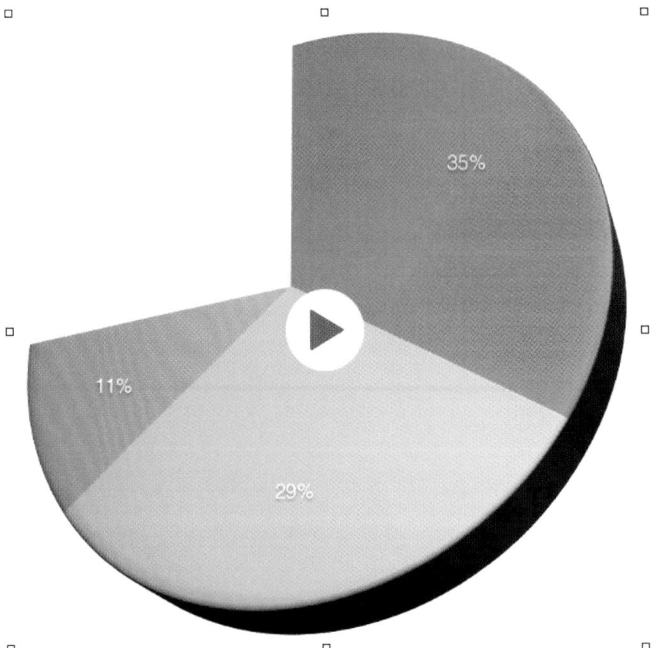

TIP ▶ The pie chart movie was made in Keynote. Creating a title slide in Keynote to act as a poster frame might be better than using a poster frame. Creating slides in Keynote is covered in Part III of this book.

11 On page 9, select **engine321-movie.m4v**.

12 In the Movie inspector, click Play. You can drag the Volume slider to adjust the volume of the video as it plays.

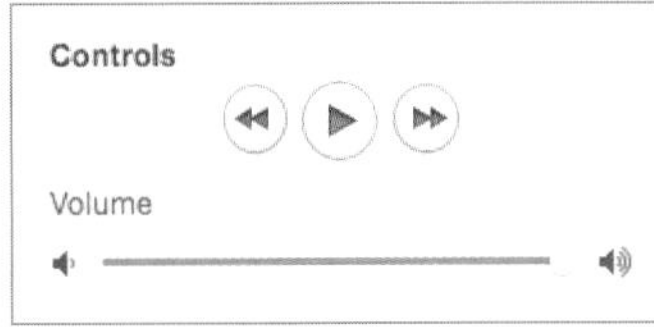

NOTE ▶ You can use the Media Browser to add video to a document. To enable a video to appear in your Media Browser, place it in your Movies folder, which is inside your Home folder.

Adding Audio to Pages

You can add audio files in Pages just as you would any other media. To make an audio file available via the Media Browser, you must add it to your iTunes library. Rather than add audio to iTunes, you'll access it directly from within Pages.

1 Go to page 10 of engine321_epub.pages.

2 Click at the end of the first paragraph, and press Return to insert an empty line.

3 Choose Insert > Choose.

4 Open APTS Pages Numbers Keynote > Lesson_07 > **railroad-audio.m4a**. An audio media button appears.

NOTE ▶ The position of the text anchor determines where the audio controls appear in the ePub, but the position of the media icon is not important. You use the audio icon in Pages only to select and manipulate the media as you work on your document.

5 Click the audio media button to open the Audio inspector.

6 In the Audio inspector, click the Play button.

You'll hear a knock on the microphone a few seconds into the recording. It's distracting and unwanted, but you can easily remove it.

7 Click the Rewind button to return to the start of the clip.

8 Drag the start point Trim slider to the right to approximately 1.4 seconds. This sets the start point for the audio just after the knock.

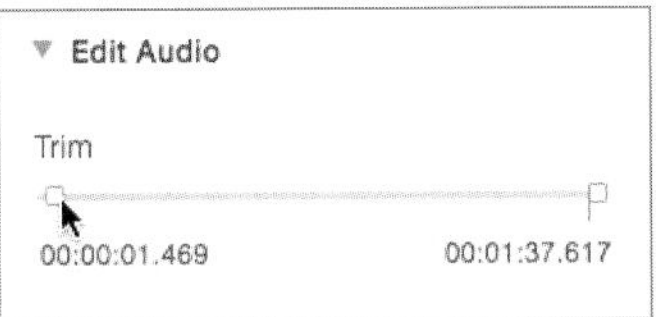

9 Click the Play button again. The knock sound has been trimmed.

NOTE ▶ Clicking the play button on the audio media button also plays the audio clip. This is an alternative to clicking the play button in the Audio inspector.

Exporting to ePub

Throughout this lesson you have been preparing the Pages document for export to ePub. Now that you've included video and audio, an optional step could be to choose File > Optimize Movies for iOS, which converts the movies in your document to H.264 (720p) so they play on iOS devices.

The movies placed in engine321_epub have been optimized using QuickTime Player to resolutions lower than 720p to save file size.

If your ePub is full of movies, it will take a long time for users to download. A balance needs to be struck between quality and size.

1 Choose File > Export To > ePub, and in the export dialog set the following:

Title—*Engine 321 Report*

Author—Will be automatically filled based on your Pages preferences, though you can change it here.

Primary Category—From the pop-up menu, choose Professional & Technical. This helps cataloguing by adding metadata tags to the book. If an appropriate category is not available, you can create your own.

Language—In the Advanced Options, from the pop-up menu, choose English.

Select "Use the first page as the book cover image."

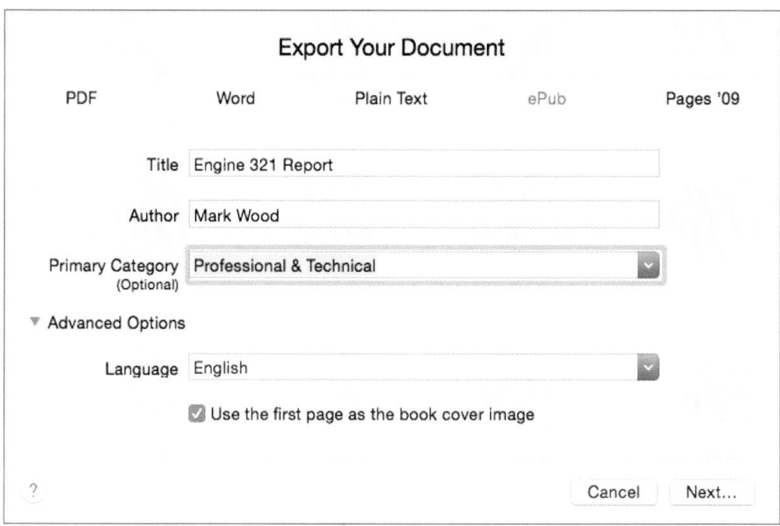

2 Click Next. In the Save dialog, name the document *engine321_report.epub*, and export it to your desktop.

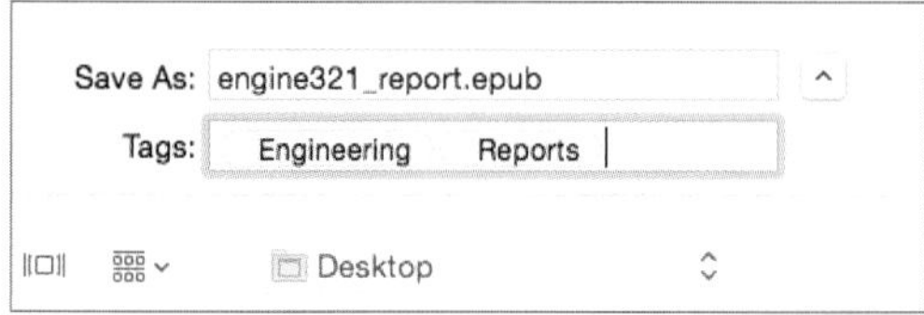

NOTE ▸ When OS X Mavericks is being used, the data field to add tags is available.

3 Click Export. A dialog appears.

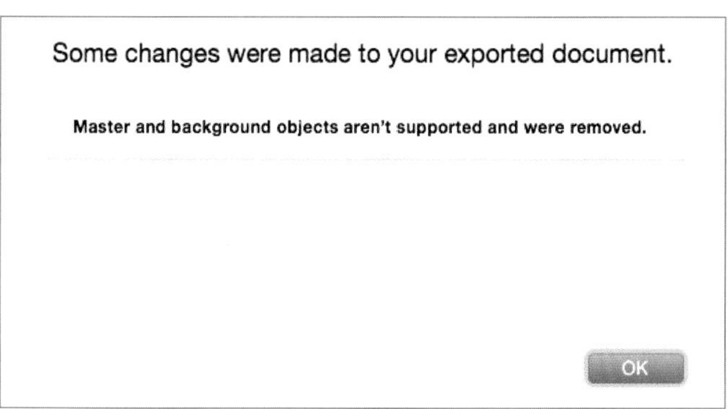

The Pages document had a logo at the top of each page; these were set as master objects, which aren't supported so they have been removed. The headers and footers, plus the table of contents have also been removed, but the preparation you've performed on the Pages document ensures that your ePub shouldn't present any nasty surprises.

4 Click OK.

You've created an e-book! Let's see what it looks like.

Previewing in iBooks

Beginning with OS X Mavericks, the Apple iBooks app is an ideal application for reviewing your ePub document. But if you are going to distribute it to users on other platforms, you might want to download a free ePub reader, such as Adobe Digital Editions or Calibre, to see how your ePub formatting holds up. Calibre has the added benefit of being able to convert ePubs to other e-book formats.

Let's take a look at your new ePub.

1 In the Finder, navigate to your desktop and Control-click engine321_report.epub.

NOTE ▶ The file extension .epub may be hidden.

2 In the shortcut menu, choose Open With > iBooks.

iBooks saves the ePub file to the desktop and copies the book to the iBooks library.

NOTE ▶ Step 2 ensures that your ePub opens in iBooks even if it is not your default ePub reader.

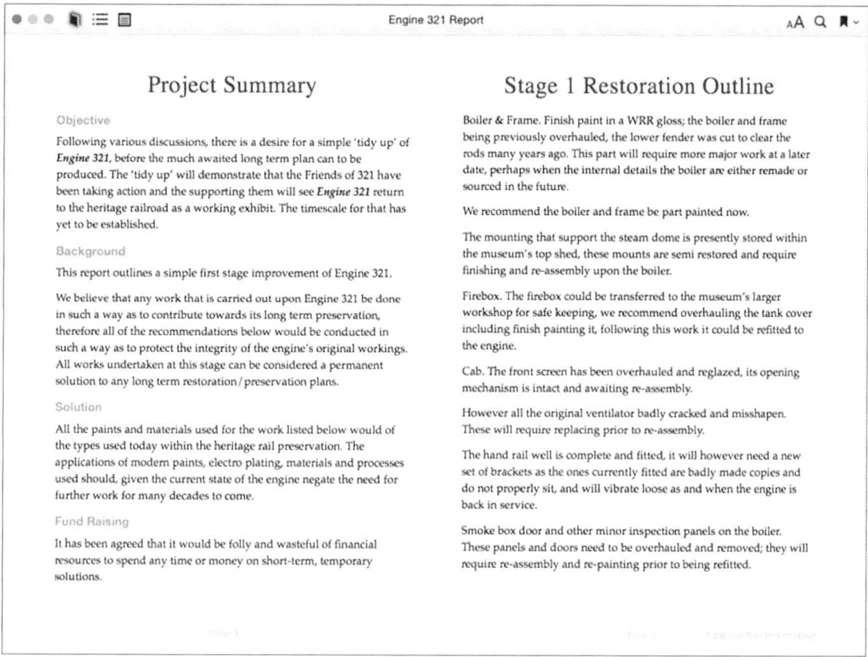
Engine 321 Report

Project Summary

Objective

Following various discussions, there is a desire for a simple 'tidy up' of ***Engine 321***, before the much awaited long term plan can to be produced. The 'tidy up' will demonstrate that the Friends of 321 have been taking action and the supporting them will see ***Engine 321*** return to the heritage railroad as a working exhibit. The timescale for that has yet to be established.

Background

This report outlines a simple first stage improvement of Engine 321.

We believe that any work that is carried out upon Engine 321 be done in such a way as to contribute towards its long term preservation, therefore all of the recommendations below would be conducted in such a way as to protect the integrity of the engine's original workings. All works undertaken at this stage can be considered a permanent solution to any long term restoration / preservation plans.

Solution

All the paints and materials used for the work listed below would of the types used today within the heritage rail preservation. The applications of modern paints, electro plating, materials and processes used should, given the current state of the engine negate the need for further work for many decades to come.

Fund Raising

It has been agreed that it would be folly and wasteful of financial resources to spend any time or money on short-term, temporary solutions.

Stage 1 Restoration Outline

Boiler & Frame. Finish paint in a WRR gloss; the boiler and frame being previously overhauled, the lower fender was cut to clear the rods many years ago. This part will require more major work at a later date, perhaps when the internal details the boiler are either remade or sourced in the future.

We recommend the boiler and frame be part painted now.

The mounting that support the steam dome is presently stored within the museum's top shed, these mounts are semi restored and require finishing and re-assembly upon the boiler.

Firebox. The firebox could be transferred to the museum's larger workshop for safe keeping, we recommend overhauling the tank cover including finish painting it, following this work it could be refitted to the engine.

Cab. The front screen has been overhauled and reglazed, its opening mechanism is intact and awaiting re-assembly.

However all the original ventilator badly cracked and misshapen. These will require replacing prior to re-assembly.

The hand rail well is complete and fitted, it will however need a new set of brackets as the ones currently fitted are badly made copies and do not properly sit, and will vibrate loose as and when the engine is back in service.

Smoke box door and other minor inspection panels on the boiler. These panels and doors need to be overhauled and removed; they will require re-assembly and re-painting prior to being refitted.

3 Skim through the pages to examine the formatting. The style sheets were exported correctly, although the font and type sizes are dictated by the options set in iBooks.

The table of contents has been removed from the body of the document, but its hierarchy can be seen in the iBooks contents menu.

4 Click the Table of Contents button to review the contents hierarchy.

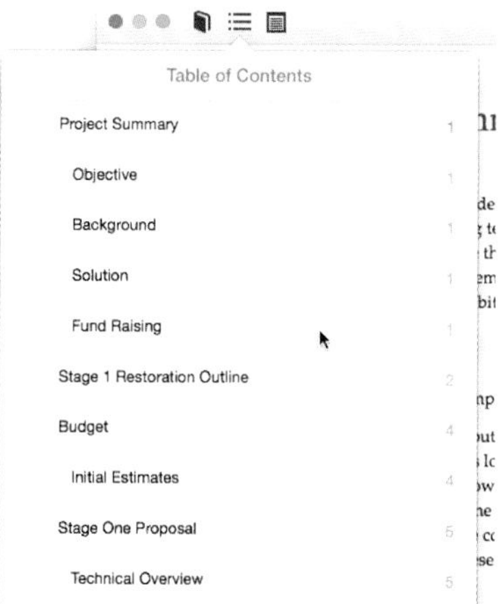

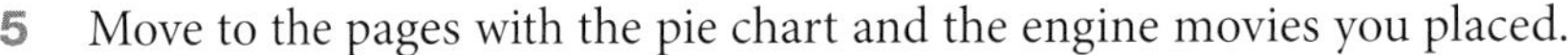

5 Move to the pages with the pie chart and the engine movies you placed.

6 Play the movies.

A controller is set on each movie. Experiment with using the movie controls. You can play and pause, as expected; and by dragging the movie progress slider, you can skim the movie. You'll also find a button to enable fullscreen view. A similar controller can be found for the audio file you inserted.

7 In iBooks, click the Appearance icon in the toolbar. Experiment with changing the font and type size. As the type changes size, the design scales perfectly on most pages, and the inline text and media files reflow.

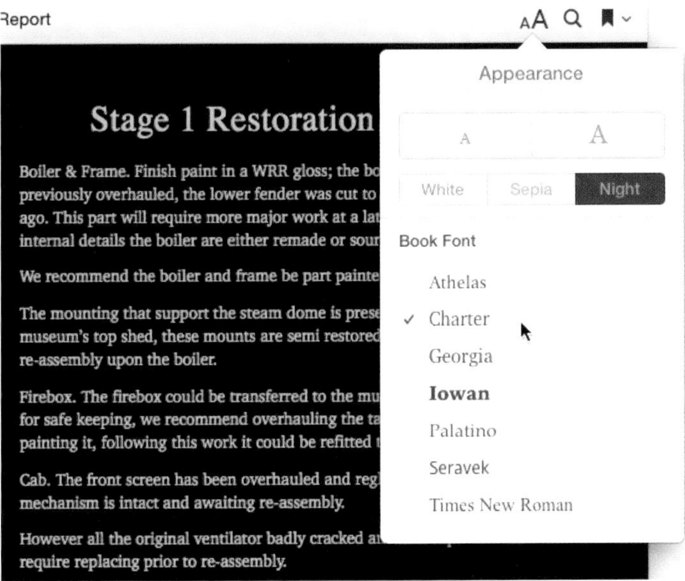

If you are able to sync your iOS device with a Mac, try the following steps.

NOTE ▶ If you are using a Mac in a training center or school situation, you are not likely to have access to your personal user account, so iTunes syncing won't be available.

8 Connect your iOS device to your Mac.

9 On the Mac, open iTunes. In the toolbar, click Devices and select your iOS device.

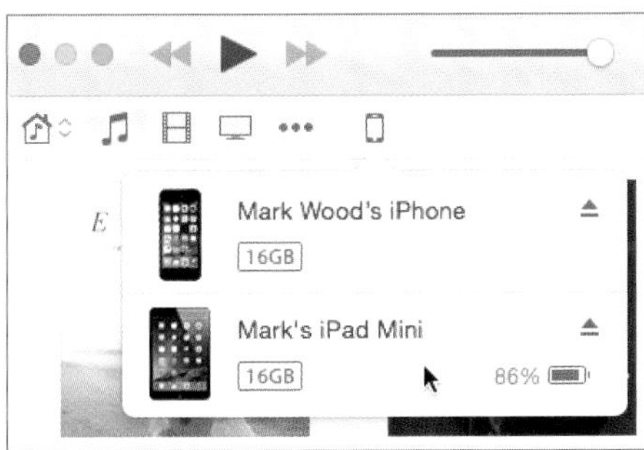

10 Click the Books tab.

11 Select Sync Books, and then for the purpose of this exercise, choose "Selected books" to sync only a selected documents with your iOS device.

12 In the Books tab, select Engine 321 Report.

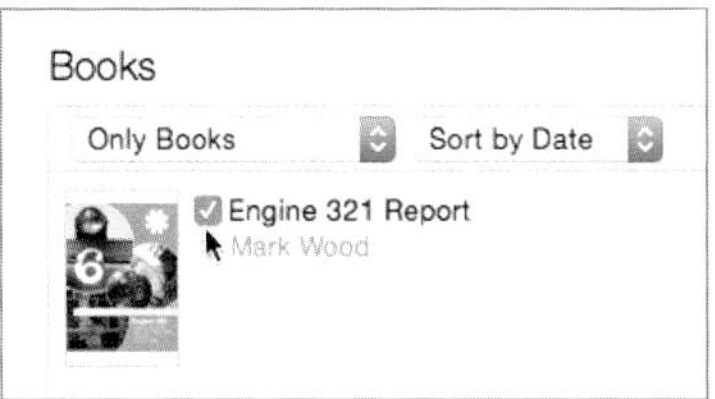

13 Click Sync.

When the sync is complete, you'll be able to open Engine 321 Report from iBooks on your iOS device.

14 Review the ePub. The styles have been honored again.

The table on the Budget page may display a few problems depending on the type size. If the text does not wrap properly in the cells, try changing the font or type sizes or both.

Budget

Initial Estimates

Rafiq Darzi will confirm the figures, before we commence stage one. Sociis mauris in integer, a dolor netus non dui aliquet, sagittis felis sodales, dolor sociis mauris, vel eu libero cras. Faucibus at. Arcu habitasse elementum est, ipsum purus pede porttitor class, ut adipiscing, aliquet sed auctor, imperdiet arcu per diam dapibus libero duis. Enim eros in vel, volutpat nec pellentesque leo, temporibus nec.

Description	Quantity	Unit Price	Cost
Item 1	55	$ 120	$ 6,600
Item 2	13	$ 95	$ 1,235
Item 3	25	$ 60	$ 1,500
Total			**$ 9,335**

Problems like this are not a fault as such, but rather a consequence of the flexible viewing and reflowing options in ePub readers.

Lesson Review

1. To what parts of text can you apply character and paragraph styles?
2. Why is "Move with Text" selected for objects placed in a document destined to become an ePub?
3. What type of objects can be locked in word processing mode?
4. What are the pros and cons of choosing File > Reduce File Size?
5. Name three Pages features that are removed when converting to ePub.

Answers

1. Character styles can be applied to words, or any run of text, within a paragraph. Paragraph styles can be applied only to whole paragraphs.
2. "Move with Text" objects retain their relative positions in an ePub's text flow.
3. All objects set to "Stay on Page" can be locked.
4. Reducing file size enables documents to download faster, but reducing file size also reduces image resolution, which can compromise image quality.
5. Table of contents are removed from the body of ePubs; headers and footers; and background objects and master objects.

Organizing and Illustrating Data Using Numbers

8

Lesson Files APTS Pages Numbers Keynote > Lesson_08 > agata-budget.numbers

Time This lesson takes approximately 75 minutes to complete.

Goals

Open and develop Numbers documents

Understand key spreadsheet terms

Create and manage sheets

Add functions to a table

Print Numbers documents

Lesson **8**

Organizing Data Using Numbers

Numbers is a spreadsheet application that presents a flexible, freeform canvas on which you can place tables, text, photos, and rich media. You can use tables in Numbers to organize data, manage lists, and generate charts; and the application supports over 250 math functions to support its data processing power.

In this lesson, you will discover the essential Numbers features of pages, sheets, and tables; and explore how the Numbers interface helps you focus on key tasks. You'll begin by reviewing a template before building a budget planner for a prospective business.

Assessing Templates

By examining the Numbers templates, you can get some great insights into the application's functions and how to apply them to real-world tasks such as personal finance or business planning.

As you learned in Lesson 2, you have several ways to open an application. If Numbers isn't already open, follow these steps:

1 In the Finder, choose Go > Applications.

2 Double-click the Numbers icon to open the program.

NOTE ▶ If you skipped Lessons 1 and 2, you will need to install the lesson files as described in Lesson 1, and be familiar with the Numbers interface and its basic controls as covered in Lesson 2.

3 Choose File > New to open the Template Chooser.

4 Click through the categories—Basic, Personal Finance, Personal, Business, and Education—and review the titles for the templates. In the Personal Finance category, the template titles—Loan Comparison, Mortgage Calculator, and Net Worth—suggest the uses for these templates.

5 In the Personal category, double-click Travel Planner.

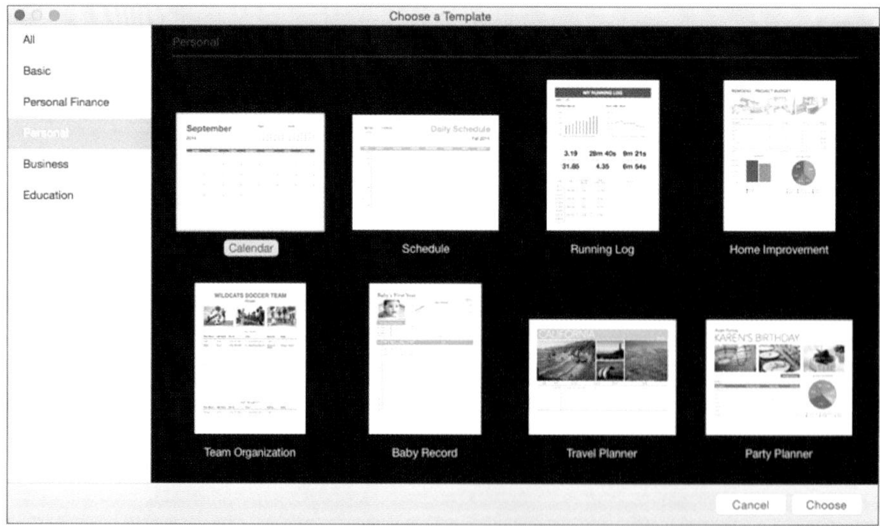

6 Choose File > Save. In the Save As field, type *vacation*.

7 Save it on the desktop.

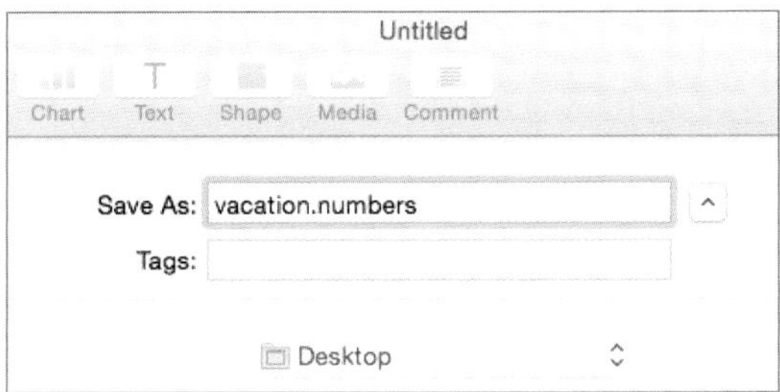

NOTE ► Saving to iCloud Drive is a great way to share Numbers documents with iOS devices, as explained in Lesson 17.

Working with Sheets

This Numbers document was created using a template with three sheets and several tables, text boxes, and image placeholders. Let's take a closer look.

Beneath the toolbar are three tabs, labeled Itinerary, Reservations, and Packing List. These represent the three sheets.

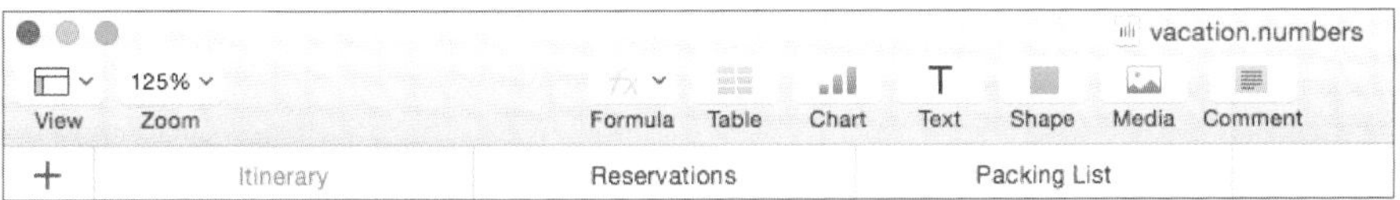

NOTE ► To the left of the sheet tabs is an Add (+) button you can use to add blank sheets.

1 Click the Reservations tab.

You'll find four tables on the Reservations sheet. These can be selected by clicking them, as described in previous lessons, but Numbers also has an extra menu you can use.

2 Move your pointer over the Reservations tab. When a disclosure triangle appears, click it.

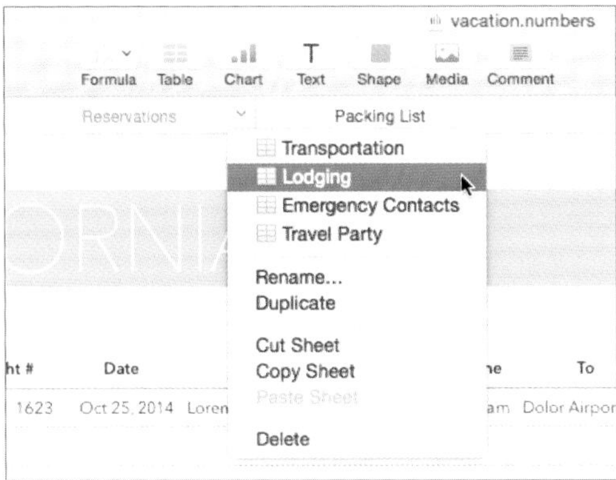

The menu includes four tables: Transportation, Lodging, Emergency Contacts, and Travel Party.

NOTE ▶ You use this menu to rename, cut, copy, and delete sheets. The Duplicate function is an ideal way to replicate a sheet. It's often better to use a single spreadsheet with multiple sheets, rather than split a project across several Numbers documents. To the left of the Sheet tabs is an Add (+) button you can use to add blank sheets.

3 Click Lodging to select that table.

4 In the toolbar, you can click the Format button to open and close the inspector. Make sure that the inspector is open.

5 In the Table inspector, deselect Table Name.

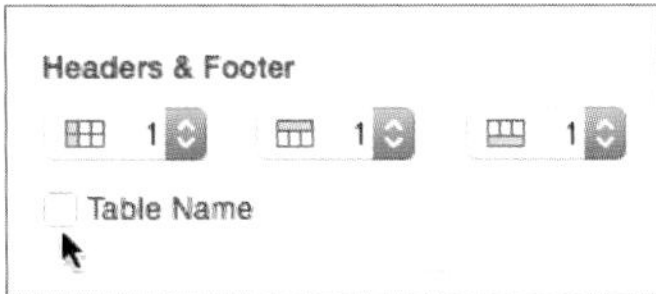

This removes the label, Lodging, from the table. However, the table is still listed as Lodging in the Sheets menu.

NOTE ▶ The Lodging table has one header for the columns and rows, and a footer row, as indicated in the Table inspector. These headers are invaluable when you have to scroll tables to navigate their length and breadth, as you'll see shortly

Objects on sheets are layered, so a table can sit in front of a graphic, as you're about to find out. When an object is under another element, that object may be difficult to select and edit.

Behind each of the tables on the Reservations sheet are icons. For the Lodging table, it's a bed. By changing the layer order, you can select the icon and move it into position.

6 In the Arrange pane, click Back. This places the icons as the uppermost layer and makes them easier to select.

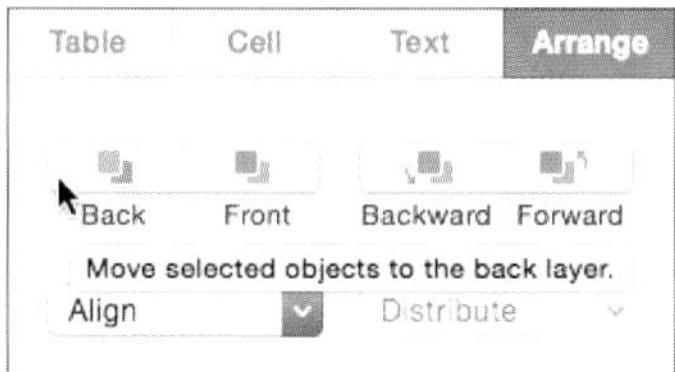

7 Drag the logo so that it appears over the Accommodations cell. Use the alignment guides for positioning.

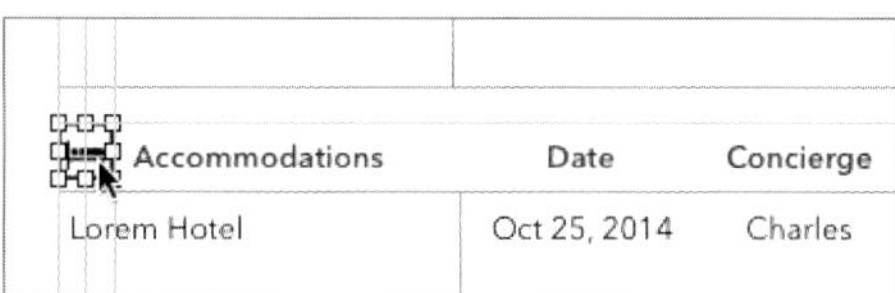

NOTE ► If the alignment guides are not visible when you drag the bed icon, choose Numbers > Preferences and select all the Alignment Guides checkboxes.

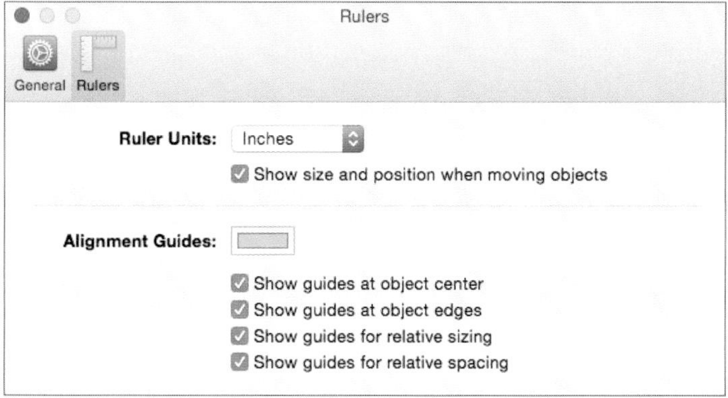

8 Click the Packing List tab to jump to that sheet.

It contains three tables, each with checkboxes.

9 Click the Clothes table, then click the checkbox in cell C2 to indicate that your bathing suits are packed.

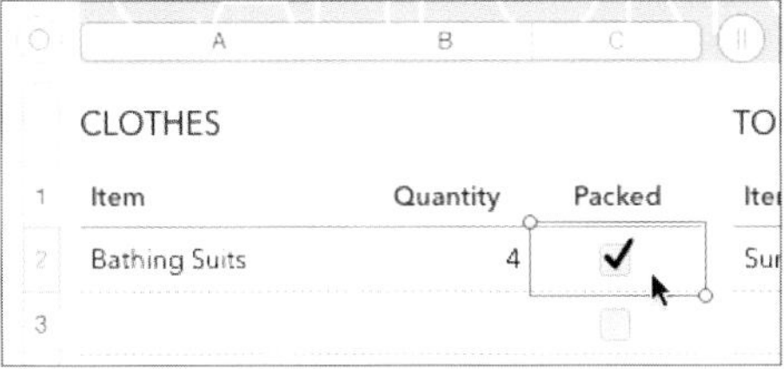

Numbers includes several cell formats not available in either Pages or Keynote. The checkbox is one of them. The others are star rating, slider, stepper, and pop-up menu.

10 In the Cell inspector, from the Data Format pop-up menu, choose Slider.

11 The Maximum slider defaults to 1. Feel free to set your own value. Press Return.

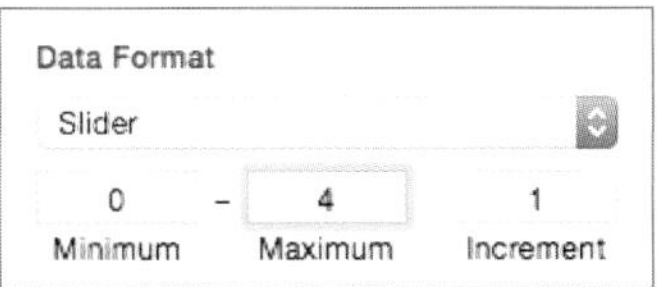

A slider appears against cell C2.

12 Drag the slider up and down to adjust the number of packed items.

The interactive data formats have many uses. The pop-up menu option was illustrated in the Ju Jitsu register in Lesson 2. You'll be using various data formats throughout these Numbers lessons.

13 Click the Itinerary tab.

It contains image placeholders. Using Numbers, you can create beautiful spreadsheets that include photos, video, and audio. In this respect it mirrors the Pages and Keynote design tools.

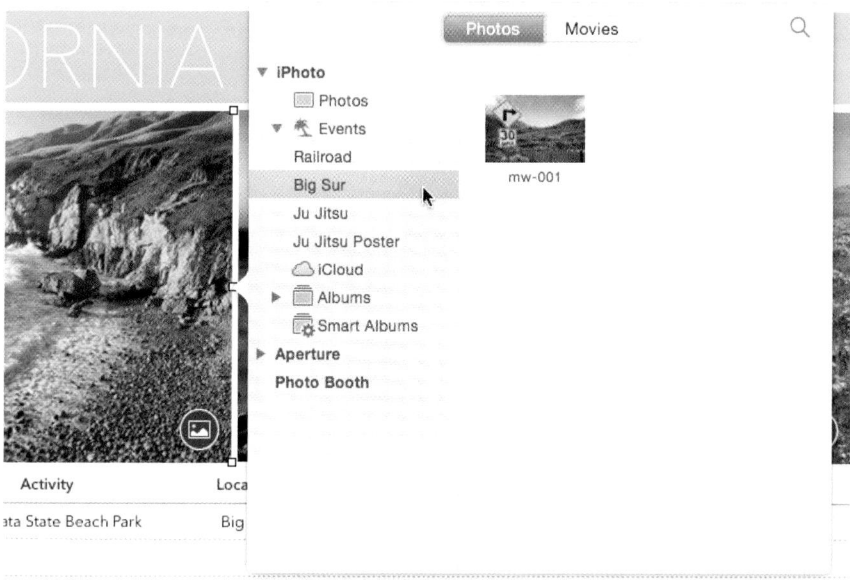

14 Click an image placeholder icon to open the Media Browser.

15 In the Media Browser, click a photo to replace the placeholder image.

NOTE ► You can use any photo but the photograph inside the Big Sur event suits the design.

16 Choose File > Close.

Making a Budget Sheet

Choosing a specialized template, such as Personal Budget, to be the foundation of a Numbers project can be a good idea, as some templates have the calculations you need built in. You can customize and create your own templates that not only contain essential calculations, but also incorporate design elements that reflect your personal or business style.

In this exercise you'll take a different approach to set up a budget sheet from a basic template. You don't need to focus on making the document look good; instead you'll be concentrating on its functionality.

1. Choose File > New, and in the Template Chooser, double-click the Blank template to open it.

   A document with a single sheet appears.

2. Click the table to select it.

3. In the toolbar, set the Zoom level to 75%.

   This zoom level should leave empty space around the table. If not, zoom out to 50%.

4. Drag the icon at the bottom right of the table, so that you have 13 columns and 10 rows. The resulting table will have columns labeled A to M, and rows labeled 1 to 10.

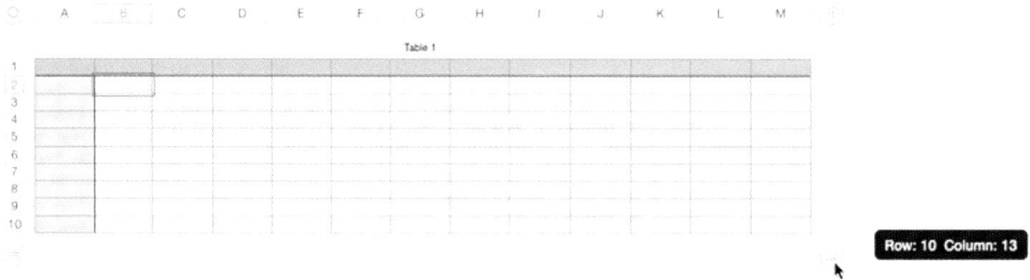

NOTE ▶ Depending on your display resolution, you may want to zoom in again to 125% or greater to see the cells more clearly.

5. Click cell B1, and type *January*. Drag the yellow circle on the right edge of the cell to the right. The months of the year appear. Keep dragging until the row ends with December.

As this is a budget sheet, you'll need to add rows for income and expense items.

6 Click cell A2, and type *Income*. Press Return.

Cell A3 is highlighted.

7 Type *Expenses* and press Return.

8 In cell A4, type *Cash Flow*. Press Tab.

NOTE ▶ Pressing Tab moves one cell to the right, while pressing Return moves down a column. Press Shift-Return to move up a column, and press Shift-Tab to move to the left. You can also press the keyboard's arrow keys to navigate through a sheet.

9 With cell B4 selected, press = (equal sign). Then, click cell B2, and press – (minus sign).

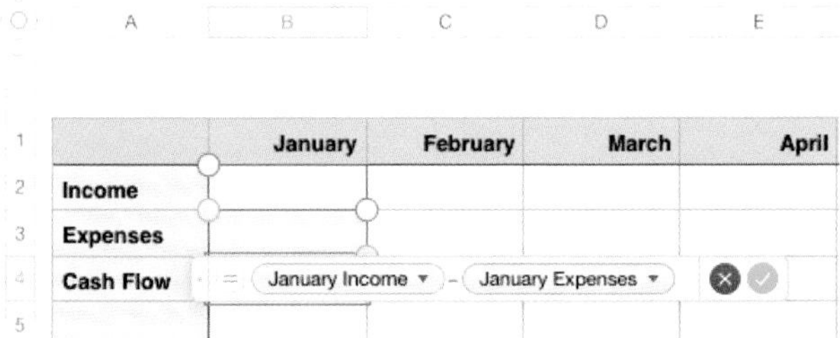

To calculate the cash flow, expenses are subtracted from income. This calculation determines whether the budget is in credit or deficit.

10 Click cell B3, and then click the checkmark button to apply the formula.

Cell B4 now shows the figure zero because there are no values in the column.

11 Click cell B2, and then Shift-click cell M4.

12 In the Cell inspector, change the Data Format to Currency, and select the Accounting Style option.

Accounting style places negative values in parentheses, a format favored by bookkeepers and auditors.

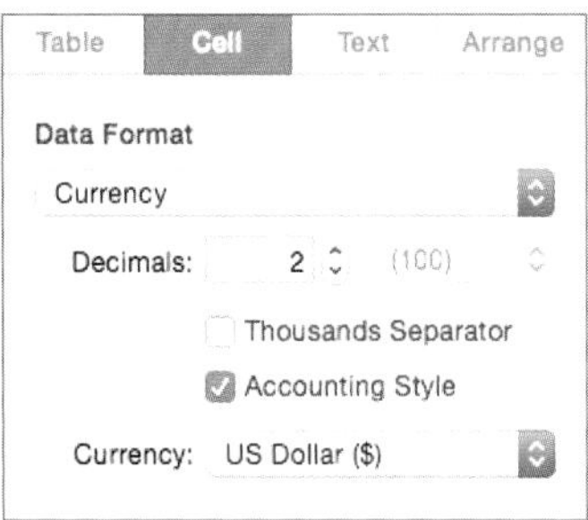

The decimal points default to two. You also have the options to add thousands separators and to change the type of currency.

13 Click cell B4, and drag the yellow circle on the cell's right edge all the way to the December column to populate the Cash Flow row with the results of the calculation you created in steps 9 and 10.

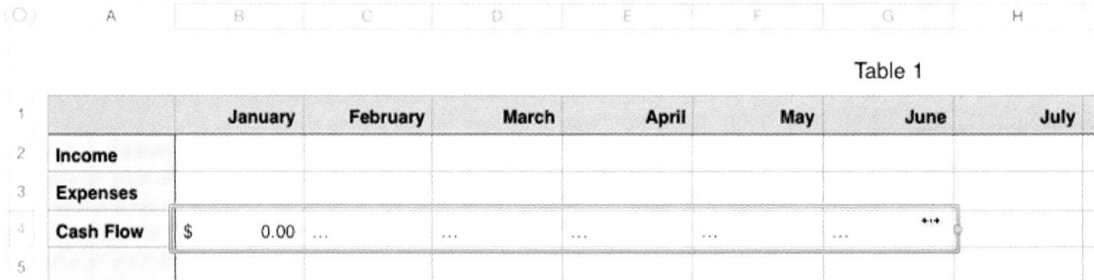

This is a very crude budget sheet, and we'll move things on in a moment by opening a planner with lots of additional figures; but before leaving this document, let's add a few figures right now.

14 In cell B2, type *2500*, as an example of income

15 Use the method described in step 13 to drag the value of cell B2 across the row to December's income in cell M2.

16 In cell B3, type *2300*, as an example for expenses.

17 Use the method described in step 13 to drag the value of cell B3 across the row to December's expenses in cell M3.

The cash flow cells perform their calculations and, hey, there's an extra $200 each month. Income and expenses could be set higher or lower.

18 In cell F3, change May's expenses to *$3000.*

The cash flow for May shows the negative amount of $500 in parentheses, which reflects the accounting style you set earlier.

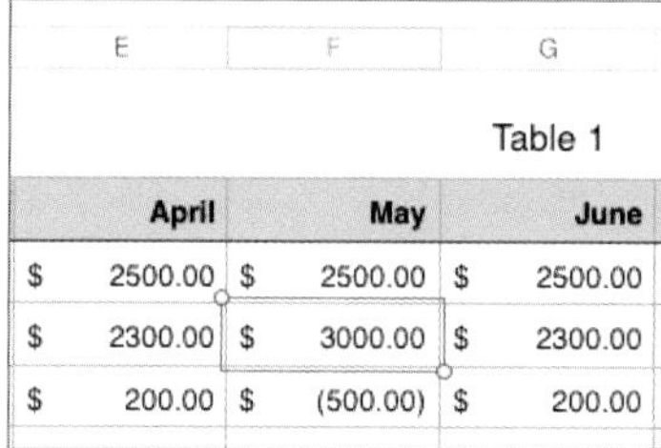

To simulate what happens when a table has so many rows or columns that it no longer fits in your document window, let's zoom in.

19 In the toolbar, set the Zoom level to 200%.

20 Scroll the document down and to the right.

The table contents disappear, but the columns and row titles remain in view. By default, header rows and columns are set to freeze and remain visible no matter where you scroll on a sheet.

This menu option is found in the row and column reference numbers.

21 Click the disclosure triangle for the row 1 reference header. From the pop-up menu, verify that Freeze Header Rows is chosen.

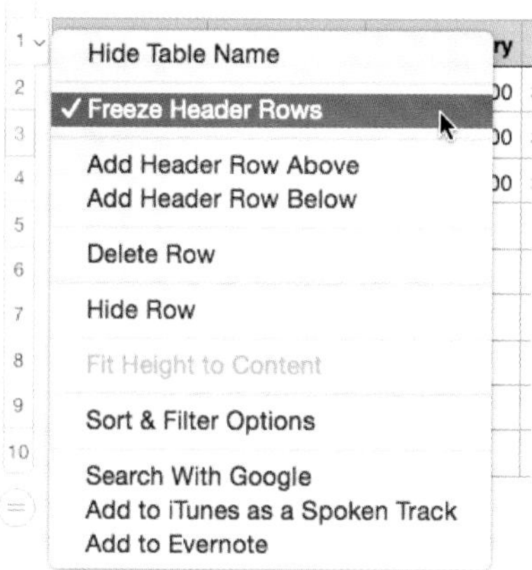

22 You're done modifying this sheet, so choose File > Close. When prompted you can give the document a name and save it, or click Delete.

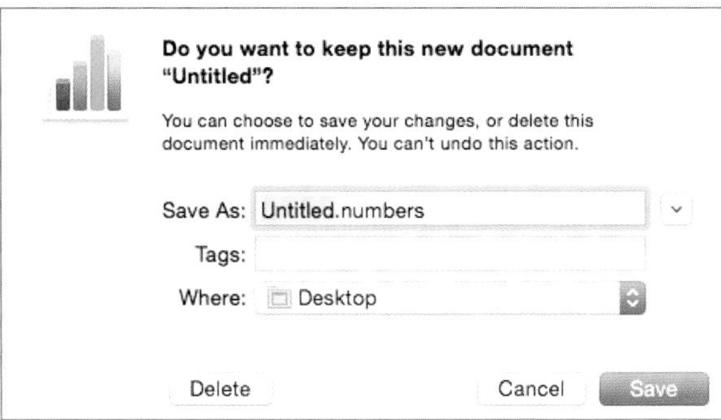

Adding Calculations

In this exercise, you are going to add functions to a budget planner. This will illustrate methods for using multiple tables to present data.

1 Open APTS Pages Numbers Keynote > Lesson_08 > **agata-budget.numbers**.

   This document has two sheets. The second sheet, Completed Projections, is the finished budget planner. You'll be working on Sheet 1.

2 From the Sheet 1 pop-up menu, choose Rename, and type *My Projections*. Press Enter.

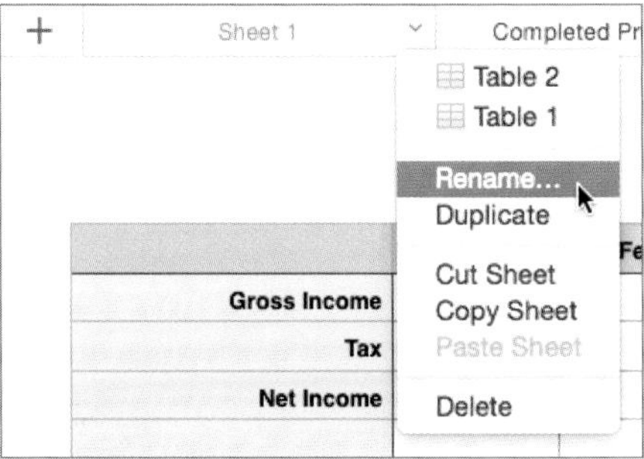

   The sheet name changes. Now let's name the tables.

3 On the sheet, select the words "Table 1." Rename the table to *Income Required.*

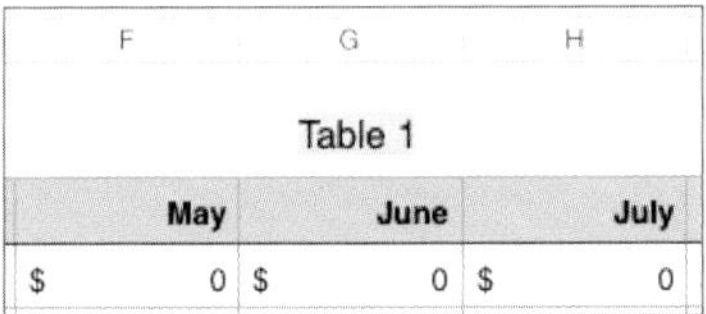

Table 1

May	June	July
$ 0	$ 0	$ 0

4 On the sheet, select the Table 2 title, and rename it to *Rate Card.*

Both tables are renamed. If you were to deselect the Table Name option in the inspector, the Sheet menu could be used to identify and select tables.

5 In the Income Required table, click cell B19. Press = (equal sign) to open the Formula Editor.

6 Click cell B6.

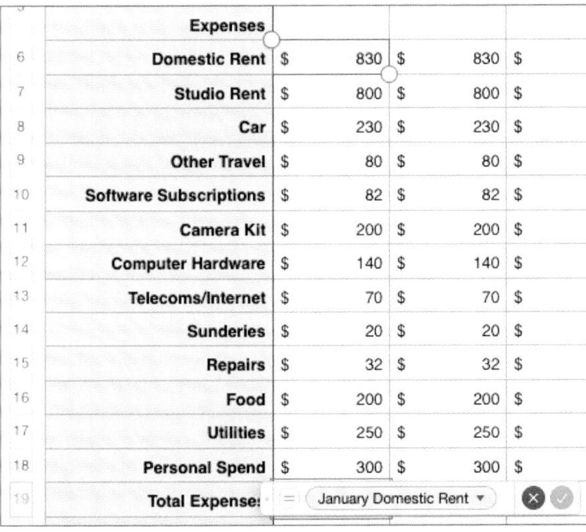

	Expenses			
6	Domestic Rent	$ 830	$ 830	$
7	Studio Rent	$ 800	$ 800	$
8	Car	$ 230	$ 230	$
9	Other Travel	$ 80	$ 80	$
10	Software Subscriptions	$ 82	$ 82	$
11	Camera Kit	$ 200	$ 200	$
12	Computer Hardware	$ 140	$ 140	$
13	Telecoms/Internet	$ 70	$ 70	$
14	Sunderies	$ 20	$ 20	$
15	Repairs	$ 32	$ 32	$
16	Food	$ 200	$ 200	$
17	Utilities	$ 250	$ 250	$
18	Personal Spend	$ 300	$ 300	$
19	Total Expense:	= January Domestic Rent ▾		

Cell B6 is selected as indicated by blue circles in the upper left and lower right of the cell.

7 In the lower right, drag the circle down the column to cell B18. Click the checkmark to accept this calculation.

	Expenses					
6	Domestic Rent	$	830	$	830	$
7	Studio Rent	$	800	$	800	$
8	Car	$	230	$	230	$
9	Other Travel	$	80	$	80	$
10	Software Subscriptions	$	82	$	82	$
11	Camera Kit	$	200	$	200	$
12	Computer Hardware	$	140	$	140	$
13	Telecoms/Internet	$	70	$	70	$
14	Sundries	$	20	$	20	$
15	Repairs	$	32	$	32	$
16	Food	$	200	$	200	$
17	Utilities	$	250	$	250	$
18	Personal Spend	$	300	$	300	$
19	Total Expenses	= SUM ▾	B6:B18 ▾			

NOTE ▶ Typing = *sum (B6:B18* would be another way of entering this formula. Numbers automatically capitalizes the function SUM and closes off the parentheses for you. In more complex equations, typing the expressions and brackets in full is a good idea.

8 Use the method you learned earlier to drag the formula across the entire row.

9 Double-click cell M19.

Its equation reads "=SUM (M6:M18)". This formula was duplicated with cell references relative to its column. If you click any of the other SUMs in row 19, you'll see that this is true for all the cells. Later you'll encounter a situation in which you'll want to change this default behavior.

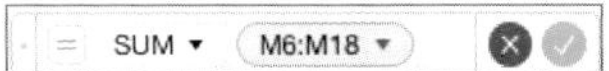

10 Click the control to the right of column M to add a new column.

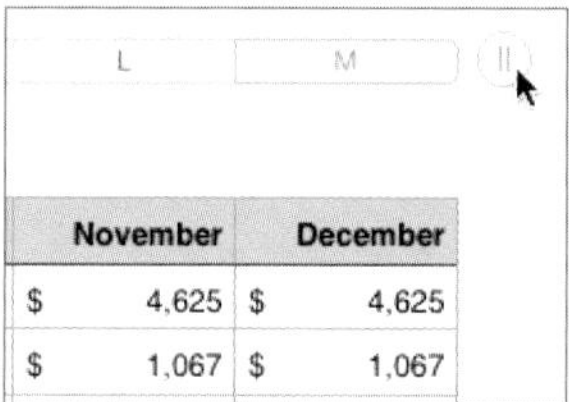

November	December
$ 4,625	$ 4,625
$ 1,067	$ 1,067

The new column automatically includes any formulas in the preceding rows. On this occasion you'll need to overwrite these calculations with a SUM of each row.

11 Click cell N2, and press Backspace, to clear the cell.

12 Press = (equal sign), and then type *SUM(B2:M2).*

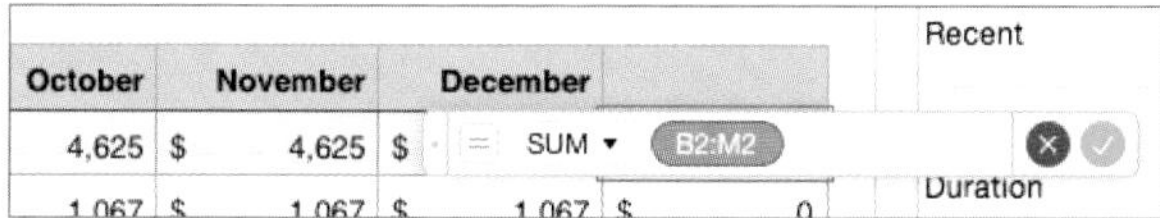

13 Click the checkmark in the Formula Editor, or press Enter to apply the function.

TIP Alternatively, you could type =*SUM*, and then click cell B2 and drag the cell handle across the row, much as you used SUM in the columns.

14 Click cell N2, and drag the lower edge of the cell down to row N20. Doing so makes column N the year totalizer for each row.

Working with Multiple Tables

Let's add some context to this exercise, as it should help explain what you're trying to achieve. The following figures represent some guesswork by a photographer who'd like to calculate realistic hourly and day rates for his services. You can use Numbers to calculate the level of income required to break even, and to determine whether renting a studio is affordable.

1 In the Rate Card table, click cell B2.

2 Press = (equal sign), and in the Income Required table, click cell N2.

The calculations made in the Income Required table suggest an income of $55,495 is required to break even. Rather than type that figure, you have now referenced the totalizer figure in cell N2.

3 Click after the reference to Income Required::N2, and in the Formula Editor, type */48*. Forty-eight is sometimes used as the maximum working weeks in a year. Click the checkmark to apply the calculation.

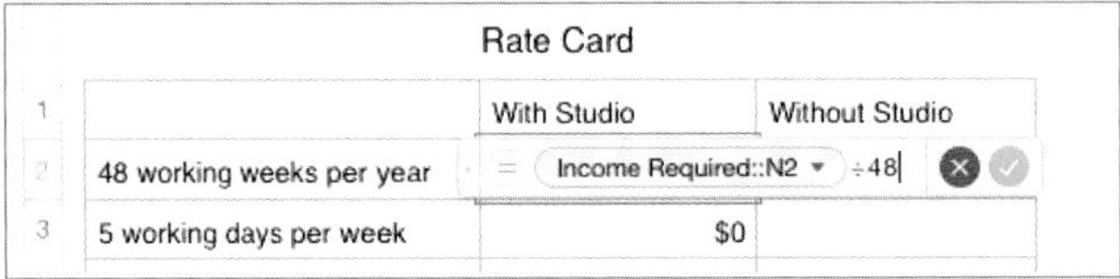

Column B of the Rate Card now calculates the income required per week (allowing for four weeks vacation) and displays it in cell B2. B3 calculates and displays the minimum day rate, and B4 the hourly rate.

4 Click cell B3, and then Shift-click cell B4.

5 Drag the right edge of the cells to the right to copy the formula to column C.

Rate Card

		With Studio	Without Studio
2	48 working weeks per year	$1156	
3	5 working days per week	$231	...
4	8 chargeable hours per day	$29	...

The cells in column C populate with the formula. The desired referencing has worked.

6 Click cell B2, and drag to copy the formula to column C. Errors appear.

Rate Card

		With Studio	Without Studio
2	48 working weeks per year	$1156	⚠
3	5 working days per week	$231	⚠
4	8 chargeable hours per day	$29	⚠

The formula in cell B2 is referencing a cell in column N of the other table. By dragging the formula to cell C2, the C2 formula is now trying to reference column O of the Income Required table. That column doesn't exist, so error symbols appear.

7 Double-click cell B2 to open the Formula Editor.

8 Click the disclosure triangle in the reference. A pop-up menu appears.

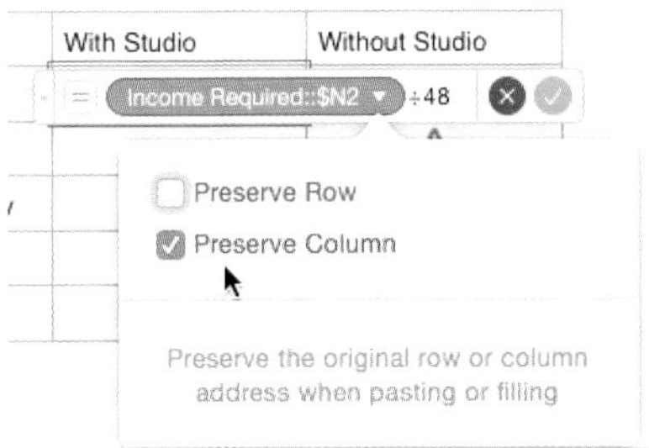

9 Select Preserve Column, and click the checkmark.

This changes the cell reference so that when you drag the formula a second time, Numbers will not point to the wrong column.

Refer to the following figure to help with steps 10, 11, and 12; or go to the Rate Card Calculations on the Complete Projections sheet and review the formulas used.

10 Drag the formula in cell B2 to cell C2 using the method described previously.

11 Double-click cell C2, and modify the formula, placing parentheses around the reference Income Required::$N2.

12 Click to the left of the closing parenthesis and press – (minus sign). Then in the Income Required table, click cell N7. Then click the checkmark.

NOTE ► The Rate Card table now references two cells in the other table. So if you were to change the expense items in the Income Required table, the level of income needed would automatically rise and the rate card would adjust accordingly.

Printing from Numbers

As you're about to see, Numbers has an easy-to-use print interface. The Numbers templates were designed with print sizes in mind, but if tables expand with hundreds of rows and columns, sheets will probably spread across multiple printed pages.

1 With APTS Pages Numbers Keynote > Lesson_08 > **agata-budget.numbers** open, click the View menu in the toolbar and zoom out to 25%.

Numbers has a vast canvas on which you can place tables, images, and charts.

2 Choose File > Print.

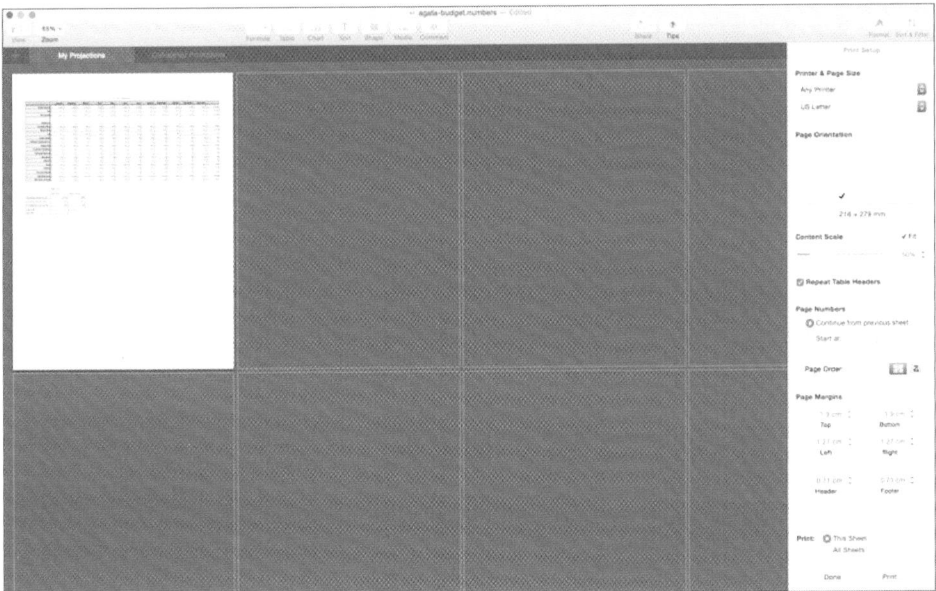

The Numbers window presents you with lots of visual feedback as to how your document will look in print.

3 In the Print Setup inspector, select a printer, if one is available, and set your paper size.

NOTE ▶ In any print dialog, setting the printer first will display only the paper sizes available for that printer.

4 Change the Page Orientation to Landscape.

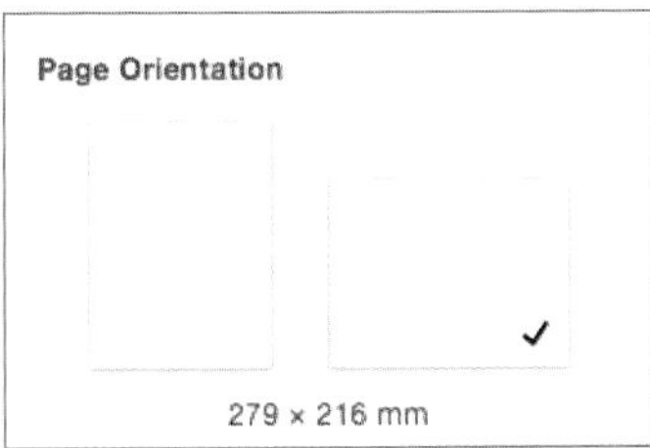

5 Change the Content Scale to 100%.

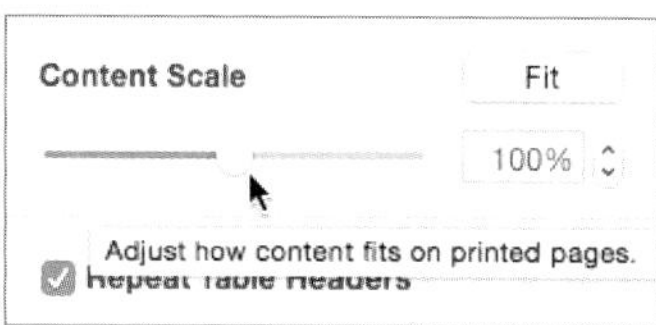

The sheet expands to three pages. The Income Required table spans two pages, and the row headers repeat on both pages, which you might find undesirable.

6 Deselect Repeat Table Headers to remove the repeated headers.

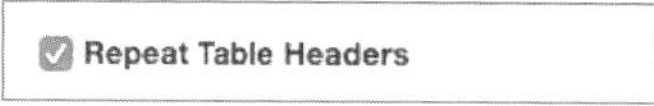

7 For the current sheet, we want the headers repeated, however, so select Repeat Table Headers.

8 To print all the current sheets, click the All Sheets radio button found at the bottom of the inspector.

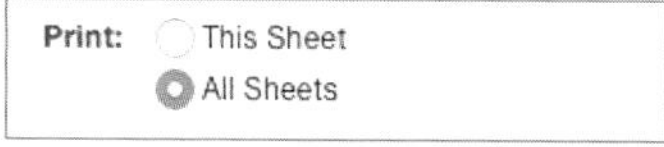

The print options in Numbers are clear, and provide great visual feedback on how your sheets will print.

9 At the bottom of the inspector, click Done to save your custom print options.

10 Choose File > Print, or press Command-P, to reopen the Print Setup inspector and verify that it remains just as you set it.

Lesson Review

1. Describe how to duplicate a sheet.
2. Name three data formats found in Numbers that are not available in Pages or Keynote.
3. How do you rename a table?
4. Describe how to repeat a formula across an entire row of a table.
5. Describe how to open the Formula Editor.

Answers

1. From the Sheet menu, choose Duplicate.
2. Five data formats are exclusive to Numbers: checkbox, star rating, slider, stepper, and pop-up menu.
3. Select the table name on the sheet and type a new name (the Table Name option must be selected in the Table inspector).
4. Click the cell containing the formula, and then drag either the left or right edge of the cell to the left or right to repeat the formula along a row.
5. Click a cell and press = (equal sign) to open the Formula Editor. (You can also click a cell and choose Insert > Formula > Create Formula.)

9

Lesson Files

APTS Pages Numbers Keynote > Lesson_09 > ju-jitsu-academy-09.numbers

APTS Pages Numbers Keynote > Lesson_09 > ju-jitsu-grading-idea.xls

APTS Pages Numbers Keynote > Lesson_09 > ju-jitsu-finished.numbers

Time

This lesson takes approximately 60 minutes to complete.

Goals

Open and upgrade a Numbers spreadsheet

Open and edit an Excel workbook

Use dynamic data formats

Add conditional highlighting

Create and apply table styles

Secure spreadsheets with passwords

Lesson **9**

Making Interactive Spreadsheets

Spreadsheets can be expanded beyond performing simple arithmetic calculation to running tailored formulas for a myriad of programming-like functions. But, let's pause here. If the thought of programming gives you a cold sweat, rest assured that this lesson introduces some basic concepts to keep things simple for most of us. For those with programming experience, this lesson will be a refresher on how to call functions and apply them in Numbers.

Two important concepts underpin this lesson. The first concerns data input. You'll be working on an assessment sheet for a Ju Jitsu club. The theme of assessment carries through all forms and levels of education, but can also be applied to an inventory or equipment checklist. You'll be using checkbox, star rating, and slider data formats to build an assessment readiness table that can be viewed and used on an iPad for even greater utility.

The second theme involves the use of conditional highlighting. This Numbers feature adds great visual feedback when reading a spreadsheet. In the assessment sheet you'll build in this lesson, complete cells will format in amber, and when a student is ready to be graded, a cell will highlight in green.

In addition, you'll add conditional formatting to indicate when annual fees are due. This kind of flagging is often used to highlight when invoices are overdue or a budget is in deficit.

		Rolls & Breakfalls	Stances	Strikes	Throws	Locks		Training Bout 1	Training Bout 2	Training Bout 3		Attendance	Ready To Grade
Abigail	Graves	✓	✓	✓	✓	✓	5	★★★••	★★★••	★★★••	9	16	30
Addison	Simmons	✓	✓	✓	✓	✓	5	★★★••	★★•••	★★★★•	9	16	30
Aiden	Fisher	✓	✓	✓	✓	✓	5	★★★••	★★★★•	★★★••	10	12	27
Alexander	Ellis	✓	✓	✓	✓	✓	5	★★•••	★★★••	★★★••	8	16	29
Alexis	Horton		✓	✓	✓	✓	4	★★★••	★★★★•	★★•••	9	16	29
Alondra	Henderson-Price	✓	✓	✓	✓	✓	5	★★★••	★★★••	★★•••	8	16	29
Andrew	Harrison	✓	✓	✓	✓	✓	5	★★★••	★★★★•	★★•••	9	16	30
Angel	Gibson	✓	✓	✓	✓	✓	5	★★★••	★★★••	★★★••	9	16	30
Anna	Barrett	✓	✓	✓			3	★★★••	★★★★•	★★•••	9	16	28
Anthony	McDonald	✓	✓		✓	✓	4	★★★••	★★★••	★★★★•	10	16	30
Ashley	O'Brien	✓	✓	✓	✓	✓	5	★★★••	★★★★•	★★★★★	12	16	33
Ava	Castro		✓	✓	✓	✓	4	★★★••	★★★••	★★★••	9	16	29
Avery	Sutton	✓	✓	✓	✓	✓	5	★★★••	★★★★•	★★•••	9	16	30
Benjamin	Cruz		✓	✓			2	★★★••	★★★★•	★★•••	9	15	26
Brayden	Marshall	✓	✓	✓	✓	✓	5	★★★••	★★★★•	★★•••	9	16	30
Brianna	Gergory	✓	✓	✓	✓	✓	5	★★★••	★★★★•	★★•••	9	16	30

Opening and Upgrading a Numbers 09 Document

Sometimes tasks get pushed down our to-do lists, so by the time you return to them, life and the software have moved on. You'll start this lesson by opening a project that was created in Numbers 09.

1 In Numbers, choose File > Open.

2 Navigate to APTS Pages Numbers Keynote > Lesson_09.

3 Double-click the **ju-jitsu-academy-09.numbers** document.

4 After the document opens in Numbers, choose File > Save.

5 In the dialog that appears, click "Edit a Copy."

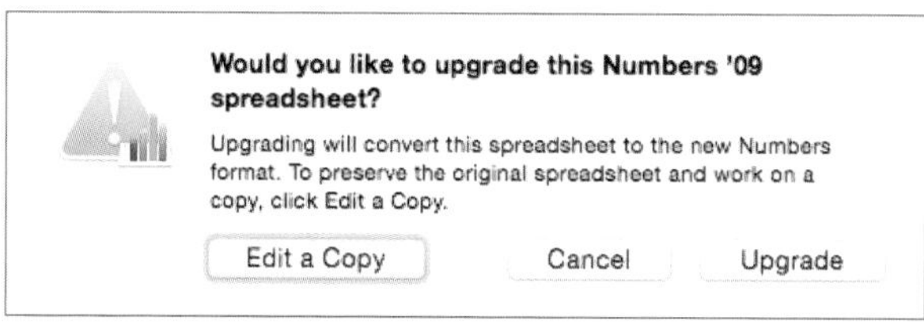
Would you like to upgrade this Numbers '09 spreadsheet?
Upgrading will convert this spreadsheet to the new Numbers format. To preserve the original spreadsheet and work on a copy, click Edit a Copy.
Edit a Copy
Cancel
Upgrade

6 Choose File > Save. In the dialog, change the name to *ju-jitsu-academy.numbers*.

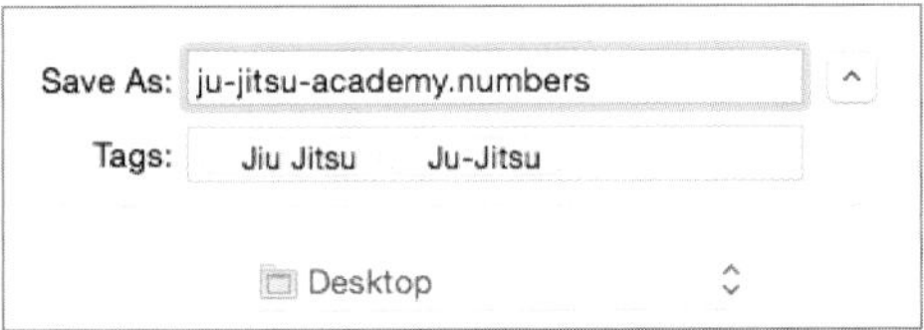

7 Click Save. Choose Desktop as the location for the spreadsheet.

You have upgraded a copy of the Numbers 09 document and left the original document untouched. The original document remains open, along with the upgraded spreadsheet.

8 In the upgraded spreadsheet, click the Grading Readiness tab.

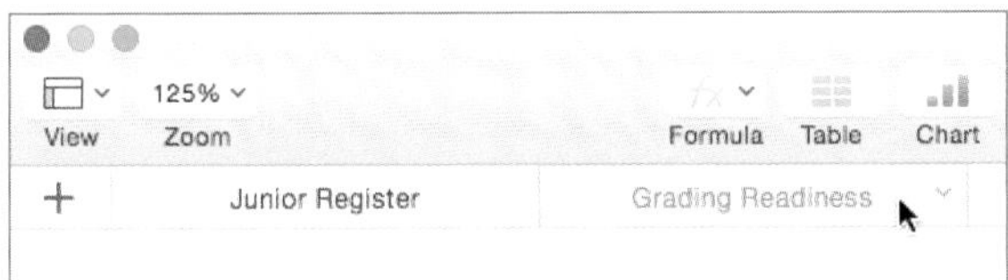

The sheet is blank. You'll now add a table to this sheet from a Microsoft Excel document.

9 Leave ju-jitsu-academy.numbers open.

Opening and Editing an Excel Workbook

Collaborating with Microsoft Excel users is a simple matter of opening, editing, and then exporting spreadsheets between the two applications, even if your colleagues are using Windows workstations. Not all Numbers formatting is maintained in Excel, however, and opening Excel workbooks in Numbers may also require changes.

1 In Numbers, choose File > Open.

2 Navigate to APTS Pages Numbers Keynote > Lesson_09.

3 Double-click the **ju-jitsu-grading-idea.xls** document.

A warning dialog may appear. Often, it concerns font substitution.

4 If necessary, close the warning dialog.

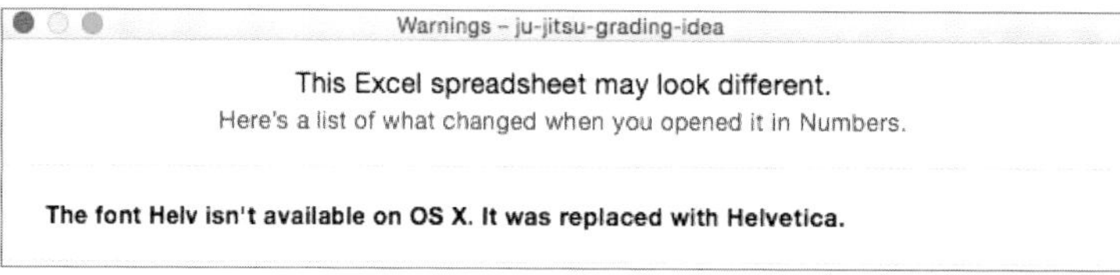

TIP If you want to examine the original layout of an Excel spreadsheet when you don't have the Excel application to do so, ask the person providing the Excel document for a PDF of it.

5 After the document opens in Numbers, choose File > Save.

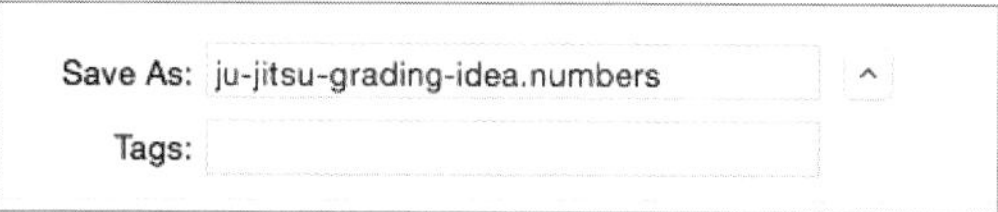

You needn't rename the document. Because you're saving a Numbers document, the original Excel document will not be overwritten.

NOTE ▶ The file will save to the lesson folder, Lesson_09. You could choose to save it to the desktop instead.

6 In ju-jitsu-grading-idea.numbers, click the Grading Readiness tab.

Excel sheets are converted to Numbers sheets. This document has two sheets. The Grading Readiness sheet contains a table.

7 From the Grading Readiness tab's pop-up menu, choose Table 1. This a reliable way to select an entire table.

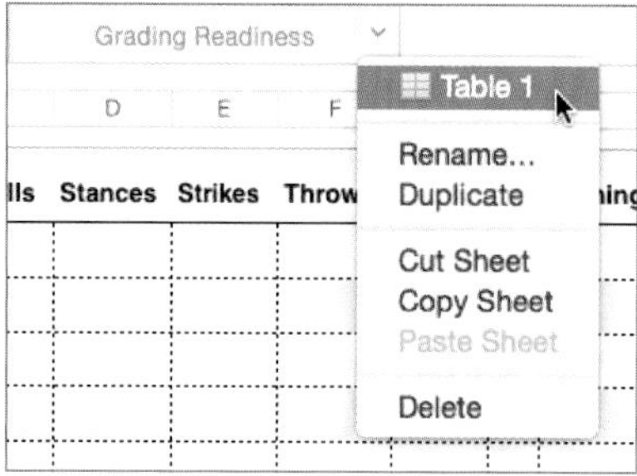

You could complete this lesson by continuing to work on the document you converted from Excel, but instead let's copy this table into the Numbers document (ju-jitsu-academy.numbers).

8 Choose Edit > Copy.

9 Choose Window > ju-jitsu-academy.

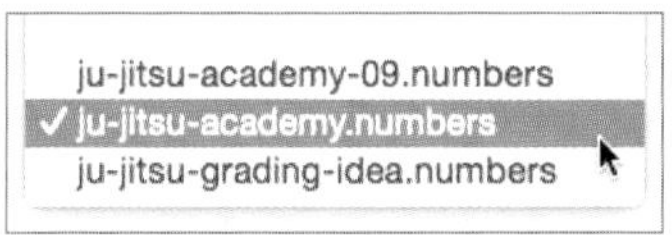

NOTE ▶ The Numbers document may contain the .numbers extension. You could use this menu to switch to ju-jitsu-academy-09.numbers to close that document.

10 In the ju-jitsu-academy.numbers document, select the Grading Readiness sheet.

11 Choose Edit > Paste.

12 Choose File > Save. Leave the document open and ready for the next exercise.

You have now prepared the foundations of an assessment table. You could have built it from scratch, but by importing from Excel you have experienced a few real-world collaboration techniques.

Formatting Tables

Good design has several meanings in the context of spreadsheets. Functionality and ease of use come from the synergy of planning functions and applying good visual design to aid readability. In this exercise, you'll apply formatting to the grading readiness table.

1 In ju-jitsu-academy.numbers, select the Register table. It's on the Junior Register sheet.

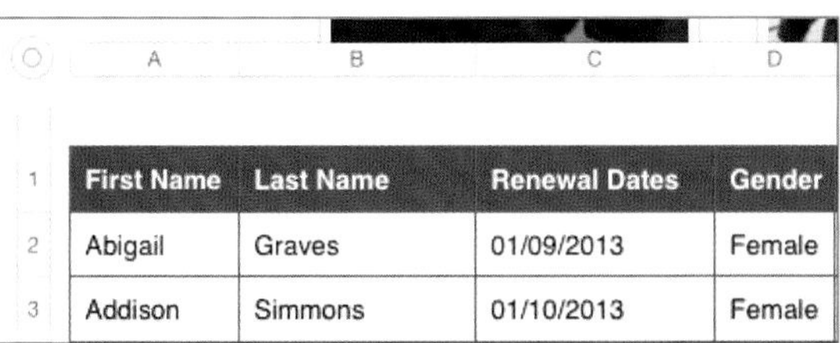

2 In Table Styles in the inspector, navigate to a pane where the + (plus sign) button is visible, and click it

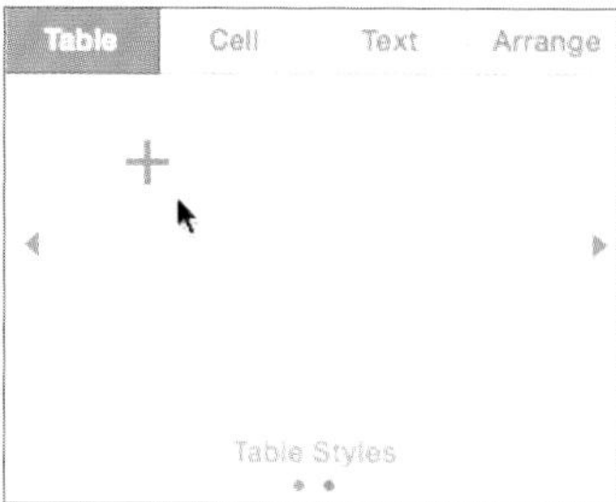

The register's formatting is added to the Table Styles pane.

3 Move to the Grading Readiness sheet, and select the table.

4 From Table Styles in the inspector, click the style you added in step 2.

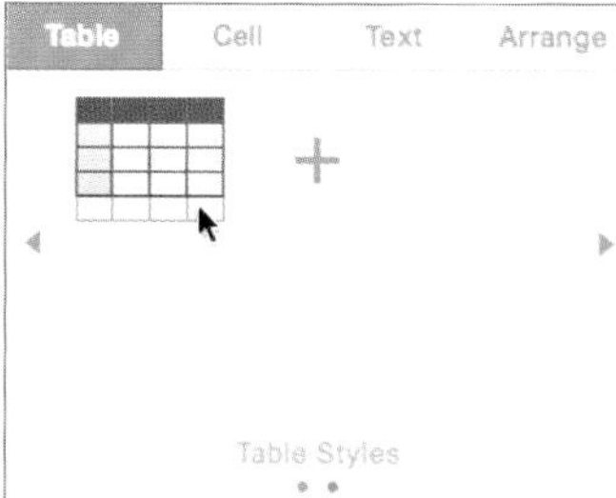

The table formatting changes, but it doesn't look like the register table yet. You'll need to delete a row and column and add header rows and columns. This process continues your look at real-world techniques. While these cross-platform formatting problems aren't hard to resolve, they can be deeply frustrating when you don't know how to fix them.

5 With the table selected, in the Table inspector, click the Fit buttons for both Row and Column.

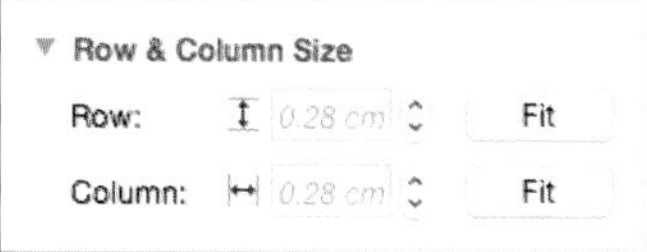

The cell borders should be clearly visible where they might have been obscured previously.

6 Click the reference header for row 1. From the pop-up menu, choose Delete Row.

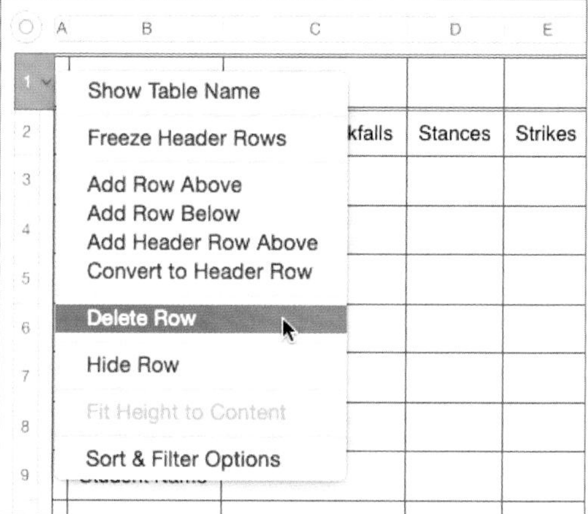

7 Click the reference header for column A. From the pop-up menu, choose Delete Column.

With the superfluous row and column removed, the table still doesn't match the applied style. You'll need to add header rows and columns.

8 Click the reference header for the new row 1. From the pop-up menu, choose Convert to Header Row.

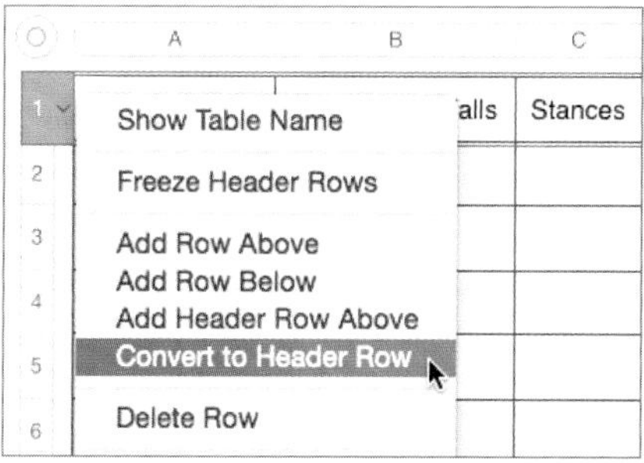

Hey presto—the header row is now correctly formatted.

9 Click the reference header for column A. From the pop-up menu, choose Convert to Header Column.

Rather than have a single column for the student names, you're going to add a new header column for the students' last names.

10 Click the reference header for column A. From the pop-up menu, choose Add Header Column After.

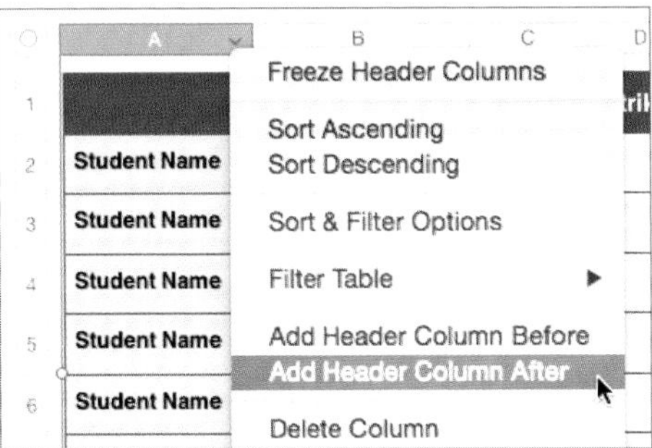

11 Click cell A1, and type *First Name*.

12 Press Tab to move to cell B1, and type *Last Name*.

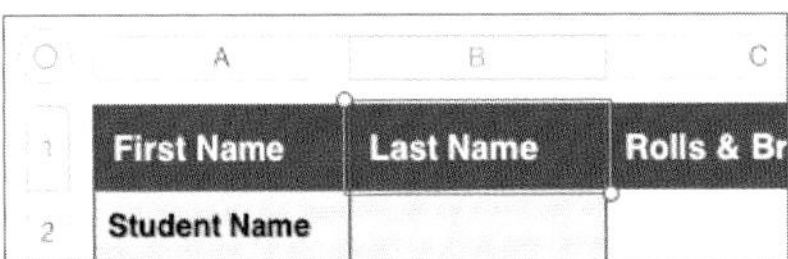

The visual formatting is complete for now. The table needs data, which you'll address in the next exercise.

Referencing Data

Many times lists can be reused (or referenced, to use the proper term) rather than retyped. The register table contains the names of the students you'll use for the grading readiness table. You will reference the names on the first table to populate the grading table.

In geek speak, the grading readiness table names will be the children of the parent table. If the name data changes on the register, the grading readiness names will automatically update in that table. Referencing is a much more productive method than retyping lists, or copying and pasting them. Actions will speak more clearly than words, so let's get to it.

1 Click cell A2, and press the = (equal sign) key.

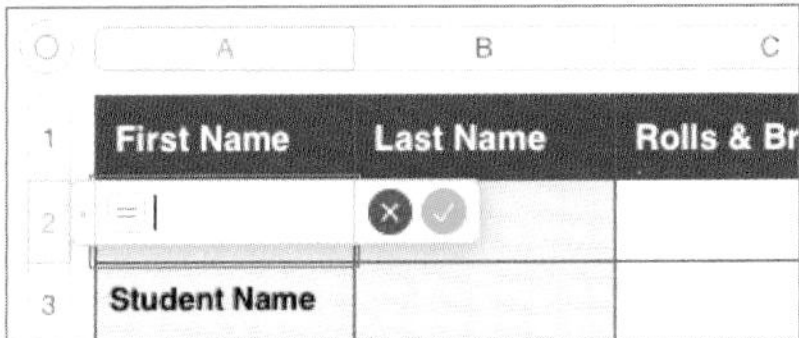

The cell clears, and the Formula Editor appears.

NOTE ▶ If you double-click the cell rather than clicking just once, the text insertion cursor becomes active, which makes clearing the cell a little lengthier. When the text insertion cursor is active, you can press Cmd-A and then press the = (equal sign) key.

2 In the Junior Register sheet, click cell A2.

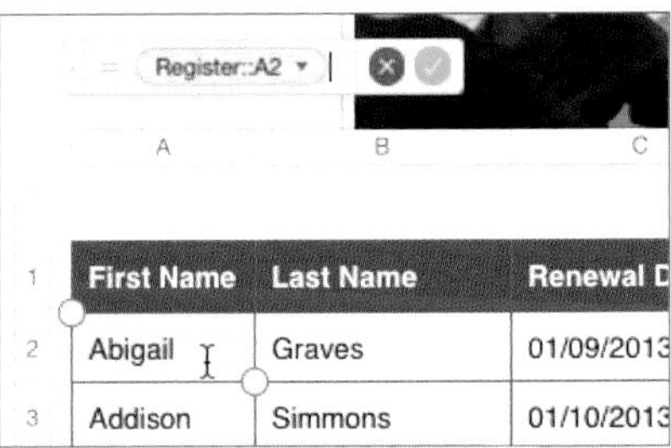

NOTE ▶ The Formula Editor remains in view.

3 Click the checkmark to accept the formula.

In the Grading Readiness sheet, Abigail's name appears in cell A2. It is referencing the register table.

4 Locate the pointer over the lower edge of cell A2, and drag the yellow handle down to fill column A with the reference formula.

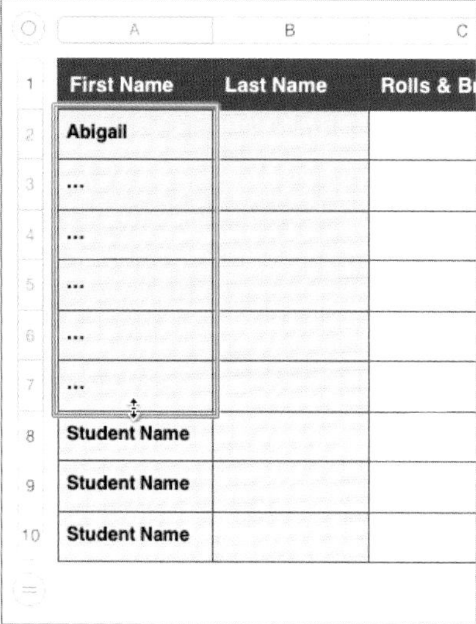

Column A is now populated with the first ten names on the referenced registered table.

NOTE ▶ This kind of referencing can be linked to tables on a single sheet or multiple sheets but not to separate Numbers documents.

5 Click cell B2 and press the = (equal sign) key.

6 In the Junior Register sheet, click cell B2.

7 Repeat steps 3 and 4 for column B, to reference the last names of the students.

8 Go to the Junior Register sheet. In cell A5 of the register, change the name of the student from Alexander to *Alexandra*.

9 Go to the Grading Readiness sheet.

Notice that the name was automatically changed.

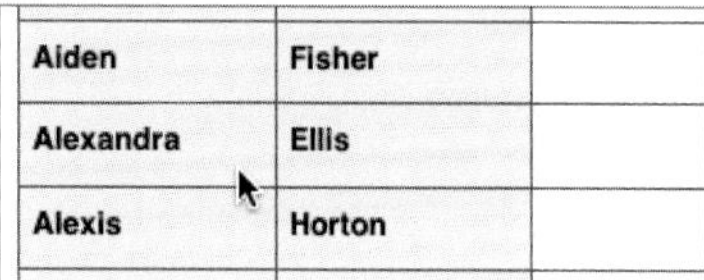

Later you'll extend the grading table to include more students, but for now you've learned a neat method for using referencing in lists.

Evaluating Data Formats

In previous lessons you worked with a variety of data formats. In this exercise, you'll add checkbox, star rating, and slider formats to the grading readiness table to enable easy data entry. Adding data entry sliders also makes your sheet appropriate for use on an iPad, thereby providing the Ju Jitsu instructor with a convenient, portable method for assessing students in class.

The techniques here can be applied to many work tasks. The methods in this exercise are centered on building functionality.

1 Click cell C2 of the grading readiness table.

2 In the Cell inspector, from the Data Format pop-up menu, choose Checkbox.

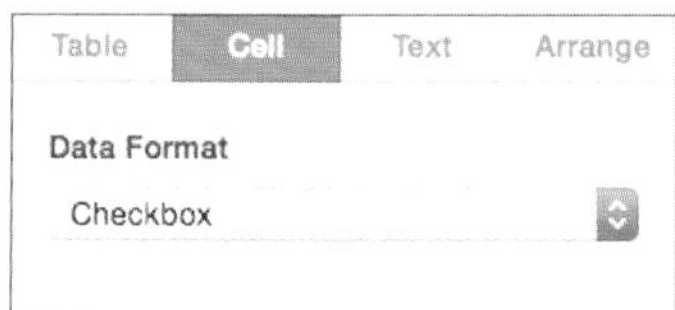

Checkboxes record "yes or no" conditions, making them ideal for this section of the grading assessment.

3 Drag the right edge of cell C2 to fill columns C to G.

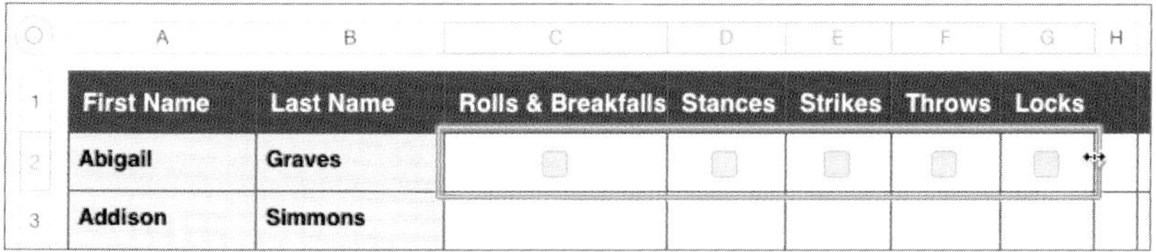

4 With cells C2 to G2 selected, drag down the bottom edge of any of the cells C to G in row 2 to row 10.

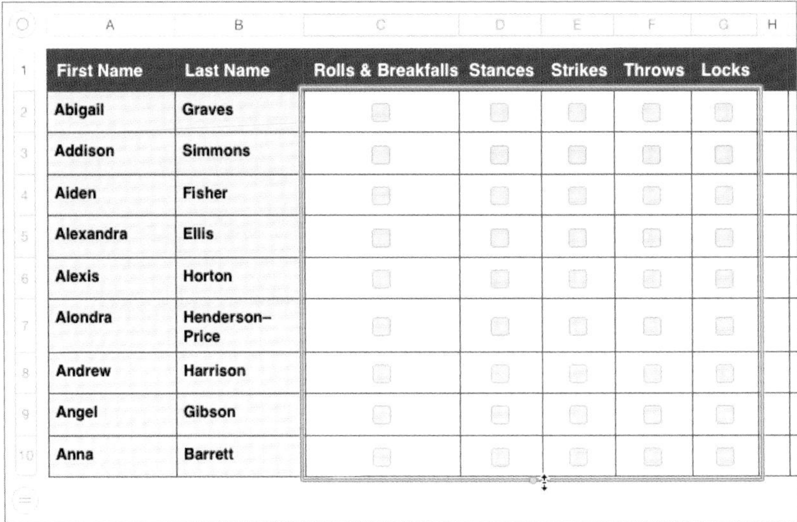

A checkbox has a numerical value of zero for deselected checkboxes and one for selected checkboxes as you'll see in the next steps.

5 Select cell H2, and press = (equal sign).

6 Click cell C2, then D2, then E2, F2, and finally G2.

7 Click the checkmark to accept the formula.

As you learned in previous lessons, this step adds together all the values in the selected cells. The sum is currently zero.

8 Click the checkbox in cell C2. The value in cell H2 returns as 1.

9 Click the checkbox in cell D2. The value in cell H2 now returns as 2.

This confirms the number values of checkboxes. You'll utilize this feature later when applying conditional highlighting.

10 Drag the formula in cell H2 down its column to cell H10.

Checkboxes work for simple "yes or no" reporting, but another data format would better suit qualitative judgments. In the next step, you'll add star ratings to the assessment sheet.

11 Click cell I2, and choose Star Rating from the Data Format pop-up menu.

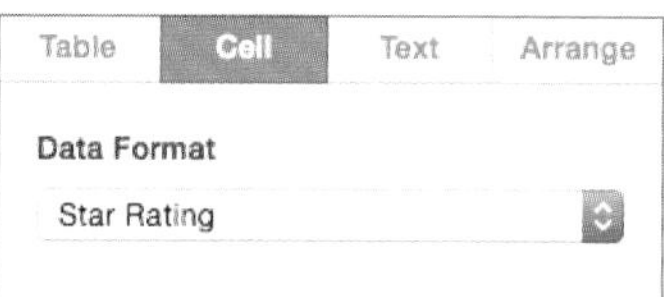

12 Drag the right edge of cell I2 to cell K2 to autofill the data format.

13 With cells I2 to K2 selected, drag the lower edge of any of the selected cells down to row 10 to fill them with the star rating data format.

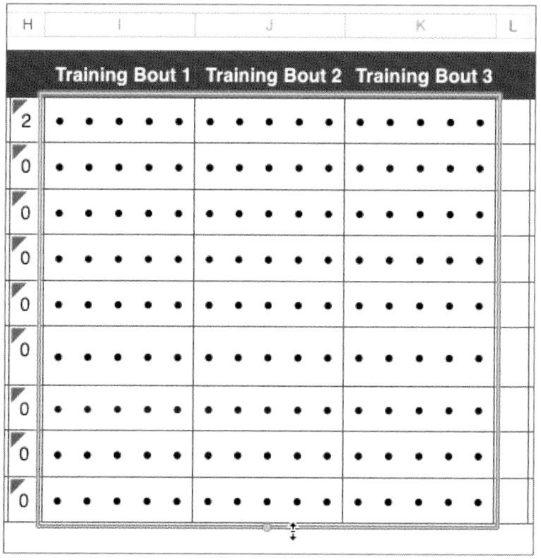

14 Click cell L2, and press = (equal sign).

15 Click cells I2, J2, and K2 to add them to the Formula Editor.

16 Click the checkmark to accept the formula.

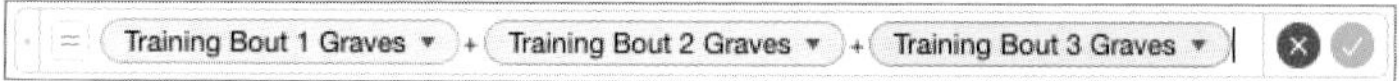

17 Drag the formula in cell L2 down to cell L10 as previously described.

NOTE ▶ You can apply star ratings by clicking one of the dots in a cell, or by selecting a cell and typing a number value from 1 to 5. Pressing 0 removes all the stars.

18 Click cell M2, and choose Slider from the Data Format pop-up menu.

Change the values in the inspector. Set the Minimum data field to 0 and the Maximum to 16. Leave the increment at 1.

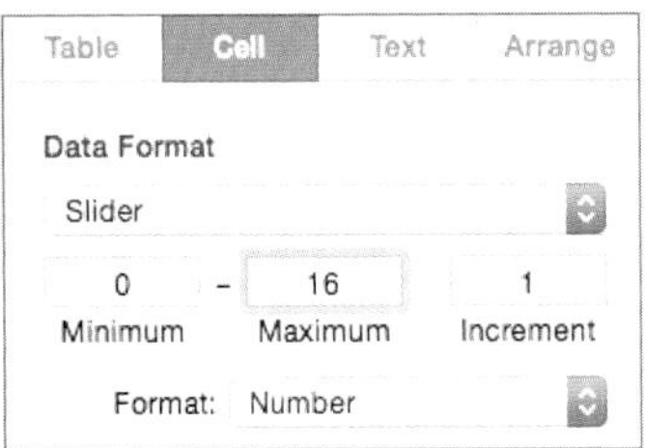

NOTE ▶ Dragging the slider up and down sets the student attendance value. Using the stepper data format would be another option for processing this kind of input, but would require a lot of clicking to set 16 starting from 0.

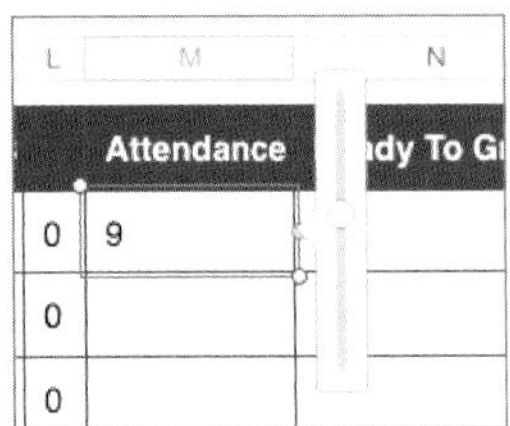

19 Using the previously described method, drag the data format in cell M2 down to fill the column down to row 10.

To complete the table's functions, you'll add a totalizer in column N.

20 Click cell N2, and press = (equal sign).

21 Click cells H2, L2, and M2 to add them to the Formula Editor. Click the checkmark to accept the formula.

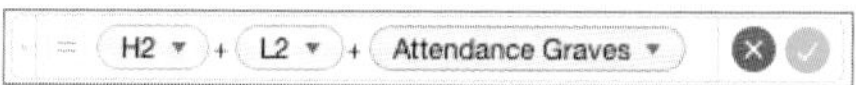

NOTE ▶ The Formula Editor's cell references can be either a letter and number, for example H2, or column name and cell contents, such as Attendance and Graves.

22 Drag the formula in cell N2 down to row N10 to apply the formula to the cells in column N.

You have created a functioning assessment table. By clicking checkboxes and star ratings and by setting attendance figures, you can change the total score for each student. At present, the value of the total score is unclear. In the next exercise, however, you'll set conditional highlighting so that when a student is ready to grade, the cells in column N will turn green.

Adding Conditional Highlighting

You have been designing a spreadsheet by mixing visual styles for clear presentation and by adding formula and data formats to create functionality. In this exercise, you'll use conditional highlighting to flag when a student is ready to grade.

These principles can be applied to an engineer's inspection schedule, a pilot's preflight check, or to budgets—the list goes on. Let's make sense of the grading table data.

1 Click cell N2. In the Cell inspector, click Conditional Highlighting.

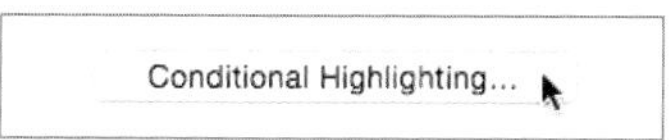

2 In the inspector, click Add a Rule.

3 Click Numbers in the popover. Choose the rule "greater than or equal to."

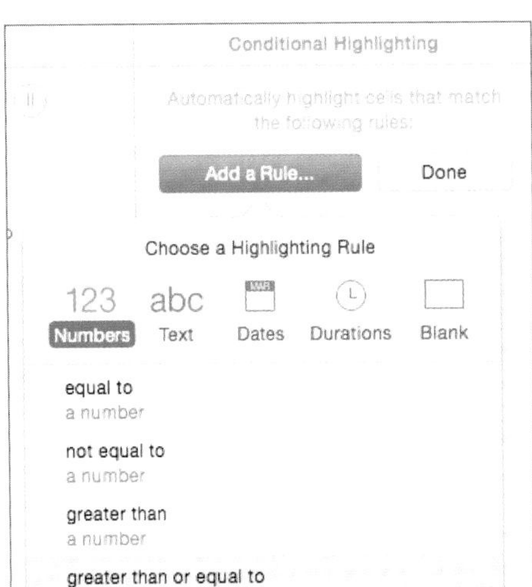

4 In the popover, set the "greater than or equal to" value to *30*. Choose a green fill.

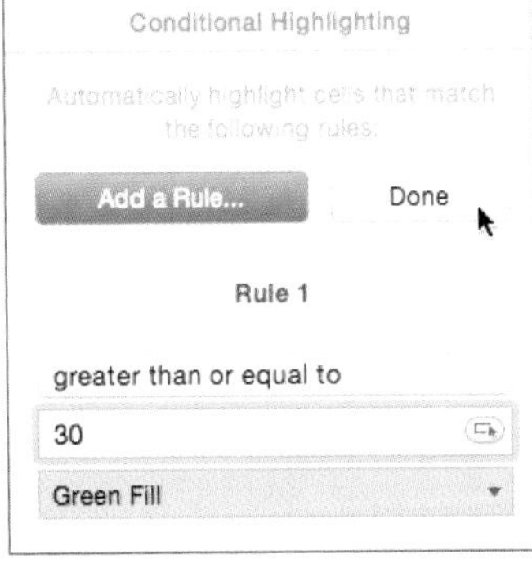

5 Click Done.

Now you have set the pass grade to 30.

6 In the lower part of cell N2, drag the yellow handle to apply the conditional highlighting to the rest of the column down to row 10.

7 In row 2, change the grades for Abigail Graves. Select all the checkboxes, give her at least three stars for each of her training bouts, and set her attendance to 16. Cell N2 turns green to indicate that she is ready to grade.

8 Click cell M2. In the Cell inspector, click Conditional Highlighting.

9 Click Add a Rule. In the Numbers tab of the popover, set the rule to be "equal to" *16* with an orange fill.

Effectively, you are flagging a student when that student has attended enough classes to be eligible to grade; but adding a second rule will provide improved visual feedback.

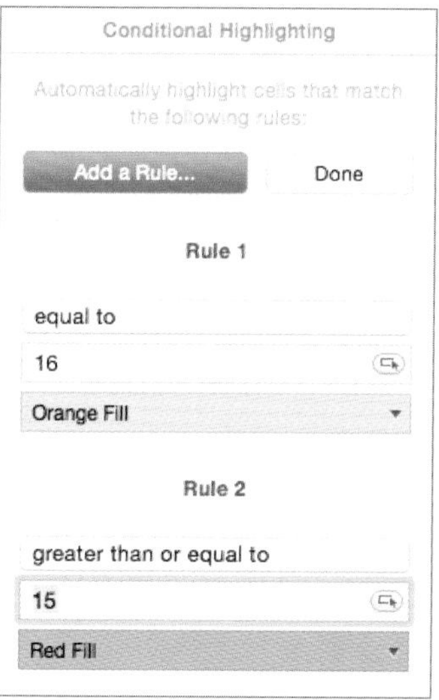

10 In the inspector, click Add a Rule. In the popover, set the rule to "less than or equal to" *15* with a red fill.

11 Click Done.

12 Drag the contents of cell M2 down to M10 to apply the conditional formatting to those cells.

NOTE ▶ The attendance value you set in cell M2 is applied to the cells you selected. You can change some of the attendance values in column M to see conditional highlighting in action.

TIP You could apply conditional highlighting to columns H and L to help flag the students' progress. A key part of spreadsheet design is to build in good visual feedback.

13 Go to the Junior Register sheet.

14 Click the reference header for column C, Renewal Dates.

15 In the Cell inspector, click Conditional Highlighting. Click Add a Rule, and then in the popover, click Dates.

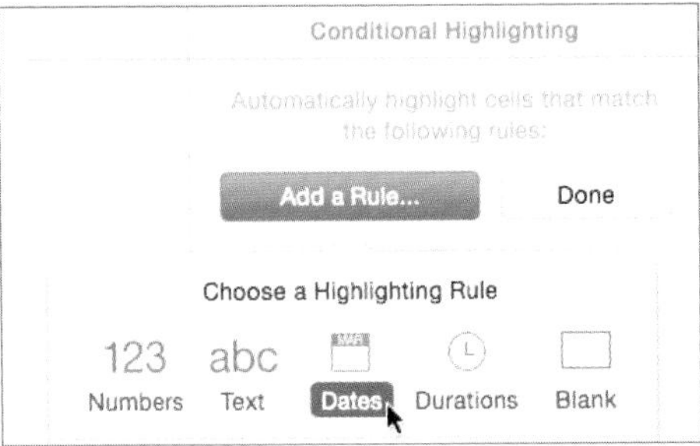

16 In the list of conditions, click Before.

17 Set Rule 1 to "date is before the date" *1* years ago, and choose a red fill.

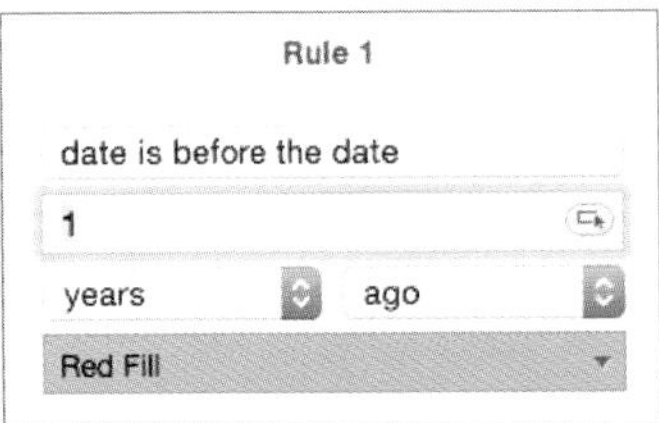

If the date in column C is over one year from the time you are working through this book, it will flag in red.

Identifying dates by using conditional highlighting is a great way to avoid missing important dates.

NOTE ▸ You can customize conditional highlighting to display colors and formats other than the presets. In the inspector, choose Custom Style at the bottom of the highlighting style options.

18 Switch to the Grading Readiness sheet. Click the grading readiness table to select it.

Notice the icon in the lower-right corner of the table.

• •	0	16	16
• •	0	16	16
• •	0	16	16

19 Drag the icon straight down to add new rows to the grading table.

The new rows contain all the formatting from the table above, and the First Name and Last Name cells automatically fill with the referenced information from the register table.

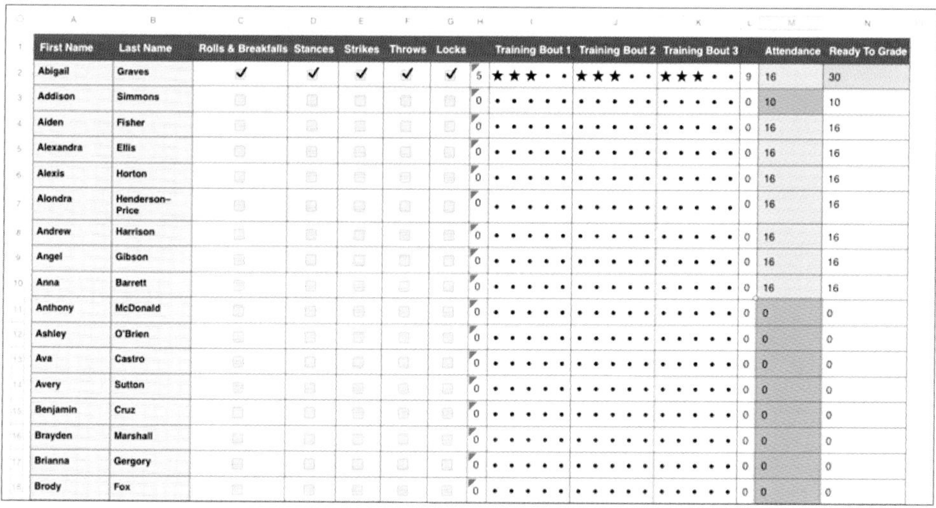

First Name	Last Name	Rolls & Breakfalls	Stances	Strikes	Throws	Locks		Training Bout 1	Training Bout 2	Training Bout 3		Attendance	Ready To Grade
Abigail	Graves	✓	✓	✓	✓	✓	5	★★★••	★★★••	★★★••	9	16	30
Addison	Simmons						0	•••••	•••••	•••••	0	10	10
Aiden	Fisher						0	•••••	•••••	•••••	0	16	16
Alexandra	Ellis						0	•••••	•••••	•••••	0	16	16
Alexis	Horton						0	•••••	•••••	•••••	0	16	16
Alondra	Henderson-Price						0	•••••	•••••	•••••	0	16	16
Andrew	Harrison						0	•••••	•••••	•••••	0	16	16
Angel	Gibson						0	•••••	•••••	•••••	0	16	16
Anna	Barrett						0	•••••	•••••	•••••	0	16	16
Anthony	McDonald						0	•••••	•••••	•••••	0	0	0
Ashley	O'Brien						0	•••••	•••••	•••••	0	0	0
Ava	Castro						0	•••••	•••••	•••••	0	0	0
Avery	Sutton						0	•••••	•••••	•••••	0	0	0
Benjamin	Cruz						0	•••••	•••••	•••••	0	0	0
Brayden	Marshall						0	•••••	•••••	•••••	0	0	0
Brianna	Gergory						0	•••••	•••••	•••••	0	0	0
Brody	Fox						0	•••••	•••••	•••••	0	0	0

20 Close the spreadsheet.

Using Password Protection

You learned about password protection in Lesson 2, but it deserves a special review in this lesson. Although all the names and contact details of the Ju Jitsu students are fictitious, when creating any document containing personal or personnel information, you may have a legal responsibility to protect the data. Regardless of the laws in your country, protecting sensitive information is still good practice.

The Numbers document that you are about to use contains some extra conditional highlighting that you can review and check your work in the previous exercises.

1 In Numbers, choose File > Open.

2 Navigate to APTS Pages Numbers Keynote > Lesson_09.

3 Double-click the **ju-jitsu-finished.numbers** document.

4 Choose File > Set Password.

5 In the dialog, enter a password, verify it, and add a hint, but for added security don't select "Remember this password in my keychain."

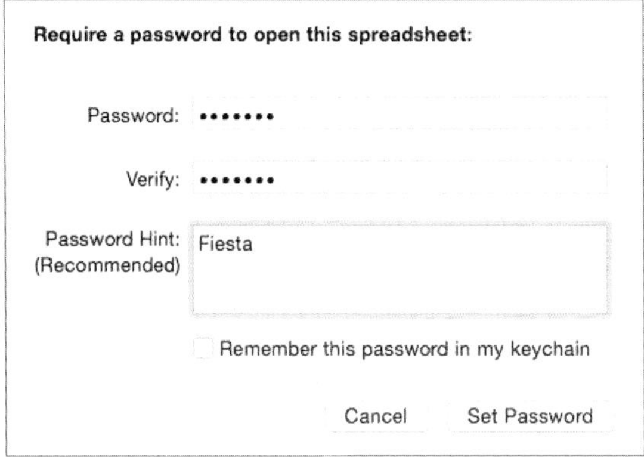

Selecting the checkbox means you won't have to input the document's password every time you open it. If the document is opened on an iOS device, such as an iPad, the user will be prompted for the password and iOS will offer to remember the password. It's your choice, but not saving passwords on a device adds an extra layer of security, particularly when those devices are shared.

Lesson Review

1. How do you open a Numbers 09 document and edit it without upgrading the original document?
2. Describe how to save a table style.
3. What is a key advantage of referencing cells when using lists?
4. Which data format has six values: 0, 1, 2, 3, 4, and 5?
5. Describe conditional highlighting.
6. Which data format is similar to slider?

Answers

1. When prompted to upgrade the 09 document, click "Edit a Copy" rather than Upgrade.
2. Select a table with the desired styles already applied. In the Table inspector, click the + (plus sign) button in Table Styles.
3. By referencing list items, any changes made in the original list are automatically reflected in the referenced list.
4. Star ratings have six values.
5. Conditional highlighting applies formatting to a cell or range of cells when rule conditions are met. For example, a cell could be set to automatically fill with a green background when its value matches the rule set.
6. Steppers are similar to sliders.

10

Lesson Files	APTS Pages Numbers Keynote > Lesson_10 > spreadsheet-concepts.numbers APTS Pages Numbers Keynote > Lesson_10 > print-pricing.numbers
Time	This lesson takes approximately 60 minutes to complete.
Goals	Add and modify formulas Concatenate cells Understand relative and absolute cell references Sort and filter tables Create custom functions

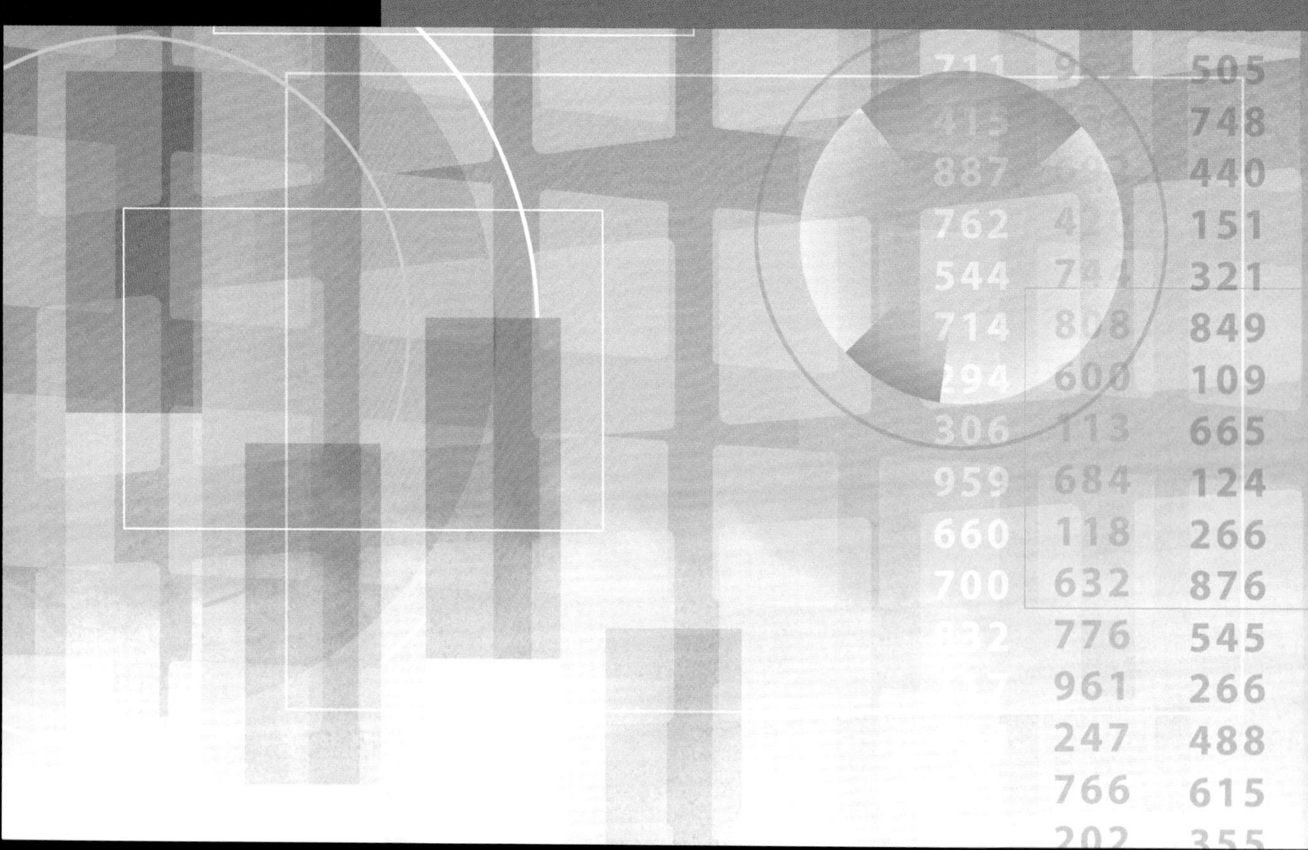

Lesson **10**

Making Customized Calculators

Now that you've learned some of the basics of creating interactive spreadsheets, let's build on those concepts to add even greater functionality to a Numbers' project.

You'll complete a spreadsheet that calculates the price of photographic prints, such as making 8x10-inch prints on glossy paper. The quantity of 5 is a number but both 8x10-inch and glossy are text items that your spreadsheet will convert to an appropriate number to determine a price for the prints.

Throughout Lesson 10 try to focus on the processes used to create formulas and don't be too concerned with the formula themselves. Try to understand the principles without becoming bogged down in the specifics. Once you understand the syntax, you can apply it to a wide range of projects. And you can use the same functions in Keynote and Pages, too.

	A	B	C	D	E	F	G	H	I	J	K	L	M
1		1	2	3	4	5	6	7	8	9	10	11	12
2	1	1	2	3	4	5	6	7	8	9	10	11	12
3	2	2	4	6	8	10	12	14	16	18	20	22	24
4	3	3	6	9	12	15	18	21	24	27	30	33	36
5	4	4	8	12	16	20	24	28	32	36	40	44	48
6	5	5	10	15	20	25	30	35	40	45	50	55	60
7	6	6	12	18	24	30	36	42	48	54	60	66	72
8	7	7	14	21	28	35	42	49	56	63	70	77	84
9	8	8	16	24	32	40	48	56	64	72	80	88	96
10	9	9	18	27	36	45	54	63	72	81	90	99	108
11	10	10	20	30	40	50	60	70	80	90	100	110	120
12	11	11	22	33	44	55	66	77	88	99	110	121	132
13	12	12	24	36	48	60	72	84	96	108	120	132	144

Understanding Relative and Absolute Cell Referencing

By default, cell references are made relative to the cell, but sometimes this will cause problems, such as when building calculators like the one you'll create in this lesson.

A key part in liberating your creative number crunching is to clarify some of the spreadsheet jargon. The terms *relative* and *absolute* cell referencing are common to most spreadsheet applications. Here's how they work.

1 In Numbers, choose File > Open.

2 Navigate to APTS Pages Numbers Keynote > Lesson_10.

3 Double-click **spreadsheet-concepts.numbers** to open it.

This Numbers document has three sheets.

4 Click the Times Tables tab.

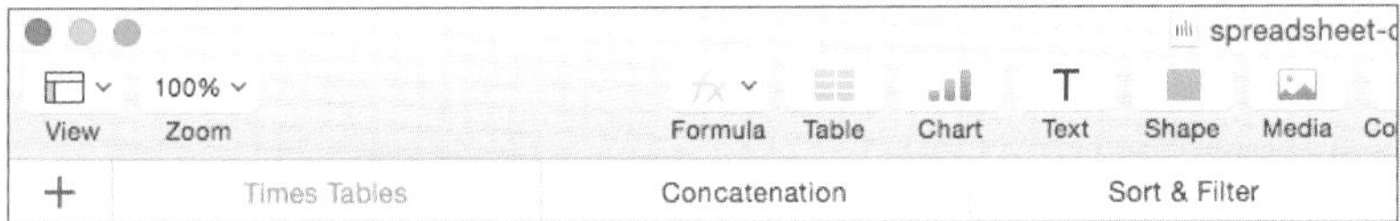

This sheet contains a single table you'll use to quickly build the times tables up to 12 × 12, and hopefully enhance your understanding of cell referencing along the way.

5 Click cell B2 and type the equal sign (=). Click cell B1 and then A2.

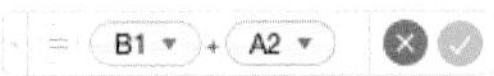

The formula automatically sets the equation's operator to addition by default. For the times table to work, the operator needs to be set to multiply.

6 Drag to select the plus symbol. Press Shift-8 to apply multiplication.

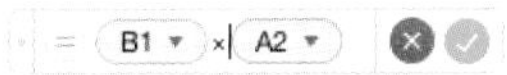

7 Click the checkmark button to apply the formula.

This formula is referencing cells relatively. To prove this you'll drag the formula to fill the remaining cells in row 2.

8 Click cell B2 and drag the yellow handle on the cell's right edge toward the right to apply the formula to all the columns from B to M.

	A	B	C	D	E	F	G	H	I	J	K	L	M
1		1	2	3	4	5	6	7	8	9	10	11	12
2	1	1	...	...	...	...	...	...	...	...	...	...	...
3	2												

This definitely did not create a times table!

9 Press Enter.

10 Click cell B2. Note the highlighted reference headers.

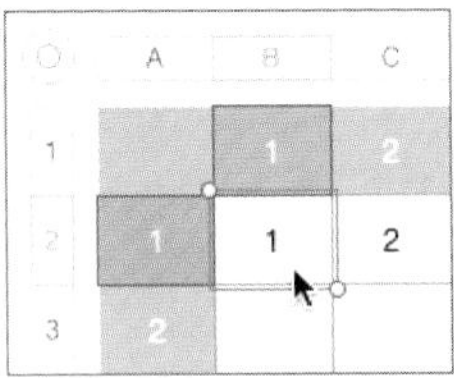

As expected, the formula is referencing the cells you selected in step 5.

11 Click cell E2.

The formula is referencing the cell immediately above and to the left of the formula.

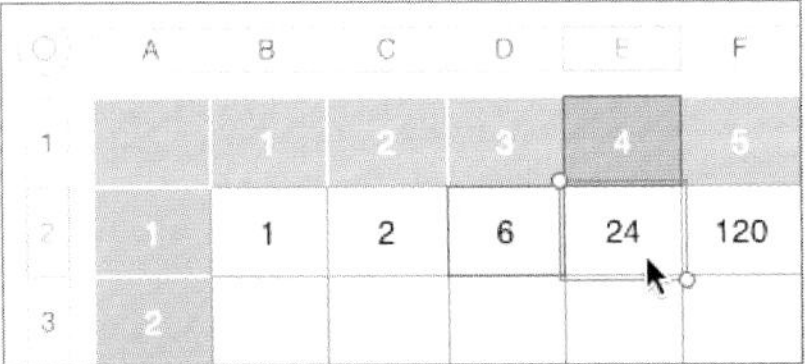

However, the formula must reference cells E1 and A1 to produce the desired result. The next steps will fix that.

12 Double-click cell B2 to open the Formula Editor.

13 In the Formula Editor, click the reference for cell B1, and from the popover select Preserve Row.

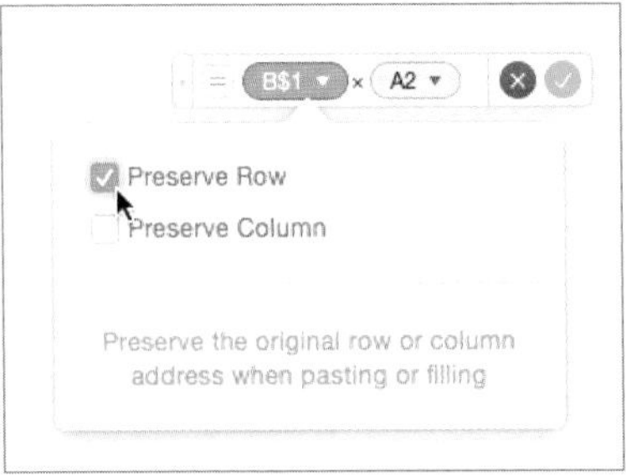

14 In the Formula Editor, click the reference for cell A2, and from the popover select Preserve Column.

The formula now reads = B$1 × $A2. The dollar signs are common spreadsheet notation.

TIP You can also type the dollar signs directly into the Formula Editor without accessing the pop-up menus.

15 Click the checkmark, or press Tab or Return, to apply your changes.

16 Click cell B2 and drag the yellow handle on the cell's right edge toward the right to apply the revised formula to all the columns from B to M.

The formula is now correct. Let's apply it to the rest of the table.

17 With cells B2 to M2 selected, drag the yellow handle on the cells' bottom edge down to row 13.

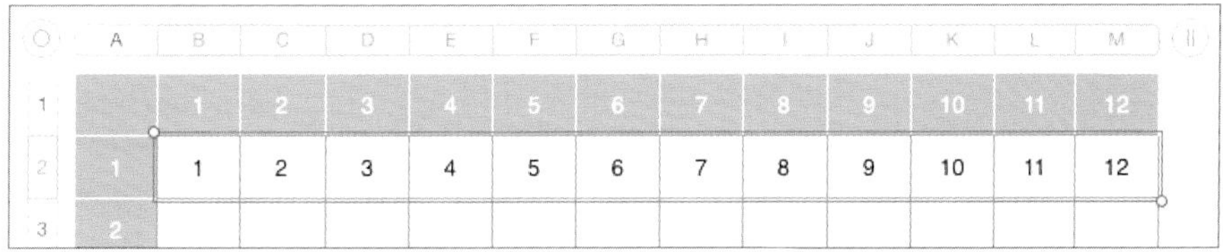

The Times Tables sheet is complete. Next you'll verify the cell references.

18 Press Enter.

19 Click cell I8. Note that it references cells I1 and A8.

	A	B	C	D	E	F	G	H	I	J
1		1	2	3	4	5	6	7	8	9
2	1	1	2	3	4	5	6	7	8	9
3	2	2	4	6	8	10	12	14	16	18
4	3	3	6	9	12	15	18	21	24	27
5	4	4	8	12	16	20	24	28	32	36
6	5	5	10	15	20	25	30	35	40	45
7	6	6	12	18	24	30	36	42	48	54
8	7	7	14	21	28	35	42	49	56	63
9	8	8	16	24	32	40	48	56	64	72

At the bottom of the application window, the formula for the selected cell is displayed as I$1 × $A8.

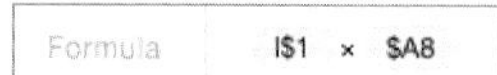

Later in this lesson you'll use cell references again in a real-world exercise.

20 Leave **spreadsheet-concepts.numbers** open for the next exercise.

Concatenating Cells

Concatenation (stringing cells together) is used to join data from two or more cells into a single cell. In this exercise you'll concatenate cells identifying fruit types and their varieties. You'll also use the sort function.

1 In **spreadsheet-concepts.numbers**, go to the Concatenation sheet. It contains a single table labeled Fruit.

2 Click the table to select it, which reveals the reference headers.

3 Click cell C2 and type the equal sign (=) to open the Formula Editor.

4 Type *co*.

Suggestions for functions appear.

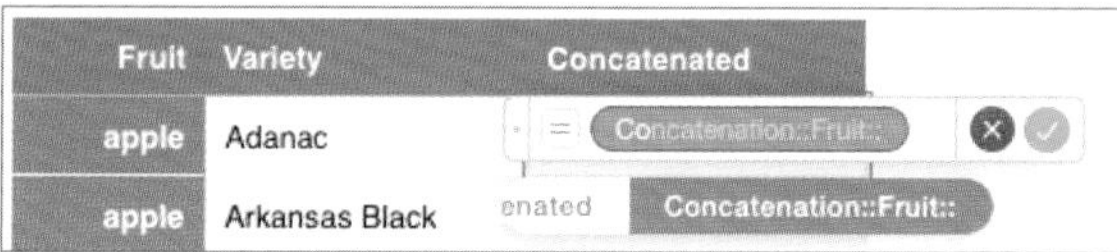

5 Press Tab to cycle through the functions beginning with "Co".

6 Type *n* to look at functions starting with "Con". Numbers helps by making suggestions as you type.

7 Press Tab to cycle through the functions until CONCATENATE is displayed.

NOTE ▸ Functions are displayed in capital letters even when you type in lowercase.

8 Press Return to choose the function.

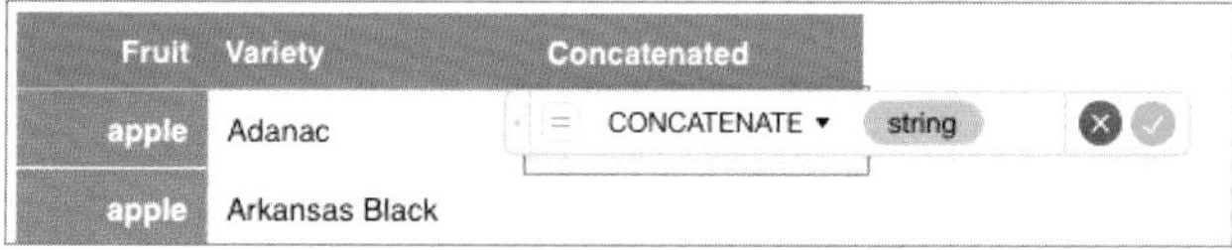

The Formula Editor displays a complete formula. In this instance, a gray button with the word "string" appears between the parentheses to suggest how the formula should be completed. To do so, you'll need to replace "string" with cell references.

In plain text, this formula would be written as = (CONCATENATE string). Numbers has set the parentheses for you because they are essential when creating formulas. Items inside a set of parentheses are known as *arguments*.

9 In the Formula Editor, click the word "string," and then click cell B2 and cell A2.

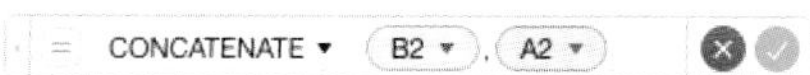

10 Press Return to apply the formula.

Cell C2 now reads "Adanacapple," but the word "apple" is invisible because the text formatting from cell A2—white text on a white background—was applied to "apple."

11 In the Text inspector, click the italic button.

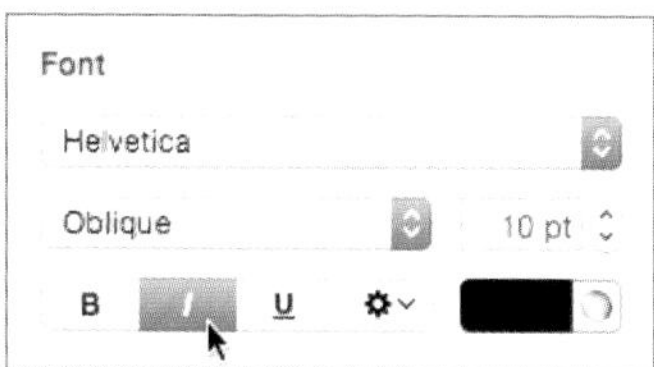

The word "apple" becomes visible. Now the second issue is revealed: no space between the concatenated words.

12 Double-click cell C2. In the Formula Editor, click between the two cell references (after the comma).

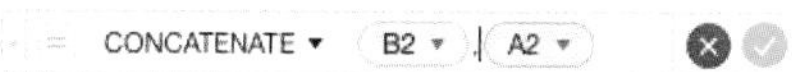

13 Type a quotation mark, and press the Spacebar. Type another quotation mark, and then type a comma.

Doing so adds the required space between the concatenated cells. Text arguments must be placed inside quotation marks.

14 Press Return to apply the formula.

15 Click cell C2, and drag the yellow handle down the column to cell C13.

All the cells from C2 to C13 are concatenated. But note that the word "apple" isn't capitalized. You'll use Sort Ascending to help fix that.

16 In columns A's reference header, click the disclosure triangle and choose Sort Ascending.

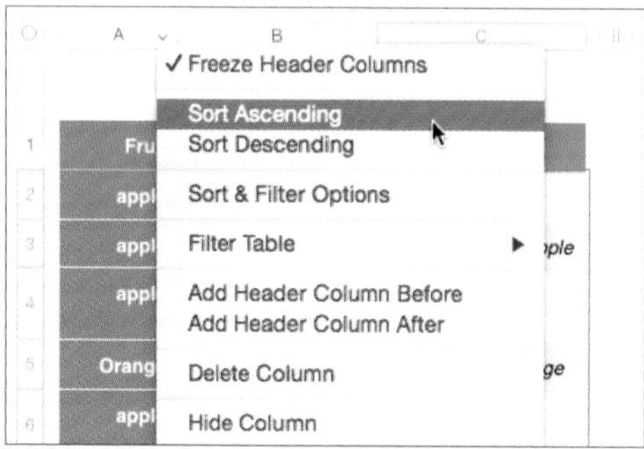

17 In cell A2 change the spelling of apple to *Apple*.

18 Drag the contents of cell A2, down to cell A8 to apply the capitalized spellings to those cells.

The word "apple" is capitalized in column C. Formulas automatically update when any cells they reference are modified.

19 Leave **spreadsheet-concepts.numbers** open for the next exercise.

Sorting Tables

Sorting and filtering are essential techniques when dealing with long tables containing dozens of columns and rows. You'll start the next set of exercises experimenting with sorting fruit varieties before filtering search results for the Ju-Jitsu club.

1 On the Concatenation sheet of **spreadsheet-concepts.numbers**, click the reference header for column B,

2 From the pop-up menu, choose Sort Descending.

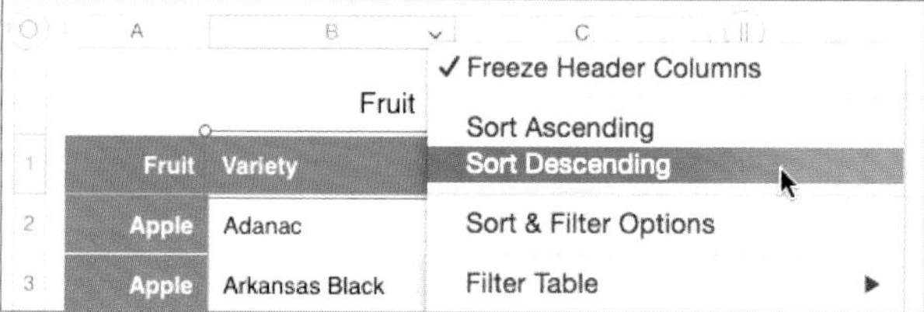

Column B, as you might expect, lists the varieties of apples and oranges in reverse order. In column A, the apples and oranges have become jumbled. In this scenario, sorting apples and oranges first and then listing their varieties alphabetically would make sense.

3 In the toolbar, click the Sort & Filter button. Make sure that the Fruit table is selected.

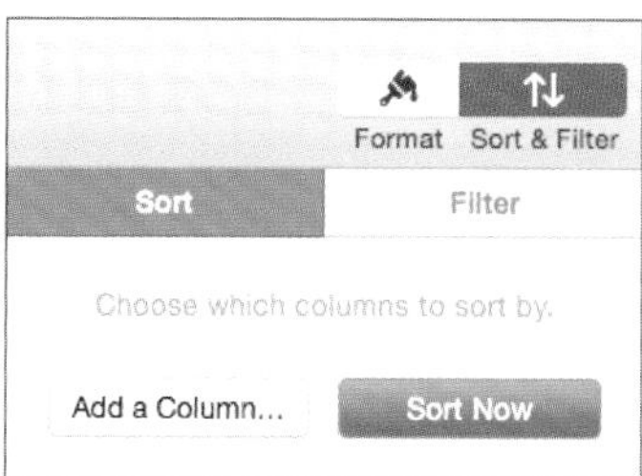

When a table is selected, the Sort inspector gives you the option to add a column.

4 Click "Add a Column," and from the pop-up menu, choose Fruit.

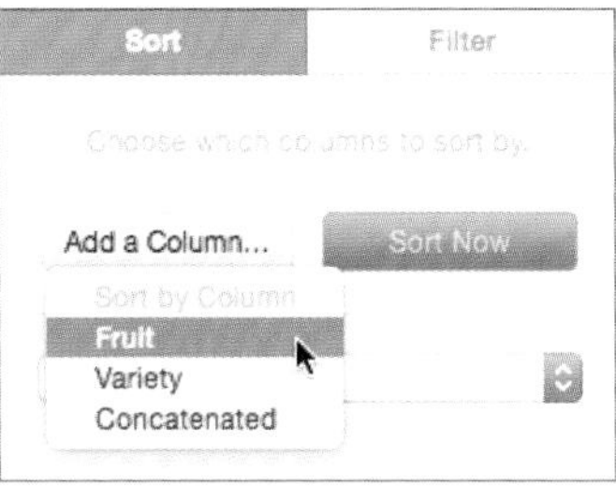

Doing so sets the first sort level. Now let's fix the second level.

5 In the Sort inspector, click "Add a Column" again, and from the pop-up menu, choose Variety.

The table automatically updates, in ascending order by default. (The Sort inspector can also sort in descending order.)

TIP Labeling tables, columns, and rows is good practice when sorting and filtering.

6 Leave **spreadsheet-concepts.numbers** open and ready for the next exercise.

Filtering Tables

Filtering a table is a form of search. After you choose your search criteria, the results are displayed, filtering out items that do not match the search. You'll work with the Ju Jitsu register because it simulates the kind of filtering you might need when working with large tables.

1 In the **spreadsheet-concepts.numbers** document, go to the Sort & Filter sheet.

It contains a Register table with 87 rows! Let's filter the table to show only those students with brown belts.

2 Select the table, and click the reference header for column E.

3 From the pop-up menu, choose Filter Table > Brown (1st Mon).

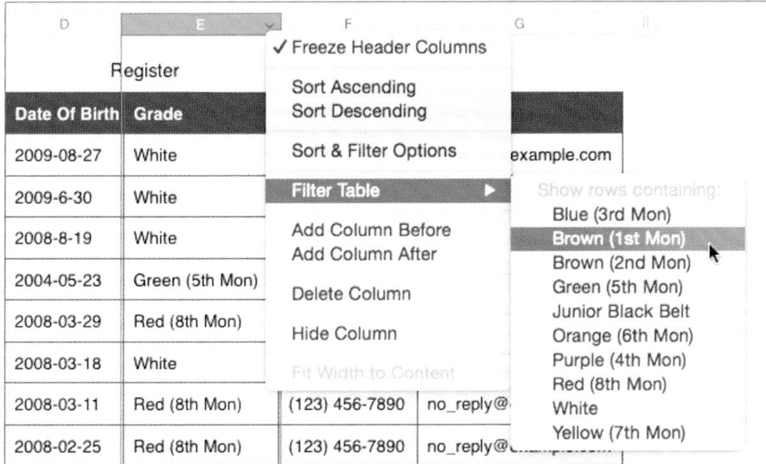

The filter returns five students at Brown Belt (1st Mon). There are two grades of brown belt. Now let's filter for Brown (2nd Mon).

4 Click the reference header for column E, and from the pop-up menu, choose Filter Table > Brown (2nd Mon).

The table now shows the eight students who are currently brown belts.

5 Go to the Filter inspector. If the Sort and Filter inspectors are not visible, click the Sort & Filter button in the toolbar, and click the Filter tab.

The Grade section displays the current filter options. Both filters are set to "text is" and will display rows that match all the filters.

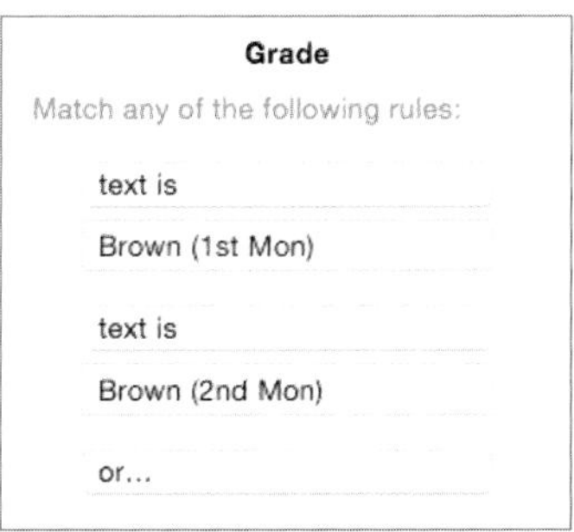

6 Click the button labeled "text is" for the Brown (2nd Mon) filter. A pop-up menu appears.

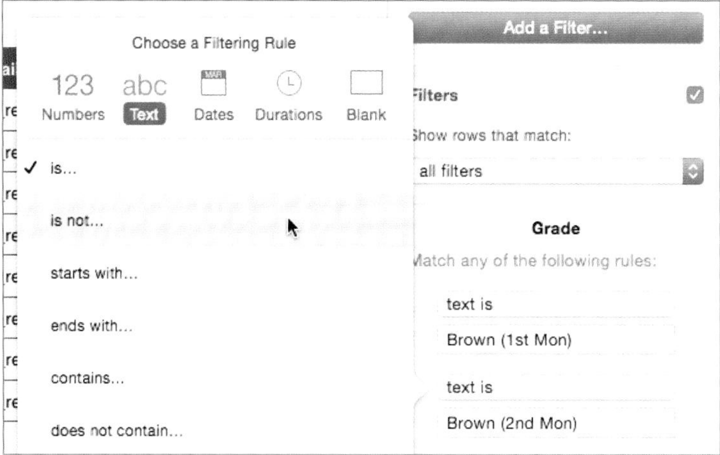

7 From the pop-up menu, choose "is not."

All the students reappear because the rules no longer filter out anything. The challenge of Boolean searches such as this is that you need to interpret the logic of search terms, but the filter options give instant results so you can experiment freely. If you no longer need a filter, you can delete it.

8 Move your pointer over the "text is not" rule. A trash icon appears. Click it to remove the rule.

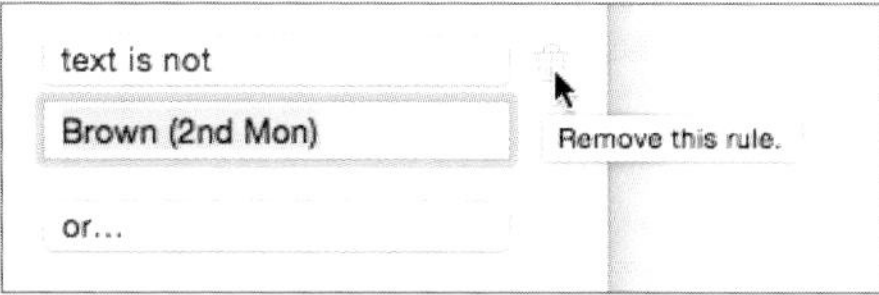

TIP Switch filters on or off in the Inspector by selecting or deselecting the Filters checkbox.

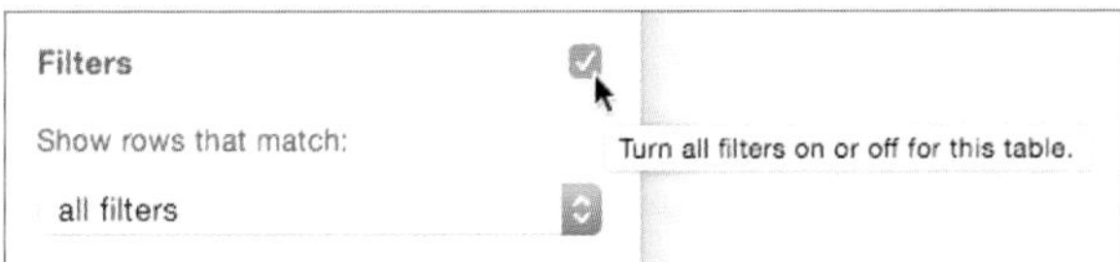

9 Delete the remaining filter rule for Brown (1st Mon) using the process described in step 8. Note that the trash icon appears adjacent to the word "Grade."

The Filter inspector is now blank. Let's add a new filter directly in the inspector.

10 Click Add a Filter. From the pop-up menu, choose Date Of Birth.

11 In the "Choose a Filtering Rule" popover, click Dates, and then scroll through the popover to choose "after the date."

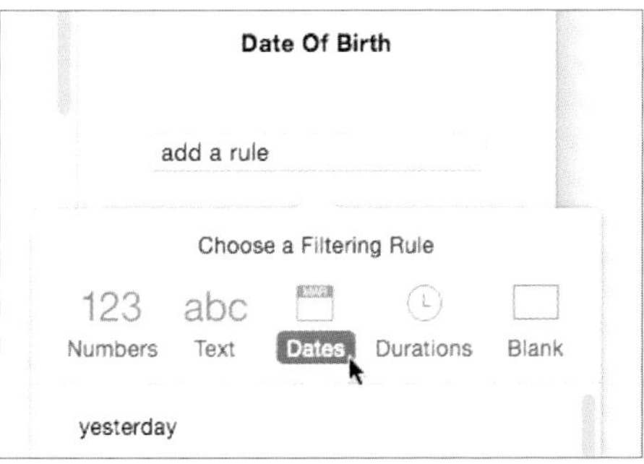

12 In the filter rule data field, type 2007-01-01. Press Return.

The table now shows the 16 youngest Ju Jitsu students.

Numbers includes many filtering options. Some will show records within a date range, others filter numbers higher or lower than a value you set. The permutations are seemingly endless.

13 Choose File > Close.

Making a Pricing Calculator

It's time to reveal the potential of Numbers for creating custom calculators. The lesson file **print-pricing.numbers** is almost complete. It contains some rather lengthy formulas for you to examine. The following exercises will help you understand the principles of applying functions. The specifics that are driving the print price calculator are less important in this lesson.

Numbers templates contain tables with built-in formulas, but the process of designing a calculator from scratch is only partially related to your Numbers prowess, in the same way that knowing how to use Pages doesn't make someone an author.

Cleaning Up a Table Design

Applying graphic design to a spreadsheet makes it easier to read by drawing attention to its key elements.

1 In Numbers, choose File > Open.

2 Navigate to APTS Pages Numbers Keynote > Lesson_10.

3 Open **print-pricing.numbers**.

The document has a single sheet, Print Price Calculator, and it contains two tables, Table 1 and Table 2. Let's give the tables descriptive names.

4 Select the Table 1 title, and change it to *Price Calculator*.

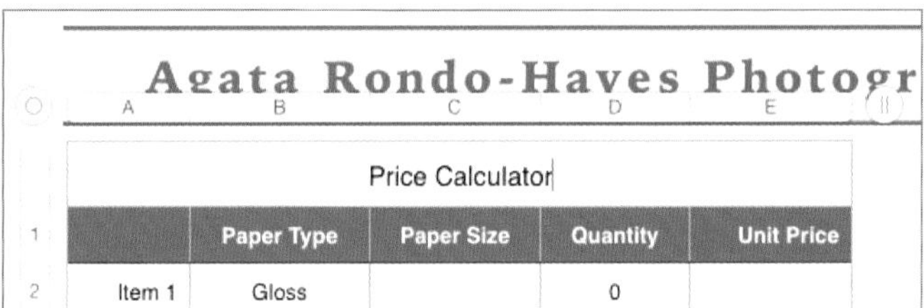

5 Select the Table 2 title, and change it to *Paper Prices*.

6 Select the Price Calculator table.

A couple of cosmetic changes are also required. In the Table inspector, note that the "Outline table name" option is selected, which places a turquoise border outside the table name.

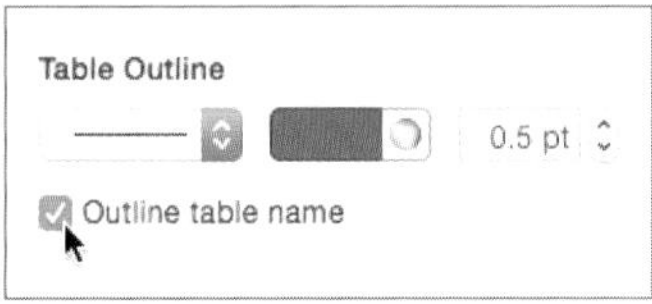

7 Deselect "Outline table name."

This price calculator is an ideal candidate for use on an iPad. To help improve iPad readability, let's make the text in the cells bigger.

8 In the Table inspector, click the Table Font Size button two times to make all the text in the table larger.

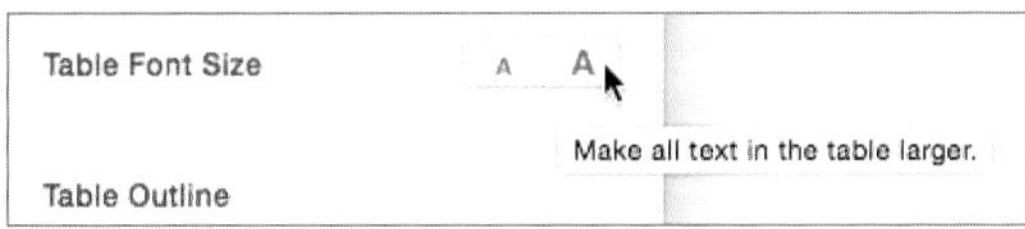

Unless you have very small fingers, larger text and cells will help you input values on an iOS device without the need to zoom in.

Let's further improve readability.

9 Click the reference header for row 12 of the Price Calculator.

10 In the Cell inspector, click the All Borders icon, and from the Border Styles pop-up menu, choose No Border.

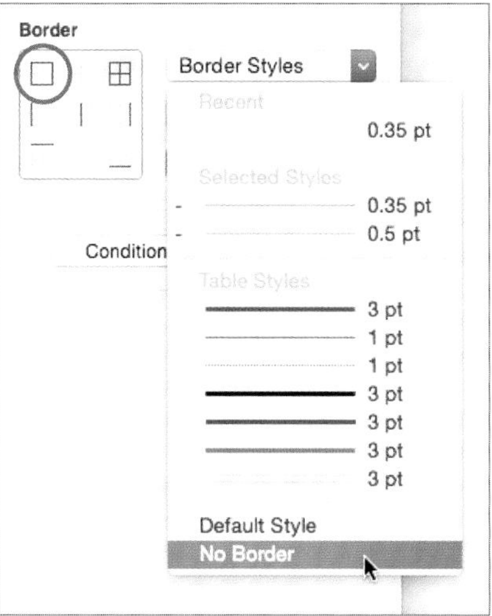

11 Click cell A13, and then Shift-click cell C13 to select cells A13, B13, and C13.

12 In the Cell inspector, in the Fill area, choose Color Fill and choose a white color.

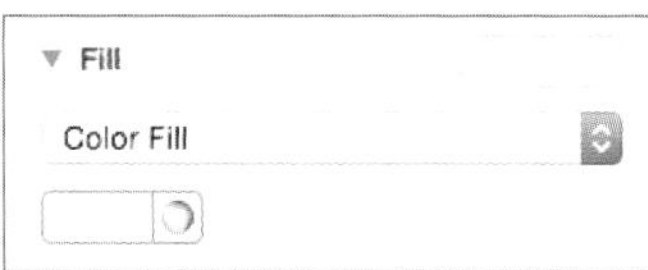

13 Click the All Borders icon, and then set the Border Styles to No Border, using the method described in step 10.

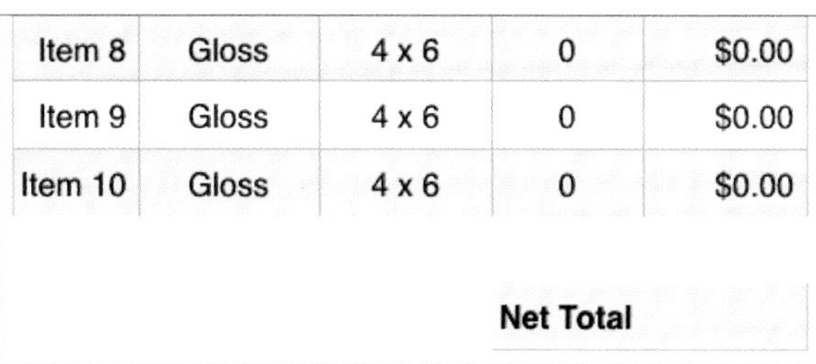

Item 8	Gloss	4 x 6	0	$0.00
Item 9	Gloss	4 x 6	0	$0.00
Item 10	Gloss	4 x 6	0	$0.00
			Net Total	

The Net Total now stands out clearly in your design. Further formatting could improve readability, but things are looking good for the next steps.

Turning Text into Numbers

Let's keep things simple for now. The Paper Prices table displays the cost price of inkjet paper.

1 In the Paper Prices table, click cell D2.

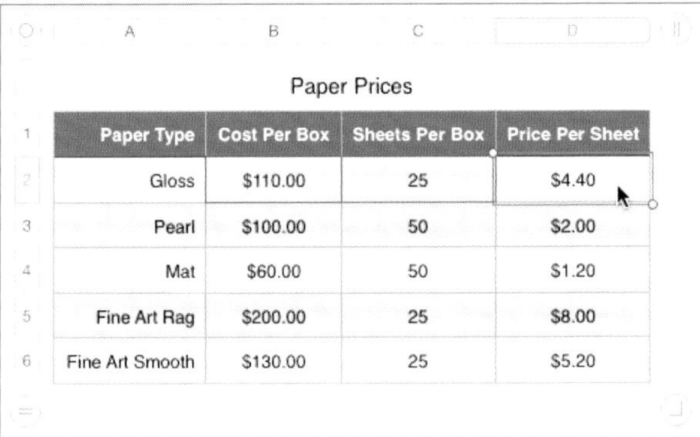

Paper Prices

Paper Type	Cost Per Box	Sheets Per Box	Price Per Sheet
Gloss	$110.00	25	$4.40
Pearl	$100.00	50	$2.00
Mat	$60.00	50	$1.20
Fine Art Rag	$200.00	25	$8.00
Fine Art Smooth	$130.00	25	$5.20

The formula bar at the bottom of the document window reveals the equation as B2 divided by C2. This table's values are numbers so the formula works, returning a value for the sheet price.

The challenge comes in the Price Calculator. In column B, you can choose a paper type: gloss, pearl, mat, fine art rag, or fine art smooth. Clearly, these are text values, so here's how to assign them a number value.

2 In the Price Calculator table, click cell E2.

3 Type = *if*. In the Formula Editor, click the word "IF", and press Enter.

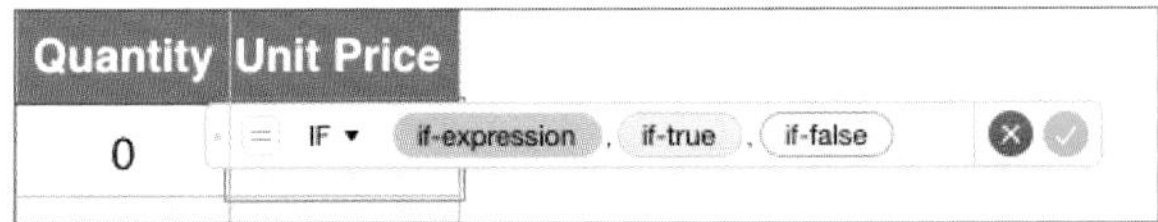

The Formula Editor fills with suggestions.

TIP Clicking the disclosure triangle for a function opens a menu in which you can choose "Show In Function Browser." The Function Browser not only defines functions, it displays examples of how to use them.

4 Select all three gray arguments, and click cell B2.

5 In the Formula Editor, after the cell reference for B2, type ="*Gloss*", (make sure to include the comma after the quotation marks), and note that yet again Numbers makes a suggestion: if-true.

6 Click "if-true" and then in the Paper Prices table click cell D2.

The Formula Editor now references the correct sheet price when Gloss is selected in the calculator.

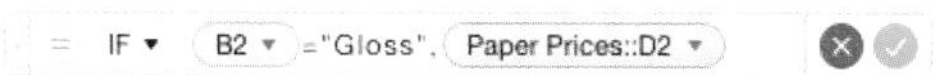

That's a good first step, but you have four other paper types to choose from. We'll add just one more to the Formula Editor to clarify how this calculator can work.

In the Formula Editor, make sure that the insertion point is blinking immediately after the reference for "Paper Prices::D2."

7 Type a comma (,).

8 In the Formula Editor, click "if-false" and press Backspace to delete it.

9 Make sure the insertion point is after the comma, and press Option-Return.

10 In the Formula Editor, type if, and then click the word "IF." Again the Formula Editor displays suggestions.

11 Select all three gray arguments, and click cell B2.

12 After the cell reference for B2, type ="*Pearl*", (make sure to include the comma after the quotation marks) and note the displayed suggestion, "if-true."

13 Click "if-true", or press Spacebar. Then in the Paper Prices table, click cell D3. Press Return to apply the formula.

You've now created two IF arguments. Let's test them.

14 In the Price Calculator table, click cell B2. In the cell pop-up menu, change the paper type to Pearl.

The price updates using the cell references you set.

Rows 2 through 11 have complete formulas applied. You'll now change the values for Item 2.

15 In cell B3, change the paper type to *Fine Art Rag*. Set the paper size to *8 x 10*, and the quality to *5*.

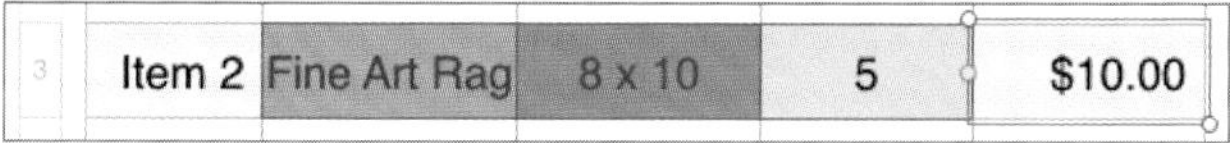

The function in cell E3 is rather involved and possibly a little frightening, but let's take a look.

16 Double-click cell E3. The Formula Editor opens. Drag the bottom edge of the Formula Editor down to view the entire formula.

```
=
(
IF B3 = "Gloss", Paper Prices::D$2 ,
    IF B3 = "Pearl", Paper Prices::D$3 ,
    IF B3 = "Mat", Paper Prices::D$4 ,
    IF B3 = "Fine Art Rag", Paper Prices::D$5 ,
    IF B3 = "Fine Art Smooth", Paper Prices::D$6
)
    ÷(
IF C3 = "4 x 6", 10,
IF C3 = "5 x 7", 8,
IF C3 = "8 x 10", 4,
IF C3 = "11 x 14", 2,
IF C3 = "11 x 17", 1,
IF C3 = "16 x 20", 1,
IF C3 = "17 x 22", 1,
)
)
× D3
```

NOTE ► The formula contains a lot of repletion. To speed things up, you can copy and paste the formula and then modify it.

The formula reads: Paper Type divided by Paper Size, multiplied by the number of prints.

Option-Tab and Option-Return were used in the Formula Editor to indent lines and place arguments on separate lines, replicating the kind of structure a programmer might use. This layout keeps formulas clear and legible.

Bracketing is important because each argument must be placed within parentheses. Here's the formula again, this time with parentheses:

(

(If the paper type is gloss, reference the gloss paper price for a sheet)

divide this by (the paper size)

) multiply the result by the number of prints

The essential learning points here are:

- Text items must be placed in quotation marks.
- Commas separate arguments.
- Parentheses set the order in which equations are evaluated.

Let's note one final bit of decoding before moving on. The argument "IF C3 = "4 x 6", 10" can be read as: If cell C3 is set to "4 x 6," divide the paper price by 10. The sheets of paper listed in the Paper Prices table are quite large so ten 4 x 6 inch prints can be made from a single sheet.

Making a Pop-Up Menu

The print price calculator uses pop-up data formats, which are ideal for this kind of work. In this exercise, you'll add a pop-up menu for paper sizes.

1 Click cell C2. In the Cell inspector, change the Data Format to Pop-Up Menu.

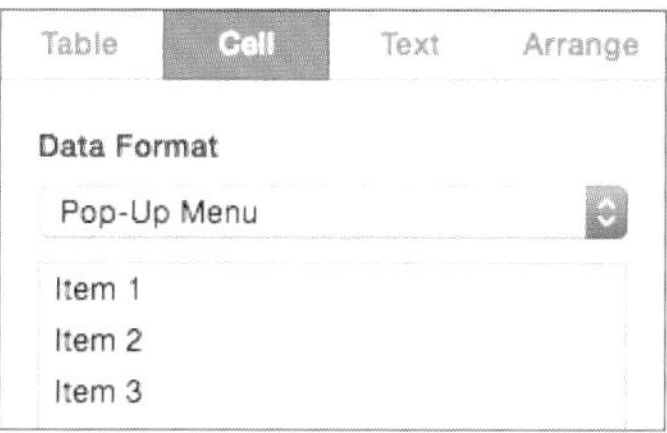

By default, three items appear. You'll need to modify these and add four more items.

2 In the inspector, double-click Item 1, and rename it to *4 x 6* (be sure to add the spaces between each character). Press Return.

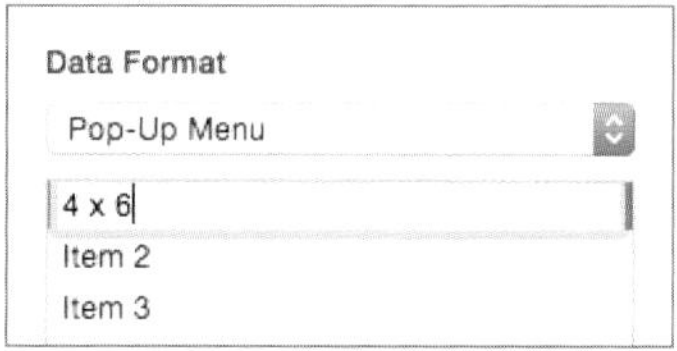

3 Rename Item 2 to *5 x 7* and Item 3 to *8 x 10*. Press Return after each rename to apply the change.

4 In the Data Format section of the inspector, click the Add Item (+) button four times to add four more items.

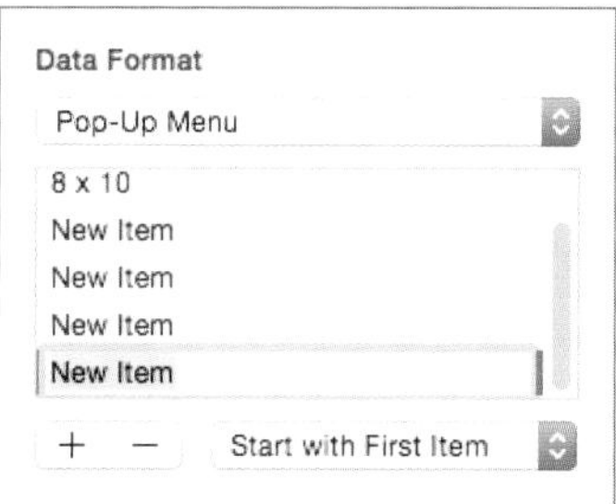

5 Change the names of the new items to *11 x 14*, *11 x 17*, *16 x 20*, and *17 x 22*.

You've made a pop-up menu.

TIP You can change the order of pop-up items by dragging them up or down in the list.

Adding a Totalizer

This pricing calculator illustrates many spreadsheet concepts. Depending on your familiarity with spreadsheets, the weight of information in this lesson could be overwhelming. But with patience, practice, and careful review of the formulas in **print-pricing.numbers** and in Numbers templates, you'll acquire plenty of useful insights.

To complete this lesson, let's add a totalizer to the price calculator.

1 Click cell E13, and type *=SUM*.

2 In the Formula Editor, click the word SUM.

3 Click the word "value," and then type *E2:E11*.

4 Press Return twice to apply the formula.

Try experimenting by setting different papers, sizes, and item quantities in the calculator. The formulas are set correctly for rows 3 to 11.

Lesson Review

1. Name the default operator.
2. Can functions be used in Pages?
3. Describe two ways to apply a filter to a table in Numbers.
4. Describe how to temporarily turn off filters.
5. What is the role of the Function Browser?
6. Text arguments need to be placed inside what kind of marks to be valid?

Answers

1. SUM or addition is the default operator.
2. Functions can be used in Numbers, Keynote, and Pages.
3. You can apply a filter by clicking a column reference header in a table and choosing Filter Table from the pop-up menu; or by using the Filter inspector.
4. In the Filter inspector, deselect Filters.
5. The Function Browser lists the available functions, explains what each does, and provides examples of their use.
6. Text arguments must be placed inside quotation marks.

11

Lesson Files

APTS Pages Numbers Keynote > Lesson_11 > new-tech-adoption.csv

APTS Pages Numbers Keynote > Lesson_11 > new-tech-adoption.numbers

APTS Pages Numbers Keynote > Lesson_11 > margin-of-error.numbers

APTS Pages Numbers Keynote > Lesson_11 > scatter-chart.numbers

Time

This lesson takes approximately 60 minutes to complete.

Goals

Open and edit a CSV file

Create and edit charts

Format chart styles

Mix chart types

Save Numbers templates

Edit data references

Lesson **11**

Illustrating Data Using Charts

You can use tables to display data in Numbers, but sometimes charts are a clearer and more concise way to illustrate data. They give form to statistics, drawing out findings and trends that can be too obscure in table form.

The exercises in this lesson were created to highlight the advantages of certain chart types. Not all data suits charts, and not all chart types are appropriate for every set of data. Selecting the wrong type of chart can present some disappointing results. However, this lesson will show you how to experiment freely and find which charts best suit the data at hand.

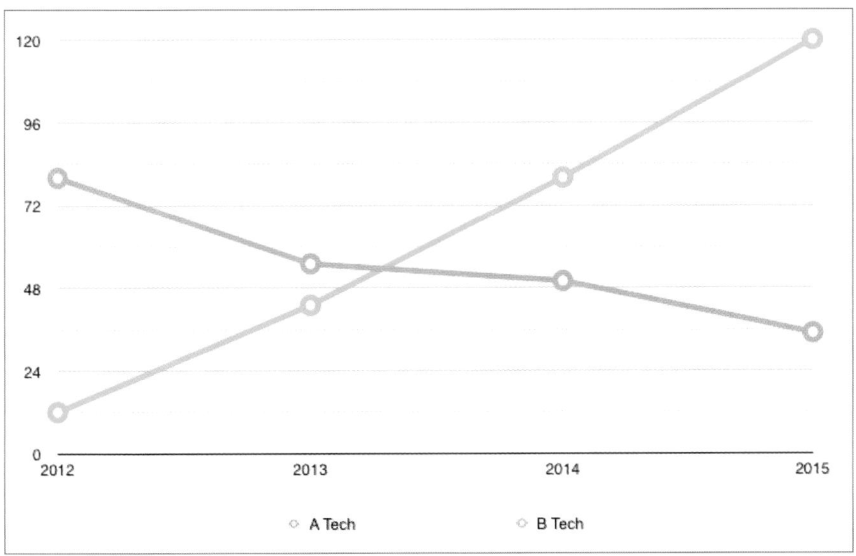

Opening a CSV File

Numbers can open and export content to several file types. (You first encountered this process in Lesson 2.) In this exercise, you'll open a CSV (comma-separated value) file—a plain text format you can create in many other applications on various computing platforms.

1 In Numbers, choose File > Open.

2 Navigate to APTS Pages Numbers Keynote > Lesson_11.

3 Double-click **new-tech-adoption.csv**.

NOTE ► In the Finder, you can Control-click a CSV file, and from the pop-up menu, choose to open it in Numbers.

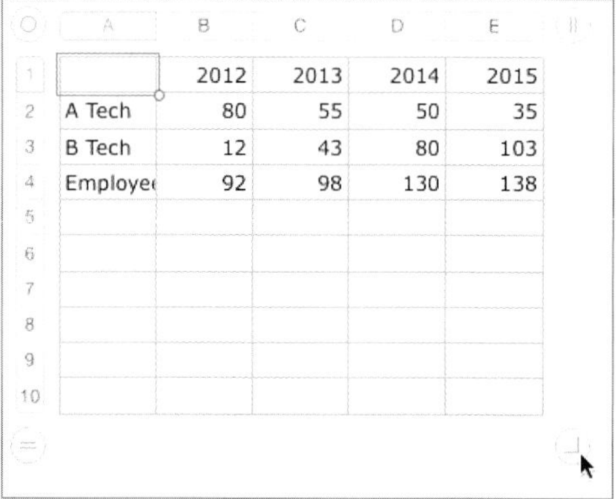

	A	B	C	D	E
1		2012	2013	2014	2015
2	A Tech	80	55	50	35
3	B Tech	12	43	80	103
4	Employe(	92	98	130	138
5					
6					
7					
8					
9					
10					

The CSV file opens seamlessly into Numbers but with some extra unwanted rows. These are a result of conversion from CSV.

4 Drag up the table handle to reduce the number of rows to 4.

This step isn't strictly necessary, but it helps keep the table lean and clean. Another option would be to click the reference header for row 1 and convert it to a header row.

5 Press Command-S.

The Save As window appears and shows that the file type is Numbers. Save the document to your desktop.

Creating a Stacked Bar Chart

Stacked bar charts combine two or more sets of data into a single bar, making them a useful alternative to standard bar charts. In this scenario you'll highlight the adoption of a new technology, B Tech, into a small firm and compare it to the total pool of users as they migrate from their previous technology, A Tech.

When comparing data sets, Numbers offers more options for creating charts than do Pages or Keynote. Here's one of them:

1 Click the reference header for row 2, and Shift-click the reference header for row 3 to select both rows.

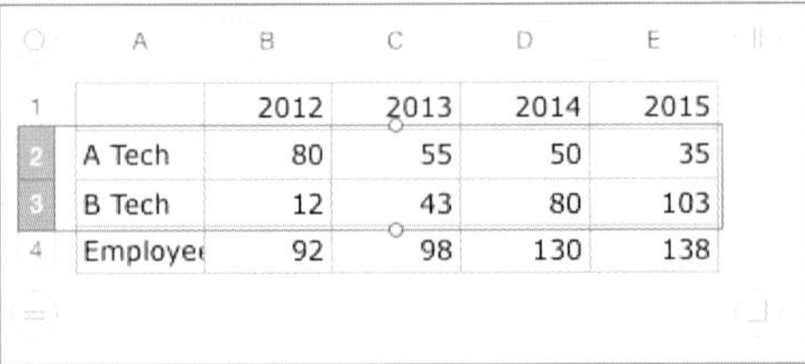

2 In the toolbar, click Chart. From the popover, select the 2D Stacked Bar chart.

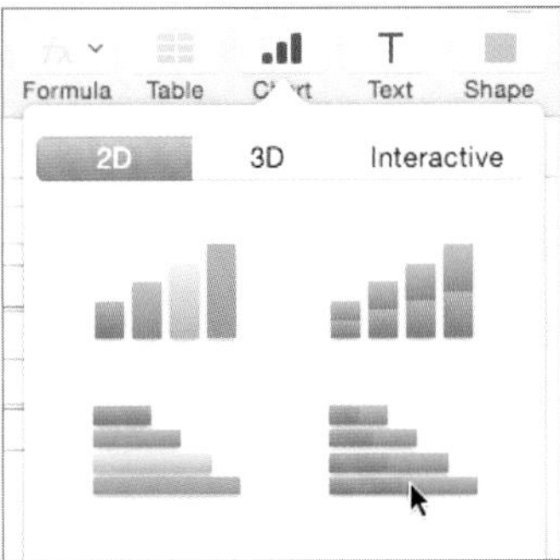

A chart appears. As you'll find out later, you can swap the chart type at any time, but for now let's stick with the 2D stacked bar chart.

3 In the Chart inspector, select the Title and Legend options.

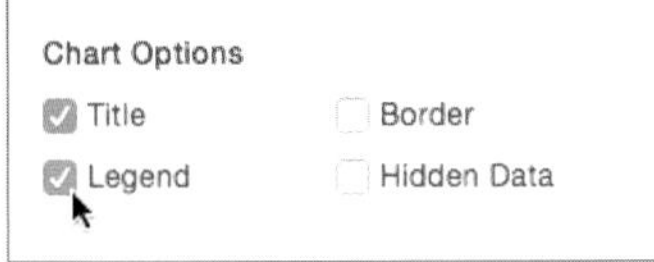

The chart updates to display these two labels, but they aren't ideally placed.

4 Click the Legend text box and drag it beneath the chart.

5 Click the Legend text box. Click Untitled 1 to select it, and then type *A Tech*.

6 Click the Legend text box. Click Untitled 2 to select it, and then type *B Tech*.

7 Change the chart title to *Personnel Adopting New Tech*.

NOTE ▶ You may have to click several times to nest down through the chart items to make the text selection.

8 Press Esc. It's a quick way to jump out of the selection.

9 Click the chart. In the Axis inspector, click the Value (X) button.

The chart axes are split into Value (X) and Category (Y). It's good to note which axis you've selected in the inspector.

10 In the Axis inspector, increase the Major Gridlines width to 1 pt. Set Minor Gridlines to dots of 1 pt.

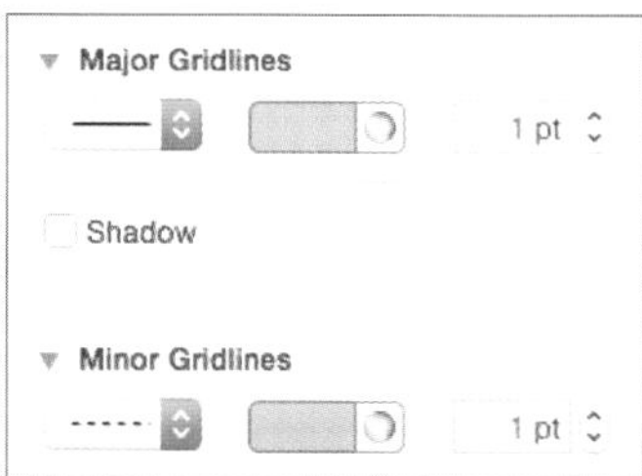

Making the gridlines stand out has improved the chart, but the values of the stacked bar chart are still hard to read.

11 Click the Series inspector to open it.

12 In the Series inspector, set Value Labels to Same As Source Data. Leave Location set to Right.

The chart is looking good, but you can experiment further.

13 Click the Chart inspector.

14 In the Chart inspector, change Chart Type to 3D Stacked Bar.

At first glance the chart may seem a little cluttered. Applying 3D and shadow effects can be distracting.

15 On the chart, drag the 3D icon to set a new view angle for the chart.

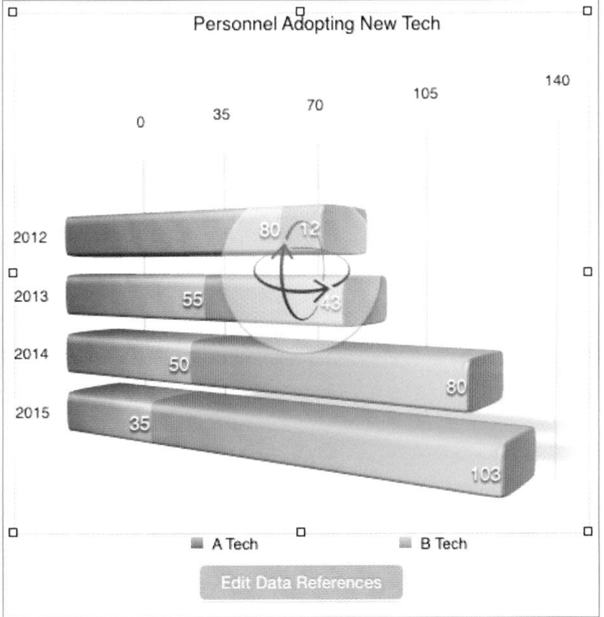

16 Adjust the parameters in the 3D Scene area of the inspector to change the look of the chart.

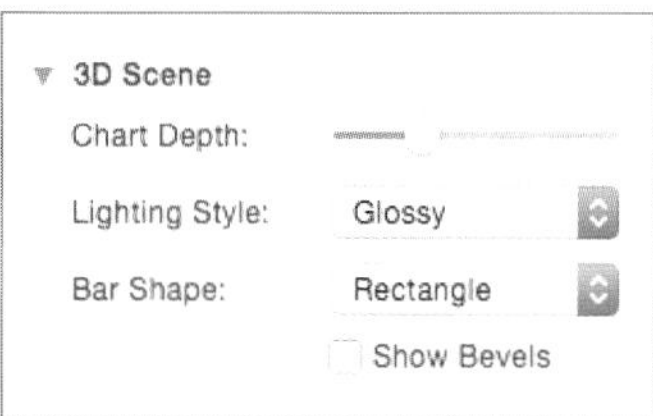

Experiment with Chart Depth, Lighting Style, and Bar Shape. Try selecting and deselecting Show Bevels, too.

NOTE ▶ At the top of the inspector are chart styles. You can create and save your own styles in the same way you created table styles.

17 When you're done experimenting, choose File > Save, and then choose File > Close.

Making a Mixed Chart

Numbers lets you mix chart types, which could add further clarity to the new technology adoption data you've been working on.

1 In Numbers, choose File > Open.

2 Navigate to APTS Pages Numbers Keynote > Lesson_11.

3 Double-click the **new-tech-adoption.numbers** document.

This version of the spreadsheet you've been working on has a 2D stacked bar chart formatted and ready for the next steps.

4 In the toolbar, set the Zoom level to 75%.

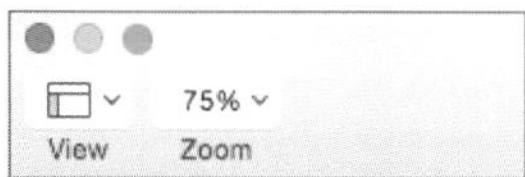

You should have free space below and to the right of the bar chart.

5 Click the bar chart, and then Option-drag the chart to the right to duplicate it. Use the alignment guides to assist in positioning the duplicate chart.

The new chart has the same color attributes as the first chart, so if you want a collection of charts to fit a design theme, it's best to set the color and design before duplicating.

NOTE ▶ Shift-dragging an object restricts its movement to the horizontal, vertical, or diagonal axis.

6 With the duplicate chart selected, in the Chart inspector change Chart Type to 2D Mixed.

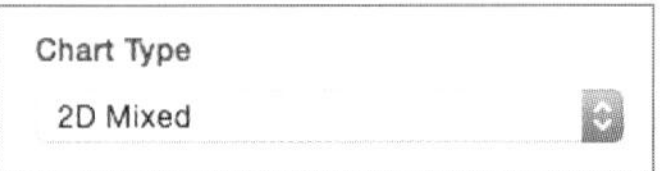

The default 2D mixed chart isn't really telling your story. You can make a couple of changes to fix that.

7 Click the green part of the column chart so that the columns are selected.

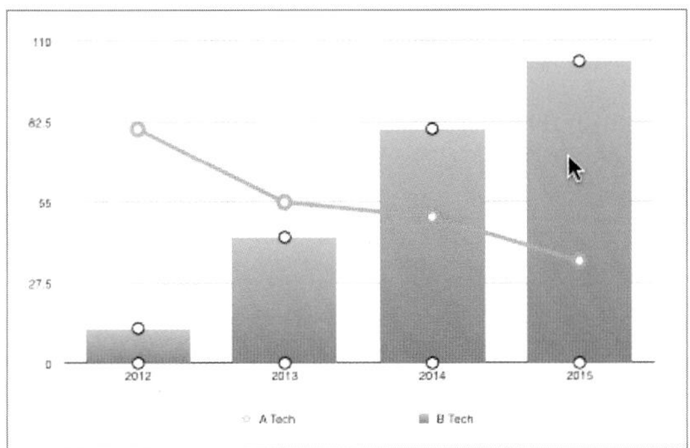

The inspector now displays series parameters.

8 In the inspector, in the "Show Series as" bar, click the Areas button.

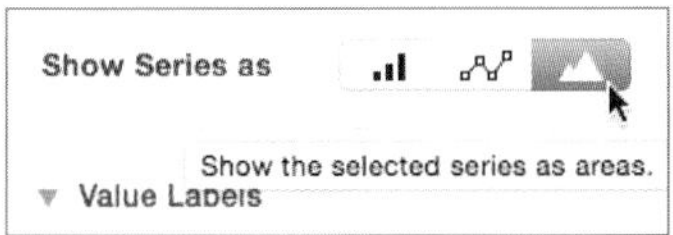

The chart now illustrates the volume of personnel moving to B Tech and the decline in A Tech usage.

NOTE ▶ A series can be shown as a column, line, or area. You'll look at all three types in this lesson.

Before making any more changes, duplicate the chart again.

9 Press Esc. Then click the 2D mixed chart.

10 Option-drag the chart down to place a copy beneath the first 2D mixed chart.

The area chart is rather bright. Let's adjust the color of the area series and add a background to the chart.

Styling a Chart

Numbers has several great chart styles, but you may wish to apply your own design scheme using personal or company colors. In this exercise, you'll continue working in the **new-tech-adoption.numbers** document.

1 In the last chart you copied, click the green area of the series.

2 In the Style inspector, choose Color Fill.

3 Click the Color button to open the Colors window.

4 In the color wheel, click a light green, or choose your own color.

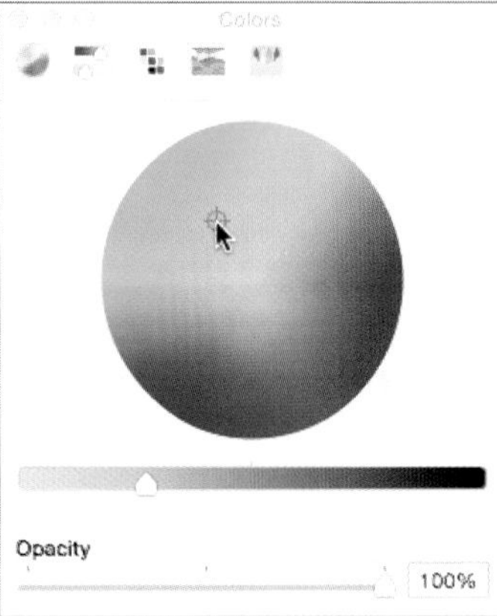

5 In the Chart inspector, display the Background & Border Style area.

6 In Background & Border Style, choose Color Fill. Then click the Color button to refresh the Colors window.

NOTE ► Although the Colors window remains open, you need to perform step 6 to target the required object

7 Click an appropriate color. Light green works well.

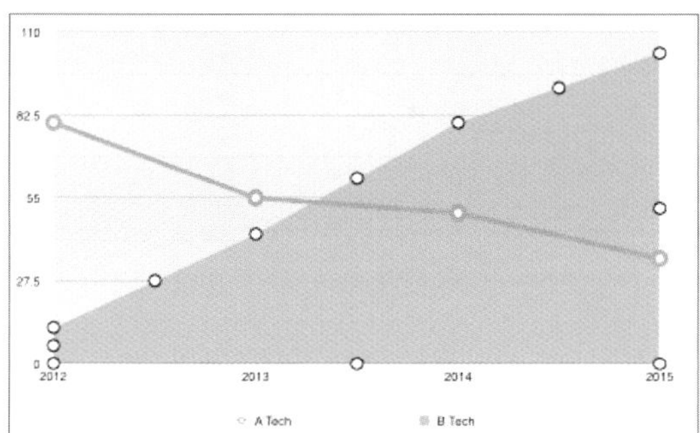

The 2D mixed chart looks OK as an area series, but to reveal the change in the usage of A and B Tech, let's set both series to a line series.

8 Click the bright green area series in the first 2D mixed chart that you created to select the green area.

9 In the Series inspector, in the "Show Series as" bar, click the Line Series button.

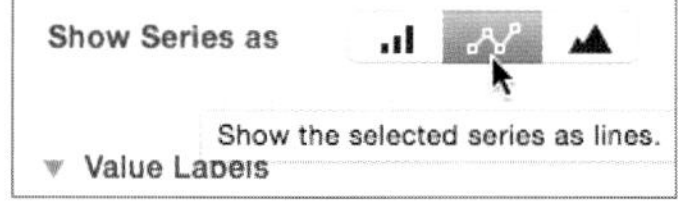

The chart now shows the classic scissor effect often observed in new technology adoption. The crossover happened in early 2013 as new employees began working with B Tech. In 2015, the trend suggests that some employees will still cling to A Tech.

The Y axis shows divisions at 27.5 and 82.5. Half a person doesn't read well.

10 Press Esc, and then click the chart to select it.

11 In the Axis inspector, for Value (Y), set the Axis Scale Steps Major data field to 5.

The sheet now contains three charts, all linked to the table.

12 Click cell E3, type 120, and press Return.

All three charts update because they are linked to the table. (Note that in Pages and Numbers, charts are created independently of tables.)

13 Choose File > Save. Leave the document open and ready for the next exercise. If necessary, close the Colors window.

Using Interactive Chart Types

The latest releases of Pages, Numbers, and Keynote include interactive charts. They can be created in any of the three Apple productivity applications, but creating them in Numbers and copying and pasting to Pages or Keynote has the advantage of linking the charts and table—an advantage that extends to all charts you create in Numbers from a table.

Let's continue working with the **new-tech-adoption.numbers** document.

1 In **new-tech-adoption.numbers**, click the 2D stacked bar chart.

2 Option-drag the duplicate chart down to the space beneath the original.

3 In the Chart inspector, change Chart Type to Interactive Column.

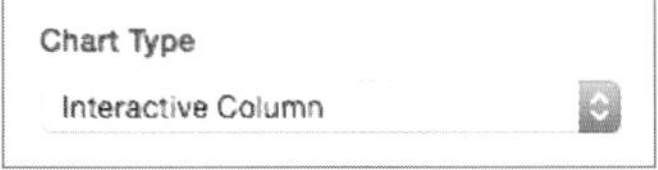

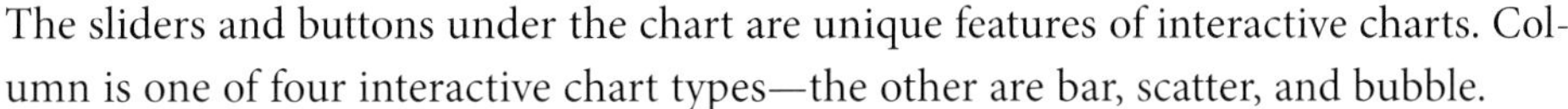
The sliders and buttons under the chart are unique features of interactive charts. Column is one of four interactive chart types—the other are bar, scatter, and bubble.

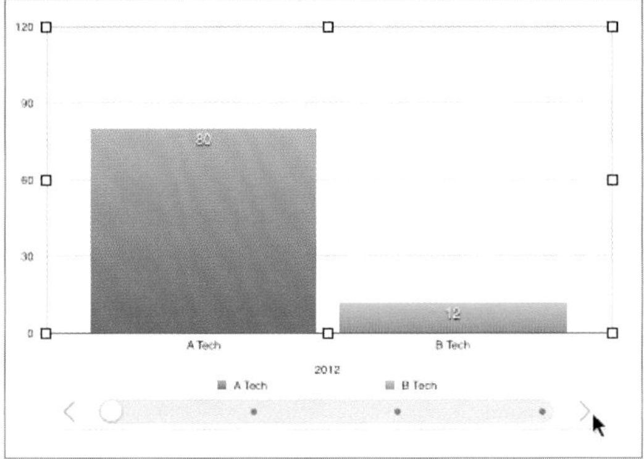

4 On the slider bar, click the arrows to jump through the series data.

5 You can also click the buttons or drag the slider to display different data points.

6 In the Interactive Chart area of the Chart inspector, choose Buttons Only and set Data Set Name to Above.

TIP To display the Data Set Name more clearly, select the Data Set Name text box, and in the inspector, increase its font size.

The interactive chart would be better if the number of employees was included as a data series.

7 With the chart selected, the Edit Data References button appears. Click it.

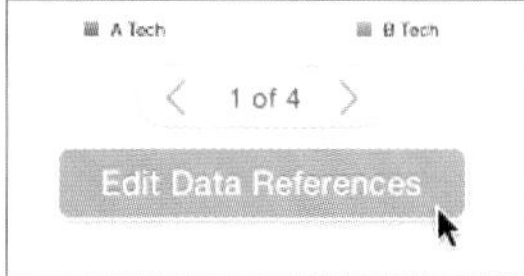

The table from which the chart was created is now highlighted and shows that rows 2 and 3 are included as data references.

	2012	2013	2014	2015
A Tech	80	55	50	35
B Tech	12	43	80	120
Employees	92	98	130	155

8 Drag down the lower-right corner of the selected data references to include the Employees row (row 4).

	2012	2013	2014	2015
A Tech	80	55	50	35
B Tech	12	43	80	120
Employees	92	98	130	155

9 Click Done (the button at the bottom of the document window).

The interactive chart now includes a column for the number of employees. This chart illustrates how the number of employees has grown over the four-year period.

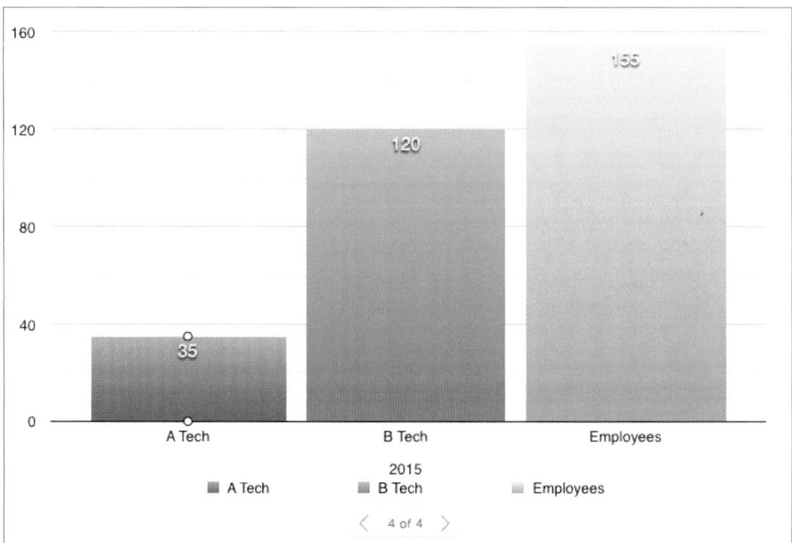

10 Choose File > Close. If prompted, save the document.

Showing a Margin of Error

Surveys and measurements are subject to error, maybe only to a small degree, but illustrating the margin of error's size is a good idea.

1 In Numbers, choose File > Open.

2 Navigate to APTS Pages Numbers Keynote > Lesson_11.

3 Double-click the **margin-of-error.numbers** document.

The document contains a single sheet with a 2D column chart generated from the Visitor Feedback table. The overall visitor satisfaction score never falls below 75%, and the greatest margin of error occurred in August.

4 Click the chart to select it.

5 In the Category (x) tab of the Axis inspector, change Label Angle to Left Diagonal.

All the months are now visible. Reducing the font size dramatically would also display the month labels, but they'd be far too small to read.

6 In the Series inspector, set Error Bars to Positive and Negative.

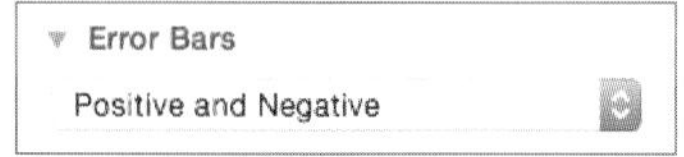

The error bars default needs to be changed to reflect the actual margin of error for this survey.

7 Set Use, in Error Bars, to Custom Values, and double-click the Positive data field.

The Formula Editor appears. Just as you did with tables, you can select specific cells here. In this case, you want to select all of column C, the +/– amounts.

8 Click the reference header for column C, and press Return.

The inspector's Formula Editor populates with the reference for column C: a +/– label.

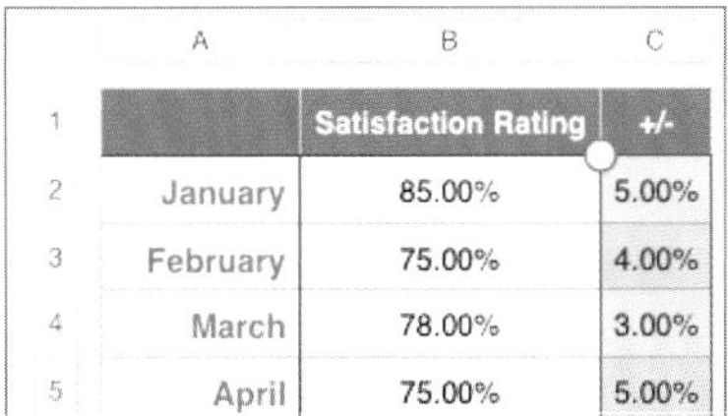

	A	B	C
1		Satisfaction Rating	+/-
2	January	85.00%	5.00%
3	February	75.00%	4.00%
4	March	78.00%	3.00%
5	April	75.00%	5.00%

9 In the Error Bars area, double-click the Negative value, 10.

10 Repeat step 8.

Now both the Positive and Negative fields are referencing the table's margin of error column.

The Satisfaction Rating chart now has error bars. Although they look great at present, you may wish to customize them.

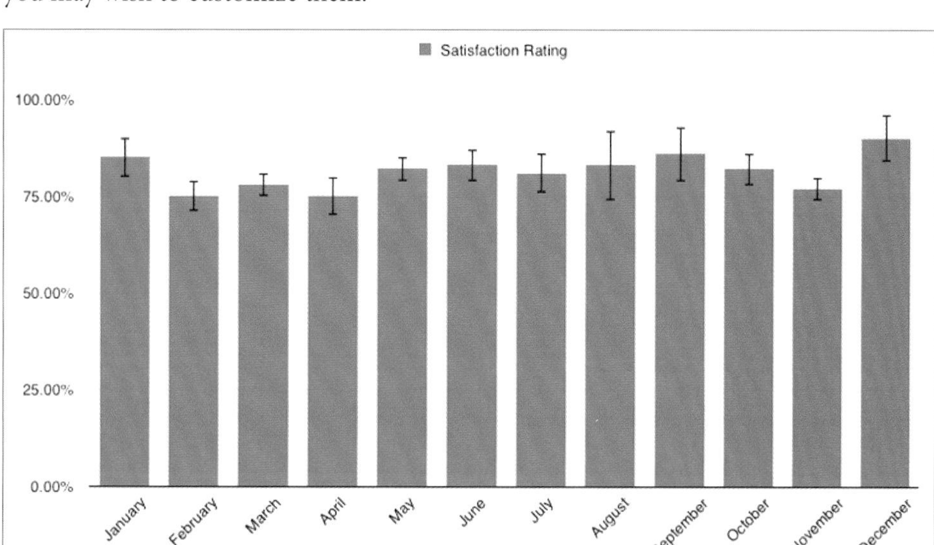

11 Click an error bar. Make sure only the error bars are selected.

The inspector displays Bar Style options. Try increasing the weight of the bar to 3 pt, and then experiment with the other options.

Because the satisfaction rating is consistent, it's hard to see the fluctuation results. You're going to modify the axis scale to focus on the difference between ratings.

12 Press Esc, and click the chart.

13 In the Axis inspector, click the Value (Y) button. In the Axis Scale area, change the Min data field to 0.5.

You are working in percentages, so the Max is 1, and you've just set the Min value to 50%.

14 Set the Steps Major value to 5 to put the horizontal divisions at 10% intervals.

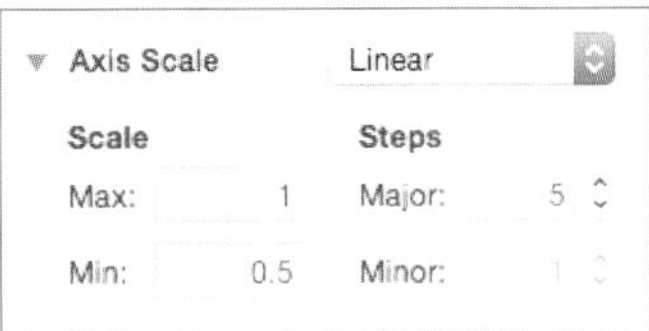

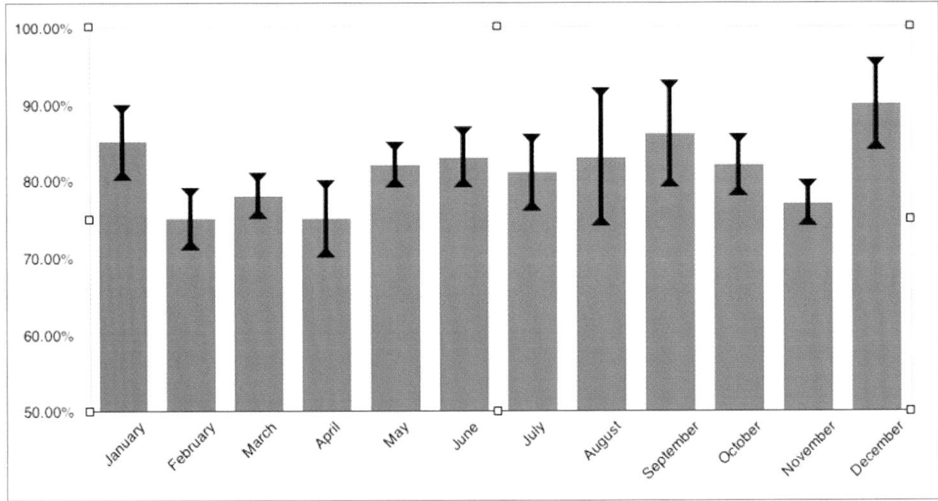

There's an old saying about lies and statistics. By changing the parameters of the chart, you can weave your own narrative.

15 Close the spreadsheet.

Building a Scatter Chart

You're about to build a scatter chart and apply trendlines. Based loosely on an experiment scenario, a test was run twice, and the results were labeled Sample 1 and Sample 2. Measurements were taken every 30 seconds. Sample 1 has already been plotted as a scatter chart.

1 In Numbers, choose File > Open.

2 Navigate to APTS Pages Numbers Keynote > Lesson_11.

3 Double-click the **scatter-chart.numbers** document.

4 Click the chart. In the Chart inspector, change Chart Type to 2D Bar, 2D Line, and then 2D Bubble to see how each type displays the data.

5 Return Chart Type to 2D Scatter.

The point of step 4 was to demonstrate that not every chart will suit every data set.

With the 2D scatter chart, you can already see that the dots of the chart suggest a trend: a linear increase over the experiment's duration.

Let's bring in the Sample 2 data.

6 Click the Edit Data References button.

7 Click above the Sample 2 column to extend the selection.

Time	Sample 1	Sample 2
00:30	0%	0%
01:00	3%	2%
01:30	8%	7%
02:00	9%	13%
02:30	14%	15%
03:00	18%	18%
03:30	22%	20%
04:00	24%	21%
04:30	27%	23%
05:00	35%	26%
05:30	36%	30%
06:00	42%	34%
X 06:30	Y	Y
07:00	47%	50%
07:30	54%	58%
08:00	55%	63%
08:30	62%	66%
09:00	69%	71%
09:30	70%	79%
10:00	75%	81%
10:30	84%	84%
11:00	85%	87%
11:30	90%	93%
12:00	95%	95%
12:30	97%	100%

The chart now displays both samples. To emphasize the increase, let's add trendlines.

8 Click Done. The chart remains selected.

9 Open the Series inspector, and in the Trendlines area, choose Polynomial.

This trendline type works well for this data. Polynomial trendlines produce a curved line that has hills and valleys to show where values rise or fall. Six types of trendlines are available. Another formatting option would be to stretch a chart either vertically or horizontally.

10 With the chart selected, drag down the bottom of the selection to stretch the chart. The type doesn't distort, only the series lines change.

Saving a Template

To conclude this look at Numbers, we'll save the current file as a template, available for future use. (If you haven't worked through the Pages lessons, you may want to go back and review how to save and use templates.)

1 With **scatter-chart.numbers** open, choose File > Save As Template.

2 In the dialog, click Add to Template Chooser.

NOTE ▶ Choosing Save gives you the option to save the template where you wish, which is ideal when you want to send the template to a colleague.

3 In the Template Chooser, in My Templates, you'll find the template you created in step 2.

   Rather than open it, you'll delete it.

4 Control-click your Numbers template, and from the shortcut menu choose Delete.

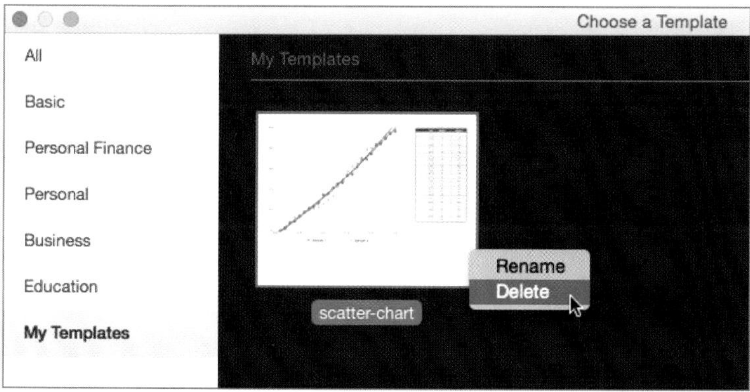

5 In the dialog that appears, click Delete.

TIP If you want Numbers to always open with a specific template, open Numbers preferences, and in the General tab, click the "Use template" radio button and then click Change Template. You then have the option to choose any template in your Template Chooser.

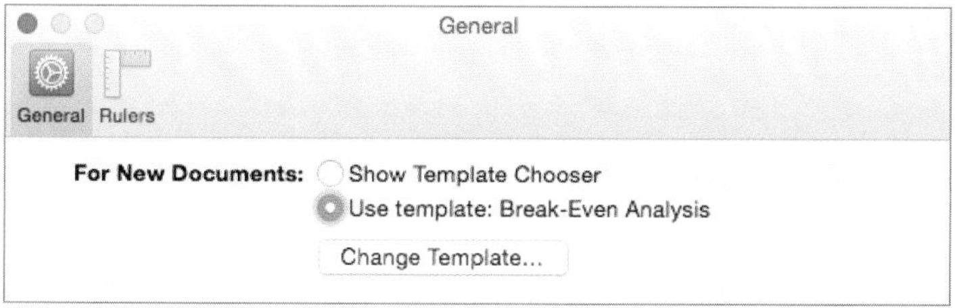

Lesson Review

1. Describe how to change a column chart to a bar chart.
2. What are data references?
3. How do you save a chart style?
4. In a mixed chart type, what are the three types of series plotting?
5. Name the four types of interactive charts.

Answers

1. Select the chart. In the Chart inspector, change Chart Type to Bar Chart.
2. When creating a chart based on an existing table, the chart series are plotted using the table data by linking or referring to the table data. These links are called data references.
3. Chart styles are created in the same way table styles are created. Click a chart with the desired formatting, and then in the Chart inspector's Chart Styles area, click the Add (+) button to save the chart style.
4. Column, line, and area
5. Interactive Column, Interactive Bar, Interactive Scatter, and Interactive Bubble

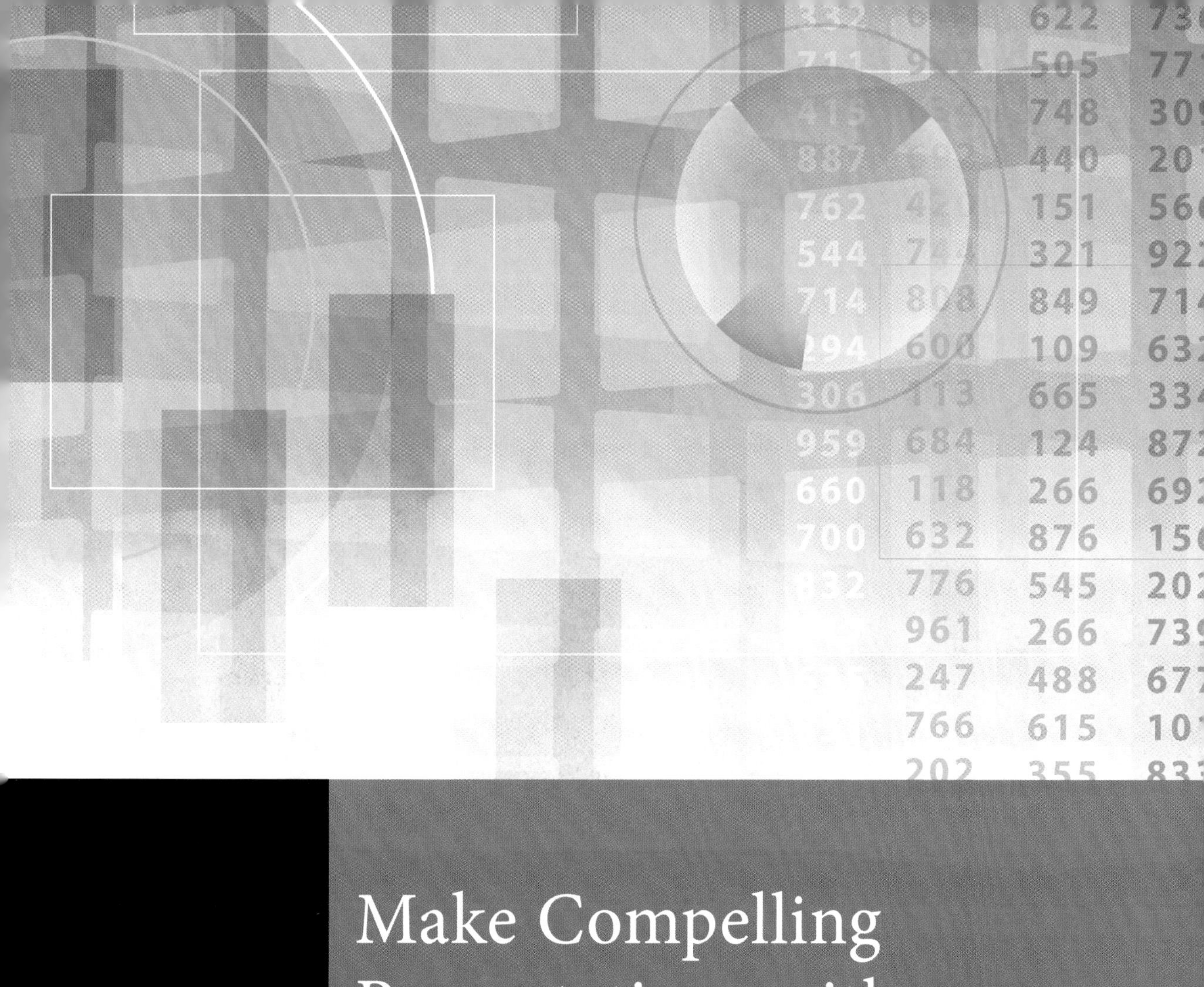

Make Compelling Presentations with Keynote

12

Lesson Files

APTS Pages Numbers Keynote > Lesson_12 > engine321-slides.ppt

APTS Pages Numbers Keynote > Lesson_12 > sophia-presentation.kth

Time

This lesson takes approximately 60 minutes to complete.

Goals

Open and create Keynote presentations

Apply templates to a presentation

Reorder slides

Work in outline view

Introduce presenter notes

Open and edit PowerPoint presentations

Add and modify slide transitions

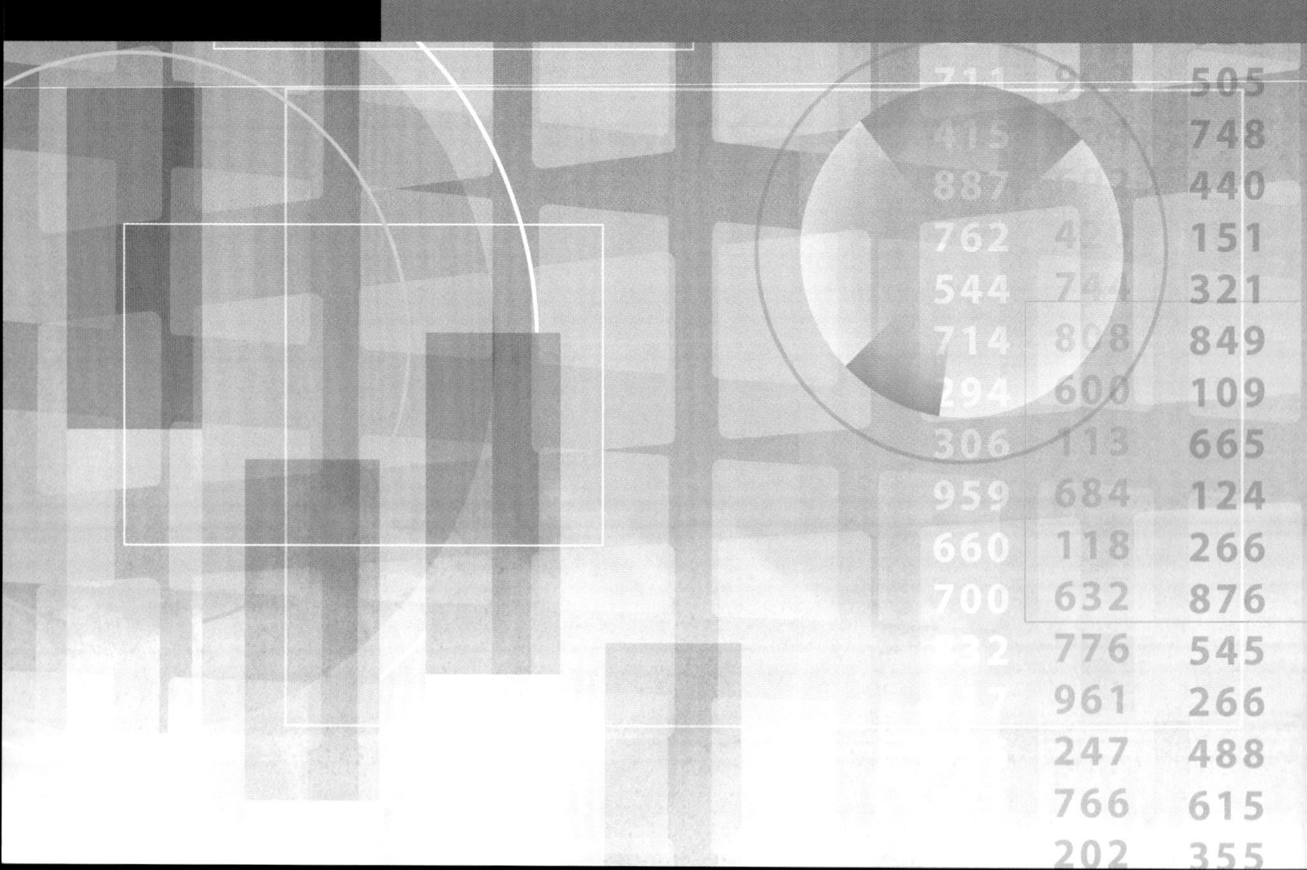

Lesson **12**

Outlining a Presentation

With Keynote you can create presentations quickly, perhaps so quickly that you may miss some very useful features and techniques, such as using themes and master slides to apply changes through a large set of slides. In this lesson you'll create a new presentation from a theme, add and modify slides, and then swap themes to understand the value of working with master slides.

You'll open a PowerPoint document in Keynote and copy slides from one presentation to another. All the topics in this lesson lay the foundation for your ongoing exploration of Keynote.

Creating a Presentation

All Keynote documents begin by selecting from one of dozens of themes in either standard or widescreen formats. You can create your own themes, too, as you'll learn in Lesson 14. In this exercise, you'll select a theme before going on to add and modify slides.

1 Open Keynote.

2 Choose File > New to open the Theme Chooser.

NOTE ▶ Unless you have changed Keynotes default preferences to open a specific theme, creating a new document will always open the Theme Chooser.

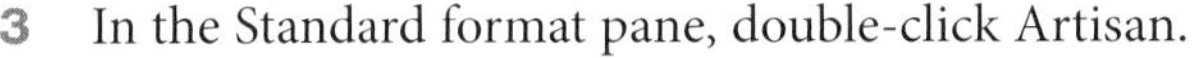

3 In the Standard format pane, double-click Artisan.

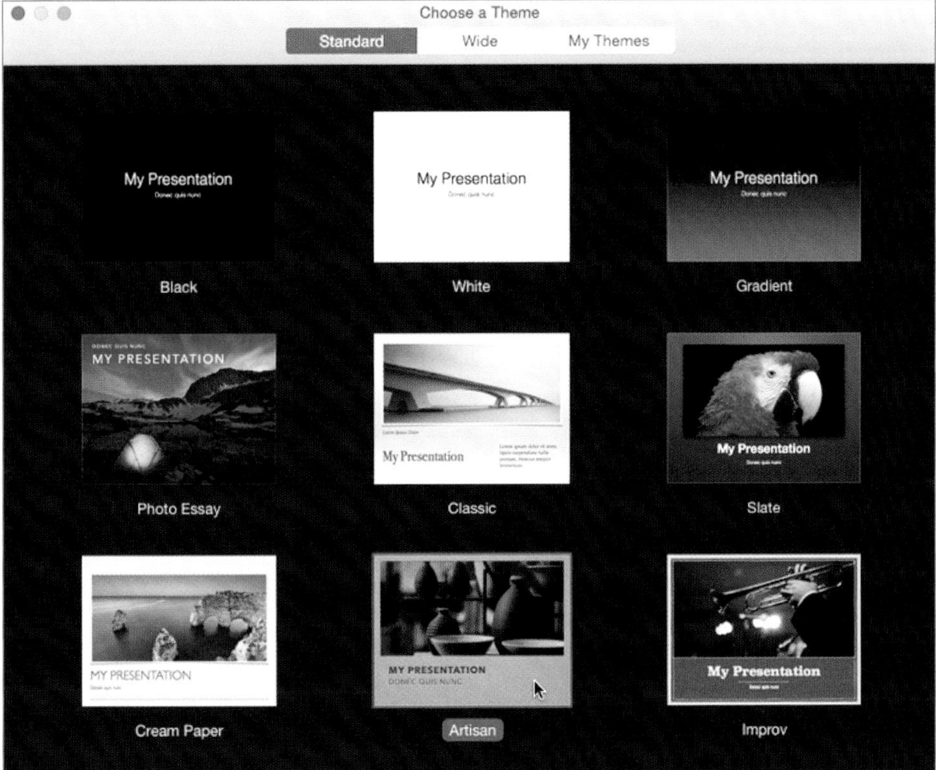

A new presentation is created with a single slide. The inspector should be visible.

4 If necessary, in the toolbar, click the Format button to open the inspector.

Depending on what you've clicked since creating this presentation, the inspector may not display options for slide layout. Let's make sure your Keynote document view matches the upcoming figures.

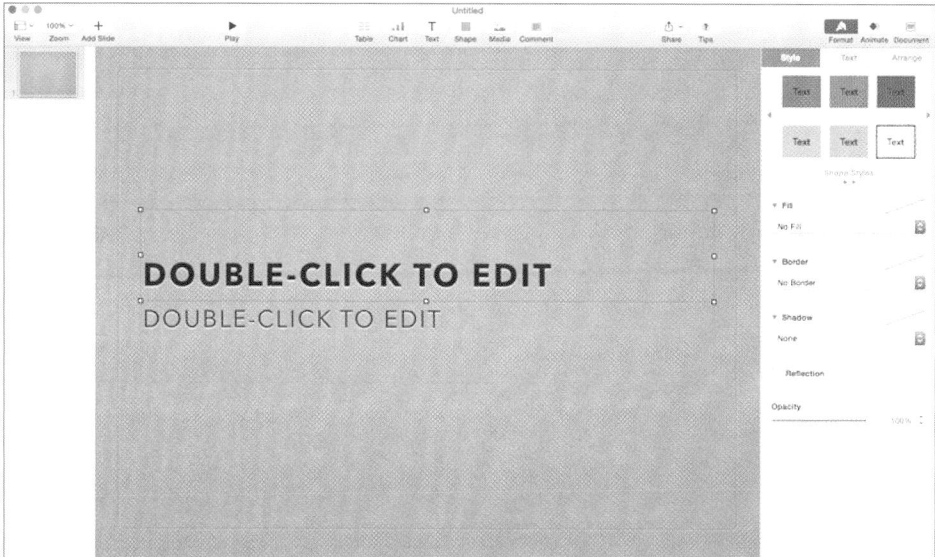

5 In the toolbar, click the View button and choose Navigator from the pop-up menu.

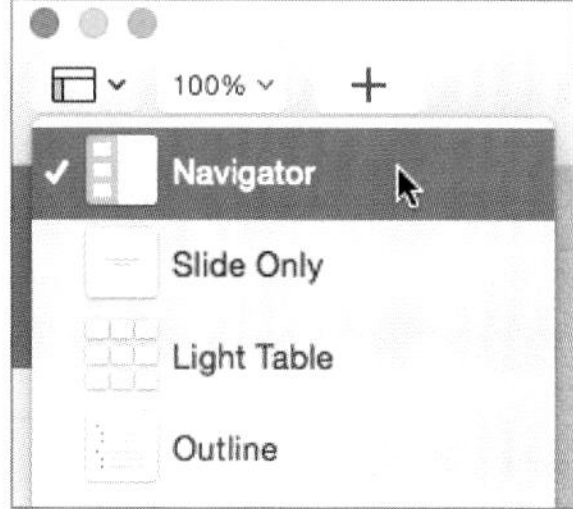

The navigator appears as a column to the left of the presentation window. This is the default option you'll use in this exercise, but feel free to later try Slide Only, Light Table, and Outline.

6 In the slide navigator, click the slide thumbnail. The inspector displays slide layout options.

7 Click the title text box, "Double-Click To Edit."

The inspector displays options for Style, Text, and Arrange.

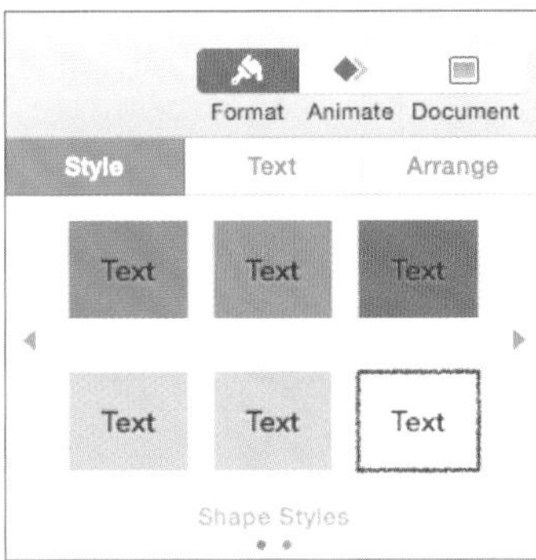

Like all the Apple productivity apps, Keynote is context aware. Selecting thumbnails or objects determines which options are available in the inspector and other menus.

8 Click "Double-Click To Edit" again. The placeholder text is replaced with a blinking text insertion pointer.

9 Type *Engine 321*.

The text appears in capital letters, regardless of whether you press Shift or Caps Lock.

10 Double-click the lower text box placeholder text. Type *Sophia Larkinson*.

11 Choose File > Save.

12 In the Save As field of the dialog, type *Engine 321 Report*.

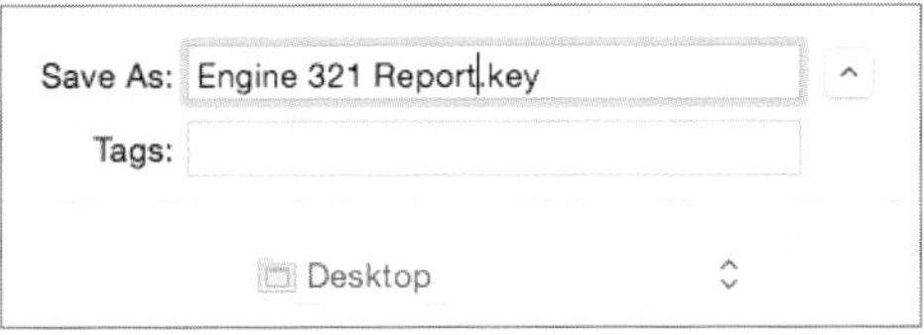

TIP Add tags to help catalog your work. For this document, appropriate tags could include *Engine 321*, *restoration*, and *reports*.

13 Save the document to your desktop, and leave it open for the next exercise.

Customizing Your Workspace

The default view in Keynote displays several essential editing options, but as you develop your presentation-building skills you may wish to add extra items to improve your workflow.

1 Control-click the toolbar and choose Customize Toolbar from the shortcut menu.

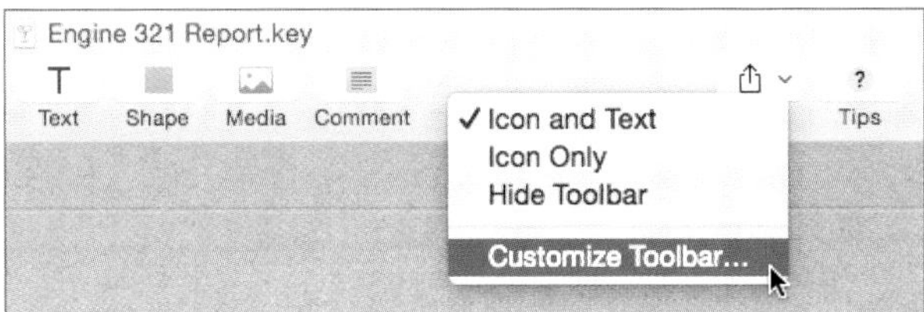

2 In the window that appears, locate the Copy Style icon, and drag it up to the toolbar.

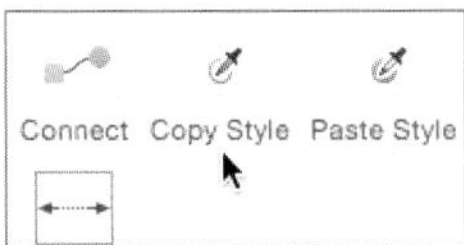

3 Drag the Paste Style and Connect icons to the toolbar. When they're in place, click Done to close the window.

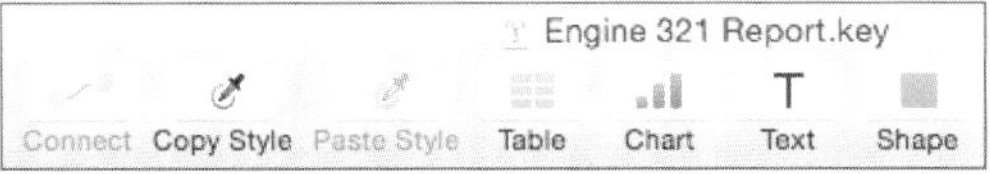

NOTE ▶ Copy Style, Paste Style, and Connect can be accessed by choosing Format > Copy Style, Format > Paste Style, or Insert > Line > Straight Connection Line.

4 In the toolbar, click the View button and choose Show Presenter Notes from the pop-up menu.

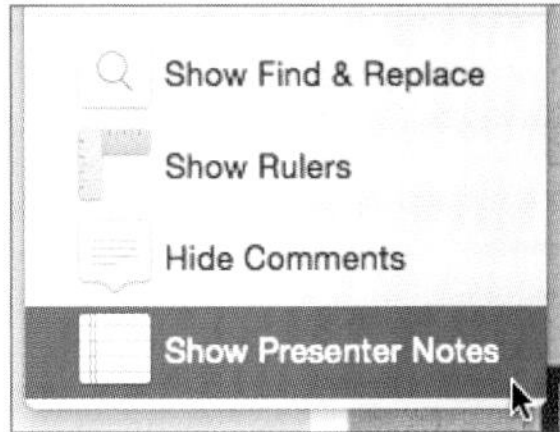

The role of presenter notes will become clearer in upcoming lessons, but adding presenter notes should be one of your first steps when developing a presentation.

5 Choose File > Save.

Keynote autosaves as you work, so choosing to save now creates a specific version that you can revert to, if necessary.

Adding Slides

Presentations rarely have a single slide. Let's add more and review the master slides available in this theme.

1 In Engine 321 Report, click the Slides thumbnail.

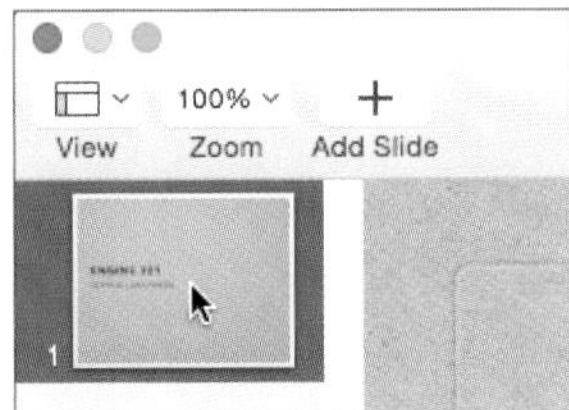

The inspector displays options for slide layout; the current slide is made from the Title & Subtitle master.

2 Choose Slide > New Slide.

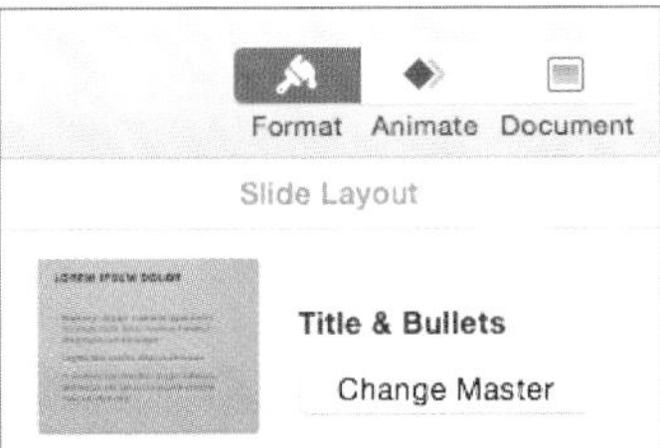

A new slide is added, but Keynote assumes you don't want another Title & Subtitle slide, so it added a Title & Bullets slide instead. You can use the Slide Layout inspector to change the slide master; however, here's another way to add a slide.

3 In the toolbar, click the Add Slide button. A popover appears showing all the currently available master slides.

4 Click any of the master slide thumbnails to add a slide to your presentation.

5 In the slide navigator, verify that the slide you just added is selected.

6 In the Slide Layout inspector, click Change Master.

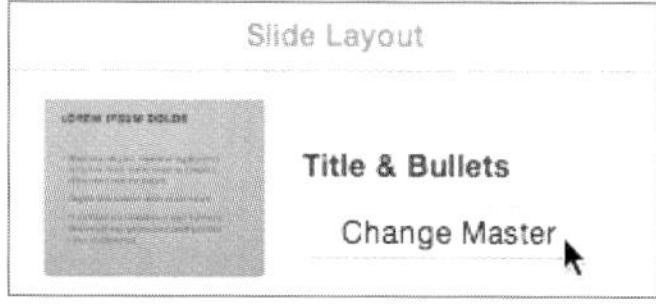

The same popover appears showing the available master slides.

7 In the popover, click the Photo – 3 up button (the thumbnail showing three photos). This changes the master slide applied to slide 3.

Your presentation now has three slides. Let's add one more.

8 In the slide navigator, Control-click slide 3's thumbnail and from the shortcut menu choose Duplicate.

9 In the slide navigator, click slide 2's thumbnail.

10 On the slide, double-click the title, and type *Stage 1: Restoration Outline* to replace its placeholder text.

11 Double-click the placeholder text for the bullets on the slide. Do the following:

Type *Budget*, and press Return.

Type *Stage One Proposal*, and press Return.

Type *Stage Two Proposal*, and press Return.

Type *Stage Three Proposal*.

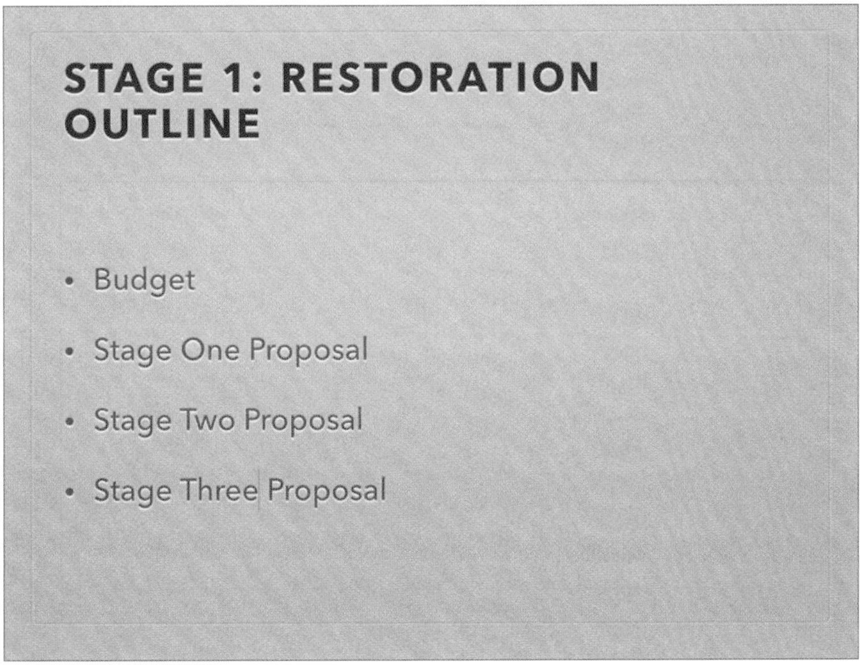

STAGE 1: RESTORATION OUTLINE

- Budget
- Stage One Proposal
- Stage Two Proposal
- Stage Three Proposal

12 Choose File > Save, and leave the presentation open for the next exercise.

The presentation now has four slides, each created from a specific master slide. You are about to add more slides, but they are currently in a PowerPoint presentation.

Opening a PowerPoint Presentation in Keynote

Keynote can open PowerPoint files in the .ppt and the newer .pptx formats. It can also export back to both those formats. Although slide formatting is generally preserved during the translation process, slide transitions and animation are often changed or lost.

1 In Keynote, choose File > Open.

2 Navigate to APTS Pages Numbers Keynote > Lesson_12.

3 Double-click **engine321-slides.ppt**.

The PowerPoint presentation opens in Keynote. You could now work on this new document just like any other Keynote presentation, but instead you'll copy slides from it into Engine 321 Report.

4 Position the engine321-slides document window over Engine 321 Report so that you can see the slide thumbnails in each presentation.

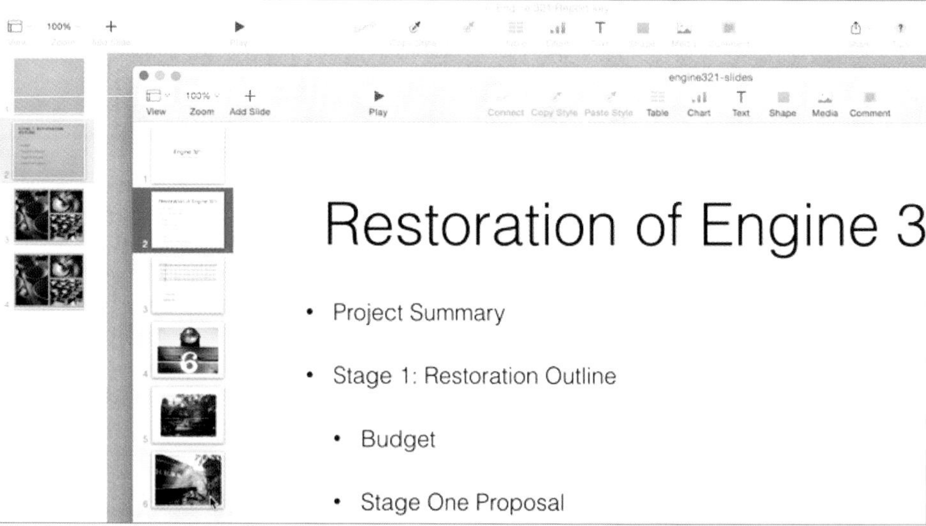

NOTE ▶ Step 4 assumes you are not working in full-screen view.

5 In engine321-slides, click the thumbnail for slide 2, and then Shift-click the thumbnail for slide 6 to select all the slides except slide 1.

In the navigator, the selected slides have a yellow border.

6 Drag the selected slides to the slide navigator of Engine 321 Report. The slides now appear in the Engine 321 Report.

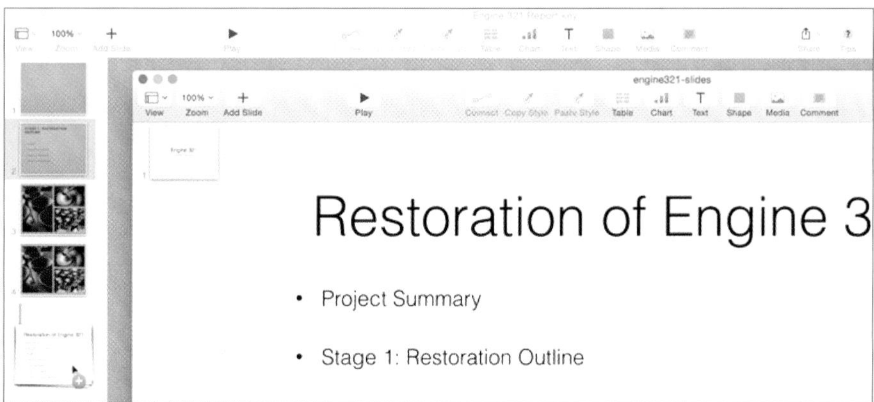

The slides are not in the desired order, however, so you'll reorder them in the next exercise.

7 Close the engine321-slides converted from the PowerPoint presentation.

Reordering and Deleting Slides

Reordering slides in Keynote is best done in either the navigator or light table views. In this exercise, you'll work in navigator view, but in Lesson 15 you'll revise a slideshow using the light table view.

1 In the navigator click slide 5. Drag the thumbnail for slide 5 to position it between slides 1 and 2.

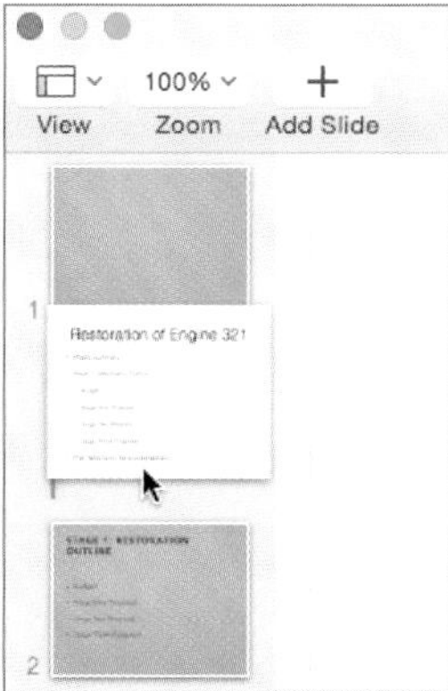

Try to keep the blue insert line aligned with the left edge of the slides. If you don't, you'll indent the slide (although doing so wouldn't create a problem in this exercise).

NOTE ▶ Indenting is a useful feature when organizing large slide decks, as you'll learn in Lesson 13.

Slides 4 and 5 aren't needed so you can delete them.

2 In the slide navigator, click the thumbnail for slide 4 and Shift-click slide 5.

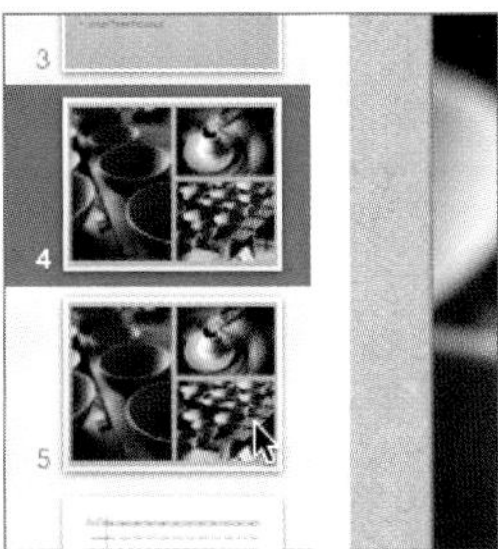

3 Press Delete to delete the two slides.

The presentation currently mixes two themes, which you'll resolve later. Note, however, that a Keynote presentation can have multiple themes. This is not a problem because once the content is completed an overall theme can be applied.

4 Press Command-S to save a version of your document.

Working in Outline View

Many Keynote presentations are planned in outline view. It allows you to write titles and bullets for a sequence of slides just as you would type the text in a word processing program such as Pages.

1 In the Engine 321 Report presentation, click slide 3.

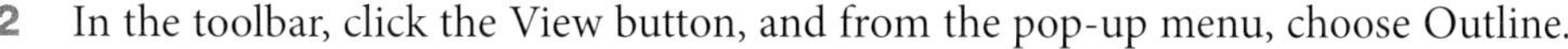

2 In the toolbar, click the View button, and from the pop-up menu, choose Outline.

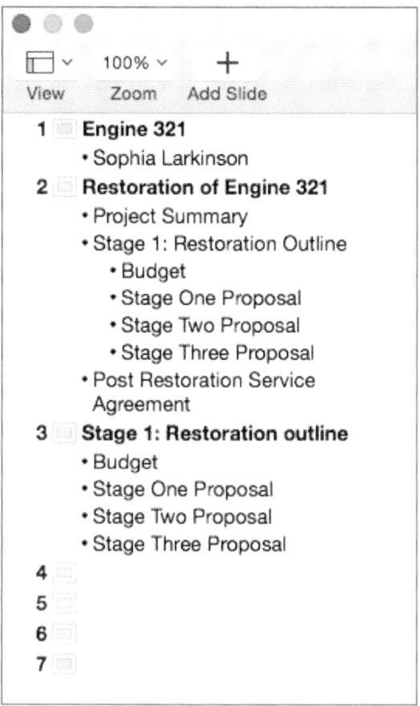

Instead of slide thumbnails, you are presented with text. The bold text elements are titles. Bullets are displayed indented in a regular font with bullet symbols. Slides 4 to 7 show no text because slide 4 contains a table and the remaining slides contain photos.

3 Press the Up and Down Arrows to move up and down the lines of text, and select the last bullet point on slide 3, Stage Three Proposal.

4 Press Return. A new bullet point is added at the same level as Stage Three Proposal.

5 Press Tab to further indent the bullet point.

6 Press Shift-Tab twice to remove the indentation of this bullet point, thereby creating a new slide 4.

You'll continue to press Return, Tab, and Shift-Tab as you type out some new slides for your presentation.

7 Type *Stage One Proposal*, and press Return. Then press Tab, and type *Phase 1*. Press Return, and type *Phase 2*. Press Return, and type *Phase 3*.

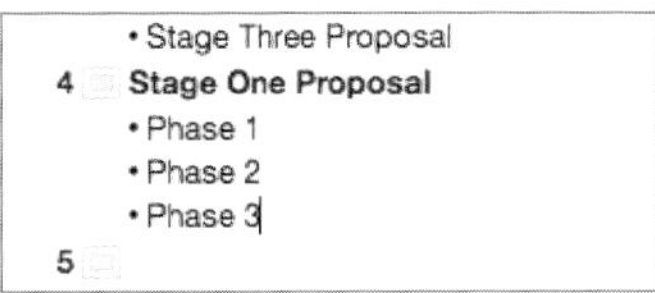

As long as you remain in outline view, you can type your presentation ideas while breaking them down into slides and bullets.

8 Press Return, and then press Shift-Tab to remove the bullet indentation and create a new slide 5.

9 Type *Stage Two Proposal*.

TIP Use outline view to type out presentation ideas as they occur to you. Then after you've generated your content, drag the text into a logical slide sequence. You can indent and "outdent" slides to create your hierarchy of ideas.

10 In the outline, click the slide icon for slide 4.

11 Press Command-D to duplicate slide 4. A new slide is created using only the title.

Slide 5 reads "Stage One Proposal" and has the three Phase bullet points.

12 In the outline, click the slide icon for slide 5. Shift-click the last bullet point of slide 5.

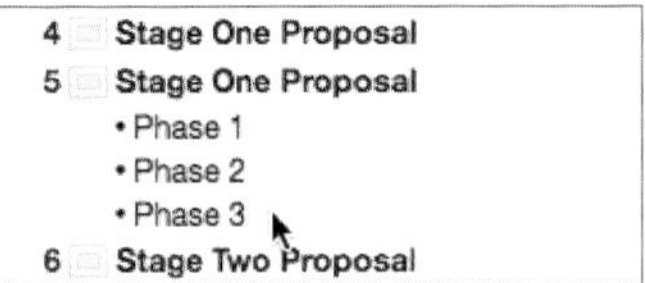

13 Press Command-D to create a new slide with the title and bullets.

14 Drag slide 6 down to position it after slide 7.

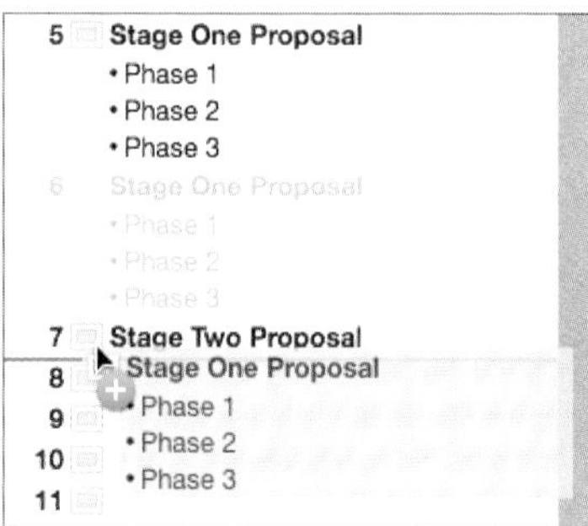

Slide 7 now needs to be retitled.

15 In the title of slide 7, double-click the word "One," and then type *Three*.

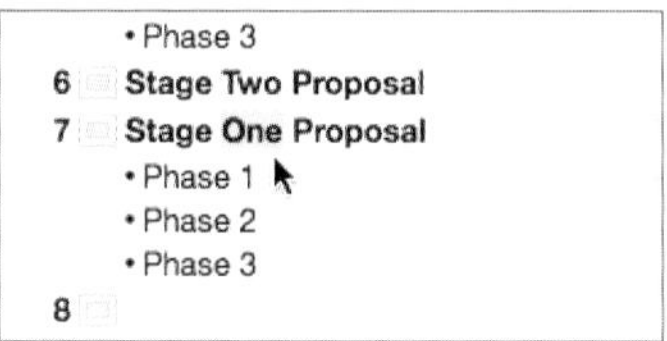

16 Click slide 4, and press Delete.

17 Choose File > Save, and leave the presentation open for the next exercise.

Adding Slide Transitions

You could remain in outline view for this exercise, but let's return to navigator view to add transitions to your presentation. Transitions can help add style and pizzazz to your work, even though overdoing the special effects can also distract an audience from your message.

In Lesson 13, you'll have a chance to fully explore the wow factor of transitions, but for now you'll keep things simple.

1 In the Engine 321 Report presentation, choose View > Navigator as an alternative to using the toolbar View button.

2 In the slide navigator, click any slide thumbnail.

3 Press Command-A to select all the slides.

4 In the toolbar, click the Animate button.

The Transitions inspector appears.

5 Click "Add an Effect."

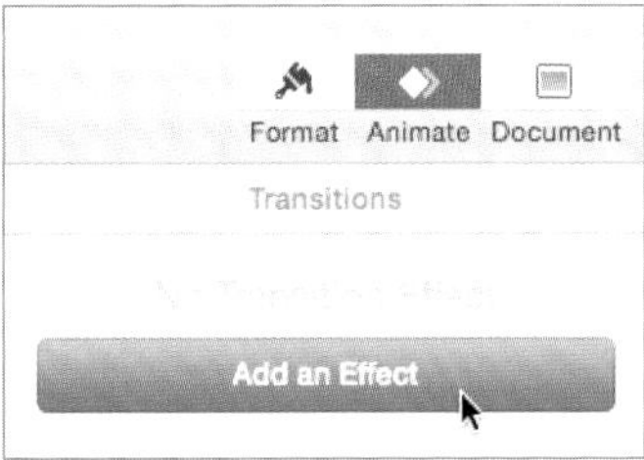

6 Choose Dissolve, and set Duration to 1.00 s.

Use either the slider or stepper to set the duration. Speeding up the transition will increase the pace of this business presentation. (In Lesson 13 you'll slow down transitions to create a more contemplative mood.)

7 Click slide 1. In the toolbar, click Play to start the slideshow.

8 Press Spacebar to move through each slide until you see a slide with a train in it. Then, press Left Arrow to back up through the slideshow.

9 Return to slide 1. Press Spacebar, or Right Arrow, to move to slide 2.

There is no tension in this slide. It just appears, enabling an audience to read the slide before the presenter has a chance to talk about it. This problem is sometimes referred to as *read-on*.

Rather than have the whole slide appear in a single click, you'll use builds to improve the flow of your presentation.

Using Builds

Builds, like transitions, can be exciting, fun, and generally very useful additions to a slideshow, but they also can be overdone. Transitions work between slides, while builds take place within a slide causing elements to appear and disappear or move around. In this exercise, you'll add a Build In effect.

1 In the Engine 321 Report presentation, press Esc to exit the slideshow. Make sure you are on slide 2.

2 Click the text box containing the bullet points.

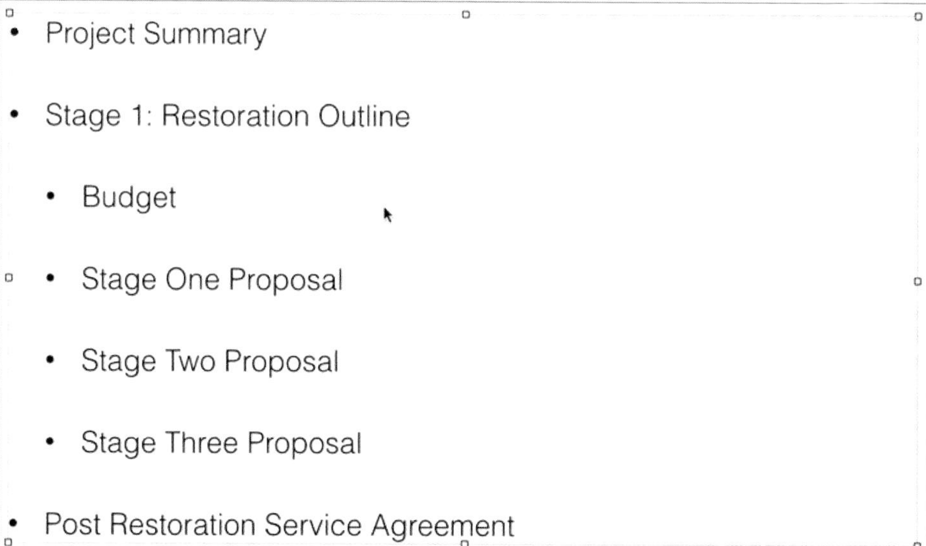

3 In the Animate inspector, the Build In tab is selected. Click "Add an Effect."

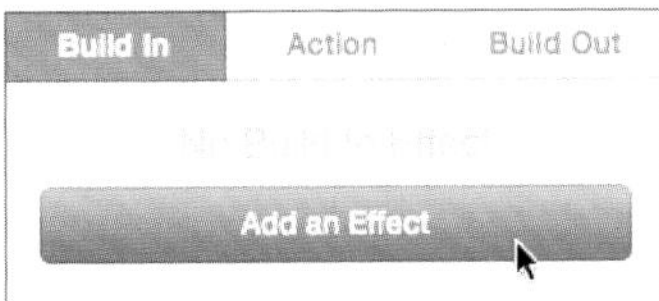

4 From the menu, in the Appear & Move section, choose Typewriter.

The inspector shows options for the Typewriter build. The options for each kind of build vary.

5 In the Build inspector, set the Delivery to By Bullet.

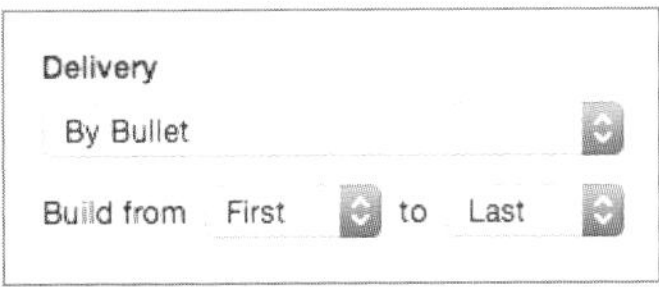

The default option would animate the build of the entire text box at once. By changing the delivery type, the build will be performed bullet by bullet.

6 In the toolbar, click Play.

The slideshow begins at slide 2.

7 Press the Spacebar. The first bullet appears.

8 Press the Spacebar again.

Imagine talking about the slide. Press the Spacebar each time you are ready to continue to the next point. Using a build like this keeps you in control of your presentations and prevents your audience from reading on.

9 Press Esc to quit the presentation.

Other slides in this presentation would benefit from this build. For extra practice, try applying it to the bullets on slide 3.

10 Press Command-S to save a version of your presentation.

Applying Themes

In this lesson, you've been outlining ideas, developing a sequence of slides, and choosing how they might be delivered. However, the overall look of the presentation has yet to be properly addressed. This has been done to make a point. If master slides are used properly, another Keynote theme can be applied at any time.

The Engine 321 Report presentation contains multiple master slides, transitions, and builds. It also contains one set of presenter notes.

1 In the Engine 321 Report presentation, click the thumbnail for slide 7.

   The slide contains two tables, and in the presenter notes area are several lines of text. They read like a script for the presentation of this slide.

   These presenter notes were added in PowerPoint and transferred when the table slide was dragged into the current presentation. (You'll learn more about presenter notes in the next lesson.)

2 In the toolbar, click the Document button.

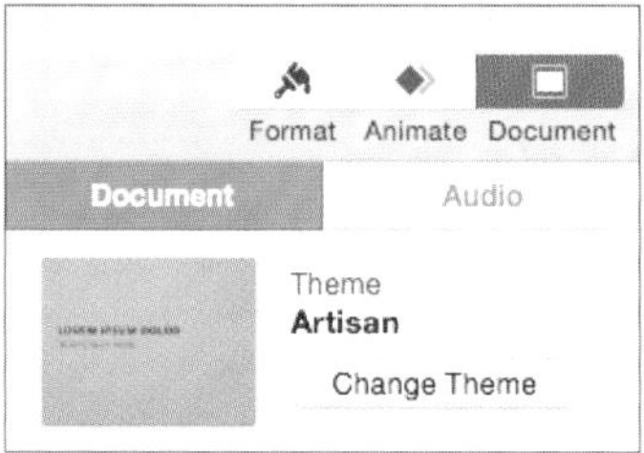

   The current document has two themes: Artisan, and a theme brought over from PowerPoint.

3 In the Document inspector, click Change Theme to open the Theme Chooser.

4 Double-click the Artisan theme to apply it to all of your slides.

Yikes! The title and bullets on slide 2 have disappeared. However, all the other slides have adopted the theme change without losing slide content. Let's fix the problem in slide 2.

5 In the slide navigator, select slide 2.

6 In the toolbar, click the Format button.

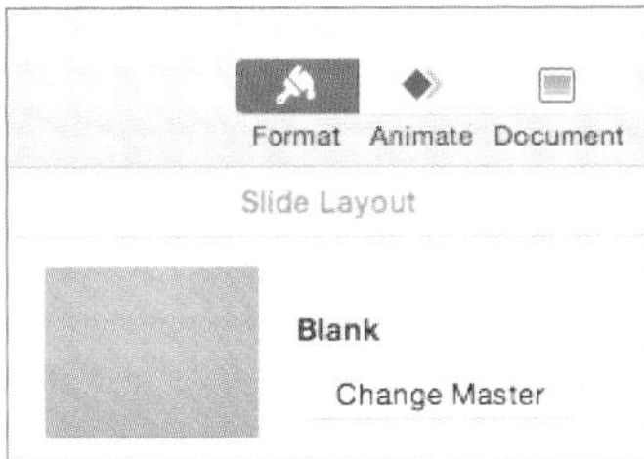

In the Slide Layout area, the master slide is shown to be blank. The master slide option was not automatically set in the translation from PowerPoint. Whether opening PowerPoint presentations in Keynote or working solely in Keynote, applying the correct masters is very important.

7 In the Slide Layout area, click Change Master, and choose Title & Bullets.

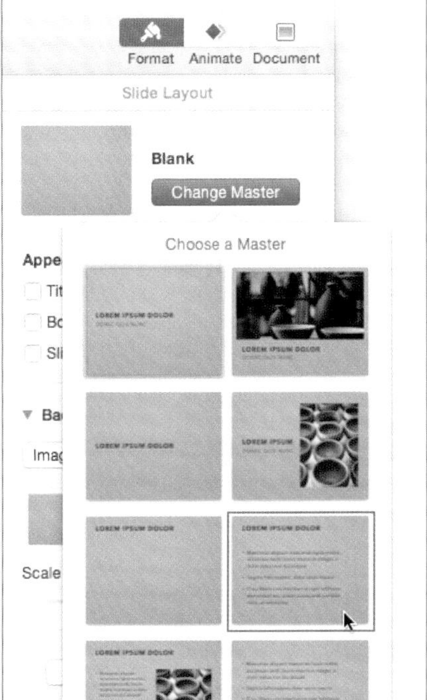

The title and bullets reappear.

8 In the toolbar, click the Document button.

9 In the Document inspector, click Change Theme.

Use the steps previously outlined to experiment by changing the theme to Improv, Renaissance, or any other themes that look appealing.

10 Press Command-S to save a version of your presentation and leave it open for the last exercise.

Applying a Custom Theme

To close out this lesson, you'll apply a custom theme. In Lesson 14 you'll learn how to build your own theme, but here you'll apply a design from Sophia Larkinson, an engineer.

1 In Keynote, choose File > Open.

2 Navigate to APTS Pages Numbers Keynote > Lesson12.

3 Double-click the **sophia-presentation.kth** template.

4 In the dialog, click "Add to Theme Chooser."

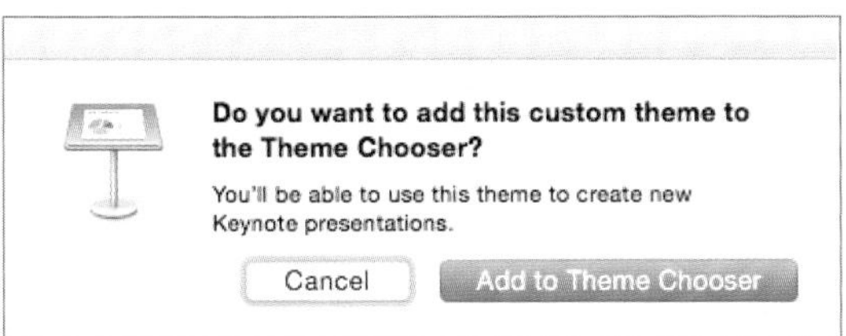

The chooser now includes a My Themes tab.

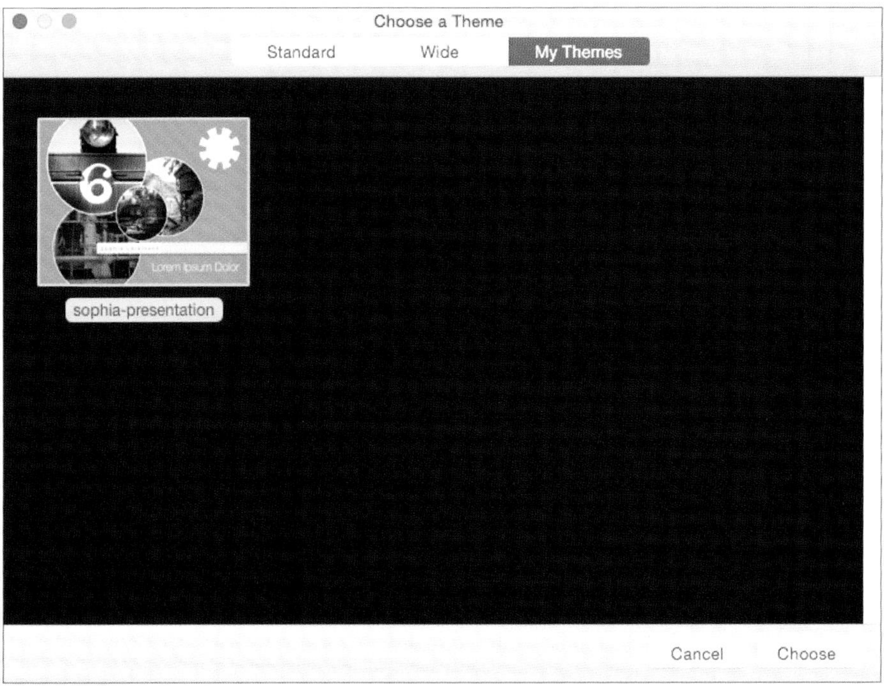

5 In the Theme Chooser, click Cancel.

NOTE ▶ If you click Choose, a new presentation is created.

In the Engine 321 Report presentation, you'll use the Document inspector to change the theme once more.

6 In the Document inspector, click Change Theme

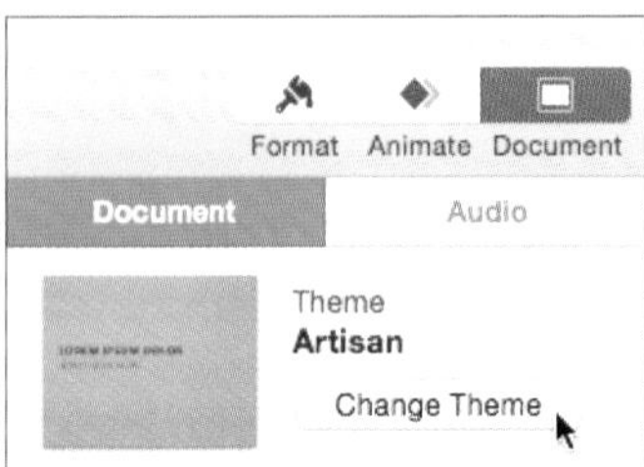

7 At the top of the Theme Chooser, click My Themes, and then double-click the sophia-presentation theme.

All the slides now have the custom theme. Some of the slides require a little editing, but for the most part, you're done.

8 Press Command-W to close your presentation.

In this lesson, you've acquired a solid foundation of techniques for building presentations in Keynote.

Lesson Review

1. In addition to navigator view, what other slide view options are available in Keynote?
2. Describe three ways to create a new slide in Keynote.
3. Which Animate option works only between slides?
4. Describe how to change a presentation's theme.
5. In outline view, if a slide title is selected and you press Tab, what happens?

Answers

1. You can also view Keynote slides in slide only, light table, and outline views.
2. To create a new slide in Keynote, you can:

   Click the Add Slide icon in the toolbar.

   Choose Slide > New Slide (or press Command-Shift-N).

   Control-click a slide in navigator, light table, or outline view, and choose New Slide from the shortcut menu.

   In the outline view pane, pressing Shift creates new slides or bullet points dependent on the level of indentation. To remove a bullet indentation, press Shift-Tab twice to create a new slide.
3. Transitions are animations that work only between slides.
4. In the Document inspector, click Change Theme and select a theme from the chooser.
5. The slide becomes a bullet point of the preceding slide.

13

Lesson Files

APTS Pages Numbers Keynote > Lesson_13 > agata-presentation.key

APTS Pages Numbers Keynote > Lesson_13 > ju-jitsu-talk-ideas.key

APTS Pages Numbers Keynote > Lesson_13 > roll-pitch-yaw.key

APTS Pages Numbers Keynote > Lesson_13 > agata-folio

APTS Pages Numbers Keynote > Lesson_13 > Doxy.m4a

APTS Pages Numbers Keynote > Lesson_13 > Kote-Cucansetsu.mp4

Time

This lesson takes approximately 75 minutes to complete.

Goals

Manage animations

Understand the difference between build in, action, and build out

Change the build order and timing

Add and trim a movie

Add a soundtrack

Add audio to individual slides

Lesson **13**

Making Media-Rich Presentations

Keynote can play slideshows that combine animation with high-quality video and audio, which is one of its great strengths. You will discover this as you add builds and actions to objects and place video and audio media into Keynote presentations.

However, whenever you use special effects—such as Swoosh, Twirl, and Fireworks—ask yourself how these effects will add to your message. Sometimes a little razzle-dazzle is called for; other times you need to exercise a little conservative reserve.

Making a Slide Background

In earlier lessons, you learned how to add photos and video to Pages. You can use the same process to do so in Keynote. You can also add an image as a slide background. In this exercise, you'll modify the first slide of a presentation to include a photograph.

1 In Keynote, choose File > Open.

2 Navigate to APTS Pages Numbers Keynote > Lesson_13.

3 Double-click the **agata-presentation.key** document to open it.

4 With slide 1 selected, in the Format Inspector under Appearance, deselect the Body checkbox.

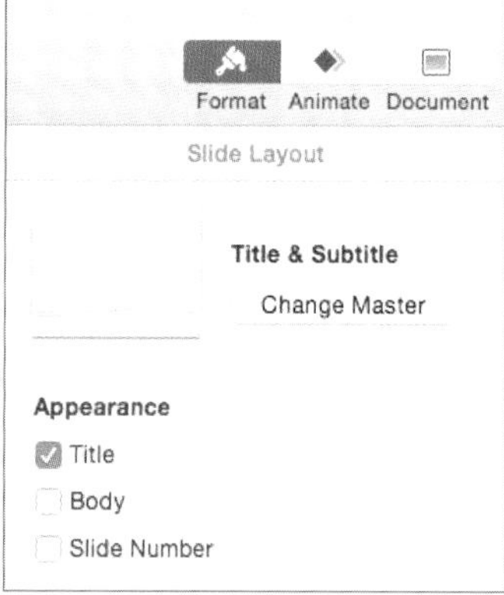

The placeholder text box under the photographer's logotype disappears.

NOTE ▸ By selecting the Slide Number checkbox, you can display slide numbers.

You are going to change the slide background, which can be a color, gradient, or an advanced gradient fill. In this instance, let's use the Image Fill option but swap the photo being used.

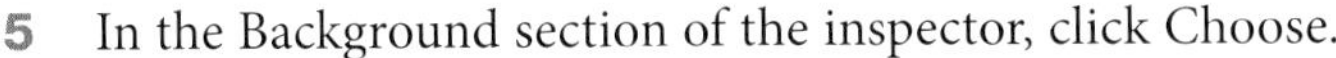

5 In the Background section of the inspector, click Choose.

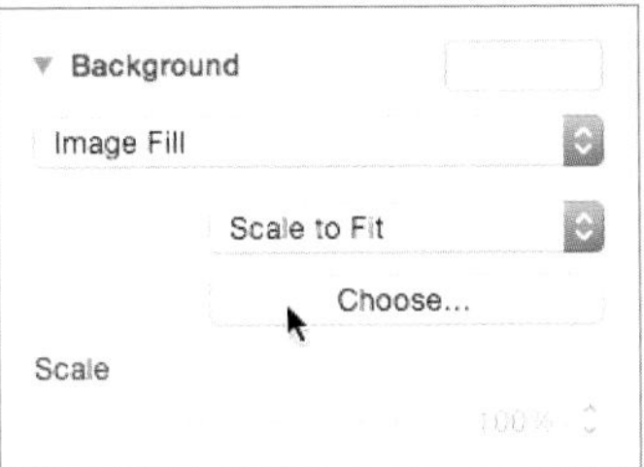

6 Navigate to APTS Pages Numbers Keynote > Lesson_13 > agata-folio, and double-click **mw-L13-cover.jpg** to replace the Image Fill background.

The photograph of the rose doesn't quite fill the slide, but you can fix that. You can choose how the image will appear on the slide.

NOTE ▶ An Advanced Image Fill allows you to select a Tint Color overlay for the image fill.

7 In the inspector, change the Background option to "Scale to Fill."

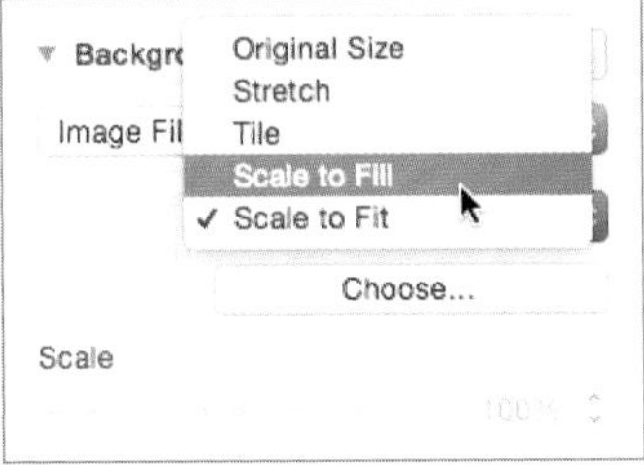

8 Choose File > Save to save a version of the presentation.

Updating a Paragraph Style

Keynote uses styles with graphic design features, as do many applications (including Pages and Numbers). All the slides in **agata-presentation.key** use the Title paragraph style. In this exercise, you'll modify an instance of this style on slide 1, and then update it to automatically change every instance of the style in the document.

1 On slide 1, triple-click the words "Agata Rhondo-Hayes Photography."

2 In the Text inspector, change the font size to 38 pt.

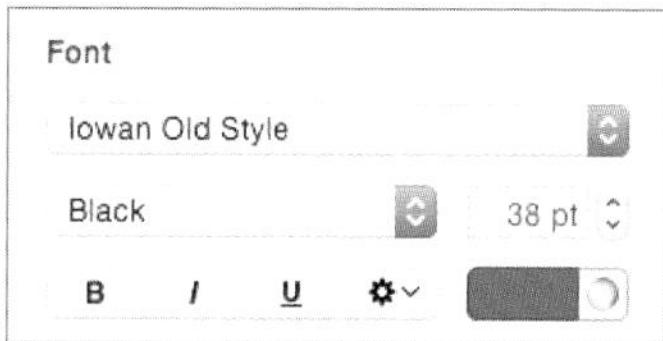

This size gives the text more presence. In the inspector, an Update button appears next to the Title style.

3 Click Update.

To the left of the slide is the slide navigator. Note the size of title text on the other slides. Because you may have missed the change in appearance due to the speedy update, let's undo and redo the paragraph style change for a before/after comparison.

4 Press Command-Z. The title style in the thumbnails reverts to its initial size.

5 Press Command-Shift-Z to redo the update, and watch the font size of the titles return to 38 pt.

You'll learn more about using styles in Lesson 14, when you'll develop a custom Keynote theme.

Creating New Slides by Dragging Files

The photography presentation you are working on needs plenty of images. In Lesson 2 you learned how to use the Media Browser to place photos, and you also directly imported a logo into a document. In Keynote, you have an additional method for importing images.

You can drag the contents of a folder containing photographs and movies from the Finder into Keynote. Doing so will automatically create a slide for each image and video.

1 In the Finder, navigate to APTS Pages Numbers Keynote > Lesson_13 > agata-folio.

2 Open the agata-folio folder in a separate Finder window.

Your window might look different from the one shown here due to your Finder preferences. You don't need to adjust your Finder, though.

3 Position the Finder so that its window and your Keynote document are both visible on your display.

4 In the Finder, press Command-A to select all the media files in the folder.

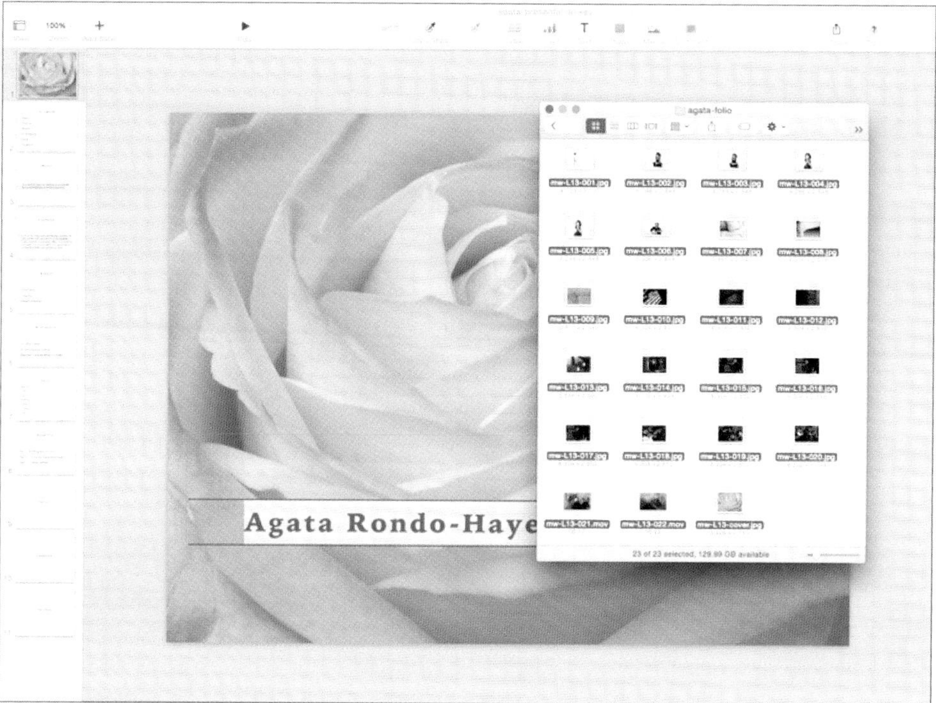

5 Drag the selected files to the Keynote slide navigator and place them after slide 11. Also make sure that the blue insertion line is in line with the far left edge of the slides.

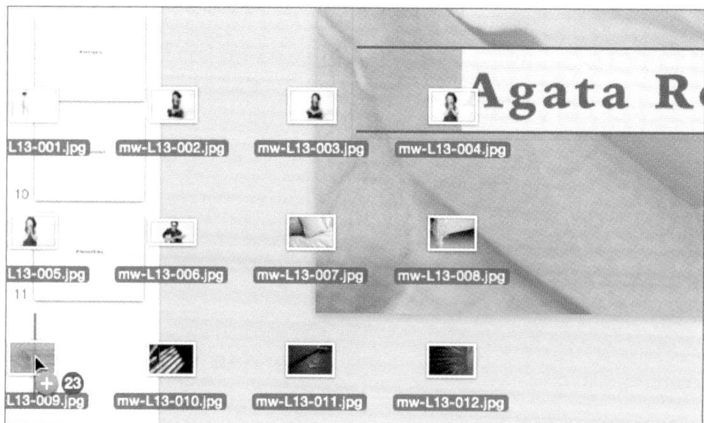

The media files populate the slide navigator, creating slides for each of the files. You can resize and reposition the images, just as you would any other image in Keynote.

6 Choose File > Save to save a version of the presentation.

Reordering Slides Using the Light Table

The photographer's presentation had its content in place, but the slides need rearranging into their proper order. To do this, you'll use the light table view. Slides 9, 10, and 11 are title slides for different types of photography: portraits, commercial, and multimedia slideshows. You'll group the images and videos under these headings to give you experience with the light table features.

1 In the slide navigator, select the thumbnails for slides 9, 10, and 11.

They are the title slides for portraits, commercial, and photofilms, respectively.

2 In the toolbar, click the View button, and from the pop-up menu, choose Light Table.

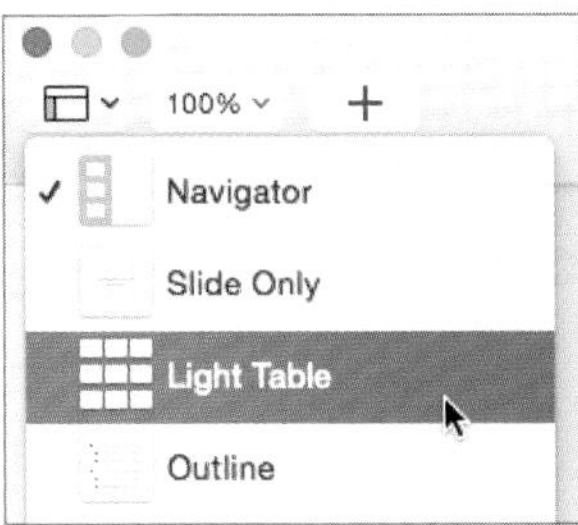

The slider at the bottom of the document window adjusts the size of the thumbnails. Dragging to the left reduces the thumbnail size; dragging to the right enlarges them.

3 Drag the thumbnail slider so that all 34 slides are visible.

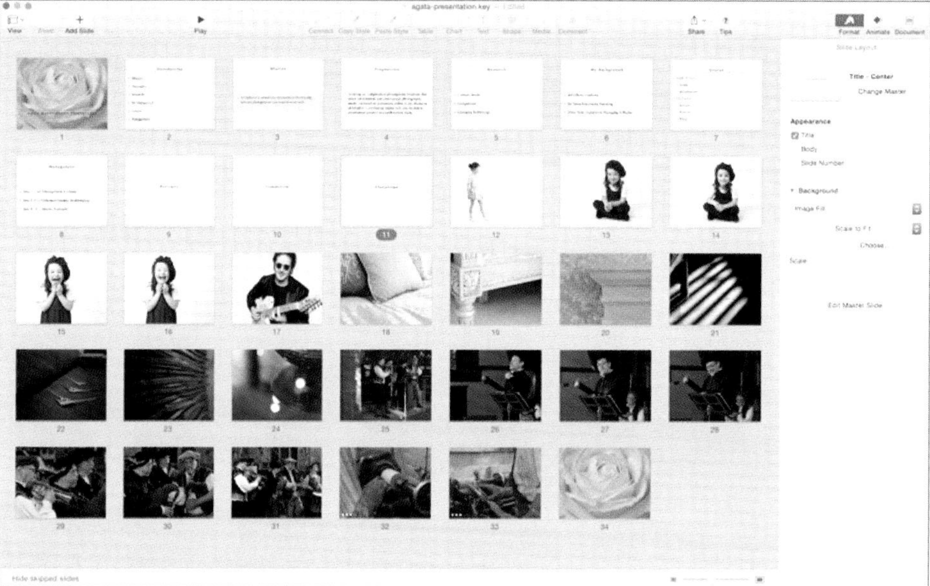

In the light table, you can create, duplicate, and delete slides just as you would in the slide navigator. Slide 34 is a duplicate image of the rose, so you can remove it.

4 Control-click slide 34, and from the shortcut menu, choose Delete.

Now you'll place the images into groups.

5 Click slide 12 and then Shift-click slide 17 to select slides 12 through 17.

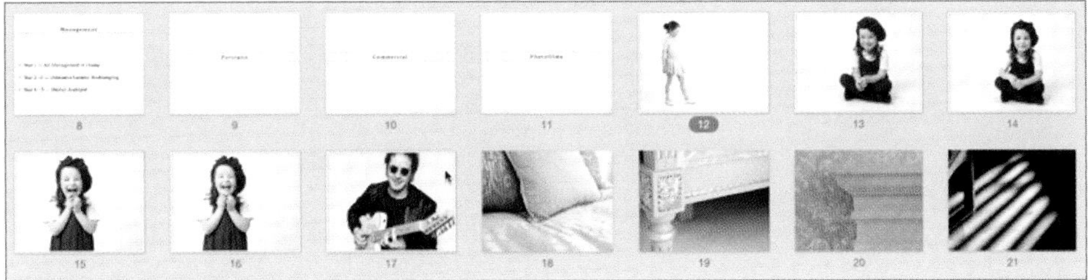

6 Drag the slides between slides 9 and 10.

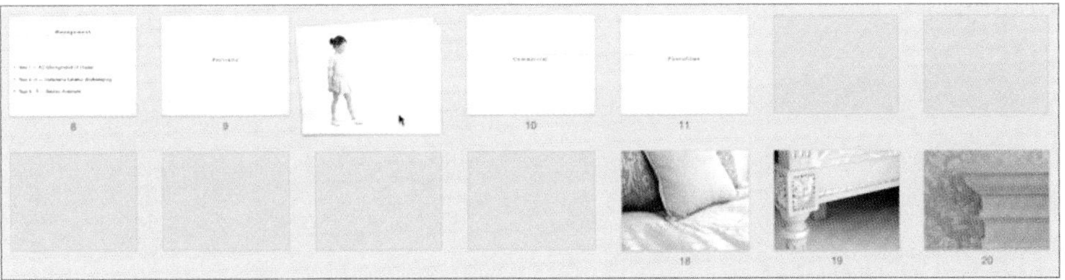

The portrait slides are in sequence. You'll now move the commercial slides.

7 Select slides 18 through 24. Drag the slides between slides 16 and 17.

Although you could continue to work in the light table, let's return to the slide navigator to create slide groups.

8 Choose View > Navigator.

9 Select slides 10 through 15, and press Tab.

The selected slides are indented and grouped with slide 9, which now displays a disclosure triangle. Grouping slides like this helps you manage large presentations.

10 Click the disclosure triangle on slide 9. The photo slides are hidden.

11 Click the disclosure triangle again to show the photo slides.

Leave the navigator open so that you're ready to add transitions in the next exercise.

Using Transitions to Create Moods

In Lesson 12, you learned how to add transitions and builds. Now you'll dig a little deeper into transition options to unlock their full creative potential. For this kind of presentation, a slow Dissolve transition would be ideal to create a contemplative mood.

1 Click anywhere in the slide navigator.

2 Press Command-A to select all the slides.

   Starting off by applying the same transition across an entire presentation is often a good idea.

3 In the toolbar, click Animate.

   Because whole slides are selected, transition effects appear.

4 Click "Add an Effect."

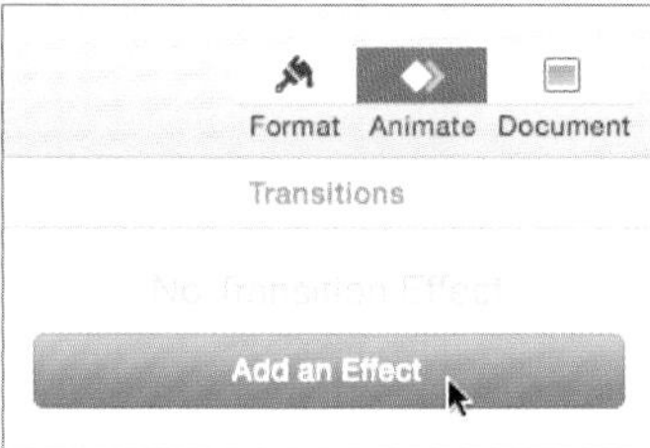

   A menu appears containing dozens of effects. As you hover the pointer over a transition, the option to preview the effect appears.

5 Click the Preview button of several transition effects to preview them.

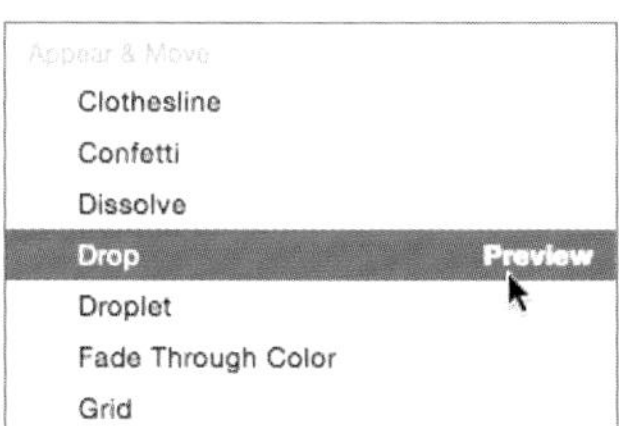

6 Select the Dissolve transition.

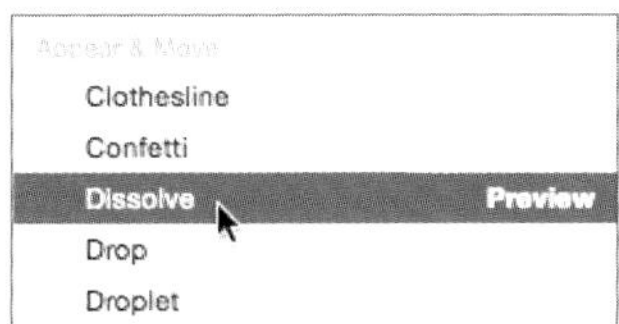

The transition is applied with a default timing of 1.5 seconds. Rather than click Preview in the inspector, let's play the entire slideshow to assess the pacing created so far.

7 In the navigator, click slide 1 then press Command-Option-P to play the slideshow. Press Spacebar to advance the slides.

After playing four or five slides, you'll see that the current timing works well for the text slides, but a slower transition for the photographs might be more effective.

8 Press Esc to stop the slideshow.

9 In the slide navigator, select slides 17 through 23.

10 In the inspector, change Duration to 3.5 seconds.

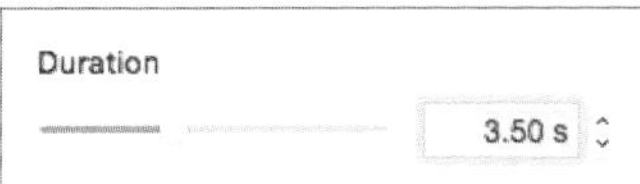

11 Press Command-Option-P to play the slideshow, and press Spacebar to advance the slides.

The slower transition is more calming, and it draws you in, which suits this set of images.

12 Keep pressing the Spacebar to play through the slides of the musicians.

They play at the default 1.5-second duration. The transition works, but there's room for improvement.

13 Press Esc to stop the slideshow.

14 In the slide navigator, select slides 25 through 27.

The three slides are a sequence of a musician speaking to an audience. The transition needs more pace.

15 In the inspector, click Change to see the menu of transitions, and choose Fade Through Color.

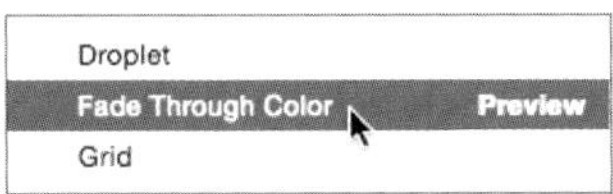

16 Change Duration to 0.3 seconds.

The default transition color is black, and with the fast transition this will look like blinking your eyes.

17 Press Command-Option-P to play the slideshow, and step through the three slides.

The transition now adds momentum to those slides. The Fade Through Color transition can be used on the studio portraits, too.

18 Press Esc to stop the slideshow.

19 In the slide navigator, select slides 10 through 15.

20 In the inspector, change the transition to Fade Through Color, and set the Duration to 0.2 seconds.

Rather than fade through black, you'll change the color to white to give the impression of a flash bulb firing.

21 In the inspector, change Color to white.

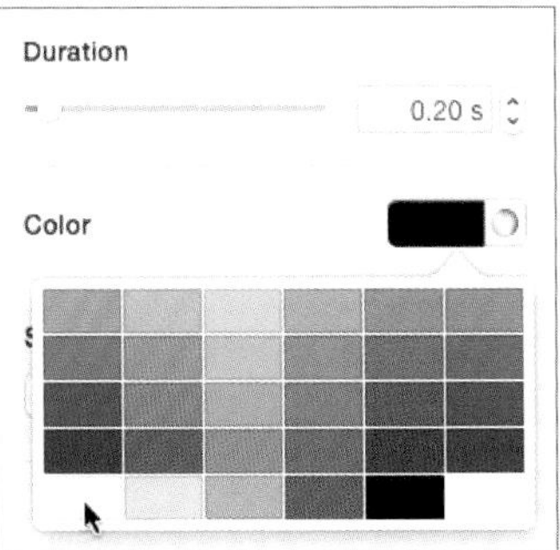

22 Press Command-Option-P to play the slideshow.

Et voilà! A studio flash effect is created. Changing the duration of a transition greatly affects its impact. Hours of time can now be spent experimenting with these fabulous effects.

23 Press Esc to end the slideshow.

Triggering Transitions

So far your transitions are triggered by clicking the mouse button or pressing the Spacebar. This is a good standard practice because you stay in control of your presentations. However, at times you may want a transition to trigger automatically. The **agata-presentation.key** document has two photofilms included. They are movie files you imported when dragging content. Let's take a look at them.

1 In the slide navigator, click slide 32.

2 Press Command-Option-P to play the slideshow.

3 Press Spacebar.

The movie, which is a series of still photographs, begins to play. The movie ends with a fade to black.

4 Press Spacebar again to advance to the next slide.

You need to press Spacebar once more to play the next movie, which isn't ideal. Removing the fade to black and getting the second movie to play seamlessly would be better.

5 Press Esc to stop the slideshow.

6 Navigate to slide 33, then click the movie on the main part of the Keynote window.

7 In the Movie tab of the Format inspector, deselect "Start movie on click."

The movie will now play automatically after the transition, but there's more work to be done.

8 Navigate to slide 32, and then click the movie on the main part of the Keynote window.

9 In the Movie inspector, drag the right Trim slider to the left and set it at 14.023 seconds.

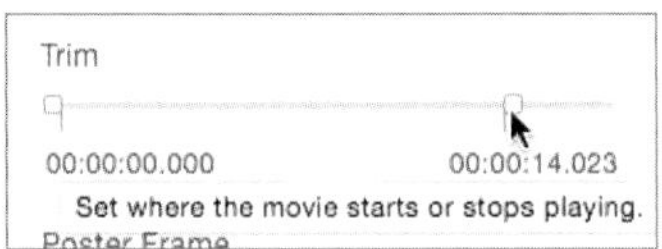

This locates the last frame before the movie starts to fade. You're almost done, but you'd still need to click to advance to the second movie slide. Here's how you can make the transition occur automatically.

10 In the slide navigator, click slide 32.

11 In the Animate inspector, change the Start Transition to Automatically.

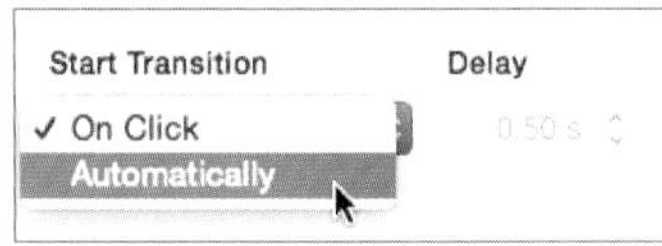

Now the two movies flow together, but slide 32 plays for only 0.5 seconds, which is the delay set in the inspector. In step 9 you set the movie to end at 14.023 seconds, which is the delay timing you want.

12 Click the movie on slide 32. In the Trim section of the inspector, triple-click the ending time value.

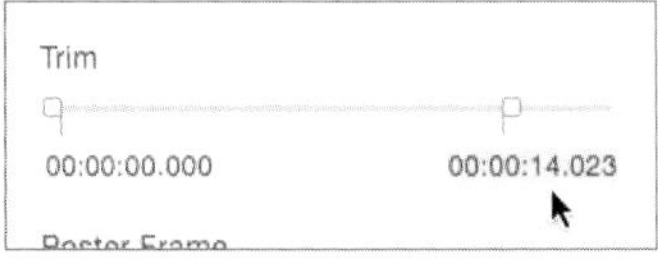

13 Press Command-C to copy the value to the clipboard.

14 In the slide navigator, click slide 32.

15 In the Animate inspector, triple-click the Delay field.

16 Press Command-V to paste the time value from the clipboard into the Delay field.

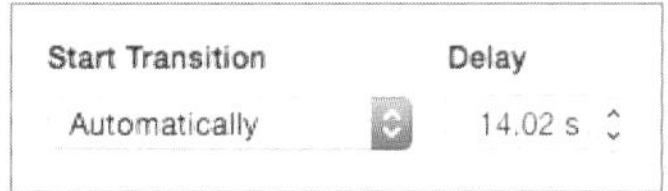

17 Press Enter.

18 Press Command-Option-P to play the slideshow, and press Spacebar.

The movie won't start until you press Spacebar. Once the movie is playing, the delay starts its countdown, and the advance to slide 33 happens automatically.

19 Press Esc to end the slideshow.

20 Choose File > Save, to save a version of the presentation.

Adding an Audio Soundtrack

You can add sound files to a presentation just as any other media such as photos or video. Like with video, you set it to play automatically or on a mouse click. However, you can also include it as a soundtrack that plays along with a slideshow.

Keynote can access your iTunes library, but including commercially available music in a public presentation is likely to be in breach of copyright law. Therefore, in this exercise, the soundtrack you'll use is a rough demo of a guitar improvisation recorded using GarageBand.

First, let's look at how to access a soundtrack in your iTunes library.

1 With the **agata-presentation.key** document open, in the toolbar, click the Document button.

2 In the Document inspector, click the Audio tab.

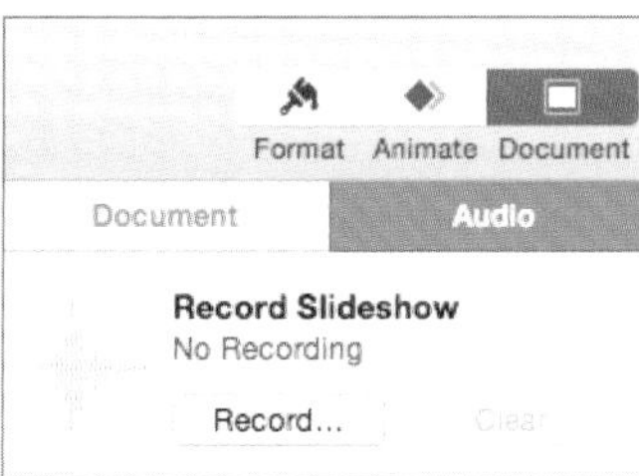

You'll see an option to record your slideshow; this feature is discussed in Lesson 15.

In the Audio inspector, you'll find a button that lets you choose an audio file.

3 Click the Add Audio button.

A pop-up menu appears showing your iTunes library. If you were to click one of the tracks listed, it would become your presentation soundtrack.

4 Click away from the pop-up menu to close it without choosing an audio clip.

Instead of using this method to add a soundtrack, you'll drag an audio clip from the Finder into your presentation.

5 Go to the Finder, and navigate to APTS Pages Numbers Keynote > Lesson_13.

6 Open the Lesson_13 folder in a separate Finder window. Position the window so that it and your Keynote document are both visible.

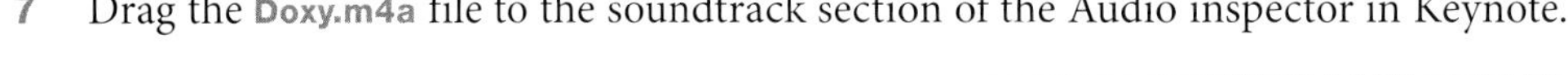

7 Drag the **Doxy.m4a** file to the soundtrack section of the Audio inspector in Keynote.

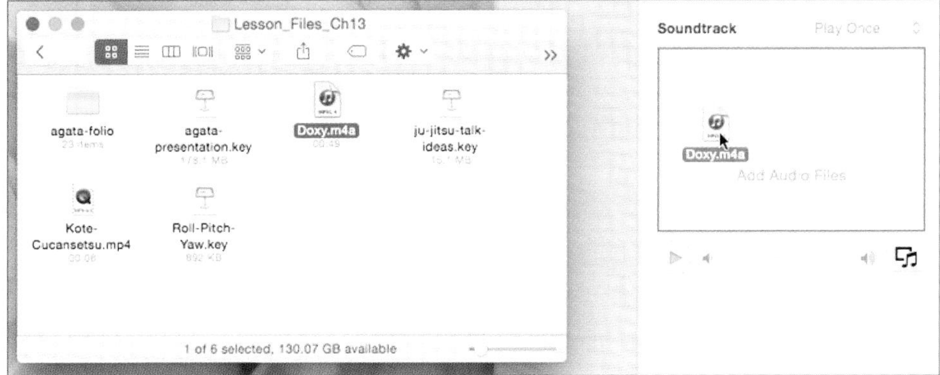

The audio clip is now in place, but it's only 49 seconds long so you'll need to loop it.

8 In the Soundtrack options, from the pop-up menu, choose Loop.

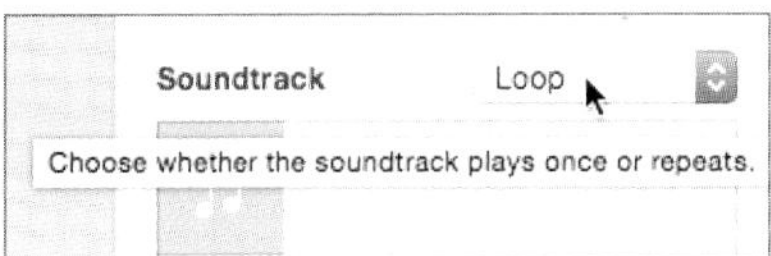

The music works best with the picture slides.

9 In the slide navigator, click slide 10.

10 Press Command-Option-P to play the slideshow.

Advance through the slideshow, playing several slides.

11 Press Esc to stop the slideshow.

You've explored ways to add a little audiovisual mood to your presentations. Of course, the choice of soundtrack will play a big part in that, as will the transitions you choose.

You can add several soundtracks to a Keynote presentation. If you want to remove a soundtrack, select it in the inspector and press Backspace to delete it.

12 Close the **agata-presentation.key** document.

Controlling a Presentation with Builds

Using builds is a great way to control your presentation, such as the Typewriter build you used on bullet points to stop your audience from reading ahead on your slides (Lesson 12). In this exercise, you'll add builds to pace a slide about grading in Ju-Jitsu.

1 In Keynote, choose File > Open.

2 Navigate to APTS Pages Numbers Keynote > Lesson_13.

3 Double-click the **ju-jitsu-talk-ideas.key** document.

4 With slide 7 selected, press Command-Option-P to play the slideshow.

5 Press Spacebar to advance. You jump immediately to slide 8.

6 Press Esc to stop the slideshow.

The idea here is to get each grade to reveal itself with a mouse click. So when the presenter has spoken about a topic, he can manually reveal the next topic.

You've learned about Build In, now you'll apply a Build Out.

7 On slide 7, drag a selection rectangle around the ten colored boxes (representing each of the Ju-Jitsu belts) partially hidden under the brown rectangles.

Take care not to select the brown rectangles in front of them.

You don't want to accidentally change these, so you'll lock them.

8 Choose Arrange > Lock. The colored boxes are locked and cannot be changed.

9 Drag a selection rectangle around the brown rectangles.

As you drag, you need only to touch part of an object to select it.

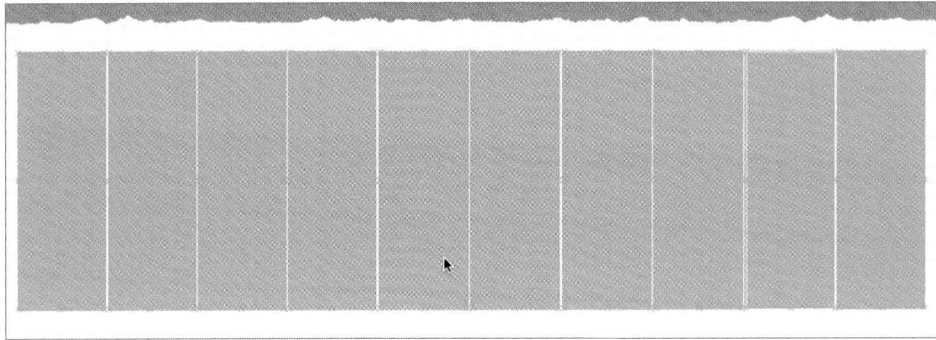

10 Drag the selected brown rectangles upward to cover the colored ones.

You are now ready to apply a build. The order in which you apply a build determines the order in which the animation will play.

11 Press Command-Shift-A to deselect all objects.

12 Click the first brown rectangle on the left to select it.

13 In the Animate inspector, click the Build Out tab.

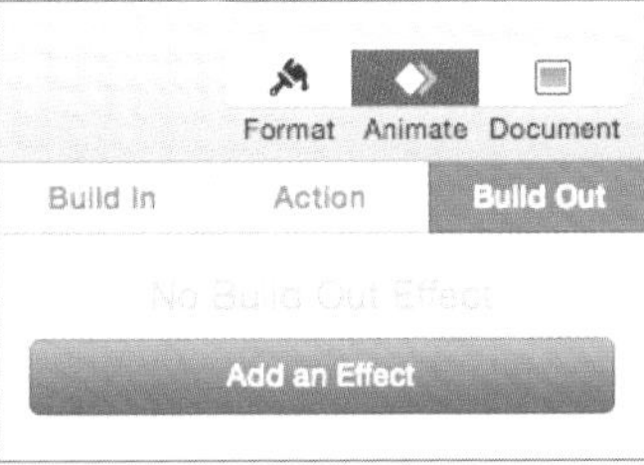

14 Click "Add an Effect," and from the menu, choose Wipe.

The default settings of a wipe from the left are ideal, and the duration is good, too.

NOTE ▶ Each build has its own set of parameters. Some will offer control over duration only. Others offer you lots of animation options.

To apply this build to the other rectangles, you'll copy and paste the animation. Whoop, whoop for this time-saver!

15 With the first rectangle selected, choose Format > Copy Animation.

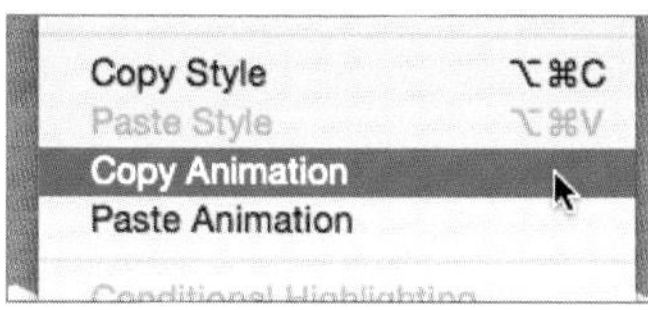

16 Select the second rectangle, and choose Format > Paste Animation.

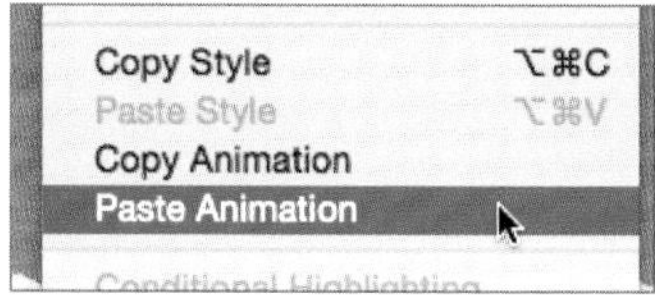

17 Repeat the selection and paste animation on the remaining rectangles.

Be sure to work left to right because the order in which you paste the animation determines the order in which the builds will play. When you're done you can preview your work.

18 Press Command-Option-P to play the slideshow from slide 7. Advance through the builds.

Imagine Sensei Takao talking about each grade using the builds to reveal the next belt when he's ready. Extend that thought to the dozens of other situations when you can use builds to control your presentations.

19 Press Esc to quit the slideshow.

20 Click the third brown rectangle. In the inspector, note its build order.

It should be 3. You can use the Order pop-up menu to change the sequence of builds. You'll work with build order at the end of this lesson.

Layering Objects with Master Slides

Master slides can contain many objects. As a consequence, they become layered, even if the objects don't overlap. As you've discovered, the layer order can be changed by moving objects forward or backward. When you place objects on a slide created from a master that has layers, you may need to perform the following steps to overcome layering problems.

Here's an example of a problem.

1 Go to slide 4 of the **ju-jitsu-talk-ideas.key** document.

It contains a movie and a partially obscured logo. You'll now add a movie to slide 6 and fix the layering problems.

2 In the slide navigator, select slide 6.

3 Choose Insert > Choose, and navigate to APTS Pages Numbers Keynote > Lesson_13 > **Kote-Cucansetsu.mp4**. Double-click the file to place the video.

A warning might appear cautioning you that this movie may not play on an iPad or iPhone. (Lesson 17 covers this easy-to-fix problem.) For now, if it has appeared, ignore it.

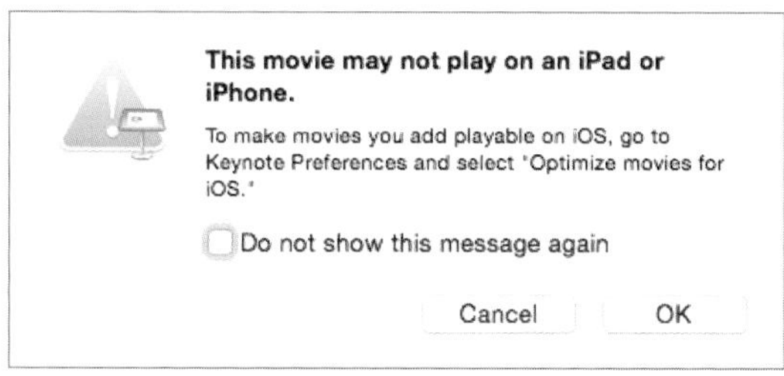

4 Click OK to close the warning. Position the movie file so that it touches the top and sides of the slide.

The slide layout should match slide 4.

5 In the slide navigator, click the thumbnail for slide 6, so that you can access the necessary options in the inspector.

6 In the Format inspector, click Edit Master Slide.

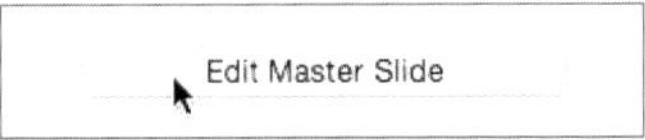

The inspector is context aware so it now shows options for the slide master.

7 In the inspector, select the "Allow objects on slide to layer with master" checkbox.

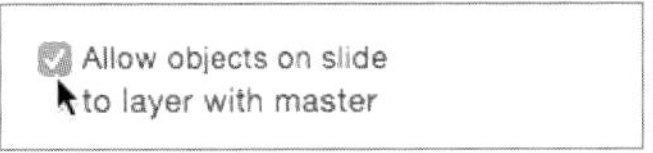

8 At the bottom of the slide window, click Done to close the slide master.

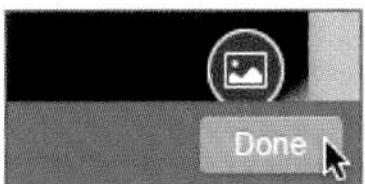

Objects on the slide can now layer with master slide objects, enabling you to change the layer order of the movie.

9 Click the movie on slide 6. In the Arrange tab of the Format inspector, click the Backward button.

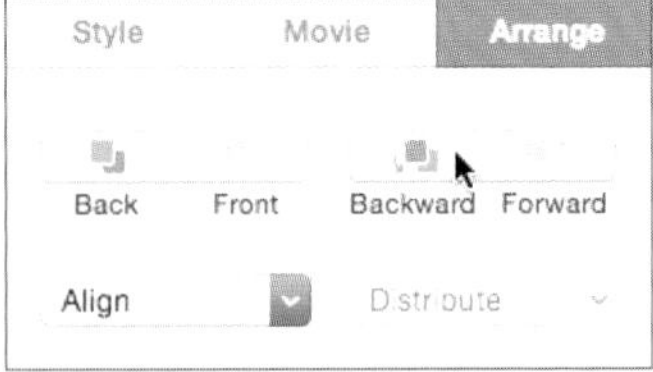

The movie now sits behind the logo. You can repeat the arrange step for the movie on slide 4 if you wish.

10 Close the **ju-jitsu-talk-ideas.key** presentation.

Building Animations Using Actions

The options for actions allow you to move objects while rotating and scaling them. You can also make objects appear and disappear. In this exercise, you'll work with a live project related to aeronautical engineering. The artwork was generated in Adobe Illustrator, which has a function called Adobe Illustrator on the Clipboard (AICB). This feature allows you to simply copy artwork from Illustrator and paste it directly into Keynote.

Previewing an Emphasis Action

Keynote has two types of action: Basic and Emphasis. You'll work with the basic options later, but here you'll preview an Emphasis effect.

1 In Keynote, choose File > Open.

2 Navigate to APTS Pages Numbers Keynote > Lesson_13.

3 Double-click the **roll-pitch-yaw.key** document.

4 On slide 1, click the aircraft silhouette.

5 In the toolbar, click Animate, and then click the Action tab.

6 Click the "Add an Effect" button.

7 Preview the Jiggle effect.

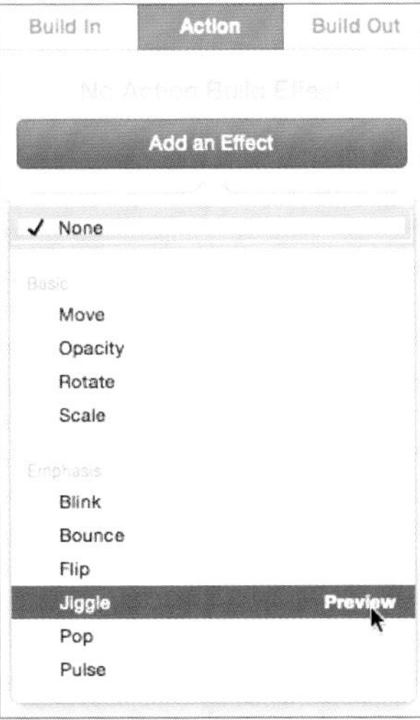

The aircraft looks like it's going to shake itself apart. Emphasis effects can draw attention to objects. Feel free to preview other emphasis effects.

8 From the Basic effects, select Rotate.

The rotate effect is ideal for illustrating how aircraft roll. In the next exercise, you'll customize this animation.

Creating Custom Animations

One of the aims of this live project is to explain the three basic axes of aircraft movement: roll, pitch, and yaw.

You'll modify the Rotate action to make the aircraft roll clockwise, then counterclockwise, and then return to center. In doing this you'll see how actions can be built up to create complex animated sequences.

1 In the Animate inspector, set the action as follows:

Duration: 1.5 seconds

Direction: Clockwise

Angle: 40°

Acceleration: Ease Both

The aircraft will roll clockwise to 40 degrees, and the acceleration easing will make the animation more realistic because the motion will accelerate and decelerate.

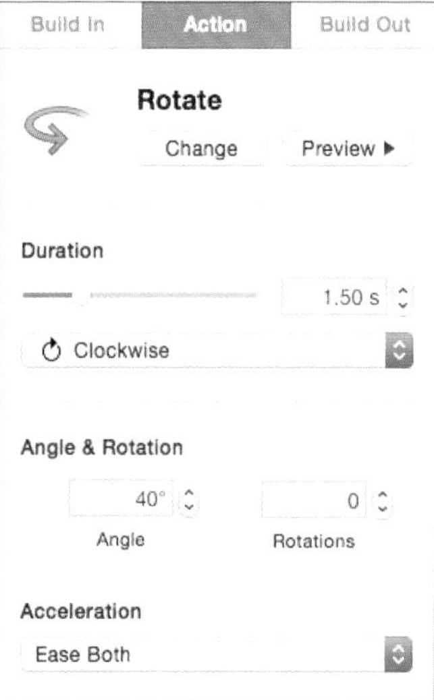

Now you'll roll the aircraft counterclockwise.

2 In the inspector, click the Add Action button. Choose Rotate.

3 In the Animate inspector, set the second action as follows:

Duration: 3.0 seconds

Direction: Counterclockwise

Angle: 80°

Acceleration: Ease Both

4 Click the Preview button.

The aircraft rolls counterclockwise back to the equivalent angle. Now you'll roll the aircraft back to center.

5 In the inspector, click the Add Action button. Choose Rotate.

6 In the Animate inspector, set the third action as follows:

Duration: 1.5 seconds

Direction: Clockwise

Angle: 40°

Acceleration: Ease Both

If you were to play the slideshow now, you'd have to click three times to get each action to play. To complete this illustration of roll, you'll modify the actions to play automatically.

7 In the Animate inspector, click the Build Order button.

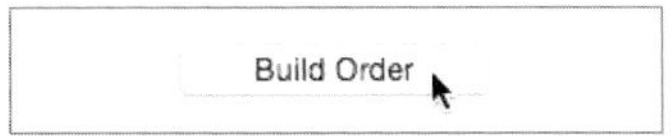

The Build Order window opens.

8 Click the second build.

This is the second action you applied. Currently, Start is set to On Click.

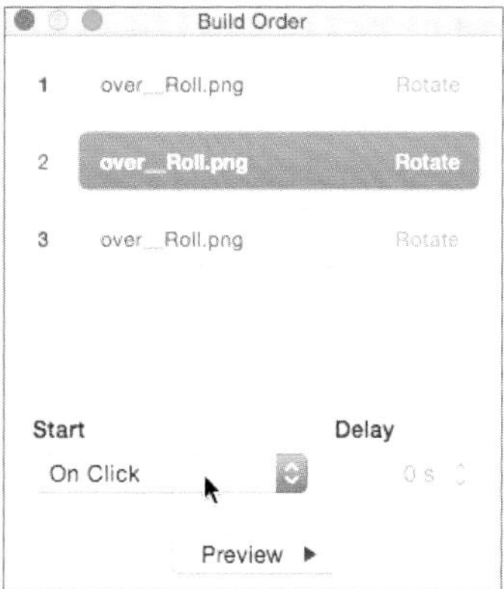

9 In the Start pop-up menu, choose After Build 1.

10 Click the third build. Change its Start to After Build 2.

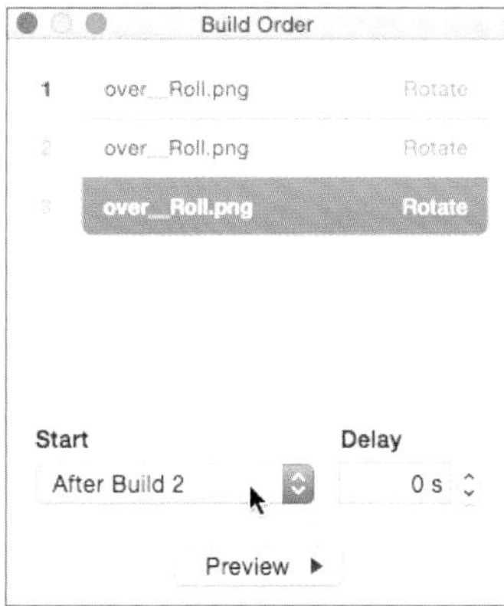

To play the animation, you will now need only a single click.

11 Press Command-Option-P to play the slideshow from slide 1. Press the Spacebar once to play the animation.

12 Press Esc to stop the slideshow.

Drawing Animation Paths

In the simplest form, you move objects in Keynote along a straight line between a start point and an end point. In this exercise, you'll take things a step further by animating along a curved line and add a Rotate action to your animation.

To preview the end result, a complete animation was included on slide 3.

1 Select slide 3. Press Command-Option-P to play the slideshow. Press the Spacebar once to play the animation.

2 Press Esc to stop the slideshow.

3 On slide 2, select the aircraft silhouette.

4 In the Action tab of the Animate inspector, click "Add an Effect."

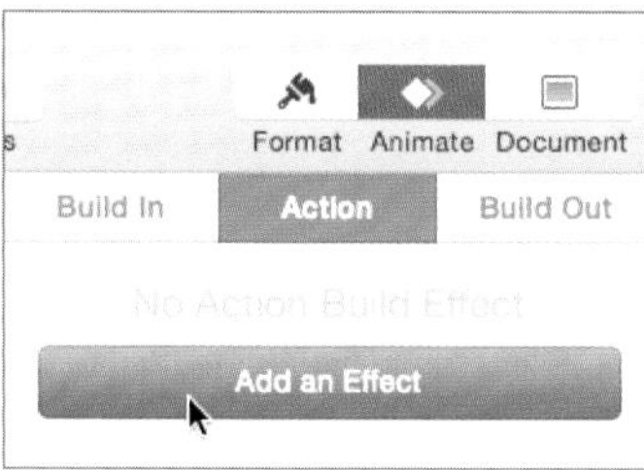

5 Choose Move.

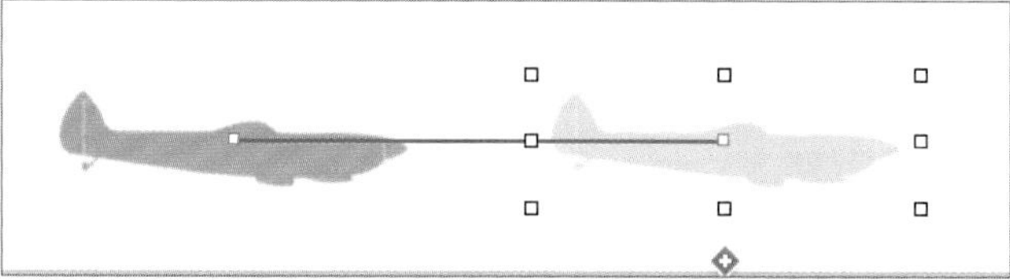

A simple straight-line move appears. You'll reposition the end point of the move to the top right of the slide.

6 Drag the ghost image of the aircraft to the upper right of the slide.

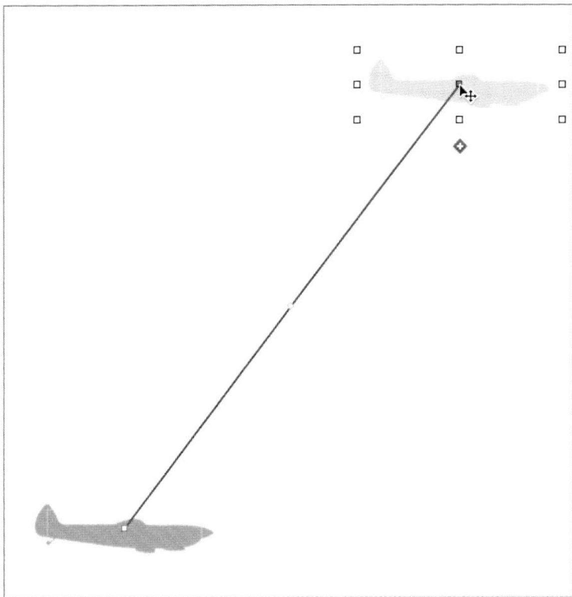

The motion is still along a straight line.

7 Drag the red line. It bends. Try dragging the line into a curve.

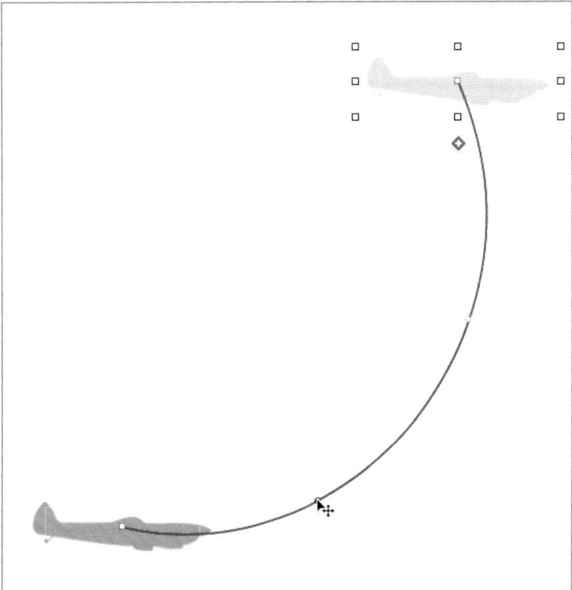

NOTE ▶ The move path has two points: a start and an end. You can Option-click the line to add anchor points, although you don't need any additional points at the moment. Control-clicking anchor points opens a shortcut menu for extra control of the path, which you can experiment with later.

8 In the inspector, change the Duration of the action to 2.5 s.

If you preview the move, the animation isn't very convincing because the aircraft needs to pitch up. You'll add a Rotate action to do this.

9 In the inspector, click Add Action, and choose Rotate.

10 Change the Rotate settings to:

Duration: 2.5 seconds (to match the move duration)

Direction: Counterclockwise

Angle: This depends on your curve. The rotation needs to align with the direction of the move path. In the illustration, the angle was set to 111°.

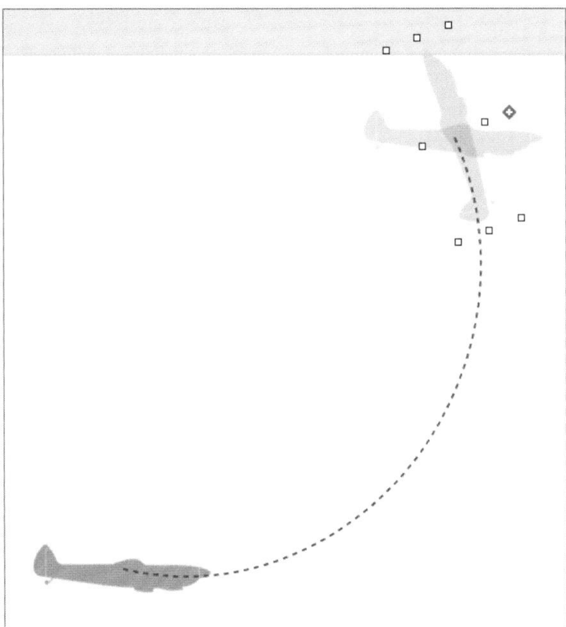

Now you have two actions that need to play together.

11 In the inspector, click Build Order.

12 In the window, click the second build, and change its Start to With Build 1.

13 Press Command-Option-P to play the slideshow from slide 2. Press the Spacebar once to play the animation.

14 Press Esc to stop the slideshow.

OK, it's not likely to win any awards, but by using the actions of move, opacity, rotate, and scale, great things can be achieved.

15 Drag the end point of the action to reposition the aircraft on the slide.

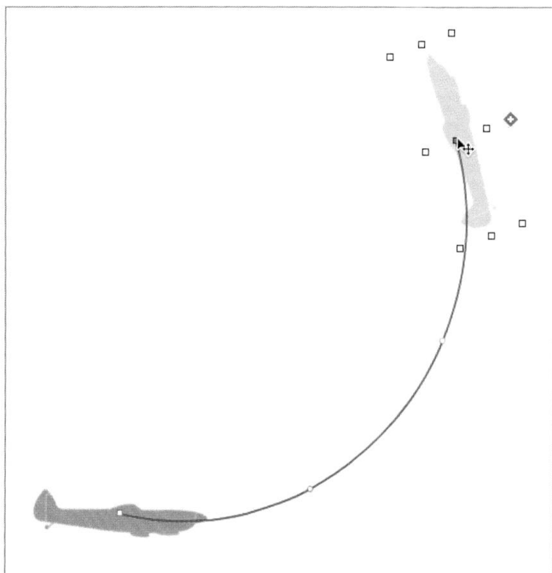

You can continue to adjust the action options at any time. Slides 4, 5, and 6 demonstrate how the simple rotate action can be used to illustrate a set of principles.

16 Close the **roll-pitch-yaw.key** presentation.

Lesson Review

1. Describe a method for dragging media files to create new slides.
2. How can you preview a transition effect without applying it to a slide?
3. If your soundtrack is too short for the expected presentation time, what option might you use to resolve the problem?
4. How do you avoid selecting objects accidentally?
5. Describe how to change a build order.

Answers

1. To create new slides from dragged media files, open a Finder window containing the media files. Select the media files and drag them to the slide navigator in Keynote. In addition you can drag media files to Keynote when it's in light table view.
2. The menu listing the transitions displays a preview option when you position the pointer over the transitions. Click the Preview button to see that transition without applying it to the slide. The menu stays open allowing you to preview other transition effects.
3. If a soundtrack is too short for the expected presentation time, set it to Loop in the Audio inspector.
4. Select them, and choose Arrange > Lock.
5. Change build orders in the Animation inspector by setting the Order pop-up menu. In addition, when the Build Order window is open, you can drag the builds up and down in the list of builds to change their order.

14

Lesson Files

APTS Pages Numbers Keynote > Lesson_14 > ju-jitsu-presentation-theme.key

APTS Pages Numbers Keynote > Lesson_14 > ju-jitsu-logo.pdf

Time

This lesson takes approximately 60 minutes to complete.

Goals

Modify master slides

Change paragraph styles

Understand which design elements are and are not saved in a theme

Learn about default OS X and iOS fonts

Create chart styles using custom colors

Make placeholder items

Save and share themes

Lesson **14**

Developing a Custom Theme

Pages and Numbers documents can be for your eyes only, but Keynote presentations are most often created for others to see.

In this lesson, you'll create a custom theme and learn which elements are saved in the theme and which are not. If you've worked through the Pages and Numbers lessons, the use of placeholders and paragraph styles will be review, but this lesson's exercises will show you how to use these time-saving features in a presentation design context.

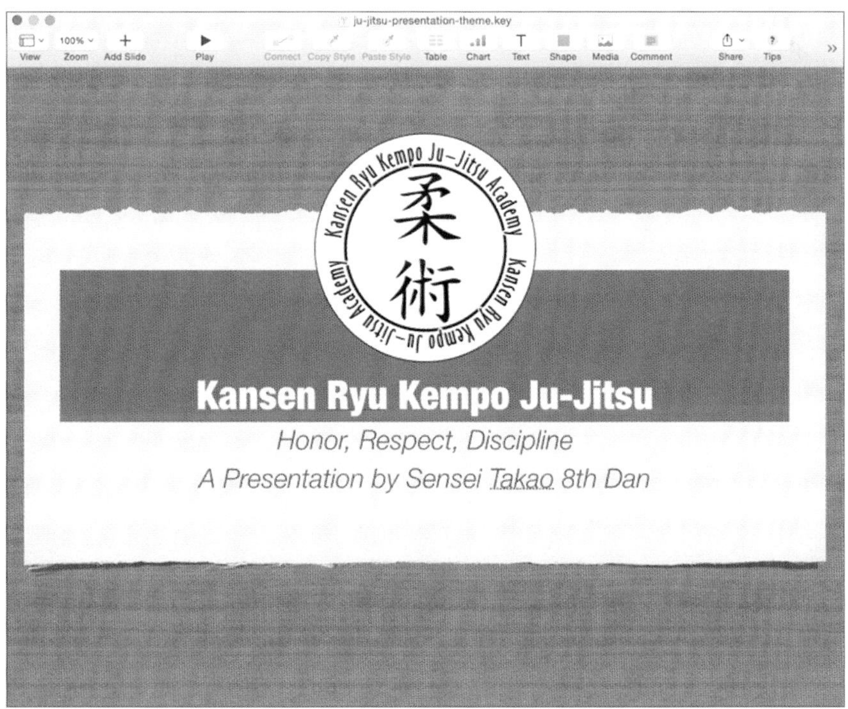

Selecting Master Slides

Keynote always creates new documents from a template (just like in Pages and Numbers), but in Keynote they're known as themes. Each theme contains several master slides, which may contain a title and subtitle, title and bullet, a set of media placeholders, or nothing at all (a blank slide). In this exercise, you'll open a presentation that uses the Kyoto theme and then modify the master slides to make a custom theme for the Ju-Jitsu club.

1 In Keynote, choose File > New.

2 In the Standard tab of the Theme Chooser, double-click the Kyoto theme to create a document using that theme.

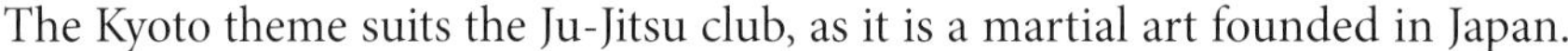

The Kyoto theme suits the Ju-Jitsu club, as it is a martial art founded in Japan.

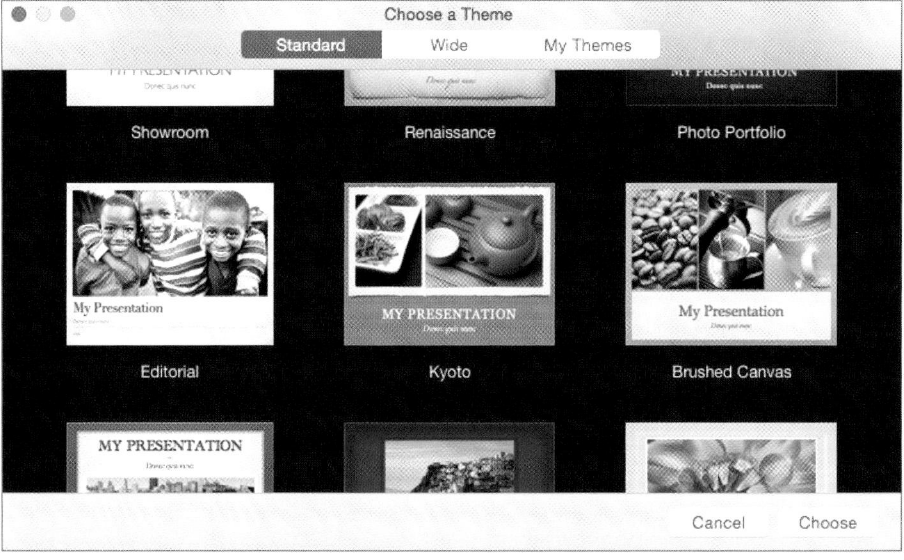

3 Choose File > Save. Name the presentation *ju-jitsu-theme-design.key*, and then save it to your desktop.

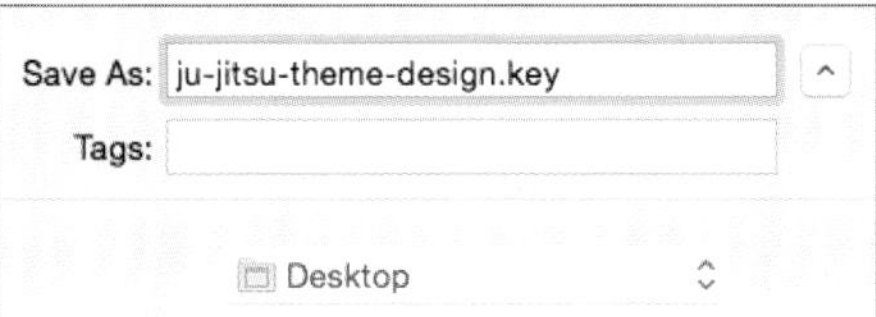

You'll modify the master slides of this presentation before saving your modifications as a custom theme.

4 In the toolbar, click the View icon, and from the pop-up menu, choose Edit Master Slides.

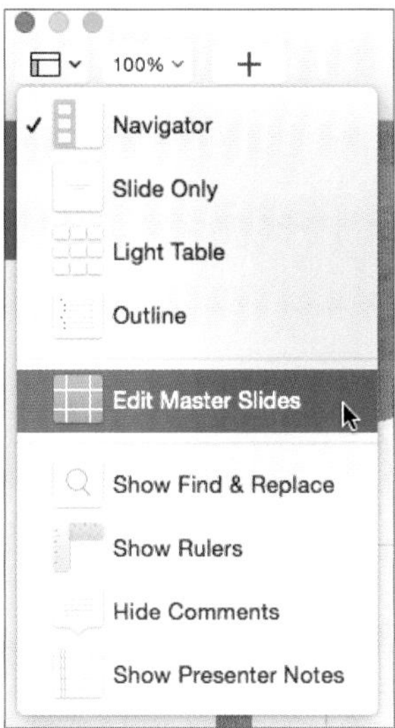

Often a theme will contain more master slides than you'll need, so deleting the redundant masters is a good idea.

5 In the slide navigator, click the thumbnail for the Title - Center master. Press Delete to delete it.

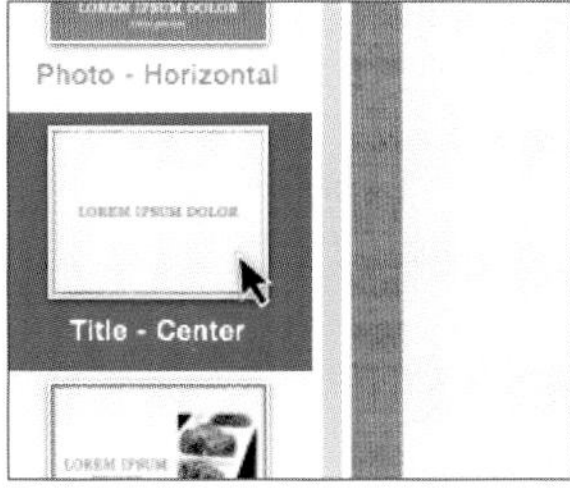

6 Using the process described in step 5, delete the following masters:

- Photo - Vertical
- Title, Bullets & Photo
- Photo - 3 Up

With the unneeded master slides removed, you can concentrate on modifying only those slides you need.

7 Choose File > Save.

Updating Paragraph Styles

Themes use placeholders for text and images. By modifying and updating the theme's placeholder styles, you'll complete the first steps toward making a custom theme.

1 In the slide navigator, click the first master slide, Title & Subtitle.

2 On the slide, select the text box containing the words "Title Text."

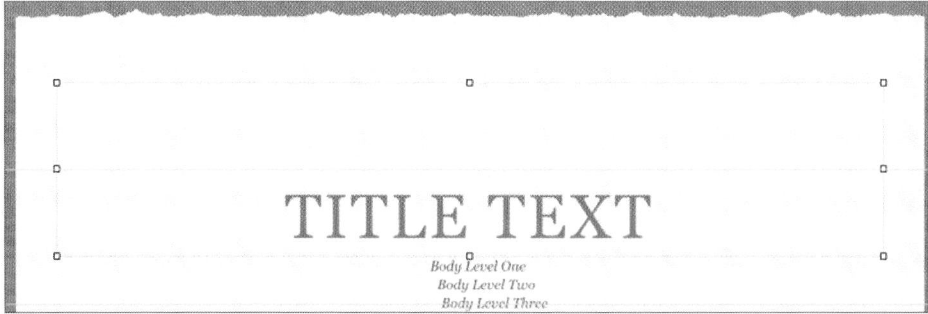

To make the title stand out, you'll apply a shape style.

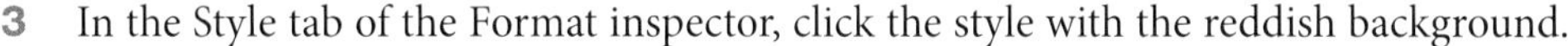

3 In the Style tab of the Format inspector, click the style with the reddish background.

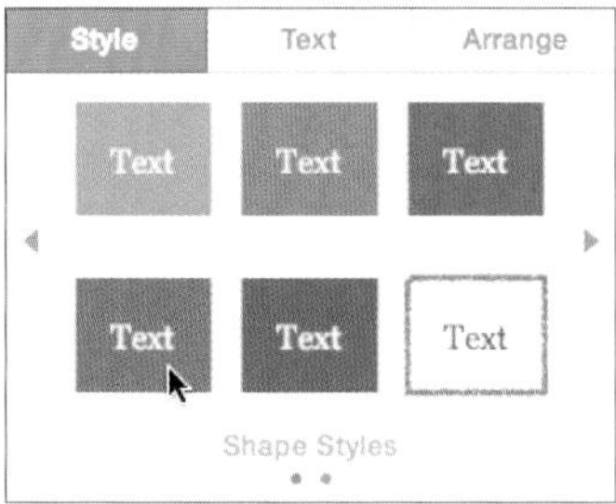

4 On the slide, double-click the text, "Title Text."

In the Text tab of the Format inspector, you'll see that this text has the Label paragraph style applied. Setting the text box's shape style changed not only the box's color but also the box's text style from Title Alt to Label. Let's return the text style to Title Alt.

5 In the Text tab, select the paragraph style. In the menu that appears, choose Title Alt.

Now let's change the typeface and font size and then update this paragraph style.

6 In the Text tab, change the Font to Helvetica Neue, Condensed Black, 48 pt.

This type color doesn't work well on the reddish background, so you can change it.

7 In the inspector, click the color wheel to open the Colors window.

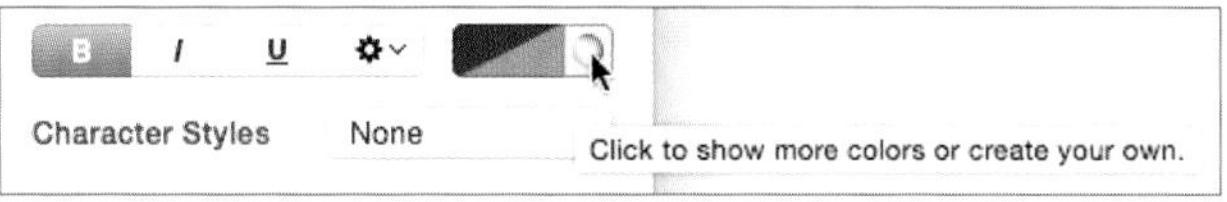

8 In the Colors window, click the eyedropper. Move the sampler over the cream paper texture on the slide and click to sample the color.

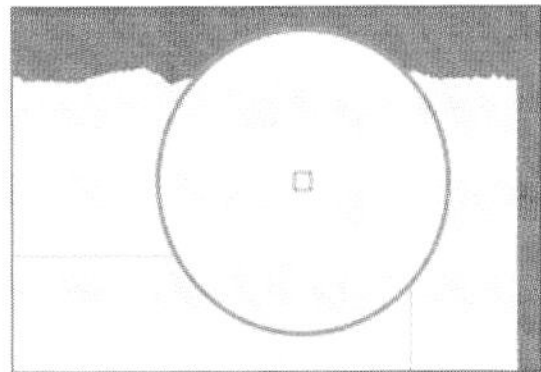

This customized text suits the design.

9 In the inspector, click Update to save your changes to the Title Alt style.

Every instance of the Title Alt style is updated, regardless of the master slide it appears on. The master slides use several paragraph styles, which would need updating in a live project. Let's update just two more.

The Photo - Horizontal, Title - Top, and Title & Bullets master slides all use the Title paragraph style.

10 On the Title & Bullets master slide, double-click the placeholder containing the words "Title Text."

11 In the inspector, change the Font to Helvetica Neue, Condensed Black, 64 pt.

12 In the inspector, click Update to save the style changes.

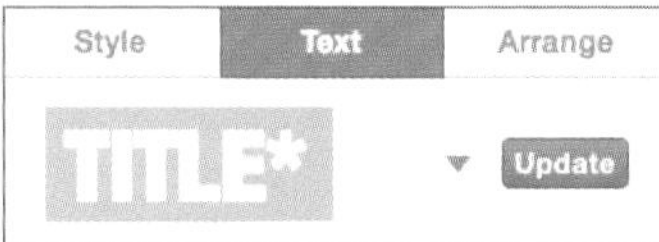

Keynote presentations often include slides with bullets. To modify those bullets, you need to edit the Body paragraph styles and change the bullet options.

13 On the Title & Bullets master slide, double-click the placeholder containing the first bullet level, Body Level One.

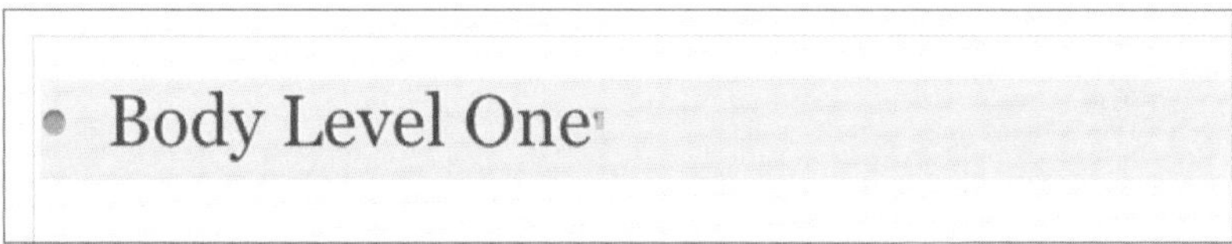

14 In the Text inspector, change the Font to Helvetica Neue, Thin, 36 pt.

The Text inspector has two tabs: Style and Layout.

15 Click the Layout tab.

The Layout tab has a "Shrink text to fit" option (selected by default), which automatically shrinks text to fit its text box. In the case of the bulleted text, you could keep adding bullet points and the text would be scaled smaller and smaller to accommodate the change.

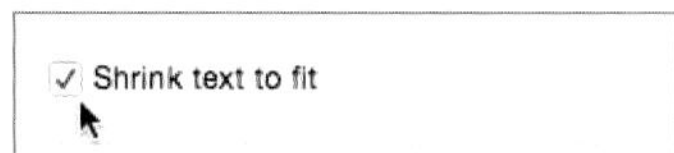

16 Deselect "Shrink text to fit."

If the bullets don't fit on a single slide, you could add them to a second or third slide. This option ensures a consistent font size.

17 In the inspector, click Update.

The text style is changed, but the bullet points need some attention.

18 In the Text inspector, click the Style tab.

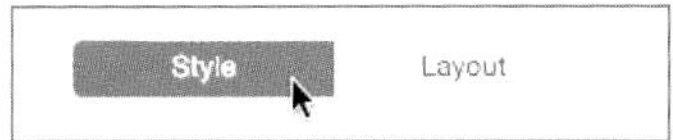

The inspector shows the options for Bullets & Lists.

19 In Bullets & Lists, click the Current Image pop-up menu, scroll to the reddish square, and select it.

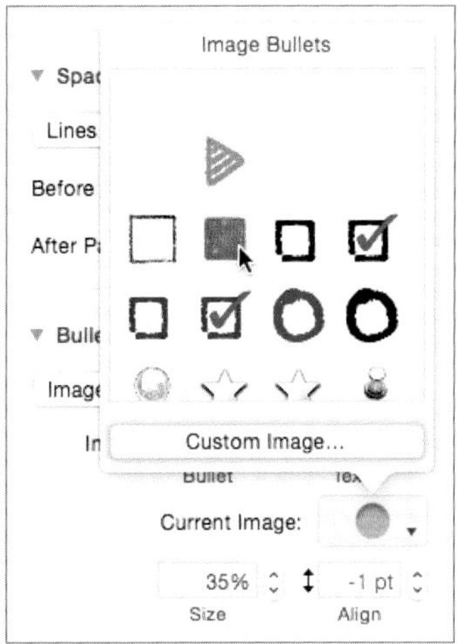

TIP The Image Bullets menu has a Custom Image button, which allows you to navigate to any custom bullet images you have available.

The reddish bullet looks too small. If you enlarge it, however, you'll also need to adjust the text indent values to maintain space between the bullet and the text.

20 In Bullets & Lists, change the Size field to 65%, and set the Indent Text field to 45 pt.

The bullet style now needs updating to save the changes you've made.

21 From the Bullets & Lists style pop-up menu, click Update, which appears adjacent to Image.

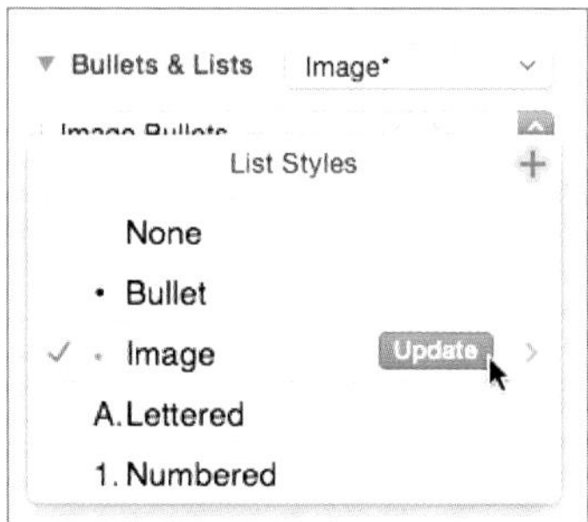

Only the first level of text bullets changes. Should you want to change all the levels of bullets simultaneously, select them all before adjusting their settings in the inspector.

You could continue to modify the existing text styles in the presentation, but for now we'll move on. An important final point to remember is that you've been updating styles rather than creating new ones. Because the master slides already have styles in place, updating existing styles is quicker than creating new styles, which would have to be placed anew on the masters.

Using System Fonts

Typefaces are classed as software and, therefore, are copyright protected. Fonts are essential items that are not included in a Keynote document, due to those copyrights. If you create a presentation in Keynote that uses nonstandard fonts, the slideshow will play correctly on the originating Mac but not on a Mac or an iOS device that doesn't have those fonts installed. In those cases, Keynote will substitute for the missing fonts, which can cause text reflow problems and alter your original design. Although additional fonts can be installed on OS X, they cannot currently be installed on iOS. Note that copying fonts may be in breach of the typeface's software license.

If you intend to run your Keynote presentations on a variety of devices, best practice is to choose a typeface installed by default on iOS devices. A list of iOS fonts are listed on Apple Support; click Support on the Apple.com site and then search for "ios fonts."

Modifying Image Placeholders

Some master slides contain media placeholders. By scaling and changing their attributes, you can create a consistent look for your images and videos.

1 In the slide navigator, select the Photo - Horizontal master slide. It contains two media placeholders.

2 Select one of the media placeholder in landscape orientation.

3 In the inspector, click through the various image styles. Select the last style in the lower right.

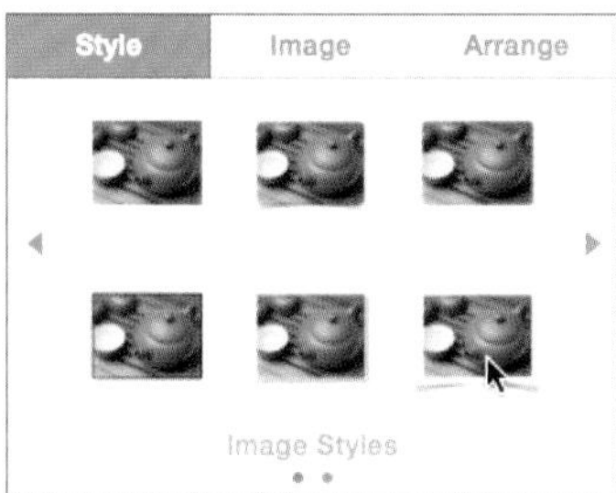

As you might expect, you can customize image styles.

4 In the Border section of the inspector, change the Scale of the picture frame to 25%.

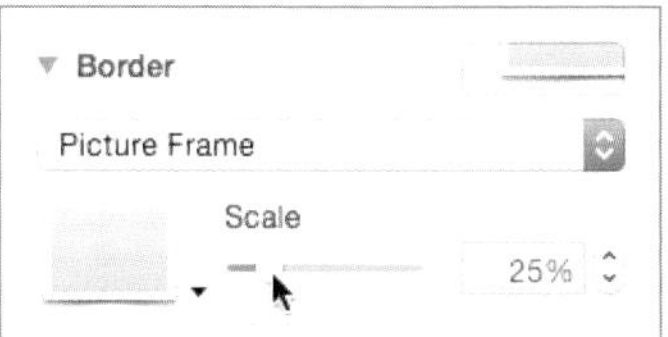

You could adjust other image attributes, but let's create a new image style.

5 In the image styles, scroll until you see the + (plus sign) button. Click it to add your customized style to the inspector.

6 Select the other media placeholder on the Photo - Horizontal master.

7 In the inspector, click the image style you just created.

NOTE ▶ The thumbnail in the inspector shows a preview of the style applied to the selected image.

Because these are media placeholders, you needn't change the images in them. Rather, you can replace them as you create your presentation. However, you may want to change these reference images.

8 In the landscape placeholder, click the media icon with the teapot photo.

The Media Browser opens. So long as you are still using the apts-pnk-photolibrary, you'll find the ju-jitsu poster images.

9 In the Media Browser, select the ju-jitsu poster album, if necessary. Click any of the images in landscape orientation to replace the current placeholder.

10 Click the media icon in the other placeholder, and repeat step 9 to replace the placeholder with a ju-jitsu photo in portrait orientation.

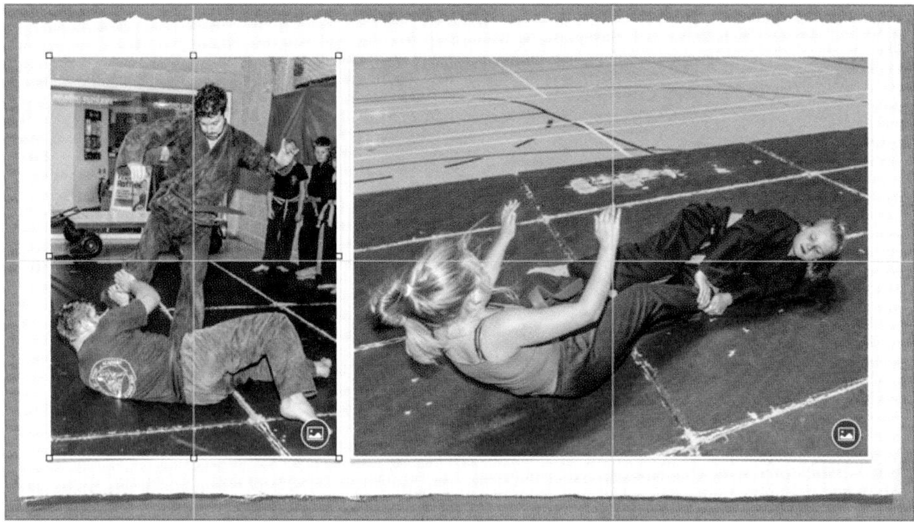

If your theme includes more master slides with media placeholders, you may also want to edit those.

Placing Objects on Master Slides

So far your customization of master slides has been restricted to editing existing objects. You'll now alter other master slide elements to include the logo for the Ju-Jitsu club.

1 In the slide navigator, select the Title & Subtitle master.

2 Choose Insert > Choose. In the dialog that appears, navigate to APTS Pages Numbers Keynote and open the Lesson 14 folder. Double-click **ju-jitsu-logo.pdf** to add it to the slide.

3 Move the logo so that it sits between the top of the slide and the placeholder text. The alignment guides will help you center the logo.

To make the logo look more like Japanese paper, you can change its opacity.

4 With the logo selected, in the Style inspector, set the Opacity to 95%.

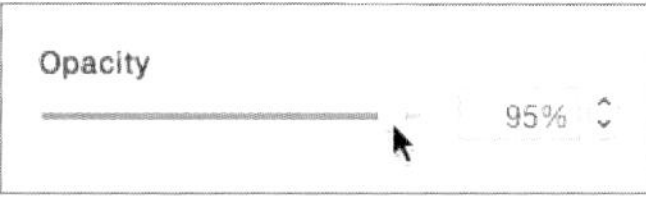

5 Press Command-C to copy the logo to the clipboard.

6 Select the Title - Top slide, and then click the slide background.

7 Press Command-V to paste the logo onto the slide.

The logo is placed into the same position from which it was copied.

8 Drag the logo to the lower right of the cream-colored box.

9 Drag the upper-left selection handles diagonally toward the opposite corner of the selection. The logo scales smaller. Drag until the logo is scaled to about 180 pt.

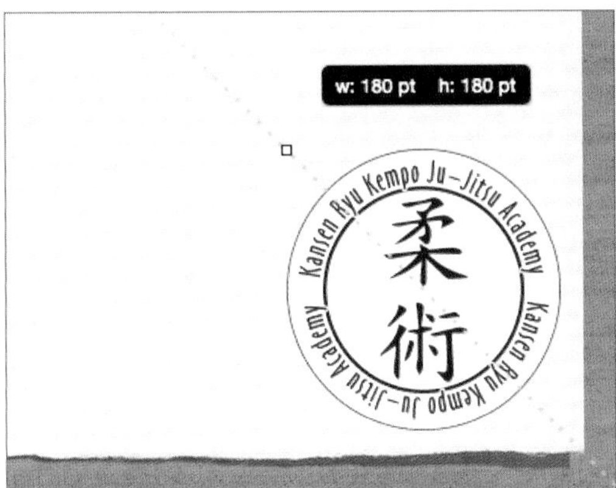

You can apply even more attributes to the logo. To make the artwork look a little more handmade, you can rotate the logo a bit.

10 In the Arrange inspector, set the Rotate Angle to 357°.

With the logo now fine-tuned for the nontitle slides, you can copy and paste it again.

11 With the logo selected, press Command-C to copy the altered logo to the clipboard.

12 In the slide navigator, select a master slide on which you want to place the logo. Then click the slide's background.

13 Press Command-V to paste the logo into position. Repeat steps 12 and 13 for all the master slides that should include the logo.

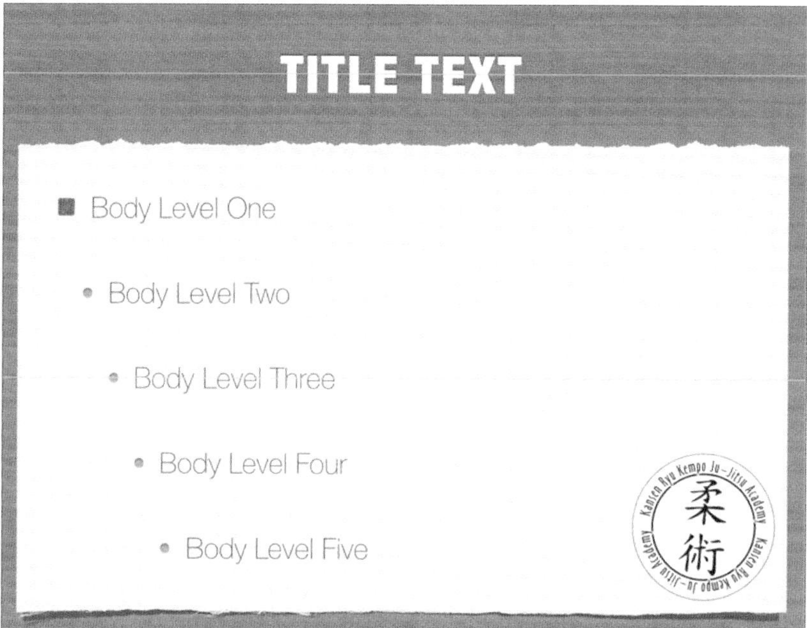

Creating a New Title Master

The current Title & Subtitle master slide has only placeholder text on it. As a result, every time the Ju-Jitsu club makes a new presentation using this theme the words "Kansen Ryu Kempo Ju-Jitsu" will have to be typed on the title slide.

Of course, there's a way to permanently add recurring text to a master.

1 In the slide navigator, Control-click the Title & Subtitle master, and from the shortcut menu, choose Duplicate.

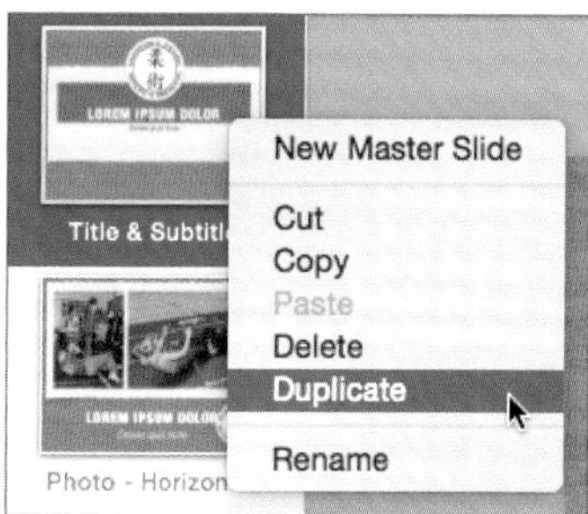

Now you'll rename this master to create a new one containing the club's name.

2 Control-click the duplicate master, and from the shortcut menu, choose Rename. Type *Title Slide* for the new name.

3 Click the reddish text box on the slide. It contains placeholder text that cannot be changed on the master.

You can type the club name in a new text box, but to save time, you'll first create a new shape style based on the reddish text box.

4 In the Format inspector's Style tab, scroll until you see a + (plus sign) button in Shape Styles. Click it to add a new shape style.

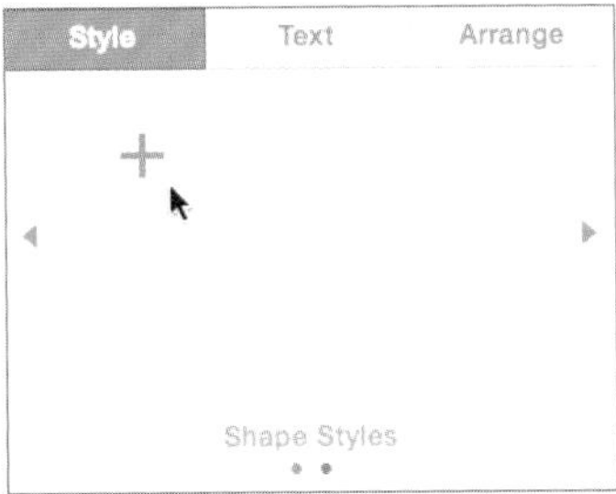

The new shape style contains the updated Title Alt paragraph style you modified previously.

5 Press Delete to delete the reddish text box.

6 In the toolbar, click the Text icon to add a new text box.

7 In the new text box, type *Kansen Ryu Kempo Ju-Jitsu*.

8 In the inspector's Shape Styles, click the style you created in step 4.

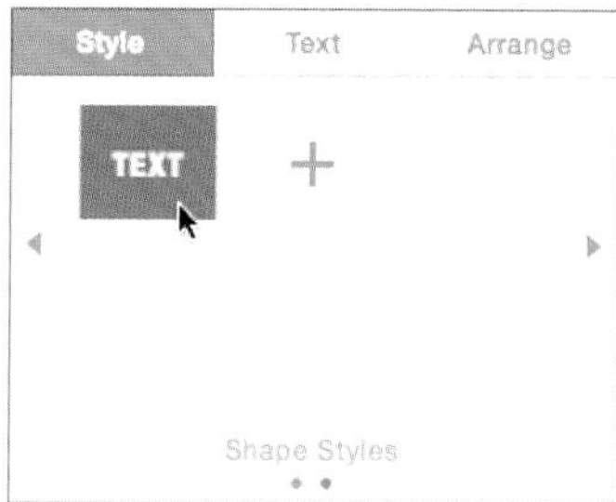

The text and shape take on the style attributes, but the box needs to be bigger. The text box can only be stretched horizontally.

9 Click outside the text box to deselect it. Then click it again to display the selection handles.

10 Drag the selection handles outward while leaving a little extra space around the text.

To create vertical space, you must add more carriage returns.

11 Double-click the placeholder text, and then click to the left of the letter K in "Kansen." The text insertion point appears.

12 Press Return twice to increase the height of the text box.

The text appears in capital letters, even if you type in lowercase. You'll turn off automatic capitalization.

13 Click outside the text box to deselect it. Then click it once more to select it again.

14 Choose Format > Font > Capitalization > None.

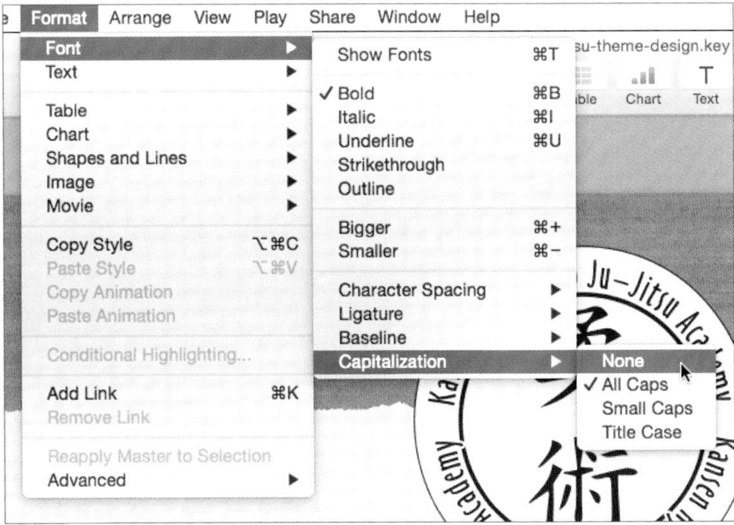

15 Drag the text box up so that it does not cover the subtitle text box.

To complete the Title Slide master, you'll need to bring the logo to the top of the layer order.

16 Select the club logo.

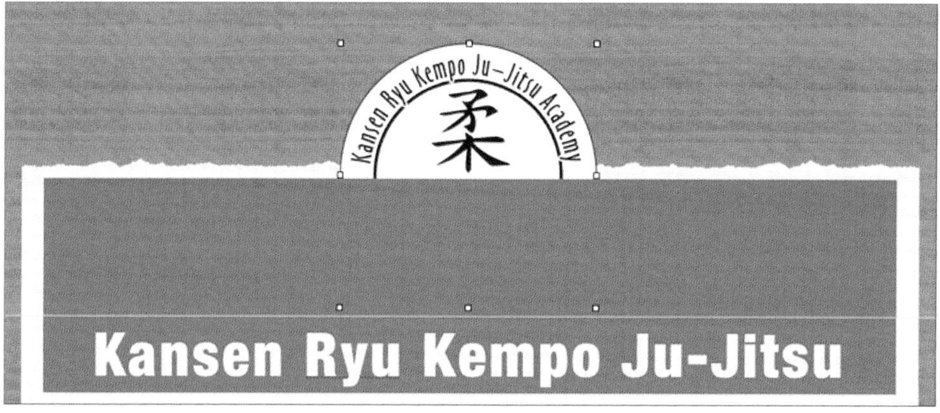

17 In the Format inspector's Arrange tab, click Front to move the logo to the front layer.

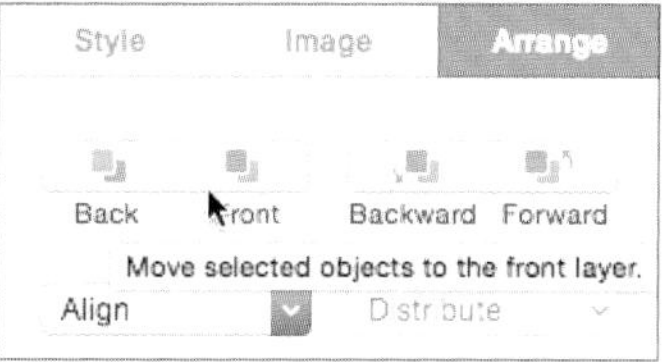

18 Click the thumbnail for the Title Slide master. In the Master Slide Layout options in the Format inspector, select "Allow objects on slide to layer with master."

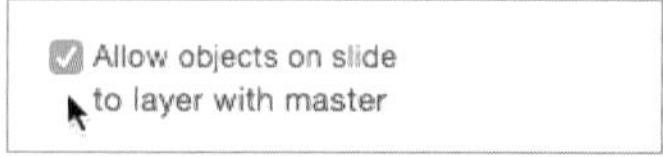

This step is necessary to keep the logo at the front of the layer order when creating slides from this master. Selecting this option is best practice for most master slides.

19 Leave the presentation open and ready for the next exercise.

Adding Charts to a Theme

Creating a theme that contains customized chart or table styles is not difficult, as you're about to learn. The process for making a table style is almost identical to creating a chart style.

To speed things along, you'll use an existing chart placed in **ju-jitsu-presentation-theme.key**.

1 In Keynote, choose File > Open.

2 Navigate to APTS Pages Numbers Keynote > Lesson_14.

3 Double-click the **ju-jitsu-presentation-theme.key** document.

4 Navigate to slide 6.

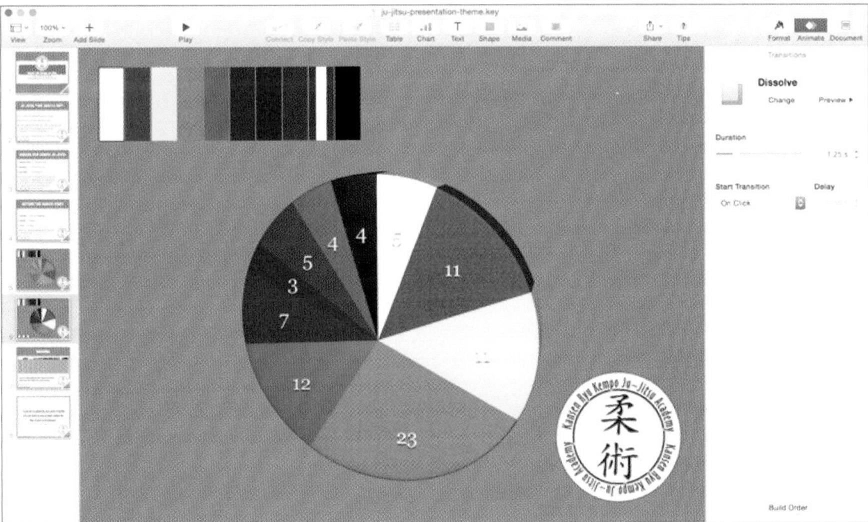

5 Press Command-Option-P to play the slideshow from slide 6.

6 Press Spacebar to advance through the builds on slide 6.

The pie chart uses the 3D Grow build, set to deliver by wedge. It's a very effective build animation for pie charts. Unfortunately, build and transition animations can't be saved as part of a theme.

7 Press Esc to quit the slideshow.

8 Go to slide 5. It contains a similar pie chart, with no animation or Ju-Jitsu grading colors applied.

NOTE ▶ You could apply an animation to this chart, or any table or object, in this exercise; but later when you save your changes as a customized theme, those animations would be lost.

9 Click the slide background to select the slide. Press Command-A to select all the objects on the slide.

10 Press Command-C to copy these objects to the clipboard.

You'll now paste these objects into your ju-jitsu-theme-design.key document.

11 Choose Window > ju-jitsu-theme-design.key to return to the presentation design.

12 In the slide navigator, select the Blank master slide.

13 Click the slide background, and choose Edit > Paste (or press Command-V) to paste the pie chart and grading color graphics onto the slide.

Creating Chart Styles Using Custom Colors

In this exercise, you will apply the grading colors to the pie chart and then save the chart as a new chart style. Chart and table styles are saved into themes. The graphic displaying the Ju-Jitsu grades will be used to color the chart.

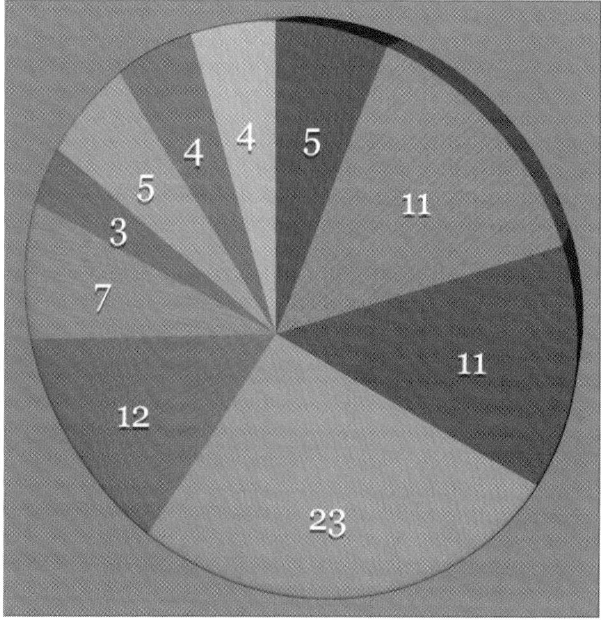

1 Choose View > Show Colors to open the Colors window.

2 In the Colors window, click the eyedropper and sample the white of the first grading color.

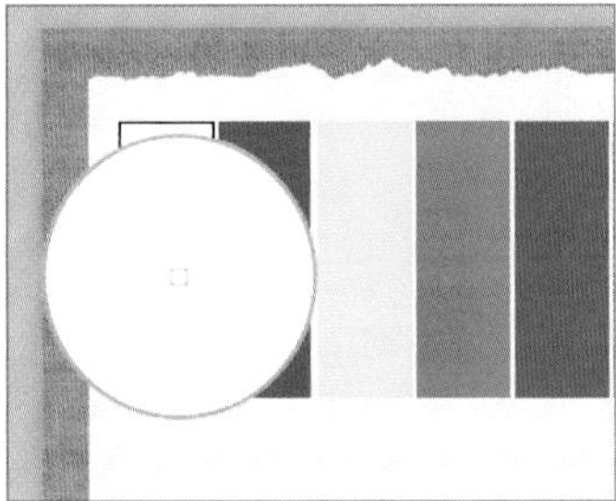

The color swatch next to the eyedropper in the Colors window changes to white. Yes, there is a quicker way to choose white, but this method shows you how to make custom colors by sampling them.

3 Drag the white swatch in the Colors window to the larger blue wedge labeled 5 in the pie chart. Two wedges change color.

4 In the Colors window, click the eyedropper, and use it to sample the red grade color.

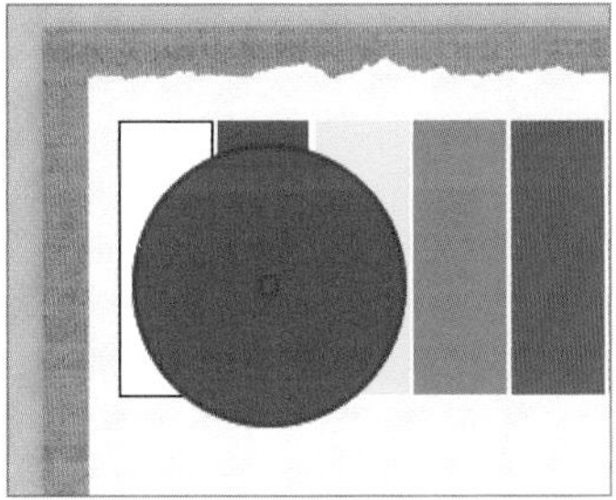

5 Drag the red swatch from the Colors window to the brown wedge labeled 11. Two wedges change to red.

6 Continue to change the wedge colors in clockwise order by sampling the grading colors moving left to right.

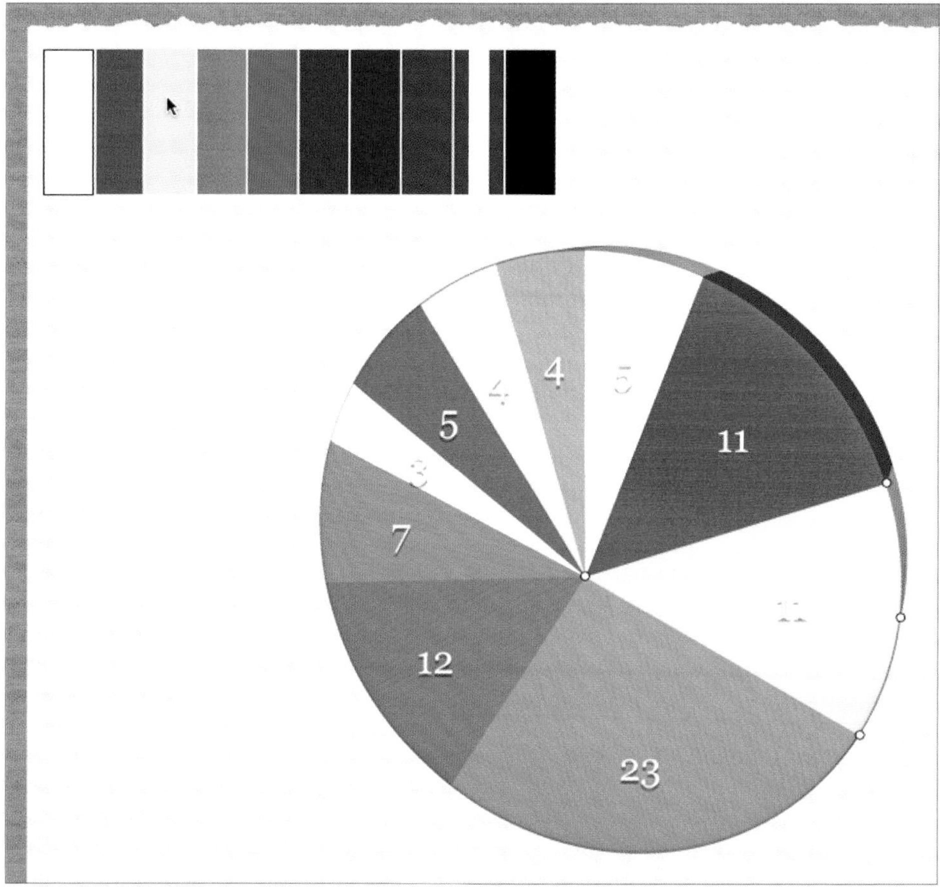

When you apply a color, two wedges change at a time until you reach the first instance of a repeated color. As you continue to update the chart colors, you'll find that all the wedges will gain a unique color, except for the Brown and Brown White belts.

7 To differentiate between these two grades, apply the brown color to both wedges.

8 After you finish applying colors, use the eyedropper to select the brown color again, and then in the Colors window, drag the lightness slider to the left to lighten that color.

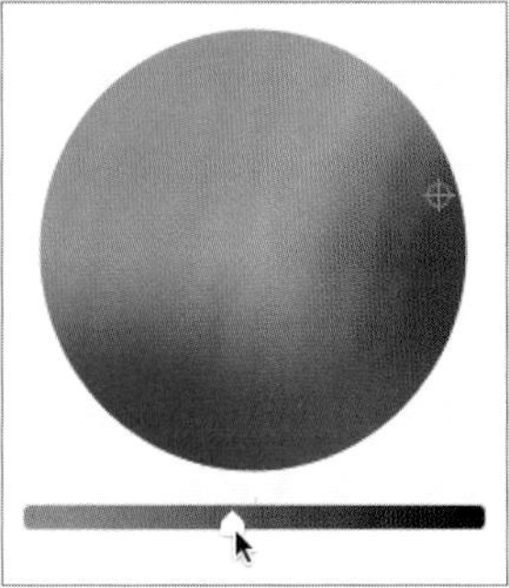

The wedge color won't change automatically. To change it to your newly mixed brown, you'll drag the color swatch to the wedge.

9 In the Colors window, drag the color swatch next to the eyedropper to the required wedge.

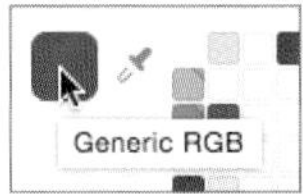

Once you've created a chart or table using custom formatting and colors, you can save it as a style and you won't need to start from scratch again.

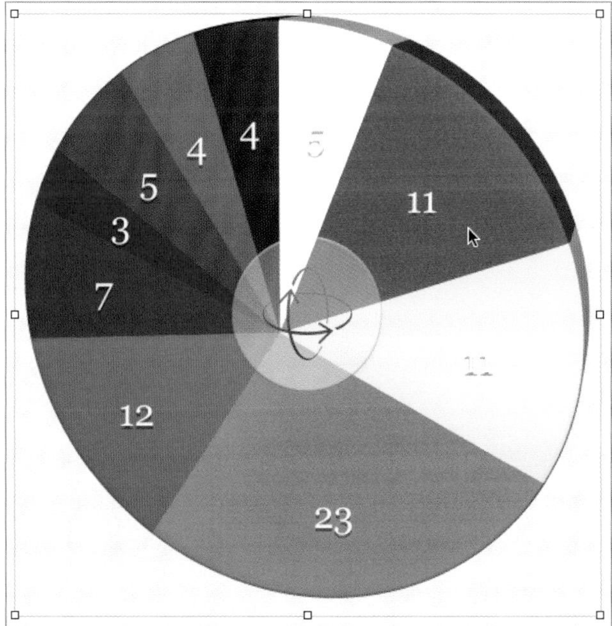

10 Select the modified chart.

11 In the Chart tab of the inspector, click the + (plus sign) in Chart Styles to add your custom chart as a new style.

12 Press Command-S to save a version of your design work.

You've completed your presentation design; now you'll create a template.

Saving Themes

A Keynote theme includes all the master slides that were used to create the theme. So anything placed on a master slide will also be included, albeit locked down. As suggested earlier, allowing objects on a slide to layer with the master is a good idea.

Any styles you've modified or created will also become part of your custom theme, whether they are paragraph, character, list, table, shape, or chart styles.

1 Choose File > Save Theme.

If you want to send the template to another user or install it on another Mac, choose Save. Doing so allows you to choose where the theme is saved.

2 Click "Add to Theme Chooser" to add the template to the Theme Chooser on your Mac.

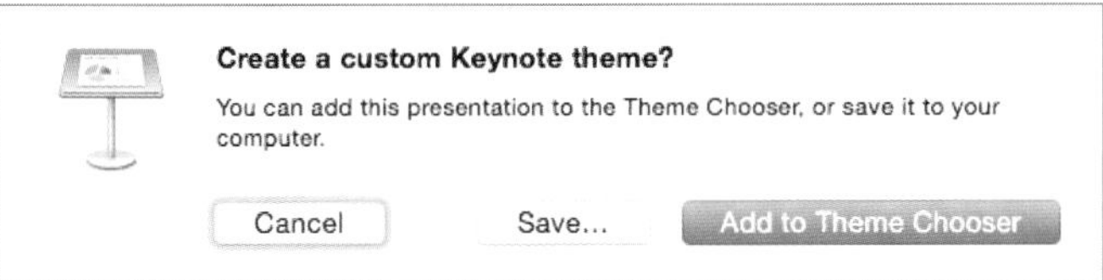

3 Name the template *Ju-Jitsu Theme*.

4 Press Enter. In the My Themes tab, you'll now find the Ju-Jitsu Theme.

Should you want to delete a theme from your chooser, Control-click it, and from the shortcut menu, choose Delete.

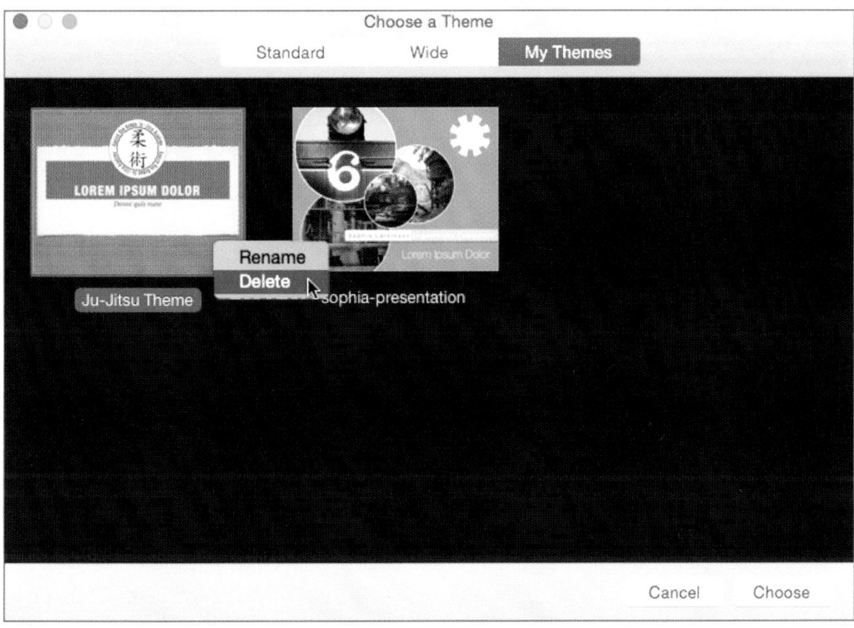

5 Double-click Ju-Jitsu Theme to open a new presentation.

Your new presentation contains all the master slides and styles you included in the theme.

6 Press Command-W, and repeat the key combination to close all open presentations.

Lesson Review

1. What are master slides?
2. Why is modifying paragraph styles rather than creating new styles a good idea?
3. When you apply an object style to a text box, what happens if its font changes?
4. A client wants you to use a custom icon as a bullet in Keynote. How do you do this?
5. In Keynote presentations, why is using fonts installed with iOS considered best practice?
6. Which Keynote functions are not included in themes?

Answers

1. Master slides are special slides from which presentation slides are created. Any objects placed on master slides appear on the slides created from them and inherit the master slide's style attributes. Objects can include placeholders for text and graphics.
2. Modifying paragraph styles is often better because most master slides contain instances of paragraph styles. If you were to modify a Title paragraph style, any master slide using that style would automatically change.
3. Paragraph styles are nested in object styles that contain text. By applying an object style, you also apply any paragraph style that might be nested within it.
4. To apply a custom icon to a bullet, use the Bullets & Lists section of the Text inspector. Set the Bullet type to Image Bullets. Click the Current Image menu. The pop-up menu that appears contains a Custom Image button. Click it, navigate to the custom icon artwork, and select it.

5. When you play a presentation on devices other than the one on which you built the presentation, Keynote uses the fonts installed on the host device. If the host device doesn't have all the fonts used in that presentation, Keynote will make font substitutions. Although additional fonts can be installed on OS X, they cannot currently be installed on iOS.
6. Animations such as transitions, builds, and actions are not included in themes.

15

Lesson Files

APTS Pages Numbers Keynote > Lesson_15 > ju-jitsu.key

APTS Pages Numbers Keynote > Lesson_15 > agata-presentation.key

Time

This lesson takes approximately 90 minutes to complete.

Goals

Understand the controls available when playing a slideshow

Rehearse presentation timings

Use an iOS device as a Keynote remote control

Record narrated self-playing presentations

Create Keynote handouts

Present on a separate screen

Lesson **15**

Rehearsing and Delivering a Presentation

As you develop a Keynote presentation, at some point you will need to assess that presentation's visual design and its pace and focus. Avoid delivering a public presentation without having a clear idea of its length or the clarity of its message.

In this lesson, you'll use Keynote's rehearsal tools and learn about the checks you should make before delivering a presentation to an audience. The emphasis here is on using Keynote, but a great presentation doesn't succeed or fail on the basis of a slideshow. It's the presenter who holds an audience's attention and reinforces the message through word choice, tone of voice, and body language. A slideshow complements the talents of a skilled presenter.

Not all presentations are delivered in person, however. Fortunately, you can also use Keynote to create self-playing presentations, which you can also narrate. There's a lot of ground to cover so let's get started.

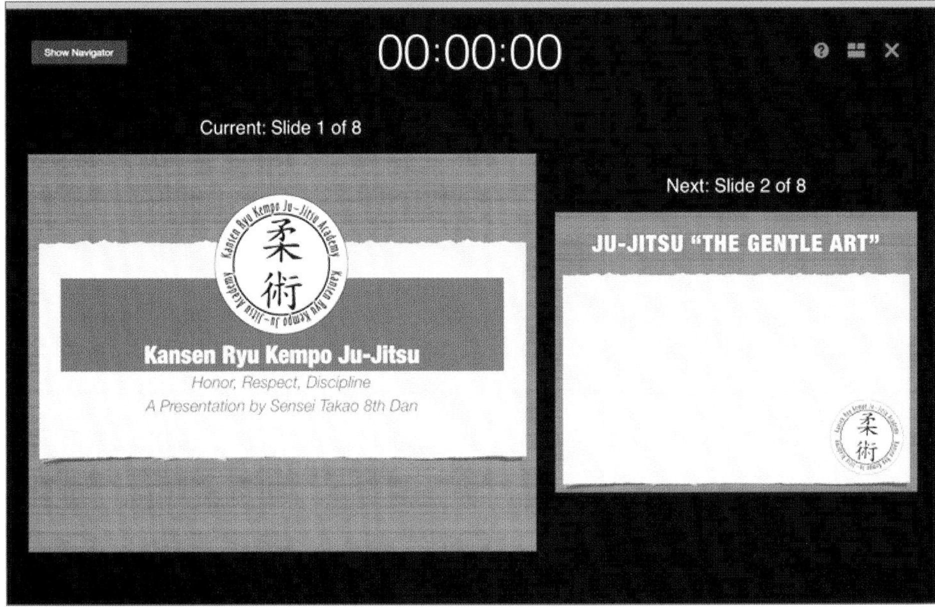

Playing a Slideshow

You've played your Keynote slideshows previously, but now you're going to mix things up a little because not all presentations proceed uninterrupted. You may have encouraged your audience to ask questions, for example, and need to jump back to an earlier slide, stop a movie, or skip to another application. You can easily manage these breaks in your presentation without quitting your Keynote slideshow.

1 Open APTS Pages Numbers Keynote > Lesson_15 > **ju-jitsu.key**.

2 Make sure you have slide 1 selected, and then press Command-Option-P to play the slideshow.

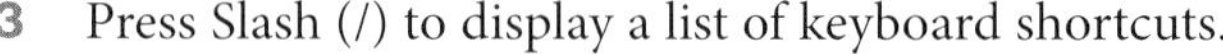

3 Press Slash (/) to display a list of keyboard shortcuts.

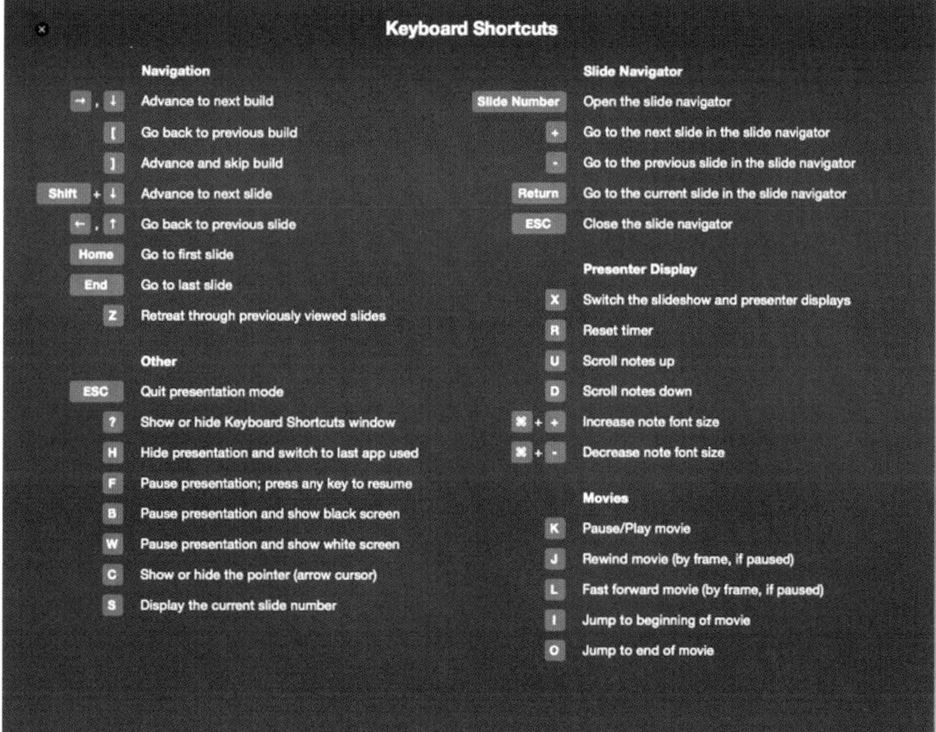

Let's see some of these shortcuts in action.

TIP Any time you're playing a slideshow and need to review the keyboard shortcuts, you can press Slash (/) to display them.

4 Press Slash (/) to close the shortcuts window.

5 Press Spacebar to advance to slide 2.

6 Press Spacebar twice more to view the first two builds on slide 2.

- Is a traditional Japanese martial arts system.
- Its roots lie in the Samurai past of Japan.

Imagine a scenario in which you're talking about the second bullet point but get a spontaneous question about the first bullet point. You want to back up and hide the second bullet point while you answer that question.

7 Press Left Bracket ([) to return to the previous build. When you're ready to continue to the second bullet point, you can advance by pressing Spacebar.

Due to the audience questions, you find you're running short of time, and you want to jump to a slide to shorten your presentation on the fly. To do this, you can type the slide number.

8 Press 6. The slide navigator appears.

9 Press Enter to jump to slide 6, which contains a movie.

10 Press Spacebar to play the movie.

11 If questions arise during the playback, you can press K to pause the movie, press J to rewind the paused movie a frame at a time, and press L to advance the paused movie a frame at a time.

TIP Using the J-K-L keys gives you access to convenient action replay and slow motion. Also note that when the movie is playing, holding down J does a fast rewind and holding down L does a fast forward.

You can open the shortcuts window and experiment to learn more, but here are two shortcuts that might require a little context.

12 Press W, and the screen turns white.

This is a great device if you're presenting in a dark auditorium using a large display or projection. The white screen will cast some light on your audience.

You can press almost any key to return to the slideshow.

13 Press W to go back to the slideshow.

14 Press B, and the screen goes black, another alternative for taking a break from your slideshow.

Although pressing H will hide your presentation, you can set up another way to jump away from your presentation without quitting it. The following technique is useful for instructors who want to demonstrate a technique point in another application.

15 Press Esc to quit the slideshow.

16 Choose Keynote > Preferences. Click Slideshow, and then in the Interacting section, enable Allow Mission Control, Dashboard and others to use the screen."

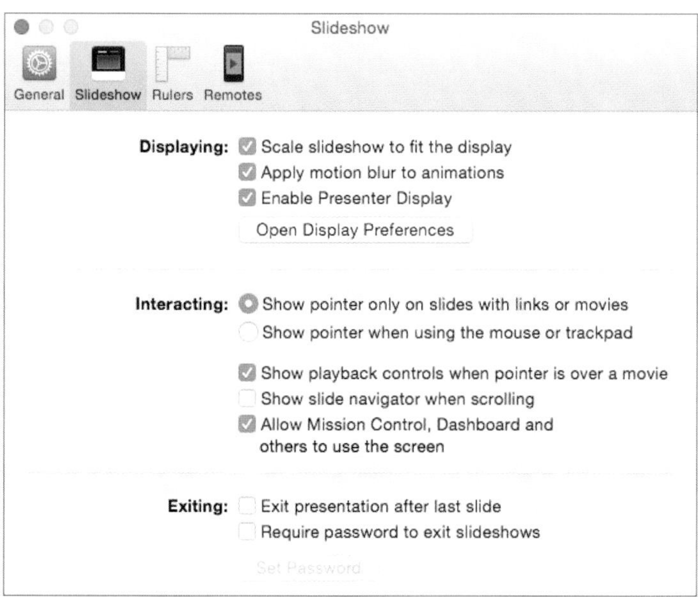

By enabling this option (which is turned off by default), you can access the Application Switcher while playing a Keynote slideshow.

17 Return to Keynote, and press Command-Option-P to play the slideshow.

18 Press Command-Tab to open the Application Switcher.

All currently opened applications are made instantly available. So, for example, a teacher instructing students in GarageBand could open that app before starting the slideshow. Then, the teacher could later interrupt the slideshow, jump to GarageBand in the switcher to demonstrate a technique, and then return straight back to Keynote by using the switcher again.

19 Press Command-Tab to switch to the Finder.

20 Press Command-Tab again to switch back to Keynote.

21 Choose File > Close to close the open presentation.

Rehearsing a Slideshow

Keynote's rehearsal tools help you calculate the length of your presentation. Rehearsing a presentation may also highlight parts of your script that look good in writing but prove perplexing to pronounce.

1 Open APTS Pages Numbers Keynote > Lesson_15 > **agata-presentation.key**.

2 With slide 1 selected, choose Play > Rehearse Slideshow.

You can advance through your slideshow with presenter display options visible.

3 Press Spacebar, read the text on the slide, and then press Spacebar again. Read the slide and bullet.

You'll see a green bar across the top of the screen that will turn red as the next build or slide loads.

TIP Slides containing large audiovisual media files can take a second or two to load. Waiting for the green bar before advancing to the movie ensures that the movie is ready to play, thereby avoiding an undesirable pause.

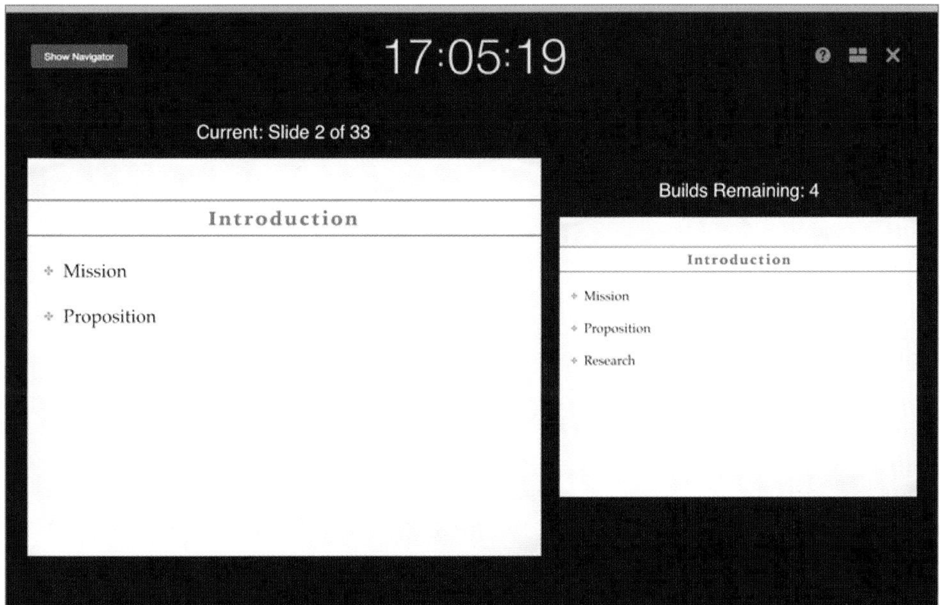

By default, the presenter display shows the current slide as it would appear to the audience, a slide representing the next build or slide, and a clock. However, you can customize this display.

4 At the upper right of the presenter display are three icons. Click the middle icon. In the popover that appears, select the Presenter Notes and Timer options.

Next you'll concentrate on the timing options.

5 In the Timer options, select Remaining, and in the time field type *1:00*. Doing so sets the target length of your presentation at one hour and instructs Keynote to display the time remaining in the presenter display.

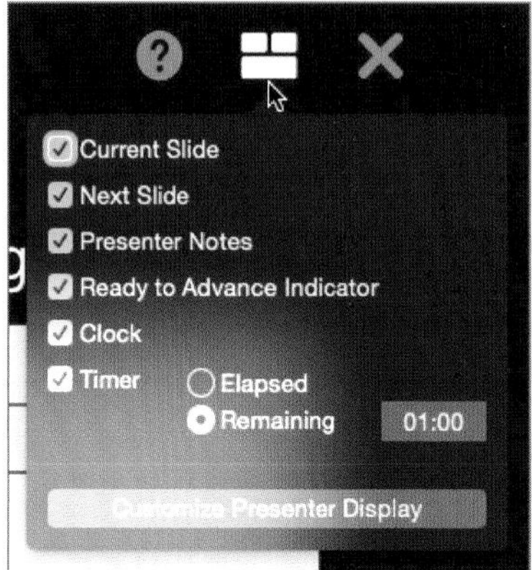

The value of 01:00 is one hour, 00:30 is 30 minutes, 01:30 is 90 minutes, and so on. You can also choose to display an elapsed time or a countdown.

The default layout of the presenter display is OK, but you might also prefer to customize it.

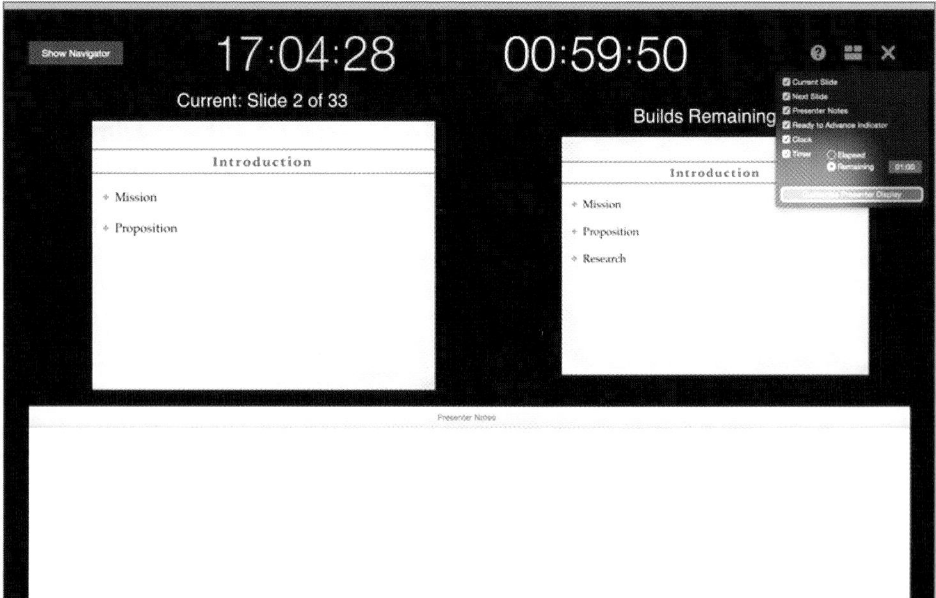

6 In the popover, click Customize Presenter Display. The Current Slide checkbox is selected. Selecting these checkboxes enables you to modify those elements in the presenter display.

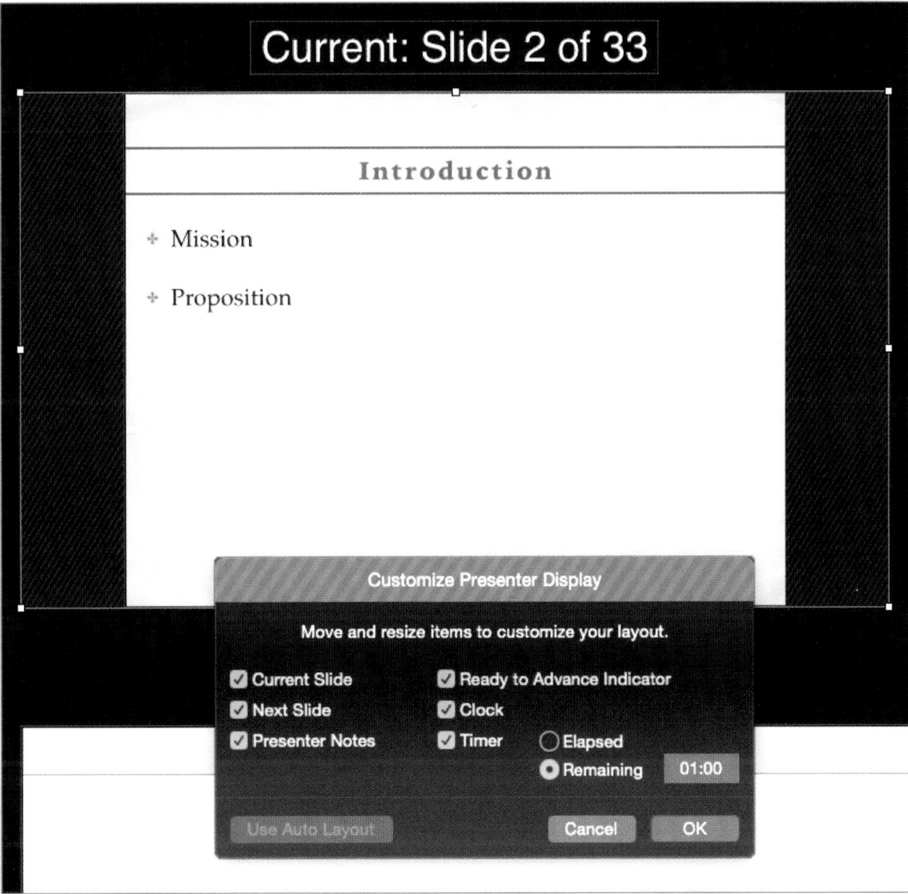

7 In the presenter display, drag the current slide item to the upper left, and then drag the edges of the slide to resize it.

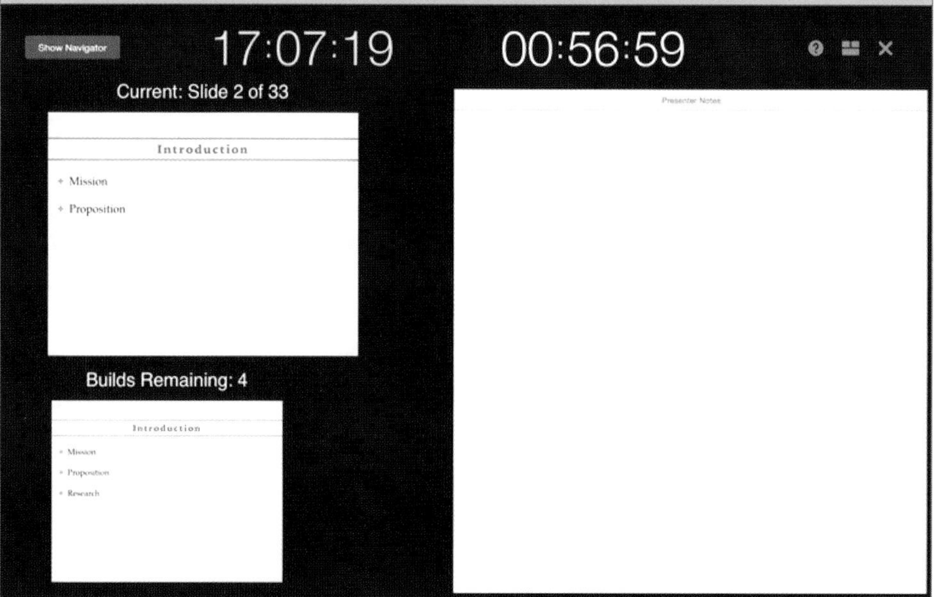

8 You can resize and reposition the other presenter items to suit yourself.

9 Click OK to close the Customize Presenter Display dialog.

NOTE ▶ You don't have to start rehearsing to customize the presenter display. You can also access this dialog by choosing Play > Customize Presenter Display.

Next you'll add presenter notes.

Add and Edit Presenter Notes

Presenter notes can help you keep on track, especially when delivering a scripted presentation. Presenter notes also can be included in handouts, which is covered later in this lesson.

1 Press Esc to quit the slideshow.

2 In the slide navigator, click slide 4.

This slide is rather wordy. When slides are as text-heavy as this one, the audience tends to read quickly rather than listening to and comprehending your comments. This text might be better placed in the presenter notes.

3 In the toolbar, click the View icon. From the pop-up menu, choose Show Presenter Notes.

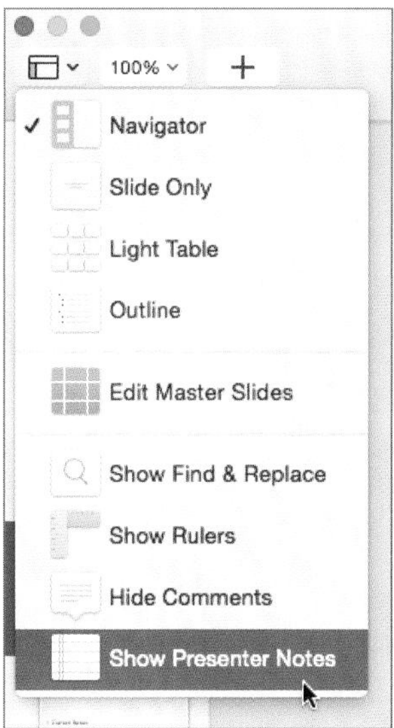

4 On slide 4, triple-click the paragraph of text to select it.

To set-up an independent photography business that caters for domestic and commercial photography needs. Centered on portraiture either in my studio or on location. Commercial clients will also be able to commission product and architecture shots.

5 Press Command-C to copy it.

6 Navigate to slide 3, and click inside the Presenter Notes window.

7 Press Command-V to paste the text into the presenter notes.

The text from slide 4 is now a presenter note on slide 3.

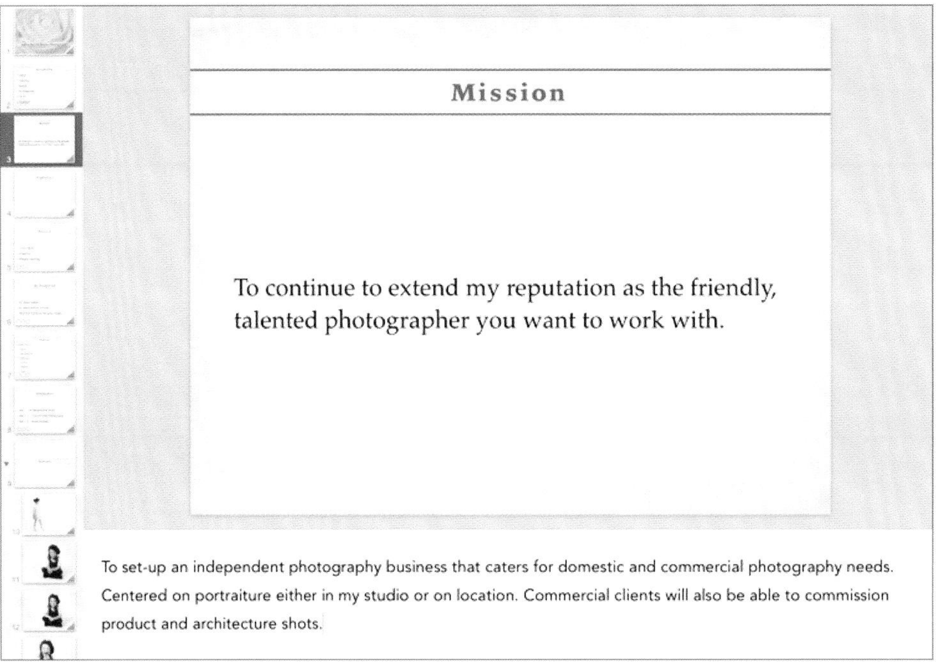

TIP Keeping key messages under 140 characters is best practice if you want your audience to spread your message via social media.

Slide 4 is now redundant, so you can delete it.

8 In the slide navigator, select slide 4. Press Delete to delete it.

9 In the slide navigator, select slide 3, and choose Play > Rehearse Slideshow.

The display shows your presenter notes.

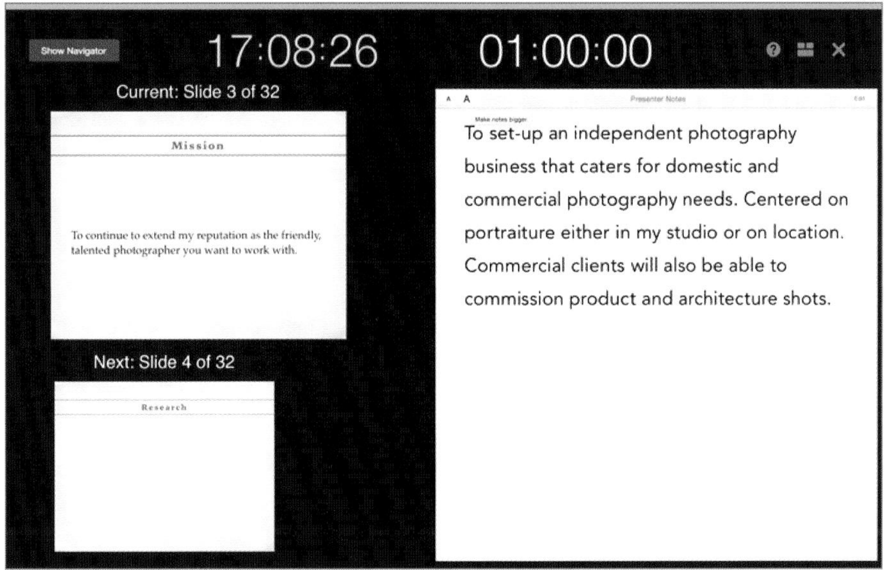

10 Locate the pointer over the presenter notes until options appear in its title bar.

Clicking the larger A button will increase the font size, and clicking the smaller A button will decrease font size. Clicking Edit allows you to alter the presenter notes.

You can configure the presenter display to help you deliver your presentation with confidence. There's one more feature you might want to enable.

11 In the upper left of the presenter display, click Show Navigator.

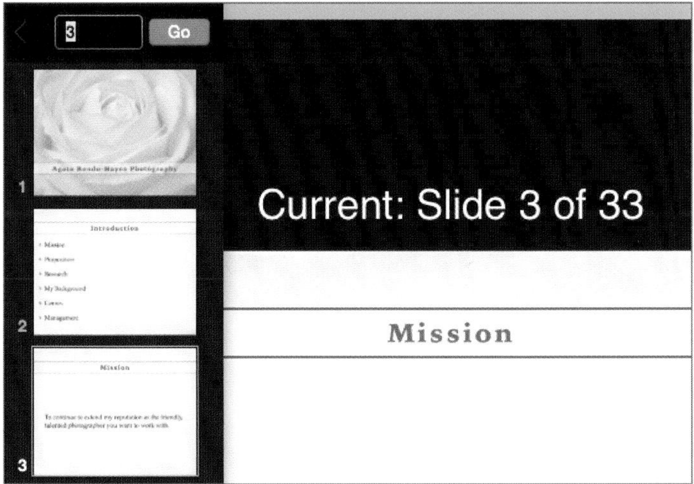

Thumbnails of the slides appear to the left of the display. You can scroll through the thumbnails to find the slide you want to jump to, or just type the slide number, as you did earlier.

12 Scroll down to slide 9. Click its thumbnail, and then press Enter. The navigator closes, and slide 9 is shown.

13 Type 23. The navigator appears, with slide 23 highlighted. Press Enter.

14 Press Esc to quit the slideshow.

Skipping Slides

During rehearsal you may discover that your presentation is too long; or even worse, you may be told just before your presentation that your 30-minute time slot has been cut to 20 minutes. Rather than delete Keynote slides to cut down (and permanently alter) your presentation, you can choose to skip them for the current presentation.

In the case of our photographer, Agata might prepare a 30-minute presentation knowing that she can skip slides when she has only 10 minutes for her pitch.

1 In the slide navigator, click slide 30.

2 Shift-click slide 32 to select the three slides to skip today.

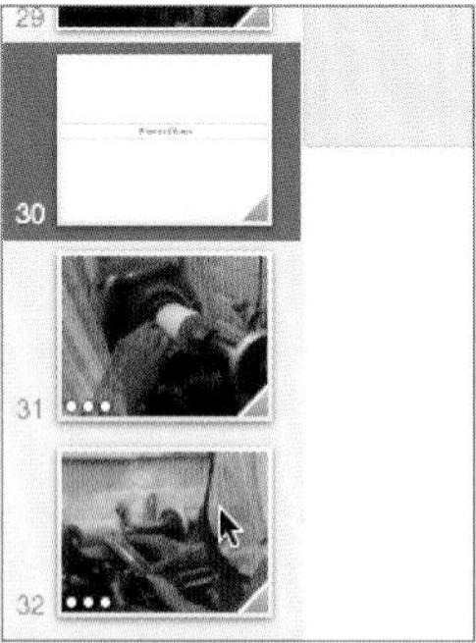

3 In the slide navigator, Control-click any of the selected slides. From the shortcut menu, choose Skip Slide.

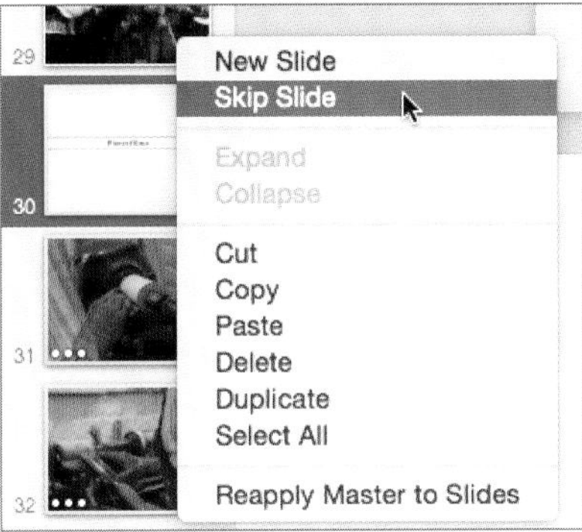

Skipped slides appear in the navigator as thin horizontal bars.

To reverse this choice for one or more slides, you can Control-click a skipped slide or set of skipped slides, and from the shortcut menu, choose Don't Skip Slide.

The light table view can help you spot slides that could be temporarily removed from a presentation.

4 In the toolbar, click the View icon, and choose Light Table.

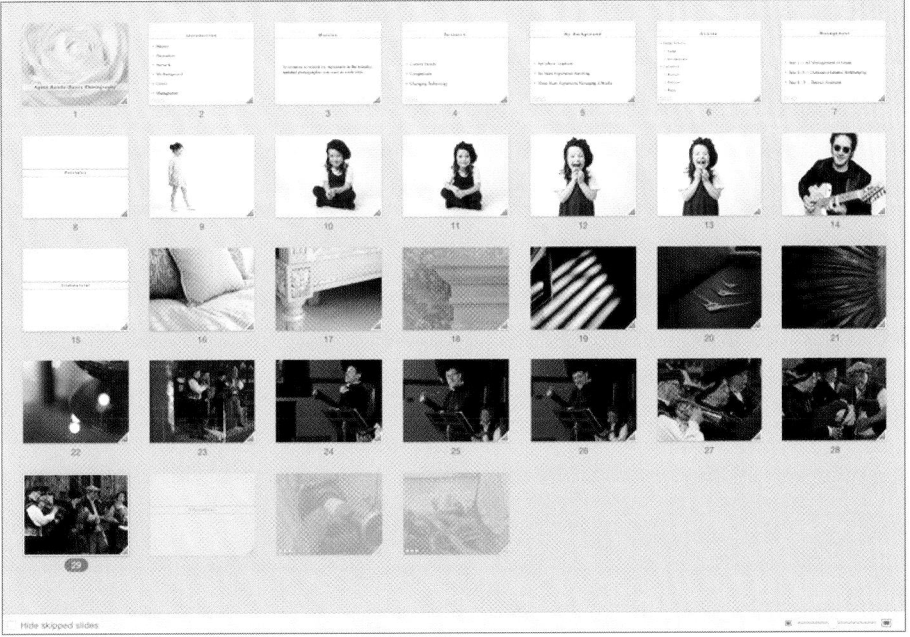

You can see that the skipped slides are dimmed. If you'd like, you can select the Hide Skipped Slides option, which can help you visualize your new presentation order by hiding the skipped slides. When you return to the navigator view, you'll see that the skipped slides are represented by lines.

5 Command-click three or four photo slides to select them.

6 Control-click any of the selected slides, and from the shortcut menu, choose Skip Slide.

7 Choose View > Navigator to return to the navigator view.

Notice how the skipped slides are represented in the slide navigator.

8 Leave **agata-presentation.key** open for the next exercise.

Using an iOS Device as a Remote Control

You can play a Keynote presentation directly from an iOS device, but you can also use an iPhone or iPad as a remote control for a slideshow running on a Mac. Having an iOS device as your remote control gives you the freedom to move around your stage, and it places a script prompt in your hand.

This exercise requires that you have the iOS Keynote application installed on an iPhone or iPad. Also, your Mac and iOS device must be on the same Wi-Fi network.

1 On your Mac, choose Apple > System Preferences. Click the Network icon.

Here you can verify that Wi-Fi is enabled and identify the name of your current network.

2 On your iOS device, tap Settings. Your current Wi-Fi status is listed along with the name of your current network.

If both devices are on the same network, you're good to go. For more information, you can review Help on your Mac and your iOS device.

3 Close the System Preferences on your Mac, and quit the iOS Settings app.

4 On your iOS device, open Keynote. If it's the first time you've opened Keynote for iOS, you'll see a Welcome screen.

Steps 5 and 6 apply only if you haven't opened Keynote for iOS before. If the Welcome screen does not appear, skip to step 7.

5 Tap Continue.

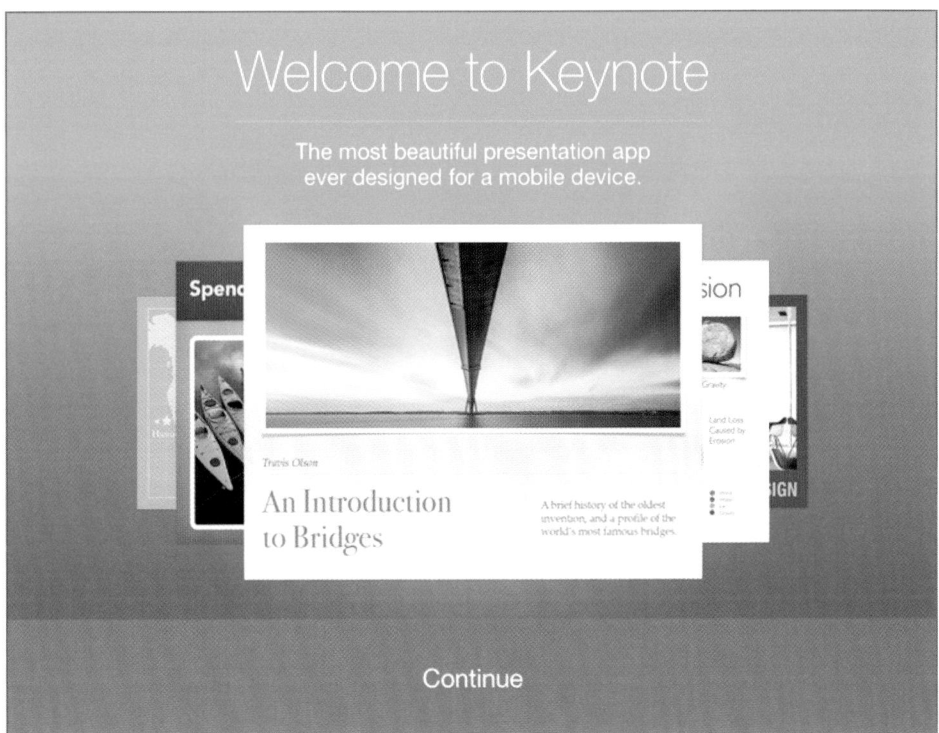

6 Keynote asks if you want to use iCloud. If you previously have signed in to your iCloud account on this device, you can tap Use iCloud. If you haven't set up an iCloud account, tap Later.

NOTE ▸ You'll learn about setting up an iCloud account in Lesson 16.

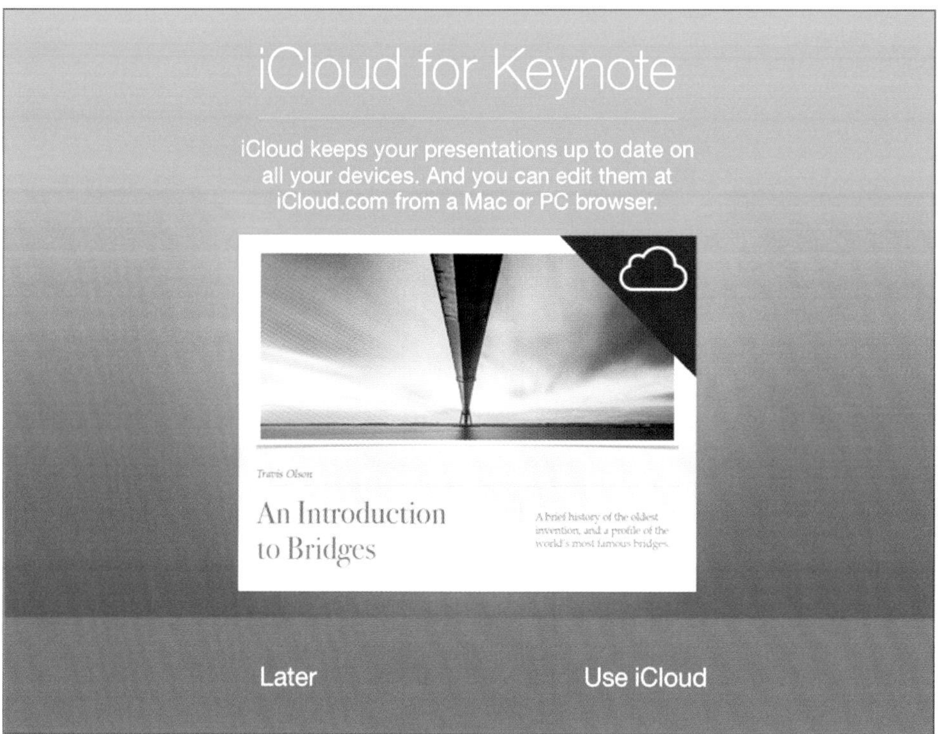

7 On Keynote for iOS, tap the iPhone-shaped icon at the upper left of the screen to open Keynote Remote.

You can follow the onscreen instructions to link your iOS device and Mac.

8 On the Welcome to Keynote Remote popover, tap Continue.

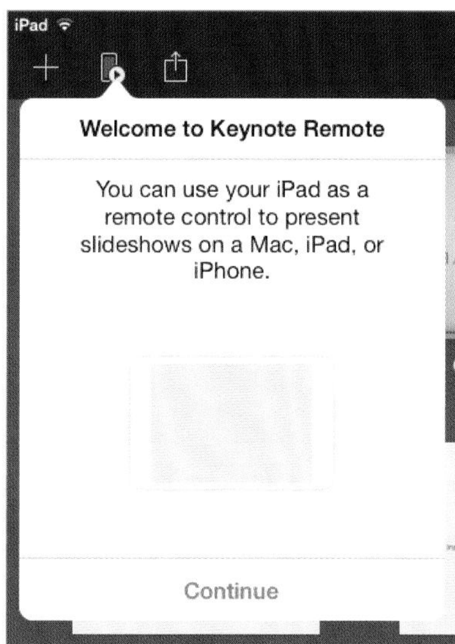

The iOS device starts looking for other networked devices running Keynote.

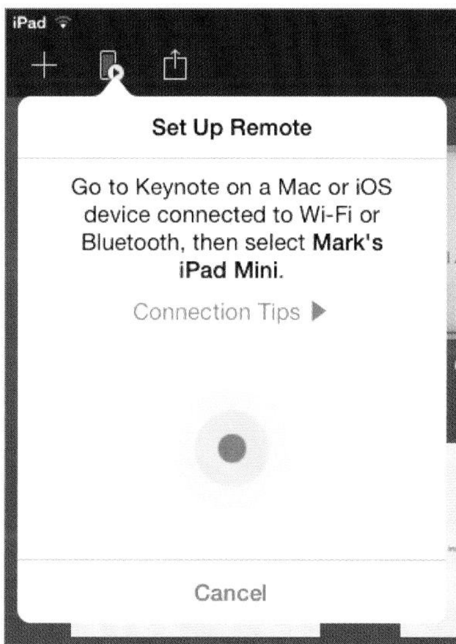

9 On your Mac, in Keynote, choose Keynote > Preferences. Click the Remotes tab.

If both devices are on the same network, the Remotes preferences will list your iOS device.

10 In Remotes preferences, select Enable, and then click Link.

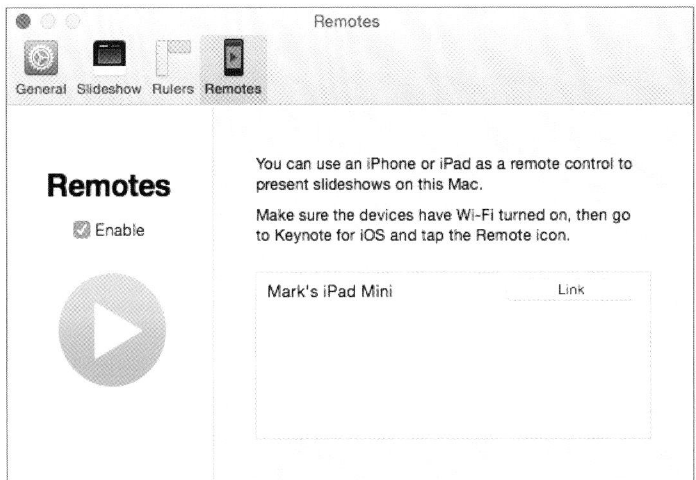

Your iOS version of Keynote displays a passcode that also appears on your Mac.

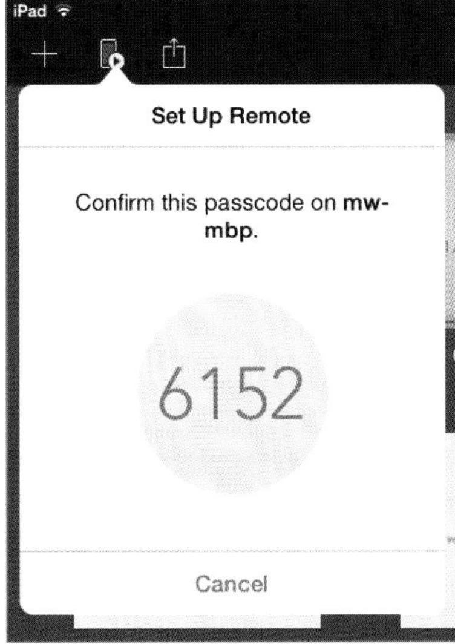

11 On the Mac, click Confirm to link your devices.

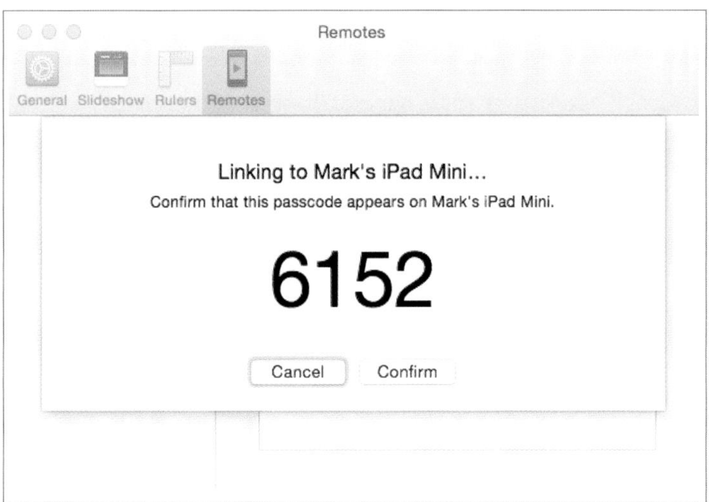

When both Keynote installations are linked, your iOS Keynote displays a large Play button.

12 Tap the Play button.

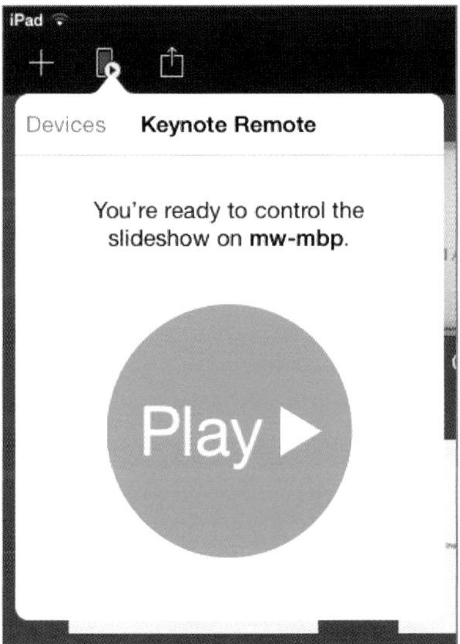

13 On the iOS device Keynote Remote, tap the screen to advance through the slides.

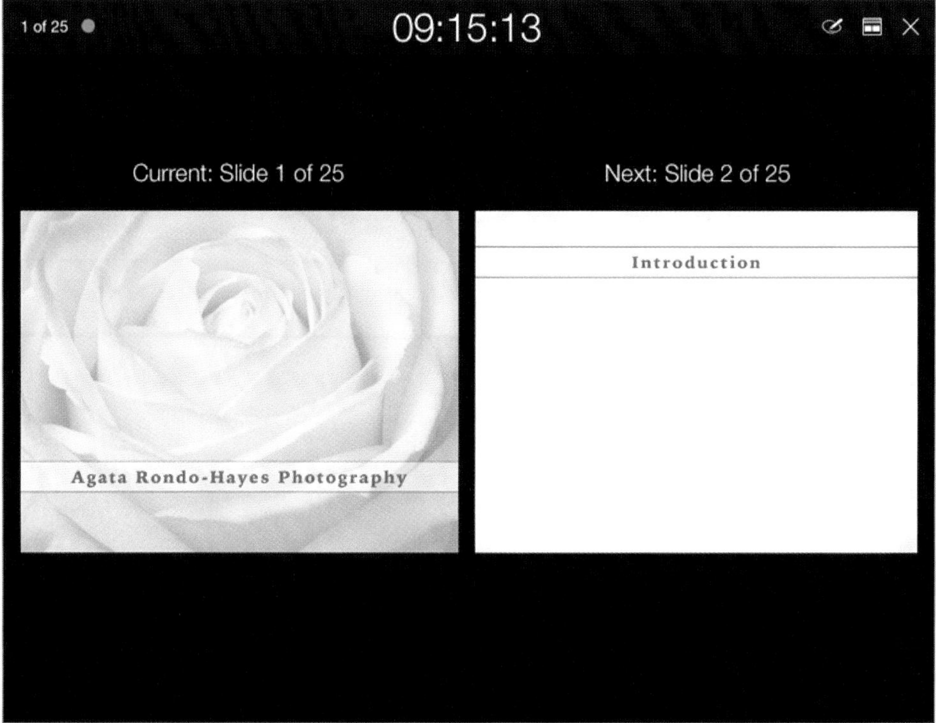

The default view can be customized.

14 At the upper right are three icons. Tap the middle icon to open Layout Options.

15 In the Layout Options popover, in the Landscape section, tap “Current and Notes.”

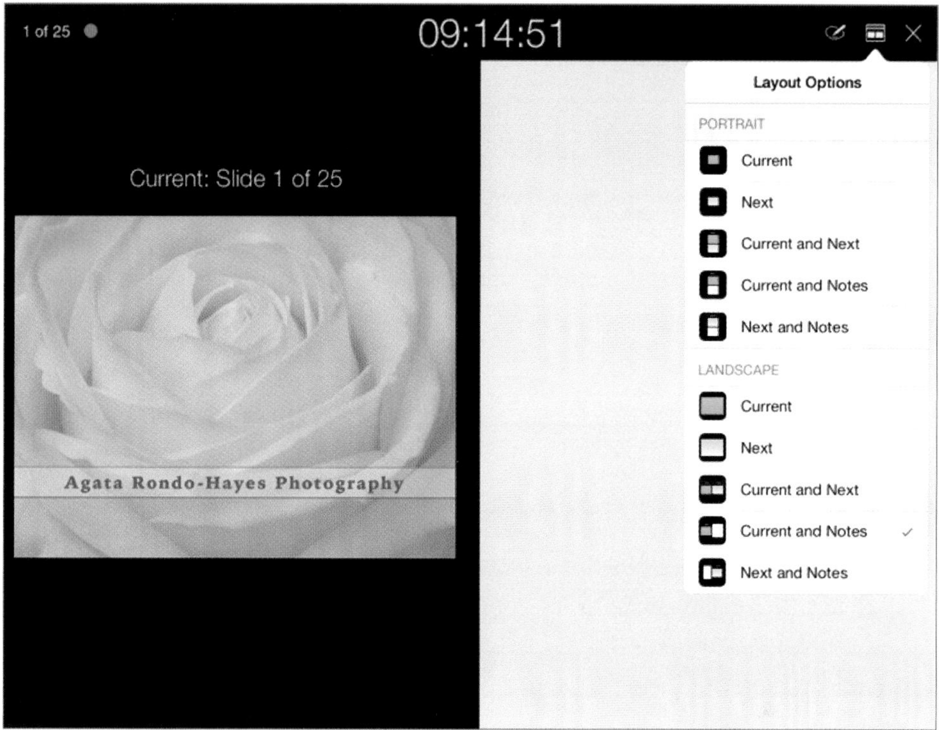

NOTE ► The layout options are available for Portrait and Landscape.

16 Tap the screen to advance to slide 3, which contains presenter notes.

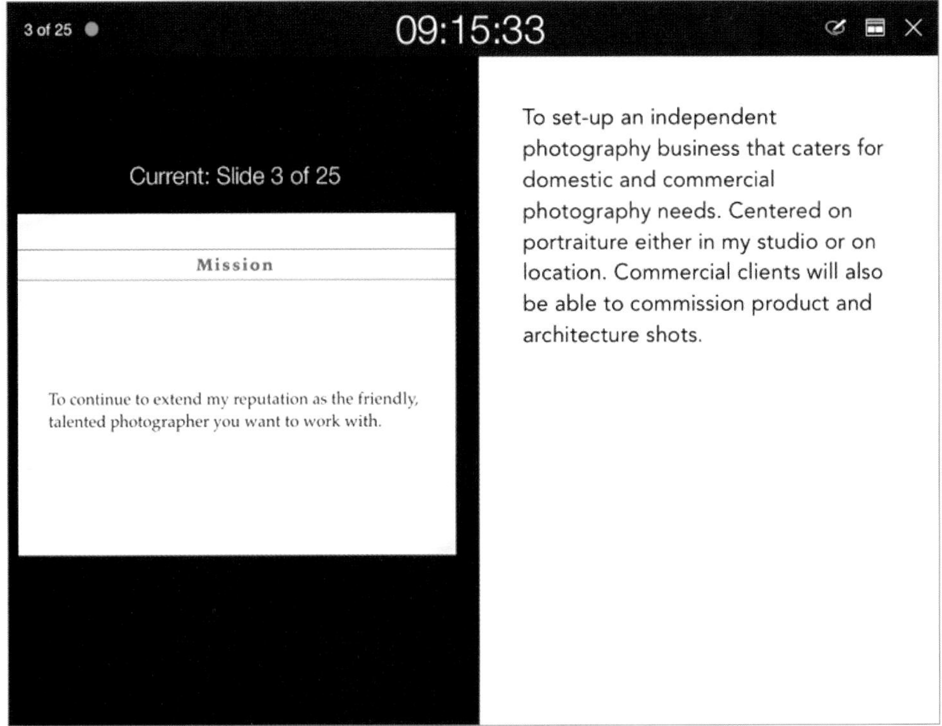

17 Leave the slideshow running.

Highlighting Slides as You Present

The Keynote Remote highlighting function lets you mark up slides as you present.

1 In the upper right of the screen, tap the Highlight button.

The display switches to a current slide view. At the bottom of this screen is a toolbar containing colored pens.

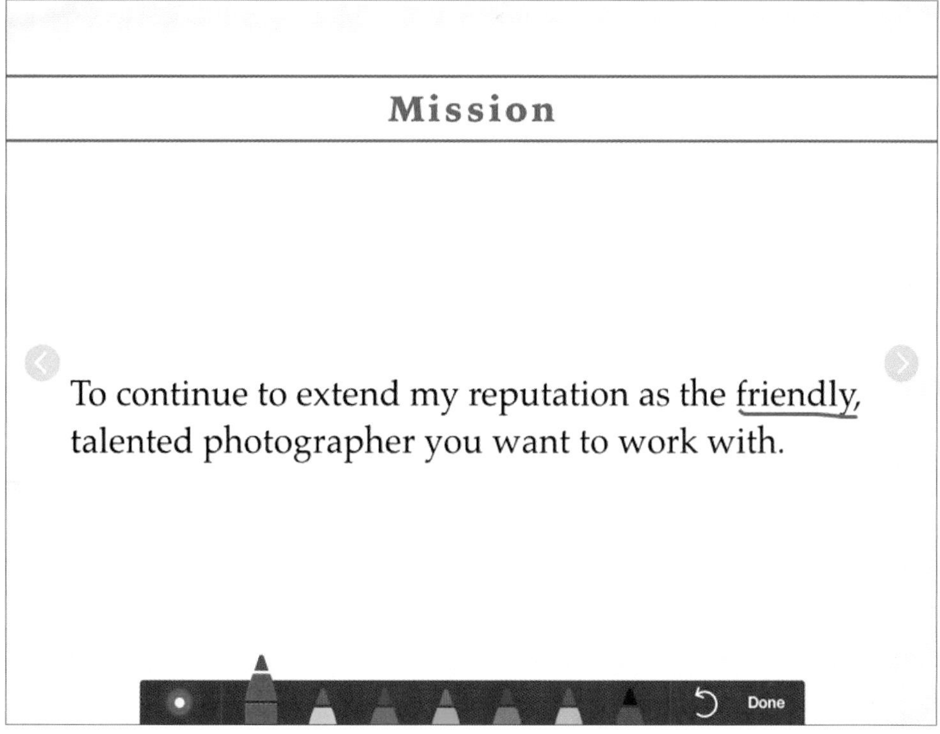

2 Tap a pen with the color you want to use for marking up your slide, and then draw with your finger on the iOS device. What you draw on the iOS device appears on the screen in your presentation.

3 Tap the Undo button to delete your marks.

4 Tap the red dot to the left of the pens.

It works like a laser pointer: As you move the red dot on the slide displayed on the iOS device, a similar red dot makes the same moves on the slide in your presentation.

5 Drag the red pointer over the slide.

6 Tap Done to close the highlighting view.

7 On Keynote Remote, tap the close button in the upper right of the screen to quit the slideshow.

Recording a Narrated, Self-Playing Presentation

Because not all presentations are delivered in person, you can use Keynote to create a self-playing slideshow with narration. You can then export the slideshow as a movie, which can then be uploaded to a server—such as YouTube or Vimeo—for playback on demand.

Although you can use your Mac computer's internal microphone to record your narration, you might want to consider using an external microphone. A USB microphone designed for podcasting is ideal because it records only those sounds that are close to the mic. Your Mac computer's internal microphone is likely to pick up ambient noise that will distract from the narration; and if you're using a laptop during the recording, the microphone may also record keyboard sounds.

You choose the microphone for recording in System Preferences.

1 On your Mac, choose Apple > System Preferences. Click the Sound icon.

2 In Sound preferences, click the Input tab, and from the list of available devices, select the desired mic.

If in doubt, select Internal Microphone.

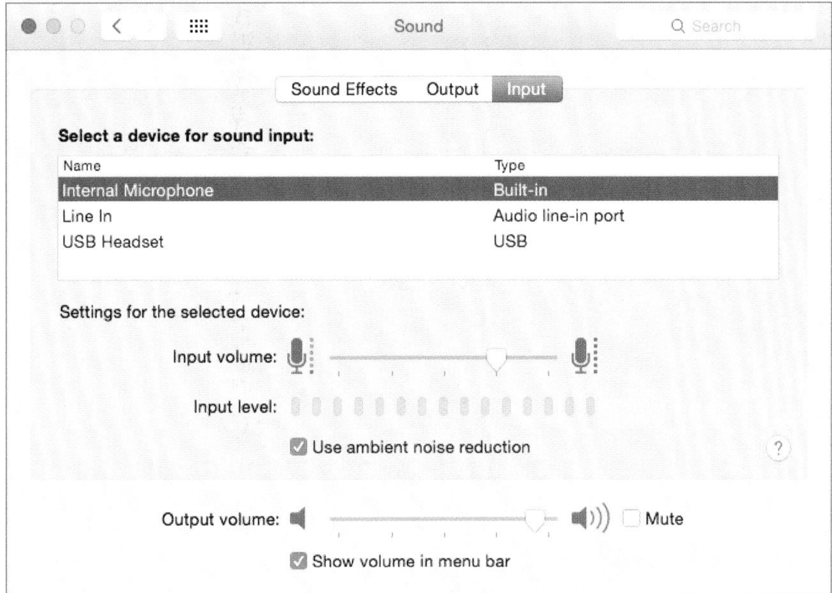

Now you'll check the mic's recording levels. Make sure you're sitting, or standing, in position for playing the slideshow.

3 Leave "Use ambient noise reduction" selected, if the option appears.

4 In your best narrator's voice, do as all good roadies do and repeatedly say "One, Two, One, Two."

5 As you do so, in Sound preferences, drag the "Input volume" slider to the left or right to reduce or increase the volume until the "Input level" bars reach to about 75% of the total input level with your loudest spoken narration.

6 Switch to Keynote, while leaving System Preferences open.

7 Go to slide 1.

8 In Keynote, select the Audio tab of the Document inspector.

9 Click Record.

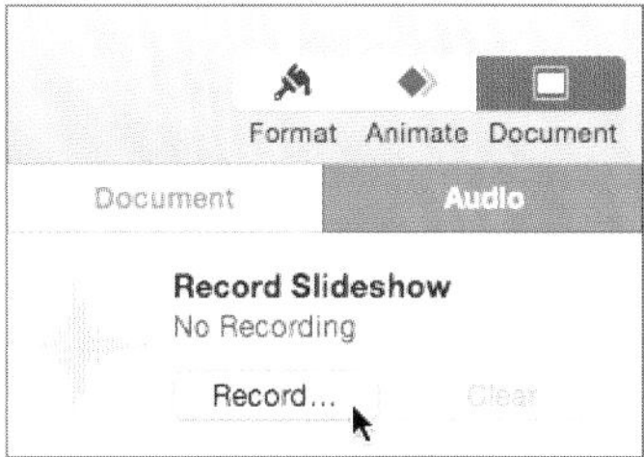

Keynote shows the presenter display with the recording controls in the lower part of the screen.

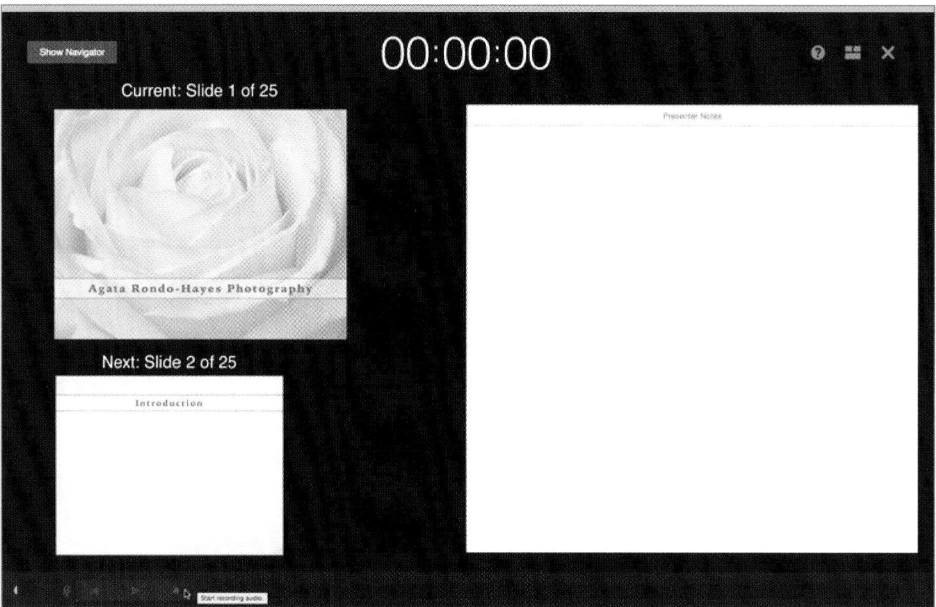

10 Say "One, Two, One, Two" again while watching the Keynote level meter.

So long as your loudest spoken narration peaks within the yellow and does not extend into the meter's red area, your recording level is good. If your loudest sounds stay entirely within the green area, however, the input level is set too low.

If you need to adjust the input levels, return to System Preferences and readjust the "Input volume" slider. When the "Input level" is properly set, you are ready to record.

11 Close System Preferences.

12 In Keynote, click the Record button. A countdown begins.

13 When the countdown is completed, start delivering your narration by reading the slide 1 text.

14 Press the Spacebar to advance through the slides and builds, narrating as you go. Try working through a couple of slides as practice. Later you'll delete this recording test.

15 Click the Pause button.

You can pause like this during your narration, perhaps to take a sip of water and gather your thoughts.

16 Click the Pause button to resume recording your narration.

For this exercise, you needn't read through all the slides.

17 Click the Record button again to stop recording.

Keynote saves your narration as part of the presentation. Now when you export your presentation to a QuickTime file (which you'll do in the next exercise), the option to use the slideshow recording will be available.

NOTE ▸ Custom timings can be recorded without narration. In the recording tools, click the Mute button while recording and continue to advance through the slideshow. Your custom timings will be recorded, but the audio will not.

18 Press Esc to quit the slideshow.

Exporting a Self-Playing Slideshow

To upload a self-playing slideshow to a streaming service, you must first export the slideshow to QuickTime.

1 Choose File > Export To > QuickTime.

The export window shows the Playback pop-up menu set to Slideshow Recording (the desired setting).

2 From the Format pop-up menu, choose 1080p.

To produce smaller files, you can choose 1024 x 768px or 720p.

3 Click Next to open the Export dialog. The default file name is OK, and you can tag the movie if you wish. Choose Desktop as the save location.

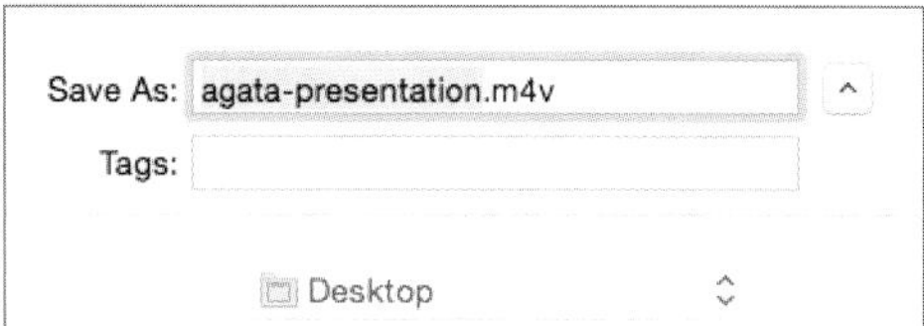

4 Click Export. Keynote creates a movie from your slideshow. This process might take a minute or two.

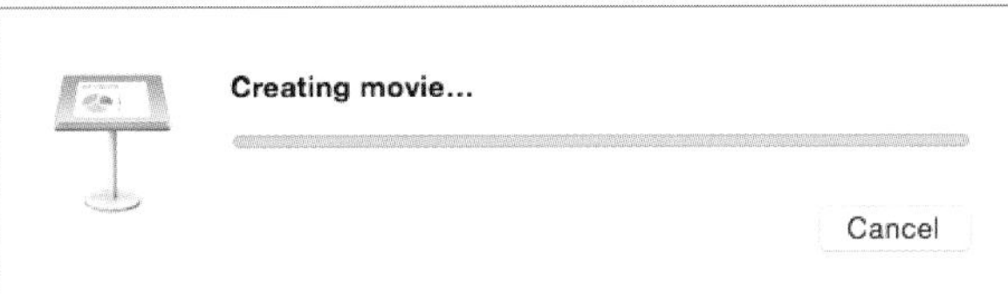

5 When the export process is completed, go to the Finder and locate the **agata-presentation.m4v** file on your desktop.

6 Control-click the **agata-presentation.m4v** file, and from the shortcut menu, choose Open With > QuickTime Player.

7 Press Spacebar to play your narrated movie.

The movie plays only the slides and builds you included in the recording.

8 Press Command-Q to quit QuickTime Player.

NOTE ▶ The compatible video file formats for each streaming service vary. The Keynote "Export To > QuickTime" command lets you customize your video settings so that you can provide the most appropriate media format.

Creating a Self-Playing Slideshow

Keynote can create self-playing slideshows that needn't be exported as a movie. In this exercise, you'll create a slideshow that plays each slide for five seconds. This type of slideshow is ideal for trade shows or shop windows, when you can use a Mac and Keynote to repeat an ongoing combination of words and pictures on an external display.

1 In the slide navigator for **agata-presentation.key**, click slide 1, and then Shift-click slide 7.

2 Control-click any of the selected slides, and from the shortcut menu, choose Skip Slide.

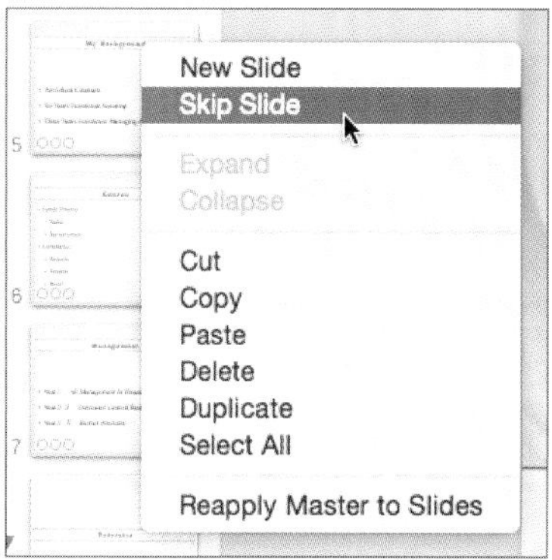

It's that easy to skip slides you don't want in your QuickTime export. But because your presentation now contains a recorded narration, skipping slides will put the narration out of sync. Adding new slides or changing animation timings will also put the narration out of sync. Fortunately, Keynote gives you the option to duplicate your presentation. You can edit this copy while preserving the original version.

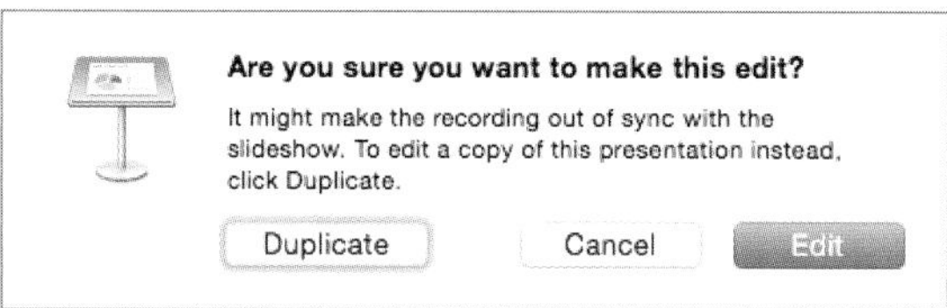

3 In the dialog that appears, click Edit. This puts the recording out of sync.

4 In the Audio inspector, click Clear to remove the recording.

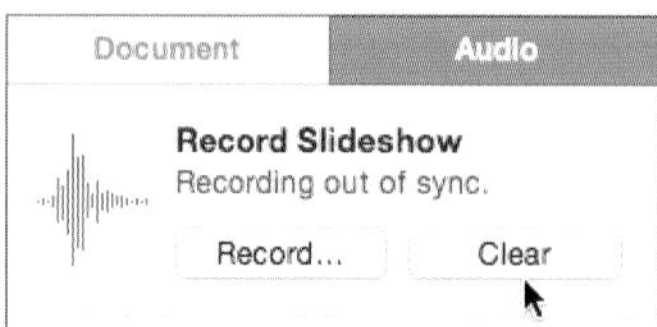

5 In the warning dialog, click Clear again to confirm the removal of your recording.

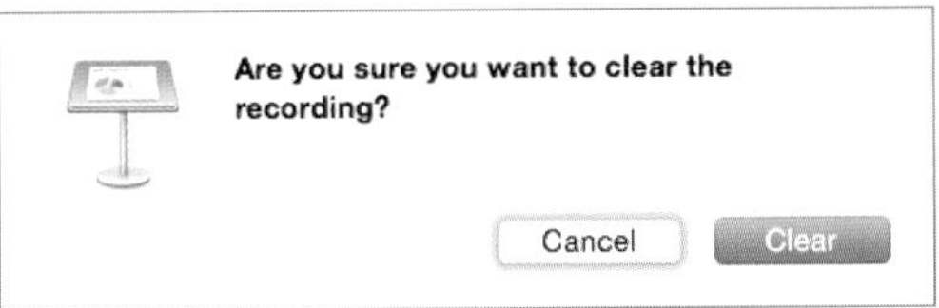

NOTE ▶ If you decide you want to use your recording, you can press Command-Z to undo the previous few steps.

To run a self-playing slideshow from Keynote, you have to make changes in both the Document inspector and Keynote preferences.

6 In the Document inspector, change the Presentation Type to Self-Playing. Leave the default timings of 5 seconds for Transitions and 2 seconds for Builds.

7 In the inspector, select "Automatically play upon open" and "Loop slideshow."

The "Restart show if idle for" option is not relevant here because a slideshow set to loop is never idle. The slideshow will now continually loop until you press Esc to quit. You can prevent unauthorized quitting by setting a password in Keynote preferences.

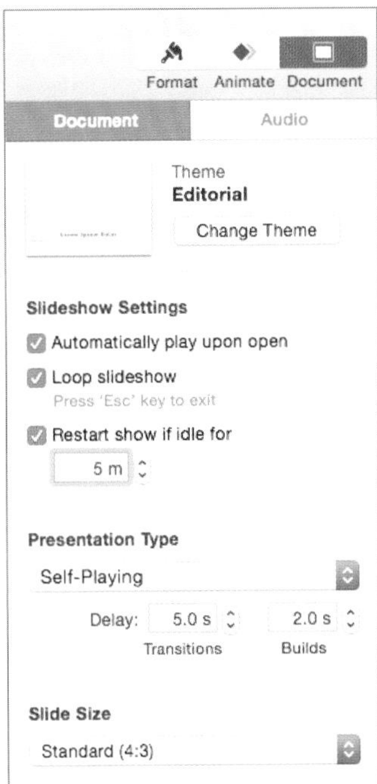

8 Choose Keynote > Preferences. In the Slideshow pane, select "Require password to exit slideshows."

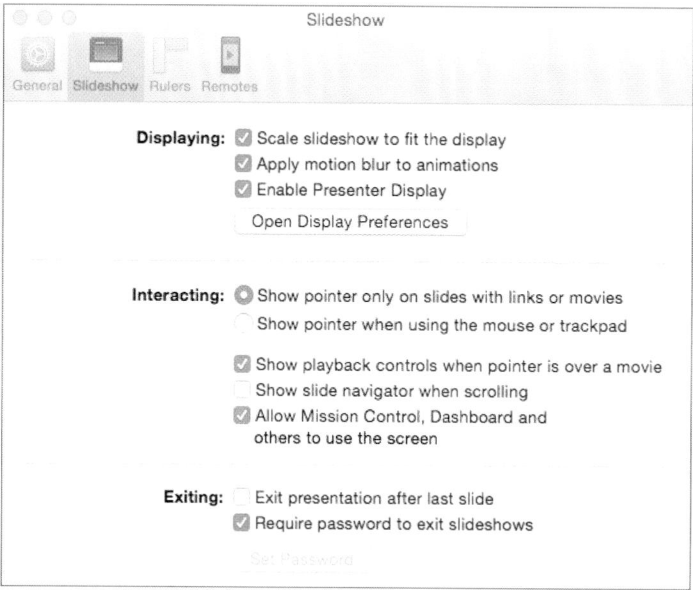

9 When prompted, enter the same password in the Password and Verify fields. Click Set Password.

You can set an exiting password only for the system on which the slideshow is playing.

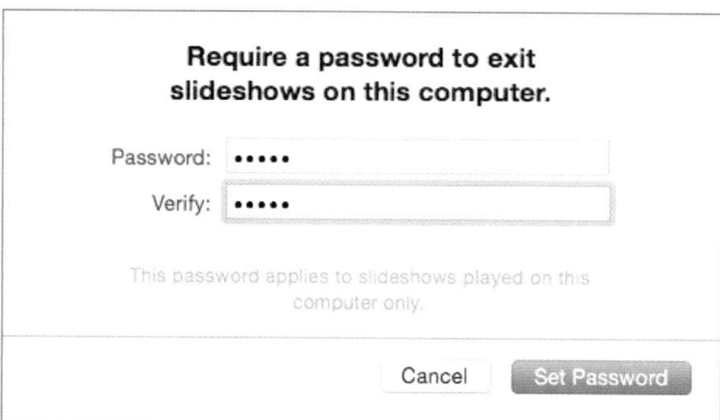

10 Press Command-Option-P to play your slideshow. Let the slideshow advance automatically.

Once you've verified that the slideshow advances automatically, you can quit the slideshow.

11 Press Esc to quit the slideshow.

12 When prompted, type your password in the Password field to exit.

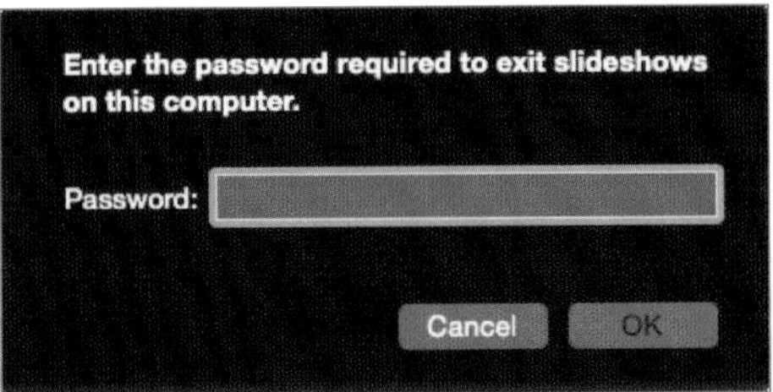

13 To remove password protection, choose Keynote > Preferences. In the Slideshow pane, deselect "Require password to exit slideshows," and then close Preferences.

Exporting a Self-Playing Slideshow to QuickTime

You can export a self-playing slideshow as a QuickTime movie in the same way you previously exported your narrated slideshow.

1 Choose File > Export To > QuickTime.

The export window shows the Playback pop-up menu set to Self-Playing (the required setting).

2 From the Format pop-up menu, choose 1024x768. Leave “Go to next slide” set to 5 seconds and “Go to next build after” set to 2 seconds.

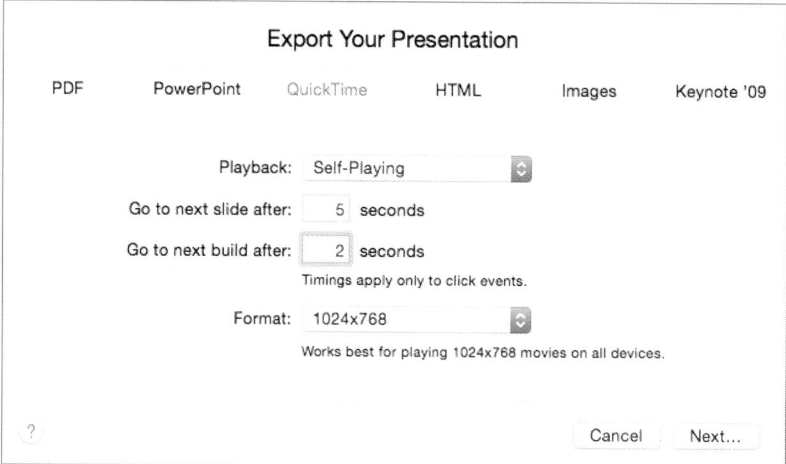

3 Click Next.

4 In the Save As field, type *agata-slides.m4v*. Save the file to the desktop.

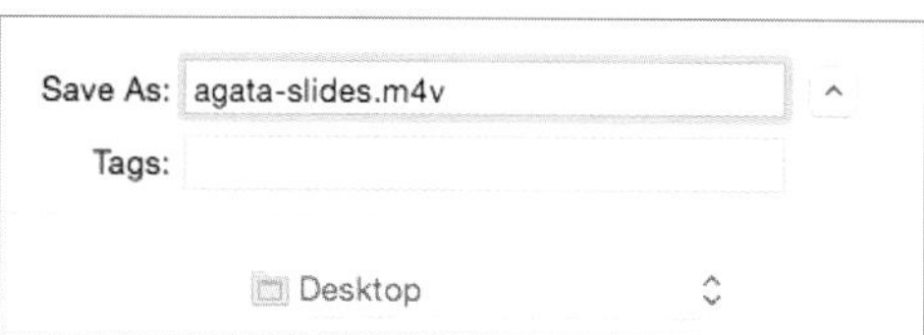

5 Once the export process is completed, return to the Finder and locate agata-slides.m4v on your desktop.

6 Control-click agata-slides.m4v, and from the shortcut menu, choose Open With > QuickTime Player.

7 Press Spacebar to play the movie. The movie advances based on the times set in step 2.

8 Press Command-Q to quit QuickTime Player.

Designing a Presentation with Links

You can design Keynote presentations to advance using only links. These kinds of presentations behave much like a website. Through navigation menus you create, users can interact with your slideshows as they would when navigating a website. You can turn text, shapes, and media into links.

This kind of kiosk presentation requires a different approach to Keynote. Let's take a brief look at how to create a presentation with links.

> **NOTE ▶** The slide navigator renumbers slides when you hide or show any slides. The eighth slide is numbered 1 because the first seven slides are skipped.

1 In the slide navigator for **agata-presentation.key**, click the line representing the first slide. Shift-click the line representing the seventh slide.

2 Control-click any of the selected slides, and from the shortcut menu, choose Don't Skip Slide.

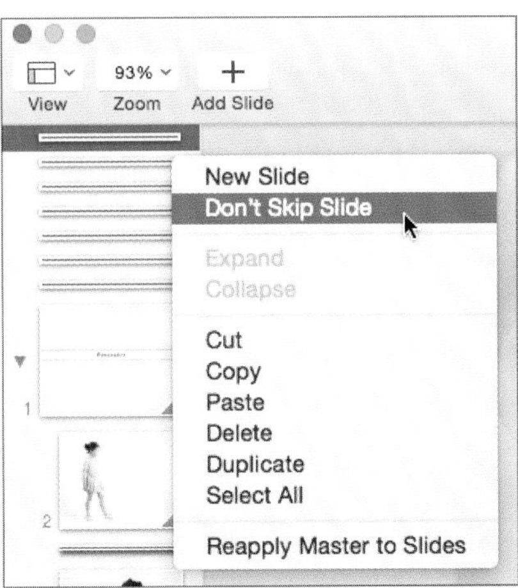

3 In the slide navigator, click slide 6. It contains suitable link candidates.

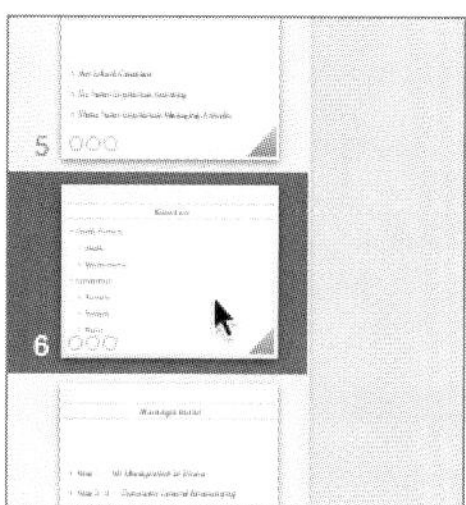

4 Double-click the word "Family."

5 Control-click the selection, and from the shortcut menu, choose Add Link.

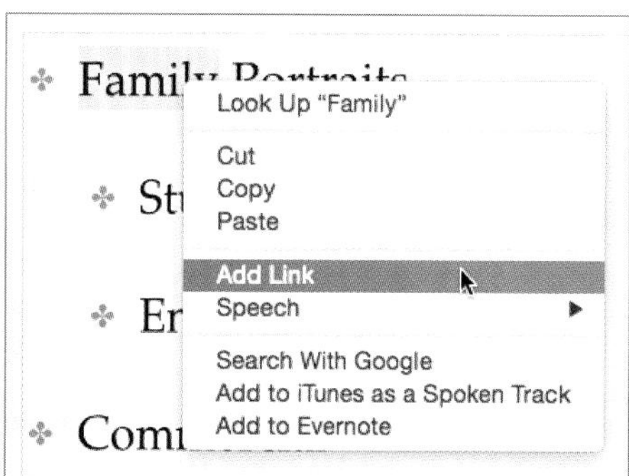

6 In the link options, choose Link to: Slide, and select the Slide option. In the Slide field, type *8*.

There are several link options you can explore.

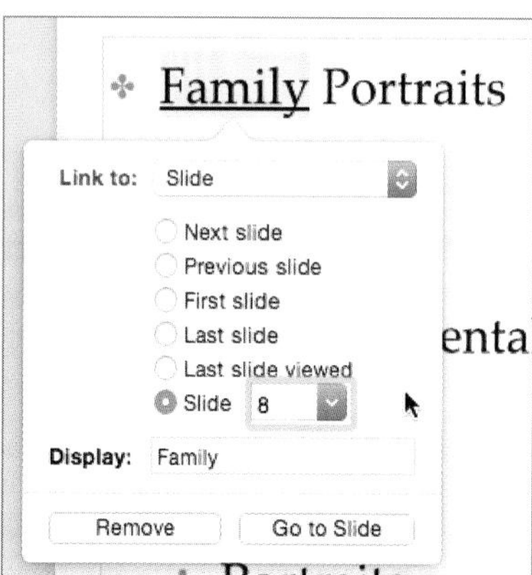

7 Click outside the link options popover to close it, but be sure to leave the word "Family" selected.

NOTE ▶ A text link can't be applied to two words in a single step. To also link the word "Portraits" to slide 8, you must apply another link separately.

The link is underlined. You could create link text style, but for now you'll just remove the underline.

8 In the Text inspector, deselect the Underline Text button to remove the underline.

It's time to play the slideshow. In this instance, the presentation type must be set to Normal because a links-only presentation demands that every slide have a link, which is the only way to advance through the slideshow.

9 In the Document inspector, set Presentation Type to Normal.

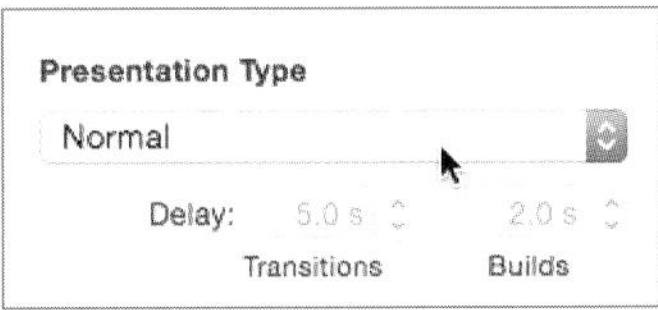

10 In the slide navigator, make sure slide 5 is selected.

11 Press Command-Option-P to play your slideshow.

12 Press Spacebar until the bullet containing the word “Family” on slide 6 appears.

The slideshow advances as expected.

13 Click the Family link. You are taken to slide 8.

14 Press Esc to quit the slideshow.

Making Keynote Handouts

You’ve used several methods to make your Keynote presentation available to others, but you have yet another way to share your presentation. Keynote can produce a variety of handouts. In this exercise, you’ll prepare a handout containing multiple slides that include space for writing notes. You can even include your presenter notes in the handouts.

1 In the **agata-presentation.key** file, choose File > Print. Then click the Show Details button at the bottom of the dialog.

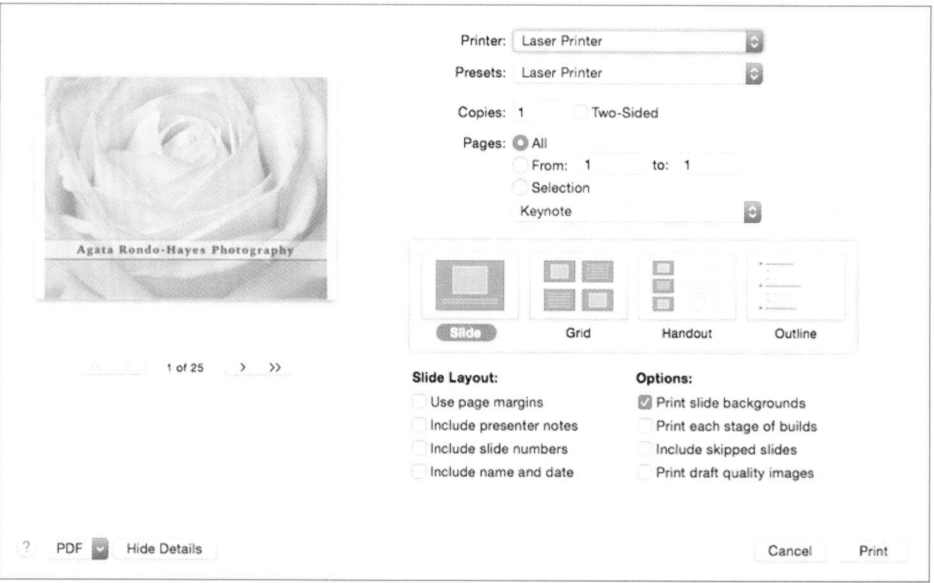

If you have a printer connected, choose it from the Printer menu. You can also select any print presets you've created.

The window is currently set to show Keynote print options. You'll need to change the page orientation in Page Attributes.

2 From the print options pop-up menu (currently displaying Keynote), choose Page Attributes.

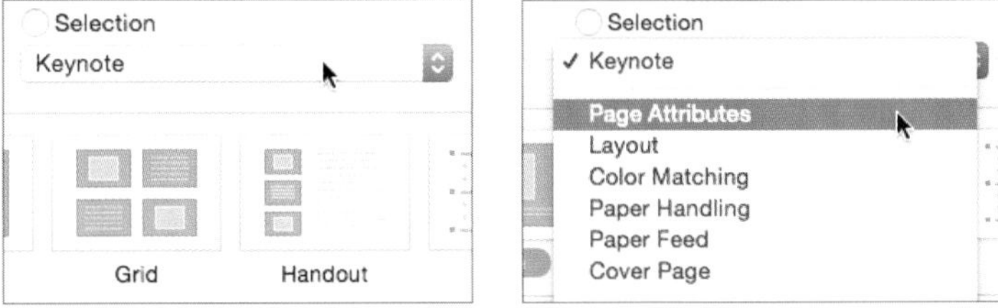

3 In Page Attributes, set Paper Size to US Letter and Orientation to Portrait.

4 From the print options pop-up menu, choose Keynote to return to the previous print dialog.

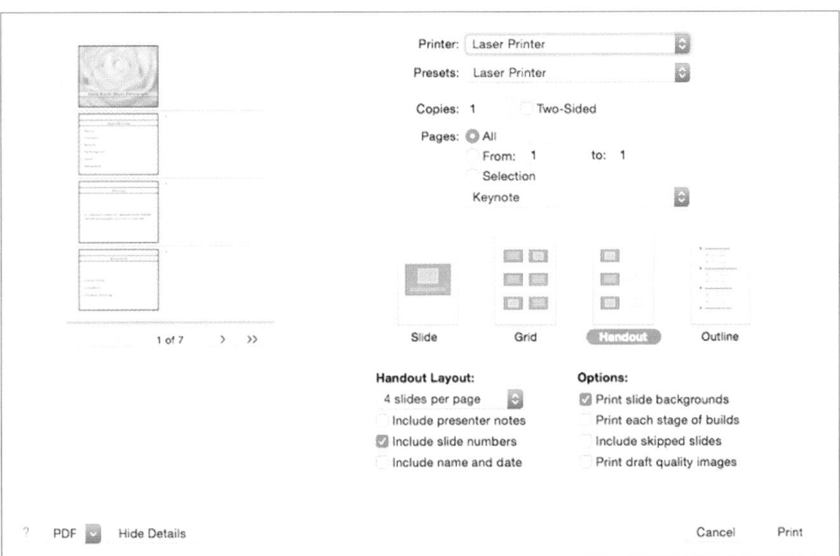

5 In the Keynote options, select Handout.

6 From the Handout Layout pop-up menu, choose "4 slides per page."

7 Select the "Include slide numbers" checkbox. If you want to print your notes as part of the handout, you can select "Include presenter notes."

Using the slide numbers as labels adds to a handout's clarity, and having four slides per page strikes a nice balance between economy of paper and legibility.

NOTE ▸ Deselecting "Print slide backgrounds" forces the handout to print in black-and-white.

You could now click Print to produce paper copies of the handouts, but saving to PDF may be a more versatile choice at this point.

Printing Notes as PDF Documents

Rather than print your handouts for distribution, why not create PDF files that people can print as they choose; or better still—and more in keeping with the ideal of the paperless office—they can read your handouts on a computer display or mobile device.

1 In the Print window, locate the PDF menu in the lower left of the window.

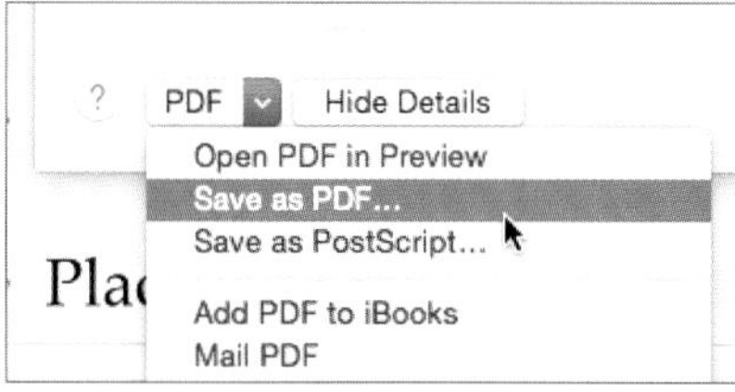

2 From the PDF pop-up menu, choose Save as PDF.

The menu also allows you to send the PDF directly to iBooks and iTunes, but you'll save a PDF to the desktop.

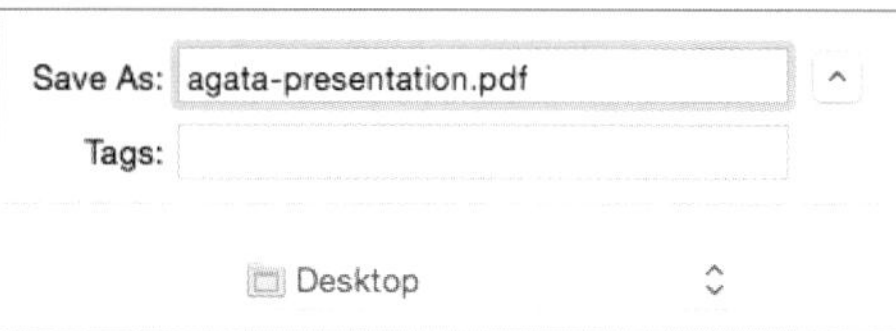

3 In the Save As field, change the filename to *agata-presentation.pdf*. Save it to the desktop.

4 Switch to the Finder, and locate agata-presentation.pdf on your desktop.

5 Control-click agata-presentation.pdf, and from the shortcut menu, choose Open With > Preview.

6 In Preview, review the PDF handout you've just created.

You can distribute or post this document for your audience to read or print on demand.

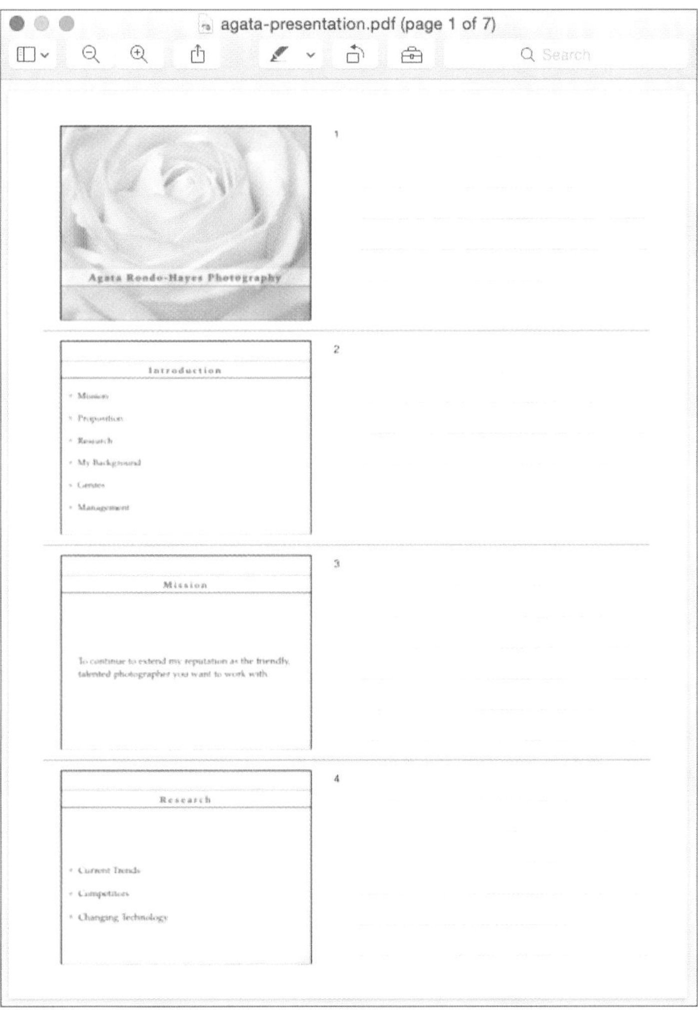

7 Press Command-W to close the PDF, and then press Command-Q to quit Preview.

Performing Presentation Preflight Checks

The clock is ticking down to zero hour, and you need to pack your bag and head off to make a presentation. The Keynote file is in good shape; your rehearsals have gone well. You elected to print handouts in advance, and they're already packed, so what else should you check before leaving your desk?

Let's assume you'll be presenting from your laptop to a data projector or large display.

- Save a copy of your presentation to a USB drive, and be sure to include any nonsystem fonts. Do this just in case you have to present using a different Mac. You also may want to include an iWork '09–formatted version of your presentation and a PowerPoint version.
- Have copies of your Keynote presentation available on iCloud and your laptop. Not all venues will allow guest users full Internet access, which means you may not be able to sign in to your iCloud account.
- Take a range of display adapters with you (for example, Mini DisplayPort to DVI and Mini DisplayPort to VGA).
- Review Keynote slideshow preferences (Keynote > Preferences), and in the Slideshow pane, check that "Scale slideshow to fit the display" is enabled. Doing so helps the slideshow scale to the resolution of the presentation display.
- A final preflight check, best made at your final destination, as you connect to the secondary display.
- You might want to temporarily switch off Energy Saver and the Screen Saver in System Preferences. With these options turned on, the data projector might switch to standby, leaving your audience to wait while you awaken the projector from its slumber.

Reducing File Size

If your Keynote presentation contains lots of high-resolution photographs and audiovisual clips, you may find that slideshow loading times are slowing down. To counter this slowdown, you can reduce the file size; but always do so on a copy of your presentation, so that you don't permanently downgrade the original media quality.

1 In **agata-presentation.key**, choose File > Duplicate.

2 Press Command-S to save a duplicate presentation.

The default file name of agata-presentation copy.key is acceptable for this purpose.

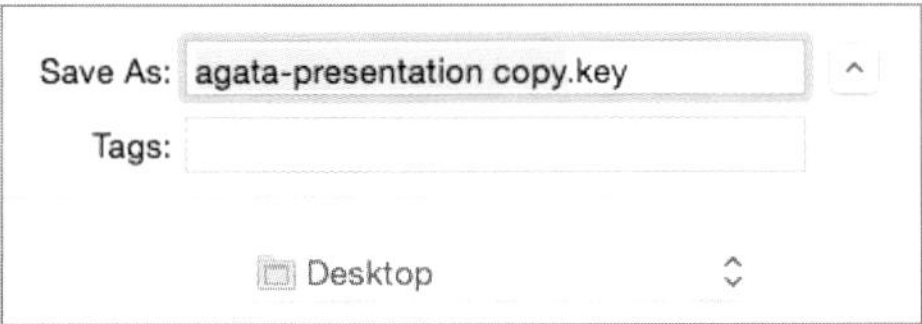

3 In the Save As window, set the file to save to the desktop, and then click Save.

4 With agata-presentation copy.key as the active document, choose File > Advanced > Reduce File Size.

A dialog appears stating what this operation will do and estimating the file size reduction.

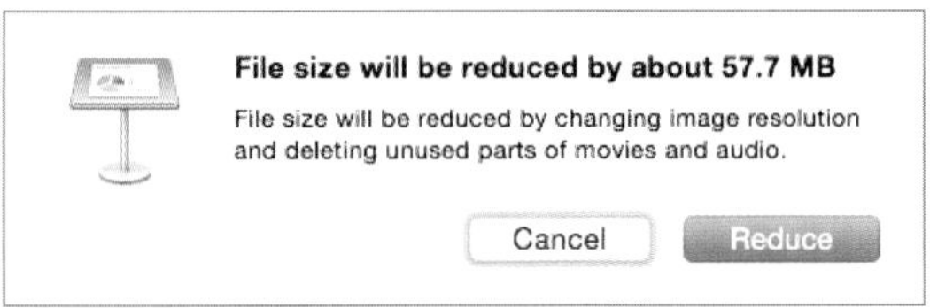

5 Click Reduce.

The reduction may take a few minutes and with some presentations may return a warning that not all images could be reduced. You can dismiss this warning because any files that could not be reduced merely remain as they were.

Presenting on an External Display

There is no substitute for experience when you need to troubleshoot the connection between your Mac and an external display. Things usually go smoothly, but here's a few tips on how to set up Keynote for a second screen.

1 Connect your Mac to the second display using the appropriate cables and adapters.

2 In Keynote, choose Keynote > Preferences. Click the Slideshow tab.

3 Make sure that "Enable Presenter Display" is selected.

4 Click Open Display Preferences to view the preferences for your display.

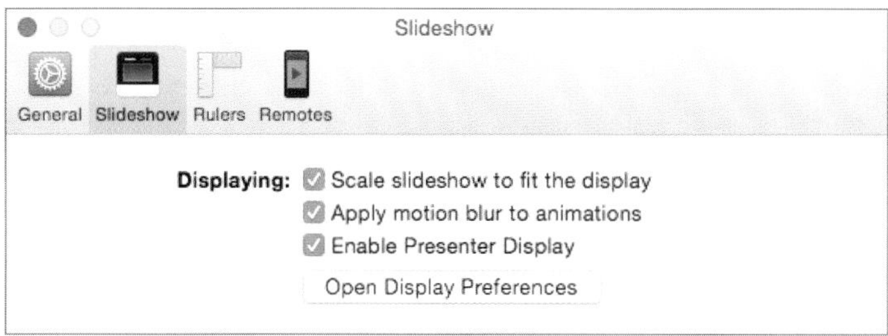

The Display preferences opens windows on both your Mac and the second display.

5 On your Mac, click Gather Windows to show both Display preferences on your Mac computer's display.

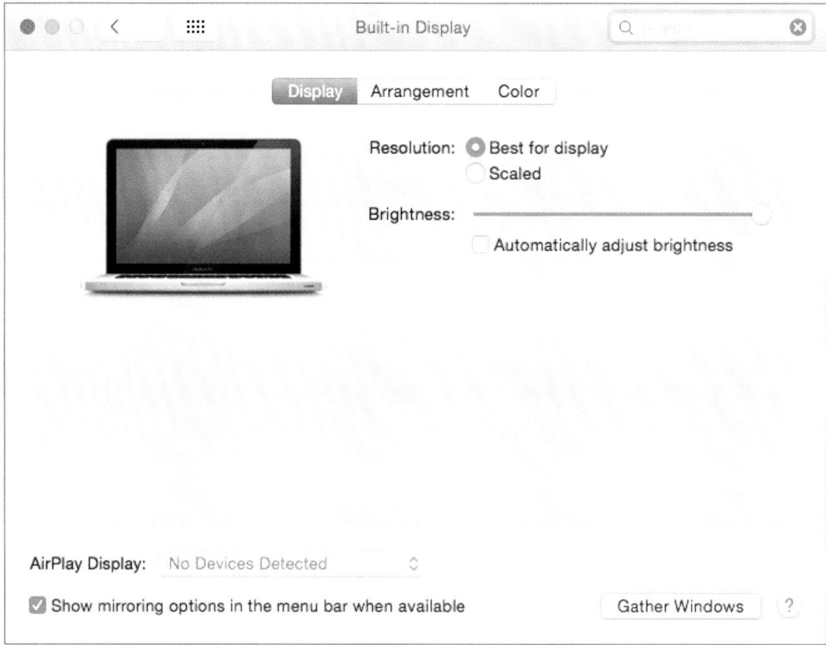

You may find that your Mac display now has a lowered resolution, but at the moment you need to pay more attention to the second display. Selecting the "Best for display" option is a good starting point. If you have time, however, selecting the Scaled option and then experimenting with different resolutions might yield a better result with higher resolution and smoother fonts.

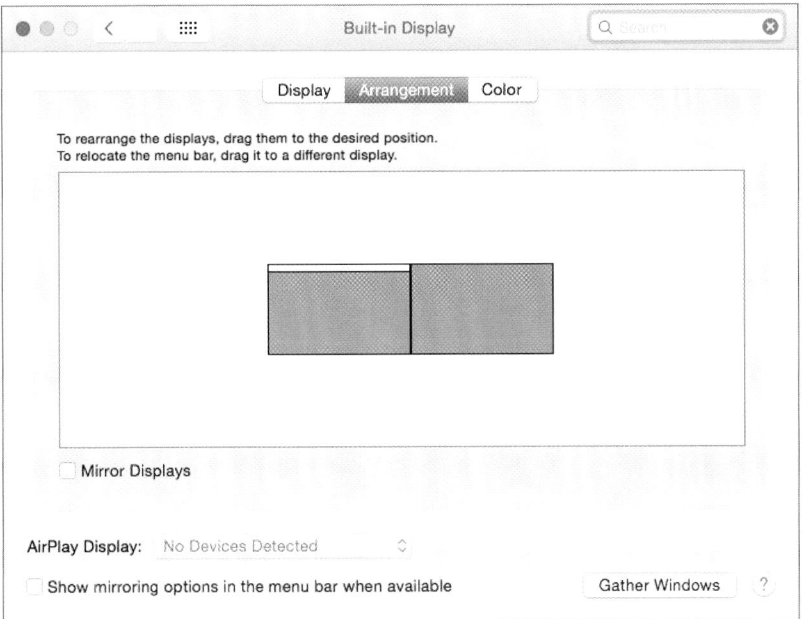

6 Click the Arrangement tab.

7 Make sure Mirror Displays is deselected.

8 Switch to Keynote.

9 Press Command-Option-P to play the slideshow.

Your Mac now shows the presenter display, and the second display shows the slides.

NOTE ▶ If your slides and notes appear on the wrong displays, you can press X to toggle which display shows the slides and which shows the notes.

10 Press Esc to quit the slideshow.

11 Choose File > Close.

12 Disconnect the second display.

13 If necessary, adjust your display settings again, and then close System preferences.

Lesson Review

1. How do you display the Keynote keyboard shortcuts?
2. Describe how to rehearse a 20-minute Keynote presentation.
3. Name two places where you can add and edit presenter notes.
4. When playing a slideshow, how do you jump to a specific slide?
5. When recording narration, which button do you click to stop recording?

Answers

1. When playing a slideshow, pressing Slash (/) will display the keyboard shortcuts. See Keynote Help for a full list of shortcuts.
2. The first rehearsal step is to play the slideshow by choosing Play > Rehearse Slideshow. In the presenter display, set the Timer to show time remaining, with a value of 20 minutes. If the presentation is running long, you can skip slides to trim the time.
3. From the View icon in the toolbar, choose Navigator, Slide Only, or Outline. You can then view and edit presenter notes. You can also edit presenter notes after choosing Play > Rehearse Slideshow.
4. To jump to a specific slide when playing a slideshow, type the slide number. Note that if you guess the wrong number, a navigator appears allowing you to scroll to the desired slide.
5. To end a recording, click the red Record button.

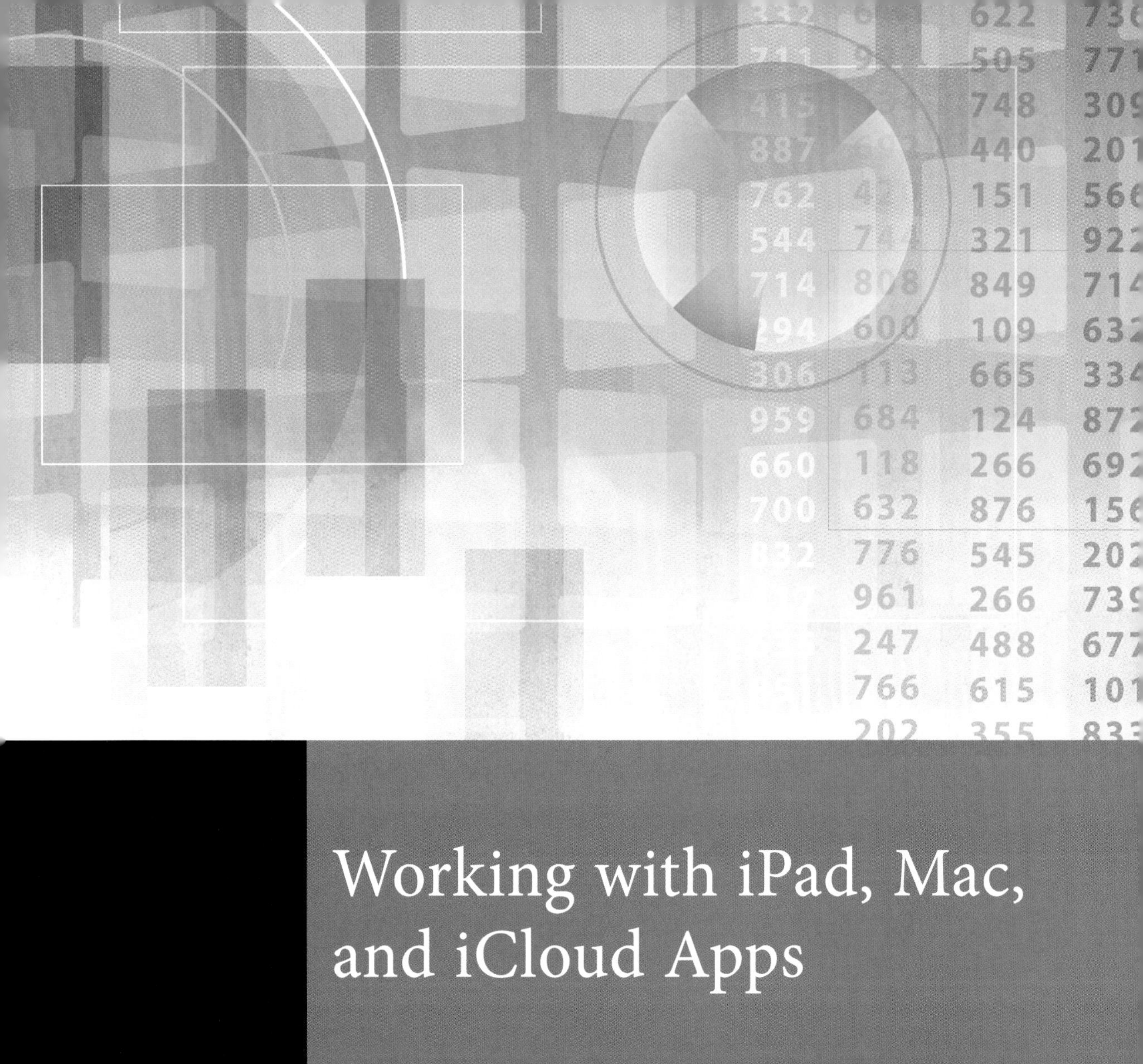

Working with iPad, Mac, and iCloud Apps

16

Lesson Files	None
Time	This lesson takes approximately 90 minutes to complete.
Goals	Open, save, and manage documents Edit text, objects, and media Understand table functions Add custom color Set password protection

Lesson **16**

Pages, Numbers, and Keynote for iOS

If you've worked through all the previous lessons, you'll be familiar with the techniques used in this lesson, but now you'll apply that knowledge of the OS X versions of Pages, Numbers, and Keynote to the iOS versions. You'll explore the interface and tool differences of the iOS apps in preparation for working across OS X, iOS, and iCloud in Lesson 17.

Although this lesson focuses on using an iPad, you could also try these exercises on an iPhone or iPod touch. Like their OS X counterparts, all three iOS apps have common tools and functions, such as document management, text formatting, and media handling.

Signing In to iCloud

You likely already have an Apple ID because it's a user account that enhances everything you do with Apple hardware and software. When you create an account for an Apple service, such as iCloud or the App Store, you create an Apple ID. If you've bought music via iTunes, you do so with an Apple ID.

> **TIP** Use just one Apple ID. Using multiple Apple IDs may cause complications when accessing purchased content or using some services.

If you don't have an Apple ID, visit Apple.com to create one. Once you have your Apple ID account, you can use it to sign in to iCloud.

Before you continue, make sure your Mac is signed in to your iCloud account.

1. On your Mac, choose Apple > System Preferences > iCloud.
2. If necessary, enter your Apple ID information into the Preferences window to enable iCloud.

   Now check the iCloud status of your iPhone, iPad, or iPod touch.
3. On your iOS device, choose Settings > iCloud.
4. If necessary, enter your Apple ID information to enable iCloud on the device.

   > **MORE INFO ▸** For additional information on setting up Apple ID and iCloud, visit Apple.com.

With iCloud enabled the documents you create in this lesson will be available on all the devices signed in to that account.

Managing Pages Documents in iOS

The iOS versions of Pages, Number, and Keynote feature clean, minimalist interfaces with few menus. They rely on gestures such as taps, swipes, and pinches. To get started, you'll open iOS Pages and make changes to placeholder text.

1. On your iOS device, open Pages.

If this is the first time you've opened Pages on this device, you'll see a Welcome screen. Perform steps 2 through 4 only if you see the Welcome screen. If not, please skip to step 5.

2 On the Welcome screen, tap Continue.

The next screen asks if you wish to use iCloud. To complete all the exercises in this lesson and to be ready for Lesson 17, you need to use iCloud.

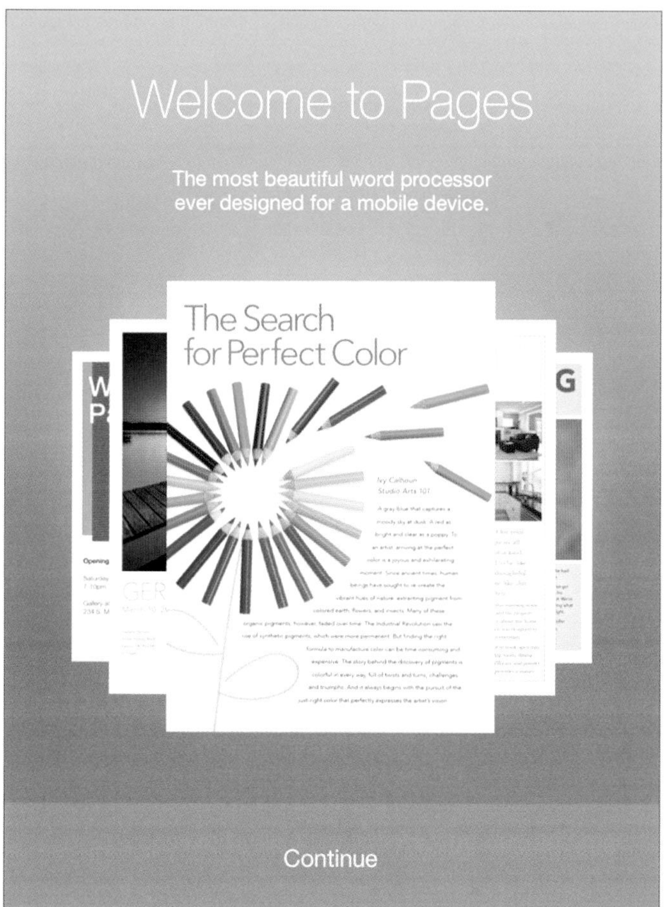

3 Tap Use iCloud to advance.

4 Tap Create a Document. Now skip to step 7.

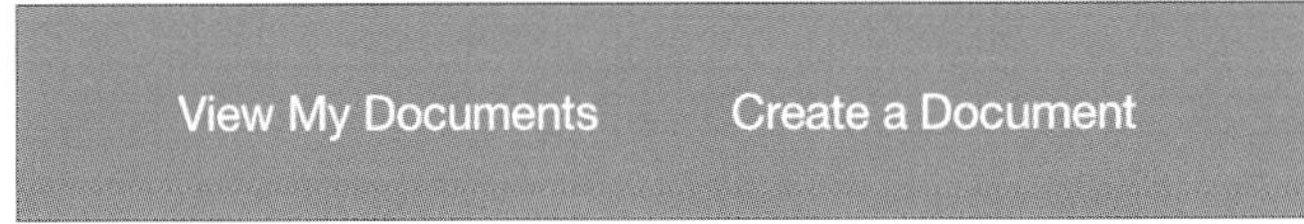

If you've opened Pages before, you'll either see the last document you worked on or the document manager.

5 If Pages opens your most recent document, tap Documents at the upper left of your screen.

6 If Pages opens in the document manager, tap the Create Document icon.

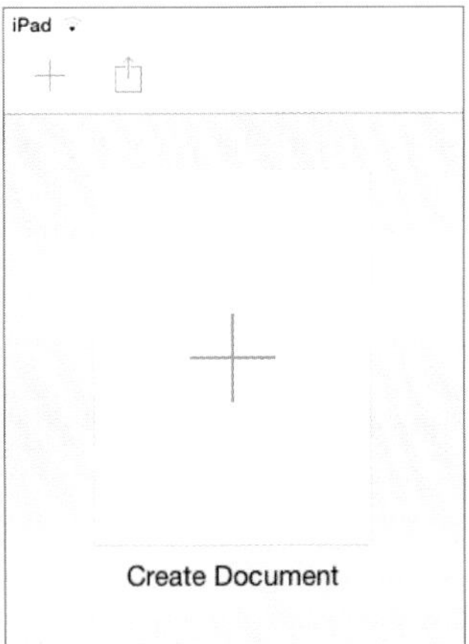

Regardless of your starting point, you now see the template chooser.

7 Rotate your iOS device to portrait orientation, then to landscape, and back to portrait.

NOTE ▶ If your iOS device has Lock Rotation enabled, step 7 will not change the orientation of the application interface. This lesson works best if Lock Rotation is not enabled.

As you work with Pages, rotate your iOS device to best suit you. Your device's orientation is independent of the document's orientation. The template you're going to open is in portrait orientation, and once a document is opened, the page's orientation cannot be changed.

TIP ▶ Choosing the most appropriate template is very important because the iOS versions of Pages, Numbers, and Keynote limit later changes. Note that Keynote always displays in landscape orientation.

8 In the template chooser, tap Modern Report.

A document opens based on the Modern Report template. A coaching tip may also appear (to let you know you can use coaching tips).

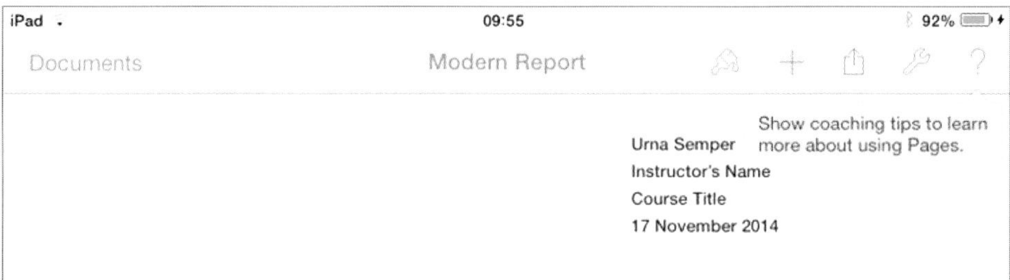

9 In the toolbar, you can tap the question mark icon in the upper right of the screen to show and hide coaching tips.

10 With coaching tips visible, note the help that is offered. Decide whether you want them on or off, and tap the question mark icon accordingly.

NOTE ▶ When enabled, you can tap the coaching tip shown in the lower-left of the screen, "Learn more about using Pages" to open Pages Help.

The document contains placeholder text so you can experiment with text editing.

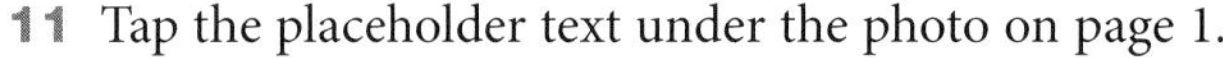
11 Tap the placeholder text under the photo on page 1.

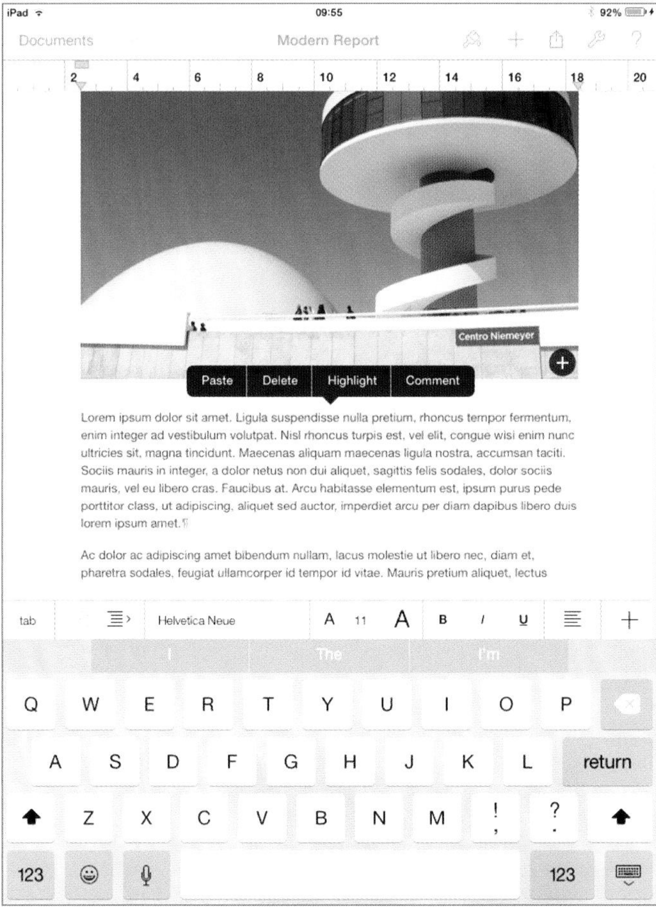

The application is context aware so appropriate menus appear. The keyboard appears, unless you're using a Bluetooth keyboard.

Across the upper part of the keyboard display are text-formatting options. Currently the font is set to Helvetica Neue.

12 Tap the font name shown above the keyboard, and from the Fonts menu that appears, choose Avenir.

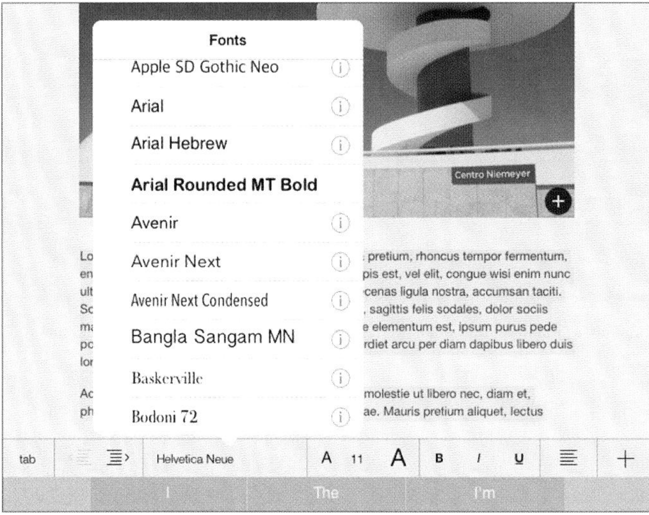

The iOS version also has several inspectors. To access these and additional tools, you can use the icons at the top of the screen.

13 Tap the wrench icon and choose Document Setup. If you've worked through the lessons on Pages for the Mac, you'll recognize many of the options shown.

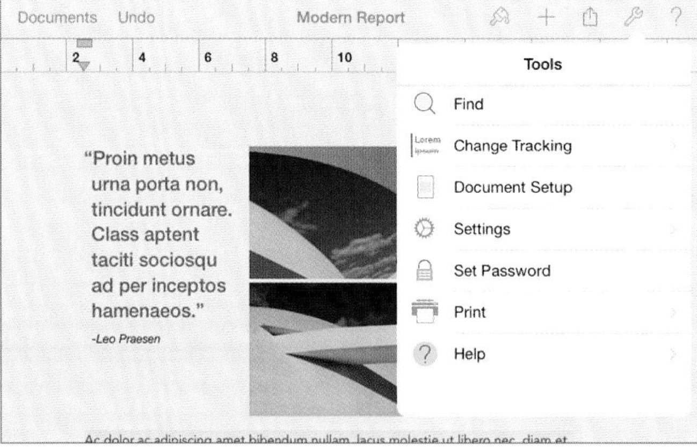

In Document Setup, you can set the page margins and edit the header and footer.

14 Adjust the page margins by dragging the page margin handles.

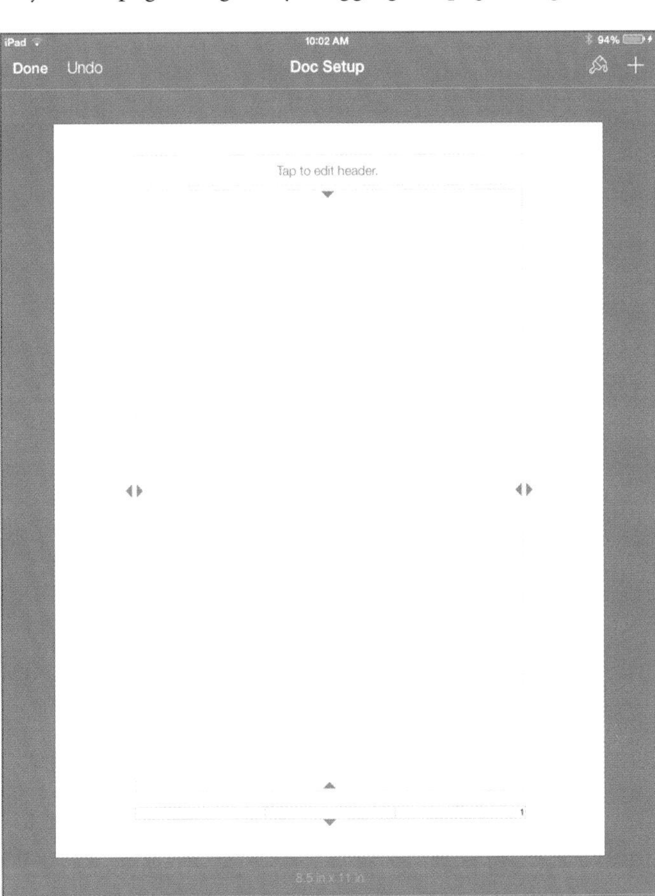

15 At the bottom of the screen, tap Change Paper Size.

Depending on the Language & Region settings on your iOS device, the paper size will be US Letter or A4. The only options available are to choose between US Letter and A4, and you cannot change the page orientation from portrait to landscape. To make a landscape document, you must choose a landscape template.

16 Tap your choice of either US Letter or A4. You are automatically returned to the previous Doc Setup screen.

17 In the Doc Setup screen, tap the footer's middle section. Tap Page Numbers to add them to the footer.

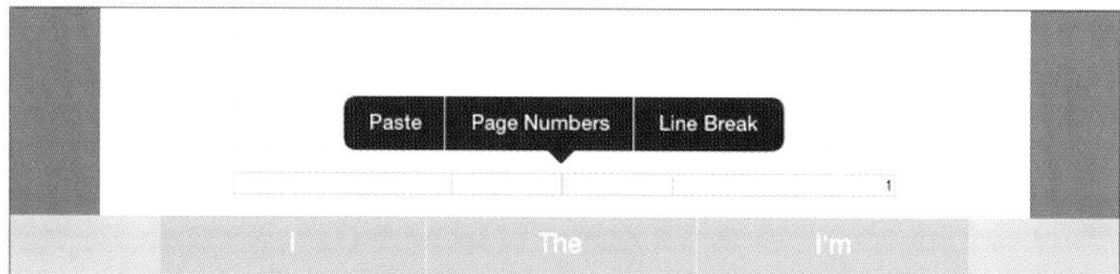

18 Tap “1 of 12” to set the page numbering format.

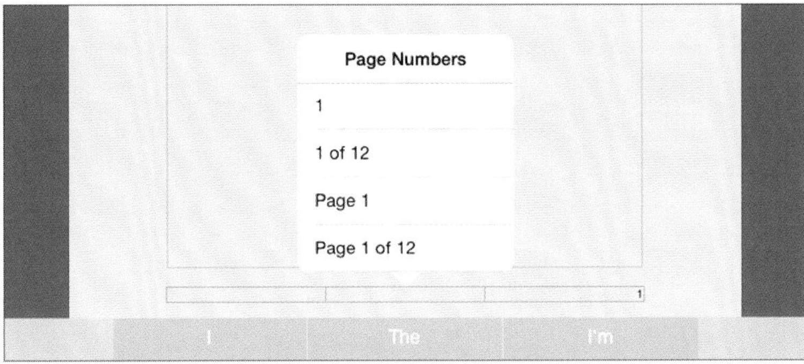

In this document, the footer section on the right already has a page number. To delete it, select it and tap the Backspace key on the virtual keyboard.

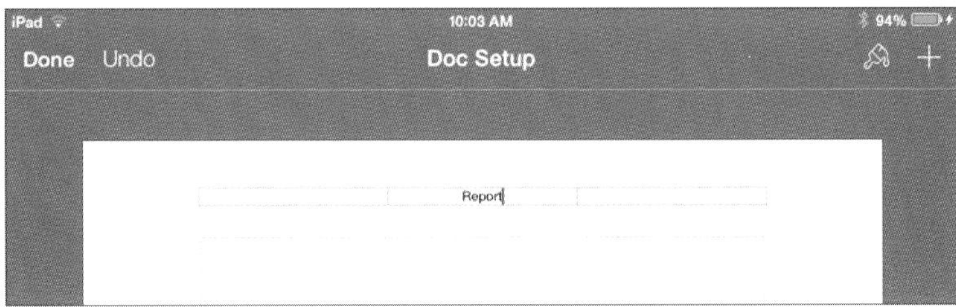

19 Tap the middle section of the header type and type *Report*.

20 In the upper left of the Doc Setup screen, tap Done when you're ready to move on.

The document has only a default name; let's change it.

21 Tap the name field and type *New Report*.

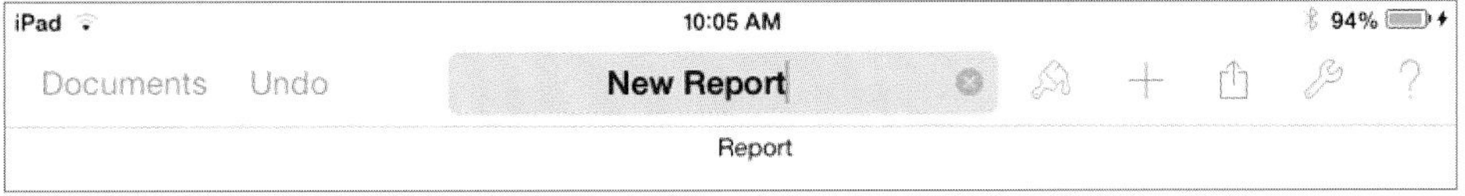

NOTE ▶ This renaming method also applies to Numbers and Keynote.

22 At the top of the screen, tap Documents to close the current document and return to the document manager.

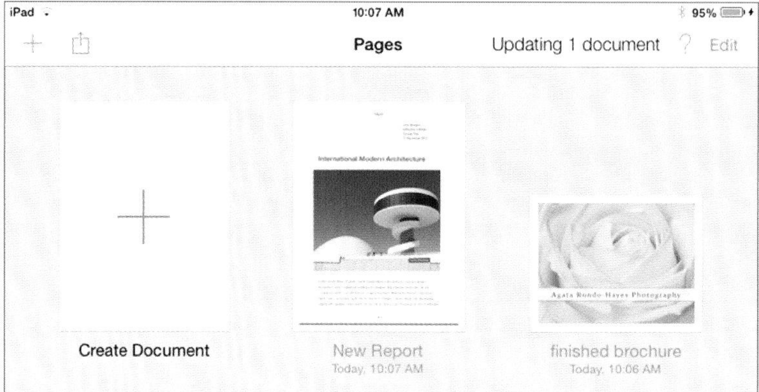

You may see a progress bar on the New Report document as a copy is sent to iCloud. However, you have other methods for sharing your document.

NOTE ▶ Although sharing and renaming options are available in the document manager, for the purpose of this exercise we'll continue to work directly in an open document.

23 In the document manager, tap the New Report icon.

24 Tap the Share icon and choose "Open in Another App."

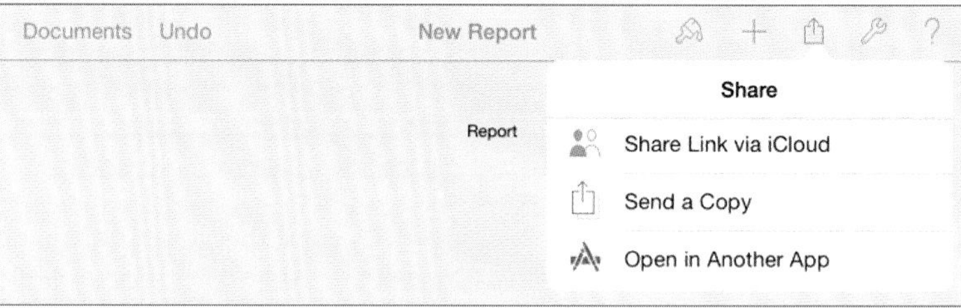

Pages opens a dialog asking in which format you want to share the document. If you were to choose "Send a Copy" from the Share menu, you'd be shown a similar dialog.

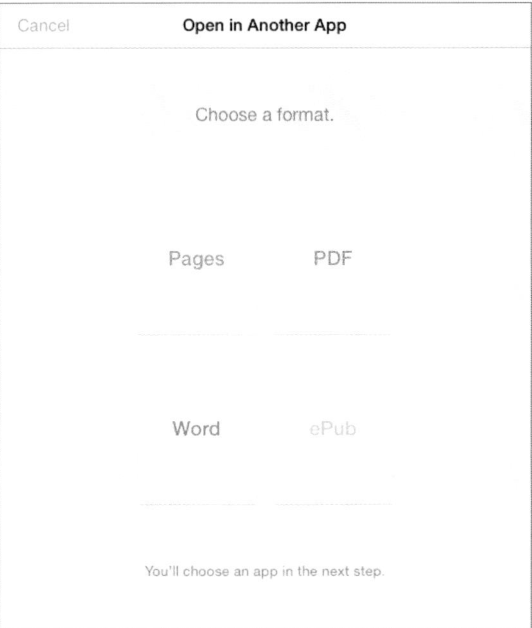

25 For now, tap Cancel.

You'll explore sharing options in Lesson 17. That concludes our brief tour of document management. Be aware that you can also use most of these methods when working in Numbers and Keynote.

Formatting Documents

Style sheets should play an important part in formatting text, but in Pages, Numbers, and Keynote for iOS they can be applied but not created or modified. This design isn't as limiting as it might seem. If you also use Pages, Numbers, and Keynote on a Mac, you can open the OS X–based custom styles you create in their iOS app counterparts, as long as the necessary fonts are available.

1 In your New Report document, on page 2, tap the text box containing a pull quote placeholder.

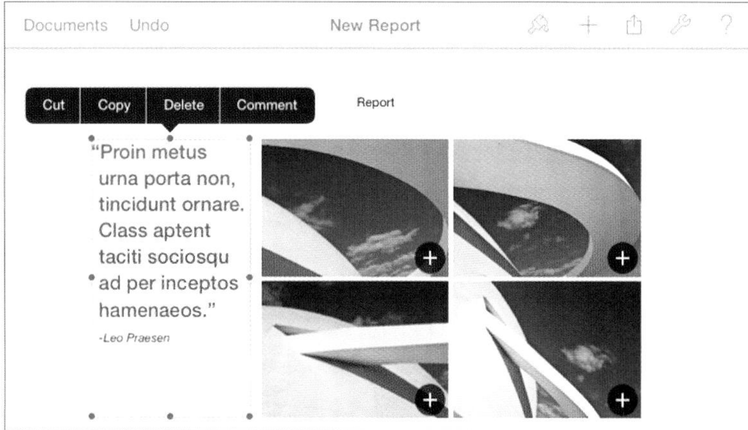

A single tap selects a text box. If you were to apply a text style now, both the pull quote and quote credit would change. To edit only the pull quote, you'll need to select just the quote.

2 Double-tap the pull quote placeholder text.

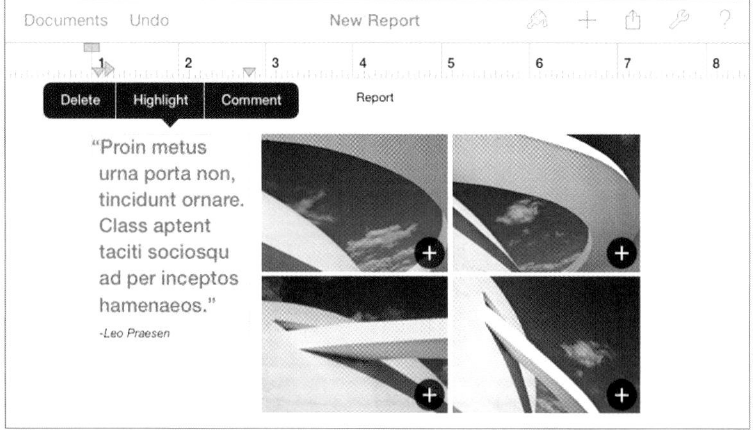

3 In the toolbar, tap Format (the paintbrush icon) to open the text formatting controls.

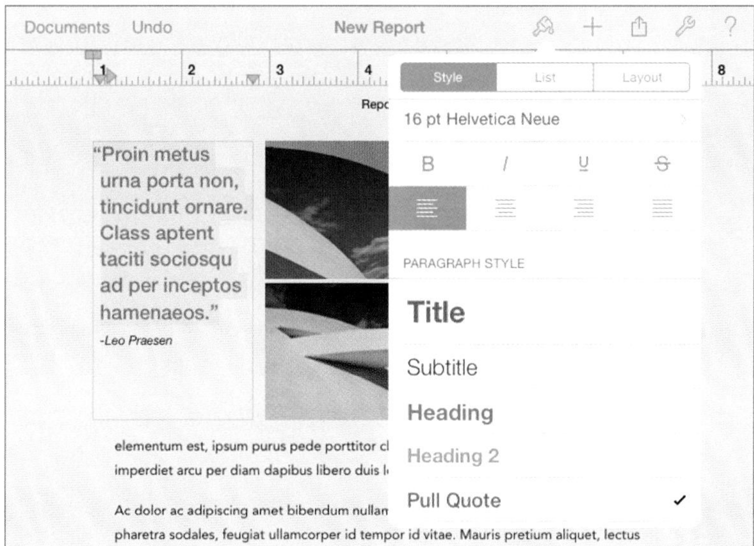

You'll see that the Pull Quote style has been applied. Any changes to the font and typestyle will affect the selected text, but the Pull Quote style won't be altered, even though Pages has tagged the text with the Pull Quote style.

4 In the Style inspector, tap "16 pt Helvetica Neue" to open the text options.

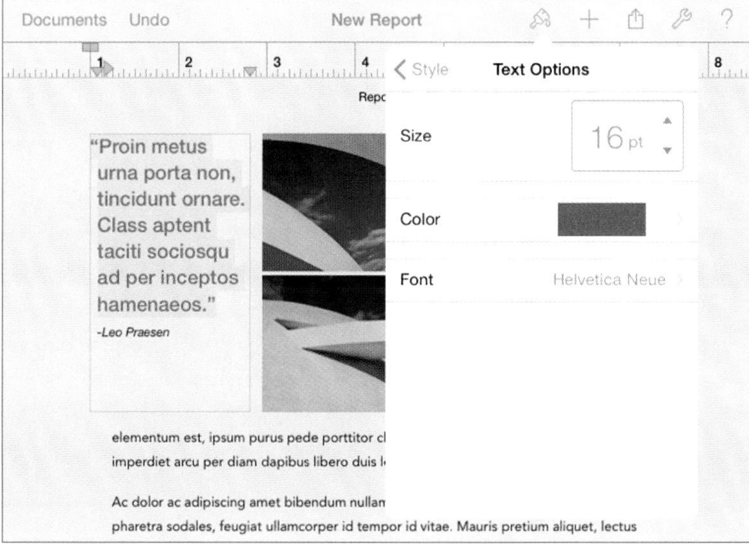

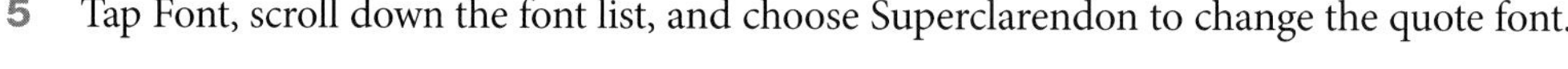

5 Tap Font, scroll down the font list, and choose Superclarendon to change the quote font.

6 Tap Text Options to return to the text options screen.

The text options are another place in which you can change font attributes. Changing colors is just as easy, but the color wheel is a little hard to locate. Let's find it.

7 Tap Color. Color swatches appear.

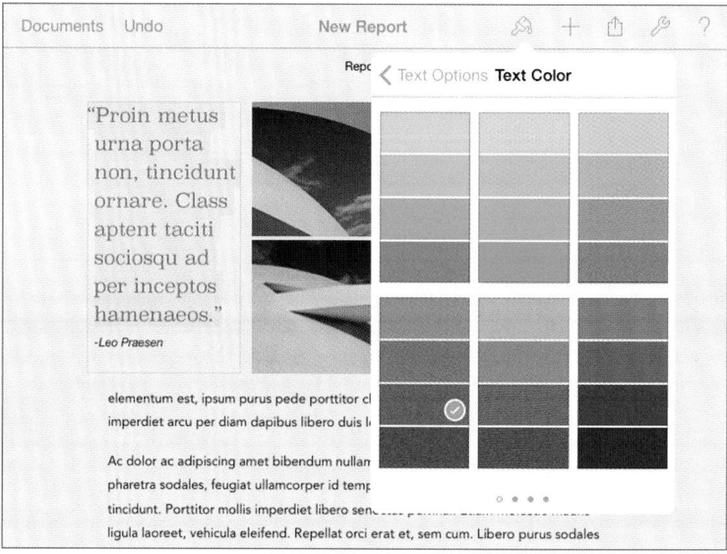

8 Swipe left to the last set of text color options, which include a color wheel and two sliders.

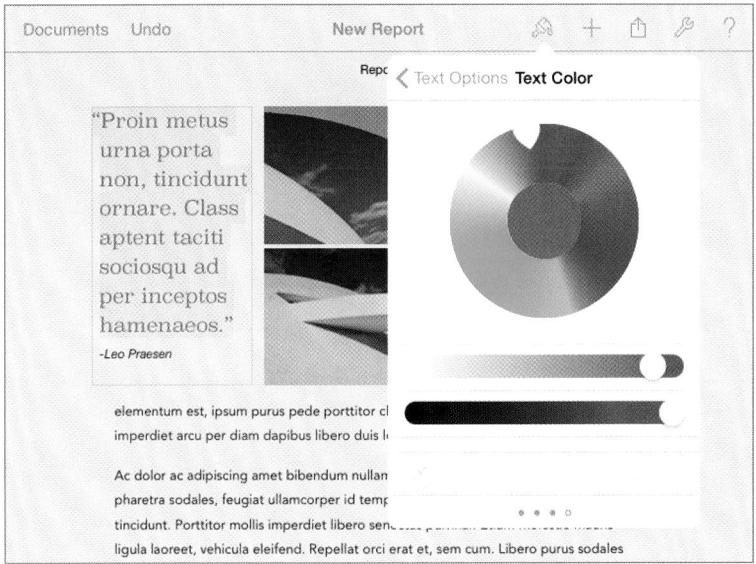

9 Drag the white pointer around the color wheel to change the hue. Drag the upper slider to the left to add white and brighten the color, and drag the bottom slider to the left to add black and darken the color.

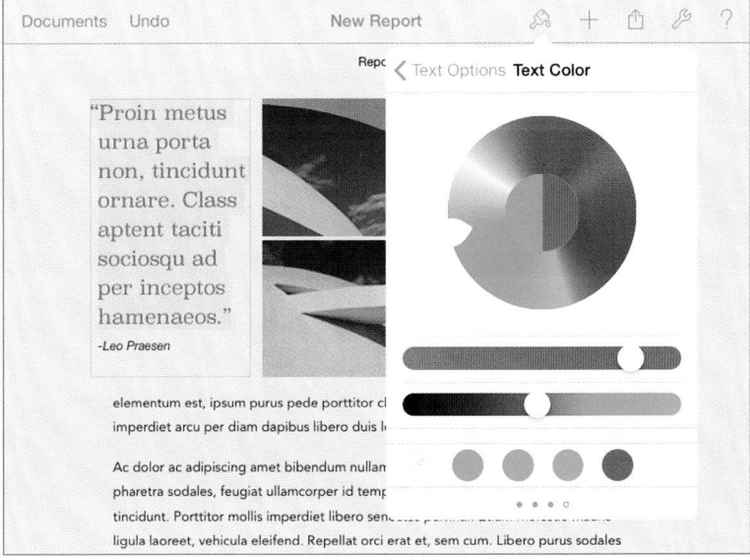

This text color options also include an eyedropper tool that works just like the eyedropper in the OS X Colors window.

10 Tap the eyedropper icon. The text color options disappear; tap the deepest blue in any of the photos next to the pull quote text.

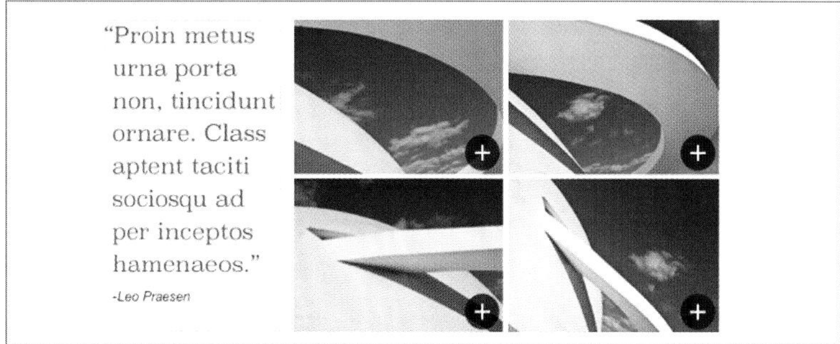

The text takes on the selected blue color.

11 Tap the Format icon again.

The Style inspector shows that the text is 16 pt Superclarendon in the blue you color selected, but the paragraph style is Pull Quote. The text has been tagged with the Pull Quote style, and you've applied additional formatting, but for now you still can't amend the style sheet to reflect this.

Undoing Changes

The toolbar contains an Undo icon you can tap to step back through your edits. Tapping and holding down Undo opens a dialog for undo and redo; you can also use gestures and shakes to open this dialog.

1 Shake your iOS device to open the Undo dialog. Tap Undo.

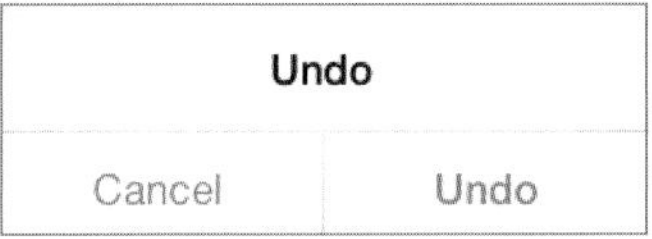

2 Shake your iOS device again. This time the dialog includes a Redo option.

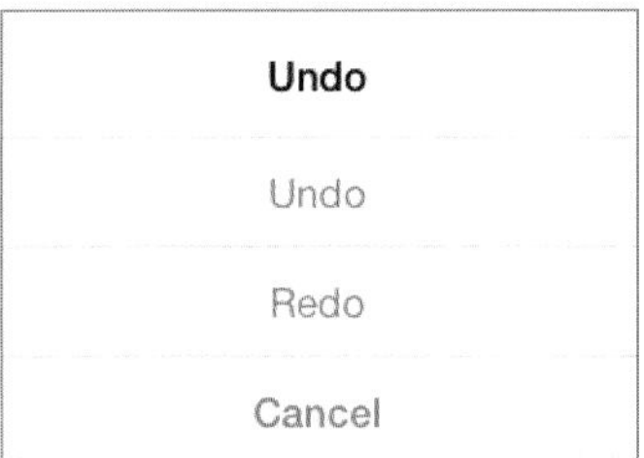

3 Tap Redo to restore the change you just removed.

iOS devices accept a wide range of input methods. Some might be a surprise, but should something unexpected happen, you're only a shake away from correcting an error.

NOTE ▶ Undo and redo remain available even in previously saved documents even after you have closed them. If you pick up a document a week after you last worked on it, you can still step back through your edits.

Modifying Text Wraps

The four photographs on page 2 have text wraps applied. In this exercise, you'll move one of these photos to see the text wrap in action, and then you'll modify the wrap.

1 On page 2 of the New Report document, tap a photo to select it.

The selection handles can be used to scale the image.

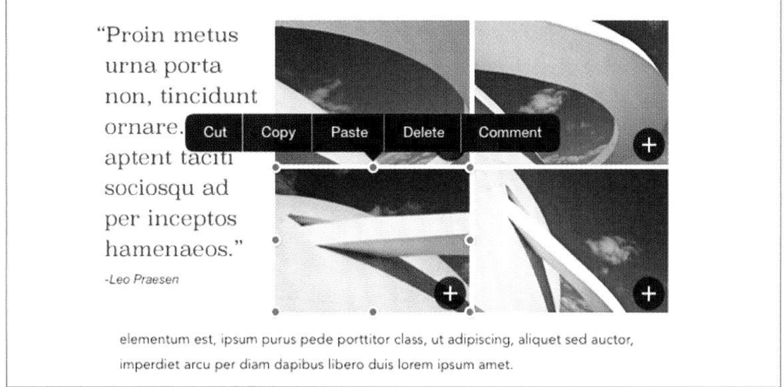

2 Drag the selected photo into the body of the second paragraph.

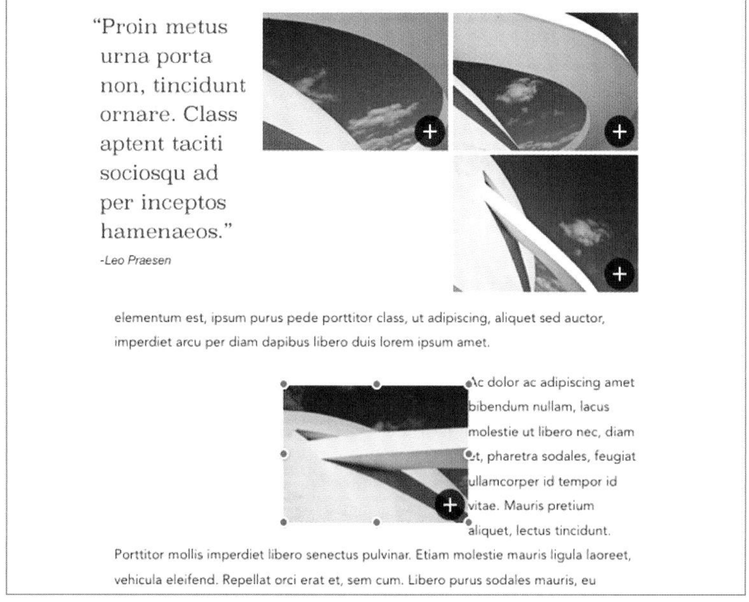

The paragraph text reflows due to the wrap feature. You can use the Format tools to style the photo, move it within the layer order, and modify the text wrap.

3 In the toolbar, tap the Format icon, and then tap Arrange and note the available options.

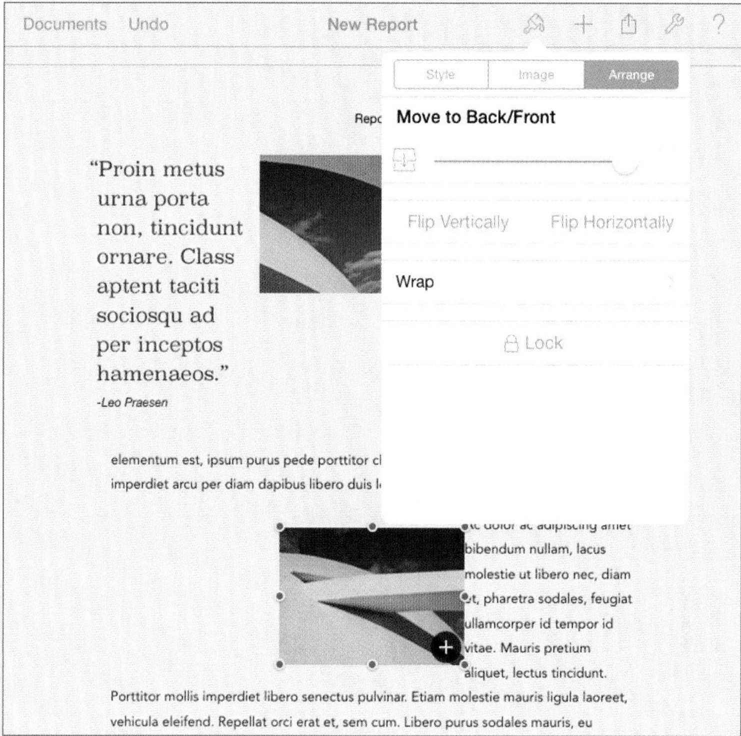

4 Tap Wrap to open the wrap options.

The options are similar to those in Pages for Mac, and as in the Mac version, you can set objects to move with the text.

5 In the Wrap options, enable "Move with Text."

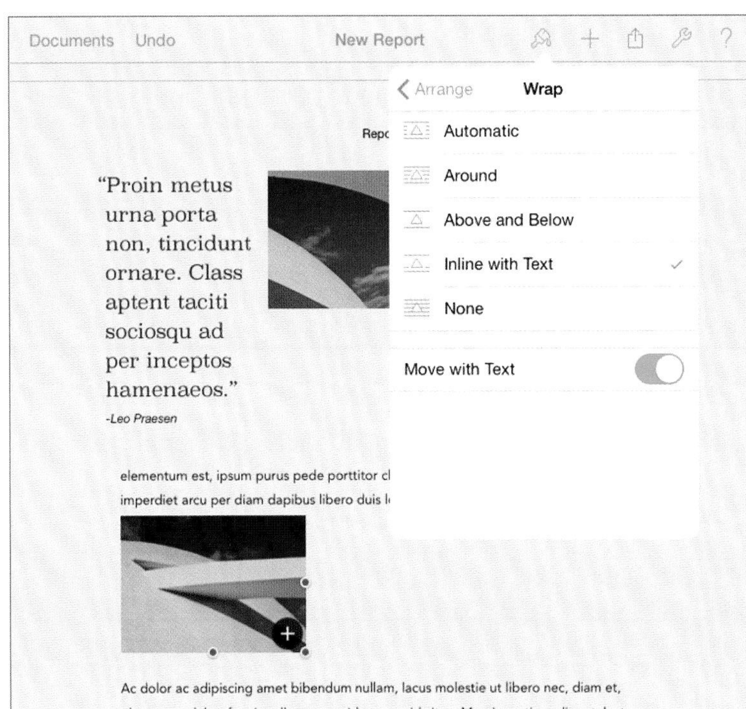

When this option is enabled, an extra wrap option appears: Inline with Text. Choosing it fixes the photo in the flow of the text, but other wrap options give you greater layout flexibility.

6 Choose "Above and Below" as the wrap option.

7 Tap away from the Wrap inspector to close it.

A text anchor, which looks like a blue pin, appears in the body of the text to indicate that the photo will remain in this position relative to the text as the document is edited.

8 Drag the photo on the page. Note that after you've finished dragging the photo the text anchor has moved, too.

Tracking Changes

Sometimes you'll need to take your work with you on the road. Reviewing documents is one of those tasks that is suited to being out and about. Marking up Pages on iOS is convenient and simple to do.

1 With the New Report document open, tap the Tools icon and choose Change Tracking.

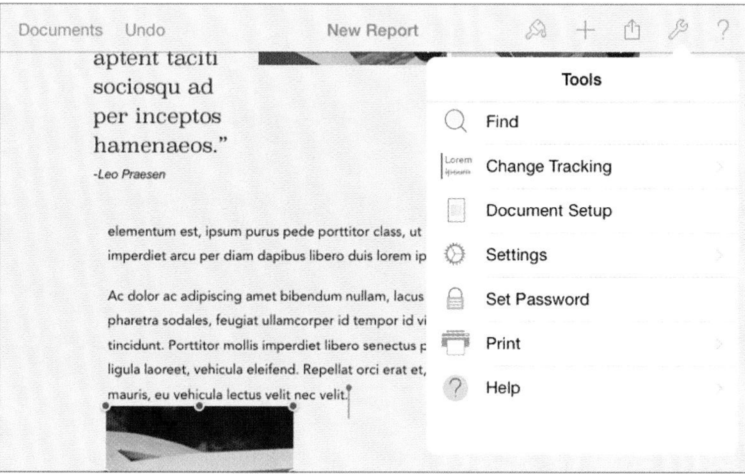

2 In the change tracking options, enable Tracking.

If this is the first time you've enabled tracking, you'll be prompted to enter an author name.

3 When prompted, type an author name into the Name field and tap Done. The name can be changed later in Settings.

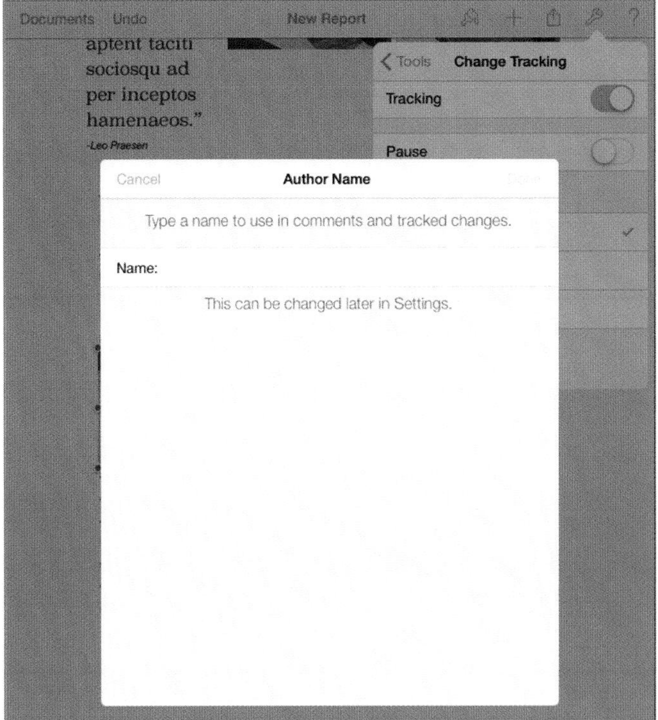

Markup is the default view setting for change tracking, but you may prefer Markup Without Deletions or Final.

4 Select a View setting for change tracking.

5 Tap the document page to close the inspector.

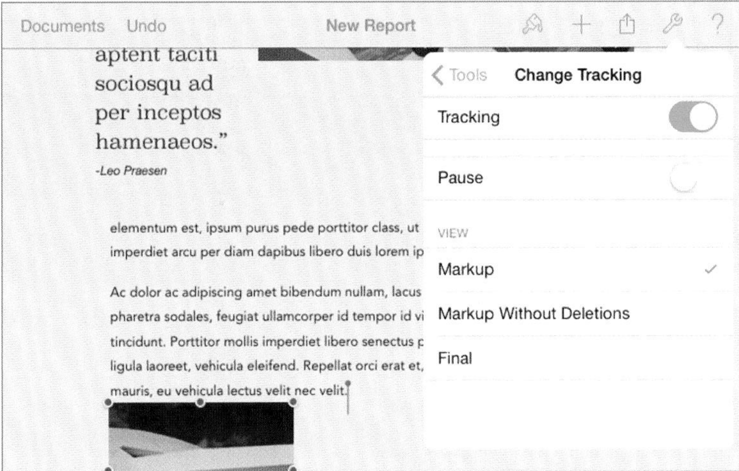

6 Go to page 1 of the document, and change the title by tapping the placeholder text and typing *A new report*.

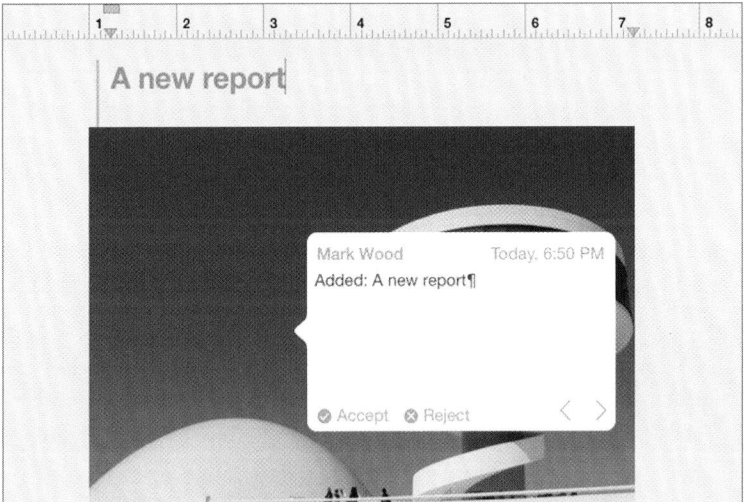

7 Tap a blank space on the page, and then tap the title text, "A new report."

A comment note appears to show who made an edit, when it was made, and what was changed. You have the option to accept or reject the change by tapping the appropriate button.

8 Tap away from the change note to close it.

Adding Comments

In addition to markups, Pages, Numbers, and Keynote lets you attach comments to text and objects.

1 On page 1, tap the placeholder text "Urna Semper" to select it.

Edit options appear. Because you've selected placeholder text, the contextual options list is reduced to Paste, Delete, Highlight, and Comment.

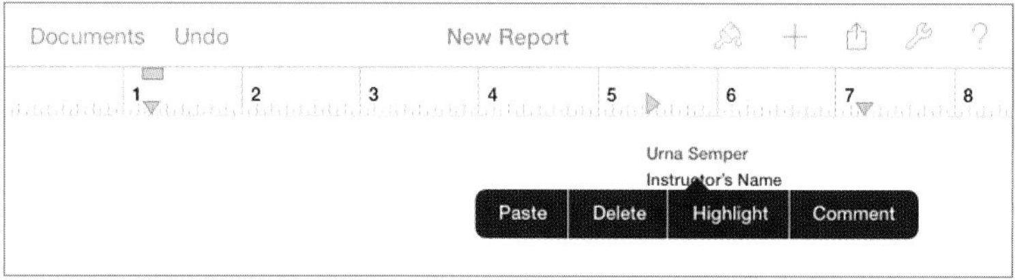

2 Tap Comment to open a note in which you can add your thoughts and advice.

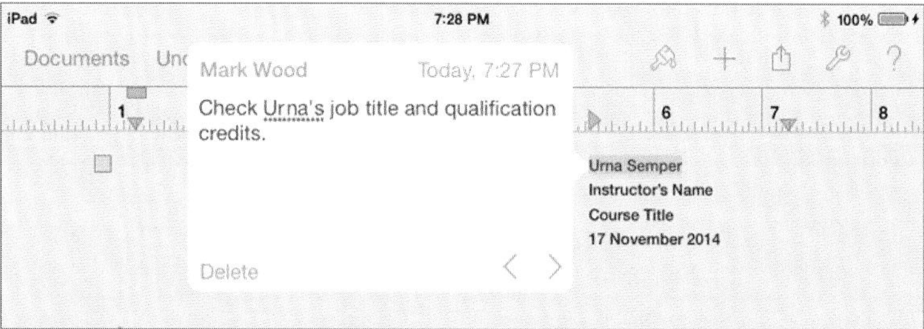

3 Tap away from the note to dismiss it.

4 Tap the photo on Page 1 to select it. Again, contextual options appear.

5 Tap Comment, and enter a note. Tap away from the comment to close it.

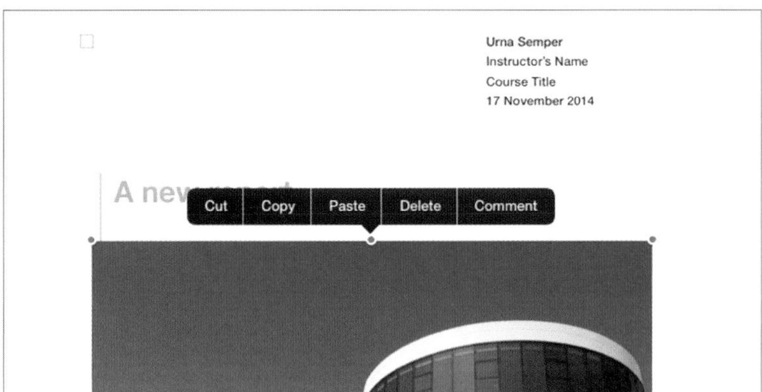

Closed comments are represented by small squares to the left of the document. Tapping a square opens the attached comment. You can tap the arrows in the lower right of the open comment to move to previous and later comments in sequence.

Working with Tables

Tables can be added to the iOS versions of Pages and Keynote, but they don't do math, unlike their Mac cousins. So, let's take a look at tables in Numbers. A table created in Numbers for iOS can be copied and pasted into Pages and Keynote for iOS, but the table will lose its math functions, so it won't be able to recalculate totals if the table data changes.

1 On your iOS device, open Numbers. If this is the first time you've opened Numbers, you'll see a Welcome screen. Choose to use iCloud.

If you've opened Numbers previously, you'll either see the most recent spreadsheet you worked on or the Spreadsheets screen. If Numbers opens a spreadsheet, tap Spreadsheets at the upper right of the screen.

2 Tap Create Spreadsheet. The template chooser appears.

NOTE ▶ Most of this exercise was prepared in landscape orientation.

3 Tap the Blank template to open it.

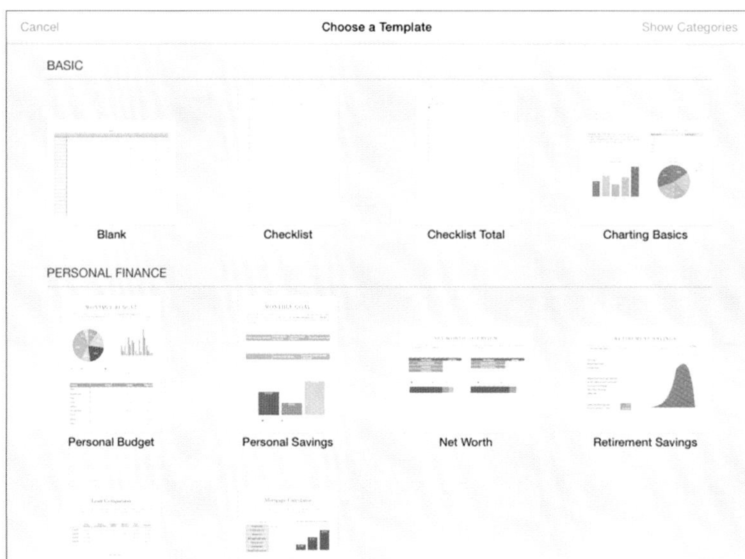

If this is your first time using Numbers for iOS, a coaching tip appears, telling you about coaching tips. This spreadsheet isn't really blank, as the template name suggests, because it includes a table (although it's very plain).

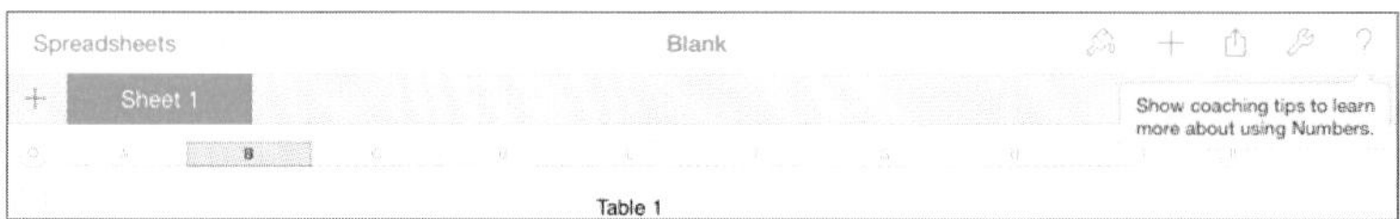

4 Tap the table, and then tap the control handle at the upper-left corner to select the entire table.

If you worked through the lessons for Numbers for Mac, you'll recognize the selection handles that appear, along with options for Cut, Copy, Delete, and Transpose.

5 Tap Delete to remove the table.

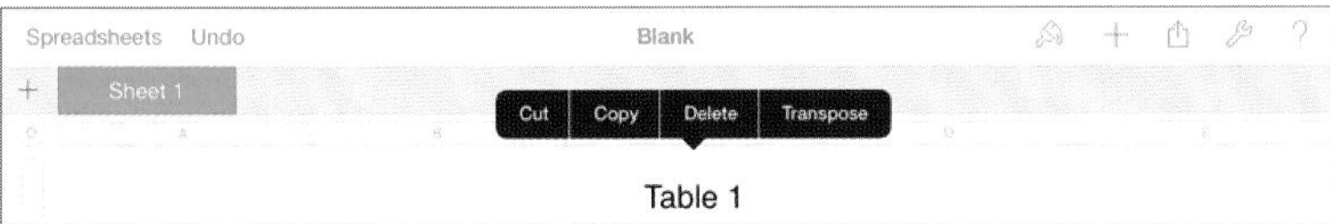

Although you can modify tables by adding columns and rows, setting fill colors, and so on, let's add a new table.

NOTE ▶ You use these same methods to add tables to Pages and Keynote, but they won't do math.

6 In the toolbar, tap the plus icon.

You can choose to add tables, charts, shapes, and media.

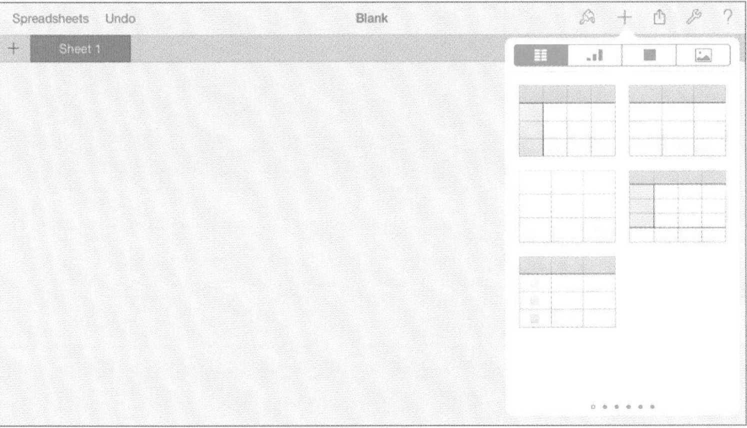

7 Tap the thumbnail of the plain table without headers.

8 Tap the header reference for the top row. Tap Insert, and then tap New Header Row.

This header is frozen, meaning that it will remain in view as you scroll around a spreadsheet that's too big to fully display on your screen.

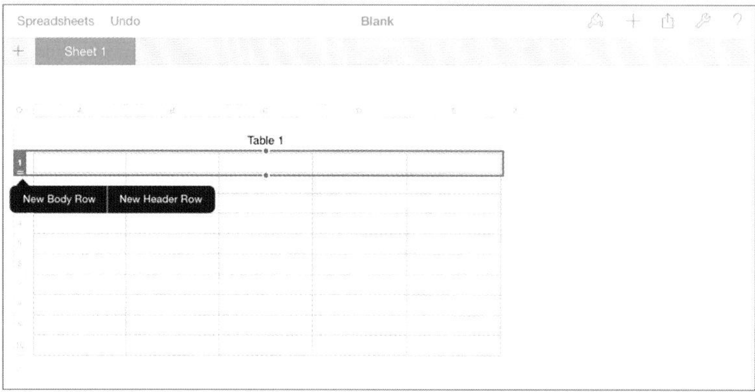

9 Double-tap cell B1. The virtual keyboard opens.

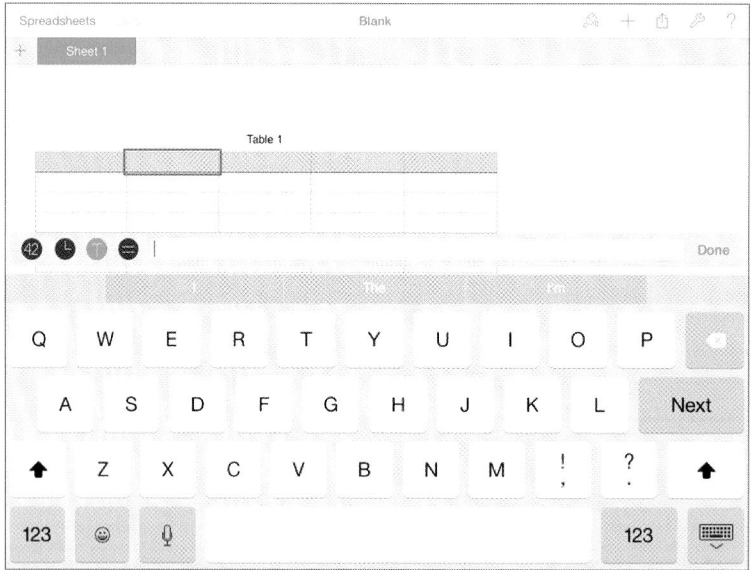

NOTE ► If you're using a Bluetooth keyboard, a data entry bar appears.

10 In cell B1, type *Monday*.

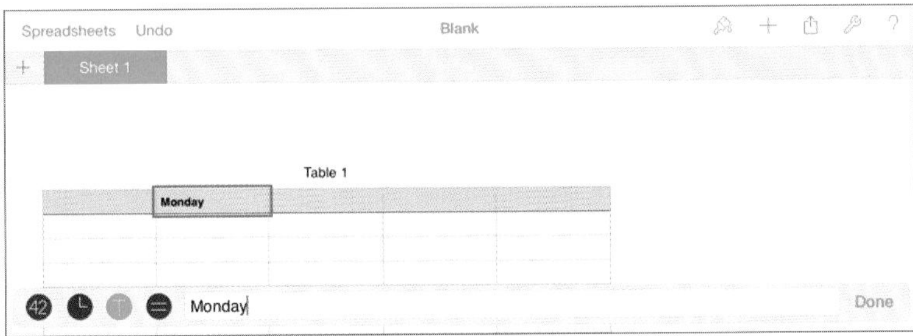

11 In the toolbar, tap the Format icon, and then tap the Format tab.

Automatic formatting is enabled for this cell. In this inspector you can set format options such as currency, duration, or pop-up menu.

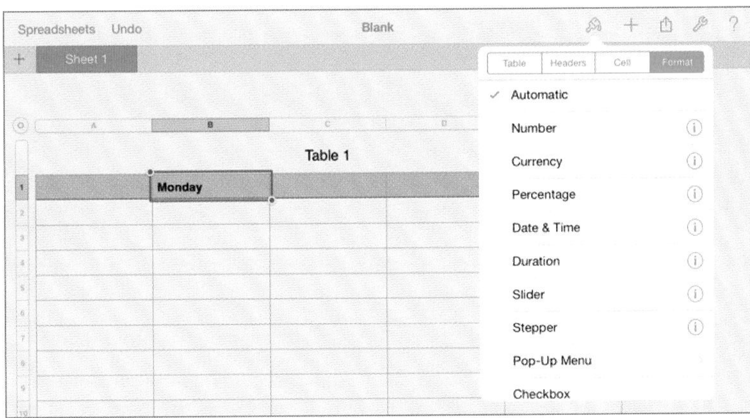

You've added straightforward text, and the keyboard configuration reflects that. Let's start to add a formula and see how the context-aware keyboard responds.

12 Tap away from the inspector to dismiss it.

13 Double-tap cell B11, and in the input bar, type = (equals sign).

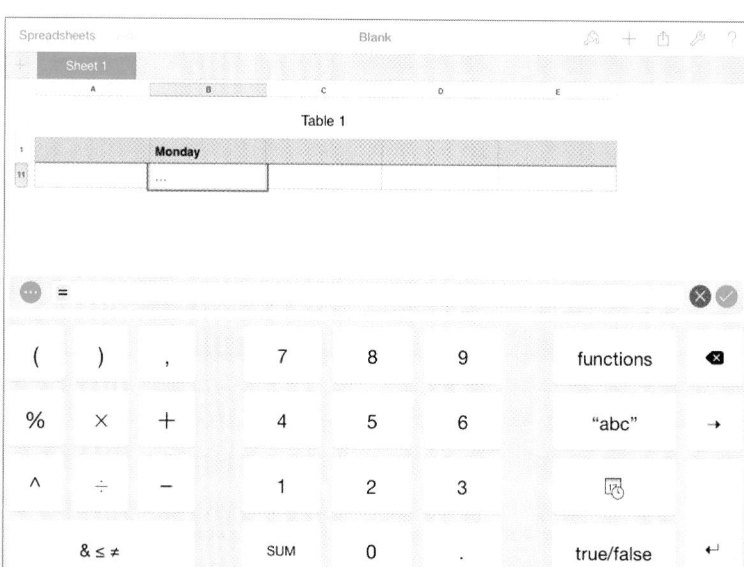

The keyboard changes to a numeric keyboard with a key for functions.

14 Tap Functions. At the top of the functions list that appears, tap Recent, and then tap SUM.

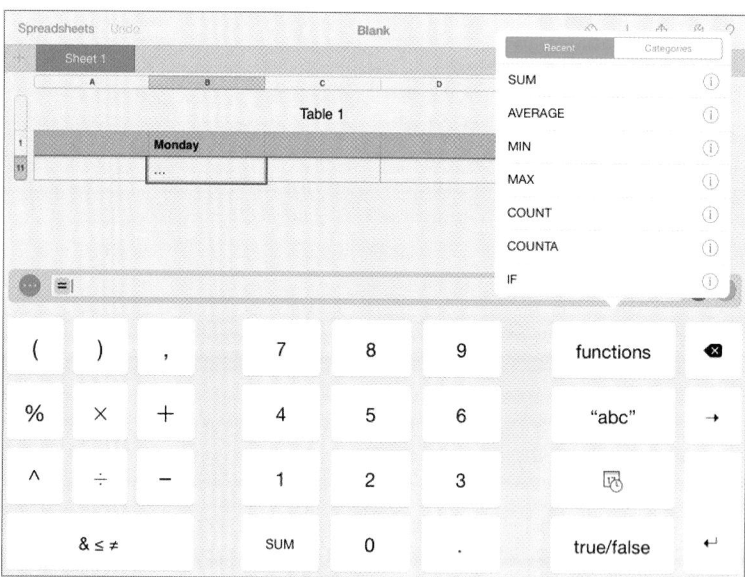

The formula editor is ready to accept the cell ranges you want to sum. Let's sum up column B.

15 If required, turn your iOS device to portrait orientation to see the entire column.

If you can't see the whole column in portrait, use the pinch gesture to zoom out.

16 Tap cell B2. It is highlighted in blue with two handles in the upper left and lower right of the cell.

17 Drag the bottom handle down the column to include every cell through cell B10 within the data range of the SUM function.

18 In the formula editor, tap the checkmark to accept the sum.

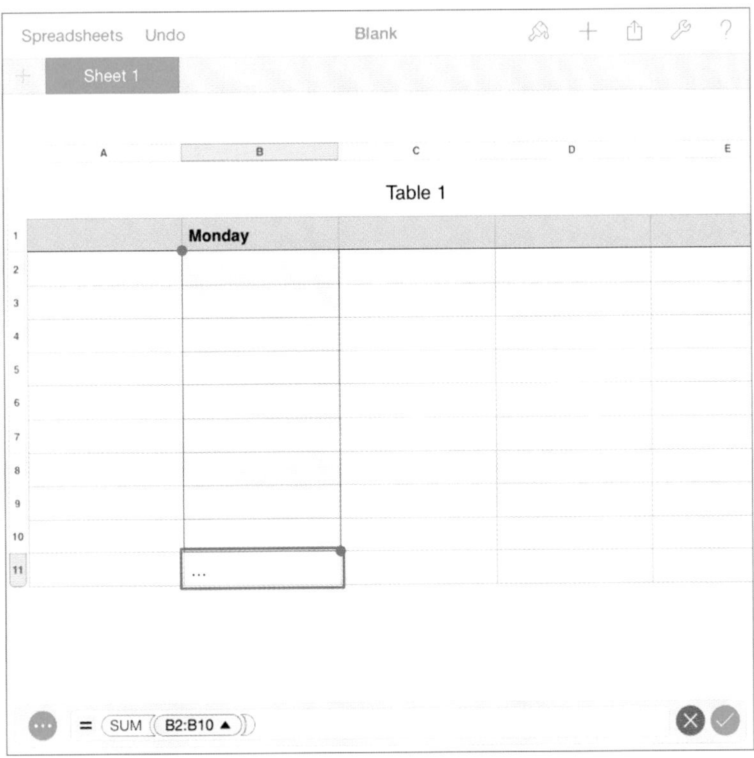

NOTE ▸ Just as in Numbers for Mac, you can also select data ranges by typing cell IDs.

This brief tour of Numbers is over. You can continue to explore by applying your knowledge of Pages for iOS to Numbers. You might want to rename the spreadsheet, or you could add and name a new sheet.

Using Keynote for iOS

Our brief tour of the iOS apps is drawing to a close. In Keynote for iOS, you can prepare and deliver presentations as you would on a Mac, but the camera in your iOS device lets you do even more. While all three apps let you add photos from your photo library, you also can use your iOS device's camera to shoot stills or video for use directly in the app. You'll investigate this feature later.

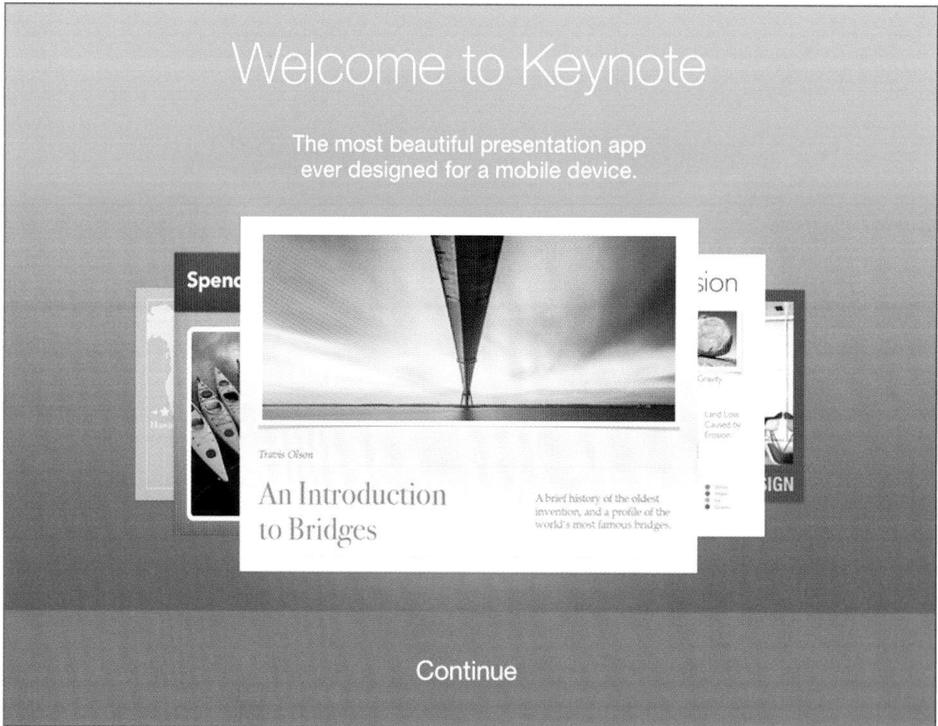

When you open Keynote for the first time, you see the Welcome screen, as you did in Pages and Numbers. If you've opened Keynote previously, it opens either your most recent presentation or the Presentations screen.

1 Using the steps previously described for creating a new document in Pages or Numbers, open the theme chooser in Keynote.

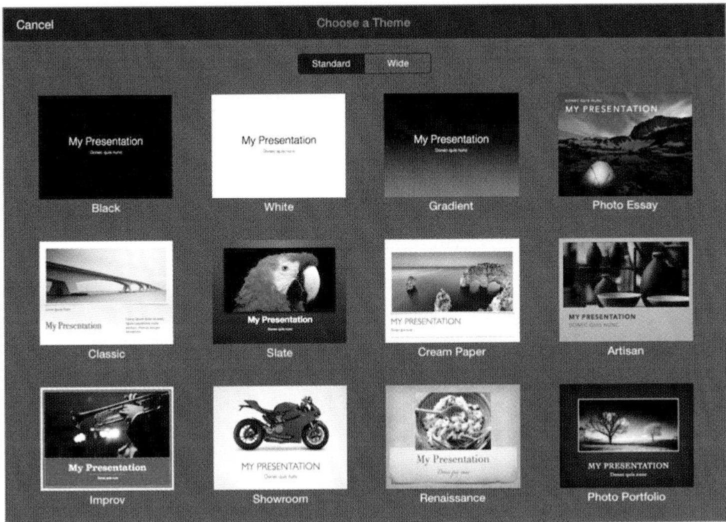

2 Tap the Improv theme to open a new presentation.

You're going to add a transition and builds to this presentation, and you'll replace the placeholder text.

3 Double-tap the title text on slide 1 to select it for editing. Type *Where I Am* as the new title.

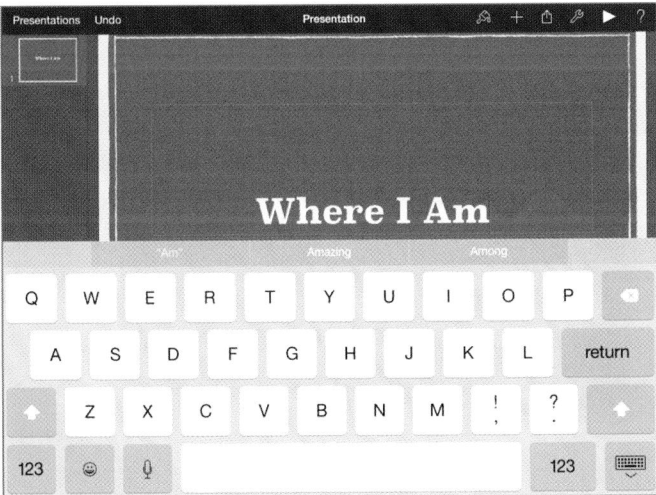

4 Tap away from the title, and then double-tap the subtitle text. Type *by <yourname>* as a credit for the presentation.

5 Tap away from subtitle to hide the keyboard.

You'll now add a slide containing media placeholders.

6 In the slide navigator, tap the Add (+) button at the bottom of the screen.

7 In the list of slide thumbnails, locate the slide with three media placeholders on a red background, and tap it to add the slide.

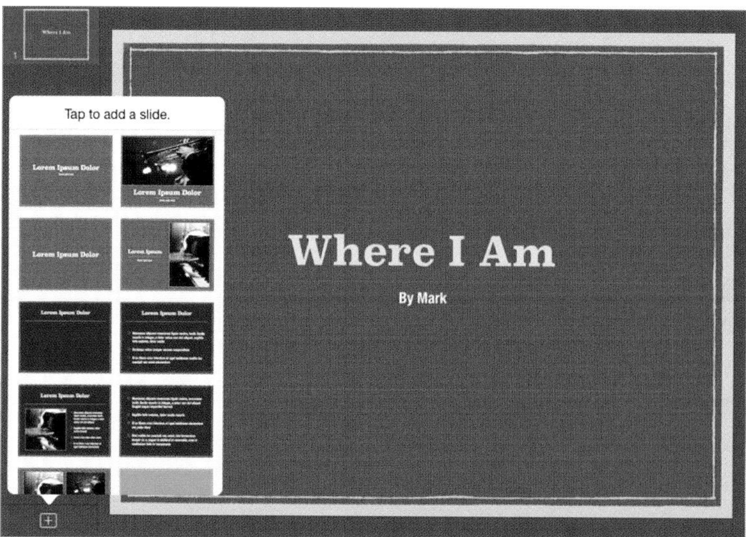

You now have enough slides and items to experiment with. Next, you'll add a transition.

8 In the slide navigator, tap and hold slide 1. Tap Transition.

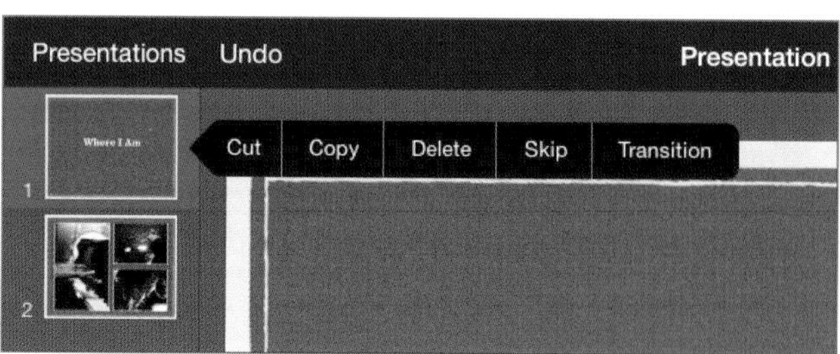

A dialog may appear explaining what you should do next.

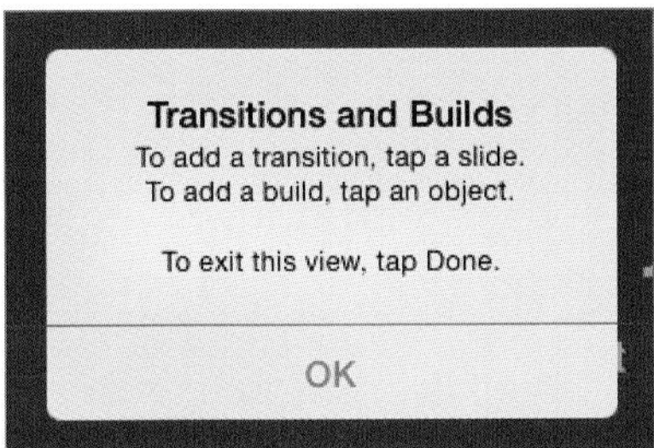

9 In the message dialog, tap OK.

The Transitions list opens. Here, you can tap an effect and tap Play to preview it.

10 Tap Color Planes to select it.

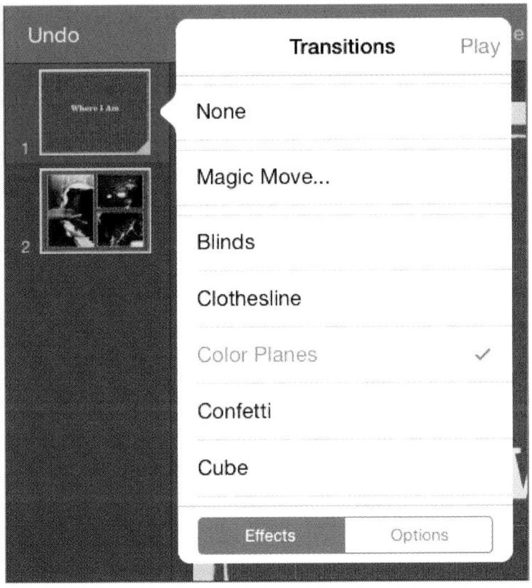

To modify an effect, you have options similar to those found in Keynote for Mac.

11 Tap Options. Each effect has its own set of variables. Experiment with Duration by dragging its slider.

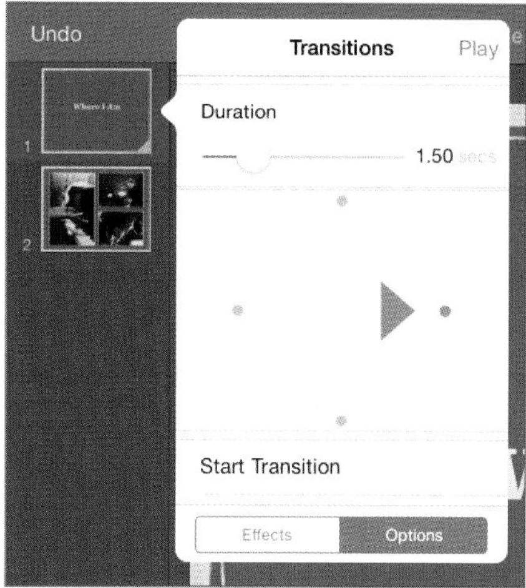

NOTE ▶ Tap Play at the upper right of the Transitions options to play the transition. When it concludes, the Transitions options reappear.

Your iOS toolbar is colored blue, indicating that you can edit animations. Remain in this mode to add a build to your slides.

12 On slide 1, tap the Title text box to select it.

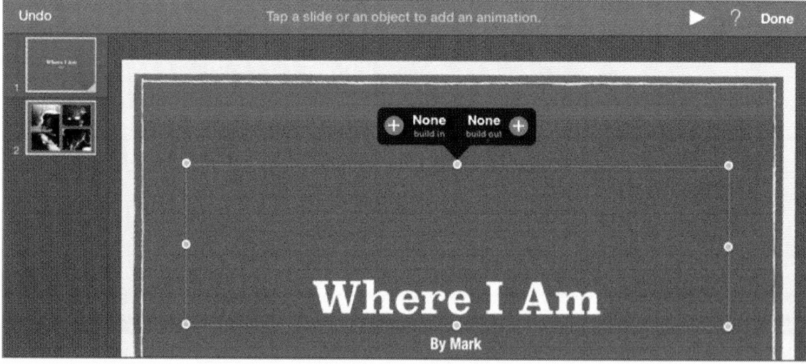

A pop-up appears letting you know that this element does not have builds.

13 Tap the plus sign for Build In. The Build In list of effects appears.

14 Tap Anvil to apply that effect.

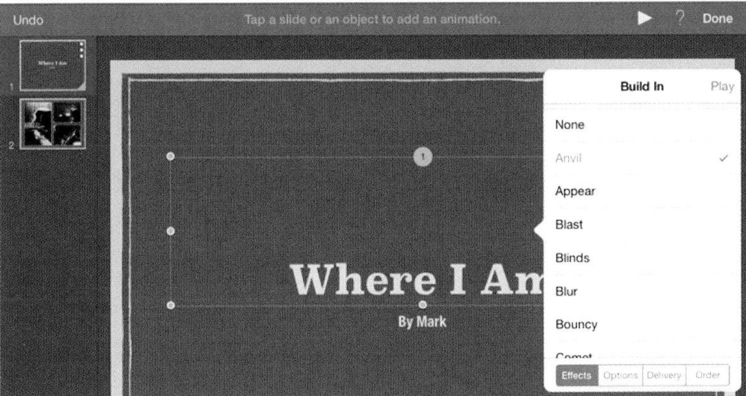

15 At the bottom of the Build In list, tap Options to review the Build In options. These are similar to the controls found in the OS X version of the app.

Feel free to experiment with other options. Tap Play at the top of the Build In options to preview your animations.

16 On slide 1, tap the second text box and, using the same method, apply a build to this text box. (Bouncy is rather fun.)

NOTE ► You can also access transitions and builds via the toolbar by tapping the Tools icon.

The presentation is ready to play.

17 In the toolbar, tap the Play button. If it's the first time you've played a slideshow on your iOS device, presentation tips appear. Tap or swipe to advance the slideshow.

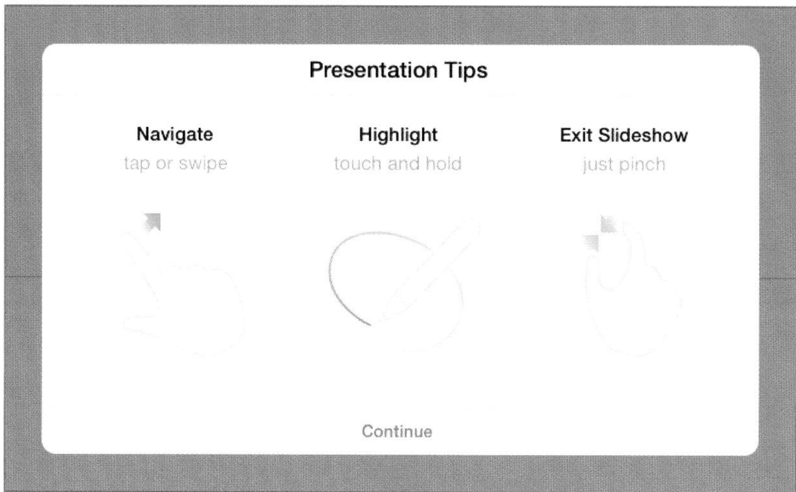

18 When you've advanced to slide 2, use the pinch gesture to exit the slideshow.

You are returned to the animation display with the blue toolbar.

19 In the toolbar, tap Done to exit the animation mode.

Adding Photos and Video

The following Keynote exercise is also applicable to Pages and Numbers. You'll first replace media placeholders using a photo from your photo library, and then you'll add video shot with your iOS device.

1 Navigate to slide 2 by tapping its thumbnail.

2 Tap the plus sign at the lower right of the first media placeholder to open your iOS device's photo library, which can contain both photos and video.

NOTE ▶ If you haven't used Keynote previously, you may see a message asking you to grant permission for Keynote to access Photos by visiting Settings > Privacy > Photos.

3 Select a photo by first tapping an album, and then tapping a photo to replace the placeholder.

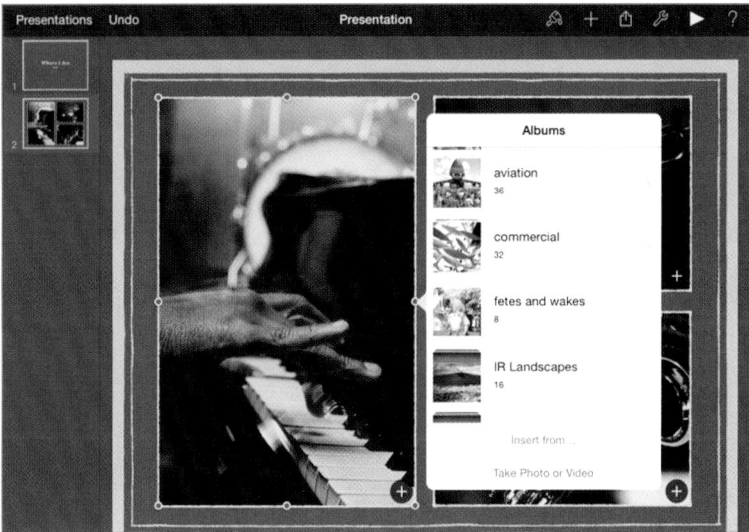

TIP Choosing the "Insert from" option allows you to find media in iCloud and other storage providers such as Dropbox.

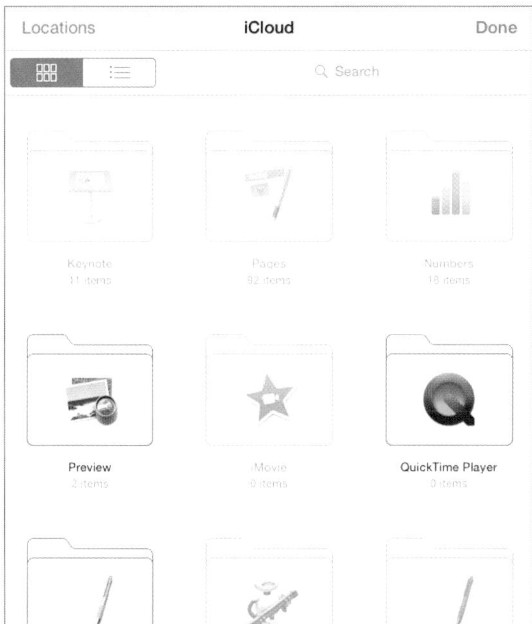

With your chosen photo in place, you can double-tap it to adjust the image mask and reposition the photo within the mask.

4 Double-tap the photo you just added. Drag the photo to reposition it within the mask.

5 Drag the mask handles to reshape the mask.

6 Tap the Format icon at the top of the screen. Tap a style to apply it.

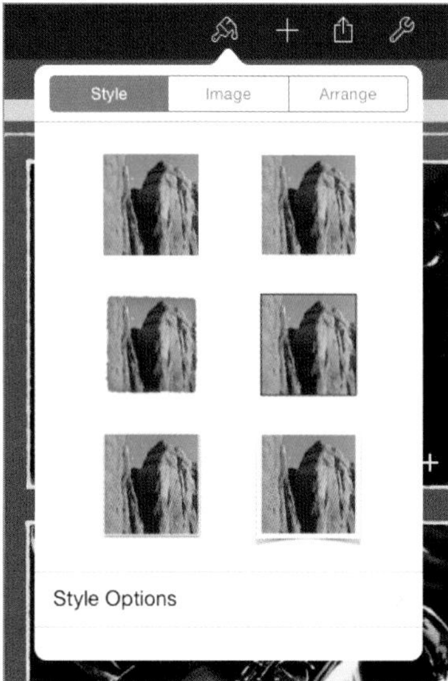

7 At the bottom of the Format inspector, tap Style Options to adjust your selected style.

8 In the Border options, drag the Width or Scale slider to the right to increase the border size, thereby giving the frame more presence.

NOTE ▶ In the style's Effects pane, you can set drop shadows and reflections.

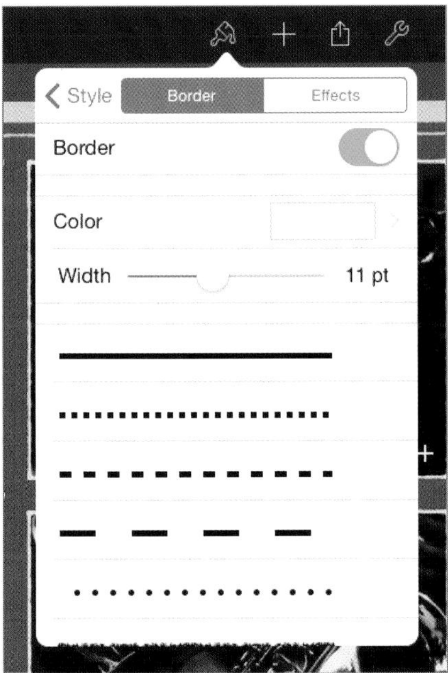

Now you'll add video by accessing your iOS device's camera from within Keynote. This technique opens up a new world of possibilities for note making. Imagine that you're on a research trip. You could work completely within Keynote to bullet important points and take photos and video as needed.

9 In the upper-right media placeholder, tap the plus sign.

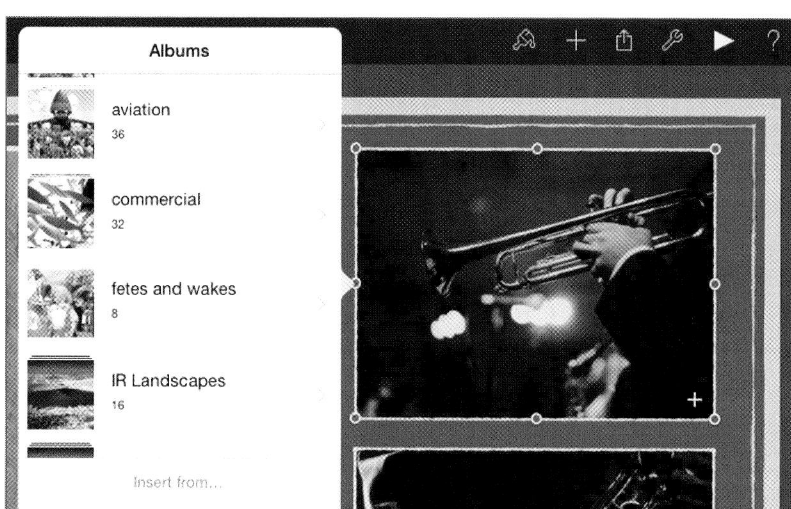

10 Tap Take Photo or Video. Keynote opens your iOS device's Camera app.

NOTE ▶ If you have not previously used this feature, Keynote requests permission to use the Camera. Similarly, in step 11 using video may cause Keynote to request permission to use the microphone.

11 In the Camera app, choose Video, frame your shot in camera, and then tap the red Record button to record a few seconds of video.

12 Tap the Record button to stop recording.

13 Tap Use Video.

Your movie replaces the placeholder directly and with no detours to other apps.

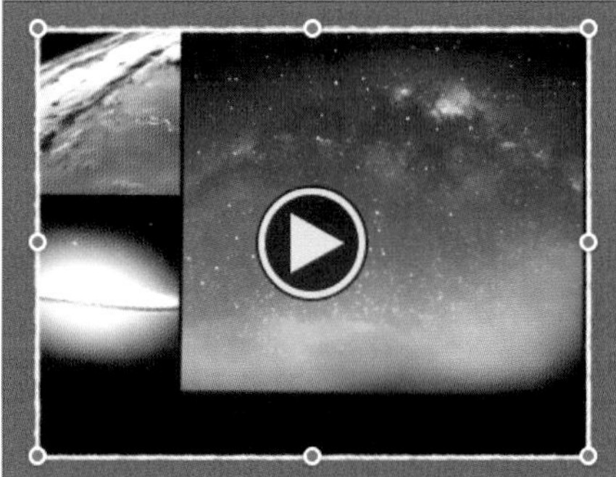

14 With the video selected, tap the Format icon, and then tap the Movie tab to review the options for the movie.

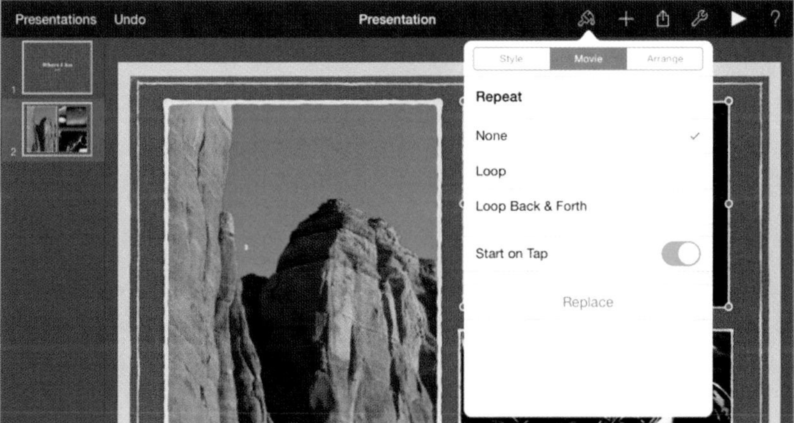

15 Turn off "Start on Tap."

16 In the slide navigator, select slide 1. Play the slideshow to review your results.

Setting a Document Password

In Lesson 17 you will draw together knowledge gleaned from this lesson as you work with both iOS and OS X versions of the productivity applications. You'll also use iCloud in greater detail. As you save files to iCloud, you may wonder about security, especially in collaborative projects. Here's how to add password protection to your iOS documents.

1 With your Keynote presentation open, tap the Tools icon at the top of the screen.

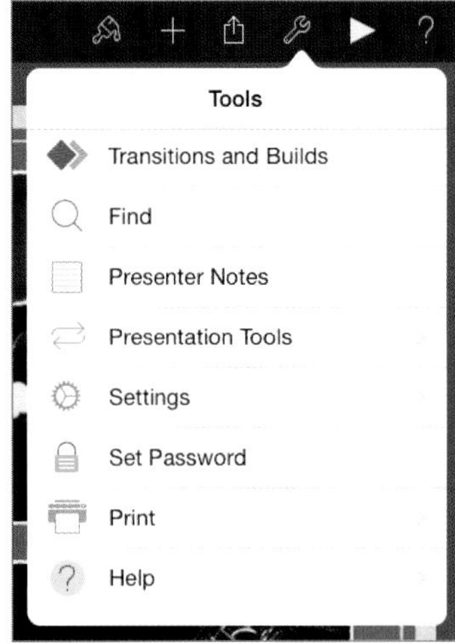

2 In the Tools list, tap Set Password.

3 In the Set Password dialog, enter a password, verify it, and enter a hint.

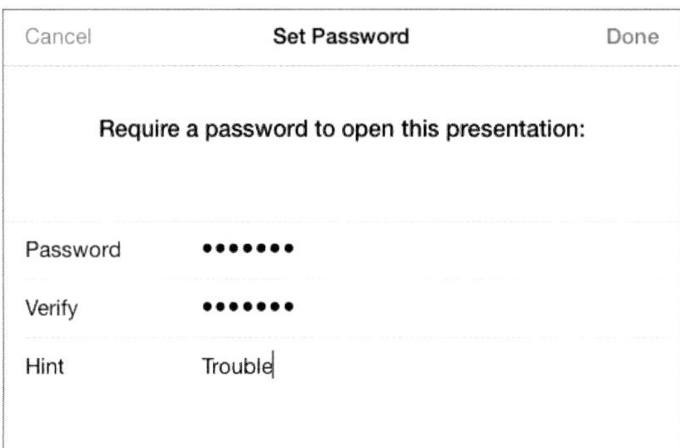

4 Tap Done to set the password.

Now let's test the password.

5 At the top of the screen, tap Presentations to close your presentation and return to the document manager.

Your presentation appears with a padlock thumbnail to indicate its secured status. You may also see the upload icon in the upper right of the thumbnail as a copy of your file is sent to iCloud.

6 Tap the locked presentation thumbnail. A password prompt appears.

7 Enter your password and tap Done.

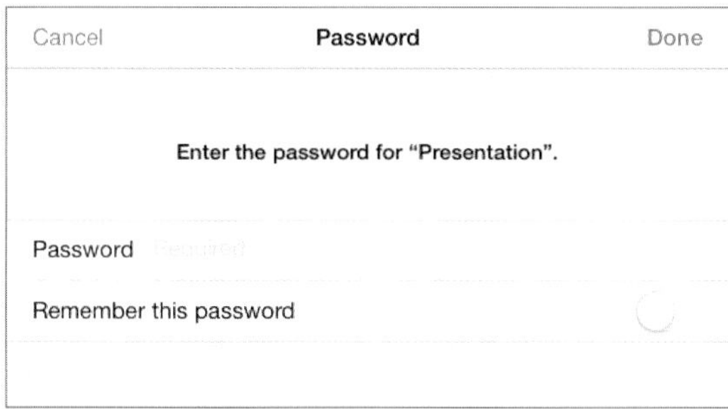

NOTE ▶ The password prompt has an option for remembering this password. With this option enabled, this presentation will be locked on other devices and the password will be required to open it; a password will not be needed on any device on which this option is enabled.

8 Leave the Keynote presentation on iCloud Drive for use in Lesson 17.

Lesson Review

1. Can you have multiple Apple IDs?
2. After you apply a style in Pages, Numbers, or Keynote in iOS, can you modify the item's appearance?
3. In Keynote for iOS, what happens when you shake your iOS device?
4. In Pages for iOS, how do you make photos and shapes move with the text?
5. Can Keynote tables perform math calculations?

Answers

1. Yes, you can have multiple Apple ID, but doing so is not recommended.
2. Yes, a text item or an object can have a preset style applied, and those attributes can be changed. However, you cannot change the style itself.
3. In Pages, Numbers, and Keynote, undo options appear when you shake your iOS device.
4. To make objects move with Pages text, select the object and on the Format inspector's Arrange pane, tap Wrap and choose Move with Text.
5. No, tables in Keynote and Pages for iOS do not perform calculations, but tables in Numbers that support math functions can be copied and pasted into Keynote or Pages where they become static table information.

17

Lesson Files

APTS Pages Numbers Keynote > Lesson_17 > sl-draft-report321.pages

APTS Pages Numbers Keynote > Lesson_17 > ju-jitsu-register.numbers

APTS Pages Numbers Keynote > Lesson_17 > sophia-presentation.kth

Time

This lesson takes approximately 75 minutes to complete.

Goals

Work with Pages, Numbers, and Keynote for iCloud

Use iCloud for document sharing and review

Apply iCloud to a collaborative workflow

Open and save documents using your Mac and iCloud

Move a document to iCloud

Lesson **17**

Moving Between iOS, iCloud, and OS X

Pages, Numbers, and Keynote can work seamlessly across the Apple ecosystem and beyond. In Lesson 16, you saved documents to your iCloud Drive, from which you could access them using other iOS devices and a Mac via Pages, Numbers, and Keynote.

In this lesson, you'll open documents saved to your iCloud Drive and learn how to manage and modify those documents across multiple devices. Using Pages, Numbers, and Keynote for OS X and iOS with iCloud maximizes their productivity-enhancing potential, overcoming the limitations of working on a single hardware platform.

Opening an iOS Document on Your Mac

In the previous lesson, you created a simple slideshow using the great-looking Improv theme in Keynote for iOS, which was automatically copied to iCloud. Now you're going to open that presentation from iCloud Drive to Keynote for OS X, and apply a custom theme, which you can do to all your iWork documents.

1 On your Mac, open Keynote.

2 Choose File > Open.

3 In the window's toolbar, click the title. (The title is derived from the current folder or drive.) From the pop-up menu, choose Keynote – iCloud.

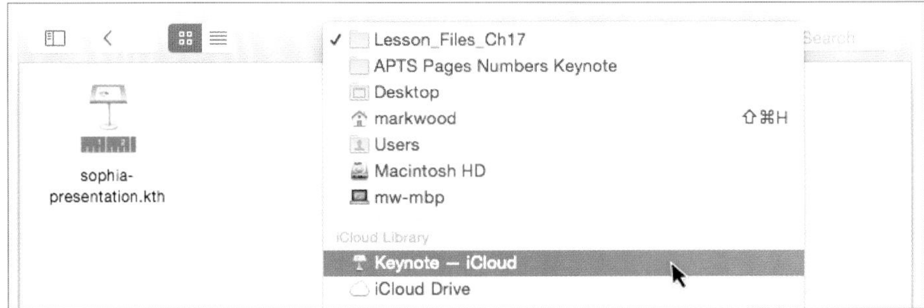

NOTE ▶ This is just one option for viewing the contents of an iCloud Drive. You can also see your iCloud Drive folders in the Finder.

4 In the window, locate the presentation you created in Lesson 16. Double-click the presentation to open it.

The presentation starts to open from iCloud on your Mac, but the document is password protected so a dialog appears.

5 Enter your password in the Password field.

TIP ▶ If you don't want to enter your password every time you open this file on this device, select "Remember this password in my keychain." Doing so retains password protection for any other devices that may access the file.

You may see a warning about fonts. By default, your Mac will have the Superclarendon typeface installed, but not its Bold or Light fonts.

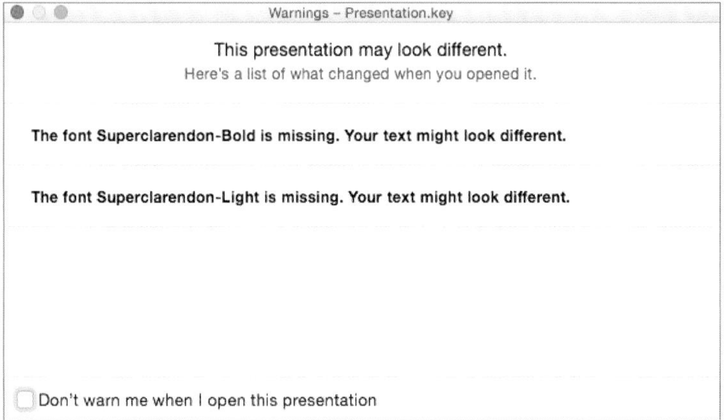

6 If necessary, close the warning window. The missing type will not affect this exercise.

NOTE ▶ To resolve problems with missing fonts, click an instance of text in which another font has been substituted for a missing font. In the inspector, select a different font or typeface, and then update the style. Repeat these steps for all styles in which missing fonts were replaced.

Applying a Custom Theme

The presentation opens with the Improv theme applied, albeit with potential font issues. You'll apply a custom theme to this presentation.

1 In the toolbar, click the Document icon, and then click the Document tab.

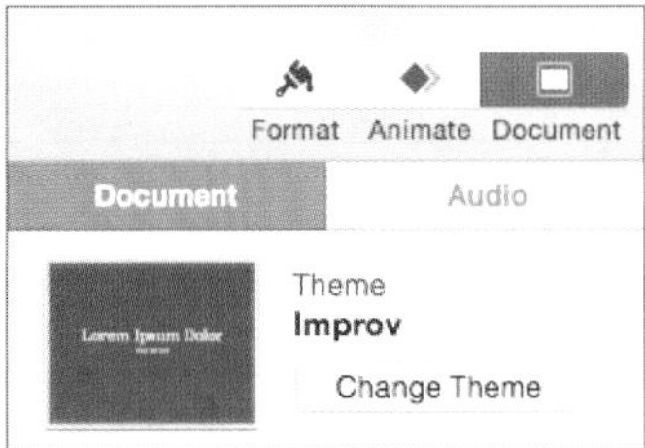

2 In the Document inspector, click Change Theme to open the Theme Chooser.

3 Click the My Themes tab to view your custom themes.

NOTE ▶ The My Themes tab is displayed only when custom themes are available.

If you skipped Lesson 12, or have deleted the sophia-presentation theme, you'll need to complete steps 4 through 9. If you see the sophia-presentation theme, you may skip to step 10.

To install the sophia-presentation theme:

4 In the Theme Chooser, click Cancel.

5 Choose File > Open, and navigate to APTS Pages Numbers Keynote > Lesson_17.

6 Double-click the **sophia-presentation.kth** template.

7 In the window that appears, click "Add to Theme Chooser."

8 In the Theme Chooser, click Cancel (you don't want to open a new presentation just now).

9 In the presentation you opened from iCloud Drive, in the Document inspector, click the Change Theme button.

The custom theme is now available in your Theme Chooser.

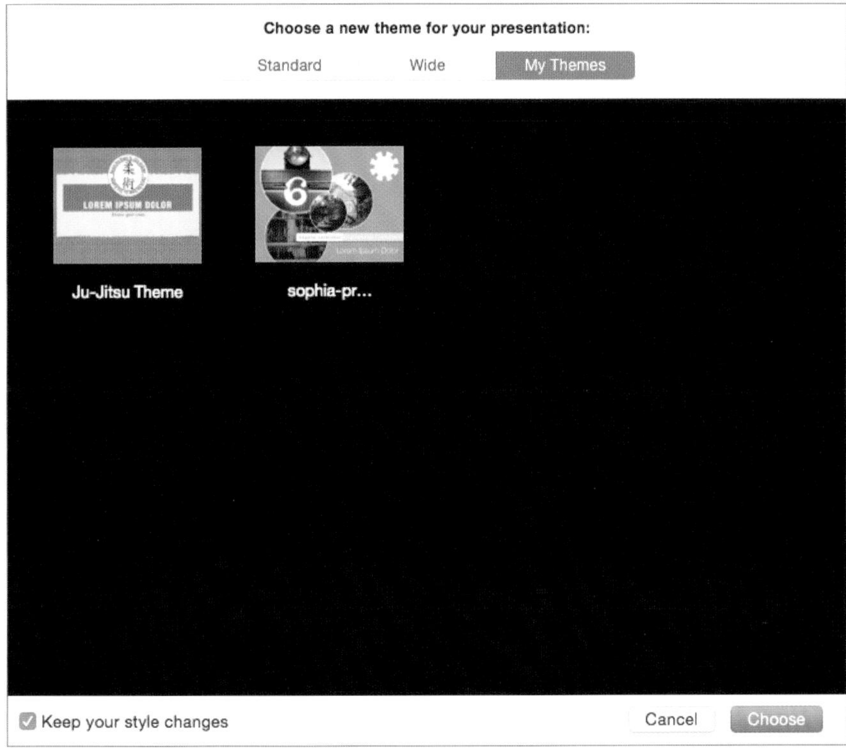

10 In the My Themes pane, double-click the sophia-presentation theme.

The presentation changes appearance as the custom theme is applied. If you work on the presentation by adding extra slides and altering text, those changes will be saved to iCloud.

11 Navigate to slide 2. The movie and photo have moved.

This move was caused by the layout used in the theme's master slide. However, the presentation has retained the transitions and builds applied with your iOS device. To verify this, you can play the slideshow.

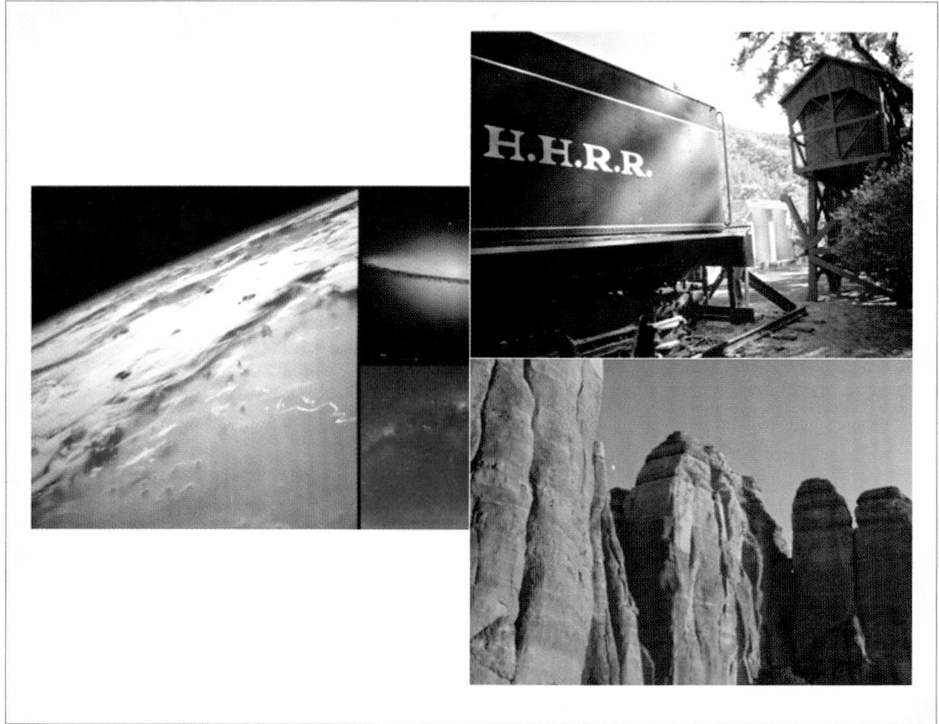

12 At the top of the document window, click the presentation name.

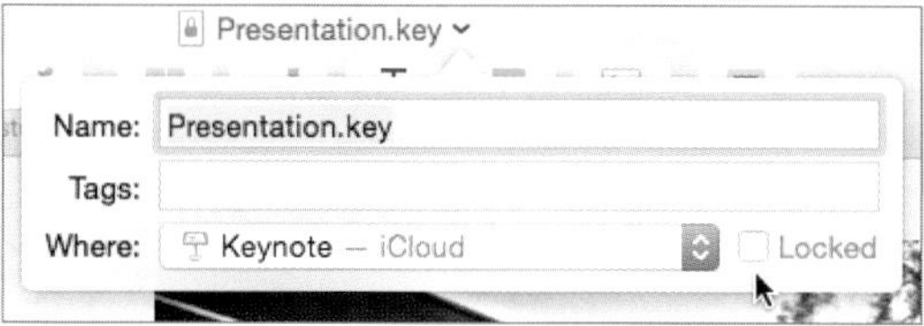

The popover shows the presentation's name, any associated tags, and of greatest relevance to this lesson, where the presentation is stored: in the Keynote folder on your iCloud Drive.

13 Click away from the popover to dismiss it.

Let's play the presentation with its new custom theme on your iOS device.

14 On your Mac, choose File > Save.

This ensures a current version of the presentation is saved to iCloud Drive.

15 On your iOS device, open Keynote.

16 In the Presentation screen, double-tap the presentation you've been editing on your Mac.

17 If prompted, enter the password.

NOTE ▶ If you're working on a busy or slow network, the file sync with iCloud may take some time to complete.

The presentation opens in Keynote for iOS with the custom theme, along with any other edits you may have made on your Mac. On your iOS device, you can continue working on the presentation, and as long as you are connected to iCloud, the presentation will regularly sync with any connected devices.

18 On your Mac, close Keynote.

Moving a Mac Document to iCloud Drive

Here's the scenario: You've been working on a Pages document on your Mac but need to head out for several hours. You'll have time between meetings to complete the document in Pages, but you want to travel light. Here's how to move that Pages document to your iCloud Drive and load it to your iPad for later polishing.

In the previous exercise, the presentation document remained on iCloud Drive. Now you'll move a document from your Mac to your iCloud Drive.

1 On your Mac, open Pages.

2 Open APTS Pages Numbers Keynote > Lesson_17 > **sl-draft-report321.pages**.

3 Navigate to page 2 of the document, and click the word "Objective."

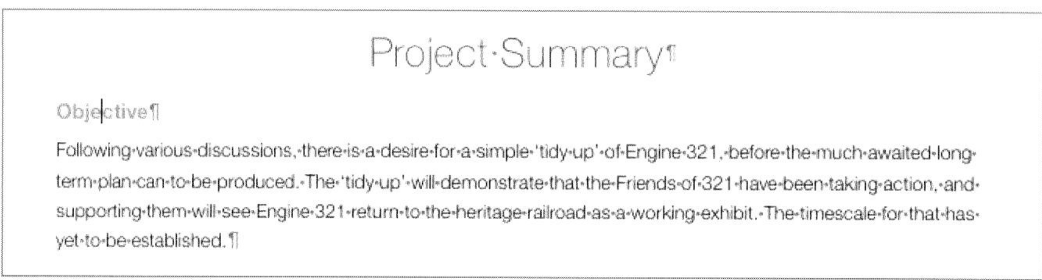

4 In the Text inspector, note that the Heading 2 paragraph style has been applied.

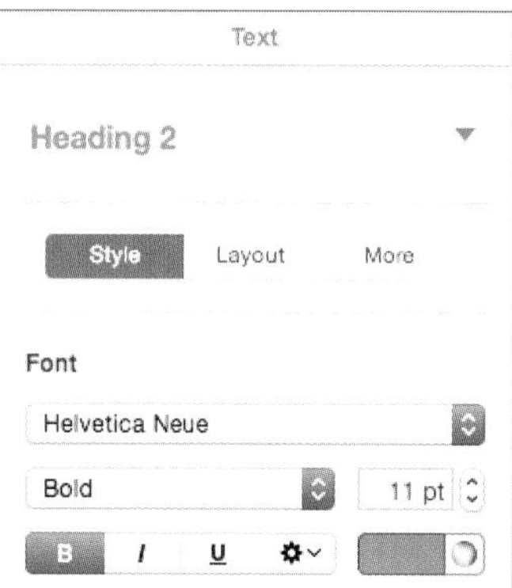

The Heading 2 style is a user-customized style. Let's see how it translates to Pages for iOS.

5 Choose File > Move to. From the Where pop-up menu, choose Pages – iCloud.

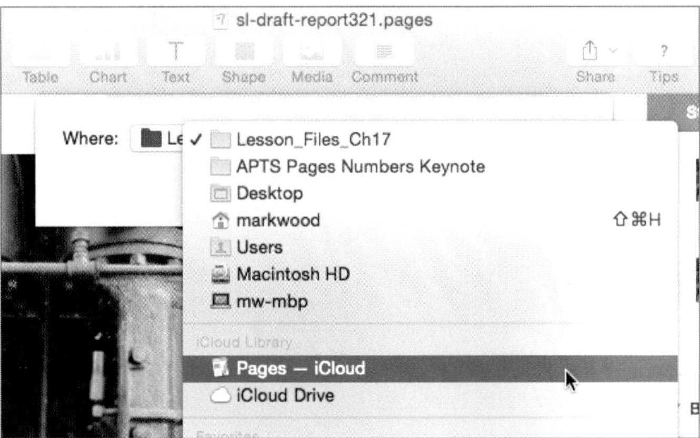

6 Click Move.

The document is transferred to iCloud. The iOS device may take more than a minute to fetch the new version of the document.

Make sure you'll be able to connect to your iCloud account with your iOS device while you're out; or make sure that your iOS device has loaded the document before you leave. The cautious user will favor the latter option.

7 On your iOS device, open Pages and go to the Documents screen. If necessary wait for the document to update.

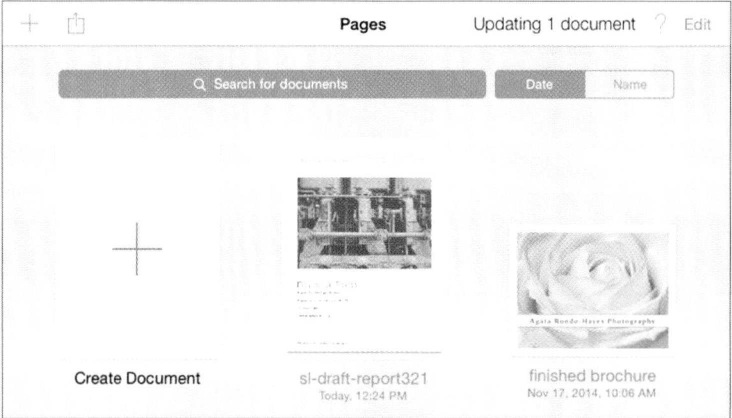

Once the update is completed, you won't need to be networked to edit the document. The same holds true for Numbers and Keynote documents on iCloud.

NOTE ▶ Documents on your iOS device will sync to iCloud only when you are networked.

8 Tap the **sl-draft-report321** document.

9 On page 2, tap the word "Objective." Use the Format tools to verify that the Heading 2 style is applied using all the type attributes that were set in Pages for OS X.

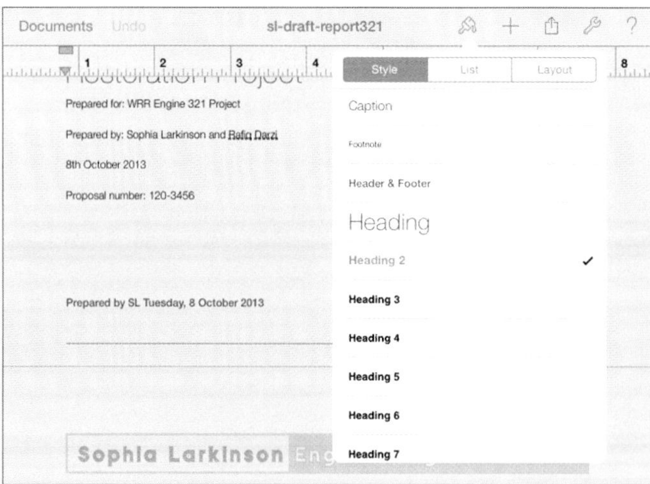

NOTE ▸ Although you cannot create custom styles on the iOS versions of iWork, any styles or templates you have created or customized on the OS X apps will be honored.

Using Handoff

OS X Yosemite and iOS 8.1 introduced Handoff, a feature you can use in Pages, Numbers, and Keynote. Handoff allows you to start a document, spreadsheet, or presentation on one device and instantly open it on other devices using your iCloud account. For this feature to work, the apps used to create the document have to appear on your lock screen and App Switcher, and also be in the Dock on your Mac.

Once you have the iOS apps positioned and your Mac computer's Dock prepared, you need to check the status of Handoff on iOS and OS X.

1 On your iOS device, open Settings. Tap General and make sure that Handoff is turned on.

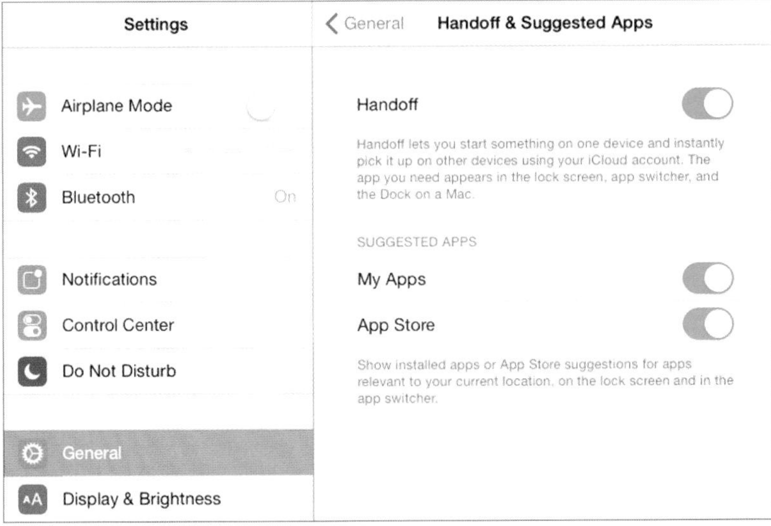

2 On your Mac in System Preferences, open General preferences and verify that "Allow Handoff between this Mac and your iCloud devices" is selected.

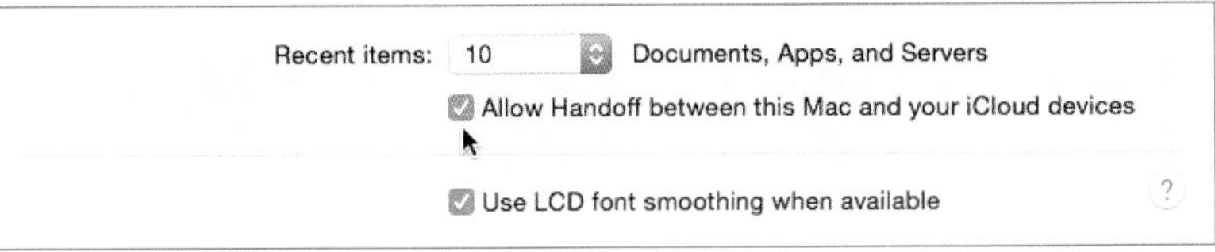

With Handoff set up properly, you can freely open and edit a document on several devices and be assured that the document will remain in sync on all of them. For example, you could use the iOS Camera app to add photos directly to a Keynote presentation on an iPhone and the photos will automatically appear in the Mac presentation.

Remember, though, Handoff works only in series as you hand off a document from one device to another. Multiple users cannot use Handoff to work on a single document at the same time in parallel. Also, network access and transfer speeds will determine how fast "instant handoff" will be.

Collaborating Using iCloud

Syncing via iCloud—with or without Handoff—increases individual productivity, but you can also use iCloud to work collaboratively. You can make an iCloud document available to other users, so they can work with you to edit documents.

1 Make sure **sl-draft-report321** is open on your Mac.

2 In the toolbar, click the Share icon, and from the pop-up menu, choose View Share Settings.

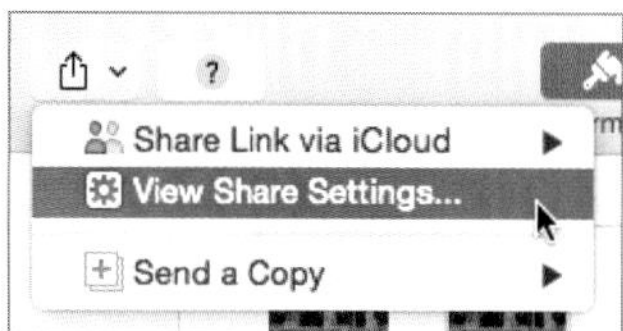

3 In the Share dialog, click the Permissions pop-up menu. It has two options: Allow Editing or View Only. Leave the menu set to Allow Editing.

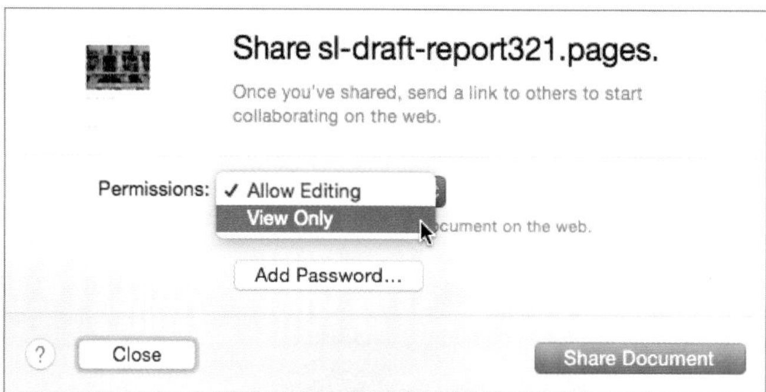

When sharing a file between users, adding a password is a wise precaution. Obviously, you'll need to share that password with your collaborators.

4 In the Share dialog, click Add Password.

5 Enter a password into the required fields.

Adding a password hint is also a good idea, especially when working with a team. By selecting "Remember this password in my keychain," you won't have to enter the password again when opening this document in Pages on your Mac.

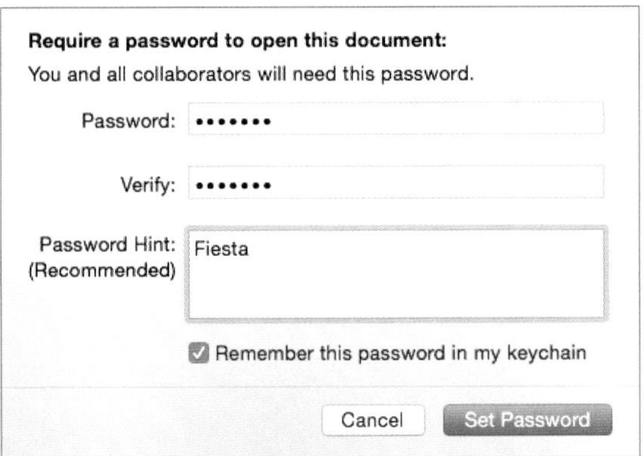

6 Click Set Password. The share dialog reappears.

7 Click Share Document

The share window confirms that the document is now shared. A Document Link field shows the link to the document on iCloud. You could copy and send that link to your colleagues, but using Send Link is easier.

8 Click the Send Link button. A pop-up menu appears with options to send the link via Mail, Messages, and several other options, including Copy Link.

9 Choose Copy Link, and then click Close to dismiss the dialog.

NOTE ▶ Best practice is to share only the link in an email, followed by a second email containing the password.

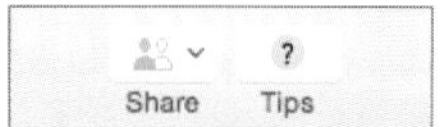

The Share icon in the Pages toolbar has changed to a green icon representing two people; a reminder that this document is now shared.

10 Quit Pages.

Editing in Pages Without an Apple Device

Exporting to alternative formats has always been an option for sharing Pages, Numbers, and Keynote documents with Windows PC users; but now you can run web-based versions of these applications on a Mac or PC via a browser. Your colleagues using PCs can use the web versions of the apps to open and edit iWork documents in their native formats.

If you have an iCloud account, you can access the productivity applications from any Windows PC with an Internet connection. This exercise works on a Mac or PC running an appropriate browser. (See the "System Requirements" section in Lesson 1 for a list of compatible browsers and versions.) You'll work with Pages for iCloud, but the lessons learned apply to Numbers and Keynote for iCloud, too.

1 On your Mac, open Safari and go to www.icloud.com.

Unless you've previously logged in to your iCloud account and chosen to remain signed in, you'll see a sign-in prompt.

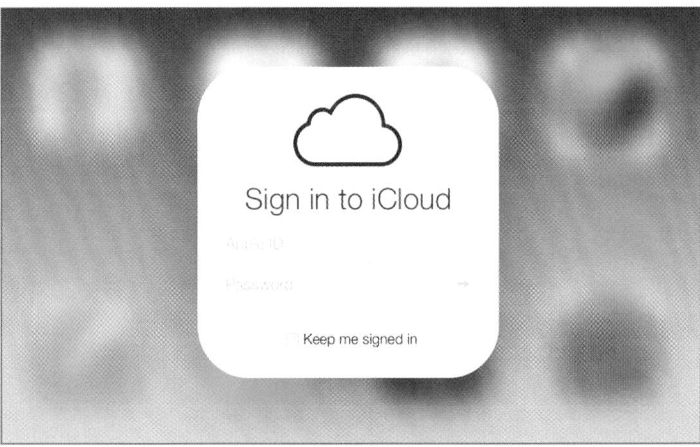

2 Enter your Apple ID and Password to sign in.

TIP If you're working on a public computer, do not select "Keep me signed in" unless you want others to have access to your iCloud account on this device.

After signing in, you see all the applications currently on iCloud.

3 Double-click the Pages icon to open the web-based version of the application.

If this is the first time you've opened Pages on iCloud, you'll see a welcome page.

4 Click Use Pages.

NOTE ▸ If you've previously used Pages for iCloud, and if the app opens the document you were working on recently, click the Tools icon and choose Go to My Documents.

5 In the Documents view, double-click **sl-draft-report321**.

Even if this is the Mac you used to create this document, you'll be prompted for a password (because you're now using the iCloud version of Pages).

6 When prompted, enter the document password, and click OK.

Enter the password for this document:
"sl-draft-report321"
Password:
Close

Pages for iCloud looks similar to the OS X and iOS versions, as do Numbers and Keynote for iCloud. You will find a simple toolbar across the top of the document window and a formatting panel down the side.

NOTE ► The iCloud versions of iWork apps do not have all the features found in their iOS and OS X counterparts.

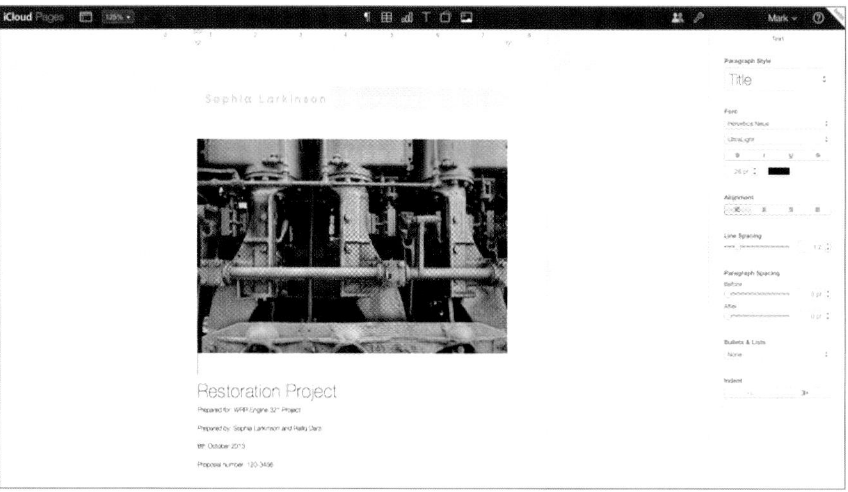

7 In the toolbar, click the Tools button.

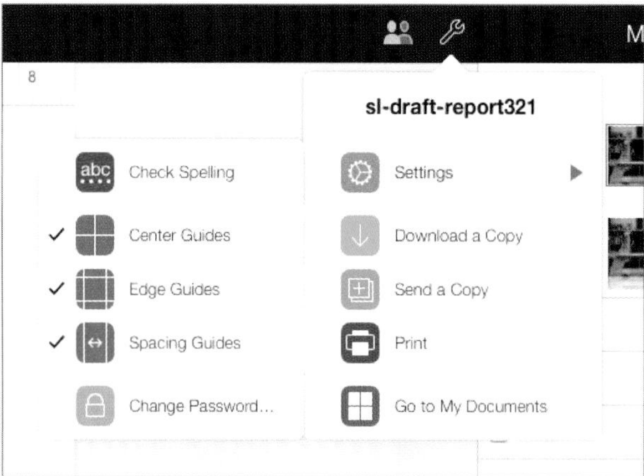

Here you'll find the options to download or send a copy of a document. As an added convenience, you can choose to download the document in Word, PDF, ePub, or Pages format. Those options are useful when you're accessing your documents from a PC and need to edit in Word, Excel, or PowerPoint.

NOTE ► Styles are honored, too, with the previously mentioned caveat about typefaces and fonts.

8 On page 2 of the document, click the word "Objective." In the formatting pane, you'll see that it remains styled as Heading 2.

Everything works as expected. Any edits you make are automatically saved. But what if you make a mistake and need to undo a change? In the toolbar, use the two arrows to undo and redo edits.

9 In the toolbar, click the Tools button, and then choose "Go to My Documents."

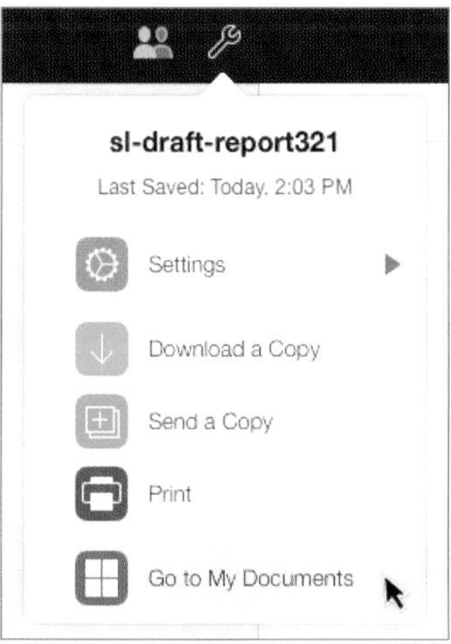

You can use the documents view to manage your files. In the center of the toolbar are three icons. Clicking the plus sign will create a new Pages document. Clicking the center button displays any shared documents you can open.

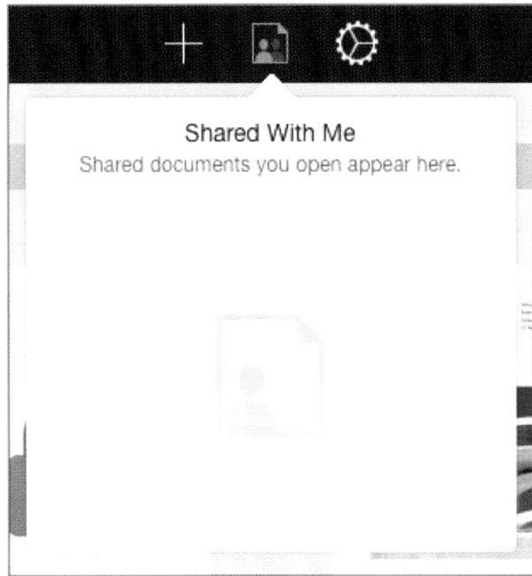

The gear button opens a menu from which you can upload files, including Word documents and PDFs. The menu also contains other file management commands.

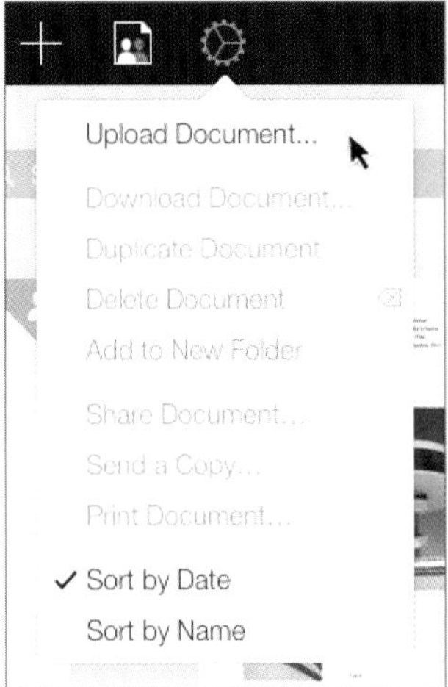

Your web browser now shows a minimum of two tabs. One of these is iCloud – Pages and another is sl-draft-report321. Open documents in Pages, Numbers, and Keynote appear as separate browser tabs.

10 In your web browser, close the sl-draft-report321 tab to close the document.

11 In the iCloud Pages browser window, control-click the **sl-draft-report321** document, and from the shortcut menu, choose Delete Document.

A warning appears stating that this document will be removed from all devices accessing it via iCloud.

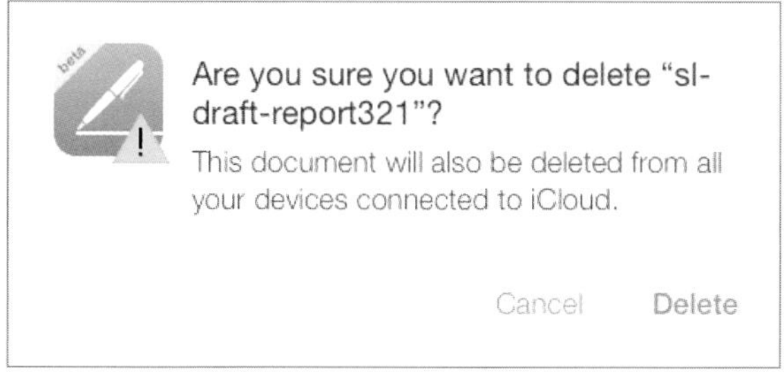

12 Click Delete to remove the document.

NOTE ► If **sl-draft-report321** was open in Pages for OS X, you will see a warning that the document was removed from iCloud. The dialog gives you a choice of deleting or saving the open document. Clicking Save As lets you save a copy of the document to a new location.

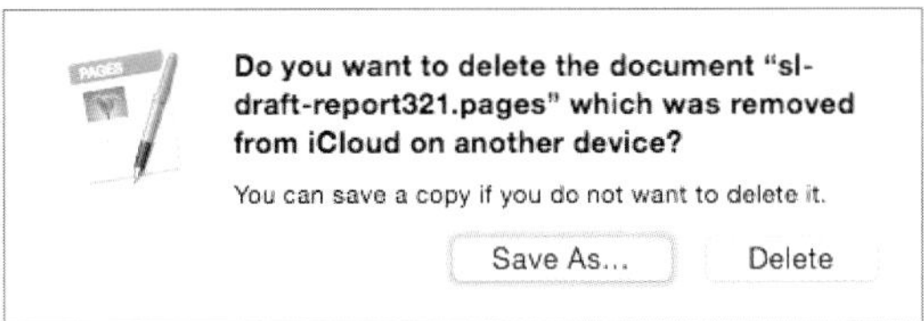

Later you'll duplicate a spreadsheet before deleting its iCloud copy.

To learn more about iWork for iCloud, click the Help (question mark) button in the Pages, Numbers, and Keynote toolbars to turn on coaching tips.

Using Numbers Forms on iOS

iPads are ideal for inputting data on the go, whether during class, in the lab, or on a factory floor. But in a spreadsheet with dozens of rows and lots of columns, you'll need to scroll around to complete each line entry. This process can lead to errors, or at the very least, a reduced efficiency as you make sure that the information goes into the right cell. Rather than resign yourself to endless scrolling, try entering data using forms.

You can create a form from any table. Let's use the Ju-Jitsu register as an example.

1 On your Mac, open Numbers.

2 Open APTS Pages Numbers Keynote > Lesson_17 > **ju-jitsu-register.numbers**.

You'll now move this spreadsheet to your iCloud Drive.

3 Click the document's title, ju-jitsu-register.numbers.

In the popover you can choose to move the spreadsheet to iCloud Drive, as an alternative to choosing File > Move To.

4 From the Where pop-up menu, choose Numbers – iCloud.

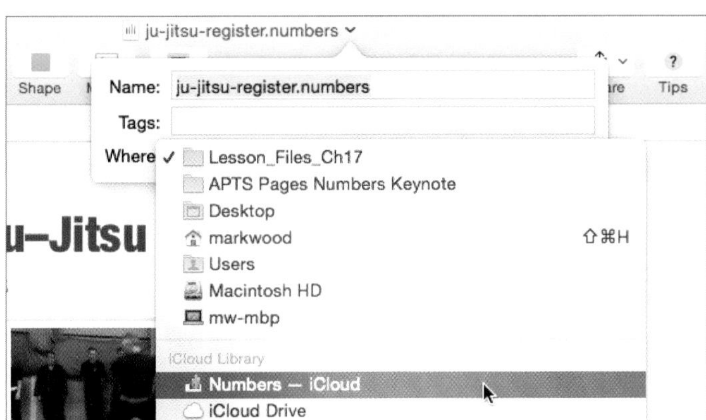

5 Click away from the popover to close it.

The spreadsheet moves to your iCloud Drive. The upload speed will depend on your network connection.

NOTE ▸ Numbers must be configured to use iCloud. To verify your settings, on your iOS Device, open Settings > Numbers and verify that "Use iCloud" is selected.

6 On your iOS device, open Numbers.

7 In the Spreadsheets window, locate and open **ju-jitsu-register**. If necessary, wait for the file to update.

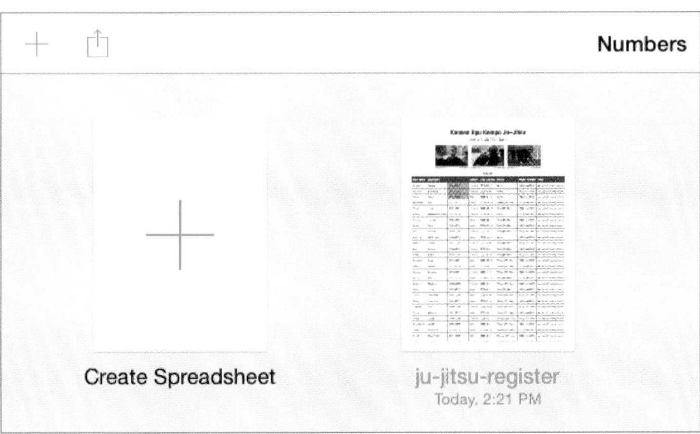

This spreadsheet has two sheets. The second, Grading Readiness, was designed to display clearly on an iPad.

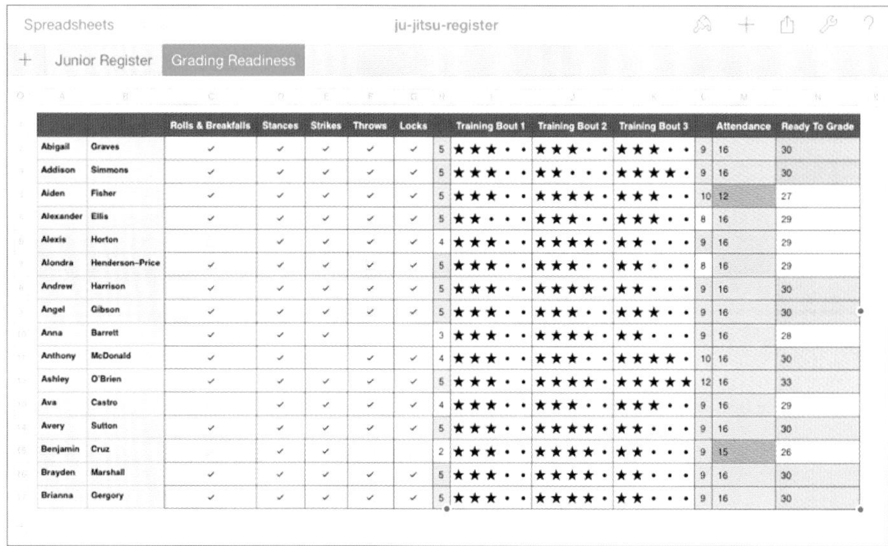

		Rolls & Breakfalls	Stances	Strikes	Throws	Locks		Training Bout 1	Training Bout 2	Training Bout 3		Attendance	Ready To Grade
Abigail	Graves	✓	✓	✓	✓	✓	5	★★★••	★★★••	★★★••	9	16	30
Addison	Simmons	✓	✓	✓	✓	✓	5	★★★••	★★•••	★★★★•	9	16	30
Aiden	Fisher	✓	✓	✓	✓	✓	5	★★★••	★★★★•	★★★••	10	12	27
Alexander	Ellis	✓	✓	✓	✓	✓	5	★★•••	★★★••	★★★••	8	16	29
Alexis	Horton		✓	✓	✓	✓	4	★★★••	★★★★•	★★•••	9	16	29
Alondra	Henderson-Price	✓	✓	✓	✓	✓	5	★★★••	★★★••	★★•••	8	16	29
Andrew	Harrison	✓	✓	✓	✓	✓	5	★★★••	★★★★•	★★•••	9	16	30
Angel	Gibson	✓	✓	✓	✓	✓	5	★★★••	★★★••	★★★••	9	16	30
Anna	Barrett	✓	✓	✓			3	★★★••	★★★★•	★★•••	9	16	28
Anthony	McDonald	✓	✓		✓	✓	4	★★★••	★★★••	★★★★•	10	16	30
Ashley	O'Brien	✓	✓	✓	✓	✓	5	★★★••	★★★★•	★★★★★	12	16	33
Ava	Castro		✓	✓	✓	✓	4	★★★••	★★★••	★★★••	9	16	29
Avery	Sutton	✓	✓	✓	✓	✓	5	★★★••	★★★★•	★★•••	9	16	30
Benjamin	Cruz		✓	✓			2	★★★••	★★★★•	★★•••	9	15	26
Brayden	Marshall	✓	✓	✓	✓	✓	5	★★★••	★★★★•	★★•••	9	16	30
Brianna	Gergory	✓	✓	✓	✓	✓	5	★★★••	★★★★•	★★•••	9	16	30

8 Tap the Junior Register sheet to open it.

First Name	Last Name		Gender	Date Of Birth	Grade	Phone Number	email
Abigail	Graves	01/09/2013	Female	2009-08-27	White	(123) 456-7890	no_reply@example.com
Addison	Simmons	01/10/2013	Female	2009-6-30	White	(123) 456-7890	no_reply@example.com
Aiden	Fisher	01/11/2013	Male	2008-8-19	White	(123) 456-7890	no_reply@example.com
Alexander	Ellis	01/12/2013	Male	2004-05-23	Green (5th Mon)	(123) 456-7890	no_reply@example.com

The register table is long, and although you can amend the student records directly within the table, using forms will make data entry faster and less error-prone.

9 Tap the plus sign adjacent to the two sheets, and then tap New Form.

Numbers asks you which table to use. The input form and the table will be linked so that data entered in one will automatically appear in the other.

10 Tap Register to choose it.

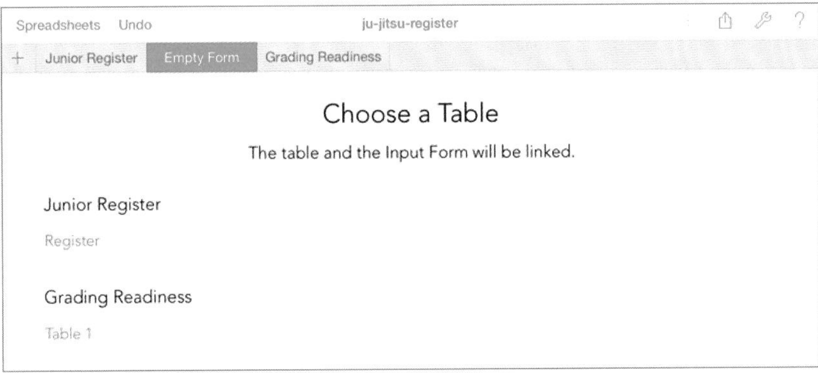

All forms have the same layout. Each row in the table appears as a record in the form.

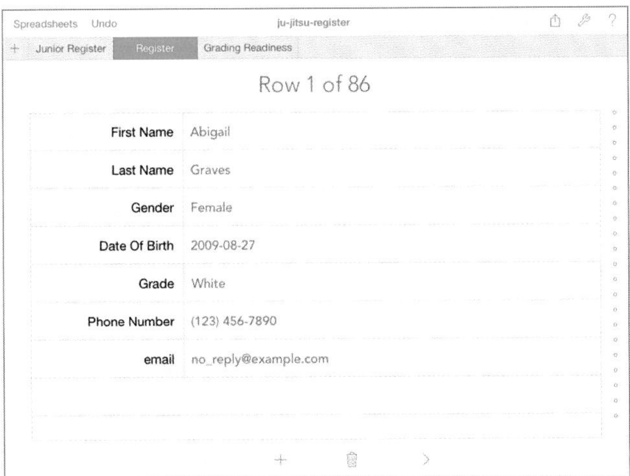

At the bottom of the form window is a plus sign (tap it to add a new record) and a Trash icon (tap it to remove the currently displayed record). You can tap the arrows to move through the records, and tap the series of dots to the right to scroll up and down.

11 On the Row 1 form, tap the Grade field and change the color from White to Red (8th Mon).

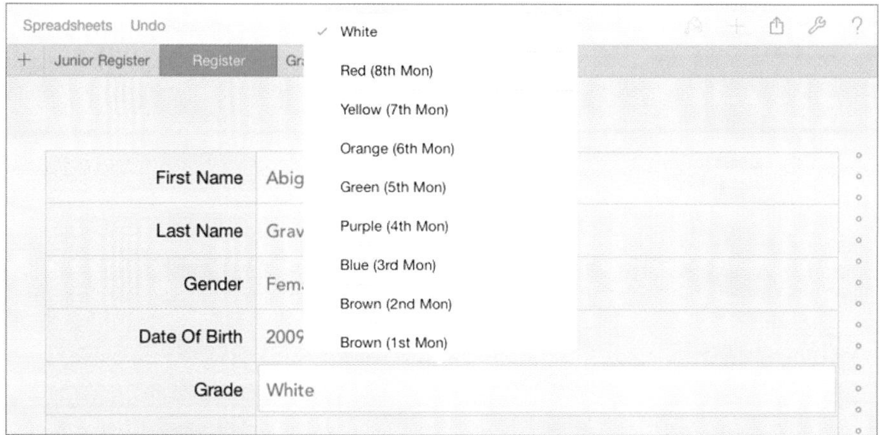

12 Tap the Junior Register sheet to see that Abigail's record, Row 1, is updated here, too.

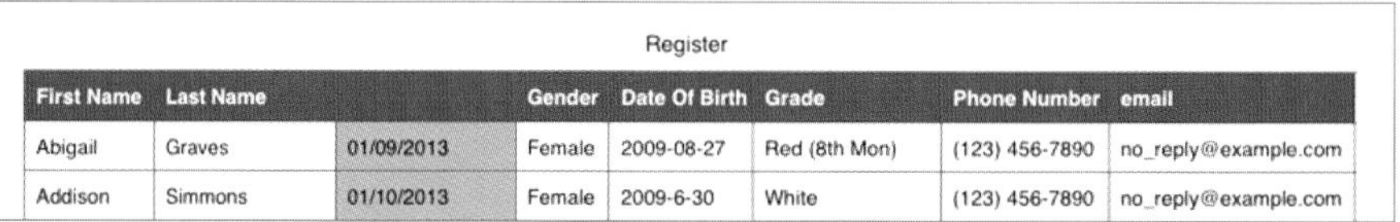

Register

First Name	Last Name		Gender	Date Of Birth	Grade	Phone Number	email
Abigail	Graves	01/09/2013	Female	2009-08-27	Red (8th Mon)	(123) 456-7890	no_reply@example.com
Addison	Simmons	01/10/2013	Female	2009-6-30	White	(123) 456-7890	no_reply@example.com

13 In the toolbar, tap Spreadsheets.

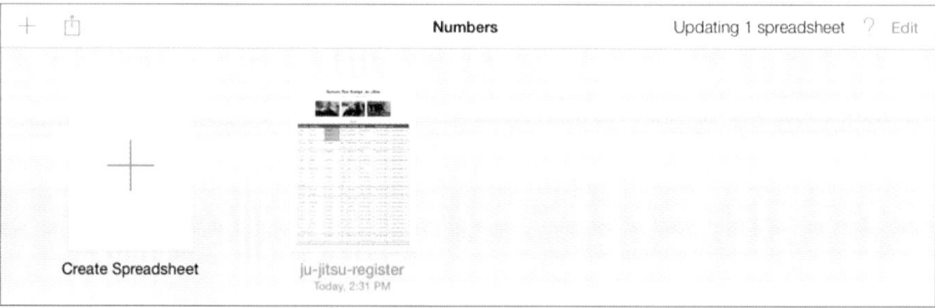

You're going to delete the spreadsheet from iCloud, but before doing so, you'll duplicate it and download it your Mac.

14 On your Mac, switch to Numbers, if necessary. The **ju-jitsu-register** spreadsheet should still be open.

15 Press Command-Shift-S to duplicate the spreadsheet.

16 Press Command-S to save a duplicate of the spreadsheet.

In the Save dialog, you can change the default name and add some tags, if you wish; but the task here is to save a copy of the spreadsheet to the Mac computer's hard disk.

17 Change the save location of the duplicate file from Numbers – iCloud to Desktop. Click Save.

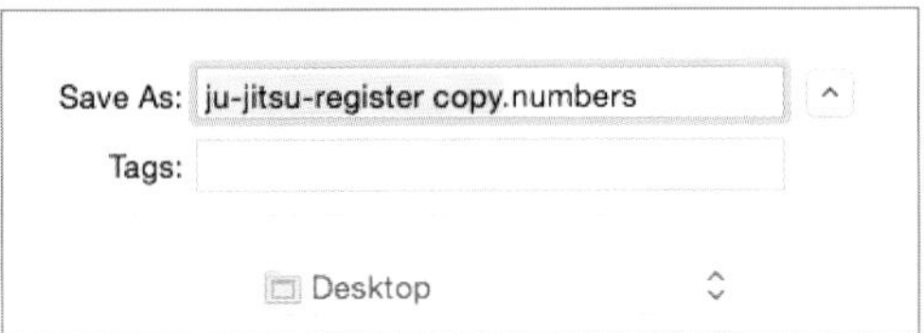

A copy of the spreadsheet is saved to your Mac. Any edits you make to this copy will not automatically update on other devices.

18 On your iOS device, tap and hold down the **ju-jitsu-register** spreadsheet icon.

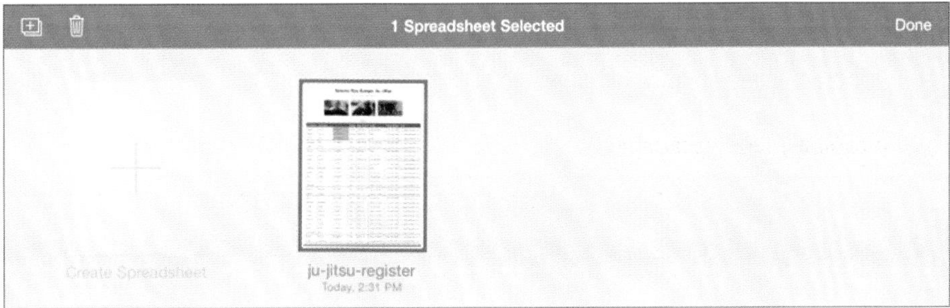

The document icon starts to jiggle. The Trash icon becomes available, as does the duplicate button next to it.

19 Tap the Trash icon to delete the file.

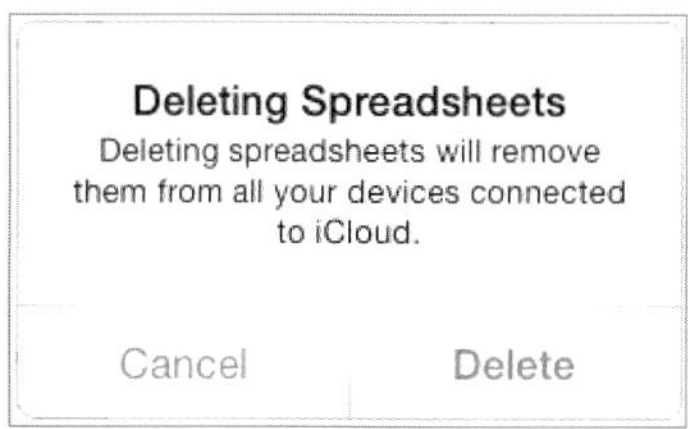
Deleting Spreadsheets
Deleting spreadsheets will remove them from all your devices connected to iCloud.
Cancel
Delete

A warning lets you know that tapping Delete now will remove the document from all connected devices.

20 Tap Delete.

Tidying Up

Not only have you finished this lesson, you've also reached the end of this book. As such, you may want to remove the tutorial files from your Mac and iCloud, along with any unwanted themes and templates.

1 On your Mac, open Pages and Keynote.

You can repeat the following steps to remove themes and templates for all three applications.

NOTE ▸ The lessons in this book did not create any Numbers templates.

2 Choose File > New.

3 In the Template Chooser or Theme Chooser, Control-click any theme or template you want to remove.

4 From the shortcut menu, choose Delete.

Rename
Delete
ntation

5 Quit Pages, Numbers, or Keynote by pressing Command-Q in each application.

To remove unwanted files from iCloud Drive, you can use the Finder.

6 Switch to the Finder.

7 In the Finder, navigate to your iCloud Drive folder.

8 Open the Pages folder.

9 Select any unwanted documents.

10 Press Command-Delete.

11 When prompted, click Delete to remove the files.

12 Repeat steps 9 through 11 for your Numbers and Keynote folders.

Throughout the lessons you've saved documents to the desktop, which was also the recommended location for the tutorial files.

13 In the Finder, navigate to your desktop. Command-click all the tutorial files and folders.

14 Press Command-Delete.

15 In the Dock, Control-click the Trash icon, and from the shortcut menu, choose Empty Trash.

And that's it, you've reached the end of the book. The lessons have led you through the interfaces of Pages, Numbers, and Keynote in all their forms. You performed real-world tasks and experiences as a foundation for applying these lessons to your own work and increasing both your productivity and enjoyment of these applications.

Lesson Review

1. When opening a password-protected document on your Mac, do you have to enter a password every time you want to open it on that Mac?
2. How can you tell whether a spreadsheet is opening from your Mac or iCloud?
3. You want to deliver a Keynote slideshow using an iPad, but you need to apply a customized theme. Describe how to do this.
4. Describe how to move an Excel spreadsheet onto an iCloud Drive using a Windows PC.
5. If you're using an iPad to enter data to a spreadsheet, which option provides a fast, reliable method for editing the data fields?

Answers

1. No, you can save passwords into your Keychain for the device. However, doing so does not save the document's password on other devices.
2. To identify the location of a current spreadsheet, click the spreadsheet's title. From the pop-up menu, the Where field entry indicates the location of the spreadsheet.
3. You must open a presentation in Keynote for OS X to apply a custom theme. Then you can copy or move it to iCloud Drive, where you can open it on Keynote for iOS.
4. You can move or copy an Excel document from a Windows PC to iCloud in several ways. The most expedient is to sign in to your iCloud account on the PC, and then open the Web app. In the document manager, click the gear icon and choose Upload Spreadsheet.
5. Using forms on Numbers for iOS provides a fast, reliable method for editing data fields.

Index

Z